Life of

Napoleon Bonaparte

By Sir Walter Scott

Volume III

SIR WALTER SCOTT

LIFE OF
NAPOLEON BONAPARTE
VOLUME III
1827

PUBLISHED BY
OMNIA VERITAS LTD

www.omnia-veritas.com

Hotel de Ville – Paris

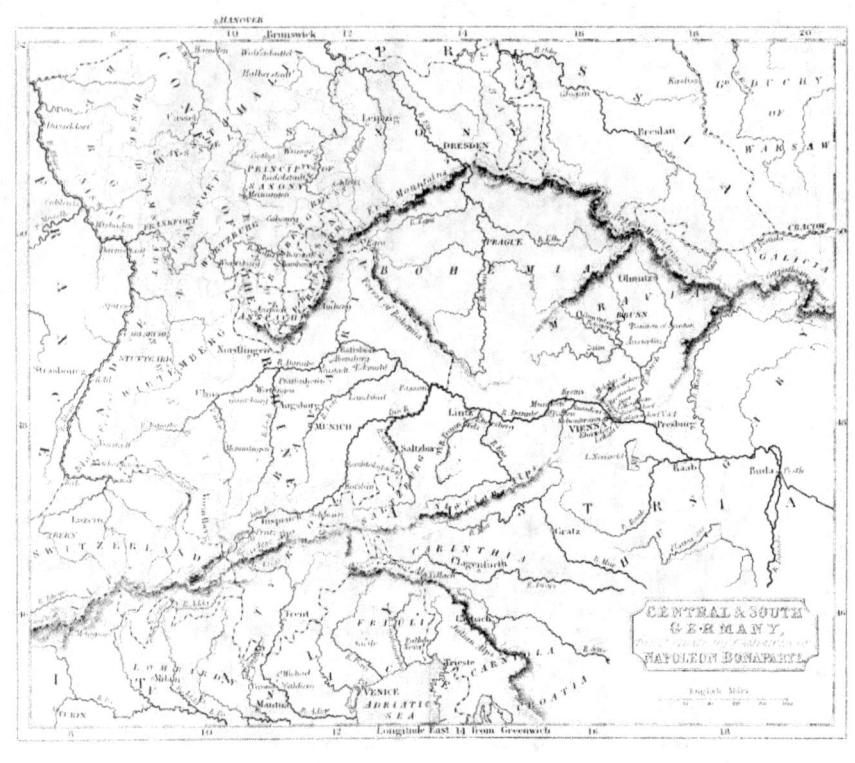

Central and South Germany, to illustrate the campaigns of Napoleon Bonaparte

CHAPTER XXV **19**

Increasing Jealousies betwixt France and England—Encroachments on the part of the former—Instructions given by the First Consul to his Commercial Agents—Orders issued by the English Ministers—Peltier's celebrated Royalist Publication, L'Ambigu—Peltier tried for a Libel against the First Consul—found Guilty—Angry Discussions respecting the Treaty of Amiens—Malta—Report of Sebastiani—Resolution of the British Government—Conferences betwixt Buonaparte and Lord Whitworth—Britain declares War against France on 18th May, 1803. 19

COMMERCIAL AGENTS. *20*
NOTE BY M. OTTO. *24*
TRIAL OF PELTIER. *26*
SEBASTIANI'S REPORT. *29*
LORD WHITWORTH. *32*

CHAPTER XXVI **41**

St. Domingo—The Negroes split into parties under different Chiefs—Toussaint L'Ouverture the most distinguished of these—Appoints a Consular Government—France sends an Expedition against St. Domingo, under General Leclerc, in December 1801—Toussaint submits—He is sent to France, where he dies—The French are assaulted by the Negroes—Leclerc is succeeded by Rochambeau—The French finally obliged to capitulate to an English squadron—Buonaparte's scheme to consolidate his power—The Consular Guard augmented—Legion of Honour—Opposition formed against the Consular Government—Application to the Count de Provence (Louis XVIII.) 41

TOUSSAINT L'OUVERTURE. *42*
DEATH OF TOUSSAINT. *45*
COURT OF THE TUILERIES. *47*
LEGION OF HONOUR. *49*
OPPOSITION TO THE GOVERNMENT. *51*
PROPOSITION TO LOUIS XVIII. *53*

CHAPTER XXVII **57**

Renewal of the War—England lays an Embargo on French Vessels—Napoleon retaliates by detaining British Subjects—Effects of this unprecedented Measure—Hanover and other places occupied by the French—Scheme of Invasion renewed—Napoleon's Preparations—Defensive Measures of England. 57

EMBARGO ON FRENCH VESSELS—DÉTENUS. *58*
HANOVER SEIZED. *61*

ARMY OF ENGLAND. 64
BOULOGNE FLOTILLA. 66
DEFENSIVE MEASURES OF ENGLAND. 69

CHAPTER XXVIII 71

Disaffection begins to arise against Napoleon among the Soldiery—Purpose of setting up Moreau against him—Character of Moreau—Causes of his Estrangement from Buonaparte—Pichegru—The Duke d'Enghien—Georges Cadoudal, Pichegru, and other Royalists, landed in France—Desperate Enterprise of Georges—Defeated—Arrest of Moreau—of Pichegru—and Georges—Captain Wright—Duke d'Enghien seized at Strasburg—Hurried to Paris—Transferred to Vincennes—Tried by a Military Commission—Condemned—and Executed—Universal Horror of France and Europe—Buonaparte's Vindication of his Conduct—His Defence considered—Pichegru found dead in his Prison—Attempt to explain his Death by charging him with Suicide—Captain Wright found with his Throat cut—A similar Attempt made—Georges and other Conspirators Tried—Condemned—and Executed—Royalists Silenced—Moreau sent into Exile. 71

DISAFFECTION OF THE SOLDIERY. 71
THE DUKE D'ENGHIEN. 75
ARREST OF PICHEGRU AND GEORGES. 78
THE DUKE D'ENGHIEN. 79
DEATH OF PICHEGRU. 89
TRIAL OF CADOUDAL AND OTHERS. 93

CHAPTER XXIX 97

General Indignation of Europe in consequence of the Murder of the Duke d'Enghien—Russia complains to Talleyrand of the Violation of Baden—and, along with Sweden, Remonstrates in a Note laid before the German Diet—but without effect—Charges brought by Buonaparte against Mr. Drake and Mr. Spencer Smith—who are accordingly Dismissed from the Courts of Stuttgard and Munich—Seizure—Imprisonment—and Dismissal—of Sir George Rumbold, the British Envoy at Lower Saxony—Treachery attempted against Lord Elgin, by the Agents of Buonaparte—Details—Defeated by the Exemplary Prudence of that Nobleman—These Charges brought before the House of Commons—and peremptorily Denied by the Chancellor of the Exchequer. 97

GENERAL INDIGNATION OF EUROPE. 97
SIR GEORGE RUMBOLD. 100
LORD ELGIN. 101

CHAPTER XXX 105

Napoleon meditates a change of title from Chief Consul to Emperor—A Motion to this purpose brought forward in the Tribunate—Opposed by Carnot—Adopted by the Tribunate and Senate—Outline of the New System—Coldly received by the People—Napoleon visits Boulogne, Aix-la-Chapelle, and the Frontiers of Germany, where he is received with respect—The Coronation—Pius VII. is summoned from Rome to perform the Ceremony at Paris—Details—Reflections—Changes that took place in Italy—Napoleon appointed Sovereign of Italy, and Crowned at Milan—Genoa annexed to France. 105

NAPOLEON MEDITATES A CHANGE OF TITLE. 105
CHANGE OF TITLE. 107
EMPEROR OF THE FRENCH. 109
THE CORONATION. 113
EMPEROR OF THE FRENCH. 114
THE IMPERIAL CONSTITUTION. 116
CHANGES IN ITALY. 121
CORONATION AT MILAN. 123

CHAPTER XXXI **127**

Napoleon addresses a Second Letter to the King of England personally—Answered by the British Secretary of State to Talleyrand—Alliance formed betwixt Russia and England—Prussia keeps aloof, and the Emperor Alexander visits Berlin—Austria prepares for War, and marches an Army into Bavaria—Her impolicy in prematurely commencing Hostilities, and in her Conduct to Bavaria—Unsoldierlike Conduct of the Austrian General Mack—Buonaparte is joined by the Electors of Bavaria and Wirtemberg, and the Duke of Baden—Skilful Manœuvres of the French Generals, and successive losses of the Austrians—Napoleon violates the Neutrality of Prussia, by marching through Anspach and Bareuth—Further Losses of the Austrian Leaders, and consequent Disunion among them—Mack is cooped up in Ulm—Issues a formidable Declaration on the 16th October—and surrenders on the following day—Fatal Results of this Man's Poltroonery, want of Skill, and probable Treachery. 127

LETTER TO THE KING OF ENGLAND. 127
THE KING OF SWEDEN. 130
PRUSSIA. 131
AUSTRIA—BAVARIA. 134
UNSOLDIERLIKE CONDUCT OF MACK. 136
MANŒUVRES OF FRENCH GENERALS. 139
CAPITULATION OF MEMMINGEN. 142
CAPITULATION OF ULM. 143

CHAPTER XXXII **149**

Position of the French Armies—Napoleon advances towards Vienna—The Emperor Francis leaves his Capital—French enter Vienna on the 13th November—Review of the French Successes in Italy and the Tyrol—Schemes of Napoleon to force on a General Battle—Battle of Austerlitz is fought on the 2d December, and the combined Austro-Russian Armies completely Defeated—Interview betwixt the Emperor of Austria and Napoleon—The Emperor Alexander retreats towards Russia—Treaty of Presburgh signed on the 26th December—Its Conditions—Fate of the King of Sweden—and of the Two Sicilies. 149

POSITION OF THE FRENCH ARMIES. 149
VIENNA TAKEN. 152
SUCCESSION OF GRAND MANŒUVRES. 155
AUSTERLITZ. 157
BATTLE OF AUSTERLITZ. 159
CONVENTION WITH PRUSSIA. 162
ARMISTICE WITH AUSTRIA. 165
NAPLES. 168
SURRENDER OF GAETA. 170

CHAPTER XXXIII 171

Relative situations of France and England—Hostilities commenced with Spain, by the Stoppage, by Commodore Moore, of four Spanish Galleons, when three of their Escort were taken, and one blew up—Napoleon's Plan of Invasion stated and discussed—John Clerk of Eldin's great System of Breaking the Line, explained—The French Admiral, Villeneuve, forms a junction with the Spanish Fleet under Gravina—Attacked and defeated by Sir Robert Calder—Nelson appointed to the Command in the Mediterranean—Battle of Trafalgar fought 21st October, 1805—Death of Nelson—Behaviour of Napoleon on learning the Intelligence of this signal Defeat—Villeneuve commits Suicide—Address of Buonaparte to the Legislative Body—Statement of M. de Champagny on the Internal Improvements of France—Elevation of Napoleon's Brothers, Louis and Joseph, to the Thrones of Holland and Naples—Principality of Lucca conferred on Eliza, the eldest Sister of Buonaparte, and that of Guastalla on Pauline, the youngest—Other Alliances made by his Family—Napoleon appoints a new Hereditary Nobility—Converts from the old Noblesse anxiously sought for and liberally rewarded—Confederation of the Rhine established, and Napoleon appointed Protector—The Emperor Francis lays aside the Imperial Crown of Germany, retaining only the Title of Emperor of Austria—Vacillating and Impolitic Conduct of Prussia. 171

WAR BETWEEN SPAIN AND ENGLAND 173
ROCHEFORT SQUADRON. 176
NELSON IN THE MEDITERRANEAN. 179
DEATH OF NELSON. 181

INTERNAL IMPROVEMENTS.	184
LOUIS, KING OF HOLLAND.	188
MURAT.	191
EUGENE, VICEROY OF ITALY.	194
SUBSIDIARY MONARCHIES.	196
NEW NOBILITY.	199
CONFEDERATION OF THE RHINE.	201

CHAPTER XXXIV 205

Death of Pitt—He is succeeded by Fox as Prime Minister—Negotiation with France—The Earl of Lauderdale sent to Paris as the British Negotiator—Negotiation broken off, in consequence of the refusal of England to cede Sicily to France—Temporizing Policy of Prussia—An attempt made by her to form a Confederacy in opposition to that of the Rhine, defeated by Napoleon—General Disposition of the Prussians to War—Legal Murder of Palm, a bookseller—The Emperor Alexander again visits Berlin—Prussia begins to arm in August 1806, and, after some Negotiation, takes the field in October, under the Duke of Brunswick—Impolicy of the Plans of the Campaign—Details—Action at Saalfeld—Battle of Auerstadt, or Jena, on 14th October—Duke of Brunswick mortally wounded—Consequences of this total Defeat—Buonaparte takes possession of Berlin on the 25th—Situations of Austria and Prussia, after their several Defeats—Reflections on the fall of Prussia. 205

DEATH OF PITT.	205
NEGOTIATION WITH ENGLAND.	207
PRUSSIA.	210
PRUSSIA ARMS AGAINST FRANCE.	216
PLANS OF THE CAMPAIGN.	218
ACTION AT SAALFIELD.	222
AUERSTADT.	223
BATTLE OF JENA.	225
PRINCE HOHENLOE—BLUCHER.	229
SURRENDER OF FORTRESSES.	231
FALL OF PRUSSIA.	233

CHAPTER XXXV 239

Ungenerous conduct of Buonaparte to the Duke of Brunswick—The approach of the French troops to Brunswick compels the dying Prince to cause himself to be carried to Altona, where he expires—Oath of revenge taken by his Son—At Potsdam and Berlin, the proceedings of Napoleon are equally cruel and vindictive—His clemency towards the Prince of Hatzfeld—His Treatment of the Lesser Powers—Jerome Buonaparte—Seizure of Hamburgh—Berlin Decrees against British Commerce—Napoleon rejects all application from the continental commercial towns to relax or repeal them—Commerce, nevertheless, flourishes in spite of them—Second anticipation called for of the Conscription for 1807—The King of Prussia applies for an Armistice, which is clogged with such harsh terms, that he refuses them. 239

THE DUKE OF BRUNSWICK. 239
THE PRINCE OF HATZFELD. 242
HESSE-CASSEL. 243
BERLIN DECREES. 247
PRUSSIA. 253

CHAPTER XXXVI 255

Retrospect of the Partition of Poland—Napoleon receives addresses from Poland, which he evades—He advances into Poland, Bennigsen retreating before him—Character of the Russian Soldiery—The Cossacks—Engagement at Pultusk, on 26th November, terminating to the disadvantage of the French—Bennigsen continues his retreat—The French go into winter quarters—Bennigsen appointed Commander-in-chief in the place of Kaminskoy, who shows symptoms of insanity—He resumes offensive operations—Battle of Eylau, 8th February, 1807—Claimed as a victory by both parties—The loss on both sides amounts to 50,000 men killed, the greater part Frenchmen—Bennigsen retreats upon Königsberg—Napoleon offers favourable terms for an Armistice to the King of Prussia, who refuses to treat, save for a general Peace—Napoleon falls back to the line of the Vistula—Dantzick is besieged, and surrenders—Russian army is poorly recruited—the French powerfully—Actions during the Summer—Battle of Heilsberg, and retreat of the Russians—Battle of Friedland, 14th June—An Armistice takes place on the 23d. 255

POLAND. 255
ADDRESSES FROM POLAND. 257
THE RUSSIAN SOLDIERY. 261
COSSACKS—ACTION OF PULTUSK. 263
ACTION OF MOHRUNGEN. 267
BATTLE OF PREUSS-EYLAU. 269
DANTZIC. 274
ACTION OF HEILSBERG. 277
BATTLE OF FRIEDLAND. 278
ARMISTICE. 282
THE KING OF PRUSSIA AT TILSIT. 285
TREATY OF TILSIT. 287
PARIS. 296

CHAPTER XXXVII 299

British Expedition to Calabria, under Sir John Stuart—Character of the People—Opposed by General Reynier—Battle of Maida, 4th July, 1806—Defeat of the French—Calabria evacuated by the British—Erroneous Commercial Views, and Military Plans, of the British Ministry—Unsuccessful Attack on Buenos Ayres—General Whitelocke—is cashiered—Expedition against Turkey, and its Dependencies—Admiral Duckworth's Squadron sent against Constantinople—Passes and repasses the Dardanelles, without accomplishing anything—Expedition against Alexandria—Rosetta attacked—British troops defeated—and withdrawn from Egypt, September, 1807—Curaçoa and Cape of Good Hope taken by England—British Expedition against Copenhagen—its Citadel, Forts, and Fleet, surrendered to the British—Effects of this proceeding upon France and Russia—Coalition of France, Russia, Austria, and Prussia, against British Commerce. 299

MAIDA. 301
PLANS OF THE BRITISH MINISTRY. 303
CONSTANTINOPLE. 305
COPENHAGEN. 308
COALITION—BRITISH COMMERCE. 312

CHAPTER XXXVIII **315**

View of the Internal Government of Napoleon at the period of the Peace of Tilsit—The Tribunate abolished—Council of State—Prefectures—Their nature and objects described—The Code Napoleon—Its Provisions—Its merits and Defects—Comparison betwixt that Code and the Jurisprudence of England—Laudable efforts of Napoleon to carry it into effect. 315

INTERNAL GOVERNMENT. 315
THE COUNCIL OF STATE. 319
PREFECTURES. 322
THE CODE NAPOLEON. 325
CIVIL CODE. 329
TAXATION—FOREIGN TRADE. 339
CAPITALISTS—MANUFACTURES. 341
PUBLIC WORKS. 345
PERSONAL AND FAMILY LIFE. 347
THE IMPERIAL COURT. 349

CHAPTER XXXIX **357**

System of Education introduced into France by Napoleon—National University—its nature and objects—Lyceums—Proposed Establishment at Meudon. 357

PUBLIC EDUCATION. 357

LYCEUMS. *359*

CHAPTER XL ***363***

>Military Details—Plan of the Conscription—Its Nature—and Effects—Enforced with unsparing rigour—Its influence upon the general Character of the French Soldiery—New mode of Conducting Hostilities introduced by the Revolution—Constitution of the French Armies, Forced Marches—La Maraude—Its Nature—and Effects—on the Enemy's Country, and on the French Soldiers themselves—Policy of Napoleon, in his personal conduct to his Officers and Soldiers—Altered Character of the French Soldiery during, and after, the Revolution. 363

>THE CONSCRIPTION. *363*
>THE CONSCRIPTION—CORPS D'ARMÉE. *367*
>LA MARAUDE. *368*
>THE FRENCH SOLDIERY. *369*

CHAPTER XLI ***373***

>Effects of the Peace of Tilsit—Napoleon's views of a State of Peace—Contrasted with those of England—The Continental System—Berlin and Milan Decrees—British Orders in Council—Spain—Retrospect of the Relations of that Country with France since the Revolution—Godoy—His Influence—Character—and Political Views—Ferdinand, Prince of Asturias, applies to Napoleon for Aid—Affairs of Portugal—Treaty of Fontainbleau—Departure of the Prince Regent for Brazil—Entrance of Junot into Lisbon—His unbounded Rapacity—Disturbances at Madrid—Ferdinand detected in a Plot against his Father, and imprisoned—King Charles applies to Napoleon—Wily Policy of Buonaparte—Orders the French Army to enter Spain. 373

>EFFECTS OF THE PEACE OF TILSIT. *375*
>MANUEL DE GODOY—SPAIN. *377*
>JUNOT ADVANCES UPON LISBON. *381*
>ROYAL FAMILY EMBARK FOR BRAZIL. *382*
>INTRIGUES AT MADRID. *385*
>PROJECTS AGAINST SPAIN. *387*

CHAPTER XLII ***391***

>Pampeluna, Barcelona, Montjouy, and St. Sebastians, are fraudulently seized by the French—King Charles proposes to sail for South America—Insurrection at Aranjuez—Charles resigns the Crown in favour of Ferdinand—Murat enters Madrid—Charles disavows his resignation—General Savary arrives at Madrid—Napoleon's Letter to Murat, touching the Invasion of Spain—Ferdinand sets out to meet Napoleon—Halts at Vittoria, and learns too late Napoleon's designs

against him—Joins Buonaparte at Bayonne—Napoleon opens his designs to Escoiquiz and Cevallos, both of whom he finds intractable—He sends for Charles, his Queen, and Godoy, to Bayonne—Ferdinand is induced to abdicate the Crown in favour of his Father, who resigns it next day to Napoleon—This transfer is reluctantly confirmed by Ferdinand, who, with his Brothers, is sent to splendid imprisonment at Vallençay—Joseph Buonaparte is appointed to the throne of Spain, and joins Napoleon at Bayonne—Assembly of Notables convoked........ 391

SEIZURE OF SPANISH FORTRESSES. 391
MURAT APPROACHES MADRID. 395
SAVARY—MURAT. 397
LETTER TO MURAT. 398
BAYONNE. 403
ESCOIQUIZ—CEVALLOS. 404
INTERVIEW AT BAYONNE. 408
LUCIEN BUONAPARTE. 411

CHAPTER XLIII 415

State of morals and manners in Spain—The Nobility—the Middle Classes—the Lower Ranks—the indignation of the People strongly excited against the French—Insurrection at Madrid on the 2d May—Murat proclaims an amnesty, notwithstanding which, many Spanish prisoners are put to death—King Charles appoints Murat Lieutenant-General of the Kingdom, and Ferdinand's resignation of the throne is announced—Murat unfolds the plan of government to the Council of Castile, and addresses of submission are sent to Buonaparte from various quarters—Notables appointed to meet at Bayonne on 15th June—The flame of resistance becomes universal throughout Spain. 415

MORALS AND MANNERS IN SPAIN. 415
INSURRECTION AT MADRID. 419
MURDER OF SOLANO—PROVISIONAL JUNTAS. 422
ARRIVAL OF JOSEPH BUONAPARTE. 425

CHAPTER XLIV 429

Plans of Defence of the Spanish Juntas—defeated by the ardour of the Insurrectionary Armies—Cruelty of the French Troops, and Inveteracy of the Spaniards—Successes of the Invaders—Defeat of Rio Secco—Exultation of Napoleon—Joseph enters Madrid—His reception—Duhesme compelled to retreat to Barcelona, and Moncey from before Valencia—Defeat of Dupont by Castanos at Baylen—His Army surrenders Prisoners of War—Effects of this Victory and Capitulation—Unreasonable Expectations of the British Public—Joseph leaves Madrid, and retires to Vittoria—Defence of Zaragossa. 429

PLANS OF THE JUNTAS. ...429
THE INSURRECTIONARY ARMIES. ...430
VALENCIA. ...434
BAYLEN. ...436
SIEGE OF ZARAGOSSA. ...440

CHAPTER XLV ...443

Zeal of Britain with regard to the Spanish struggle—It is resolved to send an Expedition to Portugal—Retrospect of what had passed in that Country—Portuguese Assembly of Notables summoned to Bayonne—Their Singular Audience of Buonaparte—Effects of the Spanish Success on Portugal—Sir Arthur Wellesley—His Character as a General—Despatched at the head of the Expedition to Portugal—Attacks and defeats the French at Roriça—Battle and victory of Vimeiro—Sir Harry Burrard Neale assumes the command, and frustrates the results proposed by Sir Arthur Wellesley from the Battle—Sir Harry Burrard is superseded by Sir Hew Dalrymple—Convention of Cintra—Its Unpopularity in England—A Court of Inquiry is held. ...443

BRITISH EXPEDITION TO PORTUGAL. ...445
PORTUGAL. ...445
SIR ARTHUR WELLESLEY. ...449
ACTION OF RORIÇA. ...452
BATTLE OF VIMEIRO. ...454
CONVENTION OF CINTRA. ...458

CHAPTER XLVI ...459

Duplicity of Buonaparte on his return to Paris—Official Statements in the Moniteur—Reports issued by Champagny, Minister of the Foreign Department—French Relations with the different Powers of Europe—Spirit of Resistance throughout Germany—Russia—Napoleon and Alexander meet at Erfurt on 27th September, and separate in apparent Friendship on 17th October—Actual feelings of the Autocrats—Their joint Letter to the King of Great Britain proposing a general peace on the principle of uti possidetis—Why rejected—Procedure in Spain—Catalonia—Return of Romana to Spain—Armies of Blake, Castanos, and Palafox—Expedition of General Moore—His desponding Views of the Spanish Cause—His Plans—Defeat of Blake—and Castanos—Treachery of Morla—Sir John Moore retreats to Corunna—Disasters on the March—Battle of Corunna, and Death of Sir John Moore. ...459

STATEMENTS IN THE MONITEUR. ...461
CHAMPAGNY'S REPORTS—CONSCRIPTION. ...462
GERMANY. ...465
CONFERENCES AT ERFURT—SPAIN. ...467

SPAIN. 469
SPANISH ARMIES—OVERTURES OF PEACE. 473
SIR JOHN MOORE. 475
BATTLE OF TUDELA. 479
THE BRITISH ARMY—MADRID. 480
RETREAT OF THE BRITISH ARMY. 482

CHAPTER XLVII **489**

General Belliard occupies Madrid—Napoleon returns to France—Cause of his hurried return—View of the Circumstances leading to a Rupture with Austria—Feelings of Russia upon this occasion—Secret intrigues of Talleyrand to preserve Peace—Immense exertions made by Austria—Counter efforts of Buonaparte—The Austrian Army enters Bavaria, 9th April, 1809—Napoleon hastens to meet them—Austrians defeated at Abensberg on the 20th—and at Eckmühl on the 22d—They are driven out of Ratisbon on the 23d—The Archduke Charles retreats into Bohemia—Napoleon pushes forward to Vienna—which, after a brief defence, is occupied by the French on the 12th of May—Retrospect of the events of the War in Poland, Italy, the North of Germany, and the Tyrol—Enterprises of Schill—of the Duke of Brunswick Oels—Movements in the Tyrol—Character and Manners of the Tyrolese—Retreat of the Archduke John into Hungary. 489

MADRID. 489
VALLADOLID. 491
AUSTRIA. 493
EXERTIONS OF AUSTRIA. 496
ACTION OF ABENSBERG. 498
RETREAT OF THE AUSTRIANS. 503
VIENNA. 505
SCHILL—KATT—DUKE OF BRUNSWICK OELS. 506
THE TYROLESE. 509

CHAPTER XLVIII **513**

Position of the French and Austrian Armies after the Battle of Eckmühl—Napoleon crosses the Danube—Great Conflict at Asperne, when victory was claimed by both parties—Battle of Wagram fought 6th July—Armistice concluded at Znaim—Close of the Career of Schill and the Duke of Brunswick Oels—Defence of the Tyrol—Its final unfortunate result—Growing resistance throughout Germany—Its effects on Buonaparte—He publishes a singular Manifesto in the Moniteur. 513

PASSAGE OF THE DANUBE. 513
BATTLE OF ESSLING. 517

DEATH OF LANNES. 520
THE DANUBE. 521
BATTLE OF WAGRAM. 524
THE DUKE OF BRUNSWICK OELS. 527
RISING IN THE TYROL. 529
REVOLUTIONARY MOVEMENTS. 531

APPENDIX. 535

No. I. 535

INSTRUCTIONS BY NAPOLEON TO TALLEYRAND, PRINCE OF BENEVENTUM.
.... 535

No. II. 538

FURTHER PARTICULARS CONCERNING THE ARREST, TRIAL, AND DEATH OF THE DUKE D'ENGHIEN. 538
ARREST OF THE DUKE D'ENGHIEN. 541
INCOMPETENCY OF THE COURT. 542
IRREGULARITIES IN THE PROCEDURE. 543
DEFECTS OF THE SENTENCE. 544
VERDICT. 549
SENTENCE. 551
EXECUTION. 556
GENERAL VIEW OF THE PROCEDURE. 557

Chapter XXV

Increasing Jealousies betwixt France and England—Encroachments on the part of the former—Instructions given by the First Consul to his Commercial Agents—Orders issued by the English Ministers—Peltier's celebrated Royalist Publication, L'Ambigu—Peltier tried for a Libel against the First Consul—found Guilty—Angry Discussions respecting the Treaty of Amiens—Malta—Report of Sebastiani—Resolution of the British Government—Conferences betwixt Buonaparte and Lord Whitworth—Britain declares War against France on 18th May, 1803.

These advances towards universal empire, made during the very period when the pacific measures adopted by the preliminaries, and afterwards confirmed by the treaty of Amiens, were in the act of being carried into execution, excited the natural jealousy of the people of Britain. They had not been accustomed to rely much on the sincerity of the French nation; nor did the character of its present chief, so full of ambition, and so bold and successful in his enterprises, incline them to feelings of greater security. On the other hand, Buonaparte seems to have felt as matter of personal offence the jealousy which the British entertained; and instead of soothing it, as policy dictated, by concessions and confidence, he showed a disposition to repress, or at least to punish it, by measures which indicated anger and irritation. There ceased to be any cordiality of intercourse between the two nations, and they began to look into the conduct of each other for causes of offence, rather than for the means of removing it.

The English had several subjects of complaint against France, besides the general encroachments which she had continued to make on the liberties of Europe. A law had been made during the times of the wildest Jacobinism, which condemned to forfeiture every vessel under a hundred tons burden, carrying British merchandise, and approaching within four leagues of France. It was now thought proper, that the enforcing a regulation of so hostile a character, made during a war of unexampled bitterness, should be the first fruits of returning peace. Several British vessels were stopped, their captains imprisoned, their cargoes confiscated, and all restitution refused. Some of these had been driven on the French coast unwillingly, and by stress of weather; but the necessity of the case created no exemption. An instance there was of a British vessel in ballast, which entered Charente, in order to load with a cargo of brandy. The plates, knives, forks, &c., used by the captain, being found to be of British manufacture, the circumstance was thought a sufficient apology for seizing the vessel. These aggressions, repeatedly made, were not, so far as appears, remedied on the most urgent remonstrances, and seemed to argue that the French were already acting on the vexatious and irritating principle which often precedes a war, but very seldom immediately follows a peace. The conduct of France was felt to be the more unreasonable and ungracious, as all restrictions on her commerce, imposed during the war, had been withdrawn on the part of Great Britain, so soon as the peace was concluded. In like manner, a stipulation of the treaty of Amiens, providing that all sequestrations imposed on the property of French or of English, in the two contending countries, should be removed, was instantly complied with in Britain, but postponed and dallied with on the part of France.

COMMERCIAL AGENTS

The above were vexatious and offensive measures, intimating little respect for the Government of England, and no desire to cultivate her good will. They were perhaps adopted by the chief consul, in hopes of inducing Britain to make some sacrifices in order to obtain from his favour a commercial treaty, the advantages of which, according to his opinion of the English nation, was a boon calculated to make them quickly forgive the humiliating restrictions from which it would emancipate their trade. If this were any part of his policy, he was ignorant of the nature of the people to whom it was applied. It is the sluggish ox alone that is governed by a goad. But what gave the deepest offence and most lively alarm to Britain, was, that while Buonaparte declined affording the ordinary facilities for English commerce, it was his purpose, nevertheless, to establish a commercial agent in every part of the British dominions, whose ostensible duty was to watch over that very trade which the first consul showed so little desire to encourage, but whose real business resembled that of an accredited and privileged spy. These official persons were not only, by their instructions, directed to collect every possible information on commercial points, but also to furnish a plan of the ports of each district, with all the soundings, and to point out with what wind vessels could go out and enter with most ease, and at what draught of water the harbour might be entered by ships of burden. To add to the alarming character of such a set of agents, it was found that those invested with the office were military men and engineers.

Consuls thus nominated had reached Britain, but had not, in general, occupied the posts assigned to them, when the British Government, becoming informed of the duties they were expected to perform, announced to them, that any one who might repair to a British seaport under such a character, should be instantly ordered to quit the island. The secrecy with which these agents had been instructed to conduct themselves was so great, that one Fauvelet, to whom the office of commercial agent at Dublin had been assigned, and who had reached the place of his destination before the nature of the appointment was discovered, could not be found out by some persons who desired to make an affidavit before him as consul of France. It can be no wonder that the very worst impression was made on the public mind of Britain respecting the further projects of her late enemies, when it was evident that they availed themselves of the first moments of returning peace to procure, by an indirect and most suspicious course of proceeding, that species of information, which would be most useful to France, and most dangerous to Britain, in the event of a renewed war.

While these grievances and circumstances of suspicion agitated the English nation, the daily press, which alternately acts upon public opinion, and is reacted upon by it, was loud and vehement. The personal character of the chief consul was severely treated; his measures of self-aggrandisement arraigned, his aggressions on the liberty of France, of Italy, and especially of Switzerland, held up to open day; while every instance of petty vexation and oppression practised upon British commerce or British subjects, was quoted as expressing his deep resentment against the only country which possessed the will and the power to counteract his acquiring the universal dominion of Europe.

There was at this period in Britain a large party of French Royalists, who, declining to return to France, or falling under the exceptions to the amnesty, regarded Buonaparte as their personal enemy, as well as the main obstacle to the restoration of the Bourbons, to which, but for him only, the people of France seemed otherwise more disposed than at any time since the commencement of the Revolution. These gentlemen found an able and active advocate of their cause in Monsieur Peltier, an emigrant, a determined royalist, and a man of that ready wit and vivacity of talent which is peculiarly calculated for periodical writing. He had opposed the democrats during the early days of the Revolution, by a publication termed the "Acts of the Apostles;"[1] in which he held up to ridicule and execration the actions, pretensions, and principles of their leaders, with such success as induced Brissot to assert, that he had done more harm to the Republican cause than all the allied armies. At the present crisis, he commenced the publication of a weekly paper in London, in the French language, called *L'Ambigu*. The decoration at the top of the sheet was a head of Buonaparte, placed on the body of a Sphinx. This ornament being objected to after the first two or three numbers, the Sphinx appeared with the neck truncated; but, being still decked with the consular emblems, continued to intimate emblematically the allusion at once to Egypt, and to the ambiguous character of the first consul. The columns of this paper were dedicated to the most severe attacks upon Buonaparte and the French Government; and as it was highly popular, from the general feelings of the English nation towards both, it was widely dispersed and generally read.

---

[1] The "Actes des Apôtres," which appeared in 1790, and in the editing of which Peltier was assisted by Riverol, Champcenetz, and the Viscount Mirabeau, was principally directed against the measures of the Constituent Assembly.

The torrent of satire and abuse poured forth from the English and Anglo-Gallican periodical press, was calculated deeply to annoy and irritate the person against whom it was chiefly aimed. In England we are so much accustomed to see characters the most unimpeachable, nay, the most venerable, assailed by the daily press, that we account the individual guilty of folly, who, if he be innocent of giving cause for the scandal, takes it to heart more than a passenger would mind the barking of a dog, that yelps at every passing sound. But this is a sentiment acquired partly by habit, partly by our knowledge, that unsubstantiated scandal of this sort makes no impression on the public mind. Such indifference cannot be expected on the part of foreigners, who, in this particular, resemble horses introduced from neighbouring counties into the precincts of forest districts, where they are liable to be stung into madness by a peculiar species of gadfly, to which the race bred in the country are from habit almost totally indifferent.

If it be thus with foreigners in general, it must be supposed that from natural impatience of censure, as well as rendered susceptible and irritable by his course of uninterrupted success, Napoleon Buonaparte must have winced under the animated and sustained attacks upon his person and government, which appeared in the English newspapers, and Peltier's *Ambigu*. He attached at all times, as we have already had occasion to remark, much importance to the influence of the press, which in Paris he had taken under his own especial superintendence, and for which he himself often condescended to compose or correct paragraphs. To be assailed, therefore, by the whole body of British newspapers, almost as numerous as their navy, seems to have provoked him to the extremity of his patience; and resentment of these attacks aggravated the same hostile sentiments against England, which, from causes of suspicion already mentioned, had begun to be engendered in the British public against France and her ruler.

Napoleon, in the meantime, endeavoured to answer in kind, and the columns of the *Moniteur* had many an angry and violent passage directed against England.[2] Answers, replies, and rejoinders

---

[2] "I made the *Moniteur* the soul and life-blood of my government; it was the intermediate instrument of my communications with public opinion, both at home and abroad. Did any

passed rapidly across the Channel, inflaming and augmenting the hostile spirit, reciprocally entertained by the two countries against each other. But there was this great disadvantage on Buonaparte's side, that while the English might justly throw the blame of this scandalous warfare on the license of a free press, the chief consul could not transfer the responsibility of the attack on his side; because it was universally known that the French periodical publications being under the most severe regulations, nothing could appear in them except what had received the previous sanction of the government. Every attack upon England, therefore, which was published in the French papers, was held to express the personal sentiments of the chief consul, who thus, by destroying the freedom of the French press, had rendered himself answerable for every such license as it was permitted to take.

NOTE BY M. OTTO

July 25.

It became speedily plain, that Buonaparte could reap no advantage from a contest in which he was to be the defendant in his own person, and to maintain a literary warfare with anonymous antagonists. He had recourse, therefore, to a demand upon the British Government, and after various representations of milder import, caused his envoy, Monsieur Otto, to state in an official note the following distinct grievances:—First, the existence of a deep and continued system to injure the character of the first consul, and prejudice the effect of his public measures, through the medium of the press: Secondly, the permission of a part of the Princes of the House of Bourbon, and their adherents, to remain in England for the purpose, (it was alleged,) that they might hatch and encourage schemes against the life and government of the chief consul. It was

---

question arise respecting certain grand political combinations, or some delicate points of diplomacy? the objects were indirectly hinted at in the *Moniteur*. They instantly attracted universal attention, and became the topics of general investigation. The *Moniteur* has been reproached for the acrimony and virulence of its notes against the enemy: but before we condemn them, we are bound to take into consideration the benefits they may have produced, the anxiety with which they occasionally perplexed the enemy, the terror with which they struck a hesitating cabinet."—Napoleon, *Las Cases*, tom. iv., p. 186.

therefore categorically demanded, 1st, That the British Government do put a stop to the publication of the abuse complained of, as affecting the head of the French Government. 2d, That the emigrants residing in Jersey be dismissed from England—that the bishops who had declined to resign their sees be also sent out of the country—that George Cadoudal be transported to Canada—that the Princes of the House of Bourbon be advised to repair to Warsaw, where the head of their family now resided—and, finally, that such emigrants who continued to wear the ancient badges and decorations of the French court, be also compelled to leave England. Lest the British ministers should plead, that the constitution of their country precluded them from gratifying the first consul in any of these demands, Monsieur Otto forestalled the objection, by reminding them that the Alien Act gave them full power to exclude any foreigners from Great Britain at their pleasure.[3]

To this peremptory mandate, Lord Hawkesbury,[4] then minister for foreign affairs, instructed the British agent, Mr. Merry, to make a reply, at once firm and conciliatory; avoiding the tone of pique and ill temper which is plainly to be traced in the French note, yet maintaining the dignity of the nation he represented. It was observed, that, if the French Government had reason to complain of the license of the English journals, the British Government had no less right to be dissatisfied with the retorts and recriminations which had been poured out from those of Paris; and that there was this remarkable feature of difference betwixt them, that the English Ministry neither had, could have, nor wished to have, any control over the freedom of the British press; whereas the *Moniteur*, in which the abuse of England had appeared, was the official organ of the French Government. But, finally, upon this point, the British Monarch, it was said, would make no concession to any foreign power, at the expense of the freedom of the press.[5] If what was published was libellous or actionable, the printers and publishers

---

[3] Annual Register, vol. xlv., p. 659.
[4] Afterwards Earl of Liverpool, and Prime Minister of England—who died early in 1827.
[5] "His Majesty cannot, and never will, in consequence of any representation or menace from a foreign power, make any concession which can be, in the smallest degree, dangerous to the liberty of the press, as secured by the constitution of the country—a liberty justly dear to every British subject."—*Annual Register*, vol. xlv., p. 664.

were open to punishment, and all reasonable facilities would be afforded for prosecuting them. To the demands so peremptorily urged, respecting the emigrants, Lord Hawkesbury replied, by special answers applying to the different classes, but summed up in the general argument, that his Majesty neither encouraged them in any scheme against the French Government, nor did he believe there were any such in existence; and that while these unfortunate princes and their followers lived in conformity to the laws of Great Britain, and without affording nations with whom she was at peace any valid or sufficient cause of complaint, his Majesty would feel it inconsistent with his dignity, his honour, and the common laws of hospitality, to deprive them of that protection, which individuals resident within the British dominions could only forfeit by their own misconduct.[6]

TRIAL OF PELTIER

To render these answers, being the only reply which an English Minister could have made to the demands of France, in some degree acceptable to Buonaparte, Peltier was brought to trial[7] for a libel against the first consul, at the instance of the Attorney-General. He was defended by Mr. Mackintosh, (now Sir James,)[8] in one of the most brilliant speeches ever made at bar or in forum, in which the jury were reminded, that every press on the continent was enslaved, from Palermo to Hamburgh, and that they were now to vindicate the right we had ever asserted, to speak of men both at home and abroad, not according to their greatness, but their crimes.

---

[6] "The French Government must have formed a most erroneous judgment of the disposition of the British nation, and of the character of its Government, if they have been taught to expect that any representation of a foreign power will ever induce them to a violation of those rights on which the liberties of the people of this country are founded."—*Ibid.*, p. 666.

[7] The trial took place in the Court of King's Bench, Feb. 21, before Lord Ellenborough and a special jury.

[8] The Right Hon. Sir James Mackintosh, died May 30, 1832.

The defendant was found guilty; but his cause might be considered as triumphant.[9] Accordingly, every part of the proceedings gave offence to Buonaparte. He had not desired to be righted by the English law, but by a vigour beyond the law. The publicity of the trial, the wit and eloquence of the advocate, were ill calculated to soothe the feelings of Buonaparte, who knew human nature, and the character of his usurped power, too well, to suppose that public discussion could be of service to him.[10] He had demanded darkness, the English Government had answered by giving him light; he had wished, like those who are conscious of flaws in their conduct, to suppress all censure of his measures, and by Peltier's trial, the British ministers had made the investigation of them a point of legal necessity. The first consul felt the consciousness that he himself, rather than Peltier,[11] was tried before the British public, with a publicity which could not fail to blaze abroad the discussion. Far from conceiving himself obliged by the species of atonement which had been offered him, he deemed the offence of the original publication was greatly aggravated, and placed it now directly to the account of the English ministers, of whom he could never be made to understand, that they had afforded him the only remedy in their power.

The paragraphs hostile to England in the *Moniteur* were continued; an English paper called the *Argus*, conducted by Irish refugees, was printed at Paris, under permission of the Government, for the purpose of assailing Britain with additional abuse, while the fire was returned from the English side of the Channel, with double vehemence and tenfold success. These were ominous precursors to

---

[9] He was never brought up to receive sentence, our quarrel with the French having soon afterwards come to an absolute rupture. [Peltier was a native of Nantes. On the restoration of the Bourbons, he returned to Paris, where he died in 1825.]

[10] "Thence the resentment which Buonaparte felt against England. 'Every wind which blows,' said he, 'from that direction, brings nothing but contempt and hatred against my person.' From that time he concluded that the peace could not benefit him; that it would not leave him sufficient facility to aggrandize his dominion externally, and would impede the extension of his internal power; that, moreover, our daily relations with England modified our political ideas and revived our thoughts of liberty."—Fouché, tom. i., p. 257.

[11] "When Napoleon was shown, at St. Helena, some numbers of *L'Ambigu*, he said, 'Ah! Peltier. He has been libelling me these twenty years: but I am very glad to get them.'"— O'Meara, vol. i., p. 385.

a state of peace, and more grounds of misunderstanding were daily added.

The new discussions related chiefly to the execution of the treaty of Amiens, in which the English Government showed no promptitude. Most of the French colonies, it is true, had been restored; but the Cape, and the other Batavian settlements, above all, the island of Malta, were still possessed by the British forces. At common law, if the expression may be used, England was bound instantly to redeem her engagement, by ceding these possessions, and thus fulfilling the articles of the treaty. In equity, she had a good defence; since in policy for herself and Europe, she was bound to decline the cession at all risks.

The recent acquisitions of France on the continent, afforded the plea of equity to which we have alluded. It was founded on the principle adopted at the treaty of Amiens, that Great Britain should, out of her conquests over the enemy's foreign settlements, retain so much as to counterbalance, in some measure, the power which France had acquired in Europe. This principle being once established, it followed that the compact at Amiens had reference to the then existing state of things; and since, after that period, France had extended her sway over Italy and Piedmont, England became thereby entitled to retain an additional compensation, in consequence of France's additional acquisitions. This was the true and simple position of the case; France had innovated upon the state of things which existed when the treaty was made, and England might, therefore, in justice, claim an equitable right to innovate upon the treaty itself, by refusing to make surrender of what had been promised in other and very different circumstances. Perhaps it had been better to fix upon this obvious principle, as the ground of declining to surrender such British conquests as were not yet given up, unless France consented to relinquish the power which she had usurped upon the continent. This, however, would have produced instant war; and the Ministers were naturally loth to abandon the prospect of prolonging the peace which had been so lately established, or to draw their pen through the treaty of Amiens, while the ink with which it was written was still moist. They yielded, therefore, in a great measure. The Cape of Good Hope and the

Dutch colonies were restored, Alexandria was evacuated, and the Ministers confined their discussions with France to the island of Malta only; and, condescending still farther, declared themselves ready to concede even this last point of discussion, providing a sufficient guarantee should be obtained for this important citadel of the Mediterranean being retained in neutral hands. The Order itself was in no respect adequate to the purpose; and as to the proposed Neapolitan garrison, (none of the most trustworthy in any case,) France, by her encroachments in Italy, had become so near and so formidable a neighbour to the King of Naples, that, by a threat of invasion of his capital, she might have compelled him to deliver up Malta upon a very brief notice. All this was urged on the part of Britain. The French Ministry, on the other hand, pressed for literal execution of the treaty. After some diplomatic evasions had been resorted to, it appeared as if the cession could be no longer deferred, when a publication appeared in the *Moniteur* [Jan. 30, 1803] which roused to a high pitch the suspicions as well as the indignation of the British nation.

SEBASTIANI'S REPORT

The publication alluded to was a report of General Sebastiani. This officer had been sent as the emissary of the first consul, to various Mahommedan courts in Asia and Africa, in all of which it seems to have been his object, not only to exalt the greatness of his master, but to misrepresent and degrade the character of England. He had visited Egypt, of which, with its fortresses, and the troops that defended them, he had made a complete survey. He then waited upon Djezzar Pacha, and gives a flattering account of his reception, and of the high esteem in which Djezzar held the first consul, whom he had so many reasons for wishing well to. At the Ionian Islands, he harangued the natives, and assured them of the protection of Buonaparte. The whole report is full of the most hostile expressions towards England, and accuses General Stuart of having encouraged the Turks to assassinate the writer. Wherever Sebastiani went, he states himself to have interfered in the factions and quarrels of the country; he inquired into its forces; renewed old intimacies, or made new ones with leading persons; enhanced his master's power, and was liberal in promises of French aid. He concludes, that a French army of six thousand men would be sufficient to conquer Egypt, and that the Ionian Islands were altogether attached to the French interest.[12]

The publication of this report, which seemed as if Buonaparte were blazoning forth to the world his unaltered determination to persist in his Eastern projects of colonization and conquest, would have rendered it an act of treason in the English Ministers, if, by the cession of Malta, they had put into his hand, or at least placed within his grasp, the readiest means of carrying into execution those gigantic schemes of ambition, which had for their ultimate, perhaps their most desired object, the destruction of the Indian commerce of Britain.

As it were by way of corollary to the gasconading journal of Sebastiani, an elaborate account of the forces, and natural advantages of France, was published at the same period, which, in order that there might be no doubt concerning the purpose of its appearance at this crisis, was summed up by the express conclusion, "that Britain was unable to contend with France single-handed."[13] This tone of defiance, officially adopted at such a moment, added not a little to the resentment of the English nation, not accustomed to decline a challenge or endure an insult.

The Court of Britain on the appearance of this Report on the State of France, together with that of Sebastiani, drawn up and subscribed by an official agent, containing insinuations totally void of foundation, and disclosing intrigues inconsistent with the preservation of peace, and the objects for which peace had been made, declared that the King would enter into no farther discussion on the subject of Malta, until his Majesty had received the most ample satisfaction for this new and singular aggression.[14]

---

[12] For a copy of Sebastiani's report to the first consul, see Annual Register, vol. xlv., p. 742.
[13] "Whatever success intrigues may experience in London, no other people will be involved in new combinations. The government says, with conscious truth, that England, single-handed, cannot maintain a struggle against France."—*View of the State of the Republic*, Feb. 22, 1803. See Annual Register, vol. xlv., p. 760.
[14] See Declaration, dated Westminster, May 18, 1803; Annual Register, vol. xlv., p. 742.

While things were thus rapidly approaching to a rupture, the chief consul adopted the unusual resolution, of himself entering personally into conference with the British ambassador. He probably took this determination upon the same grounds which dictated his contempt of customary forms, in entering, or attempting to enter, into direct correspondence with the princes whom he had occasion to treat with. Such a deviation from the established mode of procedure seemed to mark his elevation above ordinary rules, and would afford him, he might think, an opportunity of bearing down the British ambassador's reasoning, by exhibiting one of those bursts of passion, to which he had been accustomed to see most men give way.

It would have been more prudent in Napoleon, to have left the conduct of the negotiation to Talleyrand.[15] A sovereign cannot enter in person upon such conferences, unless with the previous determination of adhering precisely and finally to whatever ultimatum he has to propose. He cannot, without a compromise of dignity, chaffer or capitulate, or even argue, and of course is incapable of wielding any of the usual, and almost indispensable weapons of negotiators. If it was Napoleon's expectation, by one stunning and emphatic declaration of his pleasure, to beat down all arguments, and confound all opposition, he would have done wisely to remember, that he was not now, as in other cases, a general upon a victorious field of battle, dictating terms to a defeated enemy; but was treating upon a footing of equality with Britain, the mistress of the seas, possessing strength as formidable as his own, though of a different character, and whose prince and people were far more likely to be incensed than intimidated by any menaces which his passion might throw out.

---

[15] "The conference with Lord Whitworth proved for me a lesson which altered my method for ever. From this moment I never treated officially of political affairs, but through the intervention of my minister for foreign affairs. He, at any rate, could give a positive and formal denial, which the sovereign could not do."—Napoleon, tom. iv., p. 156.

LORD WHITWORTH

The character of the English ambassador was as unfavourable for the chief consul's probable purpose, as that of the nation he represented. Lord Whitworth was possessed of great experience and sagacity.[16] His integrity and honour were undoubted; and, with the highest degree of courage, he had a calm and collected disposition, admirably calculated to give him the advantage in any discussion with an antagonist of a fiery, impatient, and over-bearing temper.

We will make no apology for dwelling at unusual length on the conferences betwixt the first consul and Lord Whitworth, as they are strikingly illustrative of the character of Buonaparte, and were, in their consequences, decisive of his fate, and that of the world.

Their first interview of a political nature took place in the Tuileries, 17th February, 1803. Buonaparte, having announced that this meeting was for the purpose of "making his sentiments known to the King of England in a clear and authentic manner," proceeded to talk incessantly for the space of nearly two hours, not without considerable incoherence, his temper rising as he dwelt on the alleged causes of complaint which he preferred against England, though not so much or so incautiously as to make him drop the usual tone of courtesy to the ambassador.

He complained of the delay of the British in evacuating Alexandria and Malta; cutting short all discussion on the latter subject, by declaring he would as soon agree to Britain's possessing the suburb of St. Antoine as that island. He then referred to the abuse thrown upon him by the English papers, but more especially by those French journals published in London. He affirmed that Georges and other Chouan chiefs, whom he accused of designs against his life, received relief or shelter in England; and that two assassins had been apprehended in Normandy, sent over by the

---

[16] Lord Whitworth had been, successively,—in 1786, minister plenipotentiary at Warsaw,—in 1788, envoy extraordinary and minister plenipotentiary to St. Petersburgh,—and, in 1800, minister plenipotentiary to the court of Denmark.

French emigrants to murder him. This, he said, would be publicly proved in a court of justice. From this point he diverged to Egypt, of which he affirmed he could make himself master whenever he had a mind; but that he considered it too paltry a stake to renew the war for. Yet, while on this subject, he suffered it to escape him, that the idea of recovering this favourite colony was only postponed, not abandoned. "Egypt," he said, "must sooner or later belong to France, either by the falling to pieces of the Turkish government, or in consequence of some agreement with the Porte."[17] In evidence of his peaceable intentions, he asked, what he should gain by going to war, since he had no means of acting offensively against England, except by a descent, of which he acknowledged the hazard in the strongest terms. The chances, he said, were a hundred to one against him; and yet he declared that the attempt should be made if he were now obliged to go to war. He extolled the power of both countries. The army of France, he said, should be soon recruited to four hundred and eighty thousand men; and the fleets of England were such as he could not propose to match within the space of ten years at least. United, the two countries might govern the world, would they but understand each other. Had he found, he said, the least cordiality on the part of England, she should have had indemnities assigned her upon the continent, treaties of commerce, all that she could wish or desire. But he confessed that his irritation increased daily, "since every gale that blew from England, brought nothing but enmity and hatred against him."

He then made an excursive digression, in which, taking a review of the nations of Europe, he contended that England could hope for assistance from none of them in a war with France. In the total result, he demanded the instant implement of the treaty of Amiens, and the suppression of the abuse in the English papers. War was the alternative.

---

[17] "If Buonaparte had wished for the maintenance of peace, he would sedulously have avoided giving umbrage and inquietude to England, with regard to its Indian possessions, and would have abstained from applauding the rhodomontades about the mission of Sebastiani into Syria and Turkey. His imprudent conversation with Lord Whitworth accelerated the rupture. I foresaw, from that time, that he would quickly pass from a certain degree of moderation, as chief of the government, to acts of exaggeration, violence, and even rage."—Fouché, tom. i., p. 259.

During this excursive piece of declamation, which the first consul delivered with great rapidity, Lord Whitworth, notwithstanding the interview lasted two hours, had scarcely time to slide in a few words in reply or explanation. As he endeavoured to state the new grounds of mistrust which induced the King of England to demand more advantageous terms, in consequence of the accession of territory and influence which France had lately made, Napoleon interrupted him—"I suppose you mean Piedmont and Switzerland—they are trifling occurrences, which must have been foreseen while the negotiation was in dependence. You have no right to recur to them at this time of day." To the hint of indemnities which might be allotted to England out of the general spoil of Europe, if she would cultivate the friendship of Buonaparte, Lord Whitworth nobly answered, that the King of Britain's ambition led him to preserve what was his, not to acquire that which belonged to others. They parted with civility, but with a conviction on Lord Whitworth's part, that Buonaparte would never resign his claim to the possession of Malta.[18]

March 8.

The British Ministry were of the same opinion; for a Message was sent down by his Majesty to the House of Commons, stating, that he had occasion for additional aid to enable him to defend his dominions, in case of an encroachment on the part of France. A reason was given, which injured the cause of the Ministers, by placing the vindication of their measures upon simulated grounds;—it was stated, that these apprehensions arose from "military preparations carrying on in the ports of France and Holland."[19] No such preparations had been complained of during the intercourse between the ministers of France and England,—in truth, none such existed to any considerable extent,—and in so far, the British ministers gave the advantage to the French, by not resting the cause of their country on the just and true grounds. All, however, were sensible of the real merits of the dispute, which were grounded on the grasping and inordinate ambition of the French ruler, and the

---

[18] See Extract of a Despatch from Lord Whitworth to Lord Hawkesbury, dated Paris, Feb. 17; Annual Register, vol. xlv., p. 685.
[19] Annual Register, vol. xlv., p. 646.

sentiments of dislike and irritation with which he seemed to regard Great Britain.

The charge of the pretended naval preparations being triumphantly refuted by France, Talleyrand was next employed to place before Lord Whitworth the means which, in case of a rupture, France possessed of wounding England, not directly indeed, but through the sides of those states of Europe whom she would most wish to see, if not absolutely independent, yet unoppressed by military exactions. "It was *natural*," a note of this statesman asserted, "that Britain being armed in consequence of the King's message, France should arm also—that she should send an army into Holland—form an encampment on the frontiers of Hanover—continue to maintain troops in Switzerland—march others to the south of Italy, and, finally, form encampments upon the coast."[20] All these threats, excepting the last, referred to distant and to neutral nations, who were not alleged to have themselves given any cause of complaint to France; but who were now to be subjected to military occupation and exaction, because Britain desired to see them happy and independent, and because harassing and oppressing them must be in proportion unpleasing to her. It was an entirely new principle of warlike policy, which introduced the oppression of unoffending and neutral neighbours as a legitimate mode of carrying on war against a hostile power, against whom there was little possibility of using measures directly offensive.

Shortly after this note had been lodged, Buonaparte, incensed at the message of the King to Parliament, seems to have formed the scheme of bringing the protracted negotiations betwixt France and England to a point, in a time, place, and manner, equally extraordinary. At a public court held at the Tuileries, on the 13th March, the chief consul came up to Lord Whitworth in considerable agitation, and observed aloud, and within hearing of the circle,—"You are then determined on war?"—and, without attending to the disclamations of the English ambassador, proceeded,—"We have been at war for fifteen years—you are determined on hostility for

---

[20] Annual Register, vol. xlv., p. 697.

fifteen years more—and you force me to it."[21] He then addressed Count Marcow and the Chevalier Azara—"The English wish for war; but if they draw the sword first, I will be the last to return it to the scabbard. They do not respect treaties, which henceforth we must cover with black crape."[22] He then again addressed Lord Whitworth—"To what purpose are these armaments? Against whom do you take these measures of precaution? I have not a single ship of the line in any port in France: But if you arm, I too will take up arms—if you fight, I will fight—you may destroy France, but you cannot intimidate her."

"We desire neither the one nor the other," answered Lord Whitworth, calmly: "We desire to live with her on terms of good intelligence."

"You must respect treaties, then," said Buonaparte, sternly. "Woe to those by whom they are not respected! They will be accountable for the consequences to all Europe."

So saying, and repeating his last remark twice over, he retired from the levee, leaving the whole circle surprised at the want of decency and dignity which had given rise to such a scene.[23]

This remarkable explosion may be easily explained, if we refer it entirely to the impatience of a fiery temper, rendered, by the most extraordinary train of success, morbidly sensitive to any obstacle which interfered with a favourite plan; and, doubtless, it is not the least evil of arbitrary power, that he who possesses it is naturally tempted to mix up his own feelings of anger, revenge, or mortification, in affairs which ought to be treated under the most calm and impartial reference to the public good exclusively. But it

---

[21] "Nous avons," said he, "dejà fait la guerre pendant quinze ans." As he seemed to wait for an answer, I observed only, "C'en est dejà trop."—"Mais," said he, "vous voulez la faire encore quinze années; et vous m'y forcez."—Lord Whitworth to Lord Hawkesbury; see Annual Register, vol. xlv., p. 696.
[22] "Ils ne respectent pas les traités: il faut dorénavant les couvrir de crêpe noir."
[23] "The ambassador made a respectful bow, and gave no reply. The first consul left that part of the saloon; but whether he had been a little heated by this explosion of ill-humour, or from some other cause, he ceased his round, and withdrew to his own apartments. Madame Buonaparte followed; and in an instant the saloon was cleared of company."—Savary, tom. i., p. 307.

has been averred by those who had best opportunity to know Buonaparte, that the fits of violent passion which he sometimes displayed, were less the bursts of unrepressed and constitutional irritability, than means previously calculated upon to intimidate and astound those with whom he was treating at the time. There may, therefore, have been policy amid the first consul's indignation, and he may have recollected, that the dashing to pieces Cobentzel's china jar in the violent scene which preceded the signing of the treaty of Campo Formio,[24] was completely successful in its issue. But the condition of Britain was very different from that of Austria, and he might have broken all the porcelain at St. Cloud without making the slightest impression on the equanimity of Lord Whitworth. This "angry parle," therefore, went for nothing, unless in so far as it was considered as cutting off the faint remaining hope of peace, and expressing the violent and obstinate temper of the individual, upon whose pleasure, whether originating in judgment or caprice, the fate of Europe at this important crisis unhappily depended. In England, the interview at the Tuileries, where Britain was held to be insulted in the person of her ambassador, and that in the presence of the representatives of all Europe, greatly augmented the general spirit of resentment.[25]

Talleyrand, to whom Lord Whitworth applied for an explanation of the scene which had occurred, only answered, that the first consul, publicly affronted, as he conceived himself, desired to exculpate himself in presence of the ministers of all the powers of Europe.[26] The question of peace or war came now to turn on the subject of Malta. The retention of this fortress by the English could infer no danger to France; whereas, if parted with by them under an insecure guarantee, the great probability of its falling into the hands

---

[24] See *ante*, vol. ii., pp. 175, 176. "It is to be remarked, that all this passed loud enough to be heard by two hundred people who were present; and I am persuaded that there was not a single person who did not feel the impropriety of the first consul's conduct, and the total want of dignity, as well as of decency, on the occasion."—Lord Whitworth.
[25] "It is utterly incorrect, that any thing occurred in the course of our interview which was not in conformity with the common rules of decorum. Lord Whitworth himself, after our conference, being in company with other ambassadors, expressed himself perfectly satisfied, and added, that he had no doubt all things would be satisfactorily settled."—Napoleon, *Las Cases*, tom. iv., p. 157.
[26] For a copy of Napoleon's Instructions to Talleyrand, see Appendix to this Volume, No. I.

of France, was a subject of the most legitimate jealousy to Britain, who must always have regarded the occupation of Malta as a preliminary step to the recapture of Egypt. There seemed policy, therefore, in Napoleon's conceding this point, and obtaining for France that respite, which, while it regained her colonies and recruited her commerce, would have afforded her the means of renewing a navy, which had been almost totally destroyed during the war, and consequently of engaging England, at some future and propitious time, on the element which she called peculiarly her own. It was accordingly supposed to be Talleyrand's opinion, that, by giving way to England on the subject of Malta, Napoleon ought to lull her suspicions to sleep.

Yet there were strong reasons, besides the military character of Buonaparte, which might induce the first consul to break off negotiation. His empire was founded on the general opinion entertained of his inflexibility of purpose, and of his unvaried success, alike in political objects as in the field of battle. Were he to concede the principle which England now contested with him in the face of Europe, it would have in a certain degree derogated from the pre-eminence of the situation he claimed, as autocrat of the civilized world. In that character he could not recede an inch from pretensions which he had once asserted. To have allowed that his encroachment on Switzerland and Piedmont rendered it necessary that he should grant a compensation to England, by consenting to her retention of Malta, would have been to grant that Britain had still a right to interfere in the affairs of the continent, and to point her out to nations disposed to throw off the French yoke, as a power to whose mediation he still owed some deference. These reasons were not without force in themselves, and, joined to the natural impetuosity of Buonaparte's temper, irritated and stung by the attacks in the English papers, had their weight probably in inducing him to give way to that sally of resentment, by which he endeavoured to cut short the debate, as he would have brought up his guard in person to decide the fate of a long-disputed action.

Some lingering and hopeless attempts were made to carry on negotiations. The English Ministry lowered their claim of retaining Malta in perpetuity to their right of holding it for ten years.

Buonaparte, on the other hand, would listen to no modification of the treaty of Amiens, but offered, as the guarantee afforded by the occupation of Neapolitan troops was objected to, that the garrison should consist of Russians or Austrians. To this proposal Britain would not accede. Lord Whitworth left Paris, and, on the 18th May, 1803, Britain declared war against France.

Before we proceed to detail the history of this eventful struggle, we must cast our eyes backwards, and review some events of importance which had happened in France since the conclusion of the treaty of Amiens.

Chapter XXVI

St. Domingo—The Negroes split into parties under different Chiefs—Toussaint L'Ouverture the most distinguished of these—Appoints a Consular Government—France sends an Expedition against St. Domingo, under General Leclerc, in December 1801—Toussaint submits—He is sent to France, where he dies—The French are assaulted by the Negroes—Leclerc is succeeded by Rochambeau—The French finally obliged to capitulate to an English squadron—Buonaparte's scheme to consolidate his power—The Consular Guard augmented—Legion of Honour—Opposition formed against the Consular Government—Application to the Count de Provence (Louis XVIII.)

When the treaty of Amiens appeared to have restored peace to Europe, one of Buonaparte's first enterprises was to attempt the recovery of the French possessions in the large, rich, and valuable colony of St. Domingo, the disasters of which island form a terrible episode in the history of the war.

The convulsions of the French Revolution had reached St. Domingo, and, catching like fire to combustibles, had bred a violent feud between the white people in the island, and the mulattoes, the latter of whom demanded to be admitted into the privileges and immunities of the former; the newly established rights of men, as they alleged, having no reference to the distinction of colour. While the whites and the people of colour were thus engaged in a civil war, the negro slaves, the most oppressed and most numerous class of the population, rose against both parties, and rendered the whole island one scene of bloodshed and conflagration. The few planters who remained invited the support of the British arms, which easily effected a temporary conquest. But the European soldiery perished so fast through the influence of the climate, that, in 1798, the

English were glad to abandon an island which had proved the grave of so many of her best and bravest, who had fallen without a wound, and void of renown.

TOUSSAINT L'OUVERTURE

The negroes, left to themselves, divided into different parties, who submitted to the authority of chiefs more or less independent of each other, many of whom displayed considerable talent. Of these, the principal leader was Toussaint L'Ouverture, who, after waging war like a savage, appears to have used the power which victory procured him with much political skill. Although himself a negro, he had the sagacity to perceive how important it was for the civilisation of his subjects, that they should not be deprived of the opportunities of knowledge, and examples of industry, afforded them by the white people. He, therefore, protected and encouraged the latter, and established, as an equitable regulation, that the blacks, now freemen, should nevertheless continue to labour the plantations of the white colonists, while the produce of the estate should be divided in certain proportions betwixt the white proprietor and the sable cultivator.

The least transgressions of these regulations he punished with African ferocity. On one occasion, a white female, the owner of a plantation, had been murdered by the negroes by whom it was laboured, and who had formerly been her slaves. Toussaint marched to the spot at the head of a party of his horse-guards, collected the negroes belonging to the plantation, and surrounded them with his black cavalry, who, after a very brief inquiry, received orders to charge and cut them to pieces; of which order our informant witnessed the execution. His unrelenting rigour, joined to his natural sagacity, soon raised Toussaint to the chief command of the island; and he availed himself of the maritime peace, to consolidate his authority by establishing a constitution on the model most lately approved of in France, which being that of the year Eight, consisted of a consular government. Toussaint failed not, of course, to assume the supreme government to himself, with power to name his successor. The whole was a parody on the procedure of Buonaparte, which, doubtless, the latter was not highly pleased with;[27] for there are many cases in which an imitation by others, of the conduct we ourselves have held, is a matter not of compliment, but of the most severe satire. The constitution of St. Domingo was instantly put in force, although, with an ostensible deference to France, the sanction of her Government had been ceremoniously required. It was evident that the African, though not unwilling to acknowledge some nominal degree of sovereignty on the part of France, was determined to retain in his own hands the effective government of the colony. But this in no respect consisted with the plans of Buonaparte, who was impatient to restore to France those possessions of which the British naval superiority had so long deprived her—colonies, shipping, and commerce.[28]

A powerful expedition was fitted out at the harbours of Brest, L'Orient, and Rochefort, destined to restore St. Domingo in full subjection to the French empire. The fleet amounted to thirty-four ships bearing forty guns and upwards, with more than twenty frigates and smaller armed vessels. They had on board above twenty thousand men, and General Leclerc, the brother-in-law of the first consul, was named commander-in-chief of the expedition, having a staff composed of officers of acknowledged skill and bravery.

It is said that Buonaparte had the art to employ a considerable proportion of the troops which composed the late army of the Rhine, in this distant expedition to an insalubrious climate.[29] But he

---

[27] "To give an idea of the indignation which the first consul must have felt, it may suffice to mention, that Toussaint not only assumed authority over the colony during his life, but invested himself with the right of naming his successor; and pretended to hold his authority, not from the mother-country, but from a *soi-disant* colonial assembly which he had created."—Napoleon, *Montholon*, tom. i., p. 203.

[28] "The party of the colonists was very powerful in Paris: public opinion required the possession of St. Domingo. On the other hand, the first consul was not sorry to dissipate the apprehensions of the English, by sending 15,000 men to St. Domingo. These 15,000 men would have succeeded, had it not been for the yellow fever. If Toussaint, Dessalines, and Christophe had chosen to submit, they would have secured their liberty, rank, and fortune, as well as those of the people of their colour; the freedom of the blacks would have been securely confirmed."—Napoleon, *Montholon*, tom. ii., p. 218.

[29] "The first consul ardently seized the happy opportunity of sending away a great number of officers, formed in the school of Moreau, whose reputation pained him, and whose influence with the army, if not a subject of alarm, was at least to him one of restraint and inquietude. 'Well,' said Buonaparte to me one day, 'your Jacobins malignantly say, that they

would not permit it to be supposed, that there was the least danger; and he exercised an act of family authority on the subject, to prove that such were his real sentiments. His sister, the beautiful Pauline, afterwards the wife of Prince Borghese, showed the utmost reluctance to accompany her present husband, General Leclerc, upon the expedition, and only went on board when actually compelled to do so by the positive orders of the first consul, who, although she was his favourite sister, was yet better contented that she should share the general risk, than, by remaining behind, leave it to be inferred that he himself augured a disastrous conclusion to the expedition.

The armament set sail on the 14th of December, 1801, while an English squadron of observation, uncertain of their purpose, waited upon and watched their progress to the West Indies. The French fleet presented themselves before Cape François, on the 29th of January, 1802.

Toussaint, summoned to surrender, seemed at first inclined to come to an agreement, terrified probably by the great force of the expedition, which time and the climate could alone afford the negroes any chance of resisting. A letter was delivered to him from the first consul, expressing esteem for his person; and General Leclerc offered him the most favourable terms, together with the situation of lieutenant-governor. Ultimately, however, Toussaint could not make up his mind to trust the French, and he determined upon resistance, which he managed with considerable skill. Nevertheless, the well-concerted military operations of the whites soon overpowered for the present the resistance of Toussaint and his followers. Chief after chief surrendered, and submitted themselves to General Leclerc. At length, Toussaint L'Ouverture himself seems to have despaired of being able to make further or more effectual resistance. He made his formal submission, and received and accepted Leclerc's pardon, under the condition that he should retire to a plantation at Gonaives, and never leave it without permission of the commander-in-chief.

---

are the soldiers and friends of Moreau whom I am sending to perish at St. Domingo; they are grumbling maniacs; let them talk on.'"—Fouché, tom. i., p. 217.

DEATH OF TOUSSAINT

The French had not long had possession of the colony, ere they discovered, or supposed they had discovered, symptoms of a conspiracy amongst the negroes, and Toussaint was, on very slight grounds, accused as encouraging a revolt. Under this allegation, the only proof of which was a letter, capable of an innocent interpretation, the unfortunate chief was seized upon, with his whole family, and put on board of a vessel bound to France. Nothing official was ever learned concerning his fate, farther than that he was imprisoned in the Castle of Joux, in Franche Compté, where the unhappy African fell a victim to the severity of an Alpine climate,[30] to which he was unaccustomed, and the privations of a close confinement. The deed has been often quoted and referred to as one of the worst actions of Buonaparte, who ought, if not in justice, in generosity at least, to have had compassion on the man, whose fortunes bore, in many respects, a strong similarity to his own. It afforded but too strong a proof, that though humanity was often in Napoleon's mouth, and sometimes displayed in his actions, yet its maxims were seldom found sufficient to protect those whom he disliked or feared, from the fate which tyranny most willingly assigns to its victims, that of being silently removed from the living world, and enclosed in their prison as in a tomb, from which no complaints can be heard, and where they are to await the slow approach of death, like men who are literally buried alive.

The perfidy with which the French had conducted themselves towards Toussaint, was visited by early vengeance. That scourge of Europeans, the yellow fever, broke out among their troops, and in

---

[30] Anxiety, age, and a climate too severe for his constitution, soon put an end to his days. He died on April 27, 1803, after a captivity of ten months. His mysterious fate excited great interest—witness the noble sonnet of Wordsworth:— "Toussaint! the most unhappy man of men! Whether the all-cheering sun be free to shed His beams around thee, or thou rest thy head Pillow'd in some dark dungeon's noisome den— O, miserable chieftain! where and when Wilt thou find patience?—Yet die not; do thou Wear rather in thy bonds a cheerful brow: Though fallen thyself, never to rise again, Live and take comfort. Thou hast left behind Powers that will work for thee—Air, Earth, and Skies; There's not a breathing of the common wind That will forget thee; thou hast great allies; Thy friends are Exultations, Agonies, And Love, and Man's unconquerable Mind."

an incredible short space of time, swept off General Leclerc,[31] with many of his best officers and bravest soldiers. The negroes, incensed at the conduct of the governor towards Toussaint, and encouraged by the sickly condition of the French army, rose upon them in every quarter. A species of war ensued, of which we are thankful it is not our task to trace the deplorable and ghastly particulars. The cruelty which was perhaps to be expected in the savage Africans, just broke loose from the bondage of slavery, communicated itself to the civilized French. If the former tore out their prisoners' eyes with cork-screws, the latter drowned their captives by hundreds, which imitation of Carrier's republican baptism they called "deportation into the sea." On other occasions, numerous bodies of negroes were confined in hulks, and there smothered to death with the fumes of lighted sulphur. The issue of this hellish warfare was, that the cruelty of the French enraged, instead of terrifying their savage antagonists; and at length, that the numbers of the former, diminished by disease and constant skirmishing, became unequal to the defence even of the garrison towns of the island, much more so to the task of reconquering it. General Rochambeau, who succeeded Leclerc as commander-in-chief, was finally obliged to save the poor wreck of that fine army, by submitting at discretion to an English squadron, 1st December 1803. Thus was the richest colony in the West Indies finally lost to France.[32] Remaining entirely in the possession of the black population, St. Domingo will show, in process of time, how far the natives of Africa, having European civilisation within their reach, are capable of forming a state, governed by the usual rules of polity.

---

[31] "Leclerc was an officer of the first merit, equally skilful in the labours of the cabinet and in the manœuvres of the field of battle: he had served in the campaigns of 1796 and 1797 as adjutant-general to Napoleon; and in that of 1799 as a general of division under Moreau. He commanded at the battle of Freisingen, where he defeated the Archduke Ferdinand; he led into Spain an army of observation, of 20,000 men, intended to act against Portugal; finally, in this expedition of St. Domingo, he displayed great talent and activity."—Napoleon, tom. i., p. 211.
[32] "I have to reproach myself with the attempt made upon the colony during the Consulship. The design of reducing it by force was a great error. I ought to have been satisfied with governing it through the medium of Toussaint."—Napoleon, *Las Cases*, tom. iv., p. 171.

COURT OF THE TUILERIES

While Buonaparte made these strong efforts for repossessing France in this fine colony, it was not to be supposed that he was neglecting the establishment of his own power upon a more firm basis. His present situation was—like every other in life—considerably short of what he could have desired, though so infinitely superior to all that his most unreasonable wishes could at one time have aspired to. He had all the real power of royalty, and, since the settlement of his authority for life, he had daily assumed more of the pomp and circumstance with which sovereignty is usually invested. The Tuileries were once more surrounded with guards without, and filled by levees within. The ceremonial of a court was revived, and Buonaparte, judging of mankind with accuracy, neglected no minute observance by which the princes of the earth are wont to enforce their authority. Still there remained much to be done. He held the sovereignty only in the nature of a life-rent. He could, indeed, dispose of it by will, but the last wills even of kings have been frequently set aside; and, at any rate, the privilege comes short of that belonging to an hereditary crown, which descends, by the right of blood, from one possessor to another, so that, in one sense, it may be said to confer on the dynasty a species of immortality. Buonaparte knew also the virtue of names. The title of chief consul did not necessarily infer sovereign rights—it might signify every thing, or it might signify nothing—in common language, it inferred alike one of the annual executive governors of the Roman Republic, whose *fasces* swayed the world, or the petty resident who presides over commercial affairs in a foreign seaport. There were no precise ideas of power or rights necessarily and unalienably connected with it. Besides, Buonaparte had other objections to his present title of dignity. The title of first consul implied, that there were two others,—far, indeed, from being co-ordinate with Napoleon, but yet who occupied a higher rank on the steps of the throne, and approached his person more nearly than he could have desired. Again, the word reminded the hearer, even by the new mode of its application, that it belonged to a government of recent establishment, and of revolutionary origin, and Napoleon did not wish to present such ideas to the public mind; since that which was but lately erected might be easily destroyed, and that which last arose out of the revolutionary cauldron might, like the phantoms which had preceded it, give place in its turn to an apparition more potent. Policy seemed to recommend to him, to have recourse to the ancient model which Europe had been long accustomed to reverence; to adopt the form of government best known and longest established through the greater part of the world; and, assuming the title and rights of a monarch, to take his place among the ancient and recognised authorities of Europe.

It was necessary to proceed with the utmost caution in this innovation, which, whenever accomplished, must necessarily involve the French people in the notable inconsistency, of having murdered the descendant of their old princes, committed a thousand crimes, and suffered under a mass of misery, merely because they were resolved not to permit the existence of that crown, which was now to be placed on the head of a soldier of fortune. Before, therefore, he could venture on this bold measure, in which, were it but for very shame's sake, he must be certain of great opposition, Buonaparte endeavoured, by every means in his power, to strengthen himself in his government.

The army was carefully new-modelled, so as to make it as much as possible his own; and the French soldiers, who regarded the power of Buonaparte as the fruit of their own victories, were in general devoted to his cause, notwithstanding the fame of Moreau, to whom a certain part of their number still adhered. The consular guard, a highly privileged body of select forces, was augmented to the number of six thousand men. These formidable legions, which included troops of every species of arms, had been gradually formed and increased upon the plan of the corps of guides which Buonaparte introduced during the first Italian campaigns, for immediate attendance on his person and for preventing such accidents as once or twice had like to have befallen him, by unexpected encounters with flying parties of the enemy. But the guards, as now increased in numbers, had a duty much more extended. They were chosen men, taught to consider themselves as superior to the rest of the army, and enjoying advantages in pay and privileges. When the other troops were subject to privations, care was taken that the guards should experience as little of them as possible, and that by every possible exertion they should be kept in the highest degree of readiness for action. They were only employed upon service of the utmost importance, and seldom in the beginning of an engagement, when they remained in reserve under the eye of Napoleon himself. It was usually by means of his guard that the final and decisive exertion was made which marked Buonaparte's tactics, and so often achieved victory at the very crisis when it seemed inclining to the enemy. Regarding themselves as considerably superior to the other soldiers, and accustomed also to be under Napoleon's immediate command, his guards were devotedly attached to him; and a body of troops of such high character might be considered as a formidable bulwark around the throne which he meditated ascending.

LEGION OF HONOUR

The attachment of these chosen legions, and of his soldiers in general, formed the foundation of Buonaparte's power, who, of all sovereigns that ever mounted to authority, might be said to reign by dint of victory and of his sword. But he surrounded himself by another species of partisans. The Legion of Honour was destined to form a distinct and particular class of privileged individuals, whom, by honours and bounties bestowed on them, he resolved to bind to his own interest.

This institution, which attained considerable political importance, originated in the custom which Napoleon had early introduced, of conferring on soldiers, of whatever rank, a sword, fusee, or other military weapon, in the name of the state, as acknowledging and commemorating some act of peculiar gallantry. The influence of such public rewards was of course very great. They encouraged those who had received them to make every effort to preserve the character which they had thus gained, while they awakened the emulation of hundreds and thousands who desired similar marks of distinction. Buonaparte now formed the project of embodying the persons who had merited such rewards into an association, similar in many respects to those orders, or brotherhoods of chivalry, with which, during the middle ages, the feudal sovereigns of Europe surrounded themselves, and which subsist to this day, though in a changed and modified form. These, however, have been uniformly created on the feudal principles, and the honour they confer limited, or supposed to be limited, to persons of some rank and condition: but the scheme of Buonaparte was to extend this species of honourable distinction through all ranks, in the quality proper to each, as medals to be distributed among various classes of the community are struck upon metals of different value, but are all stamped with the same dye.[33] The outlines of the institution were these:—

The Legion of Honour was to consist of a great council of administration and fifteen cohorts, each of which was to have its own separate headquarters, in some distinguished town of the Republic. The council of administration was to consist of the three consuls, and four other members; a senator, namely, a member of the Legislative Body, a member of the Tribunate, and one of the Council of State, each to be chosen by the body to which he belonged. The order might be acquired by distinguished merit, either of a civil or a military nature; and various rules were laid down for the mode of selecting the members. The first consul was, in right of his office, captain-general of the legion, and president of the council of administration. Every cohort was to consist of seven grand officers, twenty commanders, thirty subaltern officers, and three hundred and fifty legionaries. Their nomination was for life, and their appointments considerable. The grand officers enjoyed a yearly pension of 5000 francs; the commanders, 2500; the officers, 1000 francs; the privates, or legionaries, 250. They were to swear upon their honour to defend the government of France, and maintain the inviolability of her empire; to combat, by every lawful means, against the re-establishment of the feudal institutions; and to concur in maintaining the principles of liberty and equality.

---

[33] "If the Legion of Honour were not the recompense of *civil* as well as *military* services, it would cease to be the *Legion of Honour*. It would be a strange piece of presumption, indeed, in the military to pretend that honours should be paid to them only. Soldiers who knew not how to read or write, were proud of bearing, in recompense for the blood they had shed, the same decoration as was given to distinguished talents in civil life; and, on the other hand, the latter attached a greater value to this reward of their labours, because it was the decoration of the brave. The Legion of Honour was the property of every one who was an honour to his country, stood at the head of his profession, and contributed to the national prosperity and glory."—Napoleon, *Montholon*, tom. ii., p. 145.

Notwithstanding these last words, containing, when properly understood, the highest political and moral truth, but employed in France originally to cover the most abominable cruelties, and used more lately as mere words of course, the friends of liberty were not to be blinded, regarding the purpose of this new institution. Their number was now much limited; but amidst their weakness they had listened to the lessons of prudence and experience, and abandoning these high-swoln, illusory, and absurd pretensions, which had created such general disturbance, seem to have set themselves seriously, and at the same time moderately to work, to protect the cause of practical and useful freedom, by such resistance as the constitution still permitted them to offer, by means of the Tribunate and the Legislative Body.

OPPOSITION TO THE GOVERNMENT

Among the statesmen who associated to form an Opposition, which, on the principle of the constitutional Opposition of England, were to act towards the executive government rather as to an erring friend, whom they desired to put right, than as an enemy, whom they meant to destroy, were Benjamin Constant, early distinguished by talent and eloquence, Chenier, author of the hymn of the Marseilloise, Savoye-Rollin, Chauvelin, and others, among whose names that of Carnot was most distinguished. These statesmen had learned apparently, that it is better in human affairs to aim at that minor degree of good which is practicable, than to aspire to a perfection which is unattainable. In the opinion of most of them, the government of Buonaparte was a necessary evil, without which, or something of the same strength, to control the factions by which she was torn to pieces, France must have continued to be a prey to a succession of such anarchical governments as had already almost ruined her. They, therefore, entertained none of the usual views of conspirators. They considered the country as in the condition of a wounded warrior, compelled for a short time to lay aside her privileges, as he his armour; but they hoped, when France had renewed her strength and spirit by an interval of repose, they might see her, under better auspices than before, renew and assert her claims to be free from military law. Meantime, they held it their duty, professing, at the same time, the highest respect to the government and its head, the first consul, to keep alive as far as was permitted the spirit of the country, and oppose the encroachments of its ruler. They were not long allowed to follow the practical and useful path which they had sketched out; but the French debates were never so decently or respectably conducted as during this period.

The opposition, as they may be called, had not objected to the reappointment of Buonaparte to the Consulate for life. Probably they were reluctant to have the appearance of giving him personal offence, were aware they would be too feebly supported, and were sensible, that struggling for a point which could not be attained, was unlikely to lead to any good practical results. The institution of the Legion of Honour offered a better chance to try their new opposition tactics.

Rœderer, the orator by whom the measure was proposed to the Tribunate, endeavoured to place it in the most favourable light. It was founded, he said, upon the eighty-seventh article of the Constitutional Declaration, which provided that national recompenses should be conferred on those soldiers who had distinguished themselves in their country's service. He represented the proposed order as a moral institution, calculated to raise to the highest the patriotism and gallantry of the French people. It was a coin, he said, of a value different from, and far more precious than that which was issued from the treasury—a treasure of a quality which could not be debased, and of a quantity which was inexhaustible, since the mine consisted in the national sense of honour.

To this specious argument, it was replied by Rollin and others, that the law was of a nature dangerous to public liberty. It was an abuse, they said, of the constitutional article, on which it was alleged to be founded, since it exhausted at once, by the creation of a numerous corps, the stock of rewards which the article referred to held in frugal reserve, to recompense great actions as they should occur. If everything was given to remunerate merits which had been already ascertained, what stock, it was asked, remained for compensating future actions of gallantry, excepting the chance of a tardy admission into the corps as vacancies should occur? But especially it was pleaded, that the establishment of a military body, distinguished by high privileges and considerable pay, yet distinct and differing from all the other national forces, was a direct violation of the sacred principles of equality. Some reprobated the intermixture of the civil officers of the state in a military institution. Others were of opinion that the oath proposed to be taken was superfluous, if not ridiculous; since, how could the members of the Legion of Honour be more bound to serve the state, or watch over the constitution, than any other citizens; or, in what manner was it proposed they should exert themselves for that purpose? Other arguments were urged; but that which all felt to be the most cogent, was rather understood than even hinted at. This was the immense additional strength which the first consul must attain, by having at his command the distribution of the new honours, and being thus enabled to form a body of satellites entirely dependent upon himself, and carefully selected from the bravest and ablest within the realm.

The institution of the Legion of Honour was at length carried in the Tribunate, by a majority of fifty-six voices over thirty-eight, and sanctioned in the Legislative Body by one hundred and sixty-six over an hundred and ten. The strong divisions of the opposition on this trying question, showed high spirit in those who composed that party; but they were placed in a situation so insulated and separated from the public, so utterly deprived of all constitutional guarantees for the protection of freedom, that their resistance, however honourable to themselves, was totally ineffectual, and without advantage to the nation.[34]

PROPOSITION TO LOUIS XVIII

Meanwhile, Buonaparte was deeply engaged in intrigues of a different character, by means of which he hoped to place the sovereign authority which he had acquired, on a footing less anomalous, and more corresponding with that of the other

---

[34] Montgaillard, tom. v., p. 573.

monarchs in Europe, than it was at present. For this purpose an overture was made by the Prussian minister Haugwitz, through the medium of M. de Meyer, President of the Regency of Warsaw, proposing to the Comte de Provence (since Louis XVIII.,) that he should resign his rights to the crown of France to the successful general who occupied the throne, in which case the exiled princes were to be invested with dominions in Italy, and restored to a brilliant existence. The answer of Louis was marked at once by moderation, sense, and that firmness of character which corresponded with his illustrious birth and high pretensions. "I do not confound Monsieur Buonaparte," said the exiled monarch, "with those who have preceded him; I esteem his bravery and military talents; I owe him good-will for many acts of his government, for the good which is done to my people I will always esteem done to me. But he is mistaken if he thinks that my rights can be made the subjects of bargain and composition. The very step he is now adopting would go to establish them, could they be otherwise called in question. I know not what may be the designs of God for myself and my family, but I am not ignorant of the duties imposed on me by the rank in which it was his pleasure I should be born. As a Christian, I will fulfil those duties to my last breath. As a descendant of Saint Louis, I will know by his example how to respect myself, even were I in fetters. As the successor of Francis the First, I will at least have it to say with him, 'We have lost all excepting our honour!'"

Such is the account which has been uniformly given by the Princes of the House of Bourbon, concerning this communication, which is said to have taken place on the 26th February, 1803.[35] Buonaparte has, indeed, denied that he was accessory to any such transaction, and has said truly enough, that an endeavour to acquire an interest in the Bourbon's title by compromise, would have been an admission on his part that his own, flowing, as he alleged, from the people, was imperfect, and needed repairs. Therefore, he denied having taken any step which could, in its consequences, have inferred such an admission.

---

[35] Montgaillard, tom. v., p. 5.

But, in the first place, it is not to be supposed that such a treaty would have been published by the Bourbon family, unless it had been proposed by Meyer; and it is equally unlikely that either Haugwitz or Meyer would have ventured on such a negotiation, excepting at the instigation of Buonaparte, who alone could make good the terms proposed on the one side, or derive advantage from the concessions stipulated on the other. Secondly, without stopping to inquire how far the title which Buonaparte pretended to the supreme authority, was of a character incapable of being improved by a cession of the Comte de Provence's rights in his favour, it would still have continued an object of great political consequence to have obtained a surrender of the claims of the House of Bourbon, which were even yet acknowledged by a very considerable party within the kingdom. It was, therefore, worth while to venture upon a negotiation which might have had the most important results, although, when it proved fruitless, we can see strong reasons for Napoleon concealing and disowning his accession to a step, which might be construed as implying some sense of deficiency of his own title, and some degree of recognition of that of the exiled prince.

It may be remarked, that, up to this period, Napoleon had manifested no particular spleen towards the family of Bourbon. On the contrary, he had treated their followers with lenity, and spoken with decency of their own claims. But the rejection of the treaty with *Monsieur* Buonaparte, however moderately worded, has been reasonably supposed to have had a deep effect on his mind, and may have been one remote cause of a tragedy, for which it is impossible to find an adequate one—the murder, namely, of the Duke d'Enghien. But, before we approach this melancholy part of Napoleon's history, it is proper to trace the events which succeeded the renewal of the war.

Chapter XXVII

Renewal of the War—England lays an Embargo on French Vessels—Napoleon retaliates by detaining British Subjects—Effects of this unprecedented Measure—Hanover and other places occupied by the French—Scheme of Invasion renewed—Napoleon's Preparations—Defensive Measures of England.

The bloody war which succeeded the short peace of Amiens, originated, to use the words of the satirist, in high words, jealousies, and fears. There was no special or determinate cause of quarrel, which could be removed by explanation, apology, or concession.

The English nation were jealous, and from the strides which Buonaparte had made towards universal power, not jealous without reason, of the farther purposes of the French ruler, and demanded guarantees against the encroachments which they apprehended; and such guarantees he deemed it beneath his dignity to grant. The discussion of these adverse claims had been unusually violent and intemperate; and as Buonaparte conceived the English nation to be his personal enemies, so they, on the other hand, began to regard his power as totally incompatible with the peace of Europe, and independence of Britain. To Napoleon, the English people, tradesmen and shopkeepers as he chose to qualify them, seemed assuming a consequence in Europe, which was, he conceived, far beyond their due. He was affected by feelings similar to those with which Haman beheld Mordecai sitting at the King's gate;—all things availing him nothing, while Britain held such a high rank among the nations, without deigning to do him reverence or worship. The English people, on the other hand, regarded him as the haughty and proud oppressor who had the will at least, if not the power, to root Britain out from among the nations, and reduce them to a state of ignominy and bondage.

When, therefore, the two nations again arose to the contest, it was like combatants whose anger against each other has been previously raised to the highest pitch by mutual invective. Each had recourse to the measures by which their enemy could be most prejudiced.

England had at her command the large means of annoyance arising out of her immense naval superiority, and took her measures with the decision which the emergency required. Instant orders were despatched to prevent the cession of such colonies as yet remained to be given up, according to the treaty of Amiens, and to seize by a *coup-de-main* such of the French settlements as had been ceded, or were yet occupied by her. France, on the other hand, in consequence of her equally great superiority by land, assembled upon her extensive line of sea-coast a very numerous army, with which she appeared disposed to make good her ruler's threats of invasion. At the same time, Buonaparte occupied without ceremony the territory of Naples, Holland, and such other states as Britain must have seen in his hands with feelings of keen apprehension, and thus made good the previous menaces of Talleyrand in his celebrated Note.[36]

But besides carrying to the utmost extent all the means of annoyance which the ordinary rules of hostility afford, Napoleon, going beyond these, had recourse to strange and unaccustomed reprisals, unknown as yet to the code of civilized nature, and tending only to gratify his own resentment, and extend the evils of war, already sufficiently numerous.

EMBARGO ON FRENCH VESSELS—DÉTENUS

The English had, as is the universal custom, laid an embargo on all French vessels in their ports, at the instant the war was proclaimed, and the loss to France was of course considerable. Buonaparte took a singular mode of retaliating, by seizing on the persons of the English of every description, who chanced to be at

---

[36] See *ante*

Paris, or travelling in the dominions of France, who, trusting to the laws of good faith hitherto observed by all civilized nations, expected nothing less than an attack upon their personal freedom. The absurd excuse at first set up for this extraordinary violation of humanity, at once, and of justice, was, that some of these individuals might be liable to serve in the English militia, and were therefore to be considered as prisoners of war. But this flimsy pretext could not have excused the seizing on the English of all ranks, conditions, and ages. The measure was adopted without the participation of the first consul's ministers; at least we must presume so, since Talleyrand himself encouraged some individuals to remain after the British ambassador had left Paris, with an assurance of safety which he had it not in his power to make good. It was the vengeful start of a haughty temper, rendered irritable, as we have often stated, by uninterrupted prosperity, and of consequence, opposing itself to all resistance, and contradiction, with an acuteness of feeling approaching to frenzy.

The individuals who suffered under this capricious and tyrannical act of arbitrary power, were treated in all respects like prisoners of war, and confined to prison as such, unless they gave their parole to abide in certain towns assigned them, and keep within particular limits.

The mass of individual evil occasioned by this cruel measure was incalculably great. Twelve years, a large proportion of human life, were cut from that of each of these *Détenus*, as they were called, so far as regarded settled plan, or active exertion. Upon many, the interruption fell with fatal influence, blighting all their hopes and prospects; others learned to live only for the passing day, and were thus deterred from habitual study or useful industry. The most tender bonds of affection were broken asunder by this despotic sentence of imprisonment; the most fatal inroads were made on family feelings and affections by this long separation between children, and husbands, and wives—all the nearest and dearest domestic relations. In short, if it was Buonaparte's desire to inflict the highest degree of pain on a certain number of persons, only because they were born in Britain, he certainly attained his end. If he hoped to gain any thing farther, he was completely baffled; and when he hypocritically imputes the sufferings of the *détenus* to the obstinacy of the English Ministry,[37] his reasoning is the same with that of a captain of Italian banditti, who murders his prisoner, and throws the blame of the crime on the friends of the deceased, who failed to send the ransom at which he had rated his life. Neither is his vindication more reasonable, when he pretends to say that the measure was taken in order to prevent England, on future occasions, from seizing, according to ancient usage, on the shipping in her ports. This outrage must therefore be recorded as one of those acts of wanton wilfulness in which Buonaparte indulged his passion at the expense of his honour, and, if rightly understood, of his real interest.

The detention of civilians, unoffending and defenceless, was a breach of those courtesies which ought to be sacred, as mitigating the horrors of war. The occupation of Hanover was made in violation of the Germanic Constitution. This patrimony of our kings had in former wars been admitted to the benefit of neutrality; a reasonable distinction being taken betwixt the Elector of Hanover, as one of the grand feudatories of the empire, and the same person in his character of King of Great Britain; in which latter capacity only he was at war with France. But Buonaparte was not disposed to recognise these metaphysical distinctions; nor were any of the powers of Germany in a condition to incur his displeasure, by asserting the constitution and immunities of the empire. Austria had paid too deep a price for her former attempts to withstand the power of France, to permit her to extend her opposition beyond a feeble remonstrance; and Prussia had too long pursued a temporizing and truckling line of politics, to allow her to break short with Napoleon by endeavouring to merit the title her monarch once claimed,—of Protector of the North of Germany.

---

[37] "Your ministers made a great outcry about the English travellers that I detained in France; although they themselves had set the example, by seizing upon all the French vessels and persons on board of them, upon whom they could lay their hands, before the declaration of war, and before I had detained the English in France. I said then, if you detain my travellers at sea, where you can do what you like, I will detain yours at land, where I am equally powerful. But after this I offered to release all the English I had seized in France before the declaration of war, provided you would in like manner release the French and their property which you had seized on board of the ships. Your ministers would not."—Napoleon, *Voice*, &c., vol. i., p. 326.

HANOVER SEIZED

Every thing in Germany being thus favourable to the views of France, Mortier, who had already assembled an army in Holland, and on the frontiers of Germany, moved forward on Hanover. A considerable force was collected for resistance under his Royal Highness the Duke of Cambridge and General Walmoden. It soon appeared, however, that, left to their own resources, and absolutely unsupported either by England or the forces of the empire, the electorate was incapable of resistance; and that any attempt at an ineffectual defence would only serve to aggravate the distresses of the country, by subjecting the inhabitants to the extremities of war. In compassion, therefore, to the Hanoverians, the Duke of Cambridge was induced to leave the hereditary dominions of his father's house; and General Walmoden had the mortification to find himself obliged to enter into a convention, by which the capital of the electorate, and all its strongholds, were to be delivered up to the French, and the Hanoverian army were to retire behind the Elbe, on condition not to serve against France and her allies till previously exchanged.[38]

The British government having refused to ratify this convention of Suhlingen, as it was termed, the Hanoverian army were summoned to surrender as prisoners of war;—hard terms, which, upon the determined resistance of Walmoden, were only thus far softened, that these tried and faithful troops were to be disbanded, and deliver up their arms, artillery, horses, and military stores. In a letter to the first consul, Mortier declares that he granted these mitigated terms from respect to the misfortunes of a brave enemy; and mentions, in a tone of creditable feeling, the distress of General Walmoden, and the despair of the fine regiment of Hanoverian guards, when dismounting from their horses to surrender them up to the French.

At the same time that they occupied Hanover, the French failed not to make a further use of their invasion of Germany, by

---

[38] Annual Register, vol. xlv., p. 283.

laying forced loans on the Hanseatic towns, and by other encroachments.

The Prince Royal of Denmark was the only sovereign who showed an honourable sense of these outrages, by assembling in Holstein an army of thirty thousand men; but being unsupported by any other power, he was soon glad to lay aside the attitude which he had assumed. Austria accepted, as current payment, the declaration of France, that by her occupation of Hanover she did not intend any act of conquest, or annexation of territory, but merely proposed to retain the electorate as a pledge for the isle of Malta, which the English, contrary, as was alleged, to the faith of treaties, refused to surrender. Prussia, naturally dissatisfied at seeing the aggressions of France extend to the neighbourhood of her own territories, was nevertheless obliged to rest contented with the same excuse.

The French ruler did not confine himself to the occupation of Hanover. Tarentum, and other seaports of the King of Naples's dominions, were seized upon, under the same pretext of their being a pledge for the restoration of Malta. In fact, by thus quartering his troops upon neutral territories, by whom he took care that they should be paid and clothed, Napoleon made the war support itself, and spared France the burden of maintaining a great proportion of his immense army; while large exactions, not only on the commercial towns, but on Spain, Portugal, and Naples, and other neutral countries, in the name of loans, filled his treasury, and enabled him to carry on the expensive plans which he meditated.

Any one of the separate manœuvres which we have mentioned, would, before this eventful war, have been considered as a sufficient object for a long campaign. But the whole united was regarded by Buonaparte only as side-blows, affecting Britain indirectly through the occupation of her monarch's family dominions, the embarrassment offered to her commerce, and the destruction of such independence as had been left to the continental powers. His great and decisive game remained to be played—that scheme of invasion to which he had so strongly pledged himself in his angry dialogue with Lord Whitworth. Here, perhaps, if ever in his life, Buonaparte, from considerations of prudence, suffered the period to elapse which would have afforded the best chance for execution of his venturous project.

It must be in the memory of most who recollect the period, that the kingdom of Great Britain was seldom less provided against invasion than at the commencement of this second war; and that an embarkation from the ports of Holland, if undertaken instantly after the war had broken out, might have escaped our blockading squadrons, and have at least shown what a French army could have done on British ground, at a moment when the alarm was general, and the country in an unprepared state. But it is probable that Buonaparte himself was as much unprovided as England for the sudden breach of the treaty of Amiens—an event brought about more by the influence of passion than of policy; so that its consequences were as unexpected in his calculations as in those of Great Britain. Besides, he had not diminished to himself the dangers of the undertaking, by which he must have staked his military renown, his power, which he held chiefly as the consequence of his reputation, perhaps his life, upon a desperate game, which, though he had already twice contemplated it, he had not yet found hardihood enough seriously to enter upon.

He now, however, at length bent himself, with the whole strength of his mind, and the whole force of his empire, to prepare for this final and decisive undertaking. The gun-boats in the bay of Gibraltar, where calms are frequent, had sometimes in the course of the former war been able to do considerable damage to the English vessels of war, when they could not use their sails. Such small craft, therefore, were supposed the proper force for covering the intended descent. They were built in different harbours, and brought together by crawling along the French shore, and keeping under the protection of the batteries, which were now established on every cape, almost as if the sea-coast of the Channel on the French side had been the lines of a besieged city, no one point of which could with prudence be left undefended by cannon. Boulogne was pitched upon as the centre port, from which the expedition was to sail. By incredible exertions, Buonaparte had rendered its harbour and roads capable of containing two thousand vessels of various descriptions. The smaller seaports of Vimereux, Ambleteuse, and Etaples,

Dieppe, Havre, St. Valeri, Caen, Gravelines, and Dunkirk, were likewise filled with shipping. Flushing and Ostend were occupied by a separate flotilla. Brest, Toulon, and Rochefort, were each the station of as strong a naval squadron as France had still the means to send to sea.

ARMY OF ENGLAND

A land army was assembled of the most formidable description, whether we regard the high military character of the troops, the extent and perfection of their appointments, or their numerical strength. The coast, from the mouth of the Seine to the Texel, was covered with forces; and Soult, Ney, Davoust, and Victor, names that were then the pride and the dread of war, were appointed to command the army of England, (for that menacing title was once more assumed,) and execute those manœuvres, planned and superintended by Buonaparte, the issue of which was to be the blotting out of Britain from the rank of independent nations.

Far from being alarmed at this formidable demonstration of force, England prepared for her resistance with an energy becoming her ancient rank in Europe, and far surpassing in its efforts any extent of military preparation before heard of in her history. To nearly one hundred thousand troops of the line, were added eighty thousand and upwards of militia, which scarce yielded to the regulars in point of discipline. The volunteer force, by which every citizen was permitted and invited to add his efforts to the defence of the country, was far more numerous than during the last war, was better officered also, and rendered every way more effective. It was computed to amount to three hundred and fifty thousand men, who, if we regard the shortness of the time and the nature of the service, had attained considerable practice in the use and management of their arms. Other classes of men were embodied, and destined to act as pioneers, drivers of waggons, and in the like services. On a sudden, the land seemed converted to an immense camp, the whole nation into soldiers, and the good old King himself into a general-in-chief. All peaceful considerations appeared for a time to be thrown aside; and the voice, calling the nation to defend their dearest rights, sounded not only in Parliament, and in meetings convoked to second the measures of defence, but was heard in the places of public amusement, and mingled even with the voice of devotion—not unbecomingly surely, since to defend our country is to defend our religion.

Beacons were erected in conspicuous points, corresponding with each other, all around and all through the island; and morning and evening, one might have said, every eye was turned towards them to watch for the fatal and momentous signal. Partial alarms were given in different places from the mistakes to which such arrangements must necessarily be liable; and the ready spirit which animated every species of troops where such signals called to arms, was of the most satisfactory description, and afforded the most perfect assurance, that the heart of every man was in the cause of his country.

Amidst her preparations by land, England did not neglect or relax her precautions on the element she calls her own. She covered the ocean with five hundred and seventy ships of war of various descriptions. Divisions of her fleet blocked up every French port in the Channel; and the army destined to invade our shores, might see the British flag flying in every direction on the horizon, waiting for their issuing from the harbour, as birds of prey may be seen floating in the air above the animal which they design to pounce upon. Sometimes the British frigates and sloops of war stood in, and cannonaded or threw shells into Havre, Dieppe, Granville, and Boulogne itself. Sometimes the seamen and marines landed, cut out vessels, destroyed signal-posts, and dismantled batteries. Such events were trifling, and it was to be regretted that they cost the lives of gallant men; but although they produced no direct results of consequence, yet they had their use in encouraging the spirits of our sailors, and damping the confidence of the enemy, who must at length have looked forward with more doubt than hope to the invasion of the English coast, when the utmost vigilance could not prevent their experiencing insults upon their own.

During this period of menaced attack and arranged defence, Buonaparte visited Boulogne, and seemed active in preparing his soldiers for the grand effort. He reviewed them in an unusual manner, teaching them to execute several manœuvres by night; and experiments were also made upon the best mode of arranging the soldiers in the flat-bottomed boats, and of embarking and disembarking them with celerity. Omens were resorted to for keeping up the enthusiasm which the presence of the first consul naturally inspired. A Roman battle-axe was said to be found when they removed the earth to pitch Buonaparte's tent or barrack; and medals of William the Conqueror were produced, as having been dug up upon the same honoured spot. These were pleasant bodings, yet perhaps did not altogether, in the minds of the soldiers, counterbalance the sense of insecurity impressed on them by the prospect of being packed together in these miserable chaloupes, and exposed to the fire of an enemy so superior at sea, that during the chief consul's review of the fortifications, their frigates stood in shore with composure, and fired at him and his suite as at a mark. The men who had braved the perils of the Alps and of the Egyptian deserts, might yet be allowed to feel alarm at a species of danger which seemed so inevitable, and which they had no adequate means of repelling by force of arms.

BOULOGNE FLOTILLA

A circumstance which seemed to render the expedition in a great measure hopeless, was the ease with which the English could maintain a constant watch upon their operations within the port of Boulogne. The least appearance of stir or preparation, to embark troops, or get ready for sea, was promptly sent by signal to the English coast, and the numerous British cruisers were instantly on the alert to attend their motions. Nelson had, in fact, during the last war, declared the sailing of a hostile armament from Boulogne to be a most forlorn undertaking, on account of cross tides and other disadvantages, together with the certainty of the flotilla being lost if there were the least wind west-north-west. "As for rowing," he adds, "that is impossible.—It is perfectly right to be prepared for a mad government," continued this most incontestible judge of maritime possibilities; "but with the active force which has been given me, I may pronounce it almost impracticable."

Buonaparte himself continued to the last to affirm that he was serious in his attempts to invade Great Britain, and that the scheme was very practicable. He did not, however, latterly, talk of forcing his way by means of armed small craft and gun-boats, while the naval forces on each side were in their present degree of comparative strength, the allowed risk of miscarriage being as ten to one to that of success;—this bravado, which he had uttered to Lord Whitworth, involved too much uncertainty to be really acted upon. At times, long after, he talked slightingly to his attendants of the causes which prevented his accomplishing his project of invasion;[39] but when speaking seriously and in detail, he shows plainly that his sole hope of effecting the invasion was by assembling such a fleet as should give him the temporary command of the Channel. This fleet was to consist of fifty vessels, which, despatched from the various ports of France and Spain, were to rendezvous at Martinico, and, returning from thence to the British Channel, protect the flotilla, upon which were to embark one hundred and fifty thousand men.[40] Napoleon was disappointed in his combinations respecting the shipping; for as it happened, Admiral Cornwallis lay before Brest; Pellew observed the harbours of Spain; Nelson watched Toulon and Genoa; and it would have been necessary for the French and Spanish navy to fight their way through these impediments, in order to form a union at Martinico.

---

[39] "On what trifles does the fate of empires depend! How petty and insignificant are our revolutions in the grand organization of the earth! If, instead of entering upon the Egyptian expedition, I had invaded Ireland; if some slight derangement of my plans had not thrown obstacles in the way of my Boulogne enterprise, what would England have been to-day? What would have been the situation of the Continent, and the whole political world?"— Napoleon, *Las Cases*, tom. iii., p. 330.

[40] See Montholon, tom. ii., p. 224. "The invasion of England," adds Napoleon, "was always regarded as practicable; and, if once the descent had been effected, London must infallibly have been taken. The French being in possession of that capital, a very powerful party would have arisen against the oligarchy. Did Hannibal look behind him when he passed the Alps? or Cæsar when he landed in Epirus, or Africa? London is situated only a few marches from Calais; and the English army, scattered for the purpose of defending the coasts, could not have joined in time to have covered that capital after once the descent had been actually made."

It is wonderful to observe how incapable the best understandings become of forming a rational judgment, where their vanity and self-interest are concerned, in slurring over the total failure of a favourite scheme. While talking of the miscarriage of this plan of invasion, Napoleon gravely exclaimed to Las Cases, "And yet the obstacles which made me fail were not of human origin— they were the work of the elements. In the south, the sea undid my plans; in the north, it was the conflagration of Moscow, the snows and ice that destroyed me. Thus, water, air, fire, all nature, in short, have been the enemies of a universal regeneration, commanded by Nature herself. The problems of Providence are inscrutable."[41]

Independent of the presumptuousness of expressions, by which an individual being, of the first-rate talents doubtless, but yet born of a woman, seems to raise himself above the rest of his species, and deem himself unconquerable save by elementary resistance, the inaccuracy of the reasoning is worth remarking. Was it the sea which prevented his crossing to England, or was it the English ships and sailors? He might as well have affirmed that the hill of Mount St. John, and the wood of Soignies, and not the army of Wellington, were the obstacles which prevented him from marching to Brussels.

Before quitting the subject, we may notice, that Buonaparte seems not to have entertained the least doubts of success, could he have succeeded in disembarking his army. A single general action was to decide the fate of England. Five days were to bring Napoleon to London, where he was to perform the part of William the Third; but with more generosity and disinterestedness. He was to call a meeting of the inhabitants, restore them what he calls their rights, and destroy the oligarchical faction. A few months would not, according to his account, have elapsed, ere the two nations, late such determined enemies, would have been identified by their principles, their maxims, their interests. The full explanation of this gibberish, (for it can be termed no better, even proceeding from the lips of Napoleon,) is to be found elsewhere, when he spoke a language more genuine than that of the *Moniteur* and the bulletins. "England," he said, "must have ended, by becoming an appendage to the France

---

[41] Las Cases, tom. ii., p. 263.

of *my* system. Nature has made it one of our islands, as well as Oleron and Corsica."[42]

It is impossible not to pursue the train of reflections which Buonaparte continued to pour forth to the companion of his exile, on the rock of Saint Helena. When England was conquered, and identified with France in maxims and principles, according to one form of expression, or rendered an appendage and dependency, according to another phrase, the reader may suppose that Buonaparte would have considered his mission as accomplished. Alas! it was not much more than commenced. "I would have departed from thence [from subjugated Britain] to carry the work of European regeneration [that is, the extension of his own arbitrary authority] from south to north, under the Republican colours, for I was then chief consul, in the same manner which I was more lately on the point of achieving it under the monarchical forms."[43] When we find such ideas retaining hold of Napoleon's imagination, and arising to his tongue after his irretrievable fall, it is impossible to avoid exclaiming, Did ambition ever conceive so wild a dream, and had so wild a vision ever a termination so disastrous and humiliating!

DEFENSIVE MEASURES OF ENGLAND

It may be expected that something should be here said, upon the chances which Britain would have had of defending herself successfully against the army of invaders. We are willing to acknowledge that the risk must have been dreadful; and that Buonaparte, with his genius and his army, must have inflicted severe calamities upon a country which had so long enjoyed the blessings of peace. But the people were unanimous in their purpose of defence, and their forces composed of materials to which Buonaparte did more justice when he came to be better acquainted with them. Of the three British nations, the English have since shown themselves possessed of the same steady valour which won the fields of Cressy and Agincourt, Blenheim and Minden—the Irish

---

[42] Las Cases, tom. iii., p. 330.
[43] Las Cases, tom. ii., p. 263.

have not lost the fiery enthusiasm which has distinguished them in all the countries of Europe—nor have the Scots degenerated from the stubborn courage with which their ancestors, for two thousand years, maintained their independence against a superior enemy. Even if London had been lost, we would not, under so great a calamity, have despaired of the freedom of the country; for the war would, in all probability, have assumed that popular and national character which, sooner or later, wears out an invading army. Neither does the confidence with which Buonaparte affirms the conviction of his winning the first battle, appear so certainly well-founded. This, at least, we know, that the resolution of the country was fully bent up to the hazard; and those who remember the period will bear us witness, that the desire that the French would make the attempt, was a general feeling through all classes, because they had every reason to hope that the issue might be such as for ever to silence the threat of invasion.[44]

---

[44] "I commanded a brigade of the army of the coasts, united at this period against England, and I remember that, when called upon to give my opinion upon this expedition, I replied, that 'a maritime expedition, unless it had the superiority at sea, appeared to me to be a contradiction.' Nevertheless, let any one imagine a French army of 200,000 men, landing upon the English territory, and seizing upon the immense city of London—would he deny that, even if the liberty of the country had not been lost, England would have suffered an immense and perhaps irreparable injury? It cannot be denied that the plan was well conceived; that the combined fleets of France and Spain were sufficient to sweep the Channel, and to command there during the time necessary to seize upon London, and even to have conveyed the whole army back to France."—Louis Buonaparte, p. 40.

Chapter XXVIII

Disaffection begins to arise against Napoleon among the Soldiery—Purpose of setting up Moreau against him—Character of Moreau—Causes of his Estrangement from Buonaparte—Pichegru—The Duke d'Enghien—Georges Cadoudal, Pichegru, and other Royalists, landed in France—Desperate Enterprise of Georges—Defeated—Arrest of Moreau—of Pichegru—and Georges—Captain Wright—Duke d'Enghien seized at Strasburg—Hurried to Paris—Transferred to Vincennes—Tried by a Military Commission—Condemned—and Executed—Universal Horror of France and Europe—Buonaparte's Vindication of his Conduct—His Defence considered—Pichegru found dead in his Prison—Attempt to explain his Death by charging him with Suicide—Captain Wright found with his Throat cut—A similar Attempt made—Georges and other Conspirators Tried—Condemned—and Executed—Royalists Silenced—Moreau sent into Exile.

DISAFFECTION OF THE SOLDIERY

While Buonaparte was meditating the regeneration of Europe, by means of conquering, first Britain, and then the northern powers, a course of opposition to his government, and disaffection to his person, was beginning to arise even among the soldiers themselves. The acquisition of the consulate for life was naturally considered as a deathblow to the Republic; and to that name many of the principal officers of the army, who had advanced themselves to promotion by means of the Revolution, still held a grateful attachment. The dissatisfaction of these military men was the more natural, as some of them might see in Buonaparte nothing more than a successful adventurer, who had raised himself high above the heads of his comrades, and now exacted their homage. As soldiers, they quickly passed from murmurs to threats; and at a festive meeting, which was prolonged beyond the limits of sobriety, a colonel of hussars proposed himself as the Brutus to remove this new Cæsar. Being expert at the use of the pistol, he undertook to hit his mark at fifty yards distance, during one of those reviews which were perpetually taking place in presence of the first consul. The affair became known to the police, but was hushed up as much as possible by the address of Fouché, who saw that Buonaparte might be prejudiced by the bare act of making public that such a thing had been agitated, however unthinkingly.[45]

The discontent spread wide, and was secretly augmented by the agents of the house of Bourbon; and, besides the constitutional Opposition, whose voice was at times heard in the Legislative Body and the Tribunate, there existed malecontents without doors, composed of two parties, one of whom considered Buonaparte as the enemy of public liberty, whilst the other regarded him as the sole obstacle to the restoration of the Bourbons; and the most eager partisans of both began to meditate on the practicability of removing him by any means, the most violent and the most secret not excepted. Those among the furious Republicans, or enthusiastic Royalists, who entertained such sentiments, excused them, doubtless, to their conscience, by Napoleon's having destroyed the liberties, and usurped the supreme authority, of the country; thus palliating the complexion of a crime which can never be vindicated.

These zealots, however, bore no proportion to the great body of Frenchmen, who, displeased with the usurpation of Buonaparte, and disposed to overthrow it, if possible, held themselves yet obliged to refrain from all crooked and indirect practices against his life. Proposing to destroy his power in the same way in which it had been built, the first and most necessary task of the discontented party was to find some military chief, whose reputation might bear to be balanced against that of Napoleon; and no one could claim such distinction excepting Moreau. If his campaigns were inferior to those of his great rival in the lightning-like brilliancy and celerity of

---

[45] Fouché, tom. i., p. 231.

their operations, and in the boldness of combination on which they were founded, they were executed at smaller loss to his troops, and were less calculated to expose him to disastrous consequences if they chanced to miscarry. Moreau was no less celebrated for his retreat through the defiles of the Black Forest, in 1796, than for the splendid and decisive victory of Hohenlinden.

Moreau's natural temper was mild, gentle, and accessible to persuasion—a man of great abilities certainly, but scarcely displaying the bold and decisive character which he ought to possess, who, in such times as we write of, aspires to place himself at the head of a faction in the state. Indeed, it rather would seem that he was forced into that situation of eminence by the influence of general opinion, joined to concurring circumstances, than that he deliberately aspired to place himself there. He was the son of a lawyer of Bretagne,[46] and in every respect a man who had risen by the Revolution. He was not, therefore, naturally inclined towards the Bourbons; yet when Pichegru's communications with the exiled family in 1795 became known to him by the correspondence which he intercepted, Moreau kept the secret until some months after,[47] when Pichegru had, with the rest of his party, fallen under the Revolution of 18th Fructidor, which installed the Directory of Barras, Reubel, and La Raveillière. After this period, Moreau's marriage with a lady[48] who entertained sentiments favourable to the Bourbons, seems to have gone some length in deciding his own political opinions.

Moreau had lent Buonaparte his sword and countenance on 18th Brumaire; but he was soon dissatisfied with the engrossing ambition of the new ruler of France, and they became gradually

---

[46] Moreau was born at Morlaix in 1763.
[47] "If Moreau's friendship for Pichegru led him into this culpable compromise, he ought not to have communicated these papers at a time when a knowledge of their contents could no longer be serviceable to the state; for, after the transactions of the 18th Fructidor, that party was defeated, and Pichegru was in chains."—Napoleon, *Montholon*, tom. i., p. 43.
[48] "The Empress Josephine married Moreau to Mademoiselle Hulot, a creole of the Isle of France. This young lady had an ambitious mother, who governed her, and soon governed her husband also. She changed his character; he was no longer the same man; he began to intrigue; his house became the rendezvous of all the disaffected. For a long time the first consul refused to notice this imprudent conduct; but at length he said, 'I wash my hands of him; let him run his head against the pillars of the Tuileries.'"—Napoleon, *Montholon*, tom. i., p. 53.

estranged from each other. This was not the fault of Buonaparte, who, naturally desirous of attaching to himself so great a general, showed him considerable attention, and complained that it was received with coldness. On one occasion, a most splendid pair of pistols had been sent to the first consul. "They arrive in a happy time," he said, and presented them to Moreau, who at that instant entered his presence chamber.[49] Moreau received the civility as one which he would willingly have dispensed with. He made no other acknowledgment than a cold bow, and instantly left the levee.

Upon the institution of the Legion of Honour, one of the grand crosses was offered to him. "The fool!" said Moreau, "does he not know that I have belonged to the ranks of honour for these twelve years?" Another pleasantry on this topic, upon which Buonaparte was very sensitive, was a company of officers, who dined together with Moreau, voting a sauce-pan of honour to the general's cook, on account of his merits in dressing some particular dish. Thus, living estranged from Buonaparte, Moreau came to be gradually regarded as the head of the disaffected party in France; and the eyes of all those who disliked Napoleon or his government, were fixed upon him, as the only individual whose influence might be capable of balancing that of the chief consul.

Meantime, the peace of Amiens being broken, the British Government, with natural policy, resolved once more to avail themselves of the state of public feeling in France, and engage the partisans of royalty in a fresh attack upon the Consular Government. They were probably in some degree deceived concerning the strength of that party, which had been much reduced under Buonaparte's management, and had listened too implicitly to the promises and projects of agents, who, themselves sanguine beyond what was warranted, exaggerated even their own hopes in communicating them to the British ministers. It seems to have been acknowledged, that little success was to be hoped for, unless Moreau

---

[49] "Moreau went to Paris during the armistice of Pahrsdorff, and alighted unexpectedly at the Tuileries. Whilst he was engaged with the first consul, the minister at war, Carnot, arrived from Versailles with a pair of pistols, enriched with diamonds, of very great value: they were intended for the first consul, who, taking the pistols, presented them to Moreau, saying, 'They come very opportunely.' This was not a thing contrived for effect."—Napoleon, *Montholon*, tom. i., p. 52.

could be brought to join the conspiracy. This, however, was esteemed possible; and notwithstanding the disagreement, personal as well as political, which had subsisted betwixt him and Pichegru, the latter seems to have undertaken to become the medium of communication betwixt Moreau and the Royalists. Escaped from the deserts of Cayenne, to which he had been exiled, Pichegru had for some time found refuge and support in London, and there openly professed his principles as a Royalist, upon which he had for a long time acted in secret.

THE DUKE D'ENGHIEN

A scheme was in agitation for raising the Royalists in the west, and the Duke de Berri was to make a descent on the coast of Picardy, to favour the insurrection. The Duke d'Enghien, grandson of the Prince of Condé, fixed his residence under the protection of the Margrave of Baden, at the chateau of Ettenheim, with the purpose, doubtless, of being ready to put himself at the head of the Royalists in the east of France, or, if occasion should offer, in Paris itself. This prince of the house of Bourbon, the destined inheritor of the name of the great Condé, was in the flower of youth, handsome, brave, and high-minded. He had been distinguished for his courage in the emigrant army, which his grandfather commanded. He gained by his valour the battle of Bortsheim; and when his army, to whom the French Republicans showed no quarter, desired to execute reprisals on their prisoners, he threw himself among them to prevent their violence. "These men," he said "are Frenchmen—they are unfortunate—I place them under the guardianship of your honour and your humanity." Such was the princely youth, whose name must now be written in bloody characters in this part of Napoleon's history.

Whilst the French princes expected on the frontier the effect of commotions in the interior of France, Pichegru, Georges Cadoudal, and about thirty other Royalists of the most determined character, were secretly landed in France, made their way to the metropolis, and contrived to find lurking places invisible to the all-seeing police. There can be no reason to doubt that a part of those agents, and Georges in particular, saw the greatest obstacle of their enterprise in the existence of Buonaparte, and were resolved to commence by his assassination. Pichegru, who was constantly in company with Georges, cannot well be supposed ignorant of this purpose, although better befitting the fierce chief of a band of Chouans than the conqueror of Holland.

In the meantime, Pichegru effected the desired communication with Moreau, then, as we have said, considered as the chief of the discontented military men, and the declared enemy of Buonaparte. They met at least twice; and it is certain that on one of these occasions Pichegru carried with him Georges Cadoudal, at whose person and plans Moreau expressed horror, and desired that Pichegru would not again bring that irrational savage into his company. The cause of his dislike we must naturally suppose to have been the nature of the measures Georges proposed, being the last to which a brave and loyal soldier like Moreau would willingly have resorted to; but Buonaparte, when pretending to give an exact account of what passed betwixt Moreau and Pichegru, represents the conduct of the former in a very different point of view. Moreau, according to this account, informed Pichegru, that while the first consul lived, he had not the slightest interest in the army, and that not even his own aides-de-camp would follow him against Napoleon; but were Napoleon removed, Moreau assured them all eyes would be fixed on himself alone—that he would then become first consul—that Pichegru should be second; and was proceeding to make farther arrangements, when Georges broke in on their deliberations with fury, accused the generals of scheming their own grandeur, not the restoration of the king, and declared that to choose betwixt *blue* and *blue*, (a phrase by which the Vendéans distinguished the Republicans,)[50] he would as soon have Buonaparte as Moreau at the head of affairs, and concluded by stating his own pretensions to be third consul at least. According to this account, therefore, Moreau was not shocked at the atrocity of Georges' enterprise, of which he himself had been the first to admit the necessity, but only disgusted at the share which the Chouan chief assorted to himself in the partition of the spoil. But we give no credit whatever to this story. Though nothing could have been so

---

[50] See Mémoires de Savary, tom. ii., p. 52.

important to the first consul at the time as to produce proof of Moreau's direct accession to the plot on his life, no such proof was ever brought forward; and therefore the statement, we have little doubt, was made up afterwards, and contains what Buonaparte might think probable, and desire that others should believe, not what he knew from certain information, or was able to prove by credible testimony.

The police was speedily alarmed, and in action. Notice had been received that a band of Royalists had introduced themselves into the capital, though it was for some time very difficult to apprehend them. Georges, meanwhile, prosecuted his attempt against the chief consul, and is believed at one time to have insinuated himself in the disguise of a menial into the Tuileries, and even into Buonaparte's apartment; but without finding any opportunity to strike the blow, which his uncommon strength and desperate resolution might otherwise have rendered decisive. All the barriers were closed, and a division of Buonaparte's guards maintained the closest watch, to prevent any one escaping from the city. By degrees sufficient light was obtained to enable the government to make a communication to the public upon the existence and tendency of the conspiracy, which became more especially necessary, when it was resolved to arrest Moreau himself. This took place on the 15th February, 1804. He was seized without difficulty or resistance, while residing quietly at his country-house. On the day following, an order of the day, signed by Murat, then Governor of Paris, announced the fact to the citizens, with the additional information, that Moreau was engaged in a conspiracy with Pichegru, Georges, and others, who were closely pursued by the police.

The news of Moreau's imprisonment produced the deepest sensation in Paris; and the reports which were circulated on the subject were by no means favourable to Buonaparte. Some disbelieved the plot entirely, while others, less sceptical, considered the chief consul as making a pretext of the abortive attempt of Pichegru and Georges for the purpose of sacrificing Moreau, who was at once his rival in military fame, and the declared opponent of his government. It was even asserted, that secret agents of

Buonaparte in London had been active in encouraging the attempts of the original conspirators, for the sake of implicating a man whom the first consul both hated and feared. Of this there was no proof; but these and other dark suspicions pervaded men's minds, and all eyes were turned with anxiety upon the issue of the legal investigations which were about to take place.

Upon the 17th February, the great judge of police, by a report[51] which was communicated to the Senate, the Legislative Body, and the Tribunate, denounced Pichegru, Georges, and others, as having returned to France from their exile, with the purpose of overthrowing the government, and assassinating the chief consul, and implicated Moreau as having held communication with them. When the report was read in the Tribunate, the brother of Moreau arose, and, recalling the merits and services of his relative, complained of the cruelty of calumniating him without proof, and demanded for him the privilege of an open and public trial.

"This is a fine display of sensibility," said Curee, one of the tribunes, in ridicule of the sensation naturally produced by this affecting incident.

"It is a display of indignation," replied the brother of Moreau, and left the assembly.

The public bodies, however, did what was doubtless expected of them, and carried to the foot of the consular throne the most exaggerated expressions of their interest in the life and safety of him by whom it was occupied.

ARREST OF PICHEGRU AND GEORGES

Meanwhile, the vigilance of the police, and the extraordinary means employed by them, accomplished the arrest of almost all the persons concerned in the plot. A false friend, whom Pichegru had trusted to the highest degree, betrayed his confidence for a large

---

[51] See Annual Register, vol. xlvi., p. 616.

bribe, and introduced the gendarmes into his apartment while he was asleep. They first secured the arms which lay beside him, and then his person, after a severe struggle. Georges Cadoudal, perhaps a yet more important capture, fell into the hands of the police soon after. He had been traced so closely, that at length he dared not enter a house, but spent many hours of the day and night in driving about Paris in a cabriolet. On being arrested, he shot one of the gendarmes dead, mortally wounded another, and had nearly escaped from them all. The other conspirators, and those accused of countenancing their enterprise, were arrested to the number of forty persons, who were of very different characters and conditions; some followers or associates of Georges, and others belonging to the ancient nobility. Among the latter were Messrs. Armand and Jules Polignac, Charles de la Rivière, and other Royalists of distinction. Chance had also thrown into Buonaparte's power a victim of another description. Captain Wright, the commander of a British brig of war, had been engaged in putting ashore on the coast of Morbihan, Pichegru and some of his companions. Shortly afterwards, his vessel was captured by a French vessel of superior force. Under pretence that his evidence was necessary to the conviction of the French conspirators, he was brought up to Paris, committed to the Temple, and treated with a rigour which became a prelude to the subsequent tragedy.

It might have been supposed, that among so many prisoners, enough of victims might have been selected to atone with their lives for the insurrection which they were accused of meditating; nay, for the attempt which was alleged to be designed against the person of the first consul. Most unhappily for his fame, Napoleon thought otherwise; and, from causes which we shall hereafter endeavour to appreciate, sought to give a fuller scope to the gratification of his revenge, than the list of his captives, though containing several men of high rank, enabled him to accomplish.

THE DUKE D'ENGHIEN

We have observed, that the residence of the Duke d'Enghien upon the French frontier was to a certain degree connected with the enterprise undertaken by Pichegru, so far as concerned the proposed insurrection of the royalists in Paris. This we infer from the duke's admission, that he resided at Ettenheim in the expectation of having soon a part of importance to play in France.[52] This was perfectly vindicated by his situation and connexions. But that the duke participated in, or countenanced in the slightest degree, the meditated attempt on Buonaparte's life, has never even been alleged, and is contrary to all the proof led in the case, and especially to the sentiments impressed upon him by his grandfather, the Prince of Condé.[53] He lived in great privacy, and amused himself principally with hunting. A pension allowed him by England was his only means of support.

On the evening of the 14th March, a body of French soldiers and gendarmes, commanded by Colonel Ordenner, acting under the direction of Caulaincourt, afterwards called Duke of Vicenza, suddenly entered the territory of Baden, a power with whom France

---

[52] The passage alluded to is in the Duke of Rovigo's (Savary's) Vindication of his own Conduct. At the same time, no traces of such an admission are to be found in the interrogations, as printed elsewhere. It is also said, that when the duke (then at Ettenheim) first heard of the conspiracy of Pichegru, he alleged that it must have been only a pretended discovery. "Had there been such an intrigue in reality," he said, "my father and grandfather would have let me know something of the matter, that I might provide for my safety." It may be added, that if he had been really engaged in that conspiracy, it is probable that he would have retired from the vicinity of the French territory on the scheme being discovered.—S.

[53] A remarkable letter from the Prince of Condé to the Comte d'Artois, dated 24th January, 1802, contains the following passage, which we translate literally:—"The Chevalier de Roll will give you an account of what has passed here yesterday. A man of a very simple and gentle exterior arrived the night before, and having travelled, as he affirmed, on foot, from Paris to Calais, had an audience of me about eleven in the forenoon, and distinctly offered to rid us of the usurper by the shortest method possible. I did not give him time to finish the details of his project, but rejected the proposal with horror, assuring him that you, if present, would do the same. I told him, we should always be the enemies of him who had arrogated to himself the power and the throne of our Sovereign, until he should make restitution: that we had combated the usurper by open force, and would do so again if opportunity offered; but that we would never employ that species of means which only became the Jacobin party; and if that faction should meditate such a crime, assuredly we would not be their accomplices." This discourse the prince renewed to the secret agent in the presence of the Chevalier de Roll, as a confidential friend of the Comte d'Artois, and, finally, advised the man instantly to leave England, as, in case of his being arrested, the prince would have afford him no countenance or protection. The person to whom the Prince of Condé addressed sentiments so worthy of himself and of his great ancestor, afterwards proved to be an agent of Buonaparte, despatched to sound the opinions of the Princes of the House of Bourbon, and if possible to implicate them in such a nefarious project as should justly excite public indignation against them.—S.

was in profound peace, and surrounded the chateau in which the unfortunate prince resided. The descendant of Condé sprung to his arms, but was prevented from using them by one of his attendants, who represented the force of the assailants as too great to be resisted. The soldiers rushed into the apartment, and, presenting their pistols, demanded to know which was the Duke d'Enghien. "If you desire to arrest him," said the Duke, "you ought to have his description in your warrant."—"Then we must seize on you all," replied the officer in command; and the prince, with his little household, were arrested and carried to a mill at some distance from the house, where he was permitted to receive some clothes and necessaries. Being now recognised, he was transferred, with his attendants, to the citadel of Strasburg, and presently afterwards separated from the gentlemen of his household, with the exception of his aide-de-camp, the Baron de St. Jacques. He was allowed to communicate with no one. He remained a close prisoner for three days; but on the 18th, betwixt one and two in the morning, he was obliged to rise and dress himself hastily, being only informed that he was about to commence a journey. He requested the attendance of his valet-de-chambre, but was answered that it was unnecessary. The linen which he was permitted to take with him amounted to two shirts only; so nicely had his worldly wants been calculated and ascertained. He was transported with the utmost speed and secrecy towards Paris, where he arrived on the 20th; and, after having been committed for a few hours to the Temple, was transferred to the ancient Gothic castle of Vincennes, about a mile from the city, long used as a state prison, but whose walls never received a more illustrious or a more innocent victim. There he was permitted to take some repose; and, as if the favour had only been granted for the purpose of being withdrawn, he was awaked at midnight, and called upon to sustain an interrogatory on which his life depended, and to which he replied with the utmost composure. On the ensuing night, at the same dead hour, he was brought before the pretended court. The law enjoined that he should have had a defender appointed to plead his cause. But none such was allotted to him.

The inquisitors before whom he was hurried, formed a military commission of eight officers, having General Hulin as their president. They were, as the proceedings express it, named by

Buonaparte's brother-in-law Murat, then governor of Paris. Though necessarily exhausted with fatigue and want of rest, the Duke d'Enghien performed in this melancholy scene a part worthy of the last descendant of the great Condé. He avowed his name and rank, and the share which he had taken in the war against France, but denied all knowledge of Pichegru or of his conspiracy. The interrogations ended by his demanding an audience of the chief consul. "My name," he said, "my rank, my sentiments, and the peculiar distress of my situation, lead me to hope that my request will not be refused."

The military commissioners paused and hesitated—nay, though selected doubtless as fitted for the office, they were even affected by the whole behaviour, and especially by the intrepidity, of the unhappy prince. But Savary, then chief of the police, stood behind the president's chair, and controlled their sentiments of compassion. When they proposed to further the prisoner's request of an audience of the first consul, Savary cut the discussion short, by saying, that was inexpedient. At length they reported their opinion, that the Duke d'Enghien was guilty of having fought against the Republic, intrigued with England, and maintained intelligence in Strasburg, for the purpose of seizing the place;—great part of which allegations, and especially the last, was in express contradiction to the only proof adduced, the admission, namely, of the prisoner himself. The report being sent to Buonaparte to know his farther pleasure, the court received for answer their own letter, marked with the emphatic words, "Condemned to death." Napoleon was obeyed by his satraps with Persian devotion. The sentence was pronounced, and the prisoner received it with the same intrepid gallantry which distinguished him through the whole of the bloody scene. He requested the aid of a confessor. "Would you die like a monk?" is said to have been the insulting reply. The duke, without noticing the insult, knelt down for a minute, and seemed absorbed in profound devotion.

"Let us go," he said, when he arose from his knees. All was in readiness for the execution; and, as if to stamp the trial as a mere mockery, the grave had been prepared ere the judgment of the court was pronounced.[54] Upon quitting the apartment in which the pretended trial had taken place, the prince was conducted by torchlight down a winding-stair, which seemed to descend to the dungeons of the ancient castle.

"Am I to be immured in an oubliette?" he said, naturally recollecting the use which had sometimes been made of those tombs for the living.—"No, Monseigneur," answered the soldier he addressed, in a voice interrupted by sobs, "be tranquil on that subject." The stair led to a postern, which opened into the castle ditch, where, as we have already said, a grave was dug, beside which were drawn up a party of the gendarmes d'élite. It was near six o'clock in the morning, and day had dawned. But as there was a heavy mist on the ground, several torches and lamps mixed their pale and ominous light with that afforded by the heavens,—a circumstance which seems to have given rise to the inaccurate report, that a lantern was tied to the button of the victim, that his slayers might take the more certain aim. Savary was again in attendance, and had taken his place upon a parapet which commanded the place of execution. The victim was placed, the fatal word was given by the future Duke de Rovigo, the party fired, and the prisoner fell. The body, dressed as it was, and without the slightest attention to the usual decencies of sepulture, was huddled into the grave with as little ceremony as common robbers use towards the carcases of the murdered.

Paris learned with astonishment and fear the singular deed which had been perpetrated so near her walls. No act had ever excited more universal horror, both in France and in foreign countries, and none has left so deep a stain on the memory of Napoleon. If there were farther proof necessary of the general opinion of mankind on the subject, the anxiety displayed by Savary, Hulin, and the other subaltern agents in this shameful transaction to diminish their own share in it, or transfer it to others, would be

---

[54] Savary has denied this. It is not of much consequence. The illegal arrest—the precipitation of the mock trial—the disconformity of the sentence from the proof—the hurry of the execution—all prove that the unfortunate prince was doomed to die long before he was brought before the military commission.—S.—See, in Savary's Memoirs, tom. ii, p. 221, the Supplementary Chapter, "On the Catastrophe of the Duke d'Enghien."

sufficient evidence of the deep responsibility to which they felt themselves subjected.

There is but justice, however, in listening to the defence which Buonaparte set up for himself when in Saint Helena, especially as it appeared perfectly convincing to Las Cases, his attendant who, though reconciled to most of his master's actions, had continued to regard the Duke d'Enghien's death as so great a blot upon his escutcheon, that he blushed even when Napoleon himself introduced the subject.[55]

His exculpation seems to have assumed a different and inconsistent character, according to the audience to whom it was stated. Among his intimate friends and followers, he appears to have represented the whole transaction as an affair not of his own device, but which was pressed upon him by surprise by his ministers. "I was seated," he said, "alone, and engaged in finishing my coffee, when they came to announce to me the discovery of some new machination. They represented it was time to put an end to such horrible attempts, by washing myself in the blood of one amongst the Bourbons; and they suggested the Duke d'Enghien as the most proper victim." Buonaparte proceeds to say, that he did not know exactly who the Duke d'Enghien was, far less that he resided so near France as to be only three leagues from the Rhine. This was explained. "In that case," said Napoleon, "he ought to be arrested." His prudent ministers had foreseen this conclusion. They had the whole scheme laid, and the orders ready drawn up for Buonaparte's signature; so that, according to this account, he was hurried into the enormity by the zeal of those about him, or perhaps in consequence of their private views and mysterious intrigues. He also charged Talleyrand with concealing from him a letter,[56] written by the unfortunate prisoner, in which he offered his services to Buonaparte, but which was intercepted by the minister. If this had reached him in time, he intimates that he would have spared the prince's life. To render this statement probable, he denies generally that Josephine had interested herself to the utmost to engage him to

---

[55] The reasoning and sentiments of Buonaparte on this subject are taken from the work of Las Cases, tom. iv., partie 7ieme, p. 249, where they are given at great length.—S.
[56] Napoleon in Exile, vol. i., p. 335.

spare the duke; although this has been affirmed by the testimony of such as declared, that they received the fact from the Empress's own lips.[57]

It is unfortunate for the truth of this statement and the soundness of the defence which it contains, that neither Talleyrand, nor any human being save Buonaparte himself, could have the least interest in the death of the Duke d'Enghien. That Napoleon should be furious at the conspiracies of Georges and Pichegru and should be willing to avenge the personal dangers he incurred; and that he should be desirous to intimidate the family of Bourbon, by "washing himself," as he expresses it, "in the blood of one of their House," was much in character. But that the sagacious Talleyrand should have hurried on a cruel proceeding, in which he had no earthly interest, is as unlikely, as that, if he had desired to do so, he could have been able to elicit from Buonaparte the powers necessary for an act of so much consequence, without his master having given the affair, in all its bearings, the most full and ample consideration. It may also be noticed, that besides transferring a part at least of the guilt from himself, Buonaparte might be disposed to gratify his revenge against Talleyrand, by stigmatizing him, from St. Helena, with a crime the most odious to his new sovereigns of the House of Bourbon. Lastly, the existence of the letter above mentioned has never been proved, and it is inconsistent with every thought and

---

[57] "The idea of the death of the Duke d'Enghien never crossed the first consul's mind, till he was astonished and confounded by the tidings communicated to him by Savary of his execution. The question was not whether he should be put to death, but whether he should be put on his trial. Joseph, Josephine, Cambacérès, Berthier, earnestly expostulated with the chief magistrate against it. Joseph, who was living at Morfontaine, and transiently in town, on the 20th of March, the day the Duke d'Enghien was taken a prisoner to Paris, spoke to his brother in his behalf, warmly urging the defence of the grandson of the Prince of Condé, who, he reminded his brother, had seven times crowned him for as many distinctions gained at the Royal School; to which expostulation the first consul's reply affords a curious proof of the state of his mind at the moment. His answer was given by declaiming the following passage from a speech of Cæsar, in Corneille's tragedy of *La Mort de Pompée*:— 'Votre zèle est faux, si seul il redoutait Ce que le monde entier à pleins vœux souhaitait: Et s'il vous a donné ces craintes trop subtiles, Qui m'ôtent tout le fruit de nos guerres civiles, Où l'honneur seul m'engage, et que pour terminer Je ne veux que celui de vaincre et pardonner; Où mes plus dangereux et plus grands adversaires, Sitôt qu'ils sont vaincus, ne sont plus que mes frères; Et mon ambition ne va qu'à les forcer, Ayant domté leur haine, à vivre et m'embrasser. Oh! combien d'allegresse une si triste guerre Aurait-elle laisée dessus toute la terre, Si l'on voyait marcher dessus un même char, Vainqueurs de leur discorde, et Pompée et César.'" Joseph Buonaparte.

sentiment of the Duke d'Enghien. It is besides said to have been dated from Strasburg; and the duke's aide-de-camp, the Baron de St. Jacques, has given his testimony that he was never an instant separated from his patron, during his confinement in that citadel; and that the duke neither wrote a letter to Buonaparte nor to any one else. But, after all, if Buonaparte had actually proceeded in this bloody matter upon the instigation of Talleyrand, it cannot be denied, that, as a man knowing right from wrong, he could not hope to transfer to his counsellor the guilt of the measures which he executed at his recommendation. The murder, like the rebellion of Absalom, was not less a crime, even supposing it recommended and facilitated by the unconscientious counsels of a modern Achitophel.

Accordingly, Napoleon has not chosen to trust to this defence; but, inconsistently with this pretence of being hurried into the measure by Talleyrand, he has, upon other occasions, broadly and boldly avowed that it was in itself just and necessary; that the Duke d'Enghien was condemned by the laws, and suffered execution accordingly under their sanction.

It is an easy task to show, that even according to the law of France, jealous and severe as it was in its application to such subjects, there existed no right to take the life of the duke. It is true he was an emigrant, and the law denounced the penalty of death against such of these as should return to France with arms in their hands. But the duke did not so return—nay, his returning at all was not an act of his own, but the consequence of violence exercised on his person. He was in a more favourable case than even those emigrants whom storms had cast on their native shore, and whom Buonaparte himself considered as objects of pity, not of punishment. He had indeed borne arms against France; but as a member of the House of Bourbon, he was not, and could not be accounted, a subject of Buonaparte, having left the country before his name was heard of; nor could he be considered as in contumacy against the state of France, for he, like the rest of the royal family, was specially excluded from the benefits of the amnesty which invited the return of the less distinguished emigrants. The act by which he was trepanned, and brought within the compass of French power, not of French law, was as much a violation of the rights of nations, as the precipitation with which the pretended trial followed the arrest, and the execution the trial, was an outrage upon humanity. On the trial no witnesses were produced, nor did any investigation take place, saving by the interrogation of the prisoner. Whatever points of accusation, therefore, are not established by the admission of the duke himself, must be considered as totally unproved. Yet this unconscientious tribunal not only found their prisoner guilty of having borne arms against the Republic, which he readily admitted, but of having placed himself at the head of a party of French emigrants in the pay of England, and carried on machinations for surprising the city of Strasburg; charges which he himself positively denied, and which were supported by no proof whatever.

Buonaparte, well aware of the total irregularity of the proceedings in this extraordinary case, seems, on some occasions, to have wisely renounced any attempt to defend what he must have been convinced was indefensible, and has vindicated his conduct upon general grounds, of a nature well worthy of notice. It seems that, when he spoke of the death of the Duke d'Enghien among his attendants, he always chose to represent it as a case falling under the ordinary forms of law, in which all regularity was observed, and where, though he might be accused of severity, he could not be charged with violation of justice. This was safe language to hearers from whom he was sure to receive neither objection nor contradiction, and is just an instance of an attempt, on the part of a conscientiously guilty party, to establish, by repeated asseverations, an innocence which was inconsistent with fact. But with strangers, from whom replies and argument might be expected, Napoleon took broader grounds. He alleged the death of the Duke d'Enghien to be an act of self-defence, a measure of state policy, arising out of the natural rights of humanity, by which a man, to save his own life, is entitled to take away that of another. "I was assailed," he said, "on all hands by the enemies whom the Bourbons raised up against me; threatened with air-guns, infernal machines, and deadly stratagems of every kind. I had no tribunal on earth to which I could appeal for protection, therefore I had a right to protect myself; and by putting to death one of those whose followers threatened my life, I was entitled to strike a salutary terror into the others."[58]

We have no doubt that, in this argument, which is in the original much extended, Buonaparte explained his real motives; at least we can only add to them the stimulus of obstinate resentment, and implacable revenge. But the whole resolves itself into an allegation of that state necessity, which has been justly called the Tyrant's plea, and which has always been at hand to defend, or rather to palliate, the worst crimes of sovereigns. The prince may be lamented, who is exposed, from civil disaffection, to the dagger of the assassin, but his danger gives him no right to turn such a weapon even against the individual person by whom it is pointed at him. Far less could the attempt of any violent partisans of the House of Bourbon authorise the first consul to take, by a suborned judgment, and the most precipitate procedure, the life of a young prince, against whom the accession to the conspiracies of which Napoleon complained had never been alleged, far less proved. In every point of view, the act was a murder; and the stain of the Duke d'Enghien's blood must remain indelibly upon Napoleon Buonaparte.

With similar sophistry, he attempted to daub over the violation of the neutral territory of Baden, which was committed for the purpose of enabling his emissaries to seize the person of his unhappy victim. This, according to Buonaparte, was a wrong which was foreign to the case of the Duke d'Enghien, and concerned the sovereign of Baden alone. As that prince never complained of this violation, "the plea," he contended, "could not be used by any other person."[59] This was merely speaking as one who has power to do wrong. To whom was the Duke of Baden to complain, or what reparation could he expect by doing so? He was in the condition of a poor man, who suffers injustice at the hands of a wealthy neighbour, because he has no means to go to law, but whose acquiescence under the injury cannot certainly change its character, or render that invasion just which is in its own character distinctly otherwise. The passage may be marked as showing Napoleon's

---

[58] See Las Cases, tom. iv., p. 269.
[59] See Las Cases, tom. iv., p. 271.

unhappy predilection to consider public measures not according to the immutable rules of right and wrong, but according to the opportunities which the weakness of one kingdom may afford to the superior strength of another.[60]

It may be truly added, that even the pliant argument of state necessity was far from justifying this fatal deed. To have retained the Duke d'Enghien a prisoner, as a hostage who might be made responsible for the Royalists' abstaining from their plots, might have had in it some touch of policy; but the murder of the young and gallant prince, in a way so secret and so savage, had a deep moral effect upon the European world, and excited hatred against Buonaparte wherever the tale was told. In the well-known words of Fouché, the duke's execution was worse than a moral crime—it was a political blunder.[61] It had this consequence, most unfortunate for Buonaparte, that it seemed to stamp his character as bloody and unforgiving; and in so far prepared the public mind to receive the worst impressions, and authorised the worst suspicions, when other tragedies of a more mysterious character followed that of the last of the race of Condé.[62]

DEATH OF PICHEGRU

The Duke d'Enghien's execution took place on the 21st March; on the 7th April following, General Pichegru was found

---

[60] See, in the Appendix to this volume, No. II., "Further Particulars concerning the Arrest, Trial, and Death of the Duke d'Enghien."
[61] "I was not the person who hesitated to express himself with the least restraint, respecting this violence against the rights of nations and humanity. 'It is more than a crime,' I said, 'it is a political blunder;' words which I record, because they have been repeated and attributed to others."—Fouché, tom. i., p. 266.
[62] "I deplore as much as any man can possibly do, the catastrophe of the Duke d'Enghien; but as Napoleon has himself spoken of it, it does not become me to add another word. I shall only observe, that this affair is far from having been cleared up—that it was impossible that my brother should have brought the prince to Paris to be immolated—that he who established a Bourbon in Tuscany, had quite a contrary design, and one which could but be favourable; else why cause so distinguished a prince to make a journey to Paris, when his presence in traversing France could but be dangerous? If it be asked, why the commendable design attributed to Napoleon was not followed up, and was so cruelly changed, I cannot explain: but I am persuaded that impartial history will one day reveal this secret."—Louis Buonaparte, p. 40.

dead in his prison. A black handkerchief was wrapped round his neck, which had been tightened by twisting round a short stick inserted through one of the folds. It was asserted that he had turned this stick with his own hands, until he lost the power of respiring, and then, by laying his head on the pillow, had secured the stick in its position. It did not escape the public, that this was a mode of terminating life far more likely to be inflicted by the hands of others than those of the deceased himself. Surgeons were found, but men, it is said, of small reputation, to sign a report upon the state of the body, in which they affirm that Pichegru had died by suicide; yet as he must have lost animation and sense so soon as he had twisted the stick to the point of strangulation, it seems strange he should not have then unclosed his grasp on the fatal tourniquet, which he used as the means of self-destruction. In that case the pressure must have relaxed, and the fatal purpose have remained unaccomplished. No human eye could see into the dark recesses of a state prison, but there were not wanting many who entertained a total disbelief of Pichegru's suicide. It was argued that the first consul did not dare to bring before a public tribunal, and subject to a personal interrogatory, a man of Pichegru's boldness and presence of mind— it was said, also, that his evidence would have been decisively favourable to Moreau—that the citizens of Paris were many of them attached to Pichegru's person—that the soldiers had not forgotten his military fame—and, finally, it was reported, that in consideration of these circumstances, it was judged most expedient to take away his life in prison. Public rumour went so far as to name, as the agents in the crime, four of those Mamelukes, of whom Buonaparte had brought a small party from Egypt, and whom he used to have about his person as matter of parade. This last assertion had a strong impression on the multitude, who are accustomed to think, and love to talk, about the mutes and bowstrings of Eastern despotism. But with well-informed persons, its improbability threw some discredit on the whole accusation. The state prisons of France must have furnished from their officials enough of men as relentless and dexterous in such a commission as those Eastern strangers, whose unwonted appearance in these gloomy regions must have at once shown a fatal purpose, and enabled every one to trace it to Buonaparte.[63]

---

[63] "M. de Bourrienne does not scruple to charge with a frightful crime the man whom he

A subsequent catastrophe, of nearly the same kind, increased by its coincidence the dark suspicions which arose out of the circumstances attending the death of Pichegru.

Captain Wright, from whose vessel Pichegru and his companions had disembarked on the French coast, had become, as we have said, a prisoner of war, his ship being captured by one of much superior force, and after a most desperate defence. Under pretext that his evidence was necessary to the conviction of Pichegru and Georges, he was brought to Paris, and lodged a close prisoner in the Temple. It must also be mentioned, that Captain Wright had been an officer under Sir Sidney Smith, and that the mind of Buonaparte was tenaciously retentive of animosity against those who had aided to withstand a darling purpose, or diminish and obscure the military renown, which was yet more dear to him. The treatment of Captain Wright was—must have been severe, even if it extended no farther than solitary imprisonment; but reports went abroad, that torture was employed to bring the gallant seaman to such confessions as might suit the purposes of the French Government. This belief became very general, when it was heard that Wright, like Pichegru, was found dead in his apartment, with his throat cut from ear to ear, the result, according to the account given by Government, of his own impatience and despair. This official account of the second suicide committed by a state prisoner, augmented and confirmed the opinions entertained concerning the death of Pichegru, which it so closely resembled. The unfortunate Captain Wright was supposed to have been sacrificed, partly perhaps

---

calls the friend of his youth, in whose service he had been for years, and by whom he sought to be again employed, as long as fortune was on his side. In my conscience, I believe there never existed a man less capable of committing such a crime than Napoleon; yet it is he whom the schoolfellow of Brienne dares to accuse. On the morning of Pichegru's death, I was in the first consul's cabinet in the Tuileries, searching for some papers, when Savary was announced, and I heard him detail the particulars of the suicide, precisely as they were afterwards published. I read on Napoleon's countenance the surprise which the event created, and little imagined that there were men so base as to charge him with so detestable and uncalled-for a murder; for the meeting between Pichegru and Moreau had been fully established."—Joseph Buonaparte.—"What advantage could accrue to me from Pichegru's assassination?—a man who was evidently guilty, against whom every proof was ready, and whose condemnation was certain. The fact is, that he found himself in a hopeless situation; his high mind could not bear to contemplate the infamy of a public execution, he despaired of my clemency, or disdained to appeal to it, and put an end to his existence."—Napoleon, *Las Cases*, tom. iv., p. 258.

to Buonaparte's sentiments of petty vengeance, but chiefly to conceal, within the walls of the Temple, the evidence which his person would have exhibited in a public court of justice, of the dark and cruel practices by which confession was sometimes extorted.

Buonaparte always alleged his total ignorance concerning the fate of Pichegru and Wright, and affirmed upon all occasions, that they perished, so far as he knew, by their own hands, and not by those of assassins. No proof has ever been produced to contradict his assertion; and so far as he is inculpated upon these heads, his crime can be only matter of strong suspicion. But it was singular that this rage for suicide should have thus infected the state prisons of Paris, and that both these men, determined enemies of the Emperor, should have adopted the resolution of putting themselves to death, just when that event was most convenient to their oppressor. Above all, it must be confessed, that, by his conduct towards the Duke d'Enghien, Buonaparte had lost that fairness of character to which he might otherwise have appealed, as in itself an answer to the presumptions formed against him. The man who, under pretext of state necessity, ventured on such an open violation of the laws of justice, ought not to complain if he is judged capable, in every case of suspicion, of sacrificing the rights of humanity to his passions or his interest. He himself has affirmed, that Wright died, long before it was announced to the public, but has given no reason why silence was preserved with respect to the event.[64] The Duke de Rovigo, also denying all knowledge of Wright's death, acknowledges that it was a dark and mysterious subject, and intimates his belief that Fouché was at the bottom of the tragedy.[65] In Fouché's real or pretended Memoirs, the subject is not mentioned. We leave, in the obscurity in which we found it, a dreadful tale, of which the truth

---

[64] See Napoleon in Exile, vol. ii., p. 215.
[65] "When, as minister of the police, the sources of information were open to me, I ascertained that Wright cut his throat in despair, after reading the account of the capitulation of the Austrian general, Mack, at Ulm, that is, while Napoleon was engaged in the campaign of Austerlitz. Can any one, in fact, without alike insulting common sense and glory, admit that the Emperor had attached so much importance to the destruction of a scurvy lieutenant of the English navy, as to send from one of his most glorious fields of battle the order for his destruction? It has been added, that it was I who received from him this commission: now I never quitted him for a single day during the whole campaign, from his departure from Paris till his return."—Savary, tom. ii., p. 61.

cannot, in all probability, be known, until the secrets of all hearts shall be laid open.

TRIAL OF CADOUDAL AND OTHERS

Rid of Pichegru, by his own hand or his jailor's, Buonaparte's government was now left to deal with Georges and his comrades, as well as with Moreau. With the first it was an easy task, for the Chouan chief retained, in the court of criminal justice before which he was conveyed, the same fearless tone of defiance which he had displayed from the beginning. He acknowledged that he came to Paris for the sake of making war personally on Napoleon, and seemed only to regret his captivity, as it had disconcerted his enterprise. He treated the judges with cool contempt, and amused himself by calling Thuriot, who conducted the process, and who had been an old Jacobin, by the name of Monsieur Tue-Roi. There was no difficulty in obtaining sentence of death against Georges and nineteen of his associates; amongst whom was Armand de Polignac, for whose life his brother affectionately tendered his own. Armand de Polignac, however, with seven others, were pardoned by Buonaparte; or rather banishment in some cases, and imprisonment in others, were substituted for a capital punishment. Georges and the rest were executed, and died with the most determined firmness.

The discovery and suppression of this conspiracy seems to have produced, in a great degree, the effects expected by Buonaparte. The Royal party became silent and submissive, and, but that their aversion to the reign of Napoleon showed itself in lampoons, satires, and witticisms, which were circulated in their evening parties, it could hardly have been known to exist. Offers were made to Buonaparte to rid him of the remaining Bourbons, in consideration of a large sum of money; but with better judgment than had dictated his conduct of late, he rejected the proposal. His interest, he was now convinced, would be better consulted by a line of policy which would reduce the exiled family to a state of insignificance, than by any rash and violent proceedings, which must necessarily draw men's attention, and, in doing so, were likely to interest them in behalf of the sufferers, and animate them against their powerful oppressor. With this purpose, the names of the exiled family were, shortly after this period, carefully suppressed in all periodical publications, and, with one or two exceptions, little allusion to their existence can be traced in the pages of the official journal of France; and, unquestionably, the policy was wisely adopted towards a people so light, and animated so intensely with the interest of the moment, as the French, to whom the present is a great deal, the future much less, and the past nothing at all.

Though Georges's part of the conspiracy was disposed of thus easily, the trial of Moreau involved a much more dangerous task. It was found impossible to procure evidence against him, beyond his own admission that he had seen Pichegru twice; and this admission was coupled with a positive denial that he had engaged to be participant in his schemes. A majority of the judges seemed disposed to acquit him entirely, but were cautioned by the president Hemart, that, by doing so, they would force the government upon violent measures. Adopting this hint, and willing to compromise matters, they declared Moreau guilty, but not to the extent of a capital crime. He was subjected to imprisonment for two years; but the soldiers continuing to interest themselves in his fate, Fouché, who about this time was restored to the administration of police, interceded warmly in his favour,[66] and seconded the applications of Madame Moreau, for a commutation of her husband's sentence.[67] His doom of imprisonment was therefore exchanged for that of exile; a mode of punishment safer for Moreau, considering the late incidents in the prisons of state; and more advantageous for Buonaparte, as removing entirely from the thoughts of the republican party, and of the soldiers, a leader, whose military talents brooked comparison with his own, and to whom the public eye would naturally be turned when any cause of discontent with their present government might incline them to look elsewhere. Buonaparte thus escaped from the consequences of this alarming conspiracy; and, like a patient whose disease is brought to a

---

[66] Mémoires de Fouché, tom. i., p. 267.
[67] "I was the person whom the first consul sent to him in the Temple to communicate his consent, and to make arrangements with him for his departure. I gave him my own carriage, and the first consul paid all the expenses of his journey to Barcelona. The general expressed a wish to see Madame Moreau; I went myself to fetch her, and brought her to the Temple."—Savary, tom. ii., p. 66.

favourable crisis by the breaking of an imposture, he attained additional strength by the discomfiture of those secret enemies.

CHAPTER XXIX

General Indignation of Europe in consequence of the Murder of the Duke d'Enghien—Russia complains to Talleyrand of the Violation of Baden—and, along with Sweden, Remonstrates in a Note laid before the German Diet— but without effect—Charges brought by Buonaparte against Mr. Drake and Mr. Spencer Smith—who are accordingly Dismissed from the Courts of Stuttgard and Munich—Seizure—Imprisonment—and Dismissal—of Sir George Rumbold, the British Envoy at Lower Saxony—Treachery attempted against Lord Elgin, by the Agents of Buonaparte—Details—Defeated by the Exemplary Prudence of that Nobleman—These Charges brought before the House of Commons—and peremptorily Denied by the Chancellor of the Exchequer.

GENERAL INDIGNATION OF EUROPE

Buonaparte, as we have seen, gained a great accession of power by the event of Pichegru's conspiracy. But this was, in some measure, counterbalanced by the diminution of character which attached to the kidnapping and murdering the Duke d'Enghien, and by the foul suspicions arising from the mysterious fate of Pichegru and Wright. He possessed no longer the respect which might be claimed by a victor and legislator, but had distinctly shown that either the sudden tempest of ungoverned passion, or the rankling feelings of personal hatred, could induce him to take the readiest means of wreaking the basest, as well as the bloodiest vengeance. Deep indignation was felt through every country on the Continent, though Russia and Sweden alone ventured to express their dissatisfaction with a proceeding so contrary to the law of nations. The court of St. Petersburg went into state mourning for the Duke d'Enghien, and while the Russian minister at Paris presented a note to M. Talleyrand, complaining of the violation of the Duke of Baden's territory, the Russian resident at Ratisbon was instructed to lay before the Diet of the Empire a remonstrance to the same effect. The Swedish minister did the same. The answer of the French minister was hostile and offensive.[68] He treated with scorn the pretensions of Russia to interfere in the affairs of France and Germany, and accused that power of being desirous to rekindle the flames of war in Europe. This correspondence tended greatly to inflame the discontents already subsisting betwixt France and Russia, and was one main cause of again engaging France in war with that powerful enemy.

The Russian and Swedish remonstrance to the Diet produced no effect. Austria was too much depressed, Prussia was too closely leagued with France to be influenced by it; and there were none of the smaller powers who could be expected to provoke the displeasure of the first consul, by seconding the complaint of the violation of the territory of Baden. The blood of the Duke d'Enghien was not, however, destined to sleep unavenged in his obscure dwelling. The Duke of Baden himself requested the matter might be left to silence and oblivion; but many of the German potentates felt as men, what they dared not, in their hour of weakness, resent as princes. It was a topic repeatedly and efficaciously resumed whenever an opportunity of resistance against the universal conqueror presented itself; and the perfidy and cruelty of the whole transaction continued to animate new enemies against him, until, in the issue, they became strong enough to work his overthrow. From the various and inconsistent pleas which Buonaparte set up in defence of his conduct—now attempting to justify, now to apologize for, now to throw on others a crime which he alone had means and interest to commit, it is believed that he felt the death of the Duke d'Enghien to be the most reprehensible as well as the most impolitic act in his life.

Already aware of the unpopularity which attached to his late cruel proceedings, Buonaparte became desirous to counterbalance it by filling the public mind with a terrific idea of the schemes of

---

[68] See Annual Register, vol. xlvi., pp. 642-656.

England, which, in framing and encouraging attempts upon his life, drove him to those unusual and extraordinary acts, which he desired to represent as measures of retaliation. Singular manœuvres were resorted to for the purpose of confirming the opinions which he was desirous to impress upon the world. The imprudence—so, at least, it seems—of Mr. Drake, British resident at Munich, enabled Buonaparte to make his charges against England with some speciousness. This agent of the British Government had maintained a secret correspondence with a person of infamous character, called Mehee de la Touche, who, affecting the sentiments of a Royalist and enemy of Buonaparte, was, in fact, employed by the first consul to trepan Mr. Drake into expressions which might implicate the English ministers, his constituents, and furnish grounds for the accusations which Buonaparte made against them. It certainly appears that Mr. Drake endeavoured, by the medium of de la Touche, to contrive the means of effecting an insurrection of the Royalists, or other enemies of Buonaparte, with whom his country was then at war; and, in doing so, he acted according to the practice of all belligerent powers, who, on all occasions, are desirous to maintain a communication with such malecontents as may exist in the hostile nation. But, unless by the greatest distortion of phrase and expression, there arises out of the letters not the slightest room to believe that Mr. Drake encouraged the party with whom he supposed himself to be in correspondence, to proceed by the mode of assassination, or any others that are incompatible with the law of nations, and acknowledged by civilized governments. The error of Mr. Drake seems to have been, that he was not sufficiently cautious respecting the sincerity of the person with whom he maintained his intercourse. Mr. Spencer Smith, the British envoy at Stuttgard, was engaged in a similar intrigue, which appears also to have been a snare spread for him by the French Government.

Buonaparte failed not to make the utmost use of these pretended discoveries, which were promulgated with great form by Regnier,[69] who held the office of grand judge. He invoked the faith of nations, as if the Duke d'Enghien had been still residing in peaceable neutrality at Ettenheim, and exclaimed against

---

[69] For the First and Second Reports of the Grand Judge to the First Consul, on the alleged Conspiracies against him, see Annual Register, vol. xlvi., pp. 619, 622.

assassination, as if his state dungeons could not have whispered of the death of Pichegru. The complaisant sovereigns of Stuttgard and Munich readily ordered Smith and Drake to leave their courts; and the latter was forced to depart on foot, and by crossroads, to avoid being kidnapped by the French gendarmes.

SIR GEORGE RUMBOLD

The fate which Mr. Drake dreaded, and perhaps narrowly escaped, actually befell Sir George Rumbold, resident at the free German city of Hamburgh, in the capacity of his British Majesty's envoy to the Circle of Lower Saxony. On the night of the 25th October, he was seized, in violation of the rights attached by the law of nations to the persons of ambassadors, as well as to the territories of neutral countries, by a party of the French troops, who crossed the Elbe for that purpose. The envoy, with his papers, was then transferred to Paris in the capacity of a close prisoner, and thrown into the fatal Temple. The utmost anxiety was excited even amongst Buonaparte's ministers, lest this imprisonment should be intended as a prelude to further violence; and both Fouché and Talleyrand exerted what influence they possessed over the mind of Napoleon, to prevent the proceedings which were to be apprehended. The King of Prussia also extended his powerful interposition; and the result was, that Sir George Rumbold, after two days' imprisonment, was dismissed to England, on giving his parole not to return to Hamburgh. It seems probable, although the *Moniteur* calls this gentleman the worthy associate of Drake and Spencer Smith, and speaks of discoveries amongst his papers which were to enlighten the public on the policy of England, that nothing precise was alleged against him, even to palliate the outrage which the French ruler had committed.

The tenor of Buonaparte's conduct in another instance, towards a British nobleman of distinction, though his scheme was rendered abortive by the sagacity of the noble individual against whom it was directed, is a striking illustration of the species of intrigue practised by the French police, and enables us to form a correct judgment of the kind of evidence upon which Buonaparte brought forward his calumnious accusation against Britain and her subjects.

LORD ELGIN

The Earl of Elgin, lately ambassador of Great Britain at the Porte, had, contrary to the usage among civilized nations, been seized upon with his family as he passed through the French territory; and during the period of which we are treating, he was residing upon his parole near Pau, in the south of France, as one of the *Détenus*. Shortly after the arrest of Moreau, Georges, &c., an order arrived for committing his lordship to close custody, in reprisal, it was said, of severities exercised in England on the French General Boyer. The truth was, that the affair of General Boyer had been satisfactorily explained to the French Government. In the Parisian papers, on the contrary, his lordship's imprisonment was ascribed to barbarities which he was said to have instigated against the French prisoners of war in Turkey—a charge totally without foundation. Lord Elgin was, however, transferred to the strong castle of Lourdes, situated on the descent of the Pyrenees, where the commandant received him, though a familiar acquaintance, with the reserve and coldness of an entire stranger. Attempts were made by this gentleman and his lieutenant to exasperate the feelings which must naturally agitate the mind of a man torn from the bosom of his family, and committed to close custody in a remote fortress, where the accommodation was as miserable as the castle itself was gloomy, strong, and ominously secluded from the world. They failed, however, in extracting from their prisoner any expressions of violence or impatience, however warranted by the usage to which he was subjected.

After a few days' confinement, a sergeant of the guard delivered to Lord Elgin a letter, the writer of which informed him, that, being his fellow prisoner, and confined in a secluded dungeon, he regretted he could not wait on his lordship, but that when he walked in the court-yard, he could have conversation with him at the window of his room. Justly suspecting this communication, Lord Elgin destroyed the letter; and while he gave the sergeant a louis-d'or, told him, that if he or any of his comrades should again bring him any secret letter or message, he would inform the commandant of the circumstance. Shortly afterwards, the commandant of the fortress, in conversation with Lord Elgin, spoke of the prisoner in question as a person whose health was suffering for want of exercise; and next day his lordship saw the individual walking in the court-yard before his window. He manifested every disposition to engage his lordship in conversation, which Lord Elgin successfully avoided.

A few weeks afterwards, and not till he had been subjected to several acts of severity and vexation, Lord Elgin was permitted to return to Pau. But he was not yet extricated from the nets in which it was the fraudulent policy of the French Government to involve him. The female, who acted as porter to his lordship's lodgings, one morning presented him with a packet, which she said had been left by a woman from the country, who was to call for an answer. With the same prudence which distinguished his conduct at Lourdes, Lord Elgin detained the portress in the apartment, and found that the letter was from the state prisoner already mentioned; that it contained an account of his being imprisoned for an attempt to burn the French fleet; and detailed his plan as one which he had still in view, and which he held out in the colours most likely, as he judged, to interest an Englishman. The packet also covered letters to the Comte d'Artois, and other foreigners of distinction, which Lord Elgin was requested to forward with his best convenience. Lord Elgin thrust the letters into the fire in presence of the portress, and kept her in the room till they were entirely consumed; explaining to her, at the same time, that such letters to him as might be delivered by any other channel than the ordinary post, should be at once sent to the governor of the town. His lordship judged it his farther duty to mention to the prefect the conspiracy detailed in the letter, under the condition, however, that no steps should be taken in consequence, unless the affair became known from some other quarter.

Some short time after these transactions, and when Buonaparte was appointed to assume the imperial crown, (at which period there was hope of a general act of grace, which should empty the prisons,) Lord Elgin's fellow-captive at Lourdes, being, it seems, a real prisoner, as well as a spy, in hopes of meriting a share in this measure of clemency, made a full confession of all which he had done or designed to do against Napoleon's interest. Lord Elgin was naturally interested in this confession, which appeared in the *Moniteur*, and was a good deal surprised to see that a detail, otherwise minute, bore no reference to, or correspondence regarding, the plan of burning the Brest fleet. He lost no time in writing an account of the particulars we have mentioned to a friend at Paris, by whom they were communicated to Monsieur Fargues, senator of the district of Bearn, whom these plots particularly interested as having his senatorie for their scene. When Lord Elgin's letter was put into his hand, the senator changed countenance, and presently after expressed his high congratulation at what he called Lord Elgin's providential escape. He then intimated, with anxious hesitation, that the whole was a plot to entrap Lord Elgin; that the letters were written at Paris, and sent down to Bearn by a confidential agent, with the full expectation that they would be found in his lordship's possession. This was confirmed by the commandant of Lourdes, with whom Lord Elgin had afterwards an unreserved communication, in which he laid aside the jailor, and resumed the behaviour of a gentleman. He imputed Lord Elgin's liberation to the favourable report which he himself and his lieutenant had made of the calm and dignified manner in which his lordship had withstood the artifices which they had been directed to use, with a view of working on his feelings, and leading him into some intemperance of expression against France or her ruler; which might have furnished a pretext for treating him with severity, and for implicating the British Government in the imprudence of one of her nobles, invested with a diplomatic character.[70]

The above narrative forms a singularly luminous commentary on the practices imputed to Messrs. Drake and Spencer, and subsequently to Sir George Rumbold; nor is it a less striking illustration of the detention of the unfortunate Captain Wright. With one iota less of prudence and presence of mind, Lord Elgin must have been entangled in the snare which was so treacherously spread

---

[70] This account is abstracted from the full details which Lord Elgin did us the honour to communicate in an authenticated manuscript.—S.

for him. Had he even engaged in ten minutes conversation with the villanous spy and incendiary, it would have been in the power of such a wretch to represent the import after his own pleasure. Or had his lordship retained the packet of letters even for half an hour in his possession, which he might have most innocently done, he would probably have been seized with them upon his person, and it must in that case have been impossible for him to repel such accusations, as Buonaparte would have no doubt founded on a circumstance so suspicious.

While Napoleon used such perfidious means, in order to attach, if possible, to a British ambassador of such distinguished rank, the charge of carrying on intrigues against his person, the British ministers, in a tone the most manly and dignified, disclaimed the degrading charges which had been circulated against them through Europe. When the topic was introduced by Lord Morpeth[71] into the British House of Commons, by a motion respecting the correspondence of Drake, the Chancellor of the Exchequer replied, "I thank the noble lord for giving me an opportunity to repel, openly and courageously, one of the most gross and most atrocious calumnies ever fabricated in one civilized nation to the prejudice of another. I affirm, that no power has been given, no instruction has been sent, by this government to any individual, to act in a manner contrary to the law of nations. I again affirm, as well in my own name as in that of my colleagues, that we have not authorised any human being to conduct himself in a manner contrary to the honour of this country, or the dictates of humanity."[72]

This explicit declaration, made by British ministers in a situation where detected falsehood would have proved dangerous to those by whom it was practised, is to be placed against the garbled correspondence of which the French possessed themselves, by means violently subversive of the law of nations; and which correspondence was the result of intrigues that would never have existed but for the treacherous suggestions of their own agents.

---

[71] Now Earl of Carlisle.
[72] See Parliamentary Debates, April 16, 1804, vol. ii., p. 131.

CHAPTER XXX

Napoleon meditates a change of title from Chief Consul to Emperor—A Motion to this purpose brought forward in the Tribunate—Opposed by Carnot—Adopted by the Tribunate and Senate—Outline of the New System—Coldly received by the People—Napoleon visits Boulogne, Aix-la-Chapelle, and the Frontiers of Germany, where he is received with respect—The Coronation—Pius VII. is summoned from Rome to perform the Ceremony at Paris—Details—Reflections—Changes that took place in Italy—Napoleon appointed Sovereign of Italy, and Crowned at Milan—Genoa annexed to France.

NAPOLEON MEDITATES A CHANGE OF TITLE

The time seemed now propitious for Buonaparte to make the last remaining movement in the great game, which he had hitherto played with equal skill, boldness, and success. The opposing factions of the state lay in a great measure prostrate before him. The death of the Duke d'Enghien and of Pichegru had intimidated the Royalists, while the exile of Moreau had left the Republicans without a leader.

These events, while they greatly injured Buonaparte's character as a man, extended, in a like proportion, the idea of his power, and of his determination to employ it to the utmost extremity against whoever might oppose him. This moment, therefore, of general submission and intimidation was the fittest to be used for transmuting the military baton of the first consul into a sceptre, resembling those of the ancient and established sovereignties of Europe; and it only remained, for one who could now dispose of France as he listed, to dictate the form and fashion of the new emblem of his sway.

The title of King most obviously presented itself; but it was connected with the claims of the Bourbons, which it was not Buonaparte's policy to recall to remembrance. That of Emperor implied a yet higher power of sovereignty, and there existed no competitor who could challenge a claim to it. It was a novelty also, and flattered the French love of change; and though, in fact, the establishment of an empire was inconsistent with the various oaths taken against royalty, it was not, in terms, so directly contradictory to them. As the re-establishment of a kingdom, so far it was agreeable to those who might seek, not indeed how to keep their vows, but how to elude, in words at least, the charge of having broken them. To Napoleon's own ear, the word King might sound as if it restricted his power within the limits of the ancient kingdom; while that of Emperor might comprise dominions equal to the wide sweep of ancient Rome herself, and the bounds of the habitable earth alone could be considered as circumscribing their extent.

The main body of the nation being passive or intimidated,[73] there was no occasion to stand upon much ceremony with the constitutional bodies, the members of which were selected and paid by Buonaparte himself, held their posts at his pleasure, had every species of advancement to hope if they promoted his schemes, and every evil, of which the least would be deprivation of office, to expect, should they thwart him.

---

[73] "I advised Buonaparte to make himself master of the crisis, and cause himself to be proclaimed Emperor, in order to terminate all our uncertainties, by the foundation of his dynasty. I knew that his resolution was taken. Would it not have been absurd, on the part of the men of the Revolution, to compromise every thing, in order to defend our principles, while we had nothing further to do but enjoy the reality?"—Fouché, tom. i., p. 268.

CHANGE OF TITLE

On the 30th of April, 1804, Curée,[74] an orator of no great note, (and who was perhaps selected on that very account, that his proposal might be disavowed, should it meet with unexpected opposition,) took the lead in this measure, which was to destroy the slight and nominal remains of a free constitution which France retained under her present form of government. "It was time to bid adieu," he said, "to political illusions. The internal tranquillity of France had been regained, peace with foreign states had been secured by victory. The finances of the country had been restored, its code of laws renovated and re-established. It was time to ascertain the possession of these blessings to the nation in future, and the orator saw no mode of doing this, save rendering the supreme power hereditary in the person and family of Napoleon, to whom France owed such a debt of gratitude. This, he stated, was the universal desire of the army and of the people. He invited the Tribunate, therefore, to give effect to the general wish, and hail Napoleon Buonaparte by the title of Emperor, as that which best corresponded with the dignity of the nation."[75]

The members of the Tribunate contended with each other who should most enhance the merits of Napoleon, and prove, in the most logical and rhetorical terms, the advantages of arbitrary power over the various modifications of popular or limited governments. But one man, Carnot, was bold enough to oppose the full tide of sophistry and adulation. This name is unhappily to be read among the colleagues of Robespierre in the Revolutionary Committee, as well as amongst those who voted for the death of the misused and unoffending Louis XVI.; yet his highly honourable conduct in the urgent crisis now under discussion, shows that the zeal for liberty which led him into such excesses was genuine and sincere; and that, in point of firmness and public spirit, Carnot equalled the ancient patriots whom he aspired to imitate. His speech was as temperate and expressive as it was eloquent. Buonaparte, he admitted, had

---

[74] Curée was born at St. André, near Lodève, in 1756. When, in 1807, the Tribunate was dissolved, he was appointed a member of the Conservative Senate. In 1808, Napoleon bestowed on him the title of Count de Labédissières.
[75] Moniteur, No. 222, An. xii.; Montgaillard, Hist. de France, tom. vi., p. 57.

saved France, and saved it by the assumption of absolute power; but this, he contended, was only the temporary consequence of a violent crisis of the kind to which republics were subject, and the evils of which could only be stemmed by a remedy equally violent. The present head of the government was, he allowed, a dictator; but in the same sense in which Fabius, Camillus, and Cincinnatus, were so of yore, who retired to the condition of private citizens when they had accomplished the purpose for which temporary supremacy had been intrusted to them. The like was to be expected from Buonaparte, who, on entering on the government of the state, had invested it with republican forms, which he had taken a solemn oath to maintain, and which it was the object of Curée's motion to invite him to violate. He allowed that the various republican forms of France had been found deficient in stability, which he contended was owing to the tempestuous period in which they had been adopted, and the excited and irritable temper of men fired with political animosity, and incapable at the moment of steady or philosophical reflection; but he appealed to the United States of America, as an example of a democratical government, equally wise, vigorous, and permanent. He admitted the virtues and talents of the present governor of France, but contended that these attributes could not be rendered hereditary along with the throne. He reminded the Tribunate that Domitian had been the son of the wise Vespasian, Caligula of Germanicus, and Commodus of Marcus Aurelius. Again, he asked, whether it was not wronging Buonaparte's glory to substitute a new title to that which he had rendered so illustrious, and to invite and tempt him to become the instrument of destroying the liberties of the very country to which he had rendered such inestimable services? He then announced the undeniable proposition, that what services soever an individual might render to the state of which he was a member, there were bounds to public gratitude prescribed by honour as well as reason. If a citizen had the means of operating the safety, or restoring the liberty of his country, it could not be termed a becoming recompense to surrender to him that very liberty, the re-establishment of which had been his own work. Or what glory, he asked, could accrue to the selfish individual who should claim the surrender of his country's independence in requital of his services, and desire to convert the state which his talents had preserved into his own private patrimony![76]

Carnot concluded his manly and patriotic speech by declaring, that though he opposed, on grounds of conscience, the alteration of government which had been proposed, he would, nevertheless, should it be adopted by the nation, give it his unlimited obedience. He kept his word accordingly, and retired to a private station, in poverty most honourable to a statesman who had filled the highest offices of the state, and enjoyed the most unlimited power of amassing wealth.[77]

When his oration was concluded, there was a contention for precedence among the time-serving speakers, who were each desirous to take the lead in refuting the reasoning of Carnot. It would be tedious to trace them through their sophistry. The leading argument turned upon the talents of Buonaparte, his services rendered to France, and the necessity there was for acknowledging them by something like a proportionate act of national gratitude. Their eloquence resembled nothing so nearly as the pleading of a wily procuress, who endeavours to persuade some simple maiden, that the services rendered to her by a liberal and gallant admirer, can only be rewarded by the sacrifice of her honour. The speaking (for it could neither be termed debate nor deliberation) was prolonged for three days, after which the motion of Curée was adopted by the Tribunate,[78] without one negative voice, excepting that of the inflexible Carnot.

EMPEROR OF THE FRENCH

The Senate, to whom the Tribunate hastened to present their project of establishing despotism under its own undisguised title, hastened to form a senatus consultum, which established the new

---

[76] Montgaillard, tom. vi., p. 76; Moniteur, No. 222, An. xii.
[77] "When a member of the Tribunate, Carnot spoke and voted against the establishment of the empire; but his conduct, open and manly, gave no uneasiness to the administration."—Napoleon, *Las Cases*, tom. iv., p. 141.
[78] For the decree, passed the Tribunate on the 3d of May, and carried up to the Conservative Senate on the following day, see Annual Register, vol. xlvi., p. 658.

constitution of France. The outline,—for what would it serve to trace the minute details of a design sketched in the sand, and obliterated by the tide of subsequent events,[79]—was as follows:—

1st, Napoleon Buonaparte was declared hereditary Emperor of the French nation. The empire was made hereditary, first in the male line of the Emperor's direct descendants. Failing these, Napoleon might adopt the sons or grandsons of his brothers, to succeed him in such order as he might point out. In default of such adoptive heirs, Joseph and Louis Buonaparte were, in succession, declared the lawful heirs of the empire. Lucien and Jerome Buonaparte were excluded from this rich inheritance, as they had both disobliged Napoleon by marrying without his consent.

2d, The members of the Imperial family were declared Princes of the Blood, and by the decree of the Senate, the offices of Grand Elector, Archchancellor of the Empire, Archchancellor of State, High Constable, and Great Admiral of the Empire, were established as necessary appendages of the empire. These dignitaries, named of course by the Emperor himself, consisting of his relatives, connexions, and most faithful adherents, formed his Grand Council. The rank of Marshal of the Empire was conferred upon seventeen of the most distinguished generals, comprehending Jourdan, Augereau, and others, formerly zealous Republicans.[80] Duroc was named Grand Marshal of the Palace; Caulaincourt, Master of the Horse; Berthier, Grand Huntsman, and the Comte de Ségur, a nobleman of the old court, Master of Ceremonies.

Thus did republican forms, at length and finally, give way to those of a court; and that nation, which no moderate or rational degree of freedom would satisfy, now contentedly, or at least passively, assumed the yoke of a military despot. France, in 1792, had been like the wild elephant in his fits of fury, when to oppose his course is death; in 1804, she was like the same animal tamed and trained, who kneels down and suffers himself to be mounted by the soldier, whose business is to drive him into the throng of the battle.

---

[79] See Organic Senatus Consultum, May 18, Annual Register, vol. xlvi., p. 664.
[80] Montgaillard, tom. vi., p. 103; Annual Register, vol. xlvi., p. 663.

Measures were taken, as on former occasions, to preserve appearances, by obtaining, in show at least, the opinion of the people, on this radical change of their system.[81] Government, however, were already confident of their approbation, which, indeed, had never been refused to any of the various constitutions, however inconsistent, that had succeeded each other with such rapidity. Secure on this point, Buonaparte's accession to the empire was proclaimed with the greatest pomp, without waiting to inquire whether the people approved of his promotion or otherwise. The proclamation was coldly received, even by the populace, and excited little enthusiasm.[82] It seemed, according to some writers, as if the shades of D'Enghien and Pichegru had been present invisibly, and spread a damp over the ceremony. The Emperor was recognised by the soldiery with more warmth. He visited the encampments at Boulogne, with the intention apparently, of receiving such an acknowledgment from the troops as was paid by the ancient Franks to their monarchs, when they elevated them on their bucklers. Seated on an iron chair, said to have belonged to King Dagobert, he took his place between two immense camps, and having before him the Channel and the hostile coasts of England. The weather, we have been assured, had been tempestuous, but no sooner had the Emperor assumed his seat, to receive the homage of his shouting host, than the sky cleared, and the wind dropt, retaining just breath sufficient gently to wave the banners. Even the elements seemed to acknowledge the imperial dignity, all save the sea, which rolled as carelessly to the feet of Napoleon as it had formerly done towards those of Canute the Dane.

---

[81] "In the army the proposed change went down of itself; this is easily accounted for. The dragoons gave the first impulse. They sent an address to the first consul, in which they alleged that their efforts would be of no service if wicked men should succeed in taking away his life; that the best way to thwart their designs, and to fix their resolute, was to put the imperial crown on his head, and to fix that dignity in his family. After the dragoons came the cuirassiers, then all the corps of infantry, and then the seamen; and lastly, those of the civil orders who wished for the change, followed the example of the army. The spirit spread in an instant to the smallest parishes; the first consul received carriages full of such addresses. A register for the reception of votes was opened in every parish in France. It was the summary of all these votes, laid before the senate, that formed the basis of the *procès-verbal* of inauguration of the Buonaparte family to the imperial dignity."—Savary, tom. ii., p. 69.

[82] "Napoleon's elevation to the imperial dignity met, from all quarters, with the most chilling reception; there were public *fêtes* without animation, and without joy."—Fouché, tom. i., p. 272.

The Emperor, accompanied with his Empress, who bore her honours both gracefully and meekly, visited Aix-la-Chapelle, and the frontiers of Germany. They received the congratulations of all the powers of Europe, excepting England, Russia, and Sweden, upon their new exaltation; and the German princes, who had every thing to hope and fear from so powerful a neighbour, hastened to pay their compliments to Napoleon in person, which more distant sovereigns offered by their ambassadors.[83]

But the most splendid and public recognition of his new rank was yet to be made, by the formal act of coronation, which, therefore, Napoleon determined should take place with circumstances of solemnity, which had been beyond the reach of any temporal prince, however powerful, for many ages. His policy was often marked by a wish to revive, imitate, and connect his own titles and interest with some ancient observance of former days; as if the novelty of his claims could have been rendered more venerable by investing them with antiquated forms, or as men of low birth, when raised to wealth and rank, are sometimes desirous to conceal the obscurity of their origin under the blaze of heraldic honours. Pope Leo, he remembered, had placed a golden crown on the head of Charlemagne, and proclaimed him Emperor of the Romans. Pius VII., he determined, should do the same for a successor to much more than the actual power of Charlemagne. But though Charlemagne had repaired to Rome to receive inauguration from the hands of the Pontiff of that day, Napoleon resolved that he who now owned the proud, and in Protestant eyes profane, title of Vicar of Christ, should travel to France to perform the coronation of the successful chief, by whom the See of Rome had been more than once humbled, pillaged, and impoverished, but by whom also her power had been re-erected and restored, not only in Italy, but in France itself.

Humiliating as the compliance with Buonaparte's request must have seemed to the more devoted Catholics, Pius VII. had already sacrificed, to obtain the Concordat, so much of the power and privileges of the Roman See, that he could hardly have been justified if he had run the risk of losing the advantages of a treaty so

---

[83] Fouché, tom. ii., p. 280.

dearly purchased, by declining to incur some personal trouble or, it might be termed, some direct self-abasement. The Pope, and the cardinals whom he consulted, implored the illumination of Heaven upon their councils; but it was the stern voice of necessity which assured them, that except at the risk of dividing the Church by a schism, they could not refuse to comply with Buonaparte's requisition. The Pope left Rome on the 5th November. He was every where received on the road with the highest respect, and most profound veneration; the Alpine precipices themselves had been secured by parapets wherever they could expose the venerable Father of the Catholic Church to danger, or even apprehension. Upon the 25th November he met Buonaparte at Fontainbleau;[84] and the conduct of the Emperor Napoleon was as studiously respectful towards him as that of Charlemagne, whom he was pleased to call his predecessor, could have been towards Leo.

THE CORONATION

On the 2d December, the ceremony of the coronation took place in the ancient cathedral of Notre Dame, with the addition of every ceremony which could be devised to add to its solemnity.[85]

---

[84] "The Emperor went to meet the Pope on the road to Nemours. To avoid ceremony, the pretext of a hunting party was assumed: the attendants, with his equipages, were in the forest. The Emperor came on horseback, and in a hunting dress, with his retinue. It was at the half moon at the top of the hill that the meeting took place. There the Pope's carriage drew up; he got out at the left door in his white costume; the ground was dirty; he did not like to step upon it with his white silk shoes, but was obliged to do so at last. Napoleon alighted to receive him. They embraced; and the Emperor's carriage, which had been purposely driven up, was advanced a few paces; but men were posted to hold the two doors open; at the moment of getting in, the Emperor took the right door, and an officer of the court handed the Pope to the left, so that they entered the carriage by the two doors at the same time. The Emperor naturally seated himself on the right; and this first step decided, without negotiation, upon the etiquette to be observed during the whole time that the Pope was to remain at Paris."—Savary, tom. ii., p. 73.

[85] "The departure of the Pope from the Tuileries for the Archiepiscopal Palace, was delayed for a short time by a singular cause. Every body was ignorant in France, that it was customary at Rome when the Pope went out to officiate in the great churches, for one of his principal chamberlains to set off a little before him, mounted on an ass, and carrying a large cross, such as is used in processions. It was not till the very moment of departure that this custom was made known. The chamberlain would not, for all the gold in the world, have derogated from the practice, and accepted a nobler animal. All the grooms of the Tuileries were instantly despatched in quest of an ass; and they were fortunate enough to find a tolerably well-looking one, which was hastily caparisoned. The chamberlain rode

Yet we have been told, that the multitude did not participate in the ceremonial with that eagerness which characterises the inhabitants of all capitals, but especially those of Paris, upon similar occasions.[86] They had, within a very few years, seen so many exhibitions, processions and festivals, established on the most discordant principles, which, though announced as permanent and unchangeable, had successively given way to newer doctrines, that they considered the splendid representation before them as an unsubstantial pageant, which would fade away in its turn. Buonaparte himself seemed absent and gloomy, till recalled to a sense of his grandeur by the voice of the numerous deputies and functionaries sent up from all the several departments of France, to witness the coronation.[87] These functionaries had been selected with due attention to their political opinions; and many of them holding offices under the government, or expecting benefits from the Emperor, made up, by the zealous vivacity of their acclamations, for the coldness of the good citizens of Paris.

EMPEROR OF THE FRENCH

The Emperor took his coronation oath, as usual on such occasions, with his hands upon the Scripture, and in the form in which it was repeated to him by the Pope. But in the act of coronation itself, there was a marked deviation from the universal custom, characteristic of the man, the age, and the conjuncture. In all other similar solemnities, the crown had been placed on the sovereign's head by the presiding spiritual person, as representing the Deity, by whom princes rule. But not even from the Head of the Catholic Church would Buonaparte consent to receive as a boon the golden symbol of sovereignty, which he was sensible he owed solely to his own unparalleled train of military and civil successes. The

---

with a composure which nothing could disturb, through the innumerable multitudes who lined the quays, and could not help laughing at this odd spectacle, which they beheld for the first time."—Savary, tom. ii., p. 75.
[86] "At the ceremony of the coronation, the acclamations, at first extremely few, were afterwards reinforced by the multitude of men in office, (*fonctionnaires*,) who were summoned from all parts of France to be present at the coronation. But upon returning to his palace, Napoleon found cold and silent spectators."—Fouché, tom. ii., p. 285.
[87] Montgaillard, tom. vi., p. 142.

crown having been blessed by the Pope, Napoleon took it from the altar with his own hands, and placed it on his brows. He then put the diadem on the head of his Empress, as if determined to show that his authority was the child of his own actions. *Te Deum* was sung; the heralds (for they also had again come into fashion) proclaimed, "that the thrice glorious and thrice august Napoleon, Emperor of the French, was crowned and installed." Thus concluded this remarkable ceremony. Those who remember having beheld it, must now doubt whether they were waking, or whether fancy had framed a vision so dazzling in its appearance, so extraordinary in its origin and progress, and so ephemeral in its endurance.[88]

The very day before the ceremony of coronation, (that is, on the 1st of December,) the Senate had waited upon the Emperor with the result of the votes collected in the departments, which, till that time, had been taken for granted. Upwards of three millions five hundred thousand citizens had given their votes on this occasion; of whom only about three thousand five hundred had declared against the proposition. The vice-president, Neufchateau, declared, "this report was the unbiassed expression of the people's choice. No government could plead a title more authentic."[89]

This was the established language of the day; but when the orator went farther, and mentioned the measure now adopted as enabling Buonaparte to guide into port the vessel of the *Republic*, one would have thought there was more irony than compliment in the expression.

Napoleon replied, by promises to employ the power which the unanimous consent of the Senate, the people, and the army, had conferred upon him, for the advantage of that nation which he himself, writing from fields of battle, had first saluted with the title of the Great. He promised, too, in name of his Dynasty, that his children should long preserve the throne, and be at once the first

---

[88] Montgaillard, tom. vi., p. 144; Annual Register, vol. xlvi., p. 680; Savary, tom. ii., p. 75.
[89] Annual Register, vol. xlvi., p. 685.

soldiers in the army of France, and the first magistrates among her citizens.[90]

As every word on such an occasion was scrupulously sifted and examined, it seemed to some that this promise, which Napoleon volunteered in behalf of children who had as yet no existence, intimated a meditated change of consort, since from his present Empress he had no longer any hope of issue. Others censured the prophetic tone in which he announced what would be the fate and conduct of unborn beings, and spoke of a reign, newly commenced, under the title of a Dynasty, which is usually applied to a race of successive princes.

THE IMPERIAL CONSTITUTION

We pause for a moment to consider the act of popular accession to the new government; because there, if any where, we are to look for something like a legal right, in virtue of which Napoleon might claim obedience. He himself, when pleading his own cause after his fall, repeatedly rests his right to be considered and treated as a legitimate monarch, upon the fact, that he was called to the crown by the voice of the people.[91]

We will not stop to inquire how the registers, in which the votes of the citizens were enrolled, were managed by the

---

[90] "I ascend the throne, to which the unanimous wishes of the senate, the people, and the army have called me, with a heart penetrated with the great destinies of that people, whom, from the midst of camps, I first saluted with the name of Great. From my youth, my thoughts have been solely fixed upon them, and I must add here, that my pleasures and my pains are derived entirely from the happiness or misery of my people. My descendants shall long preserve this throne; in the camps, they will be the first soldiers of the army, sacrificing their lives in the defence of their country. As magistrates, they will never forget that the contempt of the laws, and the confusion of social order, are only the result of the imbecility and unsteadiness of princes. You, senators, whose councils and support have never failed me in the most difficult circumstances; your spirit will be handed down to your successors. Be ever the props and first counsellors of that throne, so necessary to the welfare of this vast empire."

[91] "If I was not a legitimate sovereign, William the Third was a usurper of the throne of England, as he was brought in chiefly by the aid of foreign bayonets. George the First was placed on the throne by a faction, composed of a few nobles. I was called to that of France by the votes of nearly four millions of Frenchmen."—Napoleon, *Voice*, &c., vol. ii., p. 113.

functionaries who had the charge of them;—it is only necessary to state in passing, that these returning officers were in general accessible to the influence of government, and that there was no possibility of instituting any scrutiny into the authenticity of the returns. Neither will we repeat, that instead of waiting for the event of the popular vote, he had accepted of the empire from the Senate, and had been proclaimed Emperor accordingly. Waving those circumstances entirely, let it be remembered, that France is usually reckoned to contain upwards of thirty millions of inhabitants, and that three millions five hundred thousand, only gave their votes. This was not a third part, deducing women and children, of those who had a title to express their opinion, where it was to be held decisive of the greatest change which the state could undergo; and it must be allowed that the authority of so limited a portion of the people is far too small to bind the remainder. We have heard it indeed argued, that the question having been formally put to the nation at large, every one was under an obligation to make a specific reply; and they who did not vote, must be held to have acquiesced in the opinion expressed by the majority of such as did. This argument, being directly contrary to the presumption of law in all similar cases, is not more valid than the defence of the soldier, who, accused of having stolen a necklace from an image of the Virgin, replied to the charge, that he had first asked the Madonna's permission, and, receiving no answer, had taken silence for consent.

In another point of view, it must be remembered that this vote, by which Napoleon claimed the absolute and irredeemable cession of the liberties of France in his favour, was not a jot more solemn than those by which the people had previously sanctioned the Constitutional Monarchy of 1791, the Republic of 1792, the Directory of 1795, and the Consular Government of 1799. Now, either the vote upon all those occasions was binding and permanent, or it was capable of being denied and recalled at the pleasure of the people. If the former was the case, then the people had no right, in 1804, to resume the votes they had given, and the oaths they had sworn, to the first form of government in 1791. The others which they sanctioned in its stead, were in consequence, mere usurpations, and that now attempted the most flagrant of all; since three constitutions, each resting on the popular consent, were demolished, and three sets of oaths broken and discarded, to make room for the present model. Again, if the people, in swearing to one constitution, retained inalienably the right of substituting another whenever they thought proper, the imperial constitution remained at their mercy as much as those that preceded it; and then on what could Buonaparte rest the inviolability of his authority, guarded with such jealous precaution, and designed to descend to his successors, without any future appeal to the people? The dynasty which he supposed himself to have planted, was in that case not the oak-tree which he conceived it, but, held during the good pleasure of a fickle people, rather resembled the thistle, whose unsubstantial crest rests upon the stalk only so long as the wind shall not disturb it.

But we leave these considerations; nor do we stop to inquire how many, amid the three millions and upwards of voters, gave an unwilling signature, which they would have refused if they had dared, nor how many more attached no greater consequence to the act than to a piece of formal complaisance, which every government expected in its turn, and which bound the subject no longer than the ruler had means to enforce his obedience. Another and more formidable objection remains behind, which pervaded the whole pretended surrender by the French nation of their liberties, and rendered it void, null, and without force or effect whatever. It was, from the commencement, what jurists call a *pactum in illicito*:—the people gave that which they had no right to surrender, and Buonaparte accepted that which he had no title to take at their hands. In most instances of despotic usurpation—we need only look at the case of Cæsar—the popular party have been made the means of working out their own servitude; the government being usurped by some demagogue who acted in their name, and had the art to make their own hands the framers of their own chains. But though such consent on the part of the people, elicited from an excess of partial confidence or of gratitude, may have rendered such encroachments on the freedom of the state more easy, it did not and could not render it in any case more legal. The rights of a free people are theirs to enjoy, but not theirs to alienate or surrender. The people are in this respect like minors, to whom law assures their property, but invests them with no title to give it away or consume it; the national privileges are an estate entailed from generation to generation, and they can neither be the subject of gift, exchange, nor surrender, by those who enjoy the usufruct or temporary possession of them. No man is lord even of his person, to the effect of surrendering his life or limbs to the mercy of another; the contract of the Merchant of Venice would now be held null from the beginning in any court of justice in Europe. But far more should the report of 1804, upon Buonaparte's election, be esteemed totally void, since it involved the cession on the part of the French people of that which ought to have been far more dear to them, and held more inalienable, than "the pound of flesh nearest the heart,"[92] or the very heart itself.

As the people of France had no right to resign their own liberties, and that of their posterity, for ever, so Buonaparte could not legally avail himself of their prodigal and imprudent cession. If a blind man give a piece of gold by mistake instead of a piece of silver, he who receives it acquires no legal title to the surplus value. If an ignorant man enter unwittingly into an illegal compact, his signature, though voluntary, is not binding upon him. It is true, that Buonaparte had rendered the highest services to France by his Italian campaigns in the first instance, and afterwards by that wonderful train of success which followed his return from Egypt. Still the services yielded by a subject to his native land, like the duty paid by a child to a parent, cannot render him creditor of the country, beyond the amount which she has legal means of discharging. If France had received the highest benefits from Buonaparte, she had in return raised him as high as any subject could be advanced, and had, indeed, in her reckless prodigality of gratitude, given, or suffered him to assume, the very despotic authority, which this compact of which we treat was to consolidate and sanction under its real name of Empire. Here, therefore, we close the argument; concluding the pretended vote of the French people to be totally null, both as regarding the subjects who yielded their privileges, and the emperor who accepted of their surrender. The former could not give away rights which it was not lawful to resign, the latter could not accept an authority which it was unlawful to exercise.

---

[92] Merchant of Venice, act iv., scene 1.

An apology, or rather a palliation of Buonaparte's usurpation, has been set up by himself and his more ardent admirers, and we are desirous of giving to it all the weight which it shall be found to deserve. They have said, and with great reason, that Buonaparte, viewed in his general conduct, was no selfish usurper, and that the mode in which he acquired his power was gilded over by the use which he made of it. This is true; for we will not under-rate the merits which Napoleon thus acquired, by observing that shrewd politicians have been of opinion, that sovereigns who have only a questionable right to their authority, are compelled, were it but for their own sakes, to govern in such a manner as to make the country feel its advantage in submitting to their government. We grant willingly, that in much of his internal administration Buonaparte showed that he desired to have no advantage separate from that of France; that he conceived her interests to be connected with his own glory; that he expended his wealth in ornamenting the empire, and not upon objects more immediately personal to himself. We have no doubt that he had more pleasure in seeing treasures of art added to the Museum, than in hanging them on the walls of his own palace; and that he spoke truly, when asserting that he grudged Josephine the expensive plants with which she decorated her residence at Malmaison, because her taste interfered with the prosperity of the public botanical garden of Paris.[93] We allow, therefore, that Buonaparte fully identified himself with the country which he had rendered his patrimony; and that while it should be called by his name, he was desirous of investing it with as much external splendour, and as much internal prosperity as his gigantic schemes were able to compass. No doubt it may be said, so completely was the country identified with its ruler, that as France had nothing but what belonged to its Emperor, he was in fact improving his own estate when he advanced her public works, and could no more be said to lose sight of his own interest, than a private gentleman does, who neglects his garden to ornament his park. But it is not fair to press the motives of human nature to their last retreat, in which something like a taint of self-interest may so often be discovered. It is enough to reply, that the selfishness which embraces the interests of a whole kingdom, is of a kind so liberal, so extended, and so refined, as to be closely allied to patriotism; and

---

[93] Las Cases, tom. vii., p. 120.

that the good intentions of Buonaparte towards that France, over which he ruled with despotic sway, can be no more doubted, than the affections of an arbitrary father whose object it is to make his son prosperous and happy, to which he annexes as the only condition, that he shall be implicitly obedient to every tittle of his will. The misfortune is, however, that arbitrary power is in itself a faculty, which, whether exercised over a kingdom, or in the bosom of a family, is apt to be used with caprice rather than judgment, and becomes a snare to those who possess it, as well as a burden to those over whom it extends. A father, for example, seeks the happiness of his son, while he endeavours to assure his fortunes, by compelling him to enter into a mercenary and reluctant marriage; and Buonaparte conceived himself to be benefiting as well as aggrandizing France, when, preferring the splendour of conquest to the blessings of peace, he led the flower of her young men to perish in foreign fields, and finally was the means of her being delivered up, drained of her population,[94] to the mercy of the foreign invaders, whose resentment his ambition had provoked.

CHANGES IN ITALY

Such are the considerations which naturally arise out of Napoleon's final and avowed assumption of the absolute power, which he had in reality possessed and exercised ever since he had been created First Consul for life. It was soon after made manifest, that France, enlarged and increased in strength as she had been under his auspices, was yet too narrow a sphere for his domination. Italy afforded the first illustration of his grasping ambition.[95]

---

[94] "The Emperor constantly insisted on subjecting the whole nation to the laws of the conscription. 'The conscription,' he said, 'is the root of a nation, its moral purification, the real foundation of its habits. Organized, built up in this way, the French people might have defied the world, and might with justice have renewed the saying of the proud Gauls: 'If the sky should fall, we will keep it up with our lances.'"—Las Cases, tom. vii., p. 98.

[95] "We soon perceived that Napoleon meditated a great diversion. When he mentioned in council his idea of going to be crowned King of Italy, we all told him he would provoke a new continental war. 'I must have battles and triumphs,' replied he. And yet he did not relax his preparations for the invasion of England. One day, upon my objecting to him that he could not make war at the same time, against England and against all Europe, he replied, 'I may fail by sea, but not by land; besides, I shall be able to strike the blow before the old

The northern states of Italy had followed the example of France through all her change of models. They had become republican in a directorial form, when Napoleon's sword conquered them from the Austrians; had changed to an establishment similar to the consular, when that was instituted in Paris by the 18th Brumaire; and were now destined to receive, as a king, him who had lately accepted and exercised with regal authority the office of their president.

The authorities of the Italian (late Cisalpine) republic had a prescient guess of what was expected of them. A deputation[96] appeared at Paris, to declare the absolute necessity which they felt, that their government should assume a monarchical and hereditary form. On the 17th March, 1805, they obtained an audience of the Emperor, to whom they intimated the unanimous desire of their countrymen, that Napoleon, founder of the Italian Republic, should be monarch of the Italian Kingdom. He was to have power to name his successor, such being always a native of France or Italy. With an affectation of jealous independence, however, the authors of this "humble petition and advice" stipulated, that the crowns of France and Italy should never, save in the present instance, be placed on the head of the same monarch. Napoleon might, during his life, devolve the sovereignty of Italy on one of his descendants, either natural or adopted; but it was anxiously stipulated, that such delegation should not be made during the period while France continued to occupy the Neapolitan territories, the Russians Corfu, and the British Malta.[97]

Buonaparte granted the petition of the Italian states, and listened with indulgence to their jealous scruples. He agreed with them, that the separation of the crowns of France and Italy, which might be useful to their descendants, would be in the highest degree dangerous to themselves; and therefore he consented to bear the

---

coalition machines are ready. The people of the old school (*têtes à perruques*) understand nothing about it, and the kings have neither activity nor decision of character. I do not fear old Europe."—Fouché, tom. i., p. 285.
[96] Consisting of M. Melzi, vice-president of the Italian republic; M. Mareschalchi, ambassador of that republic; and the representatives of its principal bodies.
[97] See official proceedings relative to the assumption of the crown of Italy by Napoleon, emperor of the French.—*Annual Register*, vol. xlvii., p. 720.

additional burden which their love and confidence imposed, at least until the interest of his Italian subjects should permit him to place the crown on a younger head, who, animated by his spirit, should, he engaged, "be ever ready to sacrifice his life for the people over whom he should be called to reign, by Providence, by the constitution of the country, and by the will of Napoleon."[98] In announcing this new acquisition to the French Senate, Buonaparte made use of an expression so singularly audacious, that to utter it required almost as much courage as to scheme one of his most daring campaigns. "The power and majesty of the French empire," he said, "are surpassed by the moderation which presides over her political transactions."

CORONATION AT MILAN

Upon the 11th April, Napoleon, with his Empress, set off to go through the form of coronation, as King of Italy.[99] The ceremony almost exactly resembled that by which he had been inaugurated Emperor. The ministry of the Pope, however, was not employed on this second occasion, although, as Pius VII. was then on his return to Rome, he could scarcely have declined officiating, if he had been requested by Buonaparte to take Milan in his route for that purpose. Perhaps it was thought too harsh to exact from the Pontiff the consecration of a King of Italy, whose very title implied a possibility that his dominion might be one day extended, so as to include the patrimony of Saint Peter. Perhaps, and we rather believe it was the case, some cause of dissatisfaction had already occurred betwixt Napoleon and Pius VII. However this may be, the ministry of the

---

[98] "I shall keep this crown; but only so long as your interests shall require; and I shall with pleasure see the moment arrive, when I can place it on the head of a younger person, who, animated by my spirit, may continue my work, and be on all occasions ready to sacrifice his person and interests to the security and the happiness of the people over whom Providence, the constitutions of the kingdom, and my wish, shall have called him to reign."
[99] "Napoleon remained three weeks at Turin, and was in that city when the Pope arrived there. His holiness had lodgings provided for him in the royal palace; the Emperor went thither to see him, and set out the next day by Asti for Alexandria; the Pope took the road to Casal on his way back to Rome. At Alexandria the Emperor inspected the immense works which, by his direction, were carrying on there. He held a review on the field of Marengo; he put on that day the same coat and laced hat which he wore in the engagement; the coat was quite moth-eaten."—Savary, tom. ii., p. 80.

Archbishop of Milan was held sufficient for the occasion, and it was he who blessed the celebrated iron crown, said to have girded the brows of the ancient Kings of the Lombards. Buonaparte, as in the ceremony at Paris, placed the ancient emblem on his head with his own hands, assuming and repeating aloud the haughty motto attached to it by its ancient owners, *Dieu me l'a donné; Gare qui la touche.* "God has given it me: Let him beware who touches it."[100]

The new kingdom was, in all respects, modelled on the same plan with the French empire. An order, called "of the Iron Crown," was established on the footing of that of the Legion of Honour. A large French force was taken into Italian pay, and Eugene Beauharnois,[101] the son of Josephine by her former marriage, who enjoyed and merited the confidence of his father-in-law, was created viceroy, and appointed to represent, in that character, the dignity of Napoleon.[102]

Napoleon did not leave Italy without further extension of his empire. Genoa, once the proud and the powerful, resigned her independence, and her Doge presented to the Emperor a request that the Ligurian republic, laying down her separate rights, should be considered in future as a part of the French nation. It was but lately that Buonaparte had declared to the listening Senate, that the boundaries of France were permanently fixed, and should not be extended for the comprehension of future conquests. It is farther true, that, by a solemn alliance with France, Genoa had placed her arsenals and harbours at the disposal of the French government; engaged to supply her powerful ally with six thousand sailors, and ten sail of the line, to be equipped at her own expense; and that her

---

[100] See official account of the coronation of the Emperor of the French, as king of Italy, at Milan, 26th May, 1805.—Annual Register, vol. xlvii., p. 723. See also Botta, Storia d'Italia, tom. iv., p. 209; Jomini, Vie Politique, tom. ii., p. 86.

[101] "After the ceremony of the coronation, the Emperor went in procession to the Italian senate, where he invested Prince Eugene with the viceroyalty of Italy."—Savary, tom. ii., p. 80.

[102] "During Napoleon's stay at Milan, he directed his attention towards the embellishment of that city, with the same zeal as if it had been Paris. He had always regretted that none of the governments of that country had undertaken the completion of the cathedral of Milan, the largest edifice of the kind, after St. Peter's at Rome. He ordered the works to be immediately resumed, forbidding them to be interrupted on any pretext whatever, and created a special fund for defraying the expenses. To him the Milanese are indebted for the completion of that noble structure."—Savary, tom. ii., p. 81.

independence, or such a nominal share of that inestimable privilege as was consistent with her connexion with this formidable power, had been guaranteed by France. But neither the charge of inconsistency with his own public declarations, nor consideration of the solemn treaty acknowledging the Ligurian republic, prevented Napoleon from availing himself of the pretext afforded by the petition of the Doge. It was convenient to indulge the city and government of Genoa in their wish to become an integral part of the Great Nation.[103] Buonaparte was well aware, that, by recognising them as a department of France, he was augmenting the jealousy of Russia and Austria, who had already assumed a threatening front towards him; but, as he visited the splendid city of the Dorias, and saw its streets of marble palaces, ascending from and surrounding its noble harbours, he was heard to exclaim, that such a possession was well worth the risks of war.[104] The success of one mighty plan only induced him to form another; and while he was conscious that he was the general object of jealousy and suspicion to Europe, Napoleon could not refrain from encroachments, which necessarily increased and perpetuated such hostile sentiments towards him.[105]

---

[103] "The Doge and Senate had come to Milan to beg the Emperor to accept them, and to incorporate them with the French empire. I have no doubt that this resolution had been somewhat assisted. Such was the state of this unfortunate republic, that its inhabitants were almost famishing: the English closely blockaded it by sea; the French *douanes* cooped it up by land: it had no territory, and could not, without difficulty, procure wherewithal to subsist. Add to this, that whenever a quarrel took place in Italy, the first thing was to send it a garrison, which it had not the means of refusing. It had, therefore, all the inconveniences arising from a union with France, without possessing any of the advantages: it determined, therefore, to make application to be incorporated with the empire."—Savary, tom. ii., p. 83. See also Botta, tom. iv., p. 214; Dumas, Précis des Evénemens Militaires; and Jomini, Vie Politique, tom. ii., p. 87.

[104] "In order to show himself to his new subjects, Napoleon traversed his kingdom of Italy. Upon seeing the magnificent city of Genoa and its picturesque environs, he exclaimed—'This is indeed worth a war.'"—Fouché, tom. i., p. 286.

[105] "All the organisations of Italy were provisional. Napoleon wished to make a single power of that great peninsula; for which reason he reserved the iron crown to himself, in order to keep in his own hands the direction of the different people of Italy. He preferred uniting Genoa, Rome, Tuscany and Piedmont to the empire, rather than to the kingdom of Italy, because the people of those countries preferred it; because the imperial influence would be more powerful; because it was a means of calling a great number of the inhabitants of those countries into France, and of sending a number of French thither in exchange; and because it would bring the conscripts and sailors of those provinces to strengthen the French regiments, and the crews of Toulon."—Napoleon, *Montholon*, tom. ii., p. 234.

Chapter XXXI

Napoleon addresses a Second Letter to the King of England personally— Answered by the British Secretary of State to Talleyrand—Alliance formed betwixt Russia and England—Prussia keeps aloof, and the Emperor Alexander visits Berlin—Austria prepares for War, and marches an Army into Bavaria—Her impolicy in prematurely commencing Hostilities, and in her Conduct to Bavaria—Unsoldierlike Conduct of the Austrian General Mack—Buonaparte is joined by the Electors of Bavaria and Wirtemberg, and the Duke of Baden—Skilful Manœuvres of the French Generals, and successive losses of the Austrians—Napoleon violates the Neutrality of Prussia, by marching through Anspach and Bareuth—Further Losses of the Austrian Leaders, and consequent Disunion among them—Mack is cooped up in Ulm—Issues a formidable Declaration on the 16th October—and surrenders on the following day—Fatal Results of this Man's Poltroonery, want of Skill, and probable Treachery.

LETTER TO THE KING OF ENGLAND

Buonaparte, Consul, had affected to give a direct testimony of his desire to make peace, by opening a communication immediately and personally with the King of Great Britain. Buonaparte, Emperor, had, according to his own interpretation of his proceedings, expiated by his elevation all the crimes of the Revolution, and wiped out for ever the memory of those illusory visions of liberty and equality, which had alarmed such governments as continued to rest their authority on the ancient basis of legitimacy. He had, in short, according to his own belief, preserved in his system all that the Republic had produced of good, and done away all the memory of that which was evil.

With such pretensions, to say nothing of his absolute power, he hastened to claim admission among the acknowledged Princes of Europe; and a second time (2d January 1805,) by a letter addressed to King George III., personally, under the title of "Sir my Brother," endeavoured to prove, by a string of truisms,—on the preference of a state of peace to war, and on the reciprocal grandeur of France and England, both advanced to the highest pitch of prosperity,— that the hostilities between the nations ought to be ended.[106]

We have already stated the inconveniences which must necessarily attach to a departure from the usual course of treating between states, and to the transference of the discussions usually intrusted to inferior and responsible agents, to those who are themselves at the head of the nation. But if Napoleon had been

---

[106] "Sir and Brother,—Called to the throne of France by Providence, and by the suffrages of the senate, the people, and the army, my first sentiment is a wish for peace. France and England abuse their prosperity. They may contend for ages; but do their Governments well fulfil the most sacred of their duties, and will not so much blood, shed uselessly and without a view to any end, condemn them in their own consciences? I consider it as no disgrace to make the first step. I have, I hope, sufficiently proved to the world, that I fear none of the chances of war; it, besides, presents nothing that I need to fear: peace is the wish of my heart, but war has never been inconsistent with my glory. I conjure your majesty not to deny yourself the happiness of giving peace to the world, nor to leave that sweet satisfaction to your children; for certainly there never was a more fortunate opportunity, nor a moment more favourable, to silence all the passions, and listen only to the sentiments of humanity and reason. This moment once lost, what end can be assigned to a war which all my efforts will not be able to terminate! Your majesty has gained more within ten years, both in territory and riches, than the whole extent of Europe. Your nation is at the highest point of prosperity; what can it hope from war? To form a coalition with some powers of the continent? The continent will remain tranquil: a coalition can only increase the preponderance and continental greatness of France. To renew intestine troubles? The times are no longer the same. To destroy our finances? Finances founded on a flourishing agriculture can never be destroyed. To take from France her colonies? The colonies are to France only a secondary object; and does not your majesty already possess more than you know how to preserve? If your majesty would but reflect, you must perceive that the war is without an object, without any presumable result to yourself. Alas! what a melancholy prospect to cause two nations to fight merely for the sake of fighting. The world is sufficiently large for our two nations to live in it, and reason is sufficiently powerful to discover means of reconciling every thing, when the wish for reconciliation exists on both sides. I have, however, fulfilled a sacred duty, and one which is precious to my heart. I trust your majesty will believe in the sincerity of my sentiments, and my wish to give you every proof of it."—Napoleon.

serious in desiring peace, and saw any reason for directly communicating with the English King rather than with the English Government, he ought to have made his proposal something more specific than a string of general propositions, which, affirmed on the one side, and undisputed on the other, left the question between the belligerent powers as undecided as formerly. The question was, not whether peace was desirable, but on what terms it was offered, or could be obtained. If Buonaparte, while stating, as he might have been expected to do, that the jealousies entertained by England of his power were unjust, had agreed, that for the tranquillity of Europe, the weal of both nations, and the respect in which he held the character of the monarch whom he addressed, Malta should remain with Britain in perpetuity, or for a stipulated period, it would have given a serious turn to his overture, which was at present as vague in its tendency, as it was unusual in the form.

The answer to his letter, addressed by the British Secretary of State[107] to M. Talleyrand, declared, that Britain could not make a precise reply to the proposal of peace intimated in Napoleon's letter, until she had communicated with her allies on the continent, and in particular with the Emperor of Russia.

These expressions indicated, what was already well known to Buonaparte, the darkening of another continental storm, about to be directed against his power. On this occasion, Russia was the soul of the confederacy. Since the death of the unfortunate Paul had placed that mighty country under the government of a wise and prudent prince, whose education had been sedulously cultivated, and who had profited in an eminent degree by that advantage, her counsels had been dignified, wise, and moderate. She had offered her mediation betwixt the belligerent powers, which, accepted willingly by Great Britain, had been somewhat haughtily declined by France, whose ruler was displeased, doubtless, to find that power in the hands of a sharp-sighted and sagacious sovereign, which, when lodged in those of Paul, he might reckon upon as at his own disposal, through his influence over that weak and partial monarch.

---

[107] Lord Mulgrave. For the letter see Annual Register, vol. xlvii., p. 616.

THE KING OF SWEDEN

From this time, there was coldness betwixt the French and Russian Governments. The murder of the Duke d'Enghien increased the misunderstanding. The Emperor of Russia was too high-spirited to view this scene of perfidy and violence in silence; and as he not only remonstrated with Buonaparte himself, but appealed to the German Diet on the violation of the territories of the Empire,[108] Napoleon, unused to have his actions censured and condemned by others, how powerful soever, seems to have regarded the Emperor Alexander with personal dislike.[109] Russia and Sweden, and their monarchs, became the subject of satire and ridicule in the *Moniteur*;[110] and, as every one knew, such arrows were never discharged without Buonaparte's special authority. The latter prince withdrew his ambassador from Paris, and in a public note, delivered to the French envoy at Stockholm, expressed his surprise at the "indecent and ridiculous insolences which Monsieur *Napoleon Buonaparte* had permitted to be inserted in the *Moniteur*."[111] Gustavus was, it is true, of an irregular and violent temper, apt to undertake plans, to the achievement of which the strength of his kingdom was inadequate;[112] yet he would scarcely have expressed himself with so little veneration for the most formidable authority in Europe, had he not been confident in the support of the Czar. In fact, on the 10th

---

[108] See Note presented to M. Talleyrand, by M. d'Oubril, relative to the seizure of the Duke d'Enghien, April 20, 1804; and also Note of the Minister Resident of Russia, communicated to the Diet of Ratisbon, May 5; Annual Register, vol. xlvi., pp. 642, 654.

[109] "As to the Emperor of Russia, he possesses wit, grace, information, is fascinating; but he is not to be trusted; he is a true Greek of the Lower Empire. Would you believe what I had to discuss with him? He maintained that inheritance was an abuse of monarchy, and I had to spend more than an hour, and employ all my eloquence and logic in proving to him that this right constituted the peace and happiness of the people. It may be that he was mystifying; for he is cunning, false, and expert. If I die in St. Helena, he will be my real heir in Europe."—Napoleon, *Las Cases*, tom. i., p. 300.

[110] See Moniteur, 14th August, 1804.

[111] See Note presented by order of the King of Sweden to. M. Caillard, the French Chargé d'Affaires at Stockholm, Sept. 7, 1804; Annual Register, vol. xlvi., p. 697.

[112] "On my accession to the sovereignty, Gustavus declared himself my great antagonist; it might have been supposed, that nothing short of renewing the exploits of the great Gustavus Adolphus would have satisfied him. He ran over the whole of Germany, for the purpose of stirring up enemies against me. At the time of the catastrophe of the Duke d'Enghien, he swore he would exact vengeance in person; and at a later period, he insolently sent back the black eagle to the King of Prussia, because the latter had accepted my Legion of Honour."—Napoleon, *Las Cases*, tom. v., p. 168.

of January, 1805, the King of Sweden had signed a treaty of close alliance with Russia; and, as a necessary consequence, on the 31st of October following, he published a declaration of war against France, in terms personally insulting to Napoleon.[113]

Russia and England, in the meantime, had engaged in an alliance, the general purpose of which was to form a league upon the continent, to compel the French Government to consent to the re-establishment of the balance of Europe. The objects proposed were briefly the independence of Holland and Switzerland; the evacuation of Hanover and the north of Germany by the French troops; the restoration of Piedmont to the King of Sardinia; and the complete evacuation of Italy by the French.[114] These were gigantic schemes, for which suitable efforts were to be made. Five hundred thousand men were to be employed; and Britain, besides affording the assistance of her forces by sea and land, was to pay large subsidies for supporting the armies of the coalition.

Great Britain and Russia were the animating sources of this new coalition against France; but it was impossible, considering the insular situation of the first of those powers, and the great distance of the second from the scene of action, that they alone, without the concurrence of the Emperor of Austria and the King of Prussia, should be able to assail France with any prospect of making a successful impression. Every effort, therefore, was used to awaken those states to a sense of the daily repeated encroachments of Buonaparte, and of the extreme danger to which they, were respectively exposed by the rapidly increasing extent of his empire.

PRUSSIA

But since the unsuccessful campaign of the year 1792, Prussia had observed a cautious and wary neutrality. She had seen, not perhaps without secret pleasure, the humiliation of Austria, her natural rival in Germany, and she had taken many opportunities to make acquisition of petty objects of advantage, in consequence of

---

[113] See Annual Register, vol. xlvii., p. 717.
[114] Jomini, tom. ii., p. 82.

the various changes upon the continent; so that she seemed to find her own interest in the successes of France. It is imagined, also, that Buonaparte had found some of her leading statesmen not altogether inaccessible to influence of a different kind, by the liberal exercise of which he was enabled to maintain a strong interest in the Prussian councils.[115] But the principles of these ministers were far from being shared by the nation at large. The encroachments on the German Empire intimately concerned the safety of Prussia, and the nation saw, in the decay of the Austrian influence, the creation and increase of a strong German party in favour of France, to whom Bavaria, Wirtemberg, and almost all the petty princes upon the Rhine, and its vicinity, began now to look up with the devotion and reverence which had hitherto been paid to the great states of Austria and Prussia. The subjects of the Great Frederick also remembered his numerous victories, and, proud of the army which he had created and bequeathed to his successor, felt neither apprehension nor unwillingness at the thought of measuring forces with the Dictator of Europe. The councils, therefore, of Prussia were divided; and though those which were favourable to France prevailed so far as to prevent her immediately becoming a member of the coalition, yet, by increasing her army to the war establishment, and marching forces towards the country which appeared about to become the scene of hostilities, Prussia gave plain intimation that the continuance of her neutrality depended upon the events of war.

Oct. 25.

To animate her councils, if possible, with a more decided spirit, Alexander visited the court of Berlin in person. He was received, with the utmost distinction, and both the King of Prussia, and his beautiful and interesting queen, gave manifest tokens of the share they took personally in the success of the alliance. An oath was taken by the two sovereigns at the tomb of the Great Frederick, by which they are said to have devoted themselves to the liberation of Germany,[116]—a vow which, though at a distant period, they amply redeemed. Still, whatever might be the personal opinions of the King of Prussia, the counsels of Haugwitz continued to

---

[115] Montgaillard, tom. vi., p. 165.
[116] Montgaillard, tom. vi., p. 179; Jomini, tom. ii., p. 137.

influence his Cabinet; and the Emperor withdrew from Berlin, to place himself at the head of his troops, while the Prussian monarch, assembling an army of observation, assumed the menacing air of a neutral who feels himself able to turn the scale in favour of either of the belligerent powers at his pleasure. This was not the moment for Buonaparte to take offence at these demonstrations, as the doing so might convert a doubtful friend into an avowed and determined enemy. But the dubious policy of Prussia was not forgotten,—it was carefully treasured in Napoleon's memory, as that for which she was to be called to account at a future period. In the meantime, he had the full advantage of her hesitating councils and doubtful neutrality.

Austria was more accessible to the application of the allies. Notwithstanding the disasters of the last two wars, the loss of a large portion of Italy, the disasters of Bellegarde, Alvinzi, and Wurmser, and the disastrous defeats of Marengo and Hohenlinden, the extent and military character of her population, amongst whom a short interval of peace was sufficient to recruit the losses of the most bloody war,—above all, the haughty determination of a Cabinet remarkable for the tenacity with which they retain and act upon the principles which they have once adopted, induced her Government to accede to the alliance betwixt Russia and Great Britain. She had not forgotten the successes which her generals and armies had obtained when fighting by the side of Suwarrow, and might hope to see once more renewed the victories of Trebia and of Novi. She therefore increased her force in every quarter; and while the Archduke Charles took the command of eighty thousand men in Italy, on which country Austria always kept a wishful eye, eighty thousand more, destined to act upon the Lech, and it was hoped upon the Rhine, were placed under the charge of General Mack, whose factitious and ill-merited reputation had, unfortunately for Austria, remained unabated, notwithstanding his miserable Neapolitan campaign in 1799. The Archduke Ferdinand, a prince of great courage and hopes, was the nominal commander of the last-mentioned army, while the real authority was lodged in this old and empty professor of tactics. To conclude this detail of preparation, the Archduke John was appointed to command in the Tyrol.[117]

---

[117] Jomini, Vie Politique et Militaire, tom. ii., pp. 97-101.

It remained only to try the event of negotiation, ere finally proceeding to military extremities. It was not difficult to state the causes of the war, which was now about to break out anew. By the peace of Luneville, finally concluded between Austria and France, the independence of the Italian, Helvetian, and Batavian republics had been stipulated; but instead of such terms being complied with, Napoleon, rendering himself Grand Mediator of Switzerland and King of Italy, had at the same time filled Holland with troops, and occupied the whole three countries in such a manner, as made them virtually, and almost avowedly, the absolute dependencies of France.

Complaints on these heads, warmly urged by Austria, were sharply answered by France, who in her turn accused Austria of want of confidence, and of assuming arms in the midst of peace.[118] The Emperor of Russia interfered, and sent a special ambassador to Paris, with the purpose of coming, if possible, to an amicable accommodation, which might even yet preserve the tranquillity of Europe. But ere Novosiltzoff had reached his place of destination, the union of Genoa with the French empire was announced; an encroachment which, joined to Napoleon's influence in Switzerland, rendered the whole north-western frontier of Italy completely open for the march of French armies, and precluded the possible hope of that fine country assuming any character of independence, even if, at a future time, its crown should be vested in a person different from the ruler of France.[119]

AUSTRIA—BAVARIA

Upon hearing of this new usurpation, made at the very time when Napoleon's steps towards the aggrandisement of his power were under challenge, Russia countermanded her ambassador; and Austria, after the exchange of some more angry notes, began her daring enterprise by marching a large army upon Bavaria.[120] It would

---

[118] See two Notes, delivered on the 13th and 16th April, by M. de Talleyrand to Count Cobentzel, Annual Register, vol. xlvii., pp. 644, 648.
[119] Mémoires de Savary, tom. ii., p. 123; Jomini, tom. ii., p. 93.
[120] "The public, who had been solely occupied with the projected invasion of England, saw, with astonishment, in the *Moniteur* of the 21st September, the announcement of the invasion of Bavaria by Austria, without any rupture or previous declaration of war. What a

have been better, probably, had the Emperor Francis suspended this decisive measure, and continued to protract, if possible, the negotiation, until the Russian auxiliary armies, two in number, of fifty thousand men each, could have advanced to the assistance of their allies; or until a sense of the approaching crisis had removed the indecision in the Prussian councils, and induced the King to join the coalition. Either of these events, and more especially both, might have given a very different turn to this disastrous campaign.[121]

But Austria was not alone to be blamed for precipitating the war—she exposed herself to censure by the mode in which she conducted it. Occupying Bavaria with numerous forces, the elector was required to join the confederacy. Maximilian of Bavaria was not disinclined to unite his forces with those which proposed for their object the defence of Germany; but he pleaded that his son, now travelling in France, would be made responsible, should he join the coalition. "On my knees," he said, in a letter [September 8] to the Emperor Francis, "I implore you for permission to remain neutral."[122] His reasonable request was rejected, and the elector was required to join the confederacy with a violence of urgency, both unjust and impolitic. He was farther given to understand, that his troops would not be permitted to remain as a separate army, but must be incorporated with those of Austria. These were terms so harsh, as to render even the precarious alliance of France preferable to submission. Maximilian, retreating from his capital of Munich to Wurtzburg, and withdrawing his army into Franconia, again endeavoured to negotiate for neutrality. It was again imperiously refused; and while the Austrian Government insisted that the elector should join them with his whole forces, the Austrian troops were permitted to conduct themselves as in an enemy's country; requisitions were raised, and other measures resorted to, tending to

---

fortunate diversion for the French Emperor! It saved his maritime honour, and probably preserved him from a disaster which would have destroyed both himself and his ancient empire. The army hastened to abandon the Boulogne coast. It was a magnificent one, and felt the highest enthusiasm at quitting a state of irksome inaction to march on towards the Rhine."—Fouché, tom. i., p. 291.

[121] Jomini, tom. ii., p. 95.

[122] "I pledge," he added, "my most sacred word to your majesty, that my troops shall not, in the smallest degree, interfere with the operations of your army. It is a father, a prey to the most frightful despair, that applies for mercy in favour of his son."—See Annual Register, vol. xlvii., p. 710.

show that the invaders remembered the ancient grudge which had so long subsisted between Bavaria and Austria. It was natural that the Bavarian prince, incensed at this treatment, should regard the allies as enemies, and wait the arrival of the French as liberators.

UNSOLDIERLIKE CONDUCT OF MACK

The military manœuvres of the Austrian army were not more able, than her conduct towards the neutral state of Bavaria was politic or just. There are two errors, equally fatal, into which a general of middling or inferior talent is apt to fall, when about to encounter with an adversary of genius. If he mixes presumption with his weakness of parts, he will endeavour to calculate the probable motions of his antagonist; and having, as he supposes, ascertained what they are likely to be, will attempt to anticipate and interrupt them, and thereby expose himself to some signal disaster, by mistaking the principle on which his enemy designs to act. Or, if intimidated by the reputation of the commander opposed to him, such a general is apt to remain passive and irresolute, until the motions of the enemy make his purpose evident, at a time when it is probably impossible to prevent his attaining it. It was left for General Mack,[123] within the space of a very brief campaign, to unite both characters; and fall first into errors of rashness and presumption, afterwards into those of indecision and cowardice.

It required little experience to know, that, after two singularly unfortunate wars, every precaution should have been taken to bring the Austrian troops into contact with their enemy, under such advantages of position and numbers as might counterbalance the feelings of discouragement with which the bravest soldiers must be affected, in consequence of a course of defeat and disaster so uniform, that there seemed to be a fate in it. In this point of view, the Austrian armies ought to have halted on their own territories, where the river Inn forms a strong and excellent line of defence,

---

[123] "The Austrian army was nominally under the command of the Archduke Ferdinand; but orders had been given him to follow implicitly the advice of Mack, whom all Germany fancied a great general notwithstanding the glaring incapacity he had already shown in Flanders and at Naples."—Jomini, tom. ii., p. 101.

extending betwixt the Tyrol and the Danube, into which the Inn empties itself at Passau. Supposing Mack's large force concentrated, with this formidable barrier in front, it seems as if the Austrians might have easily maintained a defensive position until the armies of Russia appeared to support them.

If, determined upon the imperious and unjust aggression on Bavaria, Mack found it necessary to advance more to the westward than the line of the Inn, in order to secure the country of the elector, the Lech, in its turn, offered him a position in which he might have awaited the Russians, though their junction must necessarily have been protracted, in proportion to the extent of his advance. But it was the choice of this unlucky tactician to leave Bavaria also behind him, and, approaching the frontiers of France, to take possession of Ulm, Memmingen, and the line of the Iller and Danube, where he fortified himself with great care, as if to watch the defiles of the Black Forest. It can only be thought by those who judge most favourably of Mack's intentions, that, as the passes of that celebrated forest had been frequently the route by which the French invaded Germany, he had concluded it must therefore be by that road, and no other, that their approach on the present occasion was to be expected. Knowing with whom he had to contend, the Austrian general ought to have suspected the direct contrary; for Buonaparte's manœuvres were not more distinguished by talent, than by novelty and originality of design.[124]

It is not to be supposed that this great confederacy took at unawares one who had so many reasons for being alert. The Austrian forces, though they had commenced the campaign so hastily, were not more early ready for the field, than were the immense armies of the French empire. The camps at Boulogne, so long assembled on the shores of the Channel, were now to be relieved from their inactivity;[125] and serious as the danger was in

---

[124] Jomini, tom. ii., p. 107.
[125] "The Emperor, before he left Boulogne, had in haste sent orders to the banks of the Rhine to collect draught horses, and to provide as large a quantity as possible of *materiel* for artillery. We were taken quite unawares; and it required all the activity of the Emperor to supply that army, on the spur of the occasion, with what it needed for the campaign, into which it was so suddenly forced. He, however, had already calculated and foreseen every thing. The maps of England had disappeared: those of Germany alone were admitted into

which their assistance was required, Buonaparte was perhaps not displeased at finding a fair pretext to withdraw from the invasion to which he had hastily pledged himself. This formidable assemblage of troops, laying aside the appellation of the Army of England, was hereafter distinguished by that of the Grand Army. At the same time, the armies maintained in Holland, and in the North of Germany, were put into motion.

In this remarkable campaign Buonaparte commenced, for the first time, the system of issuing official bulletins, for the purpose of announcing to the French nation his accounts of success, and impressing upon the public mind what truths he desired them to know, and, at the same time, what falsehoods he was desirous they should believe. In every country, such official accounts will naturally have a partial character, as every government must desire to represent the result of its measures in as favourable a light as possible. Where there is a free press, however, the deception cannot be carried to extremity; imposture cannot be attempted, on a grand scale at least, where it can be contrasted with other sources of information, or refuted by arguments derived from evidence. But Buonaparte had the unlimited and exclusive privilege of saying what he pleased, without contradiction or commentary, and he was liberal in using a license which could not be checked. Yet his bulletins are valuable historical documents, as well as the papers in the *Moniteur*, which he himself frequently composed or superintended. Much correct information there certainly is; and that which is less accurate is interesting, since it shows, if not actual truths, at least what Napoleon desired should be received as such, and so throws considerable light both on his schemes and on his character.

Buonaparte communicated to the Senate the approach of war, by a report, dated 23d September,[126] in which, acquainting them with

---

his cabinet. He made us follow the march of the troops; and one day addressed to us these remarkable words: 'If the enemy comes to meet me, I will destroy him before he has repassed the Danube; if he waits for me, I will take him between Augsburg and Ulm.' He issued the last orders to the navy and to the army, and set out for Paris."—Savary, tom. ii., p. 91.

[126] "The wishes of the eternal enemies of the continent are accomplished; war has commenced in the midst of Germany, Austria and Russia have united with England; and our generation is again involved in all the calamities of war. But a very few days ago I cherished a hope that peace would not be disturbed. Threats and outrages only showed that

the cause of quarrel betwixt himself and the allied powers, he asked, and of course obtained, two decrees; one for ordering eighty thousand conscripts to the field, another for the organisation of the National Guard.[127] He then put himself at the head of his forces, and proceeded to achieve the destruction of Mack's army, not as at Marengo by one great general battle, but by a series of grand manœuvres, and a train of partial actions necessary to execute them, which rendered assistance and retreat alike impossible. These manœuvres we can only indicate; nor can they perhaps be well understood without the assistance of the map.

MANŒUVRES OF FRENCH GENERALS

While Mack expected the approach of the French upon his front, Buonaparte had formed the daring resolution to turn the flank of the Austrian general, cut him off from his country and his resources, and reduce him to the necessity, either of surrender, or of giving battle without a hope of success. To execute this great conception, the French army was parted into six grand divisions. That of Bernadotte, evacuating Hanover, which it had hitherto occupied, and traversing Hesse, seemed as if about to unite itself to the main army, which had now reached the Rhine on all points. But its real destination was soon determined, when, turning towards the left, Bernadotte ascended the river Maine, and at Wurtzburg formed a junction with the elector of Bavaria, who, with the troops which

---

they could make no impression upon me; but the Austrians have passed the Inn; Munich is invaded; the Elector of Bavaria is driven from his capital; *all* my hopes are therefore vanished. I tremble at the idea of the blood that must be spilt in Europe; but the French name will emerge with renovated and increased lustre."

[127] He started next day for Strasburg, and on reaching that city issued the following proclamation to the army:— "Soldiers! The war of the third coalition has begun. The Austrian army has passed the Inn, violated treaties, and has attacked and driven our ally from his capital. You yourselves have been compelled to advance by forced marches to the defence of our frontiers. Already you have passed the Rhine. We will not again make peace without a sufficient guarantee. Our policy shall no more give way to our generosity. Soldiers, your Emperor is in the midst of you. You are only the advanced guard of a great people. If it should be necessary, they will all rise at my voice to confound and dissolve this new league which has been formed by the hatred and the gold of England. But, soldiers, we shall have forced marches to make, fatigues and privations of every kind to endure. Whatever obstacles may be opposed to us, we will overcome them, and we shall take no rest until we have planted our eagles on the territory of our enemy."

had followed him into Franconia, immediately declared for the French cause.

The elector of Wirtemberg and the Duke of Baden followed the same line of politics; and thus Austria had arrayed against her those very German princes, whom a moderate conduct towards Bavaria might perhaps have rendered neutral; France, at the outset of the contest, scarce having the power to compel them to join her standard. The other five columns of French troops, under Ney, Soult, Davoust, Lannes, and Marmont, crossed the Rhine at different points, and entered Germany to the northward of Mack's position; while Murat, who made his passage at Kehl, approaching the Black Forest, manœuvred in such a manner as to confirm Mack in his belief that the main attack was to come from that quarter. But the direction of all the other divisions intimated that it was the object of the French Emperor to move round the right wing of the Austrians, by keeping on the north or left side of the Danube, and then by crossing that river, to put themselves in the rear of Mack's army, and interpose betwixt him and Vienna. For this purpose, Soult, who had crossed at Spires, directed his march upon Augsburg; while, to interrupt the communication betwixt that city and Ulm, the Austrian headquarters, Murat and Lannes had advanced to Wertingen, where a smart action took place. The Austrians lost all their cannon, and it was said four thousand men—an ominous commencement of the campaign. The action would have been termed a battle, had the armies been on a smaller scale; but where such great numbers were engaged on either side, it did not rank much above a skirmish.[128]

With the same purpose of disquieting Mack in his headquarters, and preventing him from attending to what passed on his left wing and rear, Ney, who advanced from Stutgard, attacked the bridges over the Danube at Guntzburg, which were gallantly but fruitlessly defended by the Archduke Ferdinand, who had advanced from Ulm to that place. The archduke lost many guns, and nearly three thousand men.[129]

---

[128] Jomini, tom. ii., p. 108; Savary, tom. ii., p. 99.
[129] Jomini, tom. ii., p. 112.

In the meantime, an operation took place, which marked, in the most striking manner, the inflexible and decisive character of Napoleon's councils, compared with those of the ancient courts of Europe. To accomplish the French plan, of interposing betwixt Mack and the supplies and reinforcements, both Austrian and Russian, which were in motion towards him, it was necessary that all the French divisions should be directed upon Nordlingen, and particularly that the division under Bernadotte, which now included the Bavarian troops, should accomplish a simultaneous movement in that direction. But there was no time for the last-mentioned general to get into the desired position, unless by violating the neutrality of Prussia, and taking the straight road to the scene of operations, by marching through the territories of Anspach and Bareuth, belonging to that power. A less daring general, a more timid politician than Napoleon, would have hesitated to commit such an aggression at such a moment. Prussia, undecided in her councils, was yet known to be, in point of national spirit, hostilely disposed towards France; and a marked outrage of this nature was likely to raise the indignation of the people in general to a point which Haugwitz and his party might be unable to stem. The junction of Prussia with the allies at a moment so critical, might be decisive of the fate of the campaign, and well if the loss ended there.

Yet, with these consequences before his eyes, Napoleon knew, on the other hand, that it was not want of pretexts to go to war which prevented Prussia from drawing the sword, but diffidence in the power of the allies to resist the arms and fortune of France. If, therefore, by violating the territory of Prussia, he should be able to inflict a sudden and terrible blow upon the allies, he reckoned truly, that the court of Berlin would be more astounded at his success, than irritated at the means which he had taken to obtain it. Bernadotte received, therefore, the Emperor's commands to march through the territory of Anspach and Bareuth, which were only defended by idle protests and reclamations of the rights of neutrality. The news of this aggression gave the utmost offence at the Prussian court; and the call for war, which alone could right their injured honour, became almost unanimous through the nation. But while the general irritation, which Buonaparte of course foresaw, was thus taking place on the one side, the success which he had achieved over the Austrians acted on the other as a powerful sedative.[130]

CAPITULATION OF MEMMINGEN

The spirit of enterprise had deserted Mack as soon as actual hostilities commenced. With the usual fault of Austrian generals, he had extended his position too far, and embraced too many points of defence, rendering his communications difficult, and offering facilities for Buonaparte's favourite tactics, of attacking and destroying in detail the divisions opposed to him. The defeat at Guntzburg induced Mack at length to concentrate his army around Ulm; but Bavaria and Suabia were now fully in possession of the French and Bavarians; and the Austrian General Spangenberg, surrounded in Memmingen, was compelled to lay down his arms with five thousand men.[131] The French had crossed the Rhine about the 26th September; it was now the 13th October, and they could scarcely be said to have begun the campaign, when they had made, on various points, not fewer than twenty thousand prisoners. Napoleon, however, expected that resistance from Mack's despair, which no other motive had yet engaged him to offer; and he announced to his army the prospect of a general action. He called on his soldiers to revenge themselves on the Austrians for the loss of the plunder of London, of which, but for this new continental war, they would have been already in possession. He pointed out to

---

[130] "Sir Walter Scott blames the violation of the territory of Bareuth; but, how little have these neutralities been respected by conquerors! Witness the invasion of Switzerland at the end of 1813, so fatal to France!"—Louis Buonaparte, p. 43.

[131] "This intelligence reached Napoleon in a wretched bivouac, which was so wet, that it was necessary to seek a plank for him to keep his feet out of the water. He had just received this capitulation, when Prince Maurice Lichtenstein, whom Mack had sent with a flag of truce, was announced. He came to treat for the evacuation of Ulm: the army which occupied it demanded permission permission to return to Austria. The Emperor could not forbear smiling, and said, 'What reason have I to comply with this demand? in a week you will be in my power, without conditions?' Prince Maurice protested, that without the conditions which he demanded, the army should not leave the place. 'I shall not grant them,' rejoined the Emperor; 'there is the capitulation of Memmingen; carry it to Marshal Mack, and whatever may be your resolutions in Ulm, I will never grant him any other terms: besides, I am in no hurry; the longer he delays, the worse he will render his own situation, and that of you all. For the rest, I shall have the corps which took Memmingen here to-morrow, and we shall then see.'"—Savary, tom. ii., p. 96.

them, that, as at Marengo, he had cut the enemy off from his reserves and resources, and he summoned them to signalise Ulm by a battle, which should be yet more decisive.[132]

No general action, however, took place, though several sanguinary affairs of a partial nature were fought, and terminated uniformly to the misfortune of the Austrians. In the meantime, disunion took place among their generals. The Archduke Ferdinand, Schwartzenberg, afterwards destined to play a remarkable part in this changeful history, with Collowrath and others, seeing themselves invested by toils which were daily narrowed upon them, resolved to leave Mack and his army, and cut their way into Bohemia at the head of the cavalry. The archduke executed this movement with the greatest gallantry, but not without considerable loss. Indeed, the behaviour of the Austrian princes of the blood throughout these wars was such, as if Fate had meant to mitigate the disasters of the Imperial House, by showing forth the talents and bravery of their ancient race, and proving, that although Fortune frowned on them, Honour remained faithful to their line. Ferdinand, after much fighting, and considerable damage done and received, at length brought six thousand cavalry in safety to Egra, in Bohemia.[133]

CAPITULATION OF ULM

Meanwhile, Mack found himself, with the remains of his army, cooped up in Ulm, as Wurmser had been in Mantua. He published an order of the day, which intimated an intention to imitate the persevering defence of that heroic veteran. He forbade the word surrender to be used by any one—he announced the arrival of two powerful armies, one of Austrians, one of Russians,

---

[132] "Soldiers! But for the army which is now in front of you, we should this day have been in London; we should have avenged ourselves for six centuries of insults, and restored the freedom of the seas. But bear in mind to-morrow, that you are fighting against the allies of England; that you have to avenge yourselves on a perjured prince, whose own letters breathed nothing but peace, at the moment when he was marching his army against our ally! Soldiers! to-morrow will be a hundred times more celebrated than the day of Marengo. I have placed the enemy in the same position."
[133] Jomini, tom. ii., p. 123.

whose appearance would presently raise the blockade—he declared his determination to eat horse-flesh rather than listen to any terms of capitulation. This bravado appeared on the 16th October, and the conditions of surrender were subscribed by Mack on the next day, having been probably in the course of adjustment when he was making these notable professions of resistance.[134]

The course of military misconduct which we have traced, singular as it is, might be perhaps referred to folly or incapacity on the part of Mack, though it must be owned it was of that gross kind which civilians consider as equal to fraud. But another circumstance remains to be told, which goes far to prove that this once celebrated and trusted general had ingrafted the traitor upon the fool. The terms of capitulation, as subscribed on the 17th October, bore, that there should be an armistice until 26th October at midnight; and that if, during this space, an Austrian or Russian army should appear to raise the blockade, the army at Ulm should have liberty to join them, with their arms and baggage. This stipulation allowed the Austrian soldiers some hope of relief, and in any event it was sure to interrupt the progress of Buonaparte's successes, by detaining the principal part of his army in the neighbourhood of Ulm, until the term of nine days was expired. But Mack consented to a revision of these terms, a thing which would scarcely have been proposed to a man of honour, and signed on the 19th a second capitulation, by which he consented to evacuate Ulm on the day following;[135] thus abridging considerably, at a crisis when every minute was precious, any advantage, direct or contingent, which the Austrians could have derived from the delay originally stipulated. No reason has ever been alleged for this concession. Buonaparte, indeed, had given Mack an audience[136] previous to the signing of this additional article of

---

[134] For the terms of the capitulation of Ulm, see Annual Register, vol. xlvii., p. 662.
[135] Jomini, tom. ii., p. 126.
[136] "Marshal Mack paid the Emperor a visit at the abbey of Elchingen. He kept him a long time, and made him talk a great deal. It was on this interview that he learned all the circumstances which had preceded the resolution of the Austrian cabinet to make war upon him. He was made acquainted with all the springs which the Russians had set to work to decide it; and lastly, with the plans of the coalition."—Savary, tom. ii., p. 98.

capitulation, and what arguments he then employed must be left to conjecture.[137]

The effects of Mack's poltroonery, want of skill, and probable treachery, were equal to the results of a great victory. Artillery, baggage, and military stores, were given up to an immense extent. Eight general officers surrendered upon parole, upwards of 20,000 men became prisoners of war, and were marched into France. The numbers of the prisoners taken in this campaign were so great, that Buonaparte distributed them amongst the agriculturists, that their work in the fields might make up for the absence of the conscripts, whom he had withdrawn from such labour. The experiment was successful; and from the docile habits of the Germans, and the good-humour of their French employers, this new species of servitude suited both parties, and went some length to soften the hardships of war. For not the field of battle itself, with its wounded and dead, is a more distressing sight to humanity and reflection, than prison-barracks and hulks, in which hundreds and thousands of prisoners are delivered up to idleness, and all the evils which idleness is sure to introduce, and not unfrequently to disease and death. Buonaparte meditated introducing this alteration into the usages of war upon a great scale, and thought of regimenting his prisoners for the purpose of labouring on public works. His jurists objected to the proposal as contrary to the law of nations.[138] This

---

[137] "It must be owned, that Napoleon did not think himself justified in resting his sole dependence upon his excellent troops. He recollected the saying of Machiavel: that a prudent prince must be both a fox and a lion at the same time. After having well studied his new field of battle, (for it was the first time he made war in Germany) he told us, that we should soon see that the campaigns of Moreau were nothing in comparison with his. In fact, he acted admirably in order to derange Mack's plans, who permitted himself to be petrified in his position of Ulm. All the Emperor's spies were more easily purchased than may be conceived. Almost all the Austrian staff-officers were virtually gained over. I had intrusted Savary, who was employed in the management of the *espoinage* at the grand headquarters, with all my secret notes upon Germany, and, with his hands full, he worked quickly and successfully."—Fouché, tom. i., p. 291.

[138] "I intended to enrol them in regiments, and to make them labour under military discipline, at public works and monuments. They should have received whatever money they earned, and would thus have been secured against the misery of absolute idleness, and the disorders arising out of it. They would have been well fed and clothed, and would have wanted for nothing, without being a burden on the state. But my idea did not meet the approval of the Council of State, which, in this instance, was swayed by the mistaken philanthropy, that it would be unjust and cruel to compel men to labour."—Napoleon, *Las Cases*, tom. vii., p. 45.

scruple might have been avoided, by employing only volunteers, which would also have prevented the appearance of retrograding towards those barbarous times, when the captive of the sword became the slave of his victor. But national character would, in most instances, render the scheme impracticable. Thus, an attempt was afterwards made to dispose of the Spanish prisoners in a similar way, who in most cases made their escape, and in some rose upon and destroyed their taskmasters. A French soldier would, in like manner, make an indifferent serf to an English farmer, an English prisoner a still more intractable assistant to a French agriculturist. The advantages of comparative freedom would be in both cases counterbalanced, by a feeling of degradation in the personal subjection experienced.

When the general officers of the Austrians[139] were admitted to a personal interview with the French Emperor, he behaved with courtesy to Klenau and others of reputation, whose character had become known to him in the Italian campaigns. But he complained of the politics of their court, which he said had forced him into war when he knew not what he was fighting for. He prophesied the fall of the House of Austria, unless his brother the Emperor hastened to make peace, and reprobated the policy which brought the uncivilized Russians to interfere in the decision of more cultivated countries than their own. Mack[140] had the impudence to reply, that the Emperor of Austria had been forced into the war by Russia. "Then," said Napoleon, "you no longer exist as an independent

---

[139] "The 19th October arrived. The drums beat—the bands played; the gates of Ulm opened; the Austrian army advanced in silence, filed off slowly, and went, corps by corps, to lay down its arms on a spot which had been prepared to receive them. The ceremony occupied the whole day. The Emperor was posted on a little hill in front of the centre of his army; a great fire had been lighted, and by this fire he received the Austrian generals, to the number of seventeen. They were all very dull: it was the Emperor who kept up the conversation."—Savary, tom. ii., p. 200.

[140] It will be unnecessary again to mention this man's name, of which our readers are doubtless as much tired as we ourselves are. He was committed to a state prison, in a remote part of the Austrian dominions; and whether he died in captivity, or was set at liberty, we have not learned, nor are we anxious to know.—S.—On his return to Austria, Mack was arrested, and sent to the citadel of Brunn, in Moravia, whence he was transferred to the fortress of Josephstadt, in Bohemia. He was tried by a military commission and condemned to death, but the penalty was commuted by the Emperor for two years' imprisonment, and the loss of rank.

power." The whole conversation appeared in the bulletin[141] of the day, which also insinuates, with little probability, that the Austrian officers and soldiers concurred generally in blaming the alliance between their own Emperor and Alexander.[142] From this we infer, that the union between those two powerful sovereigns was, even in the moment of this great success, a subject of apprehension to Buonaparte; whose official notes are sometimes expressed with generosity towards the vanquished, who had ceased to struggle, but always with an eager tone of reproach and offence towards those from whom an animated resistance was to be apprehended.

---

[141] Tenth Official Bulletin of the Grand Army.
[142] "This conversation was not lost upon all: none of them, however, made any reply."— Savary, tom. ii., p. 100.

Chapter XXXII

Position of the French Armies—Napoleon advances towards Vienna—The Emperor Francis leaves his Capital—French enter Vienna on the 13th November—Review of the French Successes in Italy and the Tyrol—Schemes of Napoleon to force on a General Battle—Battle of Austerlitz is fought on the 2d December, and the combined Austro-Russian Armies completely Defeated—Interview betwixt the Emperor of Austria and Napoleon—The Emperor Alexander retreats towards Russia—Treaty of Presburgh signed on the 26th December—Its Conditions—Fate of the King of Sweden—and of the Two Sicilies.

POSITION OF THE FRENCH ARMIES

The tide of war now rolled eastward, having surmounted and utterly demolished the formidable barrier which was opposed to it. Napoleon placed himself at the head of his central army.[143] Ney, upon his right, was ready to repel any descent which might be made from the passes of the Tyrol. Murat, on his left, watched the motions of the Austrians, under the Archduke Ferdinand, who, refusing to join in the unworthy capitulation of

---

[143] From Elchingen, Oct. 21, Napoleon issued the following address to the army:—"Soldiers of the Grand Army! In a fortnight we have finished a campaign: we have expelled the troops of the house of Austria from Bavaria, and re-established our ally in the sovereignty of his estates. That army which, with equal ostentation and imprudence, had posted itself on our frontiers, is annihilated. Soldiers! you owe this success to your unbounded confidence in your Emperor; to your patience in supporting fatigues and privations of every description; and to your singular intrepidity. But we will not stop here. You are impatient to commence a second campaign. We are about to make the Russian army, which the gold of England has transported from the extremities of the universe, undergo the same fate. Here there are no generals in combating against whom I can have any glory to acquire. All my care shall be to obtain the victory with the least possible effusion of blood. My soldiers are my children."

Ulm, had cut their way into Bohemia, and there united themselves with other forces, either stationed in that kingdom, or who had, like themselves, escaped thither. Lastly, the division of Augereau, (who had recently advanced from France at the head of an army of reserve,) occupying part of Swabia, served to protect the rear of the French army against any movement from the Vorarlberg; and at the same time menaced the Prussians, in case, acting upon the offence given by the violation of their territory, they should have crossed the Danube, and engaged in the war.[144]

If, however, the weight of Prussia had been thrown into the scale with sufficient energy at this decisive moment, it would not probably have been any resistance which Augereau could have offered that could have saved Napoleon from a perilous situation, since the large armies of the new enemy would have been placed in his rear, and, of course, his communications with France entirely cut off. It was a crisis of the same kind which opened to Austria in the year 1813; but she was then taught wisdom by experience, and availed herself of the golden opportunity which Prussia now suffered to escape. Buonaparte had reckoned with accuracy upon the timid and fluctuating councils of that power. The aggression on their territories of Anspach and Bareuth was learned at Berlin; but then the news of the calamity sustained by the Austrians at Ulm succeeded these tidings almost instantly, and while the first article of intelligence seemed to urge instant hostilities, the next was calculated to warn them against espousing a losing cause.

Thus, trusting to the vacillating and timid policy of Prussia,[145] Napoleon, covered on his flank and rear as we have stated, continued to push forward[146] with his central forces towards Vienna, menaced repeatedly in the former wars, but whose fate seemed

---

[144] Jomini, tom. ii., p. 133.
[145] "The conduct of Prussia at this period was conformable to the wholesome policy which had so long connected this power with France. It is not for us, Frenchmen, to reproach her inaction at this important crisis, even while criticising her raising the shield before Jena. Until then Prussia had showed herself reasonable, in not allowing herself to be drawn into new coalitions."—Louis Buonaparte, p. 44.
[146] "Napoleon was always on horseback whatever weather it might be, travelling in his carriage only when his army was two or three marches in advance. This was a calculation on his part, the point always entered into in his combinations, and to him distances were nothing: he traversed them with the swiftness of eagles."—Savary, tom. ii., p. 103.

decided after the disaster of Ulm. It is true, that an army, partly consisting of Russians and partly of Austrians, had pressed forward to prevent that disgraceful calamity, and, finding that the capitulation had taken place, were now retreating step by step in front of the advancing French; but, not exceeding forty-five thousand men, they were unable to make any effectual stand upon the Inn, the Traun, the Ens, or in any other position which might have covered Vienna. They halted, indeed, repeatedly, made a considerable show of resistance, and fought some severe though partial actions; but always ended by continuing their retreat, which was now directed upon Moravia, where the grand Russian, army had already assembled, under the command of the Emperor Alexander, and were expecting still further reinforcements under General Buxhowden.[147]

Some attempts were made to place Vienna in a state of defence, and the inhabitants were called upon to rise in mass for that purpose. But as the fortifications were ancient and in disrepair, an effort at resistance could only have occasioned the destruction of the city. The Emperor Francis saw himself, therefore, under the necessity of endeavouring to provide for the safety of his capital by negotiation, and for that of his person by leaving it. On the 7th November, accordingly, he departed from Vienna for Brunn in Moravia, in order to place himself under the protection of the Russian forces.

On the same day, but late in the evening, Count Giulay arrived at Buonaparte's headquarters, then established at Lintz, with a proposal for an armistice, previous to a general negotiation for peace. Napoleon refused to listen to the proposal, unless Venice and the Tyrol were put into his hands. These terms were too hard to be accepted.[148] Vienna, therefore, was left to its fate; and that proud capital of the proud House of Austria remained an unresisting prize to the invader.

---

[147] Jomini, tom. ii., p. 133; Savary, tom. ii., p. 101. Fourteenth and Fifteenth Bulletins of the Grand Army.
[148] Jomini, tom. ii., p. 145.

VIENNA TAKEN

On the 13th November the French took possession of Vienna, where they obtained an immense quantity of military stores, arms, and clothing;[149] a part of which spoils were bestowed by Napoleon on his ally the Elector of Bavaria, who now witnessed the humiliation of the Imperial House which had of late conducted itself so haughtily towards him. General Clarke was appointed Governor of Vienna; and by a change as rapid as if it had taken place on the stage, the new Emperor of France occupied Schonbrun, the splendid palace of the long-descended Emperor of Austria. But though such signal successes had crowned the commencement of the campaign, it was necessary to defeat the haughty Russians, in whose aid the Emperor of Austria still confided, before the object of the war could be considered as attained. The broken and shattered remnant of the Austrian forces had rallied from different quarters around the yet untouched army of Alexander; and although the latter retreated from Brunn towards Olmutz, it was only with the purpose of forming a junction with Buxhowden, before they hazarded a general battle.

In the meantime, the French army, following close on their back into Moravia, fought one or two partial actions, which, though claimed as victories, were so severely disputed as to make Napoleon aware that he had to do with a more obstinate enemy than he had of late encountered in the dispirited Austrians. He waited, therefore, until the result of his skilful combinations should have drawn around him the greatest force he could expect to collect, ere venturing upon an engagement, of which, if he failed to obtain a decisive victory, the consequences were likely to be fatal to him.

At this period, success had smiled on the French in Italy, and in the Tyrol, as well as in Germany. In the former country, it may be remembered that the Archduke Charles, at the head of seventy-five or eighty thousand men, exclusive of garrisons, was opposed to

---

[149] "In the magazines and arsenals of Vienna were found artillery and ammunition enough for two campaigns: we had no farther occasion to draw upon our stores at Strasburg or Metz: but could, on the contrary, despatch a considerable *materiel* to those two great establishments."—Savary, tom. ii., p. 107.

Massena, whose forces considerably exceeded that amount. The prince occupied the left bank of the Adige, with the purpose of maintaining a defensive warfare, until he should hear news of the campaign in Germany. Massena, however, after some fighting, succeeded in forcing the passage of the river at Verona, and in occupying the village of St. Michael. This was on the 20th October. Soon afterwards, the account of the surrender at Ulm reached the Frenchman, and determined him on a general attack along the whole Austrian line, which was strongly posted near Caldiero. The assault took place on the 30th October, and was followed by a very desperate action; for the Austrians, confident in the presence of their favourite commander, fought with the greatest courage. They were, however, defeated; and a column of five thousand men, under General Hellinger, detached for the purpose of attacking the French in the rear, failed in their purpose, and being themselves surrounded, were obliged to lay down their arms. The victors were joined by General St. Cyr, at the head of twenty-five thousand men, who had evacuated the kingdom of Naples, upon a treaty of neutrality entered into with the King, and now came to join their countrymen in Lombardy.

In the midst of his own misfortunes, the Archduke Charles received the fatal intelligence of the capitulation of Ulm, and that the French were advancing in full march towards Vienna. To cover his brother's capital became a matter of more pressing necessity than to attempt to continue the defence of Italy, which circumstances rendered almost hopeless. He commenced his retreat, therefore, on the night of the 1st of November, determining to continue it through the mountain passes of Carinthia, and so on into Hungary. If he had marched by the Tyrol, he would have found Augereau in his front, with Ney and Marmont threatening his flanks, while Massena, before whom he was now retreating, pressed on his rear.

The archduke commenced this dispiriting and distressing movement, over nearly the same ground which he had passed while retreating before Buonaparte himself in 1797. He did not, however, as on that occasion, avail himself of the Tagliamento, or Palma Nova. His purpose was retreat, not defence; and, though pursued closely by Massena, he halted no longer at these strong posts than was necessary to protect his march, and check the vivacity of the French advance. He effected at length his retreat upon Laybach, where he received tidings from his brother the Archduke John, whose situation on the Tyrol was not more agreeable than his own in Italy; and who, like Charles himself, was desirous to escape into the vicinity of Hungary with what forces remained to him.

The distress of the Archduke John was occasioned by an army of French and Bavarians, commanded by Ney, who had penetrated into the Tyrol by paths deemed impracticable; taken the forts of Schwatz, Neustadt, and Inspruck itself, and placed the archduke's army in the most precarious situation. Adopting a determination worthy of his birth, the Austrian prince resolved at all risks to effect a junction with his brother, and, though hard pressed by the enemy, he accomplished his purpose. Two considerable corps of Austrians, being left in an insulated situation by these movements of the two princes, were obliged to surrender. These were the divisions of Jellachich, in the Vorarlberg, and of the Prince of Rohan, in Lombardy. The whole of the north of Italy, with the Tyrol and all its passes, was left to the undisturbed and unresisted occupation of the French.[150]

The army of the royal brothers had, however, become formidable by their junction, and was daily growing stronger. They were in communication with Hungary, the brave inhabitants of which warlike country were universally rising in arms. They were also joined by volunteers from Croatia, the Tyrol, and all those wild and mountainous countries, which have so long supplied the Austrian army with the finest light troops in the world.

It might seem to counterbalance these advantages, that Massena had also entered into communications with the French army of Germany at Clagenfurt, the capital of Carinthia. But having left great part of his troops in Italy, he had for the time ceased to be formidable to the Austrian princes, who now meditated advancing on the French grand army, which the audacity of its leader had

---

[150] Jomini, tom. ii., p. 169; Savary, tom. ii., p. 107

placed in a situation extremely perilous to any other than French troops acting under the eye of their Emperor.

SUCCESSION OF GRAND MANŒUVRES

Nothing, it is true, could be more admirably conceived and satisfactorily accomplished than the succession of grand manœuvres, which, distinguishing the opening of the campaign, had produced the great, yet cheaply-purchased success of Ulm, and the capture of Vienna. Nor was the series of combination less wonderful, by which, clearing the Vorarlberg, the Tyrol, and the north of Italy of the enemy, Napoleon had placed almost all the subordinate divisions of his own army at his disposal, ready to assist him in the grand enterprise against the Austro-Russian forces. But he has been considered by military critics as having trusted too great a risk upon the precarious event of battle, when he crossed the Danube, and plunged into Moravia, where a defeat, or even a check, might have been attended with the most fatal consequences. The position of the Archdukes Charles and John; the organisation of the Hungarian insurrection, which proceeded rapidly; the success of the Archduke Ferdinand, in raising a similar general levy in Bohemia, threatened alarming operations in the French rear; while Prussia, with the sword drawn in her hand, and the word *war* upon her lips, watched but the slightest waning of Buonaparte's star, to pronounce the word, and to strike a blow at the same moment.

Napoleon accordingly, though he had dared the risk, was perfectly sensible that as he had distinguished the earlier part of this campaign by some of the most brilliant manœuvres which military history records, it was now incumbent upon him, without delay, to conclude it by a great and decisive victory over a new and formidable enemy. He neglected, therefore, no art by which success could be ensured. In the first place, it was necessary to determine the allies to immediate battle; for, situated in the heart of an enemy's country, with insurrection spreading wide and wider around him, an immediate action was as desirable on his part, as delay would have been advantageous to his opponents.

Some attempts at negotiation were made by the Austrians, to aid which Haugwitz, the Prussian minister, made his appearance in the French camp with the offer of his master's mediation, but with the alternative of declaring war in case it was refused. To temporize with Prussia was of the last consequence, and the French Emperor found a willing instrument in Haugwitz. "The French and Austrian outposts," said Napoleon, "are engaged; it is a prelude to the battle which I am about to fight—Say nothing of your errand to me at present—I wish to remain in ignorance of it. Return to Vienna, and wait the events of war."[151] Haugwitz, to use Napoleon's own expression, was no novice, and returned to Vienna without waiting for another hint; and doubtless the French Emperor was well pleased to be rid of his presence.[152]

Napoleon next sent Savary[153] to the Russian camp, under pretence of compliment to the Emperor Alexander, but in reality as a spy upon that monarch and his generals. He returned, having discovered, or affected to discover, that the Russian sovereign was surrounded by counsellors, whom their youth and rank rendered confident and presumptuous, and who, he concluded, might be easily misguided into some fatal act of rashness.[154]

Buonaparte acted on the hint, and upon the first movement of the Austro-Russian army in advance, withdrew his forces from the position they had occupied. Prince Dolgorucki, aide-de-camp of the Emperor Alexander, was despatched by him to return the compliments which had been brought him. He too was, doubtless, expected to use his powers of observation, but they were not so

---

[151] Montholon, tom. ii., p. 241.
[152] "I asked Napoleon, if Haugwitz had been gained by him? he replied 'No; but he was of opinion that Prussia should never play the first fiddle in the affairs of the continent; that she was only a second-rate power, and ought to act as such.'"—O'Meara, vol. i., p. 227.
[153] "Napoleon sent for me at daybreak: he had passed the night over his maps; his candles were burnt down to the sockets: he held a letter in his hand; he was silent for some moments, and then abruptly said to me, 'Be off to Olmutz; deliver this letter to the Emperor of Russia, and tell him that, having heard of his arrival at his army, I have sent you to salute him in my name. If he questions you,' added he, 'you know what answer ought to be given under such circumstances.'"—Savary, tom. ii., p. 112.
[154] "I saw at Olmutz a great number of young Russians, belonging to the different ministerial departments of their country, who talked wildly of the ambition of France; and all of whom, in their plans for reducing her to a state of harmlessness, made much the same kind of calculations as the maid with her pail of milk."—Savary, tom. ii., p. 113.

acute as those of the old officer of police. Buonaparte, as if the interior of his camp displayed scenes which he did not desire Dolgorucki to witness, met the prince at the outposts, which the soldiers were in the act of hastily covering with field-works, like an army which seeks to shelter conscious weakness under intrenchments. Encouraged by what he thought he saw of the difficulties in which the French seemed to be placed, Dolgorucki entered upon politics, and demanded in plain terms the cession of the crown of Italy. To this proposal Buonaparte listened with a patience which seemed to be the effect of his present situation. In short, Dolgorucki carried back to his imperial master the hastily conceived opinion, that the French Emperor was retreating, and felt himself in a precarious posture.[155] On this false ground the Russian council of war determined to act. Their plan was to extend their own left wing, with the purpose of turning the right of the French army, and taking them upon the flank and rear.

AUSTERLITZ

It was upon the 1st December at noon that the Russians commenced this movement, by which, in confidence of success, they abandoned a chain of heights where they might have received an attack with great advantage, descended into ground more favourable to the enemy, and, finally, placed their left wing at too great a distance from the centre. The French general no sooner witnessed this rash manœuvre, than he exclaimed, "Before to-morrow is over, that army is my own." In the meantime, withdrawing his outposts, and concentrating his forces, he continued to intimate a conscious inferiority, which was far from existing.

The two armies seem to have been very nearly of the same strength. For though the bulletin, to enhance the victory, makes the opposite army amount to 100,000 men, yet there were not actually above 50,000 Russians, and about 25,000 Austrians, in the field of battle.[156] The French army might be about the same force. But they

---

[155] Thirtieth Bulletin of the Grand Army.
[156] Jomini, tom. ii., p. 181.

were commanded by Napoleon, and the Russians by Kutousof; a veteran soldier indeed, full of bravery and patriotism, and accustomed to war as it was waged against the Turks; but deficient in general talent, as well as in the alertness of mind necessary to penetrate into and oppose the designs of his adversary, and, as is not unusual, obstinate in proportion to the narrowness of his understanding, and the prejudices of his education.

Meanwhile Buonaparte, possessed of his enemy's plan by the demonstrations of the preceding day, passed the night in making his arrangements.[157] He visited the posts in person, and apparently desired to maintain an incognito which was soon discovered. As soon as the person of the Emperor was recognised, the soldiers remembered that next day [2d December] was the anniversary of his coronation. Bunches of lighted hay, placed on the end of poles, made an extempore illumination, while the troops, with loud acclamations, protested they would present him on the following day with a bouquet becoming the occasion; and an old grenadier, approaching his person, swore that the Emperor should only have to combat with his eyes, and that, without his exposing his person, the whole colours and artillery of the Russian army should be brought to him to celebrate the festival of the morrow.[158]

In the proclamation which Napoleon, according to his custom, issued to the army, he promises that he will keep his person out of the reach of fire; thus showing the full confidence, that the assurance of his personal safety would be considered as great an encouragement to the troops, as the usual protestation of sovereigns and leaders, that they will be in the front, and share the dangers of the day.[159] This is, perhaps, the strongest proof possible of the

---

[157] "The Emperor passed the whole day of the 1st December inspecting his army himself, regiment by regiment. He spoke to the troops, viewed all the parks, all the light batteries, and gave instructions to all the officers and gunners. He returned to dine at his bivouac and sent for all his marshals; he enlarged upon all that they ought to do the next day, and all that it was possible for the enemy to attempt. He knew his ground as well as the environs of Paris. It would require a volume to detail all that emanated from his mind in those twenty-four hours."—Savary, tom. ii., p. 131.
[158] Thirtieth Bulletin of the Grand Army.
[159] "*Order of the Day. On the Field, Dec. 1.*—Soldiers! The Russian forces are before you, to avenge the Austrian army at Ulm; they are the same battalions you conquered at Hollabrun, and which you have constantly pursued. The positions we occupy are formidable, and,

complete and confidential understanding which subsisted between Napoleon and his soldiers. Yet there have not been wanting those, who have thrown the imputation of cowardice on the victor of a hundred battles, and whose reputation was so well established amongst those troops who must be the best judges, that his attention to the safety of his person was requested by them, and granted by him, as a favour to his army.

BATTLE OF AUSTERLITZ

The Battle of Austerlitz, fought against an enemy of great valour but slender experience, was not of a very complicated character. The Russians, we have seen, were extending their line to surround the French flank. Marshal Davoust, with a division of infantry, and another of dragoons, was placed behind the convent of Raygern, to oppose the forces destined for this manœuvre, at the moment when they should conceive the point carried. Soult commanded the right wing; Lannes conducted the left, which last rested upon a fortified position called Santon, defended by twenty pieces of cannon. Bernadotte led the centre, where Murat and all the French cavalry were stationed. Ten battalions of the Imperial Guard, with ten of Oudinot's division, were kept in reserve in the rear of the line, under the eye of Napoleon himself, who destined them, with forty field-pieces, to act wherever the fate of battle should render their services most necessary. Such were the preparations for this decisive battle, where three Emperors, each at the head of his own army, strove to decide the destinies of Europe. The sun rose with unclouded brilliancy; it was that sun of Austerlitz which Napoleon, upon so many succeeding occasions apostrophised, and recalled to the minds of his soldiers. As its first beams rose above the horizon, Buonaparte appeared in front of the army, surrounded

---

whilst they march to turn my right, they shall present me their flank. Soldiers! I shall direct myself all your battalions, I shall keep at a distance from the firing, if, with your accustomed bravery, you carry confusion and disorder into the enemy's ranks; but should victory be for a moment doubtful, you shall behold your Emperor expose himself to the first blow. This victory will finish our campaign, when we shall return to winter quarters, and be joined by the new armies forming in France; then the peace which I shall sanction will be worthy of my people, of you, and of myself."

by his marshals, to whom he issued his last directions, and they departed at full gallop to their different posts.[160]

The column detached from the left of the Austro-Russian army was engaged in a false manœuvre, and it was ill executed. The intervals between the regiments of which it consisted were suffered to become irregular, and the communications between this attacking column itself and the main body were not maintained with sufficient accuracy. When the Russians thought themselves on the point of turning the right flank of the French, they found themselves suddenly, and at unawares, engaged with Davoust's division, of whose position behind the convent of Raygern, they had not been aware. At the same time, Soult, at the head of the French right wing, rushed forward upon the interval between the Austro-Russian centre and left, caused by the march of the latter upon Raygern, and, completely intersecting their line, severed the left wing entirely from the centre.

The Emperor of Russia perceived the danger, and directed a desperate attempt to be made upon Soult's division by the Russian Guards, for the purpose of restoring the communication with his left. The French infantry were staggered by this charge, and one regiment completely routed. But it was in such a crisis that the genius of Buonaparte triumphed. Bessières had orders to advance with the Imperial Guard, while the Russians were disordered with their own success. The encounter was desperate, and the Russians displayed the utmost valour before they at length gave way to the discipline and steadiness of Buonaparte's veterans. Their artillery and standards were lost, and Prince Constantine, the Emperor's brother, who fought gallantly at their head, was only saved by the speed of his horse.

The centre of the French army now advanced to complete the victory, and the cavalry of Murat made repeated charges with such success, that the Emperors of Russia and Austria, from the heights

---

[160] "In passing along the front of several regiments, the Emperor said, 'Soldiers! we must finish this campaign by a thunderbolt, which shall confound the pride of our enemies;' and, instantly, hats were placed on the points of their bayonets, and cries of 'Vive l'Empereur!' were the signal for the battle."—*Thirtieth Bulletin.*

of Austerlitz, beheld their centre and left completely defeated. The fate of the right wing could no longer be protracted, and it was disastrous even beyond the usual consequences of defeat.[161] They had been actively pressed during the whole battle by Lannes, but now the troops on their left being routed, they were surrounded on all sides, and, unable to make longer resistance, were forced down into a hollow, where they were exposed to the fire of twenty pieces of cannon. Many attempted to escape across a lake, which was partially frozen; but the ice proving too weak gave way under them, or was broken by the hostile cannonade. This fatality renewed, according to Buonaparte's description, the appearance of the battle with the Turks at Aboukir, where so many thousand men, flying from the battle, perished by drowning. It was with the greatest difficulty, that, rallying the remains of their routed forces around them, and retiring in the best manner they could, the Emperors effected their personal retreat. Only the devoted bravery of the Russians, and the loyalty of the Austrian cavalry, who charged repeatedly to protect the retrograde movement, could have rendered it possible, since the sole passage to the rear lay along a causeway, extending between two lakes. The retreat was, however, accomplished, and the Emperors escaped without sustaining the loss in the pursuit which might have been expected. But in the battle, at least twenty thousand men had remained, killed, wounded, and prisoners; and forty standards, with a great proportion of the hostile artillery, were the trophies of Napoleon, whose army had thus amply redeemed their pledge. It was, however, at a high rate that they had purchased the promised bouquet. Their own ranks had lost probably

---

[161] "The Russians fled and dispersed: Alexander and the Emperor of Austria witnessed the defeat. Stationed on a height at a little distance from the field of battle, they beheld the guard, which had been expected to decide the victory, cut to pieces by a handful of brave men. Their guns and baggage had fallen into our possession, and Prince Repnin was our prisoner; unfortunately, however, we had a great number of men killed and wounded. I had myself received a sabre wound in the head; in which situation I galloped off to give an account of the affair to the Emperor. My sabre broken, my wound, the blood with which I was covered, the decided advantage we had gained with so small a force over the enemy's chosen troops, inspired Napoleon with the idea of the picture that was painted by Girard."—*Mémoires du Général Rapp*, p. 62.

five thousand men, though the bulletin diminishes the numbers to two thousand five hundred.[162]

The Austrian Emperor considered his last hope of successful opposition to Napoleon as extinguished by this defeat, and conceived, therefore, that he had nothing remaining save to throw himself upon the discretion of the victor. There, were, indeed some, who accused his councils of pusillanimity. It was said, that the levies of Prince Charles in Hungary, and of Prince Ferdinand in Bohemia, were in great forwardness—that the Emperors had still a considerable army under their own command—and that Prussia, already sufficiently disposed for war, would certainly not permit Austria to be totally overwhelmed. But it ought to be considered, on the other hand, that the new levies, however useful in a partisan war, could not be expected to redeem the loss of such a battle as Austerlitz—that they were watched by French troops, which, though inferior in number, were greatly more formidable in discipline—and that, as for Prussia, it was scarce rational to expect that she would interfere by arms, to save, in the hour of distress, those to whom she had given no assistance, when such would probably have been decisive of the contest, and that in favour of the allies.

CONVENTION WITH PRUSSIA

---

[162] Jomini, tom. ii., p. 180-191; Savary, tom. ii., p. 133. Thirtieth Bulletin of the Grand Army. On the field of battle, Napoleon issued the following proclamation:— "Headquarters, Dec. 2, 10 o'clock at night.
"Soldiers of the Grand Army! Even at this hour, before this great day shall pass away and be lost in the ocean of eternity, your Emperor must address you, and express how much he is satisfied with the conduct of all those who have had the good fortune to combat in this memorable battle. Soldiers! you are the first warriors in the world! The recollection of this exploit and of your deeds, will be eternal! thousands of ages hereafter, so long as the events of the universe continue to be related, will record, that a Russian army, of seventy-six thousand men, hired by the gold of England, was annihilated by you on the plains of Olmutz.—The miserable remains of that army, upon which the commercial spirit of a despicable nation had placed its expiring hope, are in flight, hastening to make known to the savage inhabitants of the north what the French are capable of performing; they will, likewise, tell them, that, after having destroyed the Austrian army, at Ulm, you told Vienna—'That army is no more!' To Petersburgh you shall also say—'The Emperor Alexander has no longer an army.'"

The influence of the victory on the Prussian councils was indeed soon made evident; for Count Haugwitz, who had been dismissed to Vienna till the battle should take place, now returned to Buonaparte's headquarters, having changed the original message of defiance of which he was the bearer, into a handsome compliment to Napoleon upon his victory. The answer of Napoleon intimated his full sense of the duplicity of Prussia.—"This," he said, "is a compliment designed for others, but Fortune has transferred the address to me."[163] It was, however, still necessary to conciliate a power which had a hundred and fifty thousand men in the field; and a private treaty with Haugwitz assigned the Electorate of Hanover to Prussia, in exchange for Anspach, or rather as the price of her neutrality at this important crisis.[164] Thus all hopes of Prussian interference being over, the Emperor Francis must be held justified in yielding to necessity, and endeavouring to secure the best terms which could be yet obtained, by submitting at discretion. His ally, Alexander, refused indeed to be concerned in a negotiation, which in the circumstances could not fail to be humiliating.

A personal interview took place betwixt the Emperor of Austria and Napoleon, to whose camp Francis resorted almost in the guise of a suppliant. The defeated prince is represented as having thrown the blame of the war upon the English. "They are a set of merchants," he said, "who would set the continent on fire, in order to secure to themselves the commerce of the world." The argument was not very logical, but the good prince in whose mouth it is placed, is not to be condemned for holding at such a moment the language which might please the victor. When Buonaparte welcomed him to his military hut, and said it was the only palace he had inhabited for nearly two months, the Austrian answered with a smile, "You have turned your residence, then, to such good account, that you ought to be content with it."

---

[163] Thirty-Fourth Bulletin of the Grand Army; Savary, tom. ii., p. 148.
[164] "The battle of Austerlitz took place on the 2d December, and on the 15th, Prussia, by the convention of Vienna, renounced the treaty of Potsdam and the oath of the tomb; she yielded Wesel, Bareuth, and Neuchatel to France; who, in return, consented to Frederic William's taking possession of Hanover, and uniting that country to his dominions."—Napoleon, *Montholon*, tom. ii., p. 242.

The Emperor of Austria, having satisfied himself that he would be admitted to terms of greater or less severity, next stipulated for that which Alexander had disdained to request in his own person—the unmolested retreat of the Russians to their own country.—"The Russian army is surrounded," said Napoleon; "not a man can escape me. But I wish to oblige their Emperor, and will stop the march of my columns, if your Majesty promises me that these Russians shall evacuate Germany and the Austrian and Prussian parts of Poland."—"It is the purpose of the Emperor Alexander to do so."[165]

The arrangement was communicated by Savary to the Russian Emperor, who acquiesced in the proposal to return with his army to Russia by regular marches.[166] No other engagement was required of Alexander than his word; and the respectful manner in which he is mentioned in the bulletins, indicates Buonaparte's desire to cultivate a good understanding with this powerful and spirited young monarch. On the other hand, Napoleon has not failed to place in the Czar's mouth such compliments to himself as the following:— "Tell your master," said he to Savary, "that he did miracles yesterday—that this bloody day has augmented my respect for him—He is the predestined of Heaven—it will take a hundred years ere my army equals that of France." Savary is then stated to have found Alexander, despite of his reverse of fortune, a man of heart and head. He entered into details of the battle.

"You were inferior to us on the whole," he said, "yet we found you superior on every point of action."

"That," replied Savary, "arises from warlike experience, the fruit of sixteen years of glory. This is the fortieth battle which the Emperor has fought."

---

[165] Thirty-First Bulletin of the Grand Army.
[166] "The Emperors seemed to be both in excellent humour; they laughed, which seemed to us all to be a good *omen*: accordingly, in an hour or two, the sovereigns parted with a mutual embrace. We followed Napoleon, who rode his horse at a foot-pace, musing on what he meant to do. He called me, and said, 'Run after the Emperor of Austria: tell him that I have desired you to go and wait at his headquarters for the adhesion of the Emperor of Russia to what has just been concluded between us. When you are in possession of this adhesion, proceed to the corps d'armée of Marshal Davoust, stop his movement, and tell him what has passed.'"—Savary, tom. ii., p. 140.

"He is a great soldier," said Alexander; "I do not pretend to compare myself with him—this is the first time I have been under fire. But it is enough. I came hither to the assistance of the Emperor of Austria—he has no farther occasion for my services—I return to my capital."

Accordingly, he commenced his march towards Russia, in pursuance of the terms agreed upon. The Russian arms had been unfortunate; but the behaviour of their youthful Emperor, and the marked deference shown towards him by Buonaparte, made a most favourable impression upon Europe at large.[167]

ARMISTICE WITH AUSTRIA

Dec. 6.

The Austrian monarch, left to his fate, obtained from Buonaparte an armistice[168]—a small part of the price was imposed in the shape of a military contribution of a hundred millions of francs, to be raised in the territories occupied by the French armies. The cessation of hostilities was to endure while Talleyrand on the one side, and Prince John of Lichtenstein on the other, adjusted the terms of a general pacification. Buonaparte failed not to propitiate the Austrian negotiator by the most extravagant praises in his bulletins, and has represented the Emperor of Austria as asking, "Why, possessing men of such distinguished talent, should the affairs of my cabinet be committed to knaves and fools?" Of this question we can only say, that if really asked by Francis, which we doubt, he was himself the only person by whom it could have been answered.

---

[167] "I could not help feeling a certain timidity on finding myself in Alexander's presence; he awed me by the majesty and nobleness of his look. Nature had done much for him; and it would have been difficult to find a model so perfect and so graceful; he was then twenty-six years old. He was already somewhat hard of hearing with the left ear, and he turned the right to hear what was said to him. He spoke in broken sentences; he laid great stress upon his finals, so that the discourse was never long. For the rest, he spoke the French language in all its purity, and always used its elegant academic expression. As there was no affectation in his language, it was easy to judge that this was one of the results of an excellent education."—Savary, tom. ii., p. 115.

[168] See Annual Register, vol. xlvii., p. 666.

The compliments to the Prince John of Lichtenstein, were intended to propitiate the public in favour of the treaty of peace, negotiated by a man of such talents. Some of his countrymen, on the other hand, accused him of selfish precipitation in the treaty, for the purpose of removing the scene of war from the neighbourhood of his own family estates. But what could the wisdom of the ablest negotiator, or the firmness of the most stubborn patriot have availed, when France was to dictate terms, and Austria to receive them. The treaties of Campo Formio and Luneville, though granted to Austria by Napoleon in the hour of victory, were highly advantageous compared to that of Presburgh, which was signed on the 26th of December, 1805, about a fortnight after the battle of Austerlitz.[169] By this negotiation, Francis ceded to Bavaria the oldest possession of his house, the mountains of Tyrol and of the Vorarlberg, filled with the best, bravest, and most attached of his subjects, and which, by their geographical situation, had hitherto given Austria influence at once in Germany and Italy. Venice, Austria's most recent possession, and which had not been very honourably obtained, was also yielded up, and added to the kingdom of Italy.[170] She was again reduced to the solitary seaport of Trieste, in the Adriatic.

By the same treaty, the Germanic allies of Buonaparte were to be remunerated. Wirtemberg, as well as Bavaria,[171] received large additions at the expense of Austria and of the other princes of the empire, and Francis consented that both the electors should be promoted to the kingly dignity, in reward of their adherence to the

---

[169] For a copy of the treaty, see Annual Register, vol. xlvii., p. 668.

[170] "After leaving Vienna, Napoleon, on his way to Munich, passed through Passau, where he met General Lauriston, who was returning from Cadiz; he sent him as governor to Venice."—Savary, tom. ii., p. 155.

[171] "The Emperor arrived at Munich, a few hours before New Year's-day, 1806. The Empress had come thither by his order a fortnight before. There was, as may be supposed, great rejoicing at the court of Bavaria: not only was the country saved, but almost doubled in extent. The greatest delight was therefore expressed at seeing us. It was at Munich that we began to perceive something which we had as yet only heard vaguely talked of. A courier was sent by the Tyrol with orders to the Viceroy of Italy to come immediately to Munich: accordingly, five days afterwards, he arrived. No secret was any longer made of his marriage with the Princess Augusta of Bavaria. The viceroy was much beloved, and the greatest pleasure was expressed to see him unite his destiny with that of a princess so virtuous and so lovely. The nuptials were celebrated at Munich; after which Napoleon returned to Paris."—Savary, tom. ii., p. 156.

French cause. Other provisions there were, equally inconsistent with the immunities of the Germanic body, for which scarcely a shadow of respect was retained, save by an illusory clause, or species of protest, by which Austria declared that all the stipulations to which she consented were under reservation of the rights of the empire. By the treaty of Presburgh, Austria is said to have lost upwards of 20,000 square miles of territory, two millions and a half of subjects, and a revenue to the amount of ten millions and a half of florins. And this momentous surrender was made in consequence of one unfortunate campaign, which lasted but six months, and was distinguished by only one general action.

There were two episodes in this war, of little consequence in themselves, but important considered with reference to the alterations they produced in two of the ancient kingdoms of Europe, which they proved the proximate cause of re-modelling according to the new form of government which had been introduced by Buonaparte, and sanctioned by the example of France.

The King of Sweden had been an ardent and enthusiastic member of the anti-Gallican league. He was brave, enterprising, and chivalrous, and ambitious to play the part of his namesake and progenitor, Gustavus Adolphus, or his predecessor, Charles XII.; without, however, considering, that since the time of those princes, and partly in consequence of their wars and extensive undertakings, Sweden had sunk into a secondary rank in the great European family; and without reflecting, that when great enterprises are attempted without adequate means to carry them through, valour becomes Quixotic, and generosity ludicrous. He had engaged to join in a combined effort for the purpose of freeing Hanover, and the northern parts of Germany, from the French, by means of an army of English, Russians, and Swedes. Had Prussia acceded to the confederacy, this might have been easily accomplished; especially as Saxony, Hesse, and Brunswick, would, under her encouragement, have willingly joined in the war. Nay, even without the accession of Prussia, a diversion in the north, ably conducted and strongly supported, might have at least found Bernadotte sufficient work in Hanover, and prevented him from materially contributing, by his march to the Danube, to the disasters of the Austrian army at Ulm. But, by some of those delays and misunderstandings, which are so apt to disappoint the objects of a coalition, and disconcert enterprises attempted by troops of different nations, the forces designed for the north of Europe did not assemble until the middle of November, and then only in strength sufficient to undertake the siege of the Hanoverian fortress of Hamelen, in which Bernadotte had left a strong garrison. The enterprise, too tardy in its commencement, was soon broken off by the news of the battle of Austerlitz and its consequences, and, being finally abandoned, the unfortunate King of Sweden returned to his own dominions, where his subjects received with unwillingness and terror a prince, who, on many accounts, had incurred the fatal and persevering resentment of Buonaparte. Machinations began presently to be agitated for removing him from the kingdom, as one with whom Napoleon could never be reconciled, and averting from Sweden, by such sacrifice, the punishment which must otherwise fall on the country, as well as on the King.[172]

NAPLES

While the trifling attempt against Hamelen, joined to other circumstances, was thus preparing the downfall of the ancient dynasty of Sweden, a descent, made by the Russians and English on the Neapolitan territories, afforded a good apology to Buonaparte for depriving the King of the Two Sicilies of his dominions, so far as they lay open to the power of France. Governed entirely by the influence of the Queen, the policy of Naples had been of a fickle and insincere character. Repeatedly saved from the greatest hazard of dethronement, the King or his royal consort had never omitted an opportunity to resume arms against France, under the conviction, perhaps, that their ruin would no longer be deferred than whilst political considerations induced the French Emperor to permit their possession of their power. The last interference in their behalf had been at the instance of the Emperor Paul. After this period we have seen that their Italian dominions were occupied by French troops,

---

[172] Jomini, tom. ii., p. 196; Las Cases, tom. v., p. 168; Montgaillard, tom. vi., p. 280.

who held Otranto, and other places in Calabria, as pledges (so they pretended) for the restoration of Malta.

But upon the breaking out of the war of 1805, it was agreed, by a convention entered into at Paris, 21st of September, and ratified by the King of Naples on the 8th of October, that the French should withdraw their forces from the places which they occupied in the Neapolitan territories, and the King should observe a strict neutrality. Neither of the contracting parties was quite sincere. The French troops, which were commanded by St. Cyr, were, as we have seen, withdrawn from Naples, for the purpose of reinforcing Massena, in the beginning of the campaign of Austerlitz. Their absence would probably have endured no longer than the necessity which called them away. But the court of Naples was equally insincere; for no sooner had St. Cyr left the Neapolitan territories to proceed northward, than the King, animated by the opportunity which his departure afforded, once more raised his forces to the war establishment, and received with open arms an army, consisting of 12,000 Russian troops from Corfu, and 8000 British from Malta, who disembarked in his dominions.[173]

Had this armament occupied Venice at the commencement of the war, they might have materially assisted in the campaign of the Archduke Charles against Massena. The sending them in November to the extremity of the Italian peninsula, only served to seal the fate of Ferdinand the Fourth. On receiving the news of the armistice at Austerlitz, the Russians and the British re-embarked, and not long after their departure a large French army, commanded by Joseph Buonaparte, approached, once more to enforce the doom passed against the royal family of Naples, that they should cease to reign.[174]

---

[173] "Before his departure from Vienna, Napoleon received intelligence of the entry of the Russians, jointly with some English, into Naples. He immediately made dispositions for marching troops thither. He had an old grudge against the Queen of Naples, and on receiving this news, he said, 'Ah! as for her, I am not surprised at it; but woe betide her if I enter Naples; never shall she set foot there again!' He sent from the staff of his own army officers to compose that which was about to assemble on the frontiers of Naples, and ordered Prince Joseph, his brother, whom he had left at Paris, to go and put himself at the head of it."—Savary, tom. ii., p. 152.

[174] "General St. Cyr is advancing by forced marches towards Naples, to punish the treason of the Queen, and to precipitate from the throne this culpable woman, who has violated, in so shameless a manner, all that is held sacred among men. It was endeavoured to intercede

The King and Queen fled from the storm which they had provoked. Their son, the prince royal, in whose favour they had abdicated, only made use of his temporary authority to surrender Gaeta, Pescara, and Naples itself, with its castles, to the French general. In Calabria, however, whose wild inhabitants were totally disinclined to the French yoke, Count Roger de Damas and the Duke of Calabria attempted to make a stand. But their hasty and undisciplined levies were easily defeated by the French under General Regnier, and, nominally at least, almost the whole Neapolitan kingdom was subjected to the power of Joseph Buonaparte.

SURRENDER OF GAETA

One single trait of gallantry illuminated the scene of universal pusillanimity. The Prince of Hesse Philipsthal, who defended the strong fortress of Gaeta in name of Ferdinand IV., refused to surrender it in terms of the capitulation. "Tell your general," said he, in reply to the French summons, "that Gaeta is not Ulm, nor the Prince of Hesse General Mack!" The place was defended with a gallantry corresponding to these expressions, nor was it surrendered until the 17th of July, 1806, after a long siege, in which the brave governor was wounded.[175] This heroic young prince only appeared on the public scene to be withdrawn from it by an untimely death, which has been ascribed to poison. His valour, however honourable to himself, was of little use to the royal family of Naples, whose deposition was determined on by Buonaparte, in order to place upon the throne one of his own family.

---

for her with the Emperor. He replied, 'Were hostilities to recommence, and the nation to support a thirty years' war, so atrocious an act of perfidy cannot be pardoned.' *The Queen of Naples has ceased* to reign."—*Thirty-seventh Bulletin of the Grand Army*, Dec. 26.
[175] Jomini, tom. ii., p. 237; Annual Register, vol. xlviii., p. 144.

Chapter XXXIII

Relative situations of France and England—Hostilities commenced with Spain, by the Stoppage, by Commodore Moore, of four Spanish Galleons, when three of their Escort were taken, and one blew up—Napoleon's Plan of Invasion stated and discussed—John Clerk of Eldin's great System of Breaking the Line, explained—The French Admiral, Villeneuve, forms a junction with the Spanish Fleet under Gravina—Attacked and defeated by Sir Robert Calder—Nelson appointed to the Command in the Mediterranean—Battle of Trafalgar fought 21st October, 1805—Death of Nelson—Behaviour of Napoleon on learning the Intelligence of this signal Defeat—Villeneuve commits Suicide—Address of Buonaparte to the Legislative Body—Statement of M. de Champagny on the Internal Improvements of France—Elevation of Napoleon's Brothers, Louis and Joseph, to the Thrones of Holland and Naples—Principality of Lucca conferred on Eliza, the eldest Sister of Buonaparte, and that of Guastalla on Pauline, the youngest—Other Alliances made by his Family—Napoleon appoints a new Hereditary Nobility—Converts from the old Noblesse anxiously sought for and liberally rewarded—Confederation of the Rhine established, and Napoleon appointed Protector—The Emperor Francis lays aside the Imperial Crown of Germany, retaining only the Title of Emperor of Austria—Vacillating and Impolitic Conduct of Prussia.

The triumphs of Napoleon had been greater at this period of his reign, than had ever before been recorded in history as achieved by a single man. Yet even these, like every thing earthly, had their limit. Fate, while she seemed to assign him complete domination over the land, had vested in other hands the empire of the seas; and it frequently happened, that when his victorious eagles were flying their highest pitch upon the continent, some conspicuous naval disaster warned the nations, that there was another element, where France had a rival and a superior.

It is true, that the repeated success of England, resembling almost that of the huntsman over his game, had so much diminished the French navy, and rendered so cautious such seamen as France had remaining, that the former country, unable to get opportunities of assailing the French vessels, was induced to have recourse to strange, and, as it proved, ineffectual means of carrying on hostilities. Such was the attempt at destroying the harbour of Boulogne, by sinking in the roads ships loaded with stones, and another scheme to blow up the French ships, by means of detonating machines to be affixed to them under water. The one, we believe, only furnished the inhabitants of Boulogne with a supply of useful building stone; the other, from the raft on which the machines were conveyed, was much ridiculed under the name of the catamaran expedition.[176]

Buonaparte, meanwhile, never lost sight of that combination of naval manœuvres, through means of which, by the time that the subjugation of Austria should permit the Grand Army to resume its destination for England, he hoped to assemble in the Channel such a superior fleet, as might waft his troops in safety to the devoted shores of Britain. The unbounded influence which he exercised over the court of Spain, seemed likely to facilitate this difficult enterprise. Yet, as from Spain the French Emperor derived large supplies of treasure, it would have been convenient for him, that, for a time at least, she should retain the mask of neutrality, while, in fact, she was contributing to serve France, and prejudice England, more effectually than if she had been in a state of avowed hostility with the latter power.

---

[176] These implements of destruction were afterwards used against the British cruizers in America, and were judged formidable. But such desperate courage is necessary to attach the machine to the destined vessel, and the fate of the engineer, if discovered, is so certainly fatal, that, like fire-ships, petards, and similar inventions, liable to the same inconvenience, they do not appear likely to get into general use.—S. See in the Annual Register, vol. xlvi., p. 553, Lord Keith's account of the failure of the catamaran expedition against the French flotilla outside the pier of Boulogne.

The British Government determined to bring this state of things to a decided point, by stopping four galleons, or vessels loaded with treasure, proceeding under an escort from the South Sea, and destined for Cadiz. The purpose of the English was only to detain these ships, as a pledge for the sincerity of the Government of Spain, in observing a more strict neutrality than hitherto. But unhappily the British force, under Commodore Moore, amounted only to four frigates. Spanish honour rendered the admiral unwilling to strike the national flag to an equal strength, and an action ensued, in which three of the Spanish vessels were taken, and one unfortunately blew up—an accident greatly to be regretted. Mr. Southey observes, with his usual sound sense and humanity, "Had a stronger squadron been sent, (against the Spaniards,) this deplorable catastrophe might have been saved—a catastrophe which excited not more indignation in Spain, than it did grief in those who were its unwilling instruments, in the British people and in the British government."

WAR BETWEEN SPAIN AND ENGLAND

This action took place on the 5th of October 1804; and as hostilities were of course immediately commenced betwixt Spain and Britain,[177] Buonaparte, losing the advantages he derived from the neutrality of the former power, had now only to use the naval and military means which she afforded for the advancement of his own purposes. The Court of Spain devoted them to his service, with a passive complaisance of which we shall hereafter see the reward.

Napoleon persisted to the last in asserting, that he saw clearly the means of utterly destroying the English superiority at sea. This he proposed to achieve by evading the blockades of the several ports of France and Spain, which, while weather permitted, were each hermetically sealed by the presence of a British squadron, and by finally assembling in the Channel that overwhelming force, which, according to his statement, was to reduce England to a

---

[177] See declaration of war made by Spain against England, dated Madrid, Dec. 12, 1804, and also declaration of war with Spain on the part of the King of England, Annual Register, vol. xlvi., p. 699, and vol. xlvii., p. 608.

dependency on France, as complete as that of the Isle of Oleron.[178] But men of the greatest talents must necessarily be liable to error, when they apply the principles of a science with which they are well acquainted upon one element, to the operations which are to be carried on by means of another. It is evident that he erred, when calculating his maritime combinations, in not sufficiently considering two most material differences betwixt them, and those which had exalted his glory upon land.

In the first place, as a landsman, Napoleon did not make sufficient allowance for the action of contrary winds and waves; as indeed it was perhaps his fault, even in land operations, where their influence is less essential, to admit too little consequence to the opposition of the elements. He complained, when at St. Helena, that he could never get a seaman sufficiently emancipated from the technicality of his profession, to execute or enter into any of his schemes. "If I proposed," he said, "any new idea, I had Gantheaume and all the marine department to contend with—Sir, that is impossible—Sir,—the winds—the calms—the currents, will not permit it; and thus I was stopped short."[179] We believe little dread could have been entertained of the result of naval combinations in which the influence of the winds and waves was not previously and accurately calculated; and that British seamen would have desired nothing more ardently, than that their enemies should have acted upon a system in which these casualties were neglected, even if that system had been derived from the genius of Napoleon.

But, secondly, there was this great difference betwixt the land and the sea service, to which (the vehemence of his wishes, doubtless, overpowering his judgment) Buonaparte did not give sufficient weight. Upon land, the excellence of the French troops, their discipline, and the enthusiasm arising from uninterrupted success, might be safely reckoned upon as likely to bear down any obstacle which they might unexpectedly meet with, in the execution of the movements which they were commanded to undertake. The situation of the French seamen was diametrically the contrary. Their only chance of safety consisted in their being able to elude a

---

[178] Las Cases, tom. ii., p. 264; O'Meara, vol. i., p. 351.
[179] Las Cases, tom. iii., p. 248.

rencontre with a British squadron, even of very inferior force. So much was this the case at the period of which we treat, that Linois, their admiral in the East Indian seas, commanding an eighty-four-gun ship, and at the head of a considerable squadron of ships of war, was baffled and beaten off in the straits of Malacca by a squadron of merchant vessels belonging to the British East India Company, although built, of course, for traffic, and not for war, and, as usual in war time, very imperfectly manned.[180]

Yet, notwithstanding the great and essential difference which we have pointed out between the French navy and their land forces, and that the former was even more inferior to that of England than the continental troops in general were to the French soldiers, it is evident that Buonaparte, when talking of ships of the line, was always thinking of battalions. Thus he imagines that the defeat of the Nile might have been prevented, had the headmost vessels of the French line, instead of remaining at anchor, slipped their cables, and borne down to the assistance of those which were first attacked by the British. But in urging this, the leading principle of the manœuvre of breaking the line had totally escaped the French Emperor. It was the boast of the patriotic sage,[181] who illustrated and recommended this most important system of naval tactics, that it could serve the purpose of a British fleet only. The general principle is briefly this: By breaking through the line, a certain number of ships are separated from the rest, which the remainder must either abandon to their fate by sailing away, or endeavour to save by bearing down, or doubling as it were, upon the assailants, and engaging in a close and general engagement. Now, this last alternative is what Buonaparte recommends,—what he would

---

[180] See Commodore Dance's account of the defeat of Admiral Linois' squadron in the Indian seas, Annual Register, vol. xlvi., p. 551.

[181] The late John Clerk of Eldin; a name never to be mentioned by Britons without respect and veneration, since, until his systematic Essay upon Naval Tactics appeared, the breaking of the line (whatever professional jealousy may allege to the contrary) was never practised on decided and defined principle. His suavity, nay, simplicity of manner, equalled the originality of his genius. This trifling tribute is due from one, who, honoured with his regard from boyhood, has stood by his side, while he was detailing and illustrating the system which taught British seamen to understand and use their own force, at an age so early, that he can remember having been guilty of abstracting from the table some of the little cork models by which Mr. Clerk exemplified his manœuvres; unchecked but by his good-humoured raillery, when he missed a supposed line-of-battle ship, and complained that the demonstration was crippled by its absence.—S.

certainly have practised on land,—and what he did practise, in order to extricate his right wing, at Marengo. But the relative superiority of the English navy is so great, that, while it is maintained, a close engagement with an enemy in the least approaching to equality, is equivalent to a victory; and to recommend a plan of tactics which should render such a battle inevitable, would be, in other words, advising a French admiral to lose his whole fleet, instead of sacrificing those ships which the English manœuvre had cut off, and crowding sail to save such as were yet unengaged.[182]

Under this consciousness of inferiority, the escape of a Spanish or French squadron, when a gale of wind forced, from the port in which they lay, the British blockading vessels, was a matter, the ultimate success of which depended not alone on the winds and waves, but still more upon the chance of their escaping any part of the hostile navy, with whom battle, except with the most exorbitant superiority on their side, was certain and unavoidable defeat. Their efforts to comply with the wishes of the Emperor of France, were therefore so partially conducted, so insulated, and so ineffectual, that they rather resembled the children's game of hide and seek, than any thing like a system of regular combination. A more hasty and less cautious compliance with Napoleon's earnest wishes to assemble a predominant naval force, would have only occasioned the total destruction of the combined fleets at an earlier period than when it actually took place.

ROCHEFORT SQUADRON

Upon this desultory principle, and seizing the opportunity of the blockading squadron being driven by weather from the vicinity of their harbour, a squadron of ten French vessels escaped from

---

[182] "If it were permitted to a man whose only campaign at sea was that of Egypt in the vessel of Brueyes, to speak of naval tactics, I could easily refute all that Sir Walter Scott has here said. I shall limit myself to the relation of the observations made with General Kleber, when, from the neighbouring coast, we witnessed the battle of Aboukir. The greater part of our squadron remained inactive, while the English turned the left; there was not a single spectator who was not irritated at seeing the six vessels on the right of the squadron, commanded by Brueyes, keep their line, when, if they had hoisted sail, and fallen back on the left, they would have put the English between two fires, and would certainly have gained the victory."—Louis Buonaparte, p. 46.

Rochefort on the 11th of January, 1805; and another, under Villeneuve, got out of Toulon on the 18th by a similarly favourable opportunity. The former, after rendering some trifling services in the West Indies, was fortunate enough to regain the port from which they had sailed, with the pride of a party who have sallied from a besieged town, and returned into it without loss. Villeneuve also regained Toulon without disaster, and, encouraged by his success, made a second sortie upon the 18th of March, having on board a large body of troops, designed, it was supposed, for a descent upon Ireland or Scotland. He made, however, towards Cadiz, and formed a junction there with the Spanish fleet under Gravina. They sailed for the West Indies, where the joint squadrons were able to possess themselves of a rock called Diamond, which is scarce to be discovered on the map; and with this trophy, which served at least to show they had been actually out of harbour, they returned with all speed to Europe. As for executing manœuvres, and forming combinations, as Napoleon's plans would lead us to infer was the purpose of their hurried expedition, they attempted none, save of that kind which the hare executes when the hound is at its heels. Nelson, they were aware, was in full pursuit of them, and to have attempted any thing which involved a delay, or gave a chance of his coming up with them, was to court destruction. They were so fortunate as to escape him, though very narrowly, yet did not reach their harbours in safety.

On the 22d July, the combined fleets fell in with Sir Robert Calder, commanding a British squadron. The enemy amounted to twenty sail of the line, three fifty-gun ships, and four frigates, and the British to fifteen sail of the line, and two frigates only. Under this disparity of force, nevertheless, the English admiral defeated the enemy, and took two ships of the line; yet such was the opinion in both countries of the comparative superiority of the British navy, that the French considered their escape as a kind of triumph. Buonaparte alone grumbled against Villeneuve, for not having made use of his advantages,[183] for so it pleased him to term an engagement

---

[183] "Had Villeneuve manifested more vigour at Cape Finistère, the attack on England might have been rendered practicable. I had made arrangements for his arrival, with considerable art and calculation, and in defiance of the opinions and the routine of the naval officers by whom I was surrounded. Every thing happened as I had foreseen; when the inactivity of Villeneuve ruined all."—Napoleon, *Las Cases*, tom. iii., p. 247.

in which two ships of the line were lost; whilst the English murmured at the inadequate success of Sir Robert Calder, against an enemy of such superior strength, as if he had performed something less than his duty. A court-martial ratified, to a certain extent,[184] the popular opinion; though it may be doubted whether impartial posterity will concur in the justice of the censure which was passed upon the gallant admiral. At any other period of our naval history, the action of the 22d of July would have been rated as a distinguished victory.

The combined fleets escaped into Vigo, where they refitted; and, venturing to sail from that port, they proceeded to Ferrol,[185] united themselves with the squadron which was lying there, and continued their course for Cadiz, which they entered in safety. This did not consist with the plans of Buonaparte, who would have had the whole naval force united at Brest to be in readiness to cover the descent upon England. "General terror was spread," he said, "throughout that divided nation, and never was England so near to destruction."[186] Of the general terror, few of the British, we believe, remember any thing, and of the imminent danger we were not sensible. Had the combined fleets entered the British Channel, instead of the Mediterranean, they would have found the same admiral, the same seamen, nay, in many instances, the same ships, to

---

[184] "The court are of opinion that such conduct on the part of Admiral Sir Robert Calder was not the result of cowardice or disaffection, but of error in judgment, for which he deserves to be severely reprimanded—and he is hereby severely reprimanded accordingly."—See Annual Register, vol. xlvii., p. 436. And for the Defence of Sir Robert Calder, see p. 564 of the same volume.

[185] "In 1805, M. Daru was at Boulogne, intendant general of the army. One morning, Napoleon sent for him into his cabinet: Daru there found him transported with rage, striding rapidly up and down the apartment, and breaking a sullen silence only by abrupt and short exclamations—'What a navy!—What an admiral!—What sacrifices thrown away!—My hope is destroyed!—This Villeneuve! instead of being in the Channel, he is gone into Ferrol! It is all over! he will be blockaded. Daru, sit down, listen, and write!' Napoleon had received early in the morning the news of Villeneuve's arrival in a Spanish port; he saw instantly that the conquest of England was abortive, the immense expense of the fleet and the flotilla lost for a long time, perhaps for ever. At that moment, in the transport of rage, which permits not other men to preserve their judgment, he had taken one of those bold resolutions, and traced out one of the most admirable plans of a campaign, that any other conqueror could have conceived at leisure and with coolness, without hesitation, without stopping: he then dictated the whole plan of the campaign of Austerlitz, the departure of the several corps of the army, from Hanover and Holland, even to the confines of the west and south of France."—Dupin, *Force Naval*, tom. i., p. 244.

[186] Las Cases, tom. ii., p. 263.

which Villeneuve's retreat into Cadiz gave the trouble of going to seek him there.

NELSON IN THE MEDITERRANEAN

When the certainty was known that the enemy's fleets were actually in Cadiz, Nelson was put at the head of the British naval force in the Mediterranean,[187] which was reinforced with an alertness and secrecy that did the highest honour to the Admiralty. Villeneuve, in the meantime, had, it is believed, his master's express orders to put to sea;[188] and if he had been censured for want of zeal in the action off Cape Finisterre with Calder, he was likely, as a brave man, to determine on running some risk to prove the injustice of his Emperor's reproaches. Cadiz also, being strictly blockaded by the English, the fleets of France and Spain began to be in want of necessaries. But what principally determined the French admiral on putting to sea, was his ignorance of the reinforcements received by the English, which, though they left Nelson's fleet still inferior to his own, yet brought them nearer to an equality than, had he been aware of it, would have rendered their meeting at all desirable to Villeneuve. It was another and especial point of encouragement, that circumstances led him to disbelieve the report that Nelson commanded the British fleet.[189] Under the influence of these united

---

[187] Nelson had not been a month in England when Captain Blackwood, on his way to the Admiralty with despatches, called on him at Merton, at five in the morning, and found him already dressed. Upon seeing him, he exclaimed "I am sure you bring me news of the French and Spanish fleets! I think I shall have yet to beat them!" It was as he had supposed; they had liberated the squadron from Ferrol, and being now thirty-four sail of the line, got safely into Cadiz. "Depend on it, Blackwood," he repeatedly said, "I shall yet give M. Villeneuve a drubbing!"—Southey.

[188] "Napoleon had, no doubt, ordered the minister of the marine to take from Admiral Villeneuve the command of his fleets; for the latter sent Admiral Rosilly to supersede him. He apprised Villeneuve of this by a courier: whether he added any reproaches I know not; but something of the kind must have passed, since Villeneuve quitted Cadiz without occasion, with the French and Spanish fleet, to attack the English squadron commanded by Nelson."—Savary, tom. ii., p. 112.

[189] "Villeneuve had called a council of war on hearing that Nelson had taken the command; and their determination was not to leave Cadiz unless they had reason to believe themselves one-third stronger than the British force. Many circumstances tended to deceive them into such an opinion, and an American contributed unintentionally to mislead them, by declaring that Nelson could not possibly be with the fleet, for he himself had seen him only a few days before in London."—Southey.

motives, and confiding in a plan of tactics which he had formed for resisting the favourite mode of attack practised by the English, the French admiral sailed from Cadiz on the 19th October, 1805, in an evil hour for himself and for his country.

The hostile fleets were not long in meeting, and the wind never impelled along the ocean two more gallant armaments. The advantage of numbers was greatly on the side of Villeneuve. He had thirty-three sail of the line, and seven large frigates; Nelson only twenty-seven line-of-battle ships, and three frigates. The inferiority of the English in number of men and guns was yet more considerable. The combined fleet had four thousand troops on board, many of whom, excellent rifle-men, were placed in the tops. But all odds were compensated by the quality of the British sailors, and the talents of Nelson.

Villeneuve showed no inclination to shun the eventful action. His disposition was singular and ingenious. His fleet formed a double line, each alternate ship being about a cable's length to the windward of her second a-head and a-stern, and thus the arrangements represented the chequers of a draught-board, and seemed to guard against the operation of cutting the line, as usually practised by the British. But Nelson had determined to practise the manœuvre in a manner as original as the mode of defence adopted by Villeneuve. His order for sailing was in two lines, and this was also the order for battle. An advanced squadron of eight of the fastest sailing two-deckers, was to cut off three or four of the enemy's line, a-head of their centre; the second in command, Admiral Collingwood, was to break in upon the enemy about the twelfth ship from the rear, and Nelson himself determined to bear down on the centre. The effect of these manœuvres must of course be a close and general action; for the rest Nelson knew he could trust to the determination of his officers and seamen. To his admirals and officers he explained in general, that his object was a close and decisive engagement; and that if, in the confusion and smoke of the battle, signals should not be visible, the captain would never do wrong who laid his ship alongside of the enemy.

With such dispositions on either side, the two gallant fleets met on the memorable 21st of October. Admiral Collingwood, who led the van, went down on the enemy with all his sails set, and, disdaining to furl them in the usual manner, cut the sheets, and let his canvass fly loose in the wind, as if he needed it no longer after it had borne him amidst the thickest of the enemy. Nelson run his vessel, the Victory, on board the French Redoutable; the Temeraire, a second British ship, fell on board the same vessel on the other side; another enemy's ship fell on board of the Temeraire, and the action was fiercely maintained betwixt these four vessels, which lay as close as if they had been moored together in some friendly harbour. While the Victory thus engaged the Redoutable on the starboard, she maintained from her larboard guns an incessant fire on the Bucentaur and the colossal Santa Trinidad, a vessel of four decks. The example of the admiral was universally followed by the British captains; they broke into the enemy's line on every side, engaged two or three ships at the same time, and maintained the battle at the very muzzles of the cannon. The superiority which we have claimed for our countrymen was soon made manifest. Nineteen ships of the line were captured, two were first-rate vessels, none were under seventy-four guns. Four ships of the line were taken, in a subsequent action, by Sir Richard Strachan. Seven out of the vessels which escaped into Cadiz were rendered unserviceable. The whole combined fleet was almost totally destroyed.

DEATH OF NELSON

It is twenty years and upwards since that glorious day. But the feelings of deep sorrow mingled with those of exultation, with which we first heard the tidings of the battle of Trafalgar, still agitate our bosoms, as we record, that Nelson, the darling of Britain, bought with his life this last and decided triumph over his country's enemies. A Briton himself in every word and thought, the discharge of a sailor's duty, according to his idea, was a debt involving every feat which the most exalted bravery could perform, and every risk which the extremity of danger could present. The word to which he attached such an unlimited meaning, was often in his mouth; the idea never, we believe, absent from his mind. His last signal intimated that England expected every man to do his *duty*. His first words on entering the action were, "I thank the great Disposer of events for this great opportunity of doing my *duty*;" and with his last departing breath, he was distinctly heard to repeat the same pious and patriotic sentiment, "I thank God I have done my duty."[190] That DUTY was indeed performed, even to the utmost extent of his own comprehensive interpretation of the phrase. The good servant of his country slept not before his task was fulfilled; for, by the victory in which he fell, the naval force of the enemy was altogether destroyed, and the threat of invasion silenced for ever.

It is a remarkable coincidence, that Mack's surrender having taken place the 20th October, Napoleon was probably entering Ulm in triumph upon the very day, when the united remains of his maritime force, and the means on which, according to his own subsequent account, he relied for the subjugation of England, were flying, striking, and sinking, before the banners of Nelson. What his feelings may have been on learning the news we have no certain means of ascertaining. The Memoirs of Fouché say, upon the alleged authority of Berthier, that his emotion was extreme, and that his first exclamation was, "I cannot be every where!" implying, certainly, that his own presence would have changed the scene.[191] The same idea occurs in his conversations with Las Cases.[192] It may be greatly doubted, however, whether Napoleon would have desired to have been on board the best ship in the French navy on that memorable occasion; and it seems pretty certain, that his being so

---

[190] See, for these and other particulars of the battle of Trafalgar, Southey's *Life of Nelson*, a work already repeatedly quoted. It is the history of a hero, in the narrative of which are evinced at once the judgment and fidelity of the historian, with the imagination of the poet. It well deserves to be, what already it is, the text-book of the British navy.—S.
[191] "The disaster of Trafalgar, by the ruin of our navy, completed the security of Great Britain. It was a few days after the capitulation of Ulm, and upon the Vienna road, that Napoleon received the despatch containing the first intelligence of this misfortune. Berthier has since related to me, that while seated at the same table with Napoleon, he read the fatal paper, but not daring to present it to him, he pushed it gradually with his elbows under his eyes. Scarcely had Napoleon glanced through its contents, than he started up, full of rage, exclaiming, 'I cannot be every where!' His agitation was extreme, and Berthier despaired of tranquillizing him."—Fouché, tom. i., p. 293.
[192] "It used to be remarked in the saloon of the household, that I was never accessible to any one after I had an audience with the minister of the marine. The reason was, because he never had any but bad news to communicate to me. For my part, I gave up every thing after the disaster of Trafalgar; I could not be every where, and I had enough to occupy my attention with the armies of the continent."—Napoleon, *Las Cases*, tom. iii., p. 248.

could have had no influence whatever on the fate of the day. The unfortunate Villeneuve dared not trust to his master's forgiveness. "He ought," so Buonaparte states it, "to have been victorious, and he was defeated." For this, although the mishap which usually must attend one out of the two commanders who engage in action, Villeneuve felt there was no apology to be accepted, or even offered, and the brave but unfortunate seaman committed suicide.[193] Buonaparte, on all occasions, spoke with disrespect of his memory; nor was it a sign of his judgment in nautical matters, that he preferred to this able, but unfortunate admiral, the gasconading braggart, Latouche Tréville.[194]

The unfortunate event of the battle of Trafalgar was not permitted to darken the brilliant picture, which the extraordinary campaign of Ulm and Austerlitz enabled the victor to present to the empire which he governed, and which detailed his successes in the full-blown pride of conquest. "His armies," he said, addressing the Legislative Body, the session of which he opened with great pomp on 2d March, 1806, "had never ceased to conquer, until he

---

[193] "At Rennes, 26th April, 1806, on his way from England to Paris.—Villeneuve, when taken prisoner and conveyed to England, was so much grieved at his defeat, that he studied anatomy on purpose to destroy himself. For this purpose he bought some anatomical plates of the heart, and compared them with his own body, in order to ascertain the exact situation of that organ. On his arrival in France, I ordered that he should remain at Rennes, and not proceed to Paris. Villeneuve, afraid of being tried by a court-martial, determined to destroy himself, and accordingly took his plates of the heart, and compared them with his breast. Exactly in the shape of the plate, he made a mark with a large pin, then fixed the pin as near as he could judge in the same spot in his own breast, shoved it in to the head, penetrated his heart, and expired. He need not have done it, as he was a brave man, though possessed of no talent."—Napoleon, *Voice*, &c., vol. i., p. 57.

[194] This admiral commanded at Toulon in 1804, and having stolen out of harbour with a strong squadron, when the main body of the English fleet was out of sight, had the satisfaction to see three vessels, under Rear-admiral Campbell, retreat before his superior force. This unusual circumstance so elated Monsieur Latouche Tréville, that he converted the affair into a general pursuit of the whole British fleet, and of Nelson himself, who, he pretended, fled before him. Nelson was so much nettled at his effrontery, that he wrote to his brother, "You will have seen Latouche's letter, how he chased me and how I run. I keep it, and if I take him, by God, he shall eat it." Latouche escaped this punishment by dying [19th August, 1804] of the fatigue incurred by walking so often up to the signal-post at Sepet, to watch for the momentary absence of the blockading squadron, which he pretended dared not face him. This man Buonaparte considered as the boast of the French navy.—S.—"Napoleon said, he much regretted Latouche Tréville, whom he regarded as a man of real talent. He was of opinion that that admiral would have given a different impulse to affairs. The attack on India, and the invasion of England, would by him have been at least attempted."—Las Cases, tom. iii., p. 247.

commanded them to cease to combat. His enemies were humbled and confounded—the royal house of Naples had ceased to reign *for ever*"—(the term was too comprehensive)—"the entire peninsula of Italy now made a part of the Great Empire—his generosity had permitted the return of the defeated Russians to their own country, and had re-established the throne of Austria, after punishing her by the privation of a part of her dominions." Trafalgar was then touched upon. "A tempest," he said, "had deprived him of some few vessels, after a combat imprudently entered into;"[195]—and thus he glossed over a calamitous and decisive defeat, in which so many of his hopes were shipwrecked.

INTERNAL IMPROVEMENTS

When a sovereign has not sufficient greatness of mind to acknowledge his losses, we may, without doing him wrong, suspect him of exaggerating his successes. Those of France, in her external relations, were indeed scarcely capable of being over-estimated. But when M. de Champagny, on the 4th March following, made a relation of the internal improvements of France under the government of Buonaparte, he seems to have assumed the merit of those which only existed upon paper, and of others which were barely commenced, as well as of some that were completed. All was of course ascribed to the inspiring genius of the Emperor, to whose agency France was indebted for all her prosperity. The credit of the good city of Paris was restored, and her revenue doubled—agriculture was encouraged, by the draining of immense morasses—mendicity was abolished. Beneficial results, apparently inconsistent with each other, were produced by his regulations—the expenses of legal proceedings were abridged, and the appointments of the judges were raised. Immense and most expensive improvements, which, in other countries, or rather under other sovereigns, are necessarily reserved for times of peace, were carried on by Napoleon during the most burdensome wars against entire Europe. Forty millions had been expended on public works, of which eight great canals were quoted with peculiar emphasis, as opening all the departments of the empire to the influence of internal navigation. To conclude, the

---

[195] Moniteur, 3d March, 1806.

Emperor had established three hundred and seventy schools—had restored the rites of religion—re-inforced public credit by supporting the Bank—reconciled jarring factions—diminished the public imposts—and ameliorated the condition of every existing Frenchman.[196] To judge from the rapturous expressions of M. de Champagny, the Emperor was already the subject of deserved adoration; it only remained to found temples and raise altars.

Much of this statement was unquestionably the exaggeration of flattery, which represented every thing as commenced as soon as it had been resolved upon by the sovereign, every thing finished as soon as it was begun. Other measures there were, which, like the support afforded to the Bank, merely repaired injuries which Napoleon himself had inflicted. The credit of this commercial establishment had been shaken, because, in setting off for the campaign, Napoleon had stripped it of the reserve of specie laid up to answer demands; and it was restored, because his return with victory had enabled him to replace what he had borrowed. Considering that there was no small hazard of his being unable to remedy the evil which he had certainly occasioned,[197] his conduct on the occasion scarcely deserves the name of a national benefit.

Some part of this exaggeration might even deceive Napoleon. It is one of the great disadvantages of despotism, that the sovereign himself is liable to be imposed upon by false representations of this nature; as it is said the Empress Catherine was flattered by the appearance of distant villages and towns in the desert places of her empire, which were, in fact, no more than painted representations of such objects,[198] upon the plan of those that are exhibited on the

---

[196] The Exposé also states—"The calendar of the Revolution has been abolished, because its object was found to be unattainable, and it was necessary to sacrifice it to commercial and political convenience, which requires a common system.—Indeed," it adds, "the people of fair Europe are already divided by too many varieties; they ought only to form one great family."

[197] "This embarrassment Napoleon had himself caused by carrying off from the vaults of the bank above fifty millions. Placed upon the backs of King Philip's mules, these millions had powerfully contributed to the prodigious success of this unexpected campaign."—Fouché, tom. i., p. 295.

[198] "A ridiculous story," says the Prince de Ligne, who accompanied the Empress Catherine during her tour through her southern provinces, in 1787, "has been spread, which affirms that villages of pasteboard, and paintings representing distant fleets and arsenals, and bodies of cavalry, have been so disposed as to cheat our eyes during our rapid journey. I

stage, or are erected as points of view in some fantastic pleasure gardens. It was a part of Buonaparte's character to seize with ready precision upon general ideas of improvement. Wherever he came, he formed plans of important public works, many of which never existed but in the bulletin. Having issued his general orders, he was apt to hold them as executed. It was impossible to do all himself, or even to overlook with accuracy those to whom the details were committed. There were, therefore, many magnificent schemes commenced, under feelings of the moment, which were left unfinished for want of funds, or perhaps because they only regarded some points of local interest, and there were many adopted that were forgotten amid the hurry of affairs, or postponed till the moment of peace, which was never to appear during his reign.

But with the same frankness with which history is bound to censure the immeasurable ambition of this extraordinary man, she is bound also to record that his views towards the improvement of his empire were broad, clear-sighted, and public-spirited; and we think it probable, that, had his passion for war been a less predominant point of his character, his care, applied to the objects of peace, would have done as much for France, as Augustus did for Rome. Still it must be added, that, having bereft his country of her freedom, and proposing to transmit the empire, like his own patrimony, to his heirs, the evil which he had done to France was as permanent as his system of government, while the benefits which he had conferred on her, to whatever extent they might have been realized, must have been dependent upon his own life, and the character of his successor.

But as such reflections had not prevented Napoleon from raising the fabric of supreme power, to the summit of which he had ascended, so they did not now prevent him from surrounding and strengthening it with such additional bulwarks as he could find materials for erecting, at the expense of the foes whom he subdued. Sensible of the difficulty, or rather the impossibility, of retaining all

---

believe, however, that some little contrivance is occasionally employed: that, for instance, the Empress, who cannot rove about on foot as we do, is persuaded that some towns, for the building of which she has paid considerable sums, are really finished; whereas there are, in fact, many towns without streets, streets without houses, and houses without roofs, doors, or windows."—*Lettres et Pensées*.

power in his own hands, he now bent himself so to modify and organise the governments of the countries adjacent, that they should always be dependent upon France; and to ensure this point, he determined to vest immediate relations of his own with the supreme authority in those states, which, under the name of allies, were to pay to France the same homage in peace, and render her the same services in war, which ancient Rome exacted from the countries which she had subdued. Germany, Holland, and Italy, were each destined to furnish an appanage to the princes born of the Imperial blood of Napoleon, or connected with it by matrimonial alliances. In return for these benefits, Buonaparte was disposed to subject his brothers to the ordinary monarchical restrictions, which preclude princes nearly connected with the throne from forming marriages, according to their own private inclinations, and place them in this respect entirely at the devotion of the monarch, and destined to form such political alliances as may best suit his views. They belonged, he said, in the decree creating them, entirely to the country, and must therefore lay aside every sentiment of individual feeling, when the public weal required such a sacrifice.[199]

Two of Napoleon's brothers resisted this species of authority. The services which Lucien had rendered him upon the 18th Brumaire, although without his prompt assistance that daring adventure might have altogether failed, had not saved him from falling under the Imperial displeasure. It is said that he had disapproved of the destruction of the Republic, and that, in remonstrating against the murder of the Duke d'Enghien, he had dared to tell his brother, that such conduct would cause the people to cast himself and his kindred into the common sewer, as they had done the corpse of Marat.[200] But Lucien's principal offence consisted in his refusing to part with his wife, a beautiful and affectionate woman, for the purpose of forming an alliance more

---

[199] "How does Sir Walter make these different assertions agree? The truth is, Napoleon never wished or pretended to give *appanages*, but to act as he thought right towards France, and this design was as great as it was noble and generous; exaggeration only deforms it."—Louis Buonaparte, p. 48.

[200] "One day, after a warm dispute between the two brothers, Lucien, taking out his watch, and flinging it violently on the floor, addressed Napoleon in these remarkable words: 'You will one day be smashed to pieces as I have smashed that watch; and a time will come, when your family and friends will not have a resting-place for their heads.'"—*Mémoires de Rapp*, p. 11.

suited to the views of Napoleon.[201] He remained, therefore, long in a private situation,[202] notwithstanding the talent and decision which he had evinced on many occasions during the Revolution, and was only restored to his brother's favour and countenance, when, after his return from Elba, his support became again of importance. Jerome, the youngest brother of the family, incurred also for a time his brother's displeasure, by having formed a matrimonial connexion with an American lady of beauty and accomplishments.[203] Complying with the commands of Napoleon, he was at a later period restored to his favour, but at present he too was in disgrace. Neither Lucien nor Jerome was therefore mentioned in the species of entail, which, in default of Napoleon's naming his successor, destined the French empire to Joseph and Louis in succession; nor were the former called upon to partake in the splendid provisions, which, after the campaign of Austerlitz, Napoleon was enabled to make for the other members of his family.

LOUIS, KING OF HOLLAND

Of these establishments, the most princely were the provinces of Holland, which Napoleon now converted into a kingdom, and conferred upon Louis Buonaparte. This transmutation of a republic, whose independence was merely nominal, into a kingdom, which was completely and absolutely subordinate, was effected by little more than an expression of the French Emperor's will that such an alteration should take place. The change was accomplished without attracting much attention; for the Batavian republic was placed so absolutely at Buonaparte's mercy, as to have no power whatever to

---

[201] De Bourrienne, tom. vi., p. 80.
[202] In 1805 he settled at Rome, where the Pope, calling to mind the active part he had taken in the negotiation relative to the Concordat, treated him with marked attention and kindness.
[203] Towards the close of 1803, Jerome married Miss Paterson, the daughter of a rich merchant of Baltimore. In the spring of 1805, he embarked in a neutral vessel, and landed at Lisbon, whence he set off, by land, for Paris, directing the ship to proceed to Amsterdam; from which city he intended his wife should follow him, as soon as he had obtained the requisite permission from his imperial brother. On the arrival, however, of the vessel in the Texel, Madame Jerome, not being permitted to go on shore, landed at Dover, took up her residence during the summer at Camberwell, and in the autumn returned to America.

dispute his pleasure. They had followed the French Revolution through all its phases; and under their present constitution, a Grand Pensionary, who had the sole right of presenting new laws for adoption, and who was accountable to no one for the acts of his administration, corresponded to the First Consul of the French Consular Government. This office-bearer was now to assume the name of king, as his prototype had done that of emperor; but the king was to be chosen from the family of Buonaparte.

On the 18th March, 1806, the secretary of the Dutch Legation at Paris arrived at the Hague bearing a secret commission. The States-General were convoked—the Grand Pensionary was consulted—and, finally, a deputation was sent to Paris, requesting that the Prince Louis Buonaparte should be created hereditary King of Holland. Buonaparte's assent was graciously given, and the transaction was concluded.

It is indeed probable, that though the change was in every degree contradictory of their habits and opinions, the Dutch submitted to it as affording a prospect of a desirable relief from the disputes and factions which then divided their government. Louis Buonaparte was of a singularly amiable and gentle disposition. Besides his near relationship to Napoleon, he was married to Hortensia,[204] the daughter of Josephine, step-child of course to the Emperor, and who was supposed to share a great proportion of his favour. The conquered States of Holland, no longer the High and Mighty, as they had been accustomed to style themselves, hoped in adopting a monarch so nearly and intimately connected with Buonaparte, and received from his hand, that they might be permitted to enjoy the protection of France, and be secured against the subaltern oppression exercised over their commerce and their country. The acceptance of Louis as their King, they imagined, must establish for them a powerful protector in the councils of that Autocrat, at whose disposal they were necessarily placed. Louis

---

[204] "The marriage took place on the 4th January, 1802. Louis became a husband—never was there a more gloomy ceremony—never had husband and wife a stronger presentiment of all the horrors of a forced and ill-assorted union! From this he dates the commencement of his unhappiness. It stamped on his whole existence a profound melancholy."—Louis Buonaparte, *Documens Historiques*, tom. i., p. 126.

Buonaparte was therefore received as King of Holland.[205] How far the prince and his subjects experienced fulfilment of the hopes which both naturally entertained, belongs to another page of this history.

Germany also was doomed to find more than one appanage for the Buonaparte family. The effect of the campaign of Ulm and Austerlitz had been almost entirely destructive of the influence which the House of Austria had so long possessed in the south-west districts of Germany. Stripped of her dominions in the Vorarlberg and the Tyrol, as she had formerly been of the larger portion of the Netherlands, she was flung far back from that portion of Germany bordering on the right of the Rhine, where she had formerly exercised so much authority, and often, it must be confessed, with no gentle hand.

Defeated and humbled, the Emperor of Austria was no longer able to offer any opposition to the projects of aggrandisement which Napoleon meditated in those confines of the empire which lay adjacent to the Rhine and to France, of which that river had been declared the boundary; nor indeed to his scheme of entirely new-modelling the empire itself.

Prussia, however, remained a party interested, and too formidable, from her numerous armies and high military reputation, to be despised by Napoleon. He was indeed greatly dissatisfied with her conduct during the campaign, and by no means inclined either to forget or to forgive the menacing attitude which the Court of Berlin had assumed, although finally determined by the course of events to abstain from actual hostility. Yet notwithstanding these causes of irritation, Napoleon still esteemed it more politic to purchase Prussia's acquiescence in his projects by a large sacrifice to her selfish interests, than to add her to the number of his avowed enemies. She was therefore to be largely propitiated at the expense of some other state.

---

[205] Louis pleaded the delicacy of his constitution, and the unfavourableness of the climate. "Better to die a king than to live a prince," was Napoleon's reply; and in a day or two after Talleyrand waited on him at St. Leu, and read aloud to him and Hortensia, the treaty and constitution. This took place on the 3d of June, 1806; on the 5th Louis was proclaimed King of Holland.—De Bourrienne, tom. viii., p. 126.

We have already noticed the critical arrival of Haugwitz, the prime minister of Prussia, at Vienna, and how the declaration of war against France, with which he was charged, was exchanged for a friendly congratulation to Napoleon by the event of the battle of Austerlitz. Napoleon was no dupe to the versatility of the Prussian Cabinet; but the Archduke Ferdinand had rallied a large army in Bohemia—his brother Charles was at the head of a yet larger in Hungary—Alexander, though defeated, refused to enter into any treaty, and retained a menacing attitude, and, victor as he was, Buonaparte could not wish to see the great and highly-esteemed military force of Prussia thrown into the scale against him. He entered, therefore, into a private treaty with Haugwitz, by which Prussia was to cede to France, or rather to place at her disposal, the territories of Anspach and Bareuth, and, by way of indemnification, was to have the countenance of France in occupying Hanover, from which the French troops had been withdrawn to join the Grand Army.

The conduct of the Prussian minister—for with him, rather than with his court, the fault lay—was at once mean-spirited and unprincipled. He made his country surrender to France that very territory which the French armies had so recently violated; and he accepted as an indemnification the provinces belonging to the King of Britain, with whom Prussia was so far from having any quarrel, that she had been on the point of making common cause with her against the aggressions of France; and which provinces had been seized by France in violation of the rights of neutrality claimed by the Elector of Hanover, as a member of the Germanic Body. Such gross and complicated violations of national law and justice, have often carried with them their own punishment, nor did they fail to do so in the present instance.

MURAT

Those states, Anspach and Bareuth, were united to Bavaria; that kingdom was also aggrandized by the Tyrol, at the expense of Austria; and it ceded the Grand Duchy of Berg, which, with other lordships, Napoleon erected into a Grand Duchy, and conferred as an appanage upon Joachim Murat. Originally a soldier of fortune,[206] and an undaunted one, Murat had raised himself to eminence in the Italian campaigns. On the 18th Brumaire, he commanded the party which drove the Council of Five Hundred out of their hall. In reward for this service, he obtained the command of the Consular Guard, and the hand of Marie de l'Annonciade, afterwards called Caroline, sister of Napoleon.[207] Murat was particularly distinguished as a cavalry officer; his handsome person, accomplished horsemanship, and daring bravery at the head of his squadrons, procured him the title of *Le Beau Sabreur*. Out of the field of battle he was but a weak man, liable to be duped by his own vanity, and the flattery of those around him. He affected a theatrical foppery in dress, which rather evinced a fantastic love of finery than good taste; and hence he was sometimes called King Franconi, from the celebrated mountebank of that name.[208] His wife Caroline was an able woman, and well versed in political intrigue.[209] It will presently be found that they arose to higher fortunes than the Grand Duchy of Berg. Meantime, Murat was invested with the hereditary dignity of Grand Admiral of France; for it was the policy of Buonaparte to maintain the attachment of the new princes to the Great Nation, were it but by wearing some string or tassel of his own imperial livery.

The fair territories of Naples and Sicily were conferred upon Joseph,[210] the former in possession, the latter in prospect. He was a good man, who often strove to moderate the fits of violence to which his brother gave way. In society, he was accomplished and amiable, fond of letters, and, though not possessed of any thing approaching his brother's high qualifications, had yet good judgment as well as good inclinations. Had he continued King of Naples, it is

---

[206] Murat's father was the keeper of an humble country inn, and, having once been a steward of the Talleyrands, enjoyed the protection of that ancient and wealthy family.
[207] They were married in January, 1800, at the Palace of the Luxembourg.
[208] Las Cases, tom. iv., p. 357.
[209] M. de Talleyrand said of her, that "she had Cromwell's head on the shoulders of a pretty woman."
[210] Ferdinand having embarked for Sicily, Joseph Buonaparte, in February, 1806, made his public entry into Naples, alighting at the palace which the unfortunate monarch had just quitted. He was proclaimed King of Naples and the two Sicilies on the 30th of March. The city was illuminated on the occasion, "amidst every demonstration of joy, even more on the part of the nobles than of the lower orders."—Botta, *Storia d'Italia*, tom. iv., p. 264.

probable he might have been as fortunate as Louis, in conciliating the respect of his subjects; but his transference to Spain was fatal to his reputation. In conformity with the policy which we have noticed, the King of Naples was to continue a high feudatory of the empire, under the title of the Vice-Grand Elector.

The principality of Lucca had been already conferred on Eliza, the eldest sister of Buonaparte, and was now augmented by the districts of Massa-Carara and Garfagnana. She was a woman of a strong and masculine character, which did not, however, prevent her giving way to the feminine weakness of encouraging admirers, who, it is said, did not sigh in vain.[211]

The public opinion was still less favourable to her younger sister Pauline, who was one of the most beautiful women in France, and perhaps in Europe. Leclerc, her first husband, died in the fatal expedition to St. Domingo, and she was afterwards married to the Prince Borghese. Her encouragement of the fine arts was so little limited by the ordinary ideas of decorum, that the celebrated Canova was permitted to model from her person a naked Venus, the most beautiful, it is said, of his works.[212] Scandal went the horrible length of imputing to Pauline an intrigue with her own brother; which we willingly reject as a crime too hideous to be imputed to any one, without the most satisfactory evidence.[213] The gross and guilty enormities practised by the ancient Roman emperors, do not belong to the character of Buonaparte, though such foul aspersions have been cast upon him by those who were willing to represent him as in all respects the counterpart of Tiberius or Caligula. Pauline Borghese received the principality of Guastalla, in the distribution of honours among the family of Napoleon.

---

[211] "She was haughty, nervous, passionate, dissolute, and devoured by the two passions of love and ambition—influenced, as has been said, by the poet Fontanes, in whom she was wrapped up."—Fouché, tom. i., p. 240.

[212] It is said, that being asked by a lady how she could submit to such an exposure of her person, she conceived that the question only related to physical inconvenience, and answered it by assuring her friend that the apartment was properly aired.—S.

[213] Fouché, tom. ii., p. 33. The most ridiculous reports were also circulated, respecting an improper intercourse between Napoleon and his step-daughter Hortensia:—"Such a connexion," said he, "would have been wholly repugnant to my ideas; and those who knew any thing of the morality of the Tuileries, must be aware that I need not have been reduced to so unnatural and revolting a choice."—Las Cases, tom. iii., p. 307.

EUGENE, VICEROY OF ITALY

At this period, also, Buonaparte began first to display a desire of engrafting his own family upon the ancient dynasties of Europe, with whom he had been so long at war, and the ruin of most of whom had contributed to his elevation. The Elector of Bavaria had to repay the patronage which raised him to the rank of king, and enlarged his territories with the fine country of the Tyrol, by forming an alliance which should mix his ancient blood with that of the family connexions of the fortunate soldier. Eugene Beauharnais, Viceroy of Italy, the son of Josephine by her first husband, and now the adopted son of Napoleon, was wedded to the eldest daughter of the King of Bavaria. Eugene was deservedly favoured by his father-in-law, Napoleon. He was a man of talents, probity, and honour, and displayed great military skill, particularly during the Russian Campaign of 1812. Stephanie Beauharnais,[214] the niece of Josephine, was married about the same time to the Hereditary Prince of Baden, son to the reigning duke, the neutrality of whose territories had been violated in the seizure of the Duke d'Enghien.

These various kingdoms and principalities, erected in favour of his nearest relations, imposed on the mind a most impressive image of Buonaparte's unlimited authority, who distributed crowns among his kinsfolk as ordinary men give vails to their domestics. But the sound policy of his conduct may be greatly doubted. We have elsewhere stated the obvious objections to the transference of cities and kingdoms from hand to hand, with as little ceremony as the circulation of a commercial bill payable to the holder. Authority is a plant of a slow growth, and to obtain the full veneration which renders it most effectual, must have arisen by degrees in the place

---

[214] "Stephanie Beauharnais lost her mother in childhood. She was left in the care of an English lady, who confided her *protegée* to some old nuns in the south of France. During the consulship, I had her placed in the establishment of Madame Campan, at St. Germain; all sorts of masters were appointed to superintend her education, and on her introduction into the world, her beauty, wit, accomplishments, and virtues, rendered her an object of universal admiration. I adopted her as my daughter, and gave her in marriage to the hereditary Prince of Baden. This union was, for several years, far from being happy. In course of time, however, they became attached to each other, and from that moment they had only to regret the happiness of which they had deprived themselves during the early years of their marriage."—Napoleon, *Las Cases*, tom. iii., p. 317.

which it overshadows and protects. Suddenly transferred to new regions, it is apt to pine and to perish. The theoretical evils of a long-established government are generally mitigated by some practical remedy, or those who suffer by them have grown callous from habit. The reverse is the case with a newly-established domination, which has no claim to the veneration due to antiquity, and to which the subjects are not attached by the strong though invisible chains of long habit.

Fox, in his own nervous language, has left his protest against the principle adopted at this time in Europe, of transferring the subjects of one prince to another by way of equivalents, and under the pretext of general arrangement. "The wildest schemes," he remarked, "that were ever before broached, would not go so far to shake the foundations of all established government, as this new practice. There must be in every nation a certain attachment of the people to its form of government, without which no government could exist. The system, then, of transferring the subjects of one prince to another, strikes at the foundation of every government, and the existence of every nation."[215]

These observations apply generally to violent alterations upon the European system; but other and more special objections arise to Buonaparte's system of erecting thrones in Holland, in Naples, and all through Europe, for the members of his own family. It was particularly impolitic, as marking too strongly his determination to be satisfied with nothing less than the dominion of the world; for while he governed France in his own person, the disposing of other countries to his brothers and near relations feudatories of France, and his dependents as well by blood as by allegiance, what else could be expected than that the independence of such kingdoms must be merely nominal, and their monarchs bound to act in every respect as the agents of Buonaparte's pleasure? This, indeed, was their most sacred duty, according to his own view of the matter, and he dilated upon it to Las Cases while at St. Helena. The following passage contains an express avowal of the principles on which he desired

---

[215] Speech on the King's Message, relating to Prussia, April 23, 1806; Hansard's Parliamentary Debates, vol. vi., p. 891.

and expected his brothers to regulate the governments intrusted to them:—

"At another time the Emperor recurred to the subject of his relations, the little aid he had received from them, the embarrassment and mischief which they had caused him. He dwelt especially on that false idea upon their part, that when once placed at the head of a state, they ought to identify themselves with it to such an extent, as to prefer its interests to those of the common country. He agreed, that the source of this sentiment might be in some degree honourable, but contended that they made a false and hurtful application of it, when, in their whims of absolute independence, they considered themselves as in an isolated posture, not observing that they made only parts of a great system, the movements of which it was their business to aid, and not to thwart."[216]

SUBSIDIARY MONARCHIES

This is explaining in few words the principle on which Napoleon established these subsidiary monarchies, which was not for the benefit of the people of whom they were respectively composed, but for the service of France, or more properly of himself, the sole moving principle by which France was governed. In devolving the crown of Holland on the son of Louis, after the abdication of Louis, [in July, 1810,] he repeats the same principle as a fundamental condition of its tenure. "Never forget," he said, "that in the situation to which my political system, and the interest of my empire have called you, your *first* duty is towards ME, your *second* towards France. All your other duties, even those towards the people whom I have called you to govern, rank after these."[217]

---

[216] Las Cases, tom. vii., p. 77.
[217] On the abdication of Louis, Napoleon sent an aide-de-camp for the minor, to whom he assigned a dwelling in a pavilion in the park of St. Cloud with his brother, and a few days after made him the above speech, which he caused to be inserted in the *Moniteur*. "This," says Madame de Staël, "is no libel, it is not the opinion of a faction: it is the man himself, it is Buonaparte in person, who brings against himself a severer accusation than posterity would ever have dared to do. Louis XIV. was accused of having said in private, 'I *am the*

When Napoleon censures his delegate princes for preferring the interest of the kingdoms which he had assigned them, instead of sacrificing it to him and his government, he degrades them into mere puppets, which might indeed bear regal titles and regal attendance, but, entirely dependent on the will of another, had no choice save to second the views of an ambition, the most insatiable certainly that ever reigned in a human breast.

This secret did not remain concealed from the Dutch, from the Neapolitans, or other foreigners, subjected to these pageant monarchs; and as it naturally incensed them against Napoleon's government, so it prevented the authority which he had delegated from obtaining either affection or reverence, and disposed the nations who were subjected to it to take the first opportunity of casting the yoke aside.

The erection of these kindred monarchies was not the only mode by which Napoleon endeavoured to maintain an ascendency in the countries which he had conquered, and which he desired to retain in dependence upon France, though not nominally or directly making parts of the French empire. Buonaparte had already proposed to his council the question whether the creation of Grandees of the Empire, a species of nobility whose titles were to depend, not on their descents, but on their talents and services to the state, was to be considered as a violation of the laws of liberty and equality. He was universally answered in the negative; for, having now acquired an hereditary monarch, it seemed a natural, if not an indispensable consequence, that France should have peers of the kingdom, and great officers of the crown. Such an establishment, according to Buonaparte's view, would at once place his dignity on the same footing with those of the other courts of Europe, (an assimilation to which he attached a greater degree of consequence than was consistent with policy,) and by blending the new nobles of the empire with those of the ancient kingly

---

State; and enlightened historians have with justice grounded themselves upon this language in condemning his character. But if, when that monarch placed his grandson on the throne of Spain, he had publicly taught him the same doctrine that Buonaparte taught his nephew, perhaps even Bossuet would not have dared to prefer the interests of kings to those of nations." *Consid. sur la Rév. Franç.*, tom. ii., p. 379.

government, would tend to reconcile the modern state of things with such relics of the old court as yet existed.

From respect, perhaps, to the republican opinions which had so long predominated, the titles and appanages of these grand feudatories were not chosen within the bounds of France herself, but from provinces which had experienced the sword of the ruler. Fifteen dukedoms, grand fiefs, not of France, but of the French empire, which extended far beyond France itself, were created by the fiat of the Emperor. The income attached to each amounted to the fifteenth part of the revenue of the province, which gave title to the dignitary. The Emperor invested with these endowments those who had best served him in war and in state affairs. Princedoms also were erected, and while marshals and ministers were created dukes, the superior rank of prince was bestowed on Talleyrand, Bernadotte, and Berthier, by the titles of Beneventum, Ponte-Corvo, and Neufchatel.

The transformation of Republican generals and ancient Jacobins into the peerage of a monarchical government, gave a species of incongruity to this splendid masquerade, and more than one of the personages showed not a little awkwardness in supporting their new titles. It is true, the high degree of talent annexed to some of the individuals thus promoted, the dread inspired by others, and the fame in war which many had acquired, might bear them out against the ridicule which was unsparingly heaped upon them in the saloons frequented by the ancient noblesse; but, whatever claims these dignitaries had to the respect of the public, had been long theirs, and received no accession from their new honours and titles.

In this, and on similar occasions, Napoleon overshot his aim, and diminished to a certain extent his reputation, by seeming to set a value upon honours, titles, and ceremonies, which, if matters of importance to other courts, were certainly not such as *he* ought to have rested his dignity upon. Ceremonial is the natural element of a long-established court, and etiquette and title are the idols which are worshipped there. But Buonaparte reigned by his talents and his sword. Like Mezentius in the Æneid, he ought to have acknowledged no other source of his authority.[218] It was imprudent to appear to attach consequence to points, which even his otherwise almost boundless power could not attain, since his nobility and his court-ceremonial must still retain the rawness of novelty, and could no more possess that value, which, whether real or imaginary, has been generally attached to ancient institutions and long descent, than the Emperor could, by a decree of his complaisant Senate, have given his modern coinage the value which antiquaries attach to ancient medals. It was imprudent to descend to a strife in which he must necessarily be overcome; for where power rests in a great measure on public opinion, it is diminished in proportion to its failure in objects aimed at, whether of greater or less consequence. This half-feudal half-oriental establishment of grand feudatories, with which Buonaparte now began to decorate the structure of his power, may be compared to the heavy Gothic devices with which modern architects sometimes overlay the front of their buildings, where they always encumber what they cannot ornament, and sometimes overload what they are designed to support.[219]

NEW NOBILITY

The system of the new noblesse was settled by an Imperial edict of Napoleon himself, which was communicated to the Senate 30th March, 1806, not for the purpose of deliberation or acceptance, but merely that, like the old Parliament of Paris, they might enter it upon their register.

---

[218] Dextra mihi Deus, et telum, quod missile libro, Nunc adsint——— *Æneidos, Lib. X.*—S. "Now! now! my spear, and conquering hand, he cry'd, (Mezentius owns no deity beside!) Assist my vows."—Pitt.

[219] "I had three objects in view in establishing an hereditary national nobility: 1st, to reconcile France to the rest of Europe; 2dly, to reconcile ancient with modern France; 3dly, to banish the remains of the feudal system from Europe, by attaching the idea of nobility to services rendered to the state, and detaching it from every feudal association. The old French nobles, on recovering their country and part of their wealth, had resumed their titles, not legally, but actually; they more than ever regarded themselves as a privileged race; all blending and amalgamation with the leaders of the Revolution was difficult; the creation of new titles wholly annihilated these difficulties; there was not an ancient family that did not readily form alliances with the new dukes. It was not without design that I bestowed the first title I gave on Marshal Lefebvre, who had been a private soldier, and whom every body at Paris remembered a sergeant in the French guards."—Napoleon, *Montholon*, tom. ii., p. 239.

The court of Buonaparte now assumed a character of the strictest etiquette, in which these important trifles, called by a writer on the subject the "Superstitions of Gentlemen Ushers," were treated as matters of serious import, and sometimes occupied the thoughts of Napoleon himself, and supplied the place of meditated conquests, and the future destruction or erection of kingdoms.

The possessors of ancient titles, tempted by revival of the respect paid to birth and rank, did not fail to mingle with those whose nobility rested on the new creation. The Emperor distinguished these ancient minions of royalty with considerable favour, as half-blushing for their own apostasy in doing homage to Buonaparte in the palace of the Bourbons, half-sneering at the maladroit and awkward manners of their new associates, they mingled among the men of new descent, and paid homage to the monarch of the day, "because," as one of them expressed himself to Madame de Staël, "one must serve some one or other."[220] Buonaparte encouraged these nobles of the ancient antechambers, whose superior manners seemed to introduce among his courtiers some traits of the former court, so inimitable for grace and for address, and also because he liked to rank among his retainers, so far as he could, the inheritors of those superb names which ornamented the history of France in former ages. But then he desired to make them exclusively his own; nothing less than complete and uncompromising conversion to his government would give satisfaction. A baron of the old noblesse, who had become a counsellor of state, was in 1810 summoned to attend the Emperor at Fontainbleau.

"What would you do," said the Emperor, "should you learn that the Comte de Lille was this instant at Paris?"

"I would inform against him, and have him arrested," said the candidate for favour; "the law commands it."

"And what would you do if appointed a judge on his trial?" demanded the Emperor again.

---

[220] Considerations sur la Rév. Franç., tom. ii., p. 331.

"I would condemn him to death," said the unhesitating noble; "the law denounces him."

"With such sentiments you deserve a prefecture," said the Emperor; and the catechumen, whose respect for the law was thus absolute, was made Prefect of Paris.

Such converts were searched for, and, when found, were honoured, and rewarded, and trusted. For the power of recompensing his soldiers, statesmen, and adherents, the conquered countries were again the Emperor's resource. National domains were reserved to a large amount throughout those countries, and formed funds, out of which gratifications and annuities were, at Napoleon's sole pleasure, assigned to the generals, officers, and soldiers of the French army; who might in this way be said to have all Europe for their paymaster. Thus, every conquest increased his means of rewarding his soldiers; and that army, which was the most formidable instrument of his ambition, was encouraged and maintained at the expense of those states which had suffered most from his arms.

CONFEDERATION OF THE RHINE

We have not yet concluded the important changes introduced into Europe by the consequences of the fatal campaign of Austerlitz. The Confederation of the Rhine,[221] which withdrew from the German empire so large a portion of its princes, and, transferring them from the influence of Austria, placed them directly and avowedly under the protection of France, was an event which tended directly to the dissolution of the Germanic League, which had subsisted since the year 800, when Charlemagne received the Imperial Crown from Pope Leo the Third.

By the new Federation of the Rhine, the courts of Wirtemberg and Bavaria, of Hesse d'Armstadt, with some petty princes of the right bank of the Rhine, formed among themselves an alliance

---

[221] For the "Act of Confederation of the Rhenish League, done at Paris, July 12, 1806," see Annual Register, vol. xlviii., p. 818.

offensive and defensive, and renounced their dependence upon the Germanic Body, of which they declared they no longer recognised the constitution. The reasons assigned for this league had considerable weight. It was urged, that the countries governed by these princes were, in every case of war betwixt France and Austria, exposed to all the evils of invasion, from which the Germanic Body had no longer power to defend them. Therefore, being obliged to seek for more effectual protection from so great an evil, they placed themselves directly under the guardianship of France. Napoleon, on his part, did not hesitate to accept the title of Protector of the Confederation of the Rhine. It is true, that he had engaged to his subjects that he would not extend the limits of his empire beyond that river, which he acknowledged as the natural boundary of France; but this engagement was not held to exclude the sort of seigniorie attached to the new Protectorate, in virtue of which he plunged the German states who composed the Confederacy into every war in which France herself engaged, and at pleasure carried their armies against other German states, their brethren in language and manners, or transferred them to more distant climates, to wage wars in which they had no interest, and to which they had received no provocation. It was also a natural consequence, that a number of inferior members of the empire, who had small tenures under the old constitutions, having no means of defence excepting their ancient rights, were abolished in their capacity of imperial feudatories, and reduced from petty sovereigns to the condition of private nobles. This, though certainly unjust in the abstract principle, was not in practice an inconvenient result of the great change introduced.

The military contingents, which the Confederation placed, not perhaps in words, but certainly in fact, at the disposal of their Protector, not less than sixty thousand men, were of a character and in a state of military organisation very superior to those which they had formerly furnished to the Germanic Body. These last, much fewer in number, were seldom in a complete state of equipment, and were generally very inferior in discipline. But Napoleon not only exacted, that the contingents furnished under this new federation should be complete in numbers, and perfect in discipline and appointments, but, imparting to them, and to their officers, a spark of his own military ardour, he inspired them with a spirit of bravery and confidence which they had been far from exhibiting when in the opposite ranks. No troops in his army behaved better than those of the Confederacy of the Rhine. But the strength which the system afforded to Napoleon was only temporary, and depended on the continuance of the power by which it was cheated. It was too arbitrary, too artificial, and too much opposed both to the interests and national prejudices of the Germans, not to bear within it the seeds of dissolution. When the tide of fortune turned against Buonaparte after the battle of Leipsic, Bavaria hastened to join the allies for the purpose of completing his destruction, and the example was followed by all the other princes of the Rhine. It fared with Napoleon and the German Confederation, as with a necromancer and the demon whom for a certain term he has bound to his service, and who obeys him with fidelity during the currency of the obligation; but when that is expired, is the first to tear his employer to pieces.

Francis of Austria, seeing the empire, of which his house had been so long the head, going to pieces like a parting wreck, had no other resource than to lay aside the Imperial Crown of Germany, and to declare that league dissolved which he now saw no sufficient means of enforcing. He declared the ties dissevered which bound the various princes to him as Emperor, to each other as allies; and although he reserved the Imperial title, it was only as the Sovereign of Austria, and his other hereditary states.[222]

France became therefore in a great measure the successor to the influence and dignity of the Holy Roman Empire, as that of Germany had been proudly styled for a thousand years; and the Empire of Napoleon gained a still nearer resemblance to that of Charlemagne. At least France succeeded to the Imperial influence exercised by Austria and her empire over all the south-western provinces of that powerful district of Europe. In the eastern districts, Austria, stunned by her misfortunes and her defeats, was passive and unresisting. Prussia, in the north of Germany, was halting between two very opposite set of counsellors; one of which,

---

[222] See the "Act of Resignation of the Office of Emperor of Germany, by Francis, Emperor of Austria, August 6, 1806," Annual Register, vol. xlviii., p. 824.

with too much confidence in the military resources of the country, advised war with France, for which the favourable opportunity had been permitted to escape; while the other recommended that, like the jackal in the train of the lion, Prussia should continue to avail herself of the spoils which Napoleon might permit her to seize upon, without presuming to place herself in opposition to his will. In either case, the course recommended was sufficiently perilous; but to vacillate, as the Cabinet of Berlin did, betwixt the one and the other, inferred almost certain ruin.

While Napoleon thus revelled in augmented strength, and increased honours, Providence put it once more, and for the last time, in his power to consolidate his immense empire by a general peace, maritime as well as upon the continent.

CHAPTER XXXIV

Death of Pitt—He is succeeded by Fox as Prime Minister—Negotiation with France—The Earl of Lauderdale sent to Paris as the British Negotiator—Negotiation broken off, in consequence of the refusal of England to cede Sicily to France—Temporizing Policy of Prussia—An attempt made by her to form a Confederacy in opposition to that of the Rhine, defeated by Napoleon—General Disposition of the Prussians to War—Legal Murder of Palm, a bookseller—The Emperor Alexander again visits Berlin—Prussia begins to arm in August 1806, and, after some Negotiation, takes the field in October, under the Duke of Brunswick—Impolicy of the Plans of the Campaign—Details—Action at Saalfeld—Battle of Auerstadt, or Jena, on 14th October—Duke of Brunswick mortally wounded—Consequences of this total Defeat—Buonaparte takes possession of Berlin on the 25th—Situations of Austria and Prussia, after their several Defeats—Reflections on the fall of Prussia.

DEATH OF PITT

The death of William Pitt [23d Jan.] was accelerated by the campaign of Ulm and Austerlitz, as his health had been previously injured by the defeat of Marengo. Great as he was as a statesman, ardent in patriotism, and comprehensive in his political views, it had been too much the habit of that great minister, to trust, for some re-establishment of the balance of power on the continent, to the exertions of the ancient European governments, whose efforts had gradually become fainter and fainter, and their spirits more and more depressed, when opposed to the power of Buonaparte, whose blows, like the thunderbolt, seemed to inflict inevitable ruin wherever they burst. But, while resting too much hope on coalitions, placing too much confidence in foreign armies, and too little considering, perhaps, what might have been achieved by our own, had sufficient numbers been employed on adequate objects, Pitt maintained with unabated zeal the great principle of resistance to France, unless France should be disposed to show, that, satisfied with the immense power which she possessed, her Emperor was willing to leave to the rest of Europe such precarious independence as his victorious arms had not yet bereft them of.

The British prime minister was succeeded, upon his death, by the statesman to whom, in life, he had waged the most uniform opposition. Charles Fox, now at the head of the British Government, had uniformly professed to believe it possible to effect a solid and lasting peace with France, and, in the ardour of debate, had repeatedly thrown on his great adversary the blame that such had not been accomplished. When he himself became possessed of the supreme power of administration, he was naturally disposed to realize his predictions, if Napoleon should be found disposed to admit a treaty upon any thing like equal terms. In a visit to Paris during the peace of Amiens, Mr. Fox had been received with great distinction by Napoleon. The private relations betwixt them were, therefore, of an amicable nature, and gave an opening for friendly intercourse.

The time, too, appeared favourable for negotiation; for whatever advantages had been derived by France from her late triumphant campaign on the continent, were, so far as Britain was concerned, neutralized and outbalanced by the destruction of the combined fleets. All possibility of invasion—which appears before this event to have warmly engrossed the imagination of Napoleon—seemed at an end and for ever. The delusion which represented a united navy of fifty sail of the line triumphantly occupying the British Channel, and escorting an overpowering force to the shores of England, was dispelled by the cannon of 21st October. The gay dreams, which painted a victorious army marching to London, reforming the state of England by the destruction of her aristocracy, and reducing her to her natural condition, as Napoleon termed it, of such a dependency on France as the island of Oleron or of Corsica, were gone. After the battle of Trafalgar, all hopes were extinguished, that the fair provinces of England could, in any possible event, have been cut up into new fiefs of the French empire. It was no longer to be dreamed, that *Dotations*, as they were termed, might be formed upon the Royal Exchange for the payment of annuities by hundreds of thousands, and by millions, for rewarding the soldiers of the Great Nation. To work purses for the French officers, that they might be filled with British gold, had of late been a favourite amusement among the fair ladies of France; but it was now evident that they had laboured in vain. All these hopes and projects were swallowed up in the billows which entombed the wrecks of Trafalgar.

In a word, if Austria had fallen in the contest of 1805, Britain stood more pre-eminent than ever; and it might have been rationally expected, that the desire of war, on the part of Napoleon, should have ended, when every prospect of bringing that war to the conclusive and triumphant termination which he meditated, had totally disappeared. The views of the British Cabinet, also, we have said, were now amicable, and an incident occurred for opening a negotiation, under circumstances which seemed to warrant the good faith of the English ministers.

NEGOTIATION WITH ENGLAND

A person pretending to be an adherent of the Bourbons, but afterwards pretty well understood to be an agent of the French Government, acting upon the paltry system of espionage which had infected both their internal and exterior relations, obtained an audience of Mr. Fox, for the purpose, as he pretended, of communicating to the British minister a proposal for the assassination of Buonaparte. It had happened, that Mr. Fox, in conversation with Napoleon, while at Paris, had indignantly repelled a charge of this kind, which the latter brought against some of the English Ministry. "Clear your head of that nonsense," was said to be his answer, with more of English bluntness than of French politeness. Perhaps Buonaparte was desirous of knowing whether his practice would keep pace with his principles, and on this principle had encouraged the spy. Fox, as was to be expected, not only repelled with abhorrence the idea suggested by this French agent, but caused it to be communicated to the French Emperor;[223] and this gave rise to some friendly communication, and finally to a negotiation for peace. Lord Yarmouth, and afterwards Lord Lauderdale, acted for the British Government; Champagny and General Clarke for the Emperor of France. Napoleon, who, like most foreigners, had but an inaccurate idea of the internal structure of the British constitution, had expected to find a French party in the bosom of England, and was surprised to find that a few miscreants of the lowest rank, whom he had been able to bribe, were the only English who were accessible to foreign influence; and that the party which had opposed the war with France in all its stages, were nevertheless incapable of desiring to see it cease on such terms as were dishonourable to the country.

The French commissioners made several concessions, and even intimated, in verbal conference with Lord Yarmouth, that they would be content to treat upon the principle of *uti possidetis*; that is, of allowing each party to retain such advantages as she had been able to gain by her arms during the war. But when the treaty was farther advanced, the French negotiators resisted this rule, and showed themselves disposed to deny that they had ever assented to it.

They were, indeed, willing to resign a long contested point, and consented that the island of Malta, with the Cape of Good Hope, and other possessions in the East and West Indies, should remain under the dominion of Great Britain. But then they exacted the surrender of Sicily and Naples, proposing that Frederick IV. should be indemnified at the expense of Spain by the cession of the Balearic isles. Britain could not implicitly consent to this last proposition, either in policy, or in justice to her unfortunate ally. Naples was indeed occupied by the French, and had received Joseph Buonaparte as her King; but the insular situation of Sicily rendered it

---

[223] See Mr. Fox's letter to M. Talleyrand, February 20, 1806; Hansard's Parliamentary Debates, vol. viii., p. 92; Annual Register, vol. xlviii., p. 708. After reading it, Napoleon's first words were, "I recognise here the principles of honour and of virtue, by which Mr. Fox has ever been actuated. Thank him on my part."

easy for Britain to protect that rich island, which was still in the possession of its legitimate monarch. The principle of *uti possidetis* was, therefore, in favour of the English, so far as Sicily was concerned, as it was in that of the French in the case of Naples. The English envoy, for this reason, refused an ultimatum, in which the cession of Sicily was made an indispensable article. Lord Lauderdale, at the same time, demanded his passports, which, however, he did not receive for several days, as if there had been some hopes of renewing the treaty.[224]

Buonaparte was put to considerable inconvenience by the shrewdness and tenacity of the noble negotiator, and had not forgotten them when, in 1815, he found himself on board the Bellerophon, commanded by a relation of the noble earl.[225] It is indeed probable, that, had Mr. Fox lived, the negotiation might have been renewed. That eminent statesman, then in his last illness, was desirous to accomplish two great objects—peace with France, and the abolition of the slave trade. But although Buonaparte's deference for Fox might have induced him to concede some of the points in dispute, and although the British statesman's desire of peace might have made him relinquish others on the part of England, still, while the two nations retained their relative power and positions, the deep jealousy and mutual animosity which subsisted between them would probably have rendered any peace which could have been made a mere suspension of arms—a hollow and insincere truce, which was almost certain to give way on the slightest occasion. Britain could never have seen with indifference Buonaparte making one stride after another towards universal dominion; and Buonaparte could not long have borne with patience the neighbourhood of our free institutions and our free press; the former of which must have perpetually reminded the French of the liberty they had lost, while the latter was sure to make the Emperor, his government, and his policy, the daily subject of the most severe and unsparing criticism. Even the war with Prussia and Russia, in which Napoleon was soon afterwards engaged, would, in all probability, have renewed the hostilities between France and

---

[224] For copies of the "Papers relative to the Negotiation with France," see Parliamentary Debates, vol. viii., p. 92; Annual Register, vol. xlviii., p. 708.
[225] Captain Maitland.

England, supposing them to have been terminated for a season by a temporary peace. Yet Napoleon always spoke of the death of Fox as one of the fatalities on which his great designs were shipwrecked;[226] which makes it the more surprising that he did not resume intercourse with the administration formed under his auspices, and who might have been supposed to be animated by his principles even after his decease. That he did not do so may be fairly received in evidence to show, that peace, unless on terms which he could dictate, was not desired by him.

PRUSSIA

As the conduct of Prussia had been fickle and versatile during the campaign of Austerlitz, the displeasure of Napoleon was excited in proportion against her. She had, it is true, wrenched from him an unwilling acquiescence in her views upon Hanover. By the treaty which Haugwitz had signed at Vienna, after the battle of Austerlitz, it was agreed that Prussia should receive the electoral dominions of the King of England, his ally, instead of Anspach, Bareuth, and Neufchatel, which she was to cede to France. The far superior value of Hanover was to be considered as a boon to Prussia, in guerdon of her neutrality. But Napoleon did not forgive the hostile disposition which Prussia had manifested, and it is probable he waited with anxiety for the opportunity of inflicting upon her condign chastisement. He continued to maintain a large army in Swabia and Franconia, and, by introducing troops into Westphalia, intimated, not obscurely, an approaching rupture with his ally. Meantime, under the influence of conflicting councils, Prussia proceeded in a course of politics which rendered her odious for her rapacity, and contemptible for the shortsighted views under which she indulged it.

It was no matter of difficulty for the Prussian forces to take possession of Hanover, which, when evacuated by Bernadotte and

---

[226] "Certainly the death of Fox was one of the fatalities of my career. Had his life been prolonged, affairs would have taken a totally different turn; the cause of the people would have triumphed, and we should have established a new order of things in Europe."—Napoleon, *Las Cases*, tom. vii., p. 97.

his army, lay a prey to the first invader, with the exception of the fortress of Hamelen, still occupied by a French garrison. The electorate, the hereditary dominions of the King of Great Britain, with whom Prussia was at profound peace, was accordingly seized upon, and her Cabinet pretended to justify that usurpation by alleging, that Hanover, having been transferred to France by the rights of war, had been ceded to the Prussian Government in exchange for other districts. At the same time, an order of the Prussian monarch shut his ports in the Baltic against the admission of British vessels. These measures, taken together, were looked upon by England as intimating determined and avowed hostility; and Fox described, in the House of Commons, the conduct of Prussia, as a compound of the most hateful rapacity with the most contemptible servility.[227] War was accordingly declared against her by Great Britain; and her flag being banished from the ocean by the English cruizers, the mouth of the Elbe and the Prussian seaports were declared in a state of blockade, and her trade was subjected to a corresponding degree of distress.

Meantime, it was the fate of Prussia to find, that she held by a very insecure tenure that very electorate, the price of her neutrality at Austerlitz, and which was farther purchased at the expense of war with England. Her ministers, while pressing France to confirm the cession of Hanover, had the mortification to discover that Napoleon, far from regarding the Prussian right in it as indefeasible, was in fact negotiating for a general peace upon the condition, amongst others, that the electorate should be restored to the King of England, its hereditary sovereign. While the disclosure of this double game showed Frederick William upon what insecure footing he held the premium assigned to Prussia by the treaty of Vienna, farther discovery of the projects of France seemed to impel him to change the pacific line of his policy.

Hitherto the victories of Napoleon had had for their chief consequences the depression of Austria, and the diminution of that power which was the natural and ancient rival of the House of Brandenburg. But now, when Austria was thrust back to the eastward, and deprived of her influence in the south-west of

---

[227] Parliamentary Debates, vol. vi., p. 887.

Germany, Prussia saw with just alarm that France was assuming that influence herself, and that, unless opposed, she was likely to become as powerful in the north of Germany, as she had rendered herself in the south-western circles. Above all, Prussia was alarmed at the Confederacy of the Rhine, an association which placed under the direct influence of France, so large a proportion of what had been lately component parts of the Germanic empire. The dissolution of the Germanic empire itself was an event no less surprising and embarrassing; for, besides all the other important points, in which the position of Prussia was altered by the annihilation of that ancient confederacy, she lost thereby the prospect of her own monarch being, upon the decline of Austria, chosen to wear the imperial crown, as the most powerful member of the federation.

One way remained, to balance the new species of power which France had acquired by these innovations on the state of Europe. It was possible, by forming the northern princes of the German empire into a league of the same character with the Confederacy of the Rhine, having Prussia instead of France for its protector, to create such an equilibrium as might render it difficult or dangerous for Buonaparte to use his means, however greatly enlarged, to disturb the peace of the north of Europe. It was, therefore, determined in the Prussian Cabinet to form a league on this principle.

This proposed Northern Confederacy, however, could not well be established without communication with France; and Buonaparte, though offering no direct opposition to the formation of a league, sanctioned by the example of that of the Rhine, started such obstacles to the project in detail, as were likely to render its establishment on an effectual footing impossible. It was said by his ministers, that Napoleon was to take the Hanseatic towns under his own immediate protection; that the wise prince who governed Saxony showed no desire to become a member of the proposed Confederacy; and that France would permit no power to be forced into such a measure. Finally, the Landgrave of Hesse Cassel, who was naturally reckoned upon as an important member of the proposed Northern League, was tampered with to prevail upon him to join the Confederacy of the Rhine, instead of that which was proposed to be formed under the protectorate of Prussia. This prince, afraid to decide which of these powerful nations he should adhere to, remained in a state of neutrality, notwithstanding the offers of France; and, by doing so, incurred the displeasure of Napoleon, from which in the sequel he suffered severely.

By this partial interruption and opposition, Napoleon rendered it impossible for Prussia to make any effectual efforts for combining together those remaining fragments of the German empire, over which her military power and geographical position gave her natural influence. This disappointment, with the sense of having been outwitted by the French Government, excited feelings of chagrin and resentment in the Prussian Cabinet, which corresponded with the sentiments expressed by the nation at large. In the former, the predominant feeling was, despite for disappointed hopes, and a desire of revenge on the sovereign and state by whom they had been over-reached; in the latter, there prevailed a keen and honourable sense that Prussia had lost her character through the truckling policy of her Administration.

Whatever reluctance the Cabinet of Berlin had shown to enter into hostilities with France, the court and country never appear to have shared that sensation. The former was under the influence of the young, beautiful, and high-spirited Queen, and of Louis of Prussia, a prince who felt with impatience the decaying importance of that kingdom, which the victories of the Great Frederick had raised to such a pitch of glory. These were surrounded by a numerous band of noble youths, impatient for war, as the means of emulating the fame of their fathers; but ignorant how little likely were even the powerful and well-disciplined forces of Frederick, unless directed by his genius, to succeed in opposition to troops not inferior to themselves, and conducted by a leader who had long appeared to chain victory to his chariot wheels. The sentiments of the young Prussian noblesse were sufficiently indicated, by their going to sharpen their sabres on the threshold of La Foret, the ambassador of Napoleon, and the wilder frolic of breaking the windows of the ministers supposed to be in the French interest. The Queen appeared frequently in the uniform of the regiment which bore her name, and sometimes rode at their head, to give enthusiasm to the soldiery. This was soon excited to the highest pitch; and had the military talents of the Prussian generals borne any correspondence to the gallantry of the officers and soldiers, an issue to the campaign might have been expected far different from that which took place. The manner in which the characters of the Queen, the King, and Prince Louis, were treated in the *Moniteur*, tended still more to exasperate the quarrel; for Napoleon's studious and cautious exclusion from the government paper of such political articles as had not his own previous approbation, rendered him in reason accountable for all which appeared there.

The people of Prussia at large were clamorous for war. They, too, were sensible that the late versatile conduct of their Cabinet had exposed them to the censure, and even the scorn of Europe; and that Buonaparte, seeing the crisis ended in which the firmness of Prussia might have preserved the balance of Europe, retained no longer any respect for those whom he had made his dupes, but treated with total disregard the remonstrances, which, before the advantages obtained at Ulm and Austerlitz, he must have listened to with respect and deference.

Another circumstance of a very exasperating character took place at this time. One Palm, a bookseller at Nuremberg, had exposed to sale a pamphlet,[228] containing remarks on the conduct of Napoleon, in which the Emperor and his policy were treated with considerable severity. The bookseller was seized upon for this offence by the French gendarmes, and transferred to Braunau, where he was brought before a military commission, tried for a libel on the Emperor of France, found guilty, and shot to death [Aug. 26] in terms of his sentence. The murder of this poor man, for such it literally was, whether immediately flowing from Buonaparte's mandate,[229] or the effects of the furious zeal of some of his officers, excited deep and general indignation.[230]

---

[228] The pamphlet was intitled, "L'Allemagne dans son profond Abaissement," and was attributed to the pen of M. Gentz. Palm was offered his pardon, upon condition that he gave up the author of the work; which he refused to do.
[229] "All that I recollect about Palm is, that he was arrested by order of Davoust, I believe, tried, condemned, and shot, for having, while the country was in possession of the French, and under military occupation, not only excited rebellion amongst the inhabitants, and

The constitution of many of the states in Germany is despotic; but, nevertheless, the number of independent principalities, and the privileges of the free towns, have always ensured to the nation at large the blessings of a free press, which, much addicted as they are to literature, the Germans value as it deserves. The cruel effort now made to fetter this unshackled expression of opinion, was, of course, most unfavourable to his authority by whom it had been commanded. The thousand presses of Germany continued on every possible opportunity to dwell on the fate of Palm; and, at the distance of six or seven years from his death, it might be reckoned among the leading causes which ultimately determined the popular opinion against Napoleon. It had not less effect at the time when the crime was committed; and the eyes of all Germany were turned upon Prussia, as the only member of the late Holy Roman League, by whom the progress of the public enemy of the liberties of Europe could be arrested in its course.

Amidst the general ferment of the public mind, Alexander once more appeared in person at the court of Berlin, and, more successful than on the former occasion, prevailed on the King of Prussia at length to unsheath the sword. The support of the powerful hosts of Russia was promised; and, defeated on the fatal field of Austerlitz in his attempt to preserve the south-east of Germany from French influence, Alexander now stood forth to assist Prussia as the Champion of the North. An attempt had indeed been made through means of D'Oubril, a Russian envoy at Paris, to obtain a general peace for Europe, in concurrence with that which Lord Lauderdale was endeavouring to negotiate on the part of Britain; but the treaty entirely miscarried.

While Prussia thus declared herself the enemy of France, it seemed to follow, as a matter of course, that she should become once more the friend of Britain; and, indeed, that power lost no time in manifesting an amicable disposition on her part, by recalling the order which blockaded the Prussian ports, and annihilated her

---

urged them to rise and massacre the soldiers, but also attempted to instigate the soldiers themselves to refuse obedience to their orders, and to mutiny against their generals. I believe that he met with a fair trial."—Napoleon, *Voice*, &c., vol. i., p. 432.

[230] A subscription was set on foot in Germany, and also in England, for his widow and three children.

commerce. But the Cabinet of Berlin evinced, in the moment when about to commence hostilities, the same selfish insincerity which had dictated all their previous conduct. While sufficiently desirous of obtaining British money to maintain the approaching war, they showed great reluctance to part with Hanover, an acquisition made in a manner so unworthy; and the Prussian minister, Lucchesini, did not hesitate to tell the British ambassador, Lord Morpeth, that the fate of the electorate would depend upon the event of arms.

Little good could be augured from the interposition of a power, who, pretending to arm in behalf of the rights of nations, refused to part with an acquisition which she herself had made, contrary to all the rules of justice and good faith. Still less was a favourable event to be hoped for, when the management of the war was intrusted to the same incapable or faithless ministers, who had allowed every opportunity to escape of asserting the rights of Prussia, when, perhaps, her assuming a firm attitude might have prevented the necessity of war altogether. But the resolution which had been delayed, when so many favourable occasions were suffered to escape unemployed, was at length adopted with an imprudent precipitation, which left Prussia neither time to adopt the wisest warlike measures, nor to look out for those statesmen and generals by whom such measures could have been most effectually executed.

PRUSSIA ARMS AGAINST FRANCE

About the middle of August, Prussia began to arm. Perhaps there are few examples of a war declared with the almost unanimous consent of a great and warlike people, which was brought to an earlier and more unhappy termination. On the 1st of October, Knobelsdorff, the Prussian envoy, was called upon by Talleyrand to explain the cause of the martial attitude assumed by his state. In reply, a paper was delivered, containing three propositions, or rather demands. First, That the French troops which had entered the German territory, should instantly recross the Rhine. Secondly, That France should desist from presenting obstacles to the formation of a league in the northern part of Germany, to comprehend all the states, without exception, which had not been included in the

Confederation of the Rhine. Thirdly, That negotiations should be immediately commenced, for the purpose of detaching the fortress of Wesel from the French empire, and for the restitution of three abbeys,[231] which Murat had chosen to seize upon as a part of his Duchy of Berg. With this manifesto[232] was delivered a long explanatory letter, containing severe remarks on the system of encroachment which France had acted upon. Such a text and commentary, considering their peremptory tone, and the pride and power of him to whom they were addressed in such unqualified terms, must have been understood to amount to a declaration of war. And yet, although Prussia, in common with all Europe, had just reason to complain of the encroachments of France, and her rapid strides to universal empire, it would appear that the two first articles in the King's declaration, were subjects rather of negotiation than grounds of an absolute declaration of war; and that the fortress of Wesel, and the three abbeys, were scarce of importance enough to plunge the whole empire into blood for the sake of them.

Prussia, indeed, was less actually aggrieved than she was mortified and offended. She saw she had been outwitted by Buonaparte in the negotiation of Vienna; that he was juggling with her in the matter of Hanover; that she was in danger of beholding Saxony and Hesse withdrawn from her protection, to be placed under that of France; and under a general sense of these injuries, though rather apprehended than really sustained, she hurried to the field. If negotiations could have been protracted till the advance of the Russian armies, it might have given a different face to the war; but in the warlike ardour which possessed the Prussians, they were desirous to secure the advantages which, in military affairs, belong to the assailants, without weighing the circumstances which, in their situation, rendered such precipitation fatal.

Besides, such advantages were not easily to be obtained over Buonaparte, who was not a man to be amused by words when the moment of action arrived. Four days before the delivery of the Prussian note to his minister, Buonaparte had left Paris, and was personally in the field collecting his own immense forces, and urging

---

[231] Essen, Werden, and Elten.
[232] See Annual Register, vol. xlviii., p. 800.

the contribution of those contingents which the Confederate Princes of the Rhine were bound to supply. His answer to the hostile note of the King of Prussia was addressed, not to that monarch, but to his own soldiers. "They have dared to demand," he said, "that we should retreat at the first sight of their army. Fools! could they not reflect how impossible they found it to destroy Paris, a task incomparably more easy than to tarnish the honour of the Great Nation! Let the Prussian army expect the same fate which they encountered fourteen years ago, since experience has not taught them, that while it is easy to acquire additional dominions and increase of power, by the friendship of France, her enmity, on the contrary, which will only be provoked by those who are totally destitute of sense and reason, is more terrible than the tempests of the ocean."

The King of Prussia had again placed at the head of his armies the Duke of Brunswick. In his youth, this general had gained renown under his uncle Prince Ferdinand. But it had been lost in the retreat from Champagne in 1792, where he had suffered himself to be out-manœuvred by Dumouriez and his army of conscripts. He was seventy-two years old, and is said to have added the obstinacy of age to others of the infirmities which naturally attend it. He was not communicative, nor accessible to any of the other generals, excepting Mollendorf; and this generated a disunion of councils in the Prussian camp, and the personal dislike of the army to him by whom it was commanded.

PLANS OF THE CAMPAIGN

The plan of the campaign, formed by this ill-fated prince, seems to have been singularly injudicious, and the more so, as it is censurable on exactly the same grounds as that of Austria in the late war. Prussia could not expect to have the advantage of numbers in the contest. It was, therefore, her obvious policy to procrastinate and lengthen out negotiation, until she could have the advantage of the Russian forces. Instead of this, it was determined to rush forward towards Franconia, and oppose the Prussian army alone to the whole force of France, commanded by their renowned Emperor.

The motive, too, was similar to that which had determined Austria to advance as far as the banks of the Iller. Saxony was in the present campaign, as Bavaria in the former, desirous of remaining neuter; and the hasty advance of the Prussian armies was designed to compel the Elector Augustus to embrace their cause. It succeeded accordingly; and the sovereign of Saxony united his forces, though reluctantly, with the left wing of the Prussians, under Prince Hohenloe. The conduct of the Prussians towards the Saxons bore the same ominous resemblance to that of the Austrians to the Bavarians. Their troops behaved in the country of Saxony more as if they were in the land of a tributary than an ally, and while the assistance of the good and peaceable prince was sternly exacted, no efforts were made to conciliate his good-will, or soothe the pride of his subjects. In their behaviour to the Saxons in general, the Prussians showed too much of the haughty spirit that goes before a fall.

The united force of the Prussian army, with its auxiliaries, amounted to one hundred and fifty thousand men,[233] confident in their own courage, in the rigid discipline which continued to distinguish their service, and in the animating recollections of the victorious career of the Great Frederick. There were many generals and soldiers in their ranks who had served under him; but, amongst that troop of veterans, Blucher alone was destined to do distinguished honour to the school.

Notwithstanding these practical errors, the address of the Prussian King to his army was in better taste than the vaunting proclamation of Buonaparte, and concluded with a passage, which, though its accomplishment was long delayed, nevertheless proved at last prophetic:—"We go," said Frederick William, "to encounter an enemy, who has vanquished numerous armies, humiliated monarchs, destroyed constitutions, and deprived more than one state of its independence, and even of its very name. He has threatened a similar fate to Prussia, and proposes to reduce us to the

---

[233] Jomini, tom. ii., p. 276.

dominion of a strange people, who would suppress the very name of Germans. The fate of armies, and of nations, is in the hands of the Almighty; but constant victory, and durable prosperity, are never granted, save to the cause of justice."

While Buonaparte assembled in Franconia an army considerably superior in number to that of the Prussians, the latter occupied the country in the vicinity of the river Saale, and seemed, in doing so, to renounce all the advantage of making the attack on the enemy ere he had collected his forces. Yet, to make such an attack was, and must have been, the principal motive of their hasty and precipitate advance; especially after they had secured its primary object, the accession of Saxony to the campaign. The position which the Duke of Brunswick occupied was indeed very strong as a defensive one, but the means of supporting so large an army were not easily to be obtained in such a barren country as that about Weimar; and their magazines and depôts of provisions were injudiciously placed, not close in the rear of the army, but at Naumburg, and other places, upon their extreme left, and where they were exposed to the risk of being separated from them. It might be partly owing to the difficulty of obtaining forage and subsistence, that the Prussian army was extended upon a line by far too much prolonged to admit of mutual support. Indeed, they may be considered rather as disposed in cantonments than as occupying a military position; and as they remained strictly on the defensive, an opportunity was gratuitously afforded to Buonaparte to attack their divisions in detail, of which he did not fail to avail himself with his usual talent. The headquarters of the Prussians, where were the King and Duke of Brunswick, were at Weimar; their left, under Prince Hohenloe, were at Schleitz; and their right extended as far as Muhlhausen, leaving thus a space of ninety miles betwixt the extreme flanks of their line.

Buonaparte, in the meantime, commenced the campaign, according to his custom, by a series of partial actions fought on different points, in which his usual combinations obtained his usual success; the whole tending to straiten the Prussians in their position, to interrupt their communications, separate them from their supplies, and compel them to fight a decisive battle from necessity, not choice, in which dispirited troops, under baffled and outwitted generals, were to encounter with soldiers who had already obtained a foretaste of victory, and who fought under the most renowned commanders, the combined efforts of the whole being directed by the master spirit of the age.

Upon the 8th October, Buonaparte gave vent to his resentment in a bulletin, in which he complained of having received a letter of twenty pages, signed by the King of Prussia, being, as he alleged, a sort of wretched pamphlet, such as England engaged hireling authors to compose at the rate of five hundred pounds sterling a-year. "I am sorry," he said, "for my brother, who does not understand the French language, and has certainly never read that rhapsody." The same publication contained much in ridicule of the Queen and Prince Louis.[234] It bears evident marks of Napoleon's own composition, which was as singular, though not so felicitous, as his mode of fighting; but it was of little use to censure either the style or the reasoning of the lord of so many legions. His arms soon made the impression which he desired upon the position of the enemy.

The French advanced, in three divisions, upon the dislocated and extended disposition of the large but ill-arranged Prussian army. It was a primary and irretrievable fault of the Duke of Brunswick, that his magazines, and reserves of artillery and ammunition were placed at Naumburg, instead of being close in the rear of his army, and under the protection of his main body. This ill-timed separation rendered it easy for the French to interpose betwixt the Prussians and their supplies, providing they were able to clear the course of the Saale.

---

[234] "'Marshal,' said the Emperor, on the 7th, to Berthier, 'they give us a rendezvous of honour for the 8th. They say a handsome queen is there, who desires to see battles; let us be polite, and march without delay for Saxony!' The Emperor was correctly informed; for the Queen of Prussia is with the army, equipped like an Amazon, wearing the uniform of her regiment of dragoons, and writing twenty letters a-day to all parts of the kingdom, to excite the inhabitants against the French. It appears like the conduct of the frenzied Armida, setting fire to her own palace. Next to her Majesty, Prince Louis of Prussia, a brave young man, incited by the war faction, vainly hopes to gain honours and renown in the vicissitudes of war."—*First Bulletin of the Grand Army.*

ACTION AT SAALFIELD

With this view the French right wing, commanded by Soult and Ney, marched upon Hof. The centre was under Bernadotte and Davoust, with the guard commanded by Murat. They moved on Saalburg and Schleitz. The left wing was led by Augereau against Coburg and Saalfield. It was the object of this grand combined movement to overwhelm the Prussian right wing, which was extended farther than prudence permitted; and, having beaten this part of the army, to turn their whole position, and possess themselves of their magazines. After some previous skirmishes, a serious action took place at Saalfield, where Prince Louis of Prussia commanded the advanced guard of the Prussian left wing.

In the ardour and inexperience of youth, the brave prince, instead of being contented with defending the bridge on the Saale, quitted that advantageous position, to advance with unequal forces against Lannes, who was marching upon him from Graffenthal. If bravery could have atoned for imprudence, the battle of Saalfield would not have been lost. Prince Louis showed the utmost gallantry in leading his men when they advanced, and in rallying them when they fled. He was killed fighting hand to hand with a French subaltern, who required him to surrender, and, receiving a sabre-wound for reply, plunged his sword into the prince's body. Several of his staff fell around him.[235]

The victory of Saalfield opened the course of the Saale to the French, who instantly advanced on Naumburg. Buonaparte was at Gera, within half a day's journey from the latter city, whence he sent a letter to the King of Prussia, couched in the language of a victor, (for victorious he already felt himself by his numbers and position,) and seasoned with the irony of a successful foe. He regretted his

---

[235] "Prince Louis urged and hastened hostilities, and feared to let the opportunity escape. He was, besides, a man of great courage and talent; all accounts agreed on that point. Napoleon, who did not dislike such petulant eagerness, was conversing with us one evening respecting the generals of the enemy's army; some one present happened to mention Prince Louis; 'As for him,' said he, 'I foretell that he will be killed this campaign.' Who could have thought that the prediction would so soon have been fulfilled."—*Mémoires de Rapp*, p. 66.

good brother had been made to sign the wretched pamphlet which had borne his name, but which he protested he did not impute to him as his composition. Had Prussia asked any practicable favour of him, he said he would have granted it; but she had asked his dishonour, and ought to have known there could be but one answer. In consideration of their former friendship, Napoleon stated himself to be ready to restore peace to Prussia and her monarch; and, advising his good brother to dismiss such counsellors as recommended the present war and that of 1792, he bade him heartily farewell.[236]

Buonaparte neither expected nor received any answer to this missive, which was written under the exulting sensations experienced by the angler, when he feels the fish is hooked, and about to become his secure prey. Naumburg and its magazines were consigned to the flames, which first announced to the Prussians that the French army had gotten completely into their rear, had destroyed their magazines, and, being now interposed betwixt them and Saxony, left them no alternative save that of battle, which was to be waged at the greatest disadvantage with an alert enemy, to whom their supineness had already given the choice of time and place for it. There was also this ominous consideration, that, in case of disaster, the Prussians had neither principle, nor order, nor line of retreat. The enemy were betwixt them and Magdeburg, which ought to have been their rallying point; and the army of the Great Frederick was, it must be owned, brought to combat with as little reflection or military science, as a herd of school-boys might have displayed in a mutiny.

AUERSTADT

Too late determined to make some exertion to clear their communications to the rear, the Duke of Brunswick, with the King of Prussia in person, marched with great part of their army to the recovery of Naumburg. Here Davoust, who had taken the place, remained at the head of a division of six-and-thirty thousand men, with whom he was to oppose nearly double the number. The march

---

[236] See Fifteenth Bulletin of the Grand Army.

of the Duke of Brunswick was so slow, as to lose the advantage of this superiority. He paused on the evening of the thirteenth on the heights of Auerstadt, and gave Davoust time to reinforce the troops with which he occupied the strong defile of Koesen. The next morning, Davoust, with strong reinforcements, but still unequal in numbers to the Prussians, marched towards the enemy, whose columns were already in motion. The vanguard of both armies met, without previously knowing that they were so closely approaching each other, so thick lay the mist upon the ground.

The village of Hassen-Hausen, near which the opposite armies were first made aware of each other's proximity, became instantly the scene of a severe conflict, and was taken and retaken repeatedly. The Prussian cavalry, being superior in numbers to that of the French, and long famous for its appointments and discipline, attacked repeatedly, and was as often resisted by the French squares of infantry, whom they found it impossible to throw into disorder, or break upon any point. The French, having thus repelled the Prussian horse, carried, at the point of the bayonet, some woods and the village of Spilberg, and remained in undisturbed possession of that of Hassen-Hausen. The Prussians had by this time maintained the battle from eight in the morning till eleven, and being now engaged on all points, with the exception of two divisions of the reserve, had suffered great loss. The Generalissimo, Duke of Brunswick, wounded in the face by a grape-shot, was carried off; so was General Schmettau, and other officers of distinction. The want of an experienced chief began to be felt; when, to increase the difficulties of their situation, the King of Prussia received intelligence, that General Mollendorf, who commanded his right wing, stationed near Jena, was in the act of being defeated by Buonaparte in person. The King took the generous but perhaps desperate resolution, of trying, whether in one general charge he could not redeem the fortune of the day, by defeating that part of the French with which he was personally engaged. He ordered the attack to be made along all the line, and with all the forces which he had in the field; and his commands were obeyed with gallantry enough to vindicate the honour of the troops, but not to lead to success. They were beaten off, and the French resumed the offensive in their turn.

Still the Prussian monarch, who seems now to have taken the command upon himself, endeavouring to supply the want of professional experience by courage, brought up his last reserves, and encouraged his broken troops rather to make a final stand for victory, than to retreat in face of a conquering army. This effort also proved in vain. The Prussian line was attacked every where at once; centre and wings were broken through by the French at the bayonet's point; and the retreat, after so many fruitless efforts, in which no division had been left unengaged, was of the most disorderly character. But the confusion was increased tenfold, when, as the defeated troops reached Weimar, they fell in with the right wing of their own army, fugitives like themselves, and who were attempting to retreat in the same direction. The disorder of two routed armies meeting in opposing currents, soon became inextricable. The roads were choked up with artillery and baggage waggons; the retreat became a hurried flight; and the King himself, who had shown the utmost courage during the battle of Auerstadt, was at length, for personal safety, compelled to leave the high-roads, and escape across the fields, escorted by a small body of cavalry.

BATTLE OF JENA

While the left of the Prussian army were in the act of combating Davoust at Auerstadt, their right, as we have hinted, were with equally bad fortune engaged at Jena. This second action, though the least important of the two, has always given the name to the double battle; because it was at Jena that Napoleon was engaged in person.

Oct. 14.

The French Emperor had arrived at this town, which is situated upon the Saale, on the 13th of October, and had lost no time in issuing those orders to his mareschals, which produced the demonstrations of Davoust, and the victory of Auerstadt. His attention was not less turned to the position he himself occupied, and in which he had the prospect of fighting Mollendorf, and the right of the Prussians, on the next morning. With his usual activity, he formed or enlarged, in the course of the night, the roads by which he proposed to bring up his artillery on the succeeding day, and by hewing the solid rock, made a path practicable for guns to the plateau, or elevated plain in the front of Jena, where his centre was established.[237] The Prussian army lay before them, extended on a line of six leagues, while that of Napoleon, extremely concentrated, showed a very narrow front, but was well secured both in the flanks and in the rear. Buonaparte, according to his custom, slept in the bivouac, surrounded by his guards.[238] In the morning he harangued his soldiers, and recommended to them to stand firm against the charges of the Prussian cavalry, which had been represented as very redoubtable. As before Ulm, he had promised his soldiers a repetition of the battle of Marengo, so now he pointed out to his men that the Prussians, separated from their magazines, and cut off from their country, were in the situation of Mack at Ulm. He told them, that the enemy no longer fought for honour and victory, but for the chance of opening a way to retreat; and he added, that the corps which should permit them to escape would lose their honour. The French replied with loud shouts, and demanded instantly to advance to the combat. The Emperor ordered the columns destined for the attack to descend into the plain. His centre consisted of the Imperial Guard, and two divisions of Lannes. Augereau commanded the right, which rested on a village

---

[237] "Before the Emperor lay down, he descended the hill of Jena on foot, to be certain that no ammunition-waggon had been left at the bottom. He there found the whole of Marshal Lannes's artillery sticking in a ravine, which, in the obscurity of the night had been mistaken for a road. The Emperor was excessively angry, but showed his displeasure only by a cold silence. Without wasting time in reproaches, he set to work himself to do the duty of an artillery officer. He collected the men, made them get their park-tools, and light the lanterns; one of which he held for the convenience of those whose labours he directed. Never shall I forget the expression of the countenances of the men on seeing the Emperor lighting them with a lantern, nor the heavy blows with which they struck the rocks."— Savary, tom. ii., p. 180.

[238] "The night before the battle of Jena, the Emperor said, he had run the greatest risk. He might then have disappeared without his fate being clearly known. He had approached the bivouacs of the enemy, in the dark, to reconnoitre them; he had only a few officers with him. The opinion which was then entertained of the Prussian army kept every one on the alert: it was thought that the Prussians were particularly given to nocturnal attacks. As the Emperor returned, he was fired at by the first sentinel of his camp; this was a signal for the whole line; he had no resource but to throw himself flat on his face, until the mistake was discovered. But his principal apprehension was, that the Prussian line, which was near him, would act in the same manner."—Las Cases, tom. i., p. 143.

and a forest; and Soult's division, with a part of Ney's, were upon the left.

General Mollendorf advanced on his side, and both armies, as at Auerstadt, were hid from each other by the mist, until suddenly the atmosphere cleared, and showed them to each other within the distance of half-cannon shot. The conflict instantly commenced. It began on the French right, where the Prussians attacked with the purpose of driving Augereau from the village on which he rested his extreme flank. Lannes was sent to support him, by whose succour he was enabled to stand his ground. The battle then became general; and the Prussians showed themselves such masters of discipline, that it was long impossible to gain any advantage over men, who advanced, retired, or moved to either flank, with the regularity of machines. Soult at length, by the most desperate efforts, dispossessed the Prussians opposed to him of the woods from which they had annoyed the French left; and at the same conjuncture the division of Ney, and a large reserve of cavalry, appeared upon the field of battle. Napoleon, thus strengthened, advanced the centre, consisting in a great measure of the Imperial Guard, who, being fresh and in the highest spirits, compelled the Prussian army to give way. Their retreat was at first orderly; but it was a part of Buonaparte's tactics to pour attack after attack upon a worsted enemy, as the billows of a tempestuous ocean follow each other in succession, till the last waves totally disperse the fragments of the bulwark which the first have breached. Murat, at the head of the dragoons and the cavalry of reserve, charged, as one who would merit, as far as bravery could merit, the splendid destinies which seemed now opening to him. The Prussian infantry were unable to support the shock, nor could their cavalry protect them. The rout became general.[239] Great part of the artillery was taken, and the broken troops retreated in disorder upon Weimar, where, as we

---

[239] "The Emperor, at the point where he stood, saw the flight of the Prussians, and our cavalry taking them by thousands. Night was approaching; and here, as at Austerlitz, he rode round the field of battle. He often alighted from his horse to give a little brandy to the wounded; and several times I observed him putting his hand into the breast of a soldier to ascertain whether his heart beat, because, in consequence of having seen some slight appearance of colour in his cheeks, he supposed he might not be dead. In this manner I saw him two or three times discover men who were still alive. On these occasions he gave way to a joy which it is impossible to describe."—Savary, tom. ii., p. 184.

have already stated, their confusion became inextricable, by their encountering the other tide of fugitives from their own left, which was directed upon Weimar also. All leading and following seemed now lost in this army, so lately confiding in its numbers and discipline. There was scarcely a general left to issue orders, scarcely a soldier disposed to obey them; and it seems to have been more by a sort of instinct, than any resolved purpose, that several broken regiments were directed, or directed themselves, upon Magdeburg, where Prince Hohenloe endeavoured to rally them.

The French accounts state that 20,000 Prussians were killed and taken in the course of this fatal day; that three hundred guns fell into their power, with twenty generals, or lieutenant-generals, and standards and colours to the number of sixty.[240]

The mismanagement of the Prussian generals in these calamitous battles, and in all the manœuvres which preceded them, amounted to infatuation. The troops also, according to Buonaparte's evidence, scarcely maintained their high character, oppressed probably by a sense of the disadvantages under which they combated. But it is unnecessary to dwell on the various causes of a defeat, when the vanquished seem neither to have formed one combined and general plan of attack in the action, nor maintained communication with each other while it endured, nor agreed upon any scheme of retreat when the day was lost. The Duke of Brunswick, too, and General Schmettau, being mortally wounded early in the battle, the several divisions of the Prussian army fought individually, without receiving any general orders, and consequently without regular plan or combined manœuvres. The consequences of the defeat were more universally calamitous than could have been anticipated, even when we consider, that no mode of retreat having been fixed on, or general rallying place appointed, the broken army resembled a covey of heathfowl, which the sportsman marks down and destroys in detail and at his leisure.

Next day after the action, a large body of the Prussians, who, under the command of Mollendorf had retired to Erfurt, were compelled to surrender to the victors, and the marshal, with the

---

[240] Fifth Bulletin of the Grand Army; Jomini, tom. ii., p. 281; Savary, tom. ii., p. 181.

Prince of Orange Fulda, became prisoners. Other relics of this most unhappy defeat met with the same fate. General Kalkreuth, at the head of a considerable division of troops, was overtaken and routed in an attempt to cross the Hartz mountains. Prince Eugene of Wirtemberg commanded an untouched body of sixteen thousand men, whom the Prussian general-in-chief had suffered to remain at Memmingen, without an attempt to bring them into the field. Instead of retiring when he heard all was lost, the prince was rash enough to advance towards Halle, as if to put the only unbroken division of the Prussian army in the way of the far superior and victorious hosts of France. He was accordingly attacked and defeated by Bernadotte.

PRINCE HOHENLOE—BLUCHER

The chief point of rallying, however, was Magdeburg, under the walls of which strong city Prince Hohenloe, though wounded, contrived to assemble an army amounting to fifty thousand men, but wanting every thing, and in the last degree of confusion. But Magdeburg was no place of rest for them. The same improvidence, which had marked every step of the campaign, had exhausted that city of the immense magazines which it contained, and taken them for the supply of the Duke of Brunswick's army. The wrecks of the field of Jena were exposed to famine as well as the sword. It only remained for Prince Hohenloe to make the best escape he could to the Oder, and, considering the disastrous circumstances in which he was placed, he seems to have displayed both courage and skill in his proceedings. After various partial actions, however, in all of which he lost men, he finally found himself, with the advanced guard and centre of his army, on the heights of Prenzlow, without provisions, forage, or ammunition. Surrender became unavoidable; and at Prenzlow and Passewalk, nearly twenty thousand Prussians laid down their arms.

The rear of Prince Hohenloe's army did not immediately share this calamity. They were at Boitzenburg when the surrender took place, and amounted to about ten thousand men, the relics of the battle in which Prince Eugene of Wirtemberg had engaged near

Weimar, and were under the command of a general whose name hereafter was destined to sound like a war trumpet—the celebrated Blucher.

In the extremity of his country's distresses, this distinguished soldier showed the same indomitable spirit, the same activity in execution and daringness of resolve, which afterwards led to such glorious results. He was about to leave Boitzenburg on the 29th, in consequence of his orders from Prince Hohenloe, when he learned that general's disaster at Prenzlow. He instantly changed the direction of his retreat, and, by a rapid march towards Strelitz, contrived to unite his forces with about ten thousand men, gleanings of Jena and Auerstadt, which, under the Dukes of Weimar and of Brunswick Oels, had taken their route in that direction. Thus reinforced, Blucher adopted the plan of passing the Elbe at Lauenburg, and reinforcing the Prussian garrisons in Lower Saxony. With this view he fought several sharp actions, and made many rapid marches. But the odds were too great to be balanced by courage and activity. The division of Soult which had crossed the Elbe, cut him off from Lauenburg, that of Murat interposed between him and Stralsund, while Bernadotte pressed upon his rear. Blucher had no resource but to throw himself and his diminished and dispirited army into Lubeck. The pursuers came soon up, and found him like a stag at bay. A battle was fought on the 6th of November, in the streets of Lubeck, with extreme fury on both sides, in which the Prussians were overpowered by numbers, and lost many slain, besides four thousand prisoners. Blucher fought his way out of the town, and reached Schwerta. But he had now retreated as far as he could, without violating the neutrality of the Danish territory, which would only have raised up new enemies to his unfortunate master.

On the 7th November, therefore, he gave up his good sword, to be resumed under happier auspices, and surrendered with the few thousand men which remained under his command.[241] But the

---

[241] "So jealous was Blucher of any tarnish being attached to his character, in consequence of this surrender, that the capitulation was at one time on the point of being broken off, because Bernadotte would not consent that the reasons which compelled him to surrender, viz. a want of powder and other necessaries, should be stated, as Blucher insisted, among

courage which he had manifested, like the lights of St. Elmo amid the gloom of the tempest, showed that there was at least one pupil of the Great Frederick worthy of his master, and afforded hopes, on which Prussia long dwelt in silence, till the moment of action arrived.

SURRENDER OF FORTRESSES

The total destruction, for such it might almost be termed, of the Prussian army, was scarcely so wonderful, as the facility with which the fortresses which defend that country, some of them ranking among the foremost in Europe, were surrendered by their commandants, without shame, and without resistance, to the victorious enemy. Strong towns, and fortified places, on which the engineer had exhausted his science, provided too with large garrisons, and ample supplies, opened their gates at the sound of a French trumpet, or the explosion of a few bombs. Spandau, Stettin, Custrin, Hamelen, were each qualified to have arrested the march of invaders for months, yet were all surrendered on little more than a summons. In Magdeburg was a garrison of twenty-two thousand men, two thousand of them being artillerymen; and nevertheless this celebrated city capitulated with Mareschal Ney at the first flight of shells. Hamelen was garrisoned by six thousand troops, amply supplied with provisions, and every means of maintaining a siege. The place was surrendered to a force scarcely one-third in proportion to that of the garrison. These incidents were too gross to be imputed to folly and cowardice alone. The French themselves wondered at their conquests, yet had a shrewd guess at the manner in which they were rendered so easy. When the recreant governor of Magdeburg was insulted by the students of Halle for treachery as well as cowardice, the French garrison of the place sympathized, as soldiers, with the youthful enthusiasm of the scholars, and afforded the sordid old coward but little protection against their indignation. From a similar generous impulse, Schoels, the commandant of Hamelen, was nearly destroyed by the troops under his orders. In surrendering the place, he had endeavoured to stipulate, that, in case

---

the articles drawn up between them."—See Gentz, *Journal des Quatorze Jours de la Monarchie Prussienne.*

the Prussian provinces should pass by the fortune of war to some other power, the officers should retain their pay and rank. The soldiers were so much incensed at this stipulation, which carried desertion in its front, and a proposal to shape a private fortune to himself amid the ruin of his country, that Schoels only saved himself by delivering up the place to the French before the time stipulated in the articles of capitulation.

It is believed that, on several of these occasions, the French constructed a golden key to open these iron fortresses, without being themselves at the expense of the precious metal which composed it. Every large garrison has of course a military chest, with treasure for the regular payment of the soldiery; and it is said, that more than one commandant was unable to resist the proffer, that, in case of an immediate surrender, this deposit should not be inquired into by the captors, but left at the disposal of the governor, whose accommodating disposition had saved them the time and trouble of a siege.[242]

While the French army made this uninterrupted progress, the new King of Holland, Louis Buonaparte, with an army partly composed of Dutch and partly of Frenchmen, possessed himself with equal ease of Westphalia, great part of Hanover, Emden, and East Friesland.[243]

Oct. 25.

To complete the picture of general disorder which Prussia now exhibited, it is only necessary to add, that the unfortunate King, whose personal qualities deserved a better fate, had been obliged,

---

[242] "The war with Prussia—a war which had been hatching since the battle of Austerlitz—was less caused by the counsels of the cabinet, than by the compilers of secret memoirs. They began by representing the Prussian monarchy as ready to fall at the least puff, like a house built with cards. I can affirm, that, for the last three months, this war was prepared like a *coup de théâtre*; all the chances and vicissitudes had been calculated, and weighed, with the greatest exactness. I considered it ill becoming the dignity of crowned heads, to see a cabinet so ill regulated. The Prussian monarchy, whose safeguard it should have been, depended upon the cunning of some intriguers, and the energy of a few subsidized persons, who were the very puppets of our will. Jena! history will one day develope thy secret causes."—Fouché, tom. i., p. 304.
[243] Documens sur la Hollande, tom. i., p. 282.

after the battle, to fly into East Prussia, where he finally sought refuge in the city of Königsberg. L'Estocq, a faithful and able general, was still able to assemble out of the wreck of the Prussian army a few thousand men, for the protection of his sovereign. Buonaparte took possession of Berlin on the 25th October, eleven days after the battle of Jena. The mode in which he improved his good fortune, we reserve for future consideration.

FALL OF PRUSSIA

The fall of Prussia was so sudden and so total, as to excite the general astonishment of Europe. Its prince was compared to the rash and inexperienced gambler, who risks his whole fortune on one desperate cast, and rises from the table totally ruined. That power had, for three quarters of a century, ranked among the most important of Europe; but never had she exhibited such a formidable position as almost immediately before her disaster, when, holding in her own hand the balance of Europe, she might, before the day of Austerlitz, have inclined the scale to which side she would. And now she lay at the feet of the antagonist whom she had rashly and in ill time defied, not fallen merely, but totally prostrate, without the means of making a single effort to arise. It was remembered that Austria, when her armies were defeated, and her capital taken, had still found resources in the courage of her subjects, and that the insurrections of Hungary and Bohemia had assumed, even after Buonaparte's most eminent successes, a character so formidable, as to aid in procuring peace for the defeated Emperor on moderate terms. Austria, therefore, was like a fortress repeatedly besieged, and as often breached and damaged, but which continued to be tenable, though diminished in strength, and deprived of important outworks. But Prussia seemed like the same fortress swallowed up by an earthquake, which leaves nothing either to inhabit or defend, and where the fearful agency of the destroyer reduces the strongest bastions and bulwarks to crumbled masses of ruins and rubbish.

The cause of this great distinction between two countries which have so often contended against each other for political power, and for influence in Germany, may be easily traced.

The empire of Austria combines in itself several large kingdoms, the undisturbed and undisputed dominions of a common sovereign, to whose sway they have been long accustomed, and towards whom they nourish the same sentiments of loyalty which their fathers entertained to the ancient princes of the same house. Austria's natural authority therefore rested, and now rests, on this broad and solid base, the general and rooted attachment of the people to their prince, and their identification of his interests with their own.

Prussia had also her native provinces, in which her authority was hereditary, and where the affection, loyalty, and patriotism of the inhabitants were natural qualities, which fathers transmitted to their sons. But a large part of her dominions consist of late acquisitions, obtained at different times by the arms or policy of the great Frederick; and thus her territories, made up of a number of small and distant states, want geographical breadth, while their disproportioned length stretches, according to Voltaire's well-known simile, like a pair of garters across the map of Europe. It follows as a natural consequence, that a long time must intervene betwixt the formation of such a kingdom, and the amalgamation of its component parts, differing in laws, manners, and usages, into one compact and solid monarchy, having respect and affection to their king, as the common head, and regard to each other as members of the same community. It will require generations to pass away, ere a kingdom, so artificially composed, can be cemented into unity and strength; and the tendency to remain disunited, is greatly increased by the disadvantages of its geographical situation.

These considerations alone might explain, why, after the fatal battle of Jena, the inhabitants of the various provinces of Prussia contributed no important personal assistance to repel the invader; and why, although almost all trained to arms, and accustomed to serve a certain time in the line, they did not display any readiness to exert themselves against the common enemy. They felt that they belonged to Prussia only by the right of the strongest, and therefore were indifferent when the same right seemed about to transfer their allegiance elsewhere. They saw the approaching ruin of the Prussian power, not as children view the danger of a father, which they are bound to prevent at the hazard of their lives, but as servants view that of a master, which concerns them no otherwise than as leading to a change of their employers.

There were other reasons, tending to paralyse any effort at popular resistance, which affected the hereditary states of Prussia, as well as her new acquisitions. The power of Prussia had appeared to depend almost entirely upon her standing army, established by Frederick, and modelled according to his rules. When, therefore, this army was at once annihilated, no hope of safety was entertained by those who had so long regarded it as invincible. The Prussian peasant, who would gladly have joined the ranks of his country while they continued to keep the field, knew, or thought he knew, too much of the art of war, to have any hope in the efforts which might be made in a desultory guerilla warfare; which, however, the courage, devotion, and pertinacity of an invaded people have rendered the most formidable means of opposition even to a victorious army.

The ruin of Prussia, to whatever causes it was to be attributed, seemed, in the eyes of astonished Europe, not only universal, but irremediable. The King, driven to the extremity of his dominions, could only be considered as a fugitive, whose precarious chance of restoration to the crown depended on the doubtful success of his ally of Russia, who now, as after the capture of Vienna, had upon his hands, strong as those hands were, not the task of aiding an ally, who was in the act of resistance to the common enemy, but the far more difficult one of raising from the ground a prince who was totally powerless and prostrate. The French crossed the Oder—Glogau and Breslau were invested. Their defence was respectable; but it seemed not the less certain that their fall involved almost the last hopes of Prussia, and that a name raised so high by the reign of one wise monarch, was like to be blotted from the map of Europe by the events of a single day.

Men looked upon this astonishing calamity with various sentiments, according as they considered it with relation to the Prussian administration alone, or as connected with the character of the King and kingdom, and the general interests of Europe. In the former point of view, the mind could not avoid acknowledging, with a feeling of embittered satisfaction, that the crooked and selfish policy of Prussia's recent conduct,—as shortsighted as it was grasping and unconscientious,—had met in this present hour of disaster with no more than merited chastisement. The indifference with which the Prussian Cabinet had viewed the distresses of the House of Austria, which their firm interposition might probably have prevented—the total want of conscience and decency with which they accepted Hanover from France, at the moment when they meditated war with the power at whose hand they received it— the shameless rapacity with which they proposed to detain the Electorate from its legal owner, at the very time when they were negotiating an alliance with Britain—intimated that contempt of the ordinary principles of justice, which, while it renders a nation undeserving of success, is frequently a direct obstacle to their attaining it. Their whole procedure was founded on the principles of a felon, who is willing to betray his accomplice, providing he is allowed to retain his own share of the common booty. It was no wonder, men said, that a government setting such an example to its subjects, of greediness and breach of faith in its public transactions, should find among them, in the hour of need, many who were capable of preferring their own private interests to that of their country. And if the conduct of this wretched administration was regarded in a political instead of a moral point of view, the disasters of the kingdom might be considered as the consequence of their incapacity, as well as the just remuneration of their profligacy. The hurried and presumptuous declaration of war, after every favourable opportunity had been suffered to escape, and indeed the whole conduct of the campaign, showed a degree of folly not far short of actual imbecility, and which must have arisen either from gross treachery, or something like infatuation. So far, therefore, as the ministers of Prussia were concerned, they reaped only the reward due to their political want of morality, and their practical want of judgment.

Very different, indeed, were the feelings with which the battle of Jena and its consequences were regarded, when men considered that great calamity in reference not to the evil counsellors by whom it was prepared, but to the prince and nation who were to pay the penalty. "We are human," and, according to the sentiment of the poet, on the extinction of the state of Venice,[244] "must mourn, even when the shadow of that which has once been great passes away." But the apparent destruction of Prussia was not like the departure of the aged man, whose life is come to the natural close, or the fall of a ruined tower, whose mouldering arches can no longer support the incumbent weight. These are viewed with awe indeed, and with sympathy, but they do not excite astonishment or horror. The seeming fate of the Prussian monarchy resembled the agonizing death of him who expires in the flower of manhood. The fall of the House of Brandenburgh was as if a castle, with all its trophied turrets strong and entire, should be at once hurled to the earth by a superhuman power. Men, alike stunned with the extent and suddenness of the catastrophe, were moved with sympathy for those instantly involved in the ruin, and struck with terror at the demolition of a bulwark, by the destruction of which all found their own safety endangered. The excellent and patriotic character of Frederick William, on whose rectitude and honour even the misconduct of his ministers had not brought any stain; the distress of his interesting, high-spirited, and beautiful consort; the general sufferings of a brave and proud people, accustomed to assume and deserve the name of Protectors of the Protestant Faith and of the Liberties of Germany, and whose energies, corresponding with the talents of their leader, had enabled them in former times to withstand the combined force of France, Austria, and Russia— excited deep and general sympathy.

Still wider did that sympathy extend, and more thrilling became its impulse, when it was remembered that in Prussia fell the last state of Germany, who could treat with Napoleon in the style of an equal; and that to the exorbitant power which France already possessed in the south of Europe, was now to be added an authority in the north almost equally arbitrary and equally extensive. The prospect was a gloomy one; and they who felt neither for the fallen authority of a prince, nor the destroyed independence of a kingdom, trembled at the prospect likely to be entailed on their own country

---

[244] "Men are we, and must grieve even when the shade Of that which once was great is pass'd away." Wordsworth.—S.

by a ruin, which seemed as remediless as it was extensive and astounding.

"But yet the end was NOT."—

Providence, which disappoints presumptuous hopes by the event, is often mercifully pleased to give aid when human aid seems hopeless. Whatever may be thought of the doctrine of an intermediate state of sufferance and purification in an after stage of existence, it is evident from history, that in this world, kingdoms, as well as individuals, are often subjected to misfortunes arising from their own errors, and which prove in the event conducive to future regeneration. Prussia was exposed to a long and painful discipline in the severe school of adversity, by which she profited in such a degree as enabled her to regain her high rank in the republic of Europe, with more honour perhaps to her prince and people, than if she had never been thrust from her lofty station. Her government, it may be hoped, have learned to respect the rights of other nations, from the sufferings which followed the destruction of their own— her people have been taught to understand the difference between the dominion of strangers and the value of independence. Indeed, the Prussians showed in the event, by every species of sacrifice, how fully they had become aware, that the blessing of freedom from foreign control is not to be secured by the efforts of a regular army only, but must be attained and rendered permanent by the general resolution of the nation, from highest to lowest, to dedicate their united exertions to the achievement of the public liberty at every risk, and by every act of self-devotion. Their improvement under the stern lessons which calamity taught them, we shall record in a brighter page. For the time, the cloud of misfortune sunk hopelessly dark over Prussia, of which not merely the renown, but the very national existence seemed in danger of being extinguished for ever.

CHAPTER XXXV

Ungenerous conduct of Buonaparte to the Duke of Brunswick—The approach of the French troops to Brunswick compels the dying Prince to cause himself to be carried to Altona, where he expires—Oath of revenge taken by his Son—At Potsdam and Berlin, the proceedings of Napoleon are equally cruel and vindictive—His clemency towards the Prince of Hatzfeld—His Treatment of the Lesser Powers—Jerome Buonaparte—Seizure of Hamburgh—Berlin Decrees against British Commerce—Napoleon rejects all application from the continental commercial towns to relax or repeal them—Commerce, nevertheless, flourishes in spite of them—Second anticipation called for of the Conscription for 1807—The King of Prussia applies for an Armistice, which is clogged with such harsh terms, that he refuses them.

The will of Napoleon seemed now the only law, from which the conquered country, that so late stood forth as the rival of France, was to expect her destiny; and circumstances indicated, that, with more than the fortune of Cæsar or Alexander, the Conqueror would not emulate their generosity or clemency.

THE DUKE OF BRUNSWICK

The treatment of the ill-fated Duke of Brunswick did little honour to the victor. After receiving a mortal wound on the field of battle, he was transported from thence to Altona. Upon his way to his native dominions, in the government of which his conduct had been always patriotic and praiseworthy, he wrote to Napoleon, representing that, although he had fought against him as a general in the Prussian service, he nevertheless, as a Prince of the Empire, recommended his hereditary principality to the moderation and clemency of the victor. This attempt to separate his two characters, or to appeal to the immunities of a league which Napoleon had dissolved, although natural in the duke's forlorn situation, formed a plea not likely to be attended to by the conqueror. But, on other and broader grounds, Buonaparte, if not influenced by personal animosity against the duke, or desirous to degrade, in his person, the father-in-law of the heir of the British crown, might have found reasons for treating the defeated general with the respect due to his rank and his misfortunes. The Duke of Brunswick was one of the oldest soldiers in Europe, and his unquestioned bravery ought to have recommended him to his junior in arms. He was a reigning prince, and Buonaparte's own aspirations towards confirmation of aristocratical rank should have led him to treat the vanquished with decency. Above all, the duke was defenceless, wounded, dying; a situation to command the sympathy of every military man, who knows on what casual circumstances the fate of battle depends. The answer of Napoleon was, nevertheless, harsh and insulting in the last degree. He reproached the departing general with his celebrated proclamation against France in 1792, with the result of his unhappy campaign in that country, with the recent summons by which the French had been required to retreat beyond the Rhine. He charged him as having been the instigator of a war which his counsels ought to have prevented. He announced the right which he had acquired, to leave not one stone standing upon another in the town of Brunswick; and summed up his ungenerous reply by intimating, that though he might treat the subjects of the duke like a generous victor, it was his purpose to deprive the dying prince and his family of their hereditary sovereignty.[245]

As if to fulfil these menaces, the French troops approached the city of Brunswick; and the wounded veteran, dreading the further resentment of his ungenerous victor, was compelled to cause himself to be removed to the neutral town of Altona, where he expired.[246] An application from his son, requesting permission to lay

---

[245] Sixteenth Bulletin of the Grand Army, dated 12th Oct.
[246] "The Duke of Brunswick's entry into Altona presented a new and striking proof of the instability of fortune. A sovereign prince was beheld, enjoying, right or wrong, a great military reputation, but very lately powerful and tranquil in his own capital, now beaten and mortally wounded, borne into Altona on a miserable litter, carried by ten men, without officers, without domestics, escorted by a crowd of boys and ragamuffins, who pressed

his father's body in the tomb of his ancestors, was rejected with the same sternness which had characterised Buonaparte's answer to the attempt of the duke, when living, to soften his enmity. The successor of the duke vowed, it is believed, to requite these insults with mortal hatred—did much to express it during his life—and bequeathed to his followers the legacy of revenge,[247] which the Black Brunswickers had the means of amply discharging upon the 18th of June, 1815.

Some have imputed this illiberal conduct of Buonaparte to an ebullition of spleen against the object of his personal dislike; others have supposed that his resentment was, in whole or in part, affected in order to ground upon it his resolution of confiscating the state of Brunswick, and uniting it with the kingdom of Westphalia, which, as we shall presently see, he proposed to erect as an appanage for his brother Jerome. Whether arising from a burst of temperament, or a cold calculation of interested selfishness, his conduct was equally unworthy of a monarch and a soldier.

At Potsdam and at Berlin, Napoleon showed himself equally as the sworn and implacable enemy, rather than as the generous conqueror. At Potsdam he seized on the sword, belt, and hat of the Great Frederick, and at Berlin he appropriated and removed to Paris the monument of Victory, erected by the same monarch, in consequence of the defeat of the French at Rosbach.[248] The finest paintings and works of art in Prussia were seized upon for the benefit of the French National Museum.

---

about him from curiosity, deposited in a bad inn, and so worn out with fatigue, that the morrow after his arrival, the report of his death was generally credited. His wife joined him on the 1st November; he refused all visits, and died on the 10th."—Bourrienne, tom. vii., p. 159.

[247] "Within a window'd niche of that high hall, Sate Brunswick's fated chieftain: he did hear That sound the first amidst the festival, And caught its tone with Death's prophetic ear; And when they smiled because he deem'd it near, His heart more truly knew that peal too well, Which stretch'd his Father on a bloody bier, And roused the Vengeance blood alone could quell. He rush'd into the field, and, foremost fighting, fell." *Childe Harold.*

[248] "The sword of the Great Frederick was easily found at Potsdam, together with the scarf which he wore during the Seven Years' War; also the insignia of the Black Eagle. The Emperor took these trophies with transport, saying, 'I would rather have these than twenty millions: I shall send them to my old soldiers—I shall present them to the governor of the Invalids: in that hotel they shall remain.'"—*Nineteenth Bulletin.*

The language of the victor corresponded with his actions. His bulletins and proclamations abounded with the same bitter sarcasms against the King, the Queen, and those whom he called the war faction of Prussia. Ascribing the war to the unrepressed audacity of the young nobility, he said, in one of those proclamations, he would permit no more rioting in Berlin, no more breaking of windows; and, in addressing the Count Neale, he threatened, in plain terms, to reduce the nobles of Prussia to beg their bread.[249] These, and similar expressions of irritated spleen, used in the hour of conquest, level the character of the great victor with that of the vulgar Englishman in the farce, who cannot be satisfied with beating his enemy, but must scold him also. Napoleon's constant study of the poetry ascribed to Ossian, might have taught him that wrath should fly on eagles' wings from a conquered foe. The soldiers, and even the officers, caught the example of their Emperor, and conceived they met his wishes by behaving more imperiously in quarters, and producing more distress to their hosts, than had been their custom in the Austrian campaigns. Great aggressions, perhaps, were rarely perpetrated, and would have been punished, as contrary to military discipline; but a grinding, constant, and unremitting system of vexation and requisition, was bitterly felt by the Prussians at the time, and afterwards sternly revenged.

THE PRINCE OF HATZFELD

It is but justice, however, to record an act of clemency of Napoleon amid these severities. He had intercepted a letter containing some private intelligence respecting the motions of the French, sent by Prince Hatzfeld, late the Prussian governor of Berlin, to Prince Hohenloe, then still at the head of an army. Napoleon appointed a military commission for the trial of Hatzfeld; and his doom, for continuing to serve his native prince after his capital had been occupied by the enemy, would have been not less certain than severe. His wife, however, threw herself at Napoleon's

---

[249] "The good people of Berlin have been the sacrifice of the war; while those who excited it have left them and are become fugitives; I shall reduce those noble courtiers to such extremities that they shall be compelled to beg their bread." To Prince Hatzfeld, the Emperor said, "Do not appear in my presence; I have no need of your services; retire to your estates."—*Twenty-first Bulletin.*

feet, who put into her hands the fatal document which contained evidence of what was called her husband's guilt, with permission to throw it into the fire.[250] The French Emperor is entitled to credit for the degree of mercy he showed on this occasion; but it must be granted at the same time, that to have proceeded to sentence and execution upon such a charge, would have been an act of great severity, if not of actual atrocity. If, as has been alleged, the correspondence of Prince Hatzfeld was dated before, not after the capitulation of Berlin, his death would have been an unqualified murder.[251]

HESSE-CASSEL

The victor, who had all at his disposal, was now to express his pleasure concerning those satellites of Prussia, which, till her fall,

---

[250] "I remained at the door of the Emperor's cabinet to prevent any person from being announced before the princess. Duroc soon came out and immediately introduced her. She knew not why her husband had been arrested; and, in the simplicity of her nature, demanded justice for the wrong which she supposed was done to him. When she had finished, the Emperor handed to her the letter written by her husband; when she had run it over, she seemed motionless, and looked as if she had lost sensation. She stared with haggard eyes at the Emperor; but articulated not a word. He said to her, 'Well, madam, is this a calumny—an unjust charge?' The princess, more dead than alive, was going to answer only with her tears, when the Emperor took the letter from her, and said, 'Madam, were it not for this letter there would be no proof against your husband.'—'That is very true,' she replied, 'but I cannot deny that it is his writing.'—'Well,' said the Emperor, 'there is nothing to be done but to burn it;' and he threw the letter into the fire."—Savary, tom. ii., p. 206.
The following is Napoleon's own account of what passed, in a letter to Josephine, dated 6th November, nine o'clock evening:—"I received thy letter; in which thou seemest angry with me for speaking ill of women." In the letter here referred to, Josephine had expressed her regret at the disrespectful terms in which the Queen of Prussia was spoken of in the Bulletins of the Grand Army. "It is true I utterly abominate intriguing females. I am accustomed to those who are amiable, gentle, and conciliating; and such I love. If they have spoiled me it is not my fault, but thine. But at least thou wilt see I have been very good to one, who showed herself a feeling, amiable woman—Madame Hatzfeld. When I showed her her husband's letter, she replied to me, weeping bitterly, with heartfelt sensibility and *naïveté. Alas! it is but too surely his writing.* When she read it, her accent went to my soul—her situation distressed me. I said, *Well, then, madame, throw that letter into the fire; I shall then no longer possess the means of punishing your husband.* She burnt the letter, and was happy. Her husband is restored to tranquillity: Two hours later, and he would have been a lost man. Thus thou seest, that I esteem women that are good, and ingenuous, and amiable: but this is because such alone resemble thee."—*Lettres de Napoléon à Josephine*, tom. i., p. 195.
[251] "The letter was forwarded from the post-office a few days *after* our arrival at Berlin."—Savary, tom. ii., p. 205.

had looked up to her as their natural protector and ally. Of these, Saxony and Hesse-Cassel were the principal; and, in his proceedings towards them, Buonaparte regarded the train of his own policy much more than the merits which the two electors might have respectively pleaded towards France.

Saxony had joined her arms to those of Prussia—forced, as she said, by the arguments which a powerful neighbour can always apply to a weaker—still she *had* joined her, and fought on her side at the battle of Jena. The apology of compulsion was admitted by Buonaparte; the Saxon troops were dismissed upon their parole, and their prince raised to the rank of a King, shortly afterwards admitted as a member of the Confederacy of the Rhine, and treated by Buonaparte with much personal consideration. The Dukes of Saxe-Weimar and Saxe-Gotha also were permitted to retain their dominions, on acknowledging a similar vassalage to the French empire.

The Landgrave, or Elector, of Hesse-Cassel, might have expected a still more favourable acceptance in the eyes of the victor; for he had refused to join Prussia, and, in spite of threats and persuasions, had observed neutrality during the brief contest. But Napoleon remembered, to the prejudice of the landgrave, that he had resisted all previous temptations to enter into the Confederation of the Rhine. He imputed his neutrality to fear, not choice. He alleged, that it had not been strictly observed; and, treating the inaction of Hesse, whose inclinations were with Prussia, as a greater crime than the actual hostilities of Saxony, whose will was with France, he declared, according to his usual form of dethronement, that the House of Hesse-Cassel had ceased to reign. The doom was executed even before it was pronounced. Louis Buonaparte, with Marshal Mortier, had possessed himself of Hesse-Cassel by the 1st of November.[252] The army of the landgrave made no resistance—a

---

[252] "This is not correct. I had put myself at this period at the head of my own troops and some French regiments then in Holland, because the Emperor required the King of Holland to form a combined army at Wesel, under the title of the Army of the North. Endeavouring as much as possible to reconcile my very different duties, I marched towards Cassel, at the orders of Marshal Mortier, who was advancing upon Mayence with a small number of troops. When I approached Cassel, Marshal Mortier had entered the evening before. I immediately halted the body of the army before I entered the town, and leaving

part of them passed under the banners of France, the rest were disbanded.

The real cause of seizing the territories of an unoffending prince, who was totally helpless, unless in so far as right or justice could afford him protection, was Buonaparte's previous resolution, already hinted at, to incorporate Hesse-Cassel with the adjacent territories, for the purpose of forming a kingdom to be conferred on his youngest brother Jerome. This young person bore a gay and dissipated character; and, though such men may at times make considerable sacrifices for the indulgence of transient passion, they are seldom capable of retaining for a length of time a steady affection for an object, however amiable. Jerome Buonaparte, as before stated, had married an American young lady, distinguished for her beauty and her talents, and had thus lost the countenance of Napoleon, who maintained the principle, that segregated as his kindred were from the nation at large, by their connexion with him, his rank, and his fortunes, they were not entitled to enter into alliances according to the dictates of their own feelings, but were bound to form such as were most suitable to his policy. Jerome was tempted by ambition finally to acquiesce in this reasoning, and sacrificed the connexion which his heart had chosen, to become the tool of his brother's ever-extending schemes of ambition. The reward was the kingdom of Westphalia, to which was united Hesse-Cassel, with the various provinces which Prussia had possessed in Franconia, Westphalia Proper, and Lower Saxony; as also the territories of the unfortunate Duke of Brunswick. Security could be scarcely supposed to attend upon a sovereignty, where the materials were acquired by public rapine, and the crown purchased by domestic infidelity.

About the middle of November, Mortier formally re-occupied Hanover in the name of the Emperor, and, marching upon Hamburgh, took possession of that ancient free town, so long the emporium of commerce for the north of Europe. Here, as formerly at Leipsic, the strictest search was made for British commodities and property, which were declared the lawful subject of confiscation.

---

the French troops under the command of Marshal Mortier, I took the route to Holland with the Dutch."—Louis Buonaparte, p. 50.

The *Moniteur* trumpeted forth, that these rigorous measures were accompanied with losses to British commerce which would shake the credit of the nation. This was not true. The citizens of Hamburgh had long foreseen that their neutrality would be no protection, and, in spite of the fraudful assurances of the French envoy, designed to lull them into security, the merchants had availed themselves of the last two years to dispose of their stock, call in their capital, and wind up their trade; so that the rapacity of the French was in a great measure disappointed. The strict search after British property, and the confiscation which was denounced against it at Hamburgh and elsewhere, were no isolated acts of plunder and spoliation, but made parts of one great system for destroying the commerce of England, which was shortly after laid before the world by the celebrated decrees of Berlin.[253]

It was frequently remarked of Buonaparte, that he studied a sort of theatrical effect in the mode of issuing his decrees and proclamations, the subject matter of which formed often a strange contrast with the date; the latter, perhaps, being at the capital of some subdued monarch, while the matter promulgated respected some minute regulation affecting the municipality of Paris. But there was no such discrepancy in the date and substance of the Berlin decrees against British enterprise. It was when Buonaparte had destroyed the natural bulwark which protected the independence of the north of Germany, and had necessarily obtained a corresponding power on the shores of the Baltic, that he seriously undertook to promulgate his sweeping plan of destroying the commerce of his Island foe.[254]

---

[253] "On the 19th November, Hamburgh was taken possession of in the Emperor's name. The demands which Marshal Mortier was necessitated to make were hard. But my representations suspended for a time the order given by Napoleon to seize the Bank. I cannot do otherwise than render a tribute to the uprightness of the marshal's conduct, who forwarded my representations to the Emperor at Berlin, announcing that he has delayed acting till the arrival of fresh orders. The Emperor read and approved my views."— Bourrienne, tom. vii., p. 179.

[254] "The delirium caused by the wonderful results of the Prussian campaign completed the intoxication of France. She prided herself upon having been saluted with the name of the Great Nation by her Emperor, who had triumphed over the genius and the work of Frederick. Napoleon believed himself the Son of Destiny, called to break every sceptre. Peace, and even a truce with England, was no longer thought of. The idea of destroying the power of England, the sole obstacle to universal monarchy, now became his fixed resolve.

When slight inconveniences, according to Buonaparte's expression, put an end to his hopes of invading Britain, or when, as at other times he more candidly admitted, the defeat at Trafalgar induced him "to throw helve after hatchet," and resign all hope of attaining any success by means of his navy, he became desirous of sapping and undermining the bulwark, which he found it impossible to storm; and, by directing his efforts to the destruction of British commerce, he trusted gradually to impair the foundations of her national wealth and prosperity. He erred, perhaps, in thinking that, even if his object could have been fully attained, the full consequences would have followed which his animosity anticipated. Great Britain's prosperity mainly rests on her commerce, but her existence as a nation is not absolutely dependent upon it; as those foreigners are apt to imagine, who have only seen the numerous vessels with which she covers the ocean and fills foreign ports, but have never witnessed the extent of her agricultural and domestic resources. But, entertaining the belief which Napoleon did, in regard to the indispensable connexion betwixt British commerce and British power, the policy of his war upon the former cannot be denied. It was that of the Abyssynian hunter, who, dreading to front the elephant in his fury, draws his sabre along the animal's heel-joint, and waits until the exertions of the powerful brute burst the injured sinews, and he sinks prostrate under his own weight.

BERLIN DECREES

The celebrated Decrees of Berlin appeared on the 21st November, 1806, interdicting all commerce betwixt Great Britain and the continent; which interdiction was declared a fundamental law of the French empire, until the English should consent to certain alterations in the mode of conducting hostilities by sea, which should render her naval superiority less useful to herself, and less detrimental to the enemy. This measure was justified upon the following grounds:—That England had either introduced new

---

It was with this view he established the continental system, the first decree concerning which was dated from Berlin. Napoleon persuaded himself, that by depriving England of all the outlets for its manufactures, he should reduce it to poverty, and that it must then submit to its fate. He not only thought of subjecting it, but also of effecting its destruction."—Fouché, tom. i., p. 305.

customs into her maritime code, or revived those of a barbarous age—that she seized on merchant vessels, and made their crews prisoners, just as if they had been found on board ships of war—declared harbours blockaded which were not so in reality—and extended the evils of war to the peaceful and unarmed citizen.

This induction to the celebrated project, afterwards called the Continental System of the Emperor, was false in the original proposition, and sophistical in those by which it was supported. It was positively false that Great Britain had introduced into her maritime law, either by new enactment, or by the revival of obsolete and barbarous customs, any alteration by which the rights of neutrals were infringed, or the unarmed citizen prejudiced, more than necessarily arose out of the usual customs of war. The law respecting the blockade of ports, and the capture of vessels at sea, was the same on which every nation had acted for three centuries past, France herself not excepted. It is true, that the maritime code seemed at this period to be peculiarly that of England, because no nation save herself had the means of enforcing them; but she did not in this respect possess any greater advantage by sea than Napoleon enjoyed by land.

The reasoning of the Emperor Napoleon upon the inequality and injustice of the maritime mode of exercising war, compared with the law of hostilities by land, was not more accurate than his allegation that Britain had innovated upon the former for the purpose of introducing new, or reviving old severities. This will appear plain from the following considerations:—

At an early period of society, the practice of war was doubtless the same by land or sea; and the savage slaughtered or enslaved his enemy whether he found him in his hut or in his canoe. But when centuries of civilisation began to mitigate the horrors of barbarous warfare, the restrictive rules introduced into naval hostilities were different from those adopted in the case of wars by land, as the difference of the services obviously dictated. A land army has a precise object, which it can always attain if victorious. If a general conquer a town, he can garrison it; he can levy contributions; nay, he may declare that he will appropriate it to himself in right of sovereignty. He can afford to spare the property of private individuals, when he is at liberty to seize, if he is so minded, upon all their public rights, and new-mould them at his pleasure. The seaman, on the other hand, seizes on the merchant vessel and its cargo, by the same right of superior force, in virtue of which the victor by land has seized upon castles, provinces, and on the very haven, it may be, which the vessel belongs to. If the maritime conqueror had no right to do this, he would gain nothing by his superiority except blows, when he met with vessels of force, and would be cut off from any share of the spoils of war, which form the reward of victory. The innocent and unarmed citizen, perhaps the neutral stranger, suffers in both cases; but a state of war is of course a state of violence, and its evils, unhappily, cannot be limited to those who are actually engaged in hostilities. If the spirit of philanthropy affected in the peroration to Buonaparte's decrees had been real, he might have attained his pretended purpose of softening the woes of war, by proposing some relaxation of the rights of a conqueror by land, in exchange for restrictions to be introduced into the practice of hostilities by sea. Instead of doing so, he, under the pretext of exercising the right of reprisals, introduced the following Decrees, unheard of hitherto among belligerent powers, and tending greatly to augment the general distress, which must, under all circumstances, attend a state of war.

    I. The British isles were declared in a state of blockade. II. All commerce and correspondence with England was forbidden. All English letters were to be seized in the post-houses. III. Every Englishman, of whatever rank or quality, found in France, or the countries allied with her, was declared a prisoner of war. IV. All merchandise, or property of any kind, belonging to English subjects, was declared lawful prize. V. All articles of English manufacture, and articles produced in her colonies, were in like manner declared contraband and lawful prize. VI. Half of the produce of the above confiscations was to be employed in the relief of those merchants whose vessels had been captured by the English cruisers. VII. All vessels coming from England, or the English colonies, were to be refused admission into any harbour. Four additional articles provided the mode of promulgating and enforcing the decree, and directed that it should be communicated to the allies of France.

This was the first link of a long chain of arbitrary decrees and ordinances, by which Napoleon, aiming at the destruction of British finance, interrupted the whole commerce of Europe, and destroyed for a season, and as far as lay in his power, that connexion between distant nations which unites them to each other by the most natural and advantageous means, the supply of the wants of the one country by the superfluous produce of the other. The extent of public inconvenience and distress, which was occasioned by the sudden suppression of commercial communication with England, may be judged of by reflecting, how many of the most ordinary articles of consumption are brought from foreign countries—in how many instances the use of these articles have brought them into the list of necessaries—and how, before an ordinary mechanic or peasant sits down to breakfast, distant climes must be taxed to raise the coffee and sugar which he consumes.[255]

The painful embarrassment of those deprived of their habitual comforts, was yet exceeded by the clamour and despair of the whole commercial world on the continent, who were thus, under pretext of relieving them from the vexation of the English cruizers, threatened with a total abrogation of their profession. Hamburgh, Bourdeaux, Nantes, and other continental towns, solicited, by petitions and deputations, some relaxation of decrees which inferred their general ruin. They pleaded the prospect of universal bankruptcy, which this prohibitory system must occasion. "Let it be so," answered the Emperor; "the more insolvency on the continent, the greater will be the distress of the merchants in London. The fewer traders in Hamburgh, the less will be the temptation to carry on commerce with England. Britain must be humbled, were it at the expense of

---

[255] "It is difficult, at this day, to conceive how Europe could, for a single hour, endure that fiscal tyranny which exacted the most exorbitant prices for articles, become indispensable necessaries of life, both to rich and poor, through habits of three centuries. It is so far from being the truth that such system had for its only and exclusive aim to prevent England from disposing of her merchandise, that licenses were sold at a high rate to those who had influence sufficient to procure them; and gold alone gave that influence. The quantity and the quality of articles exported from France were exaggerated with incredible impudence. It became necessary, indeed, to purchase such articles, in submission to the will of the Emperor; but they were bought only to be thrown into the sea. And yet none was found who had the conscience to tell the Emperor that England sold to the continent, but that she bought almost nothing from thence."—Bourrienne, tom. vii., p. 231.

throwing civilisation back for centuries, and returning to the original mode of trading by barter."

But, great as was Buonaparte's power, he had overrated it in supposing, that, by a mere expression of his will, he could put an end to an intercourse, in the existence of which the whole world possessed an interest. The attempt to annihilate commerce, resembled that of a child who tries to stop with his hand the stream of an artificial fountain, which escapes in a hundred partial jets from under his palm and between his fingers. The Genius of Commerce, like a second Proteus, assumed every variety of shape, in order to elude the imperial interdiction, and all manner of evasions was practised for that purpose. False papers, false certificates, false bills of lading, were devised, and these frauds were overlooked in the seaports, by the very agents of the police, and customhouse officers, to whom the execution of the decrees was committed. Douaniers, magistrates, generals, and prefects, nay, some of the kindred princes of the House of Napoleon, were well pleased to listen to the small still voice of their interest, rather than to his authoritative commands; and the British commerce, though charged with heavy expenses, continued to flourish in spite of the Continental System.[256] The new, and still more violent measures, which Napoleon had recourse to for enforcing his prohibitions, will require our notice hereafter. Meantime, it is enough to say, that such acts of increasing

---

[256] "The accusation thus brought might also fall upon me; and although I consider myself beyond the reach of such calumnies, I must declare, in answer to the frequent insinuations made during and even since the reign of my brother, that such an accusation is as untrue as it is inconceivable. I declare I was in no manner a partisan of the Continental System; first, because it injured Holland more than it did England, and it was the interest of Holland which concerned me most deeply; and, in the second place, because this system, though true in theory, was false in its application. I compare it to a sieve; a single hole is sufficient to render it incapable of containing any thing. The Continental System being acted upon in most countries, must have produced more beneficial results in those points where it was not maintained; and thus it was with respect to the advantages it conferred upon English commerce, mentioned by Sir Walter Scott. It was this which gave France the means of benefiting her merchants, to the injury of those of other countries, who had not the power to open and shut their ports at will. It will consequently be supposed that I could only lend myself partially, without zeal or pleasure, to the Continental System, since it was both against my own opinion and against the interest of the country, and I was convinced of its inefficacy against England; but at the same time I may declare, since all this is now a mere matter of history, that I did not hesitate to obey all that was required, with respect to the pretended blockade of England; but I repeat, that it was against my own opinion, and consequently without zeal and without pleasure."—Louis Buonaparte, p. 53.

severity had the natural consequence of rendering his person and power more and more unpopular; so that, while he was sacrificing the interests and the comforts of the nations under his authority to his hope of destroying England, he was, in fact, digging a mine under his own feet, which exploded to his destruction long before the security of England was materially affected.

Napoleon had foreseen, that, in order to enforce the decrees by which, without possession of any naval power, he proposed to annihilate the naval supremacy of England, it would be necessary to augment to a great extent the immense superiority of land forces which France already possessed. It was necessary, he was aware, that to enable him to maintain the prohibitions which he had imposed upon general commerce, as well as to prosecute the struggle in which he was about to be engaged with Russia, a large draught should be made on the population of France. He had, accordingly, by a requisition addressed to the Senate, dated from Bamberg, 7th of October, required a second anticipation of the conscription of 1807, amounting to a levy of eighty thousand men.

The measure was supported in the Senate by the oratory of Regnault de St. Jean d'Angely, an ancient Republican. This friend of freedom saw nothing inconsistent in advocating a measure, which the absolute monarch recommended as the necessary step to a general peace. The conscripts who had first marched had secured victory; those who were now to be put in motion were to realize the prospect of peace, the principal object of their brethren's success. The obsequious Senate readily admitted these arguments, as they would have done any which had been urged in support of a request which they dared not deny. The sole purpose of Regnault's eloquence, was to express in decent amplification the simple phrase, "Napoleon so wills it."

A deputation of the Senate,[257] carrying to Napoleon in person their warm acquiescence in the proposed measure, received in

---

[257] "This deputation thought fit to make representations to the Emperor, on the danger which he might incur by advancing beyond the Oder, and to express to him a wish to see his conquests brought to a termination. This observation offended the Emperor, and he replied to the deputation, that he would make peace as soon as he could, but in such a way as to make it once for all; and that he could not refrain from showing his dissatisfaction at

guerdon the honourable task of conveying to Paris the spoils of Potsdam and Berlin, with three hundred and forty-six stand of colours, the trophies of the war against Prussia—with the task of announcing the celebrated Decrees, by which the general commerce of Europe and of France itself was annihilated, to secure it from the aggressions of the British naval force. The military trophies were received—the Decrees were recorded; and no one dared undertake the delicate task of balancing the victories of the Emperor against the advantage which his dominions were likely to derive from them.

PRUSSIA

In the meanwhile, the unfortunate Frederick William, whose possession of his late flourishing kingdom was reduced to such territories as Prussia held beyond the Vistula, and a few fortresses on the Oder, which still held out, sent an embassy to Berlin, for the purpose of learning upon what terms he might be yet admitted to treat for peace with the victor, who had hold of his capital and the greater part of his dominions. The Marquis Lucchesini was employed on this mission, a subtle Italian, who, being employed in negotiations at Paris, had been accustomed to treat with France on a footing of equality. But these times were passed since the battle of Jena; and the only terms to which Prussia could be now admitted, were to be so dearly purchased, that even a mere temporary armistice was to cost the surrender of Graudentz, Dantzick, Colberg,—in short, all the fortresses yet remaining to Prussia, and still in a state of defence. As this would have been placing himself entirely at the mercy of Buonaparte, and in as bad circumstances as he could be reduced to even by the most unsuccessful military operations, the King refused to acquiesce in such severe terms, and determined to repose his fate in the chance of war, and in the support of the auxiliary army of Russia, which was now hastily advancing to his assistance.

---

their want of consideration, in exhibiting the shameful spectacle of disunion between the chief of the state and the first constituted body of the nation, at the very time when they knew that the Russians were advancing to join the Prussians."—Savary, tom. ii., p. 210.

Chapter XXXVI

Retrospect of the Partition of Poland—Napoleon receives addresses from Poland, which he evades—He advances into Poland, Bennigsen retreating before him—Character of the Russian Soldiery—The Cossacks—Engagement at Pultusk, on 26th November, terminating to the disadvantage of the French—Bennigsen continues his retreat—The French go into winter quarters—Bennigsen appointed Commander-in-chief in the place of Kaminskoy, who shows symptoms of insanity—He resumes offensive operations—Battle of Eylau, 8th February, 1807—Claimed as a victory by both parties—The loss on both sides amounts to 50,000 men killed, the greater part Frenchmen—Bennigsen retreats upon Königsberg—Napoleon offers favourable terms for an Armistice to the King of Prussia, who refuses to treat, save for a general Peace—Napoleon falls back to the line of the Vistula—Dantzick is besieged, and surrenders—Russian army is poorly recruited—the French powerfully—Actions during the Summer—Battle of Heilsberg, and retreat of the Russians—Battle of Friedland, 14th June—An Armistice takes place on the 23d.

POLAND

Napoleon was politically justified in the harsh terms which he was desirous to impose on Prussia, by having now brought his victorious armies to the neighbourhood of Poland in which he had a good right to conceive himself sure to find numerous followers and a friendly reception.

The partition of this fine kingdom by its powerful neighbours, Russia, Austria, and Prussia, was the first open and audacious transgression of the law of nations, which disgraced the annals of civilized Europe. It was executed by a combination of three of the most powerful states of Europe against one too unhappy in the nature of its constitution, and too much divided by factions to offer any effectual resistance. The kingdom subjected to this aggression had appealed in vain to the code of nations for protection against an outrage, to which, after a desultory and uncombined, and therefore a vain defence, she saw herself under the necessity of submitting. The Poles retained, too, a secret sense of their fruitless attempt to recover freedom in 1791, and an animated recollection of the violence by which it had been suppressed by the Russian arms. They waited with hope and exultation the approach of the French armies; and candour must allow, that, unlawfully subjected as they had been to a foreign yoke, they had a right to avail themselves of the assistance, not only of Napoleon, but of Mahomet, or of Satan himself, had he proposed to aid them in regaining the independence of which they had been oppressively and unjustly deprived.[258]

This feeling was general among the middling classes of the Polish aristocracy, who recollected with mortified pride the diminution of their independent privileges, the abrogation of their Diets, and the suppression of the *Liberum Veto*, by which a private gentleman might render null the decision of a whole assembly, unless unanimity should be attained, by putting the dissentient to death upon the spot.[259] But the higher order of nobility, gratified by

---

[258] "We have here a critique upon the policy of Napoleon towards Poland, which I shall not stop to examine. It is but too easy to criticise the actions of statesmen, when time, in its rapid course, has unveiled the causes and effects of events: when the game is finished, the spectators have no longer any credit in discovering what the players ought to have done."—Louis Buonaparte, p. 53.

[259] Most readers must be so far acquainted with the ancient form of Polish Diets as to know, that their resolutions were not legally valid if there was one dissenting voice, and that in many cases the most violent means were resorted to, to obtain unanimity. The following instance was related to our informer, a person of high rank:—On some occasion, a provincial Diet was convened for the purpose of passing a resolution which was generally acceptable, but to which it was apprehended one noble of the district would oppose his veto. To escape this interruption, it was generally resolved to meet exactly at the hour of summons, to proceed to business upon the instant, and thus to elude the anticipated attempt of the individual to defeat the purpose of their meeting. They accordingly met at the hour, with most accurate precision, and shut and bolted the doors of their place of

the rank they held, and the pleasures they enjoyed at the courts of Berlin, Vienna, and especially at Petersburgh, preferred in general the peaceful enjoyment of their immense estates to the privileges of a stormy independence, which raised the most insignificant of the numerous aristocracy to a rank and importance nearly resembling their own. They might, too, with some justice, distrust the views of Napoleon, though recommended by the most specious promises. The dominion of Russia, in particular, from similarity of manners, and the particular attention paid to their persons and interests, was not so unpopular among the higher branches of the aristocracy as might have been expected, from the unjust and arbitrary mode in which she had combined to appropriate so large a part of their once independent kingdom. These did not, therefore, so generally embrace the side of France as the minor nobles or gentry had done. As for the ordinary mass of the population, being almost all in the estate of serfage, or villanage, which had been general over Europe during the prevalence of the feudal system, they followed their respective lords, without pretending to entertain any opinion of their own.

ADDRESSES FROM POLAND

While Russia was marching her armies hastily forward, not only to support, or rather raise up once more, her unfortunate ally

---

meeting. But the dissentient arrived a few minutes afterwards, and entrance being refused, under the excuse that the Diet was already constituted, he climbed upon the roof of the hall, and, it being summer time, when no fires were lighted, descended through the vent into the stove by which, in winter, the apartment was heated. Here he lay perdu, until the vote was called, when, just as it was about to be recorded as unanimous in favour of the proposed measure, he thrust his head out of the stove, like a turtle protruding his neck from his shell, and pronounced the fatal *veto*. Unfortunately for himself, instead of instantly withdrawing his head, he looked around for an instant with exultation, to remark and enjoy the confusion which his sudden appearance and interruption had excited in the assembly. One of the nobles who stood by unsheathed his sabre, and severed at one blow the head of the dissentient from his body. Our noble informer, expressing some doubt of a story so extraordinary, was referred for its confirmation to Prince Sobieski, afterwards King of Poland, who not only bore testimony to the strange scene, as what he had himself witnessed, but declared that the head of the Dietm rolled over on his own foot almost as soon as he heard the word *veto* uttered. Such a constitution required much amelioration; but that formed no apology for the neighbouring states, who dismembered and appropriated to themselves an independent kingdom, with the faults or advantages of whose government they had not the slightest title to interfere.—S.

the King of Prussia, but to suppress any ebullition of popular spirit in Poland, Buonaparte received addresses from that country, which endeavoured to prevail on him to aid them in their views of regaining their independence. Their application was of a nature to embarrass him considerably. To have declared himself the patron of Polish independence, might have, indeed, brought large forces to his standard—might have consummated the disasters of Prussia, and greatly embarrassed even Russia herself; and so far policy recommended to Napoleon to encourage their hopes of her restored independence. But Austria had been a large sharer in the various partitions of Poland, and Austria, humbled as she had been, was still a powerful state, whose enmity might have proved formidable, if, by bereaving her of her Polish dominions, or encouraging her subjects to rebel, Buonaparte had provoked her to hostilities, at the time when he himself and the best part of his forces were engaged in the North of Europe. The same attempt would have given a very different character to the war, which Russia at present waged only in the capacity of the auxiliary of Prussia. The safety and integrity of the Russian empire, south of the Volga, depends almost entirely upon the preservation of those territories which she has acquired in Poland; and, if she had engaged in the war as a principal, Buonaparte was scarcely yet prepared to enter upon a contest with the immense power of that empire, which must be waged upon the very frontier of the enemy, and as near to their resources as he was distant from his own. It might have been difficult, also, to have stated any consistent grounds, why he, who had carved out so many new sovereignties in Europe with the point of the sword, should reprobate the principle of the partition of Poland. Influenced by these motives, the modern setter-up and puller-down of kings abstained from re-establishing the only monarchy in Europe, which he might have new-modelled to his mind, in the character not of a conqueror, but a liberator.

While Napoleon declined making any precise declaration, or binding himself by any express stipulations to the Polish delegates, the language he used to them was cautiously worded, so as to keep up their zeal and animate their exertions. Dombrowski,[260] a Polish

---

[260] "Napoleon had sent to Italy for the Polish General, Dombrowski, who joined us at Potsdam. This was an indication of his intentions, though as yet he had not allowed a word

exile in the French army, was employed to raise men for Napoleon's service, and the enthusiasm of those who entered, as well as the expectations of the kingdom at large, were excited by such oracular passages as the following, which appeared in the thirty-sixth bulletin:—"Is the throne of Poland to be re-established, and will that great nation regain her existence and independence? Will she be recalled to life, as if summoned to arise from the tomb?—God only, the great disposer of events, can be the arbiter of this great political problem."[261]

The continuance of war was now to be determined upon; a war to be waged with circumstances of more than usual horror, as it involved the sufferings of a winter campaign in the northern latitudes. The French, having completely conquered the Prussian estates to the east of the Oder, had formed the sieges of Great Glogau, of Breslau, and of Graudentz, and were at the same time pushing westward to occupy Poland. The Russian general, Bennigsen, had on his side pressed forward for the purpose of assisting the Prussians, and had occupied Warsaw. But finding that their unfortunate allies had scarcely the remnant of an army in the field, the Russian general retreated after some skirmishes, and recrossed the Vistula, while the capital of Poland, thus evacuated, was entered on the 28th November by Murat, at the head of the French vanguard.

---

on the subject to transpire in Poland. It was not until after the final refusal of the King of Prussia to negotiate, that he appealed to the patriotism of the Poles to augment his force. With a view to this object, the mere presence of Dombrowski was of great advantage."—Savary, tom. ii., p. 212.
[261] This bulletin was dated, Imperial Headquarters at Posen, December 1. On the next day, Napoleon issued the following proclamation to the army:—"Soldiers! a year ago, at the same hour, you were on the memorable field of Austerlitz. The sacred cohorts of Russia fled, defeated, before you; or, surrounded, laid down their arms at the feet of their conquerors. To the moderation, and, perhaps, blameable generosity, which overlooked the third coalition, the formation of a fourth may be ascribed. But the ally on whose military skill their principal hope rested, is already no more. His principal towns, his fortresses, his forage, and ammunition, magazines, 280 standards, 700 pieces of cannon, are in our power. Neither the Oder, nor Warta, the deserts of Poland, nor the rude season of winter, have been capable of arresting, for a moment, our progress. You have braved all dangers, surmounted them all, and every enemy has fled on your approach. In vain did the Russians wish to defend the capital of ancient and illustrious Poland. The French eagles hover over the Vistula. The unfortunate, but brave Poles, on contemplating you, fancy they behold the celebrated legions of their great Sobieski returning from a military expedition."

About the 25th, Napoleon, leaving Berlin, had established himself at Posen, a central town of Poland, which country began to manifest an agitation, partly the consequence of French intrigues, partly arising from the animating prospect of restored independence. The Poles resumed in many instances their ancient national dress and manners, and sent deputies to urge the decision of Buonaparte in their favour. The language in which they entreated his interposition, resembled that of Oriental idolatry. "The Polish nation," said Count Radyiminiski, the Palatine of Gnesna, "presents itself before your Majesty, groaning still under the yoke of German nations, and salutes with the purest joy the regenerator of their dear country, the legislator of the universe. Full of submission to your will, they adore you, and repose on you with confidence all their hopes, as upon him who has the power of raising empires and destroying them, and of humbling the proud." The address of the President of the Judicial Council-Chamber of the Regency of Poland, was not less energetic. "Already," he said, "we see our dear country saved; for in your person we adore the most just and the most profound Solon. We commit our fate and our hopes into your hands, and we implore the mighty protection of the most august Cæsar."

Not even these Eastern hyperboles could extort any thing from Buonaparte more distinctly indicative of his intentions, than the obscure hints we have already mentioned.

In the meanwhile, Warsaw was put into a state of defence, and the auxiliary forces of Saxony and the new confederates of the Rhine were brought up by forced marches, while strong reinforcements from France repaired the losses of the early part of the campaign.

The French army at length advanced in full force, and crossed successively the rivers Vistula and Bug, forcing a passage wherever it was disputed. But it was not the object of Bennigsen to give battle to forces superior to his own, and he therefore retreated behind the Wkra, and was joined by the large bodies of troops commanded by Generals Buxhowden and Kaminskoy. The latter took the general command. He was a contemporary of Suwarrow, and esteemed an excellent officer, but more skilled in the theory than the practice of war. "Kaminskoy," said Suwarrow, "knows war, but war does not know him—I do not know war, but war knows me." It appears also, that during this campaign Kaminskoy was afflicted with mental alienation.

On the 23d December, Napoleon arrived in person upon the Wkra, and ordered the advance of his army in three divisions. Kaminskoy, when he saw the passage of this river forced, determined to retreat behind the Niemen, and sent orders to his lieutenants accordingly. Bennigsen, therefore, fell back upon Pultusk, and Prince Galitzin upon Golymin, both pursued by large divisions of the French army. The Russian Generals Buxhowden and D'Anrep also retreated in different directions, and apparently without maintaining a sufficiently accurate communication either with Bennigsen, or with Galitzin. In their retrograde movements the Russians sustained some loss, which the bulletins magnified to such an extent, as to represent their army as entirely disorganised, their columns wandering at hazard in unimaginable disorder, and their safety only caused by the shortness of the days, the difficulties of a country covered with woods and intersected with ravines, and a thaw which had filled the roads with mud to the depth of five feet. It was, therefore, predicted, that although the enemy might possibly escape from the position in which he had placed himself, it must necessarily be effected at the certain loss of his artillery, his carriages, and his baggage.[262]

THE RUSSIAN SOLDIERY

These were exaggerations calculated for the meridian of Paris. Napoleon was himself sensible, that he was approaching a conflict of a different kind from that which he had maintained with Austria, and more lately against Prussia. The common soldier in both those services was too much levelled into a mere moving piece of machinery, the hundred-thousandth part of the great machine called an army, to have any confidence in himself, or zeal beyond the mere discharge of the task intrusted to him according to the word of

---

[262] Forty-fifth, forty-sixth, and forty-seventh Bulletins of the Grand Army.

command. These troops, however highly disciplined, wanted that powerful and individual feeling, which in armies possessing a strong national character, (by which the Russians are peculiarly distinguished,) induces the soldier to resist to the last moment, even when resistance can only assure him of revenge. They were still the same Russians, of whom Frederick the Great said, "that he could kill, but could not defeat them;"—they were also strong of constitution, and inured to the iron climate in which Frenchmen were now making war for the first time;—they were accustomed from their earliest life to spare nourishment and hardship;—in a word, they formed then, as they do now, the sole instance in Europe of an army, the privates of which are semi-barbarians, with the passions, courage, love of war, and devotion to their country, which is found in the earlier periods of society, while the education received by their superior officers places them on a level with those of any other nation. That of the inferior regimental officers is too much neglected; but they are naturally brave, kind to the common soldier, and united among themselves like a family of brothers,—attributes which go far to compensate the want of information. Among the higher officers, are some of the best informed men in Europe.

The Russian army was at this period deficient in its military staff, and thence imperfect in the execution of combined movements; and their generals were better accustomed to lead an army in the day of actual battle, than to prepare for victory by a skilful combination of previous manœuvres. But this disadvantage was balanced by their zealous and unhesitating devotion to their Emperor and their country. There scarcely existed a Russian, even of the lowest rank, within the influence of bribery; and an officer, like the Prussian commandant of Hamelen, who began to speculate upon retaining his rank in another service, when surrendering the charge intrusted to him by his sovereign, would have been accounted in Russia a prodigy of unexampled villany. In the mode of disciplining their forces, the Russians proceeded on the system most approved in Europe. Their infantry was confessedly excellent, composed of men in the prime of life, and carefully selected as best qualified for military service. Their artillery was of the first description, so far as the men, guns, carriages, and appointments were concerned; but the rank of General of Artillery had not the predominant weight in the Russian army, which ought to be possessed by those particularly dedicated to the direction of that arm, by which, according to Napoleon, modern battles must be usually decided. The direction of their guns was too often intrusted to general officers of the line. The service of cavalry is less natural to the Russians than that of the infantry, but their horse regiments are nevertheless excellently trained, and have uniformly behaved well.

COSSACKS—ACTION OF PULTUSK

But the Cossacks are a species of force belonging to Russia exclusively; and although subsequent events have probably rendered every reader in some degree acquainted with their national character, they make too conspicuous a figure in the history of Napoleon, to be passed over without a brief description here.

The natives on the banks of the Don and the Volga hold their lands by military service, and enjoy certain immunities and prescriptions, in consequence of which each individual is obliged to serve four years in the Russian armies. They are trained from early childhood to the use of the lance and sword, and familiarized to the management of a horse peculiar to the country—far from handsome in appearance, but tractable, hardy, swift, and surefooted, beyond any breed perhaps in the world. At home, and with his family and children, the Cossack is kind, gentle, generous, and simple; but when in arms, and in a foreign country, he resumes the predatory, and sometimes the ferocious habits of his ancestors, the roving Scythians. As the Cossacks receive no pay, plunder is generally their object; and as prisoners were esteemed a useless encumbrance, they granted no quarter, until Alexander promised a ducat for every Frenchman whom they brought in alive. In the actual field of battle, their mode of attack is singular. Instead of acting in line, a body of Cossacks about to charge, disperse at the word of command, very much in the manner of a fan suddenly flung open, and, joining in a loud yell, or *hourra*, rush, each acting individually, upon the object of attack, whether infantry, cavalry, or artillery, to all of which they have been, in this wild way of fighting, formidable assailants. But it is as light cavalry that the Cossacks are perhaps unrivalled. They and their horses have been known to march one hundred miles in twenty-four hours without halting. They plunge into woods, swim rivers, thread passes, cross deep morasses, and penetrate through deserts of snow, without undergoing material loss, or suffering from fatigue. No Russian army, with a large body of Cossacks in front, can be liable to surprise; nor, on the other hand, can an enemy surrounded by them ever be confident against it. In covering the retreat of their own army, their velocity, activity and courage, render pursuit by the enemy's cavalry peculiarly dangerous; and in pursuing a flying enemy, these qualities are still more redoubtable. In the campaign of 1806-7, the Cossacks took the field in great numbers, under their celebrated Hettman, or Attaman, Platow, who, himself a Cossack, knew their peculiar capacity for warfare, and raised their fame to a pitch which it had not attained in former European wars.

The Russians had also in their service Tartar tribes, who in irregularity resembled the Cossacks, but were not to be compared with them in discipline or courage, being, in truth, little better than hordes of roving savages.

It remains only to be mentioned, that at this time the Russian commissariat was very indifferent, and, above all, deficient in funds. The funds of the Imperial treasury were exhausted, and an aid, amounting only to eighty thousand pounds, was obtained from England with difficulty. In consequence of these circumstances, the Russians were repeatedly, during the campaign, obliged to fight at disadvantage for want of provisions.—We return to the progress of the war.

On the 25th of December, the Russian army of Bennigsen, closely concentrated, occupied a position behind Pultusk; their left, commanded by Count Ostermann, resting upon the town, which is situated on the river Narew. A corps occupied the bridge, to prevent any attack from that point. The right, under Barclay de Tolly, was strongly posted in a wood, and the centre was under the orders of General Zachen. A considerable plain extended between the town of Pultusk and the wood, which formed the right of the Russian position. They had stationed a powerful advanced guard, had occupied the plain with their cavalry, and established a strong reserve in their rear. On the 26th, the Russian position was attacked by the French divisions of Lannes and Davoust, together with the French guards. After skirmishing some time in the centre, without making the desired impression, the battle appeared doubtful, when, suddenly assembling a great strength on their own left, the French made a decisive effort to overwhelm the Russians, by turning their right wing. The attack prevailed to a certain extent. The accumulated and superior weight of fire determined Barclay de Tolly to retreat on his reserves, which he did without confusion, while the French seized upon the wood, and took several Russian guns. But Bennigsen, in spite of Kaminskoy's order to retreat, was determined to abide the brunt of battle, and to avail himself of the rugged intrepidity of the troops which he commanded. Ordering Barclay de Tolly to continue his retreat, and thus throwing back his right wing, he enticed the French, confident in victory, to pursue their success, until the Russian cavalry, which had covered the manœuvre, suddenly withdrawing, they found themselves under a murderous and well-directed fire from one hundred and twenty guns, which, extending along the Russian front, played on the French advancing columns with the utmost success. The Russian line at the same time advanced in turn, and, pushing the enemy before them, recovered the ground from which they had been driven. The approach of night ended the combat, which had been both obstinate and bloody. The French lost near eight thousand men, killed and wounded, including General Lannes and five other general officers among the latter. The Russian loss amounted to five thousand. The French retreated after nightfall with such rapidity, that on the next day the Cossacks could not find a rear-guard in the vicinity of Pultusk.[263]

The action of Pultusk raised the reputation of Bennigsen, and the character as well as the spirits of the Russian army; but its moral effect on the soldiers was its only important consequence. Had Bennigsen been joined during the action by the division of Buxhowden or D'Anrep, of whom the former was only eight miles distant, the check might have been converted into a victory, highly influential on the issue of the campaign. But either the orders of

---

[263] Forty-seventh Bulletin of the Grand Army; Jomini, tom. ii., pp. 334, 343; Savary, tom. ii., p. 15.

Kaminskoy, or some misunderstanding, prevented either of these corps from advancing to support the efforts of Bennigsen. It became impossible for him, therefore, notwithstanding the advantages he had obtained, to retain his position at Pultusk, where he must have been surrounded. He accordingly fell back upon Ostrolenka, where he was joined by Prince Galitzin, who had been engaged in action at Golymin upon the day of the battle of Pultusk; had, like Bennigsen, driven back the enemy, and like him had retreated for the purpose of concentrating his forces with those of the grand army. The French evinced a feeling of the unusual and obstinate nature of the contest in which they had been engaged at Pultusk and Golymin. Instead of pressing their operations, they retreated into winter quarters; Napoleon withdrawing his guard as far as Warsaw,[264] while the other divisions were cantoned in the towns to the eastward, but without attempting to realize the prophecies of the bulletins concerning the approaching fate of the Russian army.

The conduct of Kaminskoy began now to evince decided tokens of insanity. He was withdrawn from the supreme command, which, with the general approbation of the soldiers, was conferred upon Bennigsen. This general was not equal in military genius to Suwarrow, but he seems to have been well fitted to command a Russian army. He was active, hardy, and enterprising, and showed none of that peculiarly fatal hesitation, by which officers of other nations opposed to the French generals, and to Buonaparte in particular, seem often to have been affected, as with a sort of moral palsy, which disabled them for the combat at the very moment when it seemed about to commence. On the contrary, Bennigsen finding himself in a supreme command of ninety thousand men, was resolved not to wait for Buonaparte's onset, but determined to anticipate his motions; wisely concluding, that the desire of desisting

---

[264] "The Emperor established himself at Warsaw on the 1st January, 1807. He calculated on remaining there until the return of spring. Our halt was delightful. With the exception of theatres, the city presented all the gaieties of Paris. Twice a-week the Emperor gave a concert; after which a court was held, which led again to numerous meetings in private parties. On these occasions, the personal beauty and graceful manners of the Polish ladies were conspicuous. While time passed away thus agreeably, duty was not neglected. The Emperor made every exertion to revictual and provide for his army."—Savary, tom. ii., p. 17.

from active operations, which the French Emperor had evinced by cantoning his troops in winter quarters, ought to be a signal to the Russians again to take the field.

ACTION OF MOHRUNGEN

The situation of the King of Prussia tended to confirm that determination. This unfortunate monarch—well surely did Frederick William then deserve that epithet—was cooped up in the town of Königsberg, only covered by a small army of a few thousand men, and threatened by the gradual approach of the divisions of Ney and Bernadotte; so that the King's personal safety appeared to be in considerable danger. Graudentz, the key of the Vistula, continued indeed to hold out, but the Prussian garrison was reduced to distress, and the hour of surrender seemed to be approaching. To relieve this important fortress, therefore, and at the same time protect Königsberg, were motives added to the other reasons which determined Bennigsen to resume offensive operations. A severe and doubtful skirmish was fought near Mohrungen,[265] in which the French sustained considerable loss. The Cossacks spread abroad over the country, making numerous prisoners; and the scheme of the Russian general succeeded so well, as to enable the faithful L'Estocq to relieve Graudentz with reinforcements and provisions.

By these daring operations, Buonaparte saw himself forced into a winter campaign, and issued general orders for drawing out his forces, with the purpose of concentrating them at Willenberg, in the rear of the Russians, (then stationed at Mohrungen,) and betwixt them and their own country. He proposed, in short, to force his enemies eastward towards the Vistula, as at Jena he had compelled the Prussians to fight with their rear turned to the Rhine. Bernadotte had orders to engage the attention of Bennigsen upon the right, and detain him in his present situation, or rather, if possible, induce him

---

[265] Fifty-fifth Bulletin of the Grand Army; Savary, tom. ii., p. 25; Jomini, tom. ii., p. 353.

to advance eastward towards Thorn, so as to facilitate the operation he meditated.

The Russian general learned Buonaparte's intention from an intercepted despatch,[266] and changed his purpose of advancing on Ney and Bernadotte. Marches and counter-marches took place, through a country at all times difficult, and now covered with snow. The experience and dexterity of the French secured some advantages; but these were fully counterbalanced by the daily annoyance and loss which they in turn sustained from Platow and his Cossacks. In cases where the French retreated, the Scythian lances were always on their rear; and when the Russians retired in turn, and were pursued by the French, with the same venturous spirit which they had displayed against others, the latter seldom failed to suffer for their presumption. There was found in the spearmen of the Don and Wolga a natural and instinctive turn for military stratagem, ambuscade, and sudden assault, which compelled the French light troops to adopt a caution, very different from their usual habits of audacity.

Bennigsen was aware that it was the interest of Russia to protract the campaign in this manner. He was near his reinforcements, the French were distant from theirs; every loss, therefore, told more in proportion on the enemy, than on his army. On the other hand, the Russian army, impatient of protracted hostilities, became clamorous for battle; for the hardships of their situation were such as to give them every desire to bring the war to a crisis. We have noticed the defects of the Russian Commissariat. They were especially manifest during those campaigns, when the leader was obliged more than once, merely from want of provisions, to peril the fate of the war upon a general battle, which prudence would have induced him to avoid. In those northern latitudes, and in the month of February, the troops had no resource but to prowl

---

[266] "As ill luck would have it, the officer despatched to Bernadotte was a young man of no experience, who proceeded straight towards the place of his destination, without making any inquiries as to what might be on the road. The consequence was, he fell into the hands of some Cossacks, who carried him and his despatch to the Russian general-in-chief. This trifling accident was attended with serious consequences. But for the capture of this officer, the Russian army must inevitably have been destroyed, and peace would have been immediately concluded."—Savary, tom. ii., p. 30.

about, and dig for the hoards of provision concealed by the peasants. This labour, added to their military duty, left them scarcely time to lie down; and when they did so, they had no bed but the snow, no shelter but the wintry heaven, and no covering but their rags.[267] The distresses of the army were so extreme, that it induced General Bennigsen, against his judgment, to give battle at all risks, and for this purpose to concentrate his forces at Preuss-Eylau, which was pitched on as the field on which he proposed to await Buonaparte.

BATTLE OF PREUSS-EYLAU

In marching through Landsberg to occupy the selected ground, the Russian rear-guard was exposed to a serious attack by the French, and was only saved from great loss by the gallantry of Prince Bagration, who redeemed, by sheer dint of fighting, the loss sustained by want of conduct in defiling through the streets of a narrow village, while pursued by an enterprising enemy. The Russian army lost 3000 men. On the 7th February, the same gallant prince, with the Russian rear-guard, gained such decided advantages over the French van as nearly balanced the loss at Landsberg, and gave time for the whole army to march through the town of Preuss-Eylau, and to take up a position behind it. It had been intended to maintain the town itself, and a body of troops had been left for that purpose; but in the confusion attending the movement of so large an army, the orders issued had been misunderstood, and the division designed for this service evacuated the place so soon as the rear-guard had passed through it.

A Russian division was hastily ordered to re-occupy Preuss-Eylau. They found the French already in possession, and, although they dislodged them, were themselves driven out in turn by another division of French, to whom Buonaparte had promised the plunder of the town. A third division of Russians was ordered to advance; for Bennigsen was desirous to protract the contest for the town until the arrival of his heavy artillery, which joined him by a different route. When it came up, he would have discontinued the struggle for

---

[267] Sir Robert Wilson's Sketches of the Campaigns in Poland, in 1806 and 1807, p. 94.—S.

possession of Preuss-Eylau, but it was impossible to control the ardour of the Russian columns, who persevered in advancing with drums beating, rushed into the town, and surprising the French in the act of sacking it, put many of them to the bayonet, even in the acts of license which they were practising. Preuss-Eylau, however, proved no place of shelter. It was protected by no works of any kind; and the French, advancing under cover of the hillocks and broken ground which skirt the village, threw their fire upon the streets, by which the Russians sustained some loss. General Barclay de Tolly was wounded, and his forces again evacuated the town, which was once more and finally occupied by the French. Night fell, and the combat ceased, to be renewed with treble fury on the next day.

The position of the two armies may be easily described. That of Russia occupied a space of uneven ground, about two miles in length and a mile in depth, with the village of Serpallen on their left; in the front of their army lay the town of Preuss-Eylau, situated in a hollow, and in possession of the French. It was watched by a Russian division; which, to protect the Russian centre from being broken by an attack from that quarter, was strongly reinforced, though by doing so the right wing was considerably weakened. This was thought of the less consequence, that L'Estocq, with his division of Prussians, was hourly expected to join the Russians on that point. The French occupied Eylau with their left, while their centre and right lay parallel to the Russians, upon a chain of heights which commanded in a great measure the ground possessed by the enemy. They also expected to be reinforced by the division of Ney, which had not come up, and which was destined to form on the extreme left.

The space betwixt the hostile armies was open and flat, and intersected with frozen lakes. They might trace each other's position by the pale glimmer of the watch-lights upon the snow. The difference of numerical force was considerably to the advantage of the French. Sir Robert Wilson rates them at 90,000 men, opposed to

60,000 only; but the disproportion is probably considerably overrated.[268]

The eventful action commenced with daybreak on the 8th of February. Two strong columns of the French advanced, with the purpose of turning the right, and storming the centre, of the Russians, at one and the same time. But they were driven back in great disorder by the heavy and sustained fire of the Russian artillery. An attack on the Russian left was equally unsuccessful. The Russian infantry stood like stone ramparts—they repulsed the enemy—their cavalry came to their support, pursued the retiring assailants, and took standards and eagles. About mid-day, a heavy storm of snow began to fall, which the wind drove right in the face of the Russians, and which added to the obscurity caused by the smoke of the burning village of Serpallen, that rolled along the line.

Under cover of the darkness, six columns of the French advanced with artillery and cavalry, and were close on the Russian position ere they were opposed. Bennigsen, at the head of his staff, brought up the reserves in person, who, uniting with the first line, bore the French back at the point of the bayonet. Their columns, partly broken, were driven again to their own position, where they rallied with difficulty. A French regiment of cuirassiers, which, during this part of the action, had gained an interval in the Russian army, were charged by the Cossacks, and found their defensive armour no protection against the lance. They were all slain except eighteen.[269]

At the moment when victory appeared to declare for the Russians, it was on the point of being wrested from them. Davoust's division had been manœuvring since the beginning of the action to turn the left, and gain the rear, of the Russian line. They now made their appearance on the field of battle with such sudden effect, that Serpallen was lost, the Russian left wing, and a part of their centre, were thrown into disorder, and forced to retire and change their

---

[268] Jomini, tom. ii., p. 359, states the Russian army to have been 80,000 strong.
[269] "When the French cuirassiers made their desperate charge on the Russian centre, and passed through an interval, the Cossacks bore down on them, speared them, unhorsed them, and in a few moments 530 Cossacks reappeared on the field, equipped with the spoil of the slain."—Sir R. Wilson, p. 27.

front, so as to form almost at right angles with the right, and that part of the centre which retained their original position.

At this crisis, and while the French were gaining ground on the rear of the Russians, L'Estocq, so long expected, appeared in his turn suddenly on the field, and, passing the left of the French, and the right of the Russians, pushed down in three columns to redeem the battle on the Russian centre and rear. The Prussians, under that loyal and gallant leader, regained in this bloody field their ancient military reputation. They never fired till within a few paces of the enemy, and then used the bayonet with readiness and courage. They redeemed the ground which the Russians had lost, and drove back in their turn the troops of Davoust and Bernadotte, who had been lately victorious.

Ney, in the meanwhile, appeared on the field, and occupied Schloditten, a village on the road to Königsberg. As this endangered the communication of the Russians with that town, it was thought necessary to carry it by storm—a gallant resolution, which was successfully executed.[270] This was the last act of the bloody day. It was ten o'clock at night, and the combat was ended.[271]

Fifty thousand men perished in this dreadful battle—the best contested in which Buonaparte had yet engaged, and by far the most unsuccessful. He retired to the heights from which he had advanced in the morning, without having gained one point for which he had struggled, and after having suffered a loss considerably greater than that which he had inflicted on the enemy. But the condition of the Russian army was also extremely calamitous. Their generals held a council of war upon the field of battle, and without dismounting

---

[270] Fifty-eighth Bulletin of the Grand Army; Savary, tom. ii., p. 30; Jomini, tom. ii., p. 357.
[271] "One day, during dinner, the conversation turned on various deeds of arms. The grand marshal said, that what had most struck him in the life of Napoleon happened at Eylau, when, attended only by some officers of his staff, a column of four or five thousand Russians came almost in contact with him. The Emperor was on foot; Berthier instantly ordered up the horses: the Emperor gave him a reproachful look; then sent orders to a battalion of his guard to advance, which was a good way behind, and standing still. As the Russians advanced, he repeated several times, 'What audacity! what audacity!' At the sight of the grenadiers of the guard, the Russians stopped short. It was high time for them to do so, as Bertrand said. The Emperor had never stirred; all who surrounded him had been much alarmed."—Las Cases, tom. i., p. 143.

from their horses. The general sentiment which prevailed among them was, a desire to renew the battle on the next day, at all hazards. Tolstoy undertook to move forward on the French lines—L'Estocq urged the same counsel. They offered to pledge their lives, that, would Bennigsen advance, Napoleon must necessarily retire; and they urged the moral effect which would be produced, not on their army only, but on Germany and on Europe, by such an admission of weakness on the part of him who had never advanced but to victory. But Bennigsen conceived that the circumstances of his army did not permit him to encounter the hazard of being cut off from Königsberg, and endangering the person of the King of Prussia; or that of risking a second general action, with an army diminished by at least 20,000 killed and wounded, short of ammunition, and totally deprived of provisions. The Russians accordingly commenced their retreat on Königsberg that very night. The division of Count Ostermann did not move till the next morning, when it traversed the field in front of Preuss-Eylau, without the slightest interruption from the French, who still occupied the town.[272]

The battle of Preuss-Eylau was claimed as a victory by both parties, though it was very far from being decided in favour of either. Bennigsen had it to boast, that he had repelled the attacks of Buonaparte along the whole of his line, and that the fighting terminated unfavourably to the French. He could also exhibit the unusual spectacle of twelve imperial eagles of France, taken in one action. For many days after the battle, also, the Cossacks continued to scour the country, and bring into Königsberg great numbers of French prisoners. On the other hand, the subsequent retreat of the Russians was interpreted by the French into an acknowledgment of weakness; and they appealed to their own possession of the field of battle, with the dead and wounded, as the usual testimonials of victory.

But there were two remarkable circumstances by which Napoleon virtually acknowledged that he had received an unusual check. On the 13th February, four days after the battle, a message was despatched to the King of Prussia by Buonaparte, proposing an armistice, on grounds far more favourable to the Prince than those

---

[272] Sir Robert Wilson's Sketch of the Campaigns in Poland, p. 29.

Frederick William might have been disposed to accept, or which Buonaparte would have been inclined to grant, after the battle of Jena. It was even intimated, that in case of agreeing to make a separate peace, the Prussian King might obtain from the French Emperor the restoration of his whole dominions. True to his ally the Emperor of Russia, Frederick William, even in the extremity of his distress, refused to accede to any save a general peace. The proposal of an armistice was also peremptorily refused, and the ground on which it was offered was construed to indicate Buonaparte's conscious weakness.

Another decisive proof of the loss which Napoleon had sustained in the battle of Preuss-Eylau, was his inactivity after the battle. For eight days he remained without making any movement, excepting by means of his cavalry, which were generally worsted, and on the 19th February he evacuated the place, and prepared himself to retreat upon the Vistula, instead of driving the Russians, as he had threatened, behind the Pregel. Various actions took place, during his retreat, with different fortunes, but the Russian Cossacks and light troops succeeded in making numbers of prisoners, and collecting much spoil.

DANTZIC

The operations of Napoleon, when he had again retired to the line of the Vistula, intimated caution, and the sense of a difficult task before him. He appeared to feel, that the advance into Poland had been premature, while Dantzic remained in the hands of the Prussians, from whence the most alarming operations might take place in his rear, should he again advance to the Vistula without subduing it. The siege of Dantzic was therefore to be formed without delay. The place was defended by General Kalkreuth to the last extremity. After many unsuccessful attempts to relieve it, Dantzic finally surrendered in the end of May 1807, after trenches had been opened before it for fifty-two days.[273] If the season of the

---

[273] Seventy-seventh Bulletin of the Grand Army; Jomini, tom. ii., p. 396; Savary, tom. ii., p. 48. Dantzic surrendered on the 24th of May, and, four days after, Napoleon conferred on Marshal Lefebvre the title of Duke of Dantzic.

year had admitted, a British expedition to Dantzic might, if ably conducted, have operated in the rear of the Emperor Napoleon the relief of Prussia, and perhaps effected the liberation of Europe.

The utmost care was also taken to supply the loss which Napoleon's armies had sustained in these hard-fought campaigns. He raised the siege of Colberg, drew the greater part of his forces out of Silesia, ordered a new levy in Switzerland, urged the march of bodies of troops from Italy, and, to complete his means, demanded a new conscription of the year 1808, which was instantly complied with by the Senate as a matter of course. At length, as summer approached, the surrender of Dantzic enabled him to unite the besieging division, twenty-five thousand strong, to his main army, and to prepare to resume offensive operations. A large levy of Poles was made at the same time; and they, with other light troops of the French, were employed in making strong reconnoissances, with various fortune, but never without the exchange of hard blows. It became evident to all Europe, that whatever might be the end of this bloody conflict, the French Emperor was contending with a general and troops, against whom it was impossible to gain those overpowering and irresistible advantages, which characterised his campaigns in Italy and Germany. The bulletins, it is true, announced new successes from day to day; but as the geographical advance upon the Polish territory was by no means in proportion to the advantages claimed, it was plain that Napoleon was as often engaged in parrying as in pushing, in repairing losses as in improving victories. The Russian generals composed plans with skill, and executed them with activity and spirit, for cutting off separate divisions, and disturbing the French communications.

The Russian army had received reinforcements; but they were deficient in numerical amount, and only made up their strength, at the utmost, to their original computation of 90,000 men. This proved unpardonable negligence in the Russian Government, considering the ease with which men can there be levied to any extent by the mere will of the Emperor, and the vital importance of the war which they were now waging. It is said, however, that the poverty of the Russian Administration was the cause of this failure to recruit their forces; and that the British being applied to, to negotiate a loan of six millions, and advance one million to account, had declined the transaction, and thereby given great offence to the Emperor Alexander.

Napoleon, so much more remote from his own territories, had already, by exertions unparalleled in the history of Europe, assembled two hundred and eighty thousand men between the Vistula and Memel, including the garrison of Dantzic. With such unequal forces the war recommenced.

The Russians were the assailants, making a combined movement on Ney's division, which was stationed at Gutstadt, and in the vicinity. They pursued him as far as Deppen, where there was some fighting; but upon the 8th of June, Napoleon advanced in person to extricate his marshal, and Bennigsen was obliged to retreat in his turn. He was hardly pressed on the rear by the Grand Army of France. But even in this moment of peril, Platow, with his Cossacks, made a charge, or, in their phrase, a hourra, upon the French, with such success, that they not only dispersed the skirmishers of the French vanguard, and the advanced troops destined to support them, but compelled the infantry to form squares, endangered the personal safety of Napoleon, and occupied the attention of the whole French cavalry, who bore down on them at full speed. Musketry and artillery were all turned on them at once, but to little or no purpose; for, having once gained the purpose of checking the advance, which was all they aimed at, the cloud of Cossacks dispersed over the field, like mist before the sun, and united behind the battalions whom their demonstration had protected.

By this means Platow and his followers had got before the retreating division of the Russian army under Bagration, which they were expected to support, and had reached first a bridge over the Aller. The Cossacks were alarmed by the immense display of force demonstrated against them, and showed a disposition to throw themselves confusedly on the bridge, which must certainly have been attended with the most disastrous consequences to the rear-guard, who would thus have been impeded in their retreat by the very troops appointed to support them. The courage and devotion of Platow prevented that great misfortune. He threw himself from his horse. "Let the Cossack that is base enough," he exclaimed, "desert his Hettman!" The children of the wilderness halted around him, and he disposed them in perfect order to protect the retreat of Bagration and the rear-guard, and afterwards achieved his own retreat with trifling loss.[274]

ACTION OF HEILSBERG

The Russian army fell back upon Heilsberg, and there concentrating their forces made a most desperate stand. A very hard-fought action [10th June] here took place. The Russians, overpowered by superior numbers, and forced from the level ground, continued to defend with fury their position on the heights, which the French made equally strenuous efforts to carry by assault. The combat was repeatedly renewed, with cavalry, infantry, and artillery, but without the fiery valour of the assailants making any effectual impression on the iron ranks of the Russians.[275] The battle continued, till the approach of midnight, upon terms of equality; and when the morning dawned, the space of ground between the position of the Russians and that of the French, was not merely strewed, but literally sheeted over, with the bodies of the dead and wounded.[276] The Russians retired unmolested after the battle of Heilsberg, and crossing the river Aller, placed that barrier betwixt them and the army of Buonaparte, which, though it had suffered great losses, had, in consequence of the superiority of numbers, been less affected by them than the Russian forces. In the condition of Bennigsen's army, it was his obvious policy to protract the war, especially as reinforcements, to the number of thirty thousand men, were approaching the frontier from the interior of the empire. It was probably with this view that he kept his army on the right bank of the Aller, with the exception of a few bodies of cavalry, for the sake of observation and intelligence.

---

[274] Sir Robert Wilson's Campaigns in Poland, p. 30.
[275] Seventy-eighth Bulletin of the Grand Army; Jomini, tom. ii., p. 408; Savary, tom. ii., p. 52.
[276] "Next day, June 11, the Russians stopped all day in front of Heilsberg: both parties removed their wounded; and we had as many as though we had fought a great battle. The Emperor was very dissatisfied."—Savary, tom. ii., p. 53.

On the 13th, the Russian army reached Friedland, a considerable town on the west side of the Aller, communicating with the eastern, or right bank of the river, by a long wooden bridge. It was the object of Napoleon to induce the Russian general to pass by this narrow bridge to the left bank, and then to decoy him into a general action, in a position where the difficulty of defiling through the town, and over the bridge, must render retreat almost impossible. For this purpose he showed such a proportion only of his forces, as induced General Bennigsen to believe that the French troops on the western side of the Aller consisted only of Oudinot's division, which had been severely handled in the battle of Heilsberg, and which he now hoped altogether to destroy. Under this deception he ordered a Russian division to pass the bridge, defile through the town, and march to the assault. The French took care to offer no such resistance as should intimate their real strength. Bennigsen was thus led to reinforce this division with another—the battle thickened, and the Russian general at length transported all his army, one division excepted, to the left bank of the Aller, by means of the wooden bridge and three pontoons, and arrayed them in front of the town of Friedland, to overpower, as he supposed, the crippled division of the French, to which alone he believed himself opposed.[277]

BATTLE OF FRIEDLAND

But no sooner had he taken this irretrievable step than the mask was dropped. The French skirmishers advanced in force; heavy columns of infantry began to show themselves; batteries of cannon were got into position; and all circumstances concurred, with the report of prisoners, to assure Bennigsen, that he, with his enfeebled forces, was in presence of the grand French army. His position, a sort of plain, surrounded by woods and broken ground,

---

[277] "The Emperor ordered me to advance alone, along the wood on our right, to seek a point whence the bridge of Friedland was visible; and after observing whether the Russians were crossing over to our bank or recrossing to the right, I returned to inform him, that the Russians, instead of retiring, were all crossing to our bank of the river, and that their masses were sensibly augmenting. 'Well,' said the Emperor, 'I am ready now. I have an hour's advantage of them, and will give them battle since they wish it: this is the anniversary of Marengo, and to-day fortune is with me.'"—Savary, tom. ii., p. 56.

was difficult to defend; with the town and a large river in his rear, it was dangerous to attempt a retreat, and to advance was prevented by the inequality of his force. Bennigsen now became anxious to maintain his communication with Wehlau, a town on the Pregel, which was the original point of retreat, and where he hoped to join with the Prussians under General L'Estocq. If the enemy should seize the bridge at Allerberg, some miles lower down the Aller than Friedland, this plan would become impossible, and he found himself therefore obliged to diminish his forces, by detaching six thousand men to defend that point. With the remainder of his force he resolved to maintain his present position till night.

The French advanced to the attack about ten o'clock. The broken and wooded country which they occupied, enabled them to maintain and renew their efforts at pleasure, while the Russians, in their exposed situation, could not make the slightest movement without being observed. Yet they fought with such obstinate valour, that at noon the French seemed sickening of the contest, and about to retire. But this was only a feint, to repose such of their forces as had been engaged, and to bring up reinforcements. The cannonade continued till about half past four, when Buonaparte brought up his full force in person, for the purpose of one of those desperate and generally irresistible efforts to which he was wont to trust the decision of a doubtful day. Columns of enormous power, and extensive depth, appeared partially visible among the interstices of the wooded country, and, seen from the town of Friedland, the hapless Russian army looked as if surrounded by a deep semicircle of glittering steel. The attack upon all the line, with cavalry, infantry, and artillery, was general and simultaneous, the French advancing with shouts of assured victory; while the Russians, weakened by the loss of at least twelve thousand killed and wounded, were obliged to attempt that most dispiriting and dangerous of movements—a retreat through encumbered defiles, in front of a superior enemy. The principal attack was on the left wing, where the Russian position was at length forced. The troops which composed it streamed into the town, and crowded the bridge and pontoons; the enemy thundered on their rear, and without the valour of Alexander's Imperial Guard, the Russians would have been utterly destroyed. These brave soldiers charged with the bayonet the corps of Ney, who led the French vanguard, disordered his column, and, though they were overpowered by numbers, prevented the total ruin of the left wing.

Meanwhile, the bridge and pontoons were set on fire, to prevent the French, who had forced their way into the town, from taking possession of them. The smoke rolling over the combatants, increased the horror and confusion of the scene; yet a considerable part of the Russian infantry escaped through a ford close by the town, which was discovered in the moment of defeat. The Russian centre and right, who remained on the west bank of the Aller, effected a retreat by a circuitous route, leaving on the right the town of Friedland, with its burning bridges, no longer practicable for friend or foe, and passing the Aller by a ford considerably farther down the river. This also was found out in the very moment of extremity—was deep and dangerous, took the infantry up to the breast, and destroyed what ammunition was left in the tumbrils.

Thus were the Russians once more united on the right bank of the Aller, and enabled to prosecute their march towards Wehlau. Amid the calamities of defeat, they had saved all their cannon except seventeen, and preserved their baggage. Indeed, the stubborn character of their defence seems to have paralysed the energies of the victor, who, after carrying the Russian position, showed little of that activity in improving his success, which usually characterised him upon such occasions. He pushed no troops over the Aller in pursuit of the retreating enemy, but suffered Bennigsen to rally his broken troops without interruption. Neither, when in possession of Friedland, did he detach any force down the left bank, to act upon the flank of the Russian centre and right, and cut them off from the river. In short, the battle of Friedland, according to the expression of a French general, was a battle gained, but a victory lost.[278]

Yet the most important consequences resulted from the action, though the French success had been but partially improved. Königsberg,[279] which had been so long the refuge of the King of Prussia, was evacuated by his forces, as it became plain his Russian

---

[278] Seventy-ninth Bulletin of the Grand Army; Savary, tom. ii., p. 56; Jomini, tom. ii., p. 411.
[279] Eightieth Bulletin of the Grand Army.

auxiliaries could no longer maintain the war in Poland.[280] Bennigsen retreated to Tilsit, towards the Russian frontiers. But the moral consequences of the defeat were of far greater consequence than could have been either the capture of guns and prisoners, or the acquisition of territory. It had the effect, evidently desired by Napoleon, of disposing the Emperor Alexander to peace. The former could not but feel that he was engaged with a more obstinate enemy in Russia, than any he had yet encountered. After so many bloody battles, he was scarce arrived on the frontiers of an immense empire, boundless in its extent, and almost inexhaustible in resources; while the French, after suffering extremely in defeating an army that was merely auxiliary, could scarce be supposed capable of undertaking a scheme of invasion so gigantic, as that of plunging into the vast regions of Muscovy.

Such an enterprise would have been peculiarly hazardous in the situation in which the French Emperor now stood. The English expedition to the Baltic was daily expected. Gustavus was in Swedish Pomerania, at the head of a considerable army which had raised the siege of Stralsund. A spirit of resistance was awakening in Prussia, where the resolute conduct of Blucher had admirers and imitators, and the nation seemed to be reviving from the consternation inflicted by the defeat of Jena. The celebrated Schill, a partisan of great courage and address, had gained many advantages, and was not unlikely, in a nation bred to arms, to acquire the command of a numerous body of men. Hesse, Hanover, Brunswick, and the other provinces of Germany, deprived of their ancient princes, and subjected to heavy exactions by the conquerors, were ripe for insurrection. All these dangers were of a nature from which little could be apprehended, while the Grand Army was at a moderate distance; but were it to advance into Russia, especially

---

[280] Three days after the battle, the unfortunate Queen of Prussia wrote thus to her father, the elector of Baden:—"By the unfortunate battle of Friedland, Königsberg fell into the hands of the French. We are closely pressed by the enemy, and if the danger should become in any degree more imminent, I shall be compelled to leave Memel with my children. I shall go to Riga, should the aspect of affairs become more alarming. God will give me the power to survive the moment when I shall cross the borders: all my firmness will then be required, but I look to Heaven for support, from whence comes all good and evil; and it is my firm belief, that no more is imposed upon us than we are able to bear."

were it to meet with a check there, these sparks of fire, left in the rear, might be expected to kindle a dreadful conflagration.

Moved by such considerations, Napoleon had fully kept open the door for reconciliation betwixt the Czar and himself, abstaining from all those personal reflections against him, which he usually showered upon those who thwarted his projects, and intimating more than once, by different modes of communication, that a peace, which should enable Russia and France to divide the world betwixt them, should be placed within Alexander's reach so soon as he was disposed to accept it.

ARMISTICE

The time was now arrived when the Emperor of Russia was disposed to listen to terms of accommodation with France. He had been for some time dissatisfied with his allies. Against Frederick William, indeed, nothing could be objected, save his bad fortune; but what is it that so soon deprives us of our friends as a constant train of bad luck, rendering us always a burden more than an aid to them? The King of Sweden was a feeble ally at best, and had become so unpopular with his subjects, that his dethronement was anticipated; and it was probably remembered, that the Swedish province of Finland extended so near to St. Petersburgh, as to be a desirable acquisition, which, in the course of a treaty with Buonaparte, might be easily attained.

The principal ally of the Czar had been Britain. But he was displeased, as we have already noticed, with the economy of the English Cabinet, who had declined, in his instance, the loans and subsidies, of which they used to be liberal to allies of far less importance. A subsidy of about eighty thousand pounds, was all which he had been able to extract from them. England had, indeed, sent an army into the north to join the Swedes, in forming the siege of Stralsund; but this was too distant an operation to produce any effect upon the Polish campaign. Alexander was also affected by the extreme sufferings of his subjects. His army had been to him, as to most young sovereigns, a particular object of attention; and he was justly proud of his noble regiments of Guards, which, maltreated as they had been in the desperate actions of which we have given some account, remained scarce the shadow of themselves, in numbers and appearance. His fame, moreover, suffered little in withdrawing from a contest in which he was engaged as an auxiliary only; and Alexander was no doubt made to comprehend, that he might do more in behalf of the King of Prussia, his ally, by negotiation, than by continuation of the war. The influence of Napoleon's name, and the extraordinary splendour of his talents and his exploits, must also have had an effect upon the youthful imagination of the Russian Emperor. He might be allowed to feel pride (high as his own situation was) that the Destined Victor, who had subdued so many princes, was willing to acknowledge an equality in his case; and he might not yet be so much aware of the nature of ambition, as to know that it holds the world as inadequate to maintain two co-ordinate sovereigns.

The Russian Emperor's wish of an armistice was first hinted at by Bennigsen, on the 21st of June, was ratified on the 23d of the same month, and was soon afterwards followed, not only by peace with Russia and Prussia, on a basis which seemed to preclude the possibility of future misunderstanding, but by the formation of a personal intimacy and friendship between Napoleon and the only sovereign in Europe, who had the power necessary to treat with him on an equal footing.

The negotiation for this important pacification was not conducted in the usual style of diplomacy, but in that which Napoleon had repeatedly shown a desire to substitute for the conferences of inferior agents, by the intervention, namely, of the high-contracting parties in person.

The armistice was no sooner agreed upon, than preparations were made for a personal interview betwixt the two Emperors.[281] It

---

[281] "I saw in the hands of M. de Talleyrand, who had just arrived at Königsberg, the letter in which the Emperor directed him to come to Tilsit, and which contained this observation, 'If peace be not concluded in a fortnight, I cross the Niemen.' At the same time, I received orders to prepare the bridge-equipage. I mentioned this circumstance to M. de Talleyrand. 'Do not hurry yourself,' replied he: 'where is the utility of going beyond the Niemen? What are we to find beyond that river? the Emperor must renounce his views

took place upon a raft prepared for the purpose, and moored in the midst of the river Niemen, which bore an immense tent or pavilion. At half-past nine, 25th June, 1807, the two Emperors, in the midst of thousands of spectators, embarked at the same moment from the opposite banks of the river. Buonaparte was attended by Murat, Berthier, Bessières, Duroc, and Caulaincourt; Alexander, by his brother the Archduke Constantine, Generals Bennigsen and Ouwarrow, with the Count de Lieven, one of his aides-de-camp. Arriving on the raft, they disembarked and embraced, amid the shouts and acclamations of both armies, and entering the pavilion which had been prepared, held a private conference of two hours. Their officers, who remained at a distance during the interview, were then reciprocally introduced, and the fullest good understanding seemed to be established between the sovereigns, who had at their disposal so great a portion of the universe.[282] It is not to be doubted, that on this momentous occasion Napoleon exerted all those personal powers of attraction, which, exercised on the part of one otherwise so distinguished, rarely failed to acquire the good-will of all with whom he had intercourse, when he was disposed to employ them.[283] He possessed also, in an eminent degree, the sort of eloquence which can make the worse appear the better reason, and which, turning into ridicule the arguments derived from general principles of morality or honesty, which he was accustomed to term idiosyncrasy, makes all reasoning rest upon existing circumstances. Thus, all the maxims of truth and honour might be plausibly parried by those arising out of immediate convenience; and the direct interest, or what seemed the direct interest, of the party whom he wished to gain over, was put in immediate opposition to the dictates of moral sentiment, and of princely virtue. In this manner he might

---

respecting Poland: that country is good for nothing: we can only organize disorder there: we have now a favourable opportunity of making an end of this business, and we must not let it escape.' At first I was at a loss to comprehend all this; and it was not until our diplomatist unfolded his projects with respect to *Spain*, that I understood the hints he had thrown out."—Savary, tom. ii., p. 74.

[282] Eighty-sixth Bulletin of the Grand Army; Savary, tom. ii., p. 75; Jomini, tom. ii., p. 423.

[283] The impression which Buonaparte's presence and conversation, aided by the preconceived ideas of his talents, made on all who approached his person, was of the most striking kind. The captain of a British man-of-war, who was present at his occupying the island of Elba, disturbed on that occasion the solemnity and gravity of a levee, at which several British functionaries attended, by bearing a homely, but certainly a striking testimony to his powers of attraction, while he exclaimed, that "Boney was a d—d good fellow, after all!"—S.

plausibly represent, in many points, that the weal of Alexander's empire might require him to strain some of the maxims of truth and justice, and to do a little wrong in order to attain a great national advantage.

The town of Tilsit was now declared neutral. Entertainments of every kind followed each other in close succession, and the French and Russian, nay, even the Prussian officers, seemed so delighted with each other's society, that it was difficult to conceive that men, so courteous and amiable, had been for so many months drenching trampled snows and muddy wastes with each other's blood. The two Emperors were constantly together in public and in private, and on those occasions their intimacy approached to the character of that of two young men of rank, who are comrades in sport or frolic, as well as accustomed to be associates in affairs, and upon occasions, of graver moment. They are well known to have had private and confidential meetings, where gaiety and even gallantry seemed to be the sole purpose, but where politics were not entirely forgotten.[284]

THE KING OF PRUSSIA AT TILSIT

Upon the more public occasions, there were guests at the imperial festivities, for which they contained small mirth. On the 28th, the unfortunate King of Prussia arrived at Tilsit, and was presented to his formidable victor. Buonaparte did not admit him to the footing of equality on which he treated the Emperor Alexander, and made an early intimation, that it would only be for the purpose of obliging his brother of the North, that he might consent to relax his grasp on the Prussian territories. Those in the King's own possession were reduced to the petty territory of Memel, with the fortresses of Colberg and Graudentz. It was soon plain, that the terms on which he was to be restored to a part of his dominions, would deprive Prussia of almost all the accessions which had been made since 1773, under the system and by the talents of the Great Frederick, and reduce her at once from a first-rate power in Europe to one of the second class.

---

[284] Las Cases, tom. iv., p. 218.

The beautiful and unfortunate Queen, whose high spirit had hastened the war, was anxious, if possible, to interfere with such weight as female intercession might use to diminish the calamities of the peace. It was but on the first day of the foregoing April, that when meeting the Emperor Alexander at Königsberg, and feeling the full difference betwixt that interview and those at Berlin which preceded the war, Alexander and Frederick William had remained locked for a time in each other's arms; the former shedding tears of compassion, the latter of grief. On the same occasion, the Queen, as she saluted the Emperor, could only utter amidst her tears the words, "Dear cousin!" intimating at once the depth of their distress, and their affectionate confidence in the magnanimity of their ally. This scene was melancholy, but that which succeeded it at Tilsit was more so, for it was embittered by degradation. The Queen, who arrived at the place of treaty some days after her husband, was now not only to support the presence of Napoleon, in whose official prints she was personally abused, and who was the author of all the misfortunes which had befallen her country; but if she would in any degree repair these misfortunes, it could only be by exciting his compassion, and propitiating his favour. "Forgive us," she said, "this fatal war—the memory of the Great Frederick deceived us—we thought ourselves his equals because we are his descendants—alas, we have not proved such!" With a zeal for the welfare of Prussia, which must have cost her own feelings exquisite pain, she used towards Napoleon those arts of insinuation, by which women possessed of high rank, great beauty, wit, and grace, frequently exercise an important influence. Desirous to pay his court, Napoleon on one occasion offered her a rose of uncommon beauty. The Queen at first seemed to decline receiving the courtesy—then accepted it, adding the stipulation—"At least with Magdeburg."[285] Buonaparte, as he boasted to Josephine, was proof against these lady-like artifices, as wax-cloth is against rain. "Your Majesty will be

---

[285] "The Queen often called to her recollection that part of English history which states that Mary, the daughter of Henry VIII., after the taking of Calais, which had so long been an appanage to the English crown, and which had often been attempted in vain by the Duke of Guise, during her reign, and its subsequent cession to France,—was accustomed to say, 'That if her heart could be opened, the name of Calais would be found traced there in letters of blood.' The same might be said of the Queen of Prussia in regard to Magdeburg."—Mad. de Berg.

pleased to remember," he said, "that it is I who offer, and that your Majesty has only the task of accepting."[286]

It was discourteous to remind the unfortunate princess how absolutely she was at the mercy of the victor, and unchivalrous to dispute that a lady, accepting a courtesy, has a right to conceive herself as conferring an obligation, and is therefore entitled to annex a condition. But it is true, on the other hand, as Napoleon himself urged, that it would have been playing the gallant at a high price, if he had exchanged towns and provinces in return for civilities. It is not believed that the Queen of Prussia succeeded, to any extent, in obtaining a modification of the terms to which her husband was subjected; and it is certain, that she felt so deeply the distress into which her country was plunged, that her sense of it brought her to an untimely grave. The death of this interesting and beautiful Queen,[287] not only powerfully affected the mind of her husband and family, but the Prussian nation at large; who, regarding her as having died a victim to her patriotic sorrow for the national misfortunes, recorded her fate as one of the many injuries for which they were to call France and Napoleon to a severe accompting.

TREATY OF TILSIT

The terms imposed on Prussia by the treaty of Tilsit,[288] were briefly these:—

That portion of Poland acquired by Prussia in the partition of 1772, was disunited from that kingdom, and erected into a separate territory, to be called the Grand Duchy of Warsaw. It was to be held by the King of Saxony, under the character of Grand Duke; and it

---

[286] Las Cases, tom. iv., p. 213.
[287] The Queen of Prussia died on the 19th July, 1810. The following letter was written by her a few days after the signing of the treaty of Tilsit:—"Peace is concluded; but at how painful a price! Our frontiers will not henceforth extend beyond the Elbe: the King, however, after all, has proved himself a greater man than his adversary. He has been compelled by necessity to negotiate with his enemy, but no alliance has taken place between them. This will one day or other bring a blessing upon Prussia. Again, I say, the King's just dealing will bring good fortune to Prussia; this is my firm belief."
[288] For a copy of the Treaty of Tilsit, see Annual Register, vol. xlix., p. 720.

was stipulated that he was to have direct communication with this new acquisition by means of a military road across Silesia, a privilege likely to occasion constant jealousy betwixt the courts of Berlin and Warsaw. Thus ended the hope of the Poles to be restored to the condition of an independent nation. They merely exchanged the dominion of one German master for another—Prussia for Saxony, Frederick William for Augustus—the only difference being, that the latter was descended from the ancient Kings of Poland. They were, however, subjected to a milder and more easy yoke than that which they had hitherto borne; nor does it appear that the King (as he had been created) of Saxony derived any real addition of authority and consequence from the Grand Duchy of Warsaw. It seems, indeed, probable, that the erection of this sovereignty was the effect of a composition between the Emperors; Napoleon, on the one hand, renouncing all attempts at the liberation of Poland, which he could not have persevered in without continuing the war with Russia, and perhaps with Austria also; and Alexander consenting that Prussia should be deprived of her Polish dominions, under the stipulation that they were to be transferred to Saxony, from whose vicinity his empire could apprehend little danger.

The constitution arranged for the Grand Duchy, also, was such as was not liable to lead to disturbances among those provinces of Poland which were united with Austria and Russia. Slavery was abolished, and the equality of legal rights among all ranks of citizens was acknowledged. The Grand Duke held the executive power. A Senate, or Upper House, of eighteen members, and a Lower House of nuncios, or deputies, amounting to a hundred, passed into laws, or rejected at their pleasure, such propositions as the Duke laid before them. But the Diets, the Pospolite, the *Liberum Veto*, and all the other turbulent privileges of the Polish nobles, continued abolished, as they had been under the Prussian government.

Buonaparte made it his boast that he had returned the Prussian territories, not to the House of Brandenburgh, but to Alexander; so that if Frederick William yet reigned, it was only, he said, by the friendship of Alexander,—"a term," he added, "which he himself did not recognise in the vocabulary of sovereigns, under the head of state affairs." Alexander, however, was not altogether so disinterested as Buonaparte, with something like a sneer, thus seemed to insinuate. There was excepted from the Grand Duchy of Warsaw, and added to the territory of Russia at the expense of Prussia, the province of Bialystock, serving materially to improve the frontier of the empire. Thus the Czar, in some degree, profited by the distress of his ally. The apology for his conduct must rest, first, on the strength of the temptation to stretch his empire towards the Vistula, as a great natural boundary; secondly, on the plea, that if he had declined the acquisition from a point of delicacy, Saxony, not Prussia would have profited by his self-denial, as the territory of Bialystock would, in that event, have gone to augment the Duchy of Warsaw. Russia ceded the lordship of Jever to Holland, as an ostensible compensation for her new acquisition.[289]

Dantzic, with a certain surrounding territory, was, by the treaty of Tilsit, recognised as a free city, under the protection of Prussia and Saxony. There can be little doubt, that the farther provision, that France should occupy the town until the conclusion of a maritime peace, was intended to secure, for the use of Napoleon, a place of arms, so important in case of a new breach betwixt him and Russia.

It followed, as a matter of course, that the Emperor Alexander and the King of Prussia ratified all the changes which Napoleon had wrought on Europe, acknowledged the thrones which he had erected, and recognised the leagues which he had formed. On the other hand, out of deference to the Emperor, Buonaparte consented that the Dukes of Saxe-Coburg, Oldenburg, and Mecklenburg-Schwerin, German princes connected with Alexander, should remain in possession of their territories; the French, however, continuing to occupy the seaports of the two countries last named, until a final peace betwixt France and England.

While these important negotiations were proceeding, a radical change took place in the councils of the British nation; what was called the Fox and Grenville administration being dissolved, and

---

[289] "This does not appear to me to be correct: according to the terms of the treaty, this country was ceded personally to me, and my first act was to unite it to Holland. I establish this fact merely for the sake of truth."—Louis Buonaparte, p. 53.

their place supplied by one formed under the auspices of the Duke of Portland, and comprehending Lords Liverpool, Castlereagh, Mr. Canning, and other statesmen, professing the principles of the late William Pitt. It was an anxious object with the new cabinet to reconcile the Czar to the alliance of England, and atone for the neglect with which he considered himself as having been treated by their predecessors. With this purpose, Lord Leveson Gower[290] was despatched with power to make such offers of conciliation as might maintain or renew an amicable intercourse between Britain and Russia. But the Emperor Alexander had taken his part, at least for the present; and, being predetermined to embrace the course recommended by his new ally Buonaparte, he avoided giving audience to the British ambassador, and took his measures at Tilsit, without listening to the offers of accommodation which Lord Gower was empowered to propose.

By the treaty of Tilsit, so far as made public, Russia offered her mediation betwixt Britain and France, on condition that the first named kingdom should accept the proffer of her interference within a month. So far, therefore, the Czar appeared to a certain extent careful of the interest of his late ally. But it is now perfectly well understood, that among other private articles of this memorable treaty, there existed one by which the Emperor bound himself, in case of Britain's rejecting the proposed mediation, to recognise and enforce what Buonaparte called the Continental System, by shutting his ports against British vessels, and engaging the Northern Courts in a new coalition, having for its object the destruction of English maritime superiority. In a word, the armed Northern Neutrality, originally formed under the auspices of Catherine, and in an evil hour adopted by the unfortunate Paul, was again to be established under the authority of Alexander. Denmark, smarting under the recollections of the battle of Copenhagen, only waited, it was thought, the signal to join such a coalition, and would willingly consent to lend her still powerful navy to its support; and Sweden was in too weak and distracted a state to resist the united will of France and Russia, either regarding war with Britain, or any other stipulations which it might be intended to impose upon her. But as there is no country of Europe to which the commerce of England is

---

[290] Now Earl Granville.

so beneficial as Russia, whose gross produce she purchases almost exclusively, it was necessary to observe strict secrecy upon these further objects. The ostensible proposal of mediation was therefore resorted to, less in the hope, perhaps, of establishing peace betwixt France and England, than in the expectation of affording a pretext, which might justify in the eye of the Russian nation a rupture with the latter power. But in spite of every precaution which could be adopted, the address of the British ambassador obtained possession of the secret which France and Russia deemed it so important to conceal; and Lord Gower was able to transmit to his court an exact account of this secret article, and particularly of the two Emperors having resolved to employ the Danish fleet in the destruction of the maritime rights of Britain, which had been so lately put upon a footing, that, to Alexander at least, had, till his recent fraternization with Buonaparte, seemed entirely satisfactory.

There were, no doubt, other secret articles named in the treaty of Tilsit, by which it seems to have been the object of these two great Emperors, as they loved to term themselves, of the North and of the South, to divide the civilized world between them.[291] It may be regarded as certain, that Buonaparte opened to Alexander the course of unprincipled policy which he intended to pursue respecting the kingdom of Spain, and procured his acquiescence in that daring usurpation. And it has been affirmed, that he also stipulated for the aid of Russia to take Gibraltar, to recover Malta and Egypt, and to banish the British flag from the Mediterranean. All these enterprises were more or less directly calculated to the depression, or rather the destruction of Great Britain, the only formidable enemy who still maintained the strife against France, and so far the promised co-operation of Russia must have been in the highest degree grateful to Napoleon. But Alexander, however much he might be Buonaparte's personal admirer, did not follow his father's simplicity in becoming his absolute dupe, but took care, in return for his compliance with the distant, and in some degree visionary projects of Buonaparte's ambition, to exact his

---

[291] "In the secret treaty, Alexander and Napoleon shared between them the continental world: all the south was abandoned to Napoleon, already master of Italy and arbiter of Germany, pushing his advanced post as far as the Vistula, and making Dantzic one of the most formidable arsenals."—Fouché, tom. i., p. 310.

countenance and co-operation in gaining certain acquisitions of the highest importance to Russia, and which were found at a future period to have added powerfully to her means of defence, when she once more matched her strength with that of France. To explain this, we must look back to the ancient policy of France and of Europe, when, by supporting the weaker states, and maintaining their dependence, it was the object to prevent the growth of any gigantic and over-bearing power, who might derange the balance of the civilized world.

The growing strength of Russia used in former times to be the natural subject of jealousy to the French Government, and they endeavoured to counterbalance these apprehensions by extending the protection of France to the two weaker neighbours of Russia, the Porte and the kingdom of Sweden, with which powers it had always been the policy of France to connect herself, and which connexion was not only honourable to that kingdom, but useful to Europe. But, at the treaty of Tilsit, and in Buonaparte's subsequent conduct relating to these powers, he lost sight of this national policy, or rather sacrificed it to his own personal objects.

One of the most important private articles of the treaty of Tilsit seems to have provided, that Sweden should be despoiled of her provinces of Finland in favour of the Czar, and be thus, with the consent of Buonaparte, deprived of all effectual means of annoying Russia. A single glance at the map will show how completely the possession of Finland put a Swedish army, or the army of France as an ally of Sweden, within a short march of St. Petersburgh; and how, by consenting to Sweden's being stripped of that important province, Napoleon relinquished the grand advantage to be derived from it, in case of his ever being again obliged to contend with Russia upon Russian ground. Yet there can be no doubt, that at the treaty of Tilsit he became privy to the war which Russia shortly after waged against Sweden, in which Alexander deprived that ancient kingdom of her frontier province of Finland, and thereby obtained a covering territory of the last and most important consequence to his own capital.

The Porte was no less made a sacrifice to the inordinate anxiety, which, at the treaty of Tilsit, Buonaparte seems to have entertained, for acquiring at any price the accession of Russia to his extravagant desire of destroying England. By the public treaty, indeed, some care seems to have been taken of the interests of Turkey, since it provides that Turkey was to have the benefit of peace under the mediation of France, and that Russia was to evacuate Moldavia and Wallachia, for the acquisition of which she was then waging an unprovoked war. But by the secret agreement of the two Emperors, it was unquestionably understood, that Turkey in Europe was to be placed at the mercy of Alexander, as forming naturally a part of the Russian Empire, as Spain, Portugal, and perhaps Great Britain, were, from local position, destined to become provinces of France. At the subsequent Congress betwixt the Emperors at Erfurt, their measures against the Porte were more fully adjusted.

It may seem strange, that the shrewd and jealous Napoleon should have suffered himself to be so much over-reached in his treaty with Alexander, since the benefits stipulated for France, in the treaty of Tilsit, were in a great measure vague, and subjects of hope rather than certainty. The British naval force was not easily to be subdued—Gibraltar and Malta are as strong fortresses as the world can exhibit—the conquest of Spain was at least a doubtful undertaking, if the last war of the Succession was carefully considered. But the Russian objects were nearer, and were within her grasp. Finland was seized on with little difficulty, nor did the conquest even of Constantinople possess any thing very difficult to a Russian army, if unopposed save by the undisciplined forces of the Turkish empire. Thus it is evident, that Napoleon exchanged, for distant and contingent prospects, his acquiescence in the Russian objects, which were near, essential, and, in comparison, of easy attainment. The effect of this policy we shall afterwards advert to. Meanwhile, the two most ancient allies of France, and who were of the greatest political importance to her in case of a second war with Russia, were most unwisely abandoned to the mercy of that power, who failed not to despoil Sweden of Finland, and, but for intervening causes, would probably have seized upon Constantinople with the same ease.

If the reader should wonder how Buonaparte, able and astucious as he was, came to be overreached in the treaty of Tilsit, we believe the secret may be found in a piece of private history. Even at that early period Napoleon nourished the idea of fixing, as he supposed, the fate of his own family, or dynasty, by connecting it by marriage with the blood of one of the established monarchies of Europe. He had hopes, even then, that he might obtain the hand of one of the Archduchesses of Russia, nor did the Emperor throw any obstacle in the way of the scheme. It is well known that his suit was afterwards disappointed by the Empress Mother, who pleaded the difference of religion; but at the time of the treaty of Tilsit, Napoleon was actually encouraged, or deceived himself into an idea that he received encouragement, to form a perpetual family connexion with Russia.[292] This induced him to deal easily with Alexander in the matters which they had to discuss together, and to act the generous, almost the prodigal friend. And this also seems to have been the reason why Napoleon frequently complained of Alexander's insincerity, and often termed him *The Greek,* according to the Italian sense of the name, which signifies a trickster or deceiver.

But we must return from the secret articles of the Tilsit treaty, which opened such long vistas in futurity, to the indisputable and direct consequences of that remarkable measure.

The treaty betwixt Russia and France was signed upon the 7th—that betwixt France and Prussia on the 9th July.[293] Frederick William published upon the 24th of the same month one of the most dignified, and at the same time the most affecting proclamations, that ever expressed the grief of an unfortunate sovereign.

"Dear inhabitants of faithful provinces, districts, and towns," said this most interesting document, "my arms have been

---

[292] "It was perhaps a misfortune to me that I had not married a sister of the Emperor Alexander, as proposed to me by Alexander himself at Erfurth. But there were inconveniences in that union arising from her religion. I did not like to allow a Russian priest to be the confessor of my wife, as I considered that he would have been a spy in the Tuileries for Alexander."—Napoleon, *Voice,* &c., vol. ii., p. 150.

[293] See the treaty between Prussia and France, Annual Register, vol. xlix., p. 714.

unfortunate. The efforts of the relics of my army have been of no avail. Driven to the extreme boundaries of my empire, and having seen my powerful ally conclude an armistice, and sign a peace, no choice remained for me save to follow his example. That peace was necessarily purchased upon terms corresponding to imperious circumstances. It has imposed on me, and on my house—it has imposed upon the whole country, the most painful sacrifices. The bonds of treaties, the reciprocalities of love and duty, the work of ages, have been broken asunder. My efforts have proved in vain. Fate ordains it, and a father parts from his children. I release you completely from your allegiance to myself and to my house. My most ardent prayers for your welfare will always attend you in your relations to your new sovereign. Be to him what you have ever been to me. Neither force nor fate shall ever efface the remembrance of you from my heart."

To trace the triumphant return of the victor is a singular contrast to those melancholy effusions of the vanquished monarch. The treaty of Tilsit had ended all appearance of opposition to France upon the Continent. The British armament, which had been sent to Pomerania too late in the campaign, was re-embarked, and the King of Sweden, evacuating Stralsund, retired to the dominions which he was not very long destined to call his own. After having remained together for twenty days, during which they daily maintained the most friendly intercourse, and held together long and secret conferences, the two Emperors at last separated, with demonstrations of the highest personal esteem, and each heaping upon the other all the honours which it was in his power to bestow. The congress broke up on the 9th July; and on his return to France, Napoleon visited Saxony, and was there met at Bautzen (doomed for a very different reason to be renowned in his history) by King Augustus, who received him with the honours due to one who had, in outward appearance at least, augmented the power which he might have overthrown.

PARIS

On 29th July, Napoleon, restored to his palace at St. Cloud, received the homage of the Senate, and other official and constitutional bodies. The celebrated naturalist Lacepède, as the organ of the former body, made a pompous enumeration of the miracles of the campaign; and avowed, that the accomplishment of such wonderful actions as would seemingly have required ages, was but to Napoleon the work of a few months; while at the same time his ruling genius gave motion to all the domestic administration of his vast empire, and, although four hundred leagues distant from the capital, was present with and observant of the most complicated as well as extensive details. "We cannot," concludes the orator, "offer to your Majesty praises worthy of you. Your glory is too much raised above us. It will be the task of posterity, removed at a distance from your presence, to estimate with greater truth its real degree of elevation. Enjoy, sire, the recompense the most worthy of the greatest of monarchs, the happiness of being beloved by the greatest of nations, and may our great-grandchildren be long happy under your Majesty's reign."

So spoke the President of the French Senate; and who, that wished to retain the name of a rational being, dared have said, that, within the period of seven years, the same Senate would be carrying to the downfallen and dejected King of Prussia their congratulations on his share in the overthrow of the very man whom they were now adoring as a demigod!

The fortunes and fame of Napoleon were, indeed, such as to excite in the highest degree the veneration with which men look upon talents and success. All opposition seemed to sink before him, and Fortune appeared only to have looked doubtfully upon him during a part of the last campaign, in order to render still brighter the auspicious aspect under which she closed it. Many of his most confirmed enemies, who, from their proved attachment to the House of Bourbon, had secretly disowned the authority of Buonaparte, and doubted the continuance of his success, when they saw Prussia lying at his feet, and Russia clasping his hand in friendship, conceived they should be struggling against the decrees of Providence, did they longer continue to resist their predestined master. Austerlitz had shaken their constancy; Tilsit destroyed it: and with few and silent exceptions, the vows, hopes, and wishes of France, seemed turned on Napoleon as her Heir by Destiny. Perhaps he himself, only, could finally have disappointed their expectations. But he was like the adventurous climber on the Alps, to whom the surmounting the most tremendous precipices, and ascending to the most towering peaks only shows yet dizzier heights and higher points of elevation.

CHAPTER XXXVII

British Expedition to Calabria, under Sir John Stuart—Character of the People—Opposed by General Reynier—Battle of Maida, 4th July, 1806— Defeat of the French—Calabria evacuated by the British—Erroneous Commercial Views, and Military Plans, of the British Ministry— Unsuccessful Attack on Buenos Ayres—General Whitelocke—is cashiered— Expedition against Turkey, and its Dependencies—Admiral Duckworth's Squadron sent against Constantinople—Passes and repasses the Dardanelles, without accomplishing anything—Expedition against Alexandria—Rosetta attacked—British troops defeated—and withdrawn from Egypt, September, 1807—Curaçoa and Cape of Good Hope taken by England—British Expedition against Copenhagen—its Citadel, Forts, and Fleet, surrendered to the British—Effects of this proceeding upon France and Russia—Coalition of France, Russia, Austria, and Prussia, against British Commerce.

The treaty of Tilsit is an important point in the history of Napoleon. At no time did his power seem more steadfastly rooted, more feebly assailed. The canker-worm by which it was ultimately to be destroyed, was, like that of the forest-tree, intrenched and hidden in the bosom of him whom it was destined to sap and consume. It is a fitting time, therefore, to take a general survey of the internal character of his government, when the arrangements seemed to be at his own choice, and ere misfortune, hitherto a stranger, dictated his course of proceeding, which had before experienced no control save his own will. We propose, therefore, in the next chapter, to take a brief review of the character of Buonaparte's government during this the most flourishing period of his power.

But, ere doing so, we must shortly notice some circumstances, civil and military, which, though they had but slight immediate effect upon the general current of events, yet serve to illustrate the character of the parties concerned, and to explain future incidents which were followed by more important consequences. These we have hitherto omitted, in order to present, in a continuous and uninterrupted form, the history of the momentous warfare, in the course of which Prussia was for the time subjugated, and Russia so far tamed by the eventful struggle, as to be willing to embrace the relation of an ally to the conqueror, whose course she had proposed to stem and to repel.

Among these comparatively minor incidents, must be reckoned the attempt made by the British Government to rescue the Calabrian dominions of the Neapolitan Bourbons from the intrusive government of Joseph Buonaparte. The character of the inhabitants of that mountainous country is well known. Bigots in their religion, and detesting a foreign yoke, as is usual with natives of a wild and almost lawless region; sudden in their passions, and readily having recourse to the sword, in revenge whether of public or private injury; enticed also by the prospect of occasional booty, and retaining a wild species of attachment to Ferdinand, whose manners and habits were popular with the Italians, and especially with those of the inferior order, the Calabrians were readily excited to take arms by the agents sent over to practise among them by the Sicilian court. Lawless at the time, cruel in their mode of conducting war, and incapable of being subjected to discipline, the bands which they formed amongst themselves, acted rather in the manner, and upon the motives of banditti, than of patriots. They occasionally, and individually, showed much courage, and even a sort of instinctive skill, which taught them how to choose their ambushes, defend their passes, and thus maintain a sort of predatory war, in which the French sustained considerable losses. Yet if their efforts remained unassisted by some regular force, it was evident that these insurrectionary troops must be destroyed in detail by the disciplined and calculated exertions of the French soldiers. To prevent this, and to gratify, at the same time, the anxious wishes of the Court of Palermo, Sir John Stuart, who commanded the British troops which had been sent to defend Sicily, undertook an expedition to the neighbouring shore of Italy, and disembarked in the Gulf of St. Euphemia, near the frontier of Lower Calabria, in the beginning of July, 1806, with something short of five thousand men.

MAIDA

The disembarkation was scarcely made, ere the British commander learned that General Reynier, who commanded for Joseph Buonaparte in Calabria, had assembled a force nearly equal to his own, and had advanced to Maida, a town about ten miles distant from St. Euphemia, with the purpose of giving him battle. Sir John Stuart lost no time in moving to meet him, and Reynier, confident in the numbers of his cavalry, the quality of his troops, and his own skill in tactics, abandoned a strong position on the further bank of the river Amata, and on the 4th July came down to meet the British in the open plain. Of all Buonaparte's generals, an Englishman would have desired, in especial, to be opposed to this leader, who had published a book on the evacuation of Egypt,[294] in which he denied every claim on the part of the British to skill or courage, and imputed the loss of the province exclusively to the incapacity of Menou, under whom Reynier, the author, had served as second in command. He was now to try his own fate with the enemy, for whom he had expressed so much contempt.

At nine in the morning, the two lines were opposite to each other, when the British light infantry brigade, forming the right of the advanced line, and the 1ere Légère on the French left, a favourite regiment, found themselves confronted. As if by mutual consent, when at the distance of about one hundred yards, the opposed corps threw in two or three close fires reciprocally, and then rushed on to charge each other with the bayonet. The British commanding officer, perceiving that his men were embarrassed by the blankets which they carried at their backs, halted the line that they might throw them down. The French saw the pause, and taking it for the hesitation of fear, advanced with a quickened pace and loud acclamations. An officer, our informer, seeing their veteran appearance, moustached countenances, and regularity of order,

---

[294] "De l'Egypte après la Balle d'Héliopolis."

could not forbear a feeling of anxiety as he glanced his eye along the British line, which consisted in a great measure of young and beardless recruits. But disembarrassed of their load, and receiving the order to advance, they cheered, and in their turn hastened towards the enemy with a rapid pace and levelled bayonets. The French officers were now seen encouraging their men, whose courage began to falter when they found they were to be the assailed party, not the assailants. Their line halted; they could not be brought to advance by the utmost efforts of their officers, and when the British were within bayonet's length, they broke and ran; but too late for safety, for they were subjected to the most dreadful slaughter. An attempt made by Reynier to redeem the day with his cavalry, was totally unsuccessful.[295] He was beaten on all points, and in such a manner as left it indisputable, that the British soldier, man to man, has a superiority over his enemy, similar to that which the British seaman possesses upon his peculiar element.[296]

It would be in vain to inquire whether this superiority, which we do not hesitate to say has been made manifest, with very few exceptions, wherever the British have met foreign troops upon equal terms, arises from a stronger conformation of body, or a more determined turn of mind; but it seems certain that the British soldier, inferior to the Frenchman in general intelligence, and in individual acquaintance with the trade of war, has a decided advantage in the bloody shock of actual conflict, and especially when maintained by the bayonet, body to body. It is remarkable also, that the charm is not peculiar to any one of the three united nations, but is common to the natives of all, different as they are in habits and education. The Guards, supplied by the city of London, may be contrasted with a regiment of Irish recruited among their

---

[295] For Sir John Stuart's detail of the memorable battle of Maida, see Annual Register, vol. xlviii., p. 590; see also Jomini, tom. ii., p. 238.

[296] "The French soldiers had a great contempt for the English troops at the beginning of the war, caused, perhaps, by the failure of the expeditions under the Duke of York, the great want of alertness in the English advanced posts, and the misfortunes which befell your armies. In this they were fools, as the English were well known to be a brave nation. It was probably by a similar error that Reynier was beaten by General Stuart; as the French imagined you would run away and be driven into the sea. Reynier was a man of talent, but more fit to give counsel to an army of twenty or thirty thousand men, than to command one of five or six. It is difficult to conceive how little the French soldiers thought of yours, until they were taught the contrary."—Napoleon, *Voice*, &c., vol. ii., p. 47.

rich meadows, or a body of Scotch from their native wildernesses; and while it may be difficult to assign the palm to either over the other two, all are found to exhibit that species of dogged and desperate courage, which, without staying to measure force or calculate chances, rushes on the enemy as the bull-dog upon the bear. This great moral encouragement was the chief advantage derived from the battle of Maida; for such was the tumultuous, sanguinary, and unmanageable character of the Calabrian insurgents, that it was judged impossible to continue the war with such assistants. The *malaria* was also found to affect the British troops; and Sir John Stuart, re-embarking his little army, returned to Sicily, and the efforts of the British were confined to the preservation of that island. But the battle of Maida was valuable as a corollary to that of Alexandria. We have not learned whether General Reynier ever thought it equally worthy of a commentary.[297]

PLANS OF THE BRITISH MINISTRY

The eyes of the best-informed men in Britain were now open to the disadvantageous and timid policy, of conducting this momentous war by petty expeditions and experimental armaments, too inadequate to the service to be productive of any thing but disappointment. The paltry idea of making war for British objects, as it was called, that is, withholding from the general cause those efforts which might have saved our allies, and going in search of some petty object in which Britain might see an individual interest, was now universally acknowledged; although it became more difficult than ever to select points of attack where our limited means might command success. It was also pretty distinctly seen, that the plan of opening a market for British manufactures, by conquering distant and unhealthy provinces, was as idle as immoral. In the latter quality, it somewhat resembled the proceedings of the surgeon mentioned in Le Sage's satirical novel, who converted passengers into patients by a stroke of his poniard, and then hastened, in his medical capacity, to cure the wounds he had inflicted. In point of

---

[297] Reynier died at Paris in 1814, at the age of forty-four. Besides his work on Egypt, he published "Conjectures sur les anciens habitans de l'Egypte," and "Sur les Sphinx qui accompagnent les Pyramides."

profit, we had frequently to regret, that the colonists, whom we proposed to convert by force of arms into customers for British goods, were too rude to want, and too poor to pay for them. Nothing deceives itself so willingly as the love of gain. Our principal merchants and manufacturers, among other commercial visions, had imagined to themselves an unlimited market for British commodities, in the immense plains surrounding Buenos Ayres, which are, in fact, peopled by a sort of Christian savages called Gauchos, whose principal furniture is the skulls of dead horses, whose only food is raw beef and water, whose sole employment is to catch wild cattle, by hampering them with a Gaucho's noose, and whose chief amusement is to ride wild horses to death.[298] Unfortunately, they were found to prefer their national independence to cottons and muslins.

Two several attempts were made on this miserable country, and neither redounded to the honour or advantage of the British nation. Buenos Ayres was taken possession of by a handful of British troops on the 27th June, 1806, who were attacked by the inhabitants and by a few Spanish troops; and, surrounded in the market place of the town, under a general and galling fire, were compelled to lay down their arms and surrender prisoners of war. A small remnant of the invading forces retained possession of a town on the coast, called Maldonado. In October, 1806, an expedition was sent out to reinforce this small body, and make some more material impression upon the continent of South America, which the nation were under the delusion of considering as a measure extremely to the advantage of British trade. Monte Video was taken, and a large body of troops, under command of General Whitelocke, a man of factitious reputation, and who had risen high in the army without having seen much service, marched against Buenos Ayres. This person proved both fool and coward. He pushed his columns of attack into the streets of Buenos Ayres, knowing that the flat roofs and terraces were manned by excellent though irregular marksmen; and, that the British might have no means of retaliation, they were not permitted to load their muskets—as if stone walls could have been carried by the bayonet. One of the columns was

---

[298] See the very extraordinary account of the Pampas, published by Captain Head of the engineers.

obliged to surrender; and although another had, in spite of desperate opposition, possessed themselves of a strong position, and that a few shells might have probably ended the sort of defence which had been maintained, Whitelocke thought it best to conclude a treaty with the enemy for recovery of the British prisoners, and so to renounce all further attempts on the colony. For this misconduct he was cashiered by the sentence of a court-martial.[299]

An expedition against Turkey and its dependencies, was as little creditable to the councils of Britain, and eventually to her arms, as were her attempts on South America. It arose out of a war betwixt England and the Porte, her late ally against France; for, so singular had been the turns of chance in this extraordinary conflict, that allies became enemies, and enemies returned to a state of close alliance, almost before war or peace could be proclaimed between them. The time was long past when the Sublime Ottoman Porte could regard the quarrels and wars of Christian powers with the contemptuous indifference with which men look on the strife of the meanest and most unclean animals.[300] She was now in such close contact with them, as to feel a thrilling interest in their various revolutions.

The invasion of Egypt excited the Porte against France, and disposed them to a close alliance with Russia and England, until Buonaparte's assumption of the Imperial dignity; on which occasion the Turks, overawed by the pitch of power to which he had ascended, sent an embassy to congratulate his succession, and expressed a desire to cultivate his friendship.

CONSTANTINOPLE

Napoleon, whose eyes were sometimes almost involuntarily turned to the East, and who besides desired, at that period, to break

---

[299] See Annual Register, vol. xlix., p. 223.
[300] In the time of Louis XIV., when the French envoy at the court of Constantinople came, in a great hurry, to intimate as important intelligence, some victory of his master over the Prussians, "Can you suppose it of consequence to his Serene Highness," said the Grand Vizier, with infinite contempt, "whether the dog bites the hog, or the hog bites the dog?"

off the good understanding betwixt the Porte and the Cabinet of St. Petersburgh, despatched Sebastiani as his envoy to Constantinople; a man well known for his skill in Oriental intrigues, as was displayed in the celebrated Report which had so much influence in breaking through the peace of Amiens.

The effect of this ambassador's promises, threats, and intrigues, was soon apparent. The Turks had come under an engagement that they would not change the Hospodars, or governors, of Moldavia and Wallachia. Sebastiani easily alarmed Turkish pride on the subject of this stipulation, and induced them to break through it. The two Hospodars were removed, in defiance of the agreement made to the contrary; and although the Turks became aware of the risk to which they had exposed themselves, and offered to replace the governors whom they had dismissed, Russia, with precipitate resentment, declared war, and invaded the two provinces in question. They overran and occupied them, but to their own cost; as an army of fifty thousand men thus rashly engaged against the Turks, might have been of the last consequence in the fields of Eylau, Heilsberg, or Friedland.

In the meanwhile, Great Britain sent a squadron, under Sir Thomas Duckworth, to compel the Porte to dismiss the French ambassador, and return to the line of politics which Sebastiani had induced them to abandon. Admiral Duckworth passed the Dardanelles in spite of the immense cannon by which they are guarded, and which hurled from their enormous muzzles massive fragments of marble instead of ordinary bullets. But if ever it was intended to act against the Turks by any other means than intimidation, the opportunity was suffered to escape; and an intercourse by message and billet was permitted to continue until the Turks had completed a line of formidable fortifications, while the state of the weather was too unfavourable to allow even an effort at the destruction of Constantinople, which had been the alternative submitted to the Turks by the English admiral. The English repassed the Dardanelles in no very creditable manner, hated for the threats which they had uttered, and despised for not having attempted to make their menaces good.[301]

Neither was a subsequent expedition to Alexandria more favourable in its results. Five thousand men, under General Fraser, were disembarked, and occupied the town with much ease. But a division, despatched against Rosetta, was the cause of renewing in a different part of the world the calamity of Buenos Ayres. The detachment was, incautiously and unskilfully on our part, decoyed into the streets of an Oriental town, where the enemy, who had manned the terraces and the flat roofs of their houses, slaughtered the assailants with much ease and little danger to themselves. Some subsequent ill-combined attempts were made for reducing the same place, and after sustaining a loss of more than a fifth of their number, by climate and combat, the British troops were withdrawn from Egypt on the 23d of September, 1807.

It was no great comfort, under these repeated failures, that the British were able to secure the Dutch island of Curaçoa. But the capture of the Cape of Good Hope was an object of deep importance; and the more so, as it was taken at a small expense of lives. Its consequence to our Indian trade is so great, that we may well hope it will be at no future time given up to the enemy. Upon the whole, the general policy of England was, at this period, of an irresolute and ill-combined character. Her ministers showed a great desire to do something, but as great a doubt what that something was to be. Thus, they either mistook the importance of the objects which they aimed at, or, undertaking them without a sufficient force, failed to carry them into execution. If the wealth and means, more especially the brave troops, frittered away in the attempts at Calabria, Buenos Ayres, Alexandria, and elsewhere, had been united with the forces sent to Stralsund, and thrown into the rear of the French army before the fatal battle of Friedland, Europe might, in all probability, have escaped that severe, and, for a time, decisive blow.

---

[301] See "Particulars from Sir J. Duckworth to Lord Collingwood, relative to the affairs of the Dardanelles," Annual Register, vol. xlix., p. 659.

The evil of this error, which had pervaded our continental efforts from the beginning of the original war with France down to the period of which we are treating, began now to be felt from experience. Britain gained nothing whatever by her partial efforts, not even settlements or sugar-islands. The enemy maintained against her revenues and commerce a constant and never-ceasing war—her resistance was equally stubborn, and it was evident that the strife on both sides was to be mortal. Ministers were, therefore, called upon for bolder risks, the nation for greater sacrifices, than had yet been demanded; and it became evident to every one, that England's hope of safety lay in her own exertions, not for petty or selfish objects, but such as might have a decided influence on the general events of the war. The urgent pressure of the moment was felt by the new Administration, whose principles being in favour of the continuance of the war, their efforts to conduct it with energy began now to be manifest.

COPENHAGEN

The first symptoms of this change of measures were exhibited in the celebrated expedition to Copenhagen, which manifested an energy and determination not of late visible in the military operations of Britain on the continent. It can hardly be made matter of serious doubt, that one grand object by which Buonaparte meant to enforce the continental system, and thus reduce the power of England without battle or invasion, was the re-establishment of the great alliance of the Northern Powers, for the destruction of Britain's maritime superiority. This had been threatened towards the conclusion of the American war, and had been again acted upon in 1801, when the unnatural compact was dissolved by the cannon of Nelson, and the death of the Emperor Paul. The treaty of Tilsit, according to the information which the British ambassador had procured, certainly contained an article to this purpose, and ministers received from other quarters the most positive information of what was intended. Indeed, the Emperor Alexander had shown, by many indications, that in the new friendship which he had formed with the Emperor of the East, he was to embrace his resentment, and further his plans, against England. The unfortunate

Gustavus of Sweden could scarcely be expected voluntarily to embrace the proposed northern alliance, and his ruin was probably resolved upon. But the accession of Denmark was of the utmost consequence. That country still possessed a fleet, and the local situation of the island of Zealand gave her the key of the Baltic. Her confessed weakness could not have permitted her for an instant to resist the joint influence of Russia and France, even if her angry recollection of the destruction of her fleet by Nelson, had not induced her inclinations to lean in that direction. It was evident that Denmark would only be permitted to retain her neutrality, till it suited the purposes of the more powerful parties to compel her to throw it off. In this case, and finding the French troops approaching Holstein, Jutland, and Fiume, the British Government, acting on the information which they had received of the purpose of their enemies, conceived themselves entitled to require from Denmark a pledge as to the line of conduct which she proposed to adopt on the approach of hostilities, and some rational security that such a pledge, when given, should be redeemed.

A formidable expedition was now fitted out, humanely, as well as politically, calculated on a scale of such magnitude, as, it might be expected, would render impossible the resistance which the Danes, as a high-spirited people, might offer to such a harsh species of expostulation. Twenty-seven sail of the line, and twenty thousand men, under the command of Lord Cathcart, were sent to the Baltic, to support a negotiation with Denmark, which it was still hoped might terminate without hostilities. The fleet was conducted with great ability through the intricate passages called the Belts, and was disposed in such a manner, that ninety pendants flying round Zealand, entirely blockaded the shores of that island.

Under these auspices the negotiation was commenced. The British envoy, Mr. Jackson, had the delicate task of stating to the Crown Prince in person, the expectation of England that his royal highness should explain unequivocally his sentiments, and declare the part which he meant to take between her and France. The unpleasant condition was annexed, that, to secure any protestation which might be made of friendship or neutrality, it was required that the fleet and naval stores of the Danes should be delivered into the hands of Great Britain, not in right of property, but to be restored so soon as the state of affairs, which induced her to require possession of them, should be altered for more peaceful times. The closest alliance, and every species of protection which Britain could afford, was proffered, to obtain compliance with these proposals. Finally, the Crown Prince was given to understand, that so great a force was sent in order to afford him an apology to France, should he choose to urge it, as having been compelled to submit to the English demands; but at the same time it was intimated, that the forces would be actually employed to compel the demands, if they should be refused.

In the ordinary intercourse betwixt nations, these requisitions, on the part of Britain, would have been, with respect to Denmark, severe and unjustifiable. The apology arose out of the peculiar circumstances of the times. The condition of England was that of an individual, who, threatened by the approach of a superior force of mortal enemies, sees close beside him, and with arms in his hand, one, of whom he had a right to be suspicious, as having co-operated against him on two former occasions, and who, he has the best reason to believe, is at the very moment engaged in a similar alliance to his prejudice. The individual, in the case supposed, would certainly be warranted in requiring to know this third party's intention, nay, in disarming him, if he had strength to do so, and retaining his weapons, as the best pledge of his neutrality.

However this reasoning may be admitted to justify the British demands, we cannot wonder that it failed to enforce compliance on the part of the Crown Prince. There was something disgraceful in delivering up the fleet of the nation under a menace that violence would otherwise be employed; and although, for the sake of his people and his capital, he ought, in prudence, to have forborne an ineffectual resistance, yet it was impossible to blame a high-minded and honourable man for making the best defence in his power.

So soon as the object of the Danes was found to be delay and evasion, while they made a hasty preparation for defence, the soldiers were disembarked, batteries erected, and a bombardment commenced, which occasioned a dreadful conflagration. Some forces which had been collected in the interior of the island, were dispersed by the troops under Sir Arthur Wellesley, a name already famous in India, but now for the first time heard in European warfare. The unavailing defence was at last discontinued, and upon the 8th September the citadel and forts of Copenhagen were surrendered to the British general. The Danish ships were fitted out for sea with all possible despatch, together with the naval stores, to a very large amount; which, had they fallen into the hands of the French, must have afforded them considerable facility in fitting out a fleet.[302]

As the nature and character of the attack upon Copenhagen were attended by circumstances which were very capable of being misrepresented, France—who, through the whole war, had herself shown the most total disregard for the rights of neutral nations, with her leader Napoleon, the invader of Egypt, when in profound peace with the Porte; of Hanover, when in amity with the German empire; and who was at this very moment meditating the appropriation of Spain and Portugal—France was filled with extreme horror at the violence practised on the Danish capital. Russia was also offended, and to a degree which showed that a feeling of disappointed schemes mingled with her affectation of zeal for the rights of neutrality.[303] But the daring and energetic spirit with which England had formed and accomplished her plan, struck a wholesome terror into other nations, and showed neutrals, that if, while assuming that character, they lent their secret countenance to the enemies of Great Britain, they were not to expect that it was to be done with impunity. This was, indeed, no small hardship upon the lesser powers, many of whom would, no doubt, have been well contented to have observed a strict neutrality, but for the threats and influence of France, against whom they had no means of defence; but the furious conflict of such two nations as France and England, is like the struggle of giants, in which the smaller and more feeble, who have the misfortune to be in the neighbourhood, are sure to be borne down and trodden upon by one or both parties.

---

[302] See "Papers relating to the Expedition to Copenhagen," Parl. Debates, vol. x., p. 221; and "Proceedings before Copenhagen," Annual Register, vol. xlix., p. 681.
[303] "Russia felt severely the loss which Denmark had sustained. The Danish fleet was a good third of the guarantee of the neutrality of the Baltic."—Savary, tom. ii., p. 112.

The extreme resentment expressed by Buonaparte, when he received intelligence of this critical and decisive measure, might serve to argue the depth of his disappointment at such an unexpected anticipation of his purposes. He had only left to him the comfort of railing against Britain in the *Moniteur*; and the breach of peace, and of the law of nations, was gravely imputed to England as an inexpiable crime, by one who never suffered his regard either for his own word, or the general good faith observed amongst nations, to interfere with any wish or interest he had ever entertained.[304]

COALITION—BRITISH COMMERCE

The conduct of Russia was more singular. An English officer of literary celebrity was employed by Alexander, or those who were supposed to share his most secret counsels, to convey to the British Ministry the Emperor's expressions of the secret satisfaction which his Imperial Majesty felt at the skill and dexterity which Britain had displayed in anticipating and preventing the purposes of France, by her attack upon Copenhagen.[305] Her ministers were invited to communicate freely with the Czar, as with a prince, who, though obliged to give way to circumstances, was, nevertheless, as much attached as ever to the cause of European independence. Thus invited, the British Cabinet entered into an explanation of their views for establishing a counterbalance to the exorbitant power of France, by a northern confederacy of an offensive and defensive character. It was supposed that Sweden would enter with pleasure into such an alliance, and that Denmark would not decline it if encouraged by the example of Russia, who was proposed as the head and soul of the coalition.

Such a communication was accordingly made to the Russian ministers, but was received with the utmost coldness. It is impossible now to determine, whether there had been some over-

---

[304] "The attack upon Copenhagen by the English was the first blow given to the secret stipulations of Tilsit, in virtue of which the navy of Denmark was to be placed at the disposal of France. Since the catastrophe of Paul the First, I never saw Napoleon abandon himself to more violent transports. What most struck him in this vigorous enterprise, was the promptness of the resolution of the English ministry."—Fouché, tom. i., p. 312.
[305] Lord Hutchinson. See Parliamentary Debates, vol. x., p. 602.

confidence in the agent; whether the communication had been founded on some hasty and fugitive idea of a breach with France, which the Emperor had afterwards abandoned; or finally, whether, as is more probable, it originated in a wish to fathom the extent of Great Britain's resources, and the purposes to which she meant to devote them. It is enough to observe, that the countenance with which Russia received the British communication, was so different from that with which she had invited the confidence of her ministers, that the negotiation proved totally abortive.

Alexander's ultimate purpose was given to the world, so soon as Britain had declined the offered mediation of Russia in her disputes with France. In a proclamation, or manifesto, sent forth by the Emperor, he expressed his repentance for having entered into agreements with England, which he had found prejudicial to the Russian trade; he complained (with justice) of the manner in which Britain had conducted the war by petty expeditions, conducive only to her own selfish ends; and the attack upon Denmark was treated as a violation of the rights of nations. He therefore annulled every convention entered into between Russia and Britain, and especially that of 1801; and he avowed the principles of the Armed Neutrality, which he termed a monument of the wisdom of the Great Catherine.[306] In November 1807, an ukase, or imperial decree, was issued, imposing an embargo on British vessels and property. But, by the favour of the Russian nation, and even of the officers employed by Government, the shipmasters were made aware of the impending arrest; and not less than eighty vessels, setting sail with a favourable wind, reached Britain with their cargoes in safety.

Austria and Prussia found themselves under the necessity of following the example of Russia, and declaring war against British commerce; so that Buonaparte had now made an immense stride towards his principal object, of destroying every species of intercourse which could unite England with the continent.

---

[306] See Declaration of the Emperor of Russia, dated St. Petersburgh, 20th (31st) October, 1807, Annual Register, vol. xlix., p. 761; and Parl. Debates, vol. x., p. 218.

Chapter XXXVIII

View of the Internal Government of Napoleon at the period of the Peace of Tilsit—The Tribunate abolished—Council of State—Prefectures—Their nature and objects described—The Code Napoleon—Its Provisions—Its merits and Defects—Comparison betwixt that Code and the Jurisprudence of England—Laudable efforts of Napoleon to carry it into effect.

INTERNAL GOVERNMENT

At this period of Buonaparte's elevation, when his power seemed best established, and most permanent, it seems proper to take a hasty view, not indeed of the details of his internal government, which is a subject that would exhaust volumes; but at least of its general character, of the means by which his empire was maintained, and the nature of the relations which it established betwixt the sovereign and his subjects.

The ruling, almost the sole principle on which the government of Buonaparte rested, was the simple proposition upon which despotism of every kind has founded itself in every species of society; namely, that the individual who is to exercise the authority and power of the state, shall, on the one hand, dedicate himself and his talents exclusively to the public service of the empire, while, on the other, the nation subjected to his rule shall requite this self-devotion on his part by the most implicit obedience to his will. Some despots have rested this claim to universal submission upon family descent, and upon their right, according to Filmer's doctrine, of representing the original father of the tribe, and becoming the legitimate inheritors of a patriarchal power. Others have strained scripture and abused common sense, to establish in their own favour a right through the especial decree of Providence. To the hereditary title Buonaparte could of course assert no claim; but he founded not a little on the second principle, often holding himself out to others, and no doubt occasionally considering himself, in his own mind, as an individual destined by Heaven to the high station which he held, and one who could not therefore be opposed in his career, without an express struggle being maintained against Destiny, who, leading him by the hand, and at the same time protecting him with her shield, had guided him by paths as strange as perilous, to the post of eminence which he now occupied. No one had been his tutor in the lessons which led the way to his preferment—no one had been his guide in the dangerous ascent to power—scarce any one had been of so much consequence to his promotion, as to claim even the merit of an ally, however humble. It seemed as if Napoleon had been wafted on to this stupendous pitch of grandeur by a power more effectual than that of any human assistance, nay, which surpassed what could have been expected from his own great talents, unassisted by the especial interposition of Destiny in his favour. Yet it was not to this principle alone that the general acquiescence in the unlimited power which he asserted is to be imputed. Buonaparte understood the character of the French nation so well, that he could offer them an acceptable indemnification for servitude; first, in the height to which he proposed to raise their national pre-eminence; secondly, in the municipal establishments, by means of which he administered their government, and which, though miserably defective in all which would have been demanded by a nation accustomed to the administration of equal and just laws, afforded a protection to life and property that was naturally most welcome to those who had been so long, under the republican system, made the victims of cruelty, rapacity, and the most extravagant and unlimited tyranny, rendered yet more odious as exercised under the pretext of liberty.

To the first of these arts of government we have often adverted; and it must be always recalled to mind whenever the sources of Buonaparte's power over the public mind in France come to be treated of. He himself gave the solution in a few words, when censuring the imbecility of the Directors, to whose power he succeeded. "These men," he said, "know not how to work upon the imagination of the French nation." This idea, which, in phraseology, is rather Italian than French, expresses the chief secret of Napoleon's authority. He held himself out as the individual upon whom the fate of France depended—of whose hundred decisive victories France enjoyed the glory. It was he whose sword, hewing down obstacles which her bravest monarchs had accounted insurmountable, had cut the way to her now undeniable supremacy over Europe. He alone could justly claim to be Absolute Monarch of France, who, raising that nation from a perilous condition, had healed her discords, reconciled her factions, turned her defeats into victory, and, from a disunited people, about to become the prey to civil and external war, had elevated her to the situation of Queen of Europe. This had been all accomplished upon one condition; and, as we have stated elsewhere, it was that which the Tempter offered in the wilderness, after his ostentatious display of the kingdoms of the earth—"All these will I give thee, if thou wilt fall down and worship me."

Napoleon had completed the boastful promise, and it flattered a people more desirous of glory than of liberty; and so much more pleased with hearing of national conquests in foreign countries, than of enjoying the freedom of their own individual thoughts and actions, that they unreluctantly surrendered the latter in order that their vanity might be flattered by the former.

Thus did Napoleon avail himself of, or, to translate his phrase more literally, play upon the imagination of the French people. He gave them public festivals, victories, and extended dominion; and in return, claimed the right of carrying their children in successive swarms to yet more distant and yet more extended conquests, and of governing, according to his own pleasure, the bulk of the nation which remained behind.

To attain this purpose, one species of idolatry was gradually and ingeniously substituted for another, and the object of the public devotion was changed, while the worship was continued. France had been formerly governed by political maxims—she was now ruled by the name of an individual. Formerly the Republic was every thing— Fayette, Dumouriez, or Pichegru, were nothing. Now, the name of a successful general was of more influence than the whole code of the

Rights of Man. France had submitted to murder, spoliation, revolutionary tribunals, and every species of cruelty and oppression, while they were gilded by the then talismanic expressions—"Liberty and Equality—Fraternization—the public welfare, and the happiness of the people." She was now found equally compliant, when the watchword was, "The honour of his Imperial and Royal Majesty—the interests of the Great Empire—the splendours of the Imperial Throne." It must be owned, that the sacrifices under the last form were less enormous; they were limited to taxes at the Imperial pleasure, and a perpetual anticipation of the conscription. The Republican tyrants claimed both life and property, the Emperor was satisfied with a tithe of the latter, and the unlimited disposal of that portion of the family who could best support the burden of arms, for augmenting the conquests of France. Such were the terms on which this long-distracted country attained once more, after its Revolution, the advantage of a steady and effective government.

The character of that government, its means and principles of action, must now be briefly traced.

It cannot be forgotten that Buonaparte, the heir of the Revolution, appropriated to himself the forms and modifications of the Directorial government, altered, in some degree, by the ingenuity of Siêyes; but they subsisted as forms only, and were carefully divested of all effectual impulse on the government. The Senate and Legislative Bodies became merely passive and pensioned creatures of the Emperor's will, whom he used as a medium for promulgating the laws which he was determined to establish. The Tribunate had been instituted for the protection of the people against all acts of arbitrary power, whether by imprisonment, exile, assaults on the liberty of the press, or otherwise; but after having gradually undermined the rights and authority of this body, after having rendered its meetings partial and secret, and having deprived it of its boldest members, Buonaparte suppressed it entirely, on account, as he alleged, of the expense which it occasioned to the government. It had, indeed, become totally useless;[307] but this was because its

---

[307] "It is certain that the Tribunate was absolutely useless, while it cost nearly half a million; I therefore suppressed it. I was well aware that an outcry would be raised against the

character had been altered, and because, originating from the Senate, and not from popular election, the Tribunate never consisted of that class of persons, who are willing to encounter the frown of power when called upon to impeach its aggressions. Yet, as the very name of this body, while it subsisted, recalled some ideas of Republican freedom, the Emperor thought fit altogether to abolish it.

THE COUNCIL OF STATE

The deliberative Council of the Emperor existed in his own personal Council of State, of whose consultations, in which he himself presided, he made frequent use during the course of his reign. Its functions were of an anomalous character, comprehending political legislation, or judicial business, according to the order of the day. It was, in short, Buonaparte's resource, when he wanted the advice, or opinion, or information, of others in aid of his own; and he often took the assistance of the Council of State, in order to form those resolutions which he afterwards executed by means of his ministers. Monsieur de Las Cases, himself a member of it, has dwelt with complaisance upon the freedom which Buonaparte permitted to their debates, and the good-humour with which he submitted to contradiction, even when expressed with obstinacy or vivacity;[308] and would have us consider the Council as an important barrier afforded to the citizens against the arbitrary will of the Sovereign. What he has said, however, only amounts to this,—that Buonaparte, desirous to have the advice of his counsellors, tolerated their freedom of speech, and even of remonstrance. Mahmoud, or Amurath, seated in their divan, must have done the same, and yet would not have remained the less absolutely masters of the lives of

---

violation of the law; but I was strong; I possessed the full confidence of the people, and I considered myself a reformer."—Napoleon, *Las Cases*, tom. i., p. 289.

[308] "So little was the Council of State understood by the people in general, that it was believed no one dared utter a word in that assembly in opposition to the Emperor's opinion. Thus I very much surprised many persons, when I related the fact, that one day, during a very animated debate, the Emperor, having been interrupted three times in giving his opinion, turned towards the individual who had rather rudely cut him short, and said in a sharp tone: 'I have not yet done, I beg you will allow me to continue; I believe every one here has a right to deliver his opinion.' The smartness of his reply, notwithstanding the solemnity of the occasion, excited a general laugh, in which the Emperor himself joined."—Las Cases, tom. i., p. 280.

those who stood around them. We have no doubt that Buonaparte, on certain occasions, permitted his counsellors to take considerable freedoms, and that he sometimes yielded up his opinion to theirs without being convinced; in such cases, at least, where his own passions or interest were no way concerned.[309] But we further read of the Emperor's using, to extremely stubborn persons, such language as plainly intimated, that he would not suffer contradiction beyond a certain point, "You are very obstinate," he said to such a disputant; "what if I were to be as much so as you? You are wrong to push the powerful to extremity—you should consider the weakness of humanity." To another he said, after a scene of argumentative violence, "Pray, pay some attention to accommodate yourself a little more to my humour. Yesterday, you carried it so far as to oblige me to scratch my temple. That is a great sign with me— take care in future not to drive me to such an extremity."[310]

Such limits to the freedom of debate in the Imperial Council of State, correspond with those laid down in the festive entertainments of Sans Souci, where the Great Frederick professed to support and encourage every species of familiar raillery, but, when it attained a point that was too personal, used to hint to the facetious guests, that he heard the King's step in the gallery. There were occasions, accordingly, when, not satisfied with calling their attention to the distant murmurs of the Imperial thunder, Napoleon launched its bolts in the midst of his trembling counsellors. Such a scene was that of Portalis. This statesman, a man of talent and virtue, had been eminently useful, as we have seen, in bringing about the Concordat, and had been created, in recompense, minister of religious affairs, and counsellor of state. In the subsequent disputes

---

[309] Ségur gives example of a case in which Buonaparte deferred his own opinion to that of the Council. A female of Amsterdam, tried for a capital crime, had been twice acquitted by the Imperial Courts, and the Court of Appeal claimed the right to try her a third time. Buonaparte alone contended against the whole Council of State, and claimed for the poor woman the immunity which, in justice, she ought to have obtained, considering the prejudices that must have been excited against her. He yielded, at length, to the majority, but protesting he was silenced, and not convinced. To account for his complaisance, it may be remarked first, that Buonaparte was no way personally interested in the decision of the question; and, secondly, if it concerned him at all, the fate of the female was in his hands, since he had only to grant her a pardon if she was condemned by the Court of Appeal.— S.—See also Las Cases, tom. i., p. 278.
[310] Las Cases, tom. i., p. 281.

betwixt the Pope and Buonaparte, a relation of the minister had been accused of circulating the bulls, or spiritual admonitions of the Pope; and Portalis had failed to intimate the circumstance to the Emperor. On this account, Napoleon, in full council, attacked him in the severest terms, as guilty of having broken his oath as a counsellor and minister of state, deprived him of both offices, and expelled him from the assembly, as one who had betrayed his sovereign.[311] If any of the members of the Council of State had ventured, when this sentence rung in their ears, to come betwixt the dragon and his wrath, for the purpose of stating that a hasty charge ought not instantly to be followed with immediate censure and punishment; that it was possible M. Portalis might have been misled by false information, or by a natural desire to screen the offence of his cousin; or, finally, that his conduct might have been influenced by views of religion which, if erroneous, were yet sincere and conscientious—we should then have believed, that the Council of State of Buonaparte formed a body, in which the accused citizen might receive some protection against the despotism of the government. But when, or in what country, could the freedom of the nation be intrusted to the keeping of the immediate counsellors of the throne? It can only be safely lodged in some body, the authority of which emanates directly from the nation, and whom the nation therefore will protect and support, in the existence of their right of opposition or remonstrance.

The deliberations of the Council of State, or such resolutions as Buonaparte chose to adopt without communication with them, (for it may be easily supposed that they were not admitted to share his more secret political discussions,) were, as in other countries, adjusted with and executed by the ostensible ministers.

---

[311] Las Cases, tom. i., p. 282. At St. Helena, Napoleon reproached himself for the expulsion of M. Portalis. "I was," he said, "perhaps too severe; I should have checked myself before I ordered him to be gone. He attempted no justification, and therefore the scene should have ended, merely by my saying, *it is well.* His punishment should have awaited him at home. Anger is always unbecoming in a sovereign. But, perhaps, I was excusable in my council, where I might consider myself in the bosom of my own family; or perhaps, after all, I may be justly condemned for this act. Every one has his fault; nature will exert her sway over us all."—Las Cases, tom. iv., p. 320.

PREFECTURES

But, that part of the organisation of the Imperial government, upon which Buonaparte most piqued himself, was the establishment of the Prefectures, which certainly gave facilities for the most effectual agency of despotism that was ever exercised. There is no mistaking the object and tendency of this arrangement, since Buonaparte himself, and his most bitter opponents, hold up the same picture, one to the admiration, the other to the censure, of the world. These prefects, it must be understood, were each the supreme governor of a department, answering to the old lieutenants and governors of counties, and representing the Imperial person within the limits of the several prefectures. The individuals were carefully selected, as persons whose attachment was either to be secured or rewarded. They received large and, in some cases, exorbitant salaries, some amounting to fifteen, twenty, and even thirty thousand francs. This heavy expense Napoleon stated to be the consequence of the depraved state of moral feeling in France, which made it necessary to attach men by their interests rather than their duties; but it was termed by his enemies one of the leading principles of his government, which treated the public good as a chimera, and erected private and personal interest into the paramount motive upon which alone the state was to be served by efficient functionaries. The prefects were chosen in the general case, as men whose birth and condition were totally unconnected with that of the department in which each was to preside; *les dépayser*, to place them in a country to which they were strangers, being an especial point of Napoleon's policy. They were entirely dependent on the will of the Emperor, who removed or cashiered them at pleasure. The administration of the departments was intrusted to these important officers.

"With the authority and local resources placed at their disposal," said Buonaparte, "the prefects were themselves emperors on a limited scale; and as they had no force excepting through the impulse which they received from the throne, as they owed their whole power to their immediate commission, and as they had no authority of a personal character, they were of as much use to the crown as the former high agents of government, without any of the inconveniences which attached to their predecessors."[312] It was by means of the prefects that an impulse, given from the centre of the government, was communicated without delay to the extremities of the kingdom, and that the influence of the crown, and the execution of its commands, were transmitted, as if by magic, through a population of forty millions. It appears that Napoleon, while describing with self-complacency this terrible engine of unlimited power, felt that it might not be entirely in unison with the opinions of those favourers of liberal institutions, whose sympathy at the close of life he thought worthy of soliciting. "My creating that power," he said, "was on my part a case of necessity. I was a dictator, called to that office by force of circumstances. There was a necessity that the filaments of the government which extended over the state, should be in complete harmony with the key-note which was to influence them. The organisation which I had extended over the empire, required to be maintained at a high degree of tension, and to possess a prodigious force of elasticity, to enable it to resist the terrible blows directed against it without cessation."[313] His defence amounts to this—"The men of my time were extravagantly fond of power, exuberantly attached to place and wealth. I therefore bribed them to become my agents by force of places and pensions. But I was educating the succeeding race to be influenced by better motives. My son would have been surrounded by youths sensible to the influence of justice, honour, and virtue; and those who were called to execute public duty, would have considered their doing so as its own reward."

The freedom of France was therefore postponed till the return of a Golden Age, when personal aggrandisement and personal wealth should cease to have any influence upon regenerated humanity. In the meanwhile, she had the dictatorship and the prefects.

The *impulse*, as Napoleon terms it, by which the crown put in action these subordinate agents in the departments, was usually given by means of a circular letter or proclamation, communicating the particular measure which government desired to be enforced.

---

[312] Las Cases, tom. iv., p. 105.
[313] Las Cases, tom. iv., p. 105.

This was subscribed by the minister to whose department the affair belonged, and concluded with an injunction upon the prefect, to be active in forwarding the matter enjoined, as he valued the favour of the Emperor, or wished to show himself devoted to the interests of the crown.[314] Thus conjured, the prefect transmitted the order to the sub-prefect and mayors of the communities within his department, who, stimulated by the same motives that had actuated their principal, endeavoured each to distinguish himself by his active compliance with the will of the Emperor, and thus merit a favourable report, as the active and unhesitating agent of his pleasure.

It was the further duty of the prefects, to see that all honour was duly performed towards the head of the state, upon the days appointed for public rejoicings, and to remind the municipal authorities of the necessity of occasional addresses to the government, declaring their admiration of the talents, and devotion to the person of the Emperor. These effusions were duly published in the *Moniteur*, and, if examined closely, would afford some of the most extraordinary specimens of composition which the annals of flattery can produce. It is sufficient to say, that a mayor, we believe of Amiens, affirmed, in his ecstasy of loyal adoration, that the Deity, after making Buonaparte, must have reposed, as after the creation of the universe. This, and similar flights of rhetoric, may appear both impious and ridiculous, and it might have been thought that a person of Napoleon's sense and taste would have softened or suppressed them. But he well knew the influence produced on the public mind, by ringing the changes to different time on the same unvaried subject. The ideas which are often repeated in all variety of language and expression, will at length produce an effect on the public mind, especially if no contradiction is permitted to reach it. A uniform which may look ridiculous on a single individual, has an imposing effect when worn by a large body of men; and the empiric,

---

[314] "Your Emperor," is the usual conclusion, "relies upon the zeal which you will display on this business, in order to prove your devotion to his person, and your attachment to the interests of the throne." Each of the prefects amplifies the circular. The warmest expressions and the strongest colours are employed; no figure of rhetoric is forgotten, and the circular is transmitted to the sub-prefects of the department. The sub-prefects in their turn season it with still stronger language, and the mayors improve upon that of the sub-prefects.—Faber, *Notices sur l'Intérieur de la France*, p. 13.

whose extravagant advertisement we ridicule upon the first perusal, often persuades us, by sheer dint of repeating his own praises, to make trial of his medicine. Those who practise calumny know, according to the vulgar expression, that if they do but throw dirt sufficient, some part of it will adhere; and acting on the same principle, for a contrary purpose, Buonaparte was well aware, that the repetition of his praises in these adulatory addresses was calculated finally to make an impression on the nation at large, and to obtain a degree of credit as an expression of public opinion.

Faber, an author too impassioned to obtain unlimited credit, has given several instances of ignorance amongst the prefects; many of whom, being old generals, were void of the information necessary for the exercise of a civil office, and all of whom, having been, upon principle, nominated to a sphere of action with the local circumstances of which they were previously unacquainted, were sufficiently liable to error. But the same author may be fully trusted, when he allows that the prefects could not be accused of depredation or rapine, and that such of them as improved their fortune during the date of their office, did so by economising upon their legitimate allowances.[315]

Such was the outline of Napoleon's provincial administration, and of the agency by which it was carried on, without check or hesitation, in every province of France at the same moment. The machinery has been in a great measure retained by the royal government, to whom it appeared preferable, doubtless, to the violent alterations which an attempt to restore the old appointments, or create others of a different kind, must necessarily have occasioned.

THE CODE NAPOLEON

But a far more important change, introduced by the Emperor, though not originating with him, was the total alteration of the laws of the kingdom of France, and the introduction of that celebrated

---

[315] Faber, *Notices*, p. 31.

code to which Napoleon assigned his name, and on the execution of which his admirers have rested his claim to be considered as a great benefactor to the country which he governed. Bacon has indeed informed us, that when laws have been heaped upon laws, in such a state of confusion as to render it necessary to revise them, and collect their spirit into a new and intelligible system, those who accomplish such an heroic task have a good right to be named amongst the legislators and benefactors of mankind. It had been the reproach of France before the Revolution, and it was one of the great evils which tended to produce that immense and violent change, that the various provinces, towns, and subordinate divisions of the kingdom, having been united in different periods to the general body of the country, had retained in such union the exercise of their own particular laws and usages; to the astonishment, as well as to the great annoyance of the traveller, who, in journeying through France, found that, in many important particulars, the system and character of the laws to which he was subjected, were altered almost as often as he changed his post-horses. It followed, from this discrepancy of laws and subdivision of jurisdiction, that the greatest hardships were sustained by the subjects, more especially when, the district being of small extent, those authorities who acted there were likely neither to have experience, nor character sufficient for exercise of the trust reposed in them.

The evils attending such a state of things had been long felt, and, at various periods before the Revolution, it had been proposed repeatedly to institute a uniform system of legislation for the whole kingdom. But so many different interests were compromised, and such were, besides, the pressing occupations of the successive administrations of Louis XVI., and his grandfather, that the project was never seriously adopted or entered upon. When, however, the whole system of provinces, districts, and feudal jurisdictions, great and small, had fallen at the word of the Abbé Siêyes, like an enchanted castle at the dissolution of a spell, and their various laws, whether written or consuetudinary, were buried in the ruins, all France, now united into one single and integral nation, lay open to receive any legislative code which the National Assembly might dictate. But the revolutionary spirit was more fitted to destroy than to establish; and was more bent upon the pursuit of political objects, than upon affording the nation the protection of just and equal laws. Under the Directory, two or three attempts towards classification of the laws had been made in the Council of Five Hundred, but never had gone farther than a preliminary and general report. Cambacérès, an excellent lawyer and enlightened statesman, was one of the first to solicit the attention of the state to this great and indispensable duty. The various successive authorities had been content with passing such laws as affected popular subjects of the day, and which (like that which licensed universal divorce) partook of the extravagance that gave them origin. The project of Cambacérès, on the contrary, embraced a general classification of jurisprudence through all its branches, although too much tainted, it is said, with the prevailing revolutionary opinions of the period, to admit its being taken for a basis, when Buonaparte, after his elevation, determined to supersede the Republican by Monarchical forms of government.

After the revolution of the 18th Brumaire, Napoleon saw no way more certain of assuring the popularity of that event, and connecting his own authority with the public interests of France, than to resume a task which former rulers of the Republic had thought too heavy to be undertaken, and thus, at once, show a becoming confidence in the stability of his own power, and a laudable desire of exercising it for the permanent advantage of the nation. An order of the Consuls, dated 24th Thermidor, in the year VIII., directed the minister of justice, with a committee of lawyers of eminence, to examine the several projects, four in number, which had been made towards compiling the civil code of national law, to give their opinion on the plan most desirable for accomplishing its formation, and to discuss the bases upon which legislation in civil matters ought to be rested.

The preliminary discourse upon the first project of the Civil Code, is remarkable for the manner in which the reporters consider and confute the general and illusory views entertained by the uninformed part of the public, upon the nature of the task to which they had been called. It is the common and vulgar idea, that the system of legislation may be reduced and simplified into a few general maxims of equity, sufficient to lead any judge of understanding and integrity, to a just decision of all questions which can possibly occur betwixt man and man. It follows, as a corollary to this proposition, that the various multiplications of authorities, exceptions, particular cases, and especial provisions, which have been introduced among civilized nations, by the address of those of the legal profession, are just so many expedients to embarrass the simple course of justice with arbitrary modifications and refinements, in order to procure wealth and consequence to those educated to the law, whose assistance must be used as its interpreters, and who became rich by serving litigants as guides through the labyrinth of obscurity which had been raised by themselves and their predecessors.

Such were the ideas of the law and its professors, which occurred to the Parliament of Praise-God-Barebones, when they proposed to Cromwell to abrogate the whole common law of England, and dismiss the lawyers, as drones who did but encumber the national hive. Such was also the opinion of many of the French statesmen, who, as rash in judging of jurisprudence as in politics, imagined that a system of maxims, modified on the plan of the Twelve Tables of the ancient Romans, might serve all the purposes of a civil code in modern France. They who thought in this manner had entirely forgotten, how soon the laws of these twelve tables became totally insufficient for Rome herself—how, in the gradual change of manners, some laws became obsolete, some inapplicable—how it became necessary to provide for emerging cases, successively by the decrees of the Senate, the ordinances of the people, the edicts of the Consuls, the regulations of the Prætors, the answers or opinions of learned Jurisconsults, and finally, by the rescripts, edicts, and novels of the Emperors, until such a mass of legislative matter was assembled, as scarcely the efforts of Theodosius or Justinian were adequate to bring into order, or reduce to principle. But this, it may be said, was the very subject complained of. The simplicity of the old laws, it may be urged, was gradually corrupted; and hence, by the efforts of interested men, not by the natural progress of society, arose the complicated system, which is the object of such general complaint.

The answer to this is obvious. So long as society remains in a simple state, men have occasion for few and simple laws. But when that society begins to be subdivided into ranks; when duties are incurred, and obligations contracted, of a kind unknown in a ruder or earlier period, these new conditions, new duties, and new obligations, must be regulated by new rules and ordinances, which accordingly are introduced as fast as they are wanted, either by the course of long custom, or by precise legislative enactment. There is, no doubt, one species of society in which legislation may be much simplified; and that is, where the whole law of the country, with the power of enforcing it, is allowed to reside in the bosom of the King, or of the judge who is to administer justice. Such is the system of Turkey, where the Cadi is bound by no laws nor former precedents, save what his conscience may discover from perusing the Koran. But so apt are mankind to abuse unlimited power, and indeed so utterly unfit is human nature to possess it, that in all countries where the judge is possessed of such arbitrary jurisdiction, he is found accessible to bribes, or liable to be moved by threats. He has no distinct course prescribed, no beacon on which to direct his vessel; and trims, therefore, his sails to the pursuit of his own profit.

CIVIL CODE

The French legislative commissioners, with these views, wisely judged it their duty to produce their civil code, upon such a system as might afford, as far as possible, protection to the various kinds of rights known and acknowledged in the existing state of society. Less than this they could not do; nor, in our opinion, is their code as yet adequate to attain that principal object. By the implied social contract, an individual surrenders to the community his right of protecting and avenging himself, under the reserved and indispensable condition that the public law shall defend him, or punish those by whom he has sustained injury. As revenge has been said, by Bacon, to be a species of wild justice, so the individual pursuit of justice is often a modified and legitimate pursuit of revenge, which ought, indeed, to be qualified by the moral and religious sentiments of the party, but to which law is bound to give free way, in requital for the bridle which she imposes on the indulgence of man's natural passions. The course of litigation, therefore, cannot be stopt; it can only be diminished, by providing beforehand as many regulations as will embrace the greater number of cases likely to occur, and trusting to the authority of the judges acting upon the spirit of the law, for the settlement of such as cannot be decided according to its letter.

The organisation of this great national work was proceeded in with the caution and deliberation which the importance of the subject eminently deserved. Dividing the subjects of legislation according to the usual distinctions of jurisconsults, the commissioners commenced by the publication and application of the laws in general; passed from that preliminary subject to the consideration of personal rights under all their various relations; then to rights respecting property; and, lastly, to those legal forms of procedure, by which the rights of citizens, whether arising out of personal circumstances, or as connected with property, are to be followed forth, explicated, and ascertained. Thus adopting the division, and in some degree the forms, of the Institutes of Justinian, the commission proceeded, according to the same model, to consider each subdivision of this general arrangement, and adopt respecting each such maxims or brocards of general law, as were to form the future basis of French jurisprudence. Their general principles being carefully connected and fixed, the ingenuity of the commissioners was exerted in deducing from them such a number of corollaries and subordinate maxims, as might provide, so far as human ingenuity could, for the infinite number of questions that were likely to emerge on the practical application of the general principles to the varied and intricate transactions of human life. It may be easily supposed, that a task so difficult gave rise to much discussion among the commissioners; and as their report, when fully weighed among themselves, was again subjected to the Council of State, before it was proposed to the Legislative Body, it must be allowed, that every means which could be devised were employed in maturely considering and revising the great body of national law, which, finally, under the name of the Code Napoleon, was adopted by France, and continues, under the title of the Civil Code, to be the law by which her subjects still possess and enforce their civil rights.

It would be doing much injustice to Napoleon, to suppress the great personal interest which, amid so many calls upon his time, he nevertheless took in the labours of the commission. He frequently attended their meetings, or those of the Council of State, in which their labours underwent revision; and, though he must be supposed entirely ignorant of the complicated system of jurisprudence as a science, yet his acute, calculating, and argumentative mind enabled him, by the broad views of genius and good sense, often to get rid of those subtleties by which professional persons are occasionally embarrassed, and to treat as cobwebs, difficulties of a technical or metaphysical character, which, to the jurisconsults, had the appearance of bonds and fetters.

There were times, however, on the other hand, when Napoleon was led, by the obvious and vulgar views of a question, to propose alterations which would have been fatal to the administration of justice, and the gradual enlargement and improvement of municipal law. Such was his idea, that advocates and solicitors ought only to be paid in the event of the cause being decided in favour of their client,[316]—a regulation which, had he ever adopted it, would have gone far to close the gates of justice; since, what practitioner would have forfeited at once one large portion of the means of his existence, and consented to rest the other upon the uncertainty of a gambling transaction? A lawyer is no more answerable for not gaining his cause, than a horse-jockey for not winning the race. Neither can foretell, with any certainty, the event of the struggle, and each, in justice, can only be held liable for the utmost exertion of his skill and abilities. Napoleon was not aware that litigation is not to be checked by preventing lawsuits from coming into court, but by a systematic and sage course of trying and deciding points of importance, which, being once settled betwixt

---

[316] "What litigations would thus have been prevented! On the first examination of a cause, a lawyer would have rejected it, had it been at all doubtful. There would have been little fear that a man, living by his labour, would have undertaken to conduct a lawsuit, from mere motives of vanity; and if he had, he would himself have been the only sufferer in case of failure. But my idea was opposed by a multitude of objections, and as I had no time to lose, I postponed the further consideration of the subject. Yet I am still convinced that the scheme might, with certain modifications, have been turned to the best account."—Napoleon, *Las Cases*, tom. vii., p. 199.

two litigants, cannot, in the same shape, or under the same circumstances, be again the subject of dispute among others.

The Civil Code of Napoleon is accompanied by a code of procedure in civil cases, and a code relating to commercial affairs, which may be regarded as supplemental to the main body of municipal law. There is, besides, a Penal Code, and a code respecting the procedure against persons accused under it. The whole forms a grand system of jurisprudence, drawn up by the most enlightened men of the age, having access to all the materials which the past and the present times afford; and it is not surprising that it should have been received as a great boon by a nation who, in some sense, may be said, previous to its establishment, to have been without any fixed or certain municipal law since the date of the Revolution.

But while we admit the full merit of the Civil Code of France, we are under the necessity of observing, that the very symmetry and theoretical consistency, which form, at first view, its principal beauty, render it, when examined closely, less fit for the actual purposes of jurisprudence, than a system of national law, which, having never undergone the same operation of compression, and abridgement, and condensation, to which that of France was necessarily subjected, spreads through a multiplicity of volumes, embraces an immense collection of precedents, and, to the eye of inexperience, seems, in comparison of the compact size and regular form of the French code, a labyrinth to which no clue is afforded. It is of the greater importance to give this subject some consideration, because it has of late been fashionable to draw comparisons between the jurisprudence of England and that of France, and even to urge the necessity of new-modelling the former upon such a concise and systematic plan as the latter exhibits.

In arguing this point, we suppose it will be granted, that that code of institutions is the most perfect, which most effectually provides for every difficult case as it emerges, and therefore averts, as far as possible, the occurrence of doubt, and, of course, of litigation, by giving the most accurate and certain interpretation to the general rule, when applied to cases as they arise. Now, in this point, which comprehends the very essence and end of all jurisprudence—the protection, namely, of the rights of the individual—the English law is preferable to the French in an incalculable degree; because each principle of English law has been the subject of illustration for many ages, by the most learned and wise judges, acting upon pleadings conducted by the most acute and ingenious men of each successive age. This current of legal judgments has been flowing for centuries, deciding, as they occurred, every question of doubt which could arise upon the application of general principles to particular circumstances; and each individual case, so decided, fills up some point which was previously disputable, and, becoming a rule for similar questions, tends to that extent to diminish the debateable ground of doubt and argument with which the law must be surrounded, like an unknown territory when it is first partially discovered.

It is not the fault of the French jurisconsults, that they did not possess the mass of legal authority arising out of a regular course of decisions by a long succession of judges competent to the task, and proceeding, not upon hypothetical cases supposed by themselves, and subject only to the investigation of their own minds, but upon such as then actually occurred in practice and had been fully canvassed and argued in open court. The French lawyers had not the advantage of referring to such a train of decisions; each settling some new point, or ascertaining and confirming some one which had been considered as questionable. By the Revolution, the ancient French courts had been destroyed, together with their records; their proceedings only served as matter of history or tradition, but could not be quoted in support or explanation of a code which had no existence until after their destruction. The commissioners endeavoured, we have seen, to supply this defect in their system, by drawing from their general rules such a number of corollary propositions as might, so far as possible, serve for their application to special and particular cases. But rules, founded in imaginary cases, can never have the same weight with precedents emerging in actual practice, where the previous exertions of the lawyers have put the case in every possible light, and where the judge comes to the decision, not as the theorist, whose opinion relates only to an ideal hypothesis of his own mind, but as the solemn arbiter of justice betwixt man and man, after having attended to, and profited by, the collision and conflict of opposite opinions, urged by those best qualified to state and to illustrate them. The value of such discussion is well known to all who have experience of courts of justice, where it is never thought surprising to hear the wisest judge confess, that he came into court with a view of the case at issue wholly different from that which he was induced to form after having given the requisite attention to the debate before him. But this is an advantage which can never be gained, unless in the discussion of a real case; and therefore the opinion of a judge, given *tota re cognita*, must always be a more valuable precedent, than that which the same learned individual could form upon an abstract and hypothetical question.

It is, besides, to be considered, that the most fertile ingenuity with which any legislator can be endued, is limited within certain bounds; and that, when he has racked his brain to provide for all the ideal cases which his prolific imagination can supply, it will be found that he has not anticipated or provided for the hundredth part of the questions which are sure to occur in actual practice. To make a practical application of what we have stated, to the relative jurisprudence of France and England, it may be remarked, that the Title V. of the 1st Book of the Civil Code, upon the subject of Marriage, contains only one hundred and sixty-one propositions respecting the rights of parties, arising in different circumstances out of that contract, the most important known in civilized society. If we deduce from this gross amount the great number of rules which are not doctrinal, but have only reference to the forms of procedure, the result will be greatly diminished. The English law, on the other hand, besides its legislative enactments, is guarded, as appears from Roper's Index, by no less than a thousand decided cases, or precedents, each of which affords ground to rule any other case in similar circumstances. In this view, the certainty of the law of England compared to that of France, bears the proportion of ten to one.

It is, therefore, a vulgar, though a natural and pleasing error, to prefer the simplicity of an ingenious and philosophic code of jurisprudence, to a system which has grown up with a nation, augmented with its wants, extended according to its civilisation, and only become cumbrous and complicated, because the state of society to which it applies has itself given rise to a complication of relative situations, to all of which the law is under the necessity of adapting itself. In this point of view, the Code of France may be compared to a warehouse built with much attention to architectural uniformity, showy in the exterior, and pleasing from the simplicity of its plan, but too small to hold the quantity of goods necessary to supply the public demand; while the Common Law of England resembles the vaults of some huge Gothic building—dark, indeed, and ill-arranged, but containing an immense store of commodities, which those acquainted with its recesses seldom fail to be able to produce to such as have occasion for them. The practiques, or adjudged cases, in fact, form a breakwater, as it were, to protect the more formal bulwark of the statute law; and although they cannot be regularly jointed or dovetailed together, each independent decision fills its space on the mound, and offers a degree of resistance to innovation, and protection to the law, in proportion to its own weight and importance.

The certainty of the English jurisprudence, (for, in spite of the ordinary opinion to the contrary, it has acquired a comparative degree of certainty,) rests upon the multitude of its decisions. The views which a man is disposed to entertain of his own rights, under the general provisions of the law, are usually controlled by some previous decision on the case; and a reference to precedents, furnished by a person of skill, saves, in most instances, the expense and trouble of a lawsuit, which is thus stifled in its very birth. If we are rightly informed, the number of actions at common law, tried in England yearly, does not exceed betwixt five-and-twenty and thirty on an average, from each county; an incredibly small number, when the wealth of the kingdom is considered, as well as the various and complicated transactions incident to the advanced and artificial state of society in which we live.

But we regard the multitude of precedents in English law as eminently favourable, not only to the certainty of the law, but to the liberty of the subject; and especially as a check upon any judge, who might be disposed to innovate either upon the rights or liberties of the lieges. If a general theoretical maxim of law be presented to an unconscientious or partial judge, he may feel himself at liberty, by exerting his ingenuity, to warp the right cause the wrong way. But if he is bound down by the decisions of his wise and learned predecessors, that judge would be venturous indeed, who should attempt to tread a different and more devious path than that which is marked by the venerable traces of their footsteps; especially, as he well knows that the professional persons around him, who might be blinded by the glare of his ingenuity in merely theoretical argument, are perfectly capable of observing and condemning every departure from precedent.[317] In such a case he becomes sensible, that, fettered as he is by previous decisions, the law is in his hands, to be administered indeed, but not to be altered or tampered with; and that if the evidence be read in the court, there are and must be many present, who know as well as himself, what must, according to precedent, be the verdict, or the decision. These are considerations which never can restrain or fetter a judge, who is only called upon to give his own explanation of the general principle briefly expressed in a short code, and susceptible therefore of a variety of interpretations, from which he may at pleasure select that which may be most favourable to his unconscientious or partial purposes.

It follows, also, from the paucity of laws afforded by a code constructed not by the growth of time, but suggested by the ingenuity of theorists suddenly called to the task, and considering its immense importance, executing it in haste, that many provisions, most important for the exercise of justice, must, of course, be neglected in the French Code. For example, the whole law of evidence, the very key and corner-stone of justice between man and man, has been strangely overlooked in the French jurisprudence. It is plain, that litigation may proceed for ever, unless there be some previous adjustment (called technically an issue) betwixt the parties, at the sight of the judge, tending to ascertain their averments in point of fact, as also the relevancy of those averments to the determination of the cause. In England, chiefly during the course of last century, the Law of Evidence has grown up to a degree of perfection, which has tended, perhaps more than any other cause, at

---

[317] The intelligent reader will easily be aware, that we mean not to say that every decision of their predecessors is necessarily binding on the judges of the day. Laws themselves become obsolete, and so do the decisions which have maintained and enforced them.—S.

once to prevent and to shorten litigation. If we pass from the civil to the penal mode of procedure in France, the British lawyer is yet more shocked by a course, which seems in his view totally to invert and confound every idea which he has received upon the law of evidence. Our law, it is well known, is in nothing so scrupulous as in any conduct towards the prisoner, which may have the most indirect tendency to entrap him into bearing evidence against himself. Law sympathizes in such a case with the frailties of humanity, and, aware of the consequence which judicial inquiries must always have on the mind of the timid and ignorant, never pushes the examination of a suspected person farther than he himself, in the natural hope of giving such an account of himself as may procure his liberty, shall choose to reply to it.

In France, on the contrary, the whole trial sometimes resolves into a continued examination and cross-examination of the prisoner, who is not only under the necessity of giving his original statement of the circumstances on which he founds his defence, but is confronted repeatedly with the witnesses, and repeatedly required to reconcile his own statement of the case with that which these have averred. With respect to the character of evidence, the same looseness of practice exists. No distinction seems to be made between that which is hearsay and that which is direct—that which is spontaneously given, and that which is extracted, or perhaps suggested, by leading questions. All this is contrary to what we are taught to consider as the essence of justice towards the accused. The use of the rack is, indeed, no longer admitted to extort the confession, but the mode of judicial examination seems to us a species of moral torture, under which a timid and ignorant, though innocent man, is very likely to be involved in such contradictions and inextricable confusion, that he may be under the necessity of throwing away his life by not knowing how to frame his defence.

We shall not protract these remarks on the Code Napoleon; the rather that we must frankly confess, that the manners and customs of a country make the greatest difference with respect to its laws, and that a system may work well in France, and answer all the purposes of jurisprudence, which in England would be thought very inadequate to the purpose. The humane institution which allows the accused the benefit of counsel, is a privilege which the English law does not permit to the accused, and may have its own weight in counterbalancing some of the inconveniences to which he is subjected in France. It seems also probable, that the deficiencies in the Code, arising from its recent origin and compressed form, must be gradually remedied, as in England, by the course of decisions pronounced by intelligent and learned judges; and that what we now state as an objection to the system, will gradually disappear under the influence of time.

Considered as a production of human science, and a manual of legislative sagacity, the Code may challenge general admiration for the clear and wise manner in which the axioms are drawn up and expressed. There are but few peculiarities making a difference betwixt its principles and those of the Roman law, which has in most contracts claimed to be considered as the mother of judicial regulation. The most remarkable occurs, perhaps, in the articles regulating what is called the Family Council—a subject which does not seem of importance sufficient to claim much attention.

The Civil Code being thus ascertained, provision was made for its regular administration by suitable courts; the judges of which did not, as before the Revolution, depend for their emoluments upon fees payable by the litigants, but were compensated by suitable salaries at the expense of the public. As France does not supply that class of persons who form what is called in England the unpaid magistracy, the French justices of peace received a small salary of from 800 to 1800 francs. Above them in rank came judges in the first instance, whose salaries amounted to 3000 francs at the utmost. The judges of the supreme tribunals enjoyed about four or five thousand francs; and those of the High Court of Cassation had not more than ten thousand francs, which scarcely enabled them to live and keep some rank in the metropolis. But, though thus underpaid, the situation of the French judges was honourable in the eyes of the country, and they maintained its character by activity and impartiality in their judicial functions.

The system of juries had been introduced in criminal cases, by the acclamation of the Assembly. Buonaparte found them, however, scrupulously restive and troublesome. There may be some truth in the charge, that they were averse from conviction, where a loop-hole remained for acquitting the criminal; and that many audacious crimes remained unpunished, from the punctilious view which the juries took of their duty. But it was from other motives than those of the public weal that Napoleon made an early use of his power, for the purpose of forming special tribunals, invested with a half-military character, to try all such crimes as assumed a political complexion, with power to condemn without the suffrage of a jury.[318] We have already alluded to this infringement of the most valuable political rights of the subject, in giving some account of the trials of Georges, Pichegru, and Moreau. No jury would ever have brought in a verdict against the latter, whose sole crime was his communication with Pichegru; a point of suspicion certainly, but no proof whatever of positive guilt. Political causes being out of the field, the trial by jury was retained in the French Code, so far as regarded criminal questions; and the general administration of justice seems to have been very well calculated for protecting the right, and punishing that which is wrong.

TAXATION—FOREIGN TRADE

The fiscal operations of Buonaparte were those of which the subjects complained the most, as indeed these are generally the grievances to which the people in every country are the most sensible. High taxes were imposed on the French people, rendered necessary by the expenses of the government, which, with all its accompaniments, were very considerable; and although Buonaparte did all in his power to throw the charge of the eternal wars which he waged upon the countries he overran or subdued, yet so far does the waste of war exceed any emolument which the armed hand can wrest from the sufferers, so imperfect a proportion do the gains of the victor bear to the losses of the vanquished, that after all the

---

[318] "In the Code Napoleon, and even in the Criminal Code, some good principles remain, derived from the Constituent Assembly; the institution of juries, for instance, the anchor of French hope: but of what value were legal institutions, when extraordinary tribunals, named by the Emperor, special courts, and military commissions, judged all political offences—the very offences on which the unchangeable ægis of the law is most required."—Mad. de Staël, tom. ii., p. 364.

revenue which was derived from foreign countries, the continual campaigns of the Emperor proved a constant and severe drain upon the produce of French industry. So rich, however, is the soil of France, such are the extent of her resources, such the patience and activity of her inhabitants, that she is qualified, if not to produce at once the large capitals which England can raise upon her national credit, yet to support the payment of a train of heavy annual imposts for a much longer period, and with less practical inconvenience. The agriculture of France had been extremely improved since the breaking up of the great estates into smaller portions, and the abrogation of those feudal burdens which had pressed upon the cultivators; and it might be considered as flourishing, in spite of war taxes, and, what was worse, the conscription itself.[319] Under a fixed and secure, though a severe and despotic government, property was protected, and agriculture received the best encouragement, namely, the certainty conferred on the cultivator of reaping the crop which he sowed.

It was far otherwise with commerce, which the maritime war, carried on so long and with such unmitigated severity, had very much injured, and the utter destruction of which was in a manner perfected by Buonaparte's adherence to the continental system. This, indeed, was the instrument by which, in the long run, he hoped to ruin the commerce of his rival, but the whole weight of which fell in the first instance on that of France, whose seaports showed no other shipping save coasters and fishing vessels; while the trade of Marseilles, Bourdeaux, Nantes, and other great commercial towns, had, in a great measure, ceased to exist. The government of the Emperor was proportionally unpopular in those cities; and although men kept silence, because surrounded by the spies of a jealous and watchful despotism, their dislike to the existing state of things could not entirely be concealed.[320]

---

[319] "Agriculture was continually improving during the whole course of the Revolution. Foreigners thought it ruined in France. In 1814, however, the English were compelled to admit, that we had little or nothing to learn from them."—Napoleon, *Las Cases*, tom. iv., p. 280.

[320] "Foreign trade, which in its results is infinitely inferior to agriculture, was an object of subordinate importance in my mind. Foreign trade is made for agriculture and home industry, and not the two latter for the former. The interests of these three fundamental

CAPITALISTS—MANUFACTURES

On the other hand, capitalists, who had sums invested in the public funds, or who were concerned with the extensive and beneficial contracts for the equipment and supply of Napoleon's large armies, with all the numerous and influential persons upon whom any part of the gathering in or expenditure of the public money devolved, were necessarily devoted to a government, under which, in spite of the Emperor's vigilance, immense profits were often derived, even after those by whom they were made had rendered to the ministers, or perhaps the generals, by whom they were protected, a due portion of the spoil. Economist and calculator as he was, to a most superior degree of excellence, Napoleon seems to have been utterly unable, if he really sincerely desired, to put an end to the peculations of those whom he trusted with power. He frequently, during his conversations at St. Helena, alludes to the venality and corruption of such as he employed in the highest offices, but whose sordid practices seem never to have occurred to him in the way of objection to his making use of their talents. Fouché, Talleyrand, and others, are thus stigmatized; and as we well know how long, and upon how many different occasions, he employed those statesmen, we cannot but suppose that, whatever may have been his sentiments as to the *men*, he was perfectly willing to compound with their peculation, in order to have the advantage of their abilities. Even when practices of this kind were too gross to be passed over, Napoleon's mode of censuring and repressing them was not adapted to show a pure sense of morality on his own part, or any desire to use extraordinary rigour in preventing them in future. This conclusion we form from the following anecdote which he communicated to Las Cases:—

Speaking of generals, and praising the disinterestedness of some, he adds, Massena, Augereau, Brune, and others, were undaunted depredators. Upon one occasion, the rapacity of the first

---

cases are diverging, and frequently conflicting. I always promoted them in their natural gradation; but I could not and ought not to have ranked them all on an equality. The difficulties, and even the total stagnation of foreign trade during my reign, arose out of the force of circumstances, and the accidents of the time. One brief interval of peace would immediately have restored it to its natural level."—Napoleon, *Las Cases*, tom. iv., p. 280.

of these generals had exceeded the patience of the Emperor. His mode of punishing him was peculiar. He did not dispossess him of the command, of which he had rendered himself unworthy by such an unsoldier-like vice—he did not strip the depredator by judicial sentence of his ill-won gains, and restore them to those from whom they were plundered—but, in order to make the General sensible that he had proceeded too far, Buonaparte drew a bill upon the banker of the delinquent, for the sum of two or three millions of francs, to be placed to Massena's debit, and the credit of the drawer. Great was the embarrassment of the banker, who dared not refuse the Imperial order, while he humbly hesitated, that he could not safely honour it without the authority of his principal. "Pay the money," was the Emperor's reply, "and let Massena refuse to give you credit at his peril." The money was paid accordingly, and placed to that General's debit, without his venturing to start any objections.[321] This was not punishing peculation, but partaking in its gains; and the spirit of the transaction approached nearly to that described by Le Sage, where the Spanish minister of state insists on sharing the bribes given to his secretary.

Junot, in like manner; who, upon his return from Portugal, gave general scandal by the display of diamonds, and other wealth, which he had acquired in that oppressed country, received from Buonaparte a friendly hint to be more cautious in such exhibitions. But his acknowledged rapacity was never thought of as a reason disqualifying him for being presently afterwards sent to the government of Illyria.

We are informed, in another of the Emperor's communications, that his Council of State was of admirable use to him in the severe inquisition which he was desirous of making into the public accounts. The proceedings of this Star Chamber, and the fear of being transmitted to the cognition of the Grand Judge, usually brought the culprits to composition; and when they had disgorged one, two, or three millions, the government was enriched, or, according to Buonaparte's ideas, the laws were satisfied.[322] The truth seems to be, that Buonaparte, though he contemned wealth in

---

[321] Las Cases, tom. ii., p. 230.
[322] Las Cases, tom. ii., p. 256.

his own person, was aware that avarice, which, after all, is but a secondary and sordid species of ambition, is the most powerful motive to mean and vulgar minds; and he willingly advanced gold to those who chose to prey upon it, so long as their efforts facilitated his possessing and retaining the unlimited authority to which he had reached. In a country where distress and disaster of every kind, public and private, had enabled many to raise large fortunes by brokerage and agiotage, a monied interest of a peculiar character was soon formed, whose hopes were of course rested on the wonderful ruler, by whose gigantic ambition new schemes of speculation were opened in constant succession, and whose unrivalled talents seemed to have found the art of crowning the most difficult undertakings with success.

It might be thought that the manufacturing interest must have perished in France, from the same reasons which so strongly and unfavourably afflicted the commerce of that country. In ceasing to import, there must indeed have been a corresponding diminution of the demand for goods to be exported, whether these were the growth of the soil, or the productions of French labour. Accordingly, this result had, in a great degree, taken place, and there was a decrease to a large amount in those goods which the French were accustomed to export in exchange for the various commodities supplied to them by British trade. But, though the real and legitimate stimulus to manufactures had thus ceased, Napoleon had substituted an artificial one, which had, to a certain extent, supplied the place of the natural trade. We must remark, that Napoleon, practically and personally frugal, was totally a stranger to the science of Political Economy. He never received or acted upon the idea, that a liberal system of commerce operates most widely in diffusing the productions which are usually the subjects of exchange, and in affording to every country the greatest share of the bounties of nature, or the produce of industry at the easiest rates. On the contrary, he had proceeded to act against the commerce of England, as, in a military capacity, he would have done in regard to the water which supplied a besieged city. He strove to cut it off, and altogether to destroy it, and to supply the absence of its productions, by such substitutes as France could furnish.[323] Hence, the factitious encouragement given to the French manufactures, not by the natural demand of the country, but by the bounties and prohibitions by which they were guarded. Hence, the desperate efforts made to produce a species of sugar from various substances, especially from the beet-root. To this unnatural and unthrifty experiment, Buonaparte used to attach so much consequence, that a piece of the new composition, which, with much time and trouble, had been made to approximate the quality of ordinary loaf-sugar, was preserved in a glass-case over the Imperial mantel-piece; and a pound or two of beet-sugar, highly-refined, was sent to foreign courts, to illustrate the means by which Napoleon consoled his subjects for the evils incumbent on the continental system. No way of flattering or gratifying the Emperor was so certain, as to appear eager in supporting these views; and it is said that one of his generals, when tottering in the Imperial good graces, regained the favour of his master, by planting the whole of a considerable estate with beet-root. In these, and on similar occasions, Napoleon, in his eager desire to produce the commodity desiderated, became regardless of those considerations which a manufacturer first ascertains when about to commence his operations, namely, the expense at which the article can be produced, the price at which it can be disposed of, and its fitness for the market which it is intended to supply. The various encouragements given to the cotton manufacturers, and others, in France, by which it was designed to supply the want of British goods, proceeded upon a system equally illiberal and impolitic. Still, however, the expensive bounties, and forced sales, which the influence of government afforded, enabled these manufacturers to proceed, and furnished employment to a certain number of men, who were naturally grateful for the protection which they received from the Emperor. In the same manner, although no artificial jet-d'eau, upon the grandest scale of expense, can so much refresh the face of nature, as the gentle and general influence of a natural shower, the former will nevertheless have the effect of feeding and nourishing such vegetable

---

[323] "The system of commercial licenses was no doubt mischievous. Heaven forbid that I should have laid it down as a principle. It was the invention of the English; with me it was only a momentary resource. Even the continental system, in its extent and rigour, was by me regarded as a measure occasioned by the war and temporary circumstances."—Napoleon, *Las Cases*, tom. iv., pp. 280, 283.

productions as are within the reach of its limited influence. It was thus, that the efforts of Napoleon at encouraging arts and manufactures, though proceeding on mistaken principles, produced, in the first instance, results apparently beneficial.[324]

PUBLIC WORKS

We have already had occasion to observe the immense public works which were undertaken at the expense of Buonaparte's government. Temples, bridges, and aqueducts, are, indeed, the coin with which arbitrary princes, in all ages, have endeavoured to compensate for the liberty of which the people are deprived. Such monuments are popular with the citizens, because the enjoyment of them is common to all, and the monarch is partial to a style of expenditure promising more plausibly than any other, to extend the memory of his present greatness far into the bosom of futurity. Buonaparte was not, and could not be insensible to either of these motives. His mind was too much enlarged to seek enjoyment in any of the ordinary objects of exclusive gratification; and undoubtedly, he who had done so much to distinguish himself during his life above ordinary mortals, must have naturally desired that his public works should preserve his fame to future ages. Accordingly, he undertook and executed some of the most splendid labours of modern times. The road over the Simplon, and the basins at Antwerp, may be always appealed to as gigantic specimens of his public spirit.

On the other hand, as we have before hinted, Napoleon sometimes aimed at producing immediate effect, by proposals and plans hastily adopted, as hastily decreed, and given in full form to the government journal; but which were either abandoned immediately after having been commenced, or perhaps, never advanced farther than the plan announced in the *Moniteur*. Buonaparte's habits of activity, his powers of deciding with a single

---

[324] "Industry or manufactures, and internal trade, made immense progress during my reign. The application of chemistry to the manufactures, caused them to advance with giant strides. I gave an impulse, the effects of which extended throughout Europe."—Napoleon, *Las Cases*, tom. iv., p. 280.

glance upon most points of either military or civil engineering, were liberally drawn upon to strike his subjects with wonder and admiration. During the few peaceful intervals of his reign, his impatience of inaction found amusement in traversing, with great rapidity, and often on the shortest notice, the various departments in France. Travelling with incredible celerity, though usually accompanied by the Empress Josephine, he had no sooner visited any town of consequence, than he threw himself on horseback, and, followed only by his aide-de-camp and his Mameluke Rustan, who with difficulty kept him in view, he took a flying survey of the place, its capacities of improvement, or the inconveniences which attached to it. With this local knowledge, thus rapidly acquired, he gave audience to the municipal authorities, and overwhelmed them very often with liberal and long details concerning the place round which he had galloped for the first time, but in which they had spent their days. Amazement at the extent and facility of the Emperor's powers of observation, was thus universally excited, and his hints were recorded in the *Moniteur*, for the admiration of France. Some public work, solicited by the municipality, or suggested by the enlightened benevolence of the Emperor himself, was then projected, but which, in many, if not most cases, remained unexecuted; the imperial funds not being in all circumstances adequate to the splendour of Napoleon's undertakings, or, which was the more frequent case, some new absorbing war, or project of ambition, occasioning every other object of expenditure to be postponed.

Even if some of Buonaparte's most magnificent works of public splendour had been completed, there is room to doubt whether they would have been attended with real advantage to his power, bearing the least proportion to the influence which their grandeur necessarily produces upon the imagination. We look with admiration, and indeed with astonishment, on the splendid dockyards of the Scheldt; but, had they been accomplished, what availed the building of first-rates, which France could hardly find sailors to man; which being manned, dared not venture out of the river; or, hazarding themselves upon the ocean, were sure to become the prizes of the first British men-of-war with whom they chanced to encounter? Almost all this profuse expense went to the mere purposes of vain glory; for more mischief would have been done to

British commerce, which Buonaparte knew well was the assailable point, by six privateers from Dunkirk, than by all the ships of the line which he could build at the new and most expensive dock-yard of Antwerp, with Brest and Toulon to boot.

In such cases as these, Napoleon did, in a most efficient manner, that which he ridiculed the Directory for being unable to do—he wrought on the imagination of the French nation, which indeed had been already so dazzled by the extraordinary things he had accomplished, that, had he promised them still greater prodigies than were implied in the magnificent works which he directed to be founded, they might still have been justified in expecting the performance of his predictions. And it must be admitted, looking around the city of Paris, and travelling through the provinces of France, that Buonaparte has, in the works of peaceful grandeur, left a stamp of magnificence, not unworthy of the soaring and at the same time profound spirit, which accomplished so many wonders in warfare.

PERSONAL AND FAMILY LIFE

The personal and family life of Napoleon was skilfully adapted to his pre-eminent station. If he had foibles connected with pleasure and passion, they were so carefully veiled to remain unknown to the world—at least, they were not manifested by any of those weaknesses which might serve to lower the Emperor to the stamp of common men. His conduct towards the Empress Josephine was regular and exemplary. From their accession to grandeur till the fatal divorce, as Napoleon once termed it, they shared the privacy of the same apartment, and for many years partook the same bed. Josephine is said, indeed, to have given her husband, upon whom she had many claims, some annoyance by her jealousy, to which he patiently submitted, and escaped the reproach thrown on so many heroes and men of genius, that, proof to every thing else, they are not so against the allurements of female seduction. What amours he had were of a passing character. No woman, excepting Josephine and her successor, who exercised their lawful and rightful influence, was ever known to possess any power over him.[325]

The dignity of his throne was splendidly and magnificently maintained, but the expense was still limited by that love of order which arose out of Buonaparte's powers of arithmetical calculation, habitually and constantly employed, and the trusting to which, contributed, it may be, to that external regularity and decorum which he always supported. In speaking of his own peculiar taste, Buonaparte said that his favourite work was a book of logarithms, and his choicest amusement was working out the problems. The individual to whom the Emperor made this singular avowal mentioned it with surprise to an officer near his person, who assured him, that not only did Napoleon amuse himself with arithmetical ciphers, and the theory of computation, but that he frequently brought it to bear on his domestic expenses, and diverted himself with comparing the price at which particular articles were charged to him, with the rate which they ought to have cost at the fair market price, but which, for reasons unnecessary to state, was in general greatly exceeded. Las Cases mentions his detecting such an overcharge in the gold fringe which adorned one of his state apartments. A still more curious anecdote respects a watch, which the most eminent artist of Paris had orders to finish with his utmost skill, in a style which might become a gift from the Emperor of France to his brother the King of Spain. Before the watch was out of the artist's hands, Napoleon received news of the battle of Vittoria. "All is now over with Joseph," were almost his first words after receiving the intelligence. "Send to countermand the order for the watch."[326]

Properly considered, this anecdote indicates no indifference as to his brother's fate, nor anxiety about saving a petty sum; it was the rigid calculation of a professed accountant, whose habits of accuracy induce him to bring every loss to a distinct balance, however trivial the off-set may be. But although the Emperor's economy descended to minute trifles, we are not to suppose that among such was its

---

[325] Las Cases, tom. iii., p. 297.
[326] The watch, half completed, remained in the hands of the artist, and is now the property of the Duke of Wellington.—S.

natural sphere. On the contrary, in the first year of the Consulate, he discovered and rectified an error in the statement of the revenue, to the amount of no less than two millions of francs, to the prejudice of the state. In another instance, with the skill which only a natural taste for calculation brought to excellence by constant practice could have attained, he discovered an enormous overcharge of more than sixty thousand francs in the pay-accounts of the garrison of Paris. Two such discoveries, by the head-magistrate, must have gone far to secure regularity in the departments in which they were made, in future.

Attending to this remarkable peculiarity throws much light on the character of Buonaparte. It was by dint of his rapid and powerful combinations that he succeeded as a general; and the same laws of calculation can be traced through much of his public and private life.

The palace charges, and ordinary expenses of the Emperor, were completely and accurately regulated by his Imperial Majesty's own calculation. He boasted to have so simplified the expenditure of the ancient kings of France, that his hunting establishment, though maintained in the utmost splendour, cost a considerable sum less than that of the Bourbons. But it must be recollected, first, that Napoleon was free from the obligation which subjected the Bourbons to the extravagant expenses which attended the high appointments of their household; secondly, that under the Imperial government, the whole establishment of falconry was abolished; a sport which is, in the opinion of many, more strikingly picturesque and interesting than any other variety of the chase, and which, as it infers a royal expense, belongs properly to sovereign princes.

THE IMPERIAL COURT

The Imperial court was distinguished not only by a severe etiquette, but the grandees, by whom its principal duties were discharged, were given to understand, that the utmost magnificence of dress and equipage was required from them upon public occasions. It was, indeed, a subject of complaint amongst the servants of the Crown, that though Buonaparte was in many respects attentive to their interests, gave them opportunities of acquiring wealth, invested them with large dotations and endowments, and frequently assisted them with an influence not easily withstood in the accomplishment of advantageous marriages; yet still the great expenditure at which they were required to support their appearance at the Imperial court, prevented their realizing any fortune which could provide effectually for their family. This expense Buonaparte loved to represent, as a tax which he made his courtiers pay to support the manufactures of France; but it was extended so far as to show plainly, that, determined as he was to establish his nobility on such a scale as to grace his court, it was far from being his purpose to permit them to assume any real power, or to form an existing and influential barrier between the crown and the people. The same inference is to be drawn from the law of France concerning succession in landed property, which is in ordinary cases equally divided amongst the children of the deceased; a circumstance which must effectually prevent the rise of great hereditary influence. And although, for the support of dignities granted by the Crown, and in some other cases; an entail of a portion of the favoured person's estate, called a *Majorat*, is permitted to follow the title, yet the proportion is so small as to give no considerable weight to those upon whom it devolves.

The composition of Buonaparte's court was singular. Amid his military dukes and mareschals were mingled many descendants of the old noblesse, who had been struck out of the lists of emigration. On these Buonaparte spread the cruel reproach, "I offered them rank in my army—they declined the service;—I opened my antechambers to them—they rushed in and filled them." In this the Emperor did not do justice to the ancient noblesse of France. A great many resumed their natural situation in the military ranks of their country, and a still greater number declined, in any capacity, to bend the knee to him, whom they could only consider as a successful usurper.

The ceremonial of the Tuileries was upon the most splendid scale, the public festivals were held with the utmost magnificence, and the etiquette was of the most strict and indefeasible character.

To all this Buonaparte himself attached consequence, as ceremonies characterising the spirit and dignity of his government; and he had drilled even his own mind into a veneration for all those outward forms connected with royalty, as accurately as if they had been during his whole life the special subject of his attention. There is a curious example given by Monsieur Las Cases. Buonaparte, in good-humoured trifling, had given his follower the titles of your highness, your lordship, and so forth, amidst which it occurred to him, in a fit of abstraction, to use the phrase, "Your Majesty." The instant that the word, sacred to his own ears, had escaped him, the humour of frolic was ended, and he resumed a serious tone, with the air of one who feels that he has let his pleasantry trespass upon an unbecoming and almost hallowed subject.

There were many of Buonaparte's friends and followers, bred, like himself, under the influence of the Revolution, who doubted the policy of his entering into such a strain of imitation of the ancient courts of Europe, and of his appearing anxious to emulate them in the only points in which he must necessarily fail, antiquity and long observance giving to ancient usages an effect upon the imagination, which could not possibly attach to the same ceremonial introduced into a court of yesterday. These would willingly have seen the dignity of their master's court rested upon its real and pre-eminent importance, and would have desired, that though republican principles were abandoned, something of the severe and manly simplicity of Republican manners should have continued to characterise a throne whose site rested upon the Revolution. The courtiers who held such opinions were at liberty to draw consolation from the personal appearance and habits of Napoleon. Amid the gleam of embroidery, of orders, decorations, and all that the etiquette of a court demands to render ceremonial at once accurate and splendid, the person of the Emperor was to be distinguished by his extreme simplicity of dress and deportment. A plain uniform, with a hat having no other ornament than a small three-coloured cockade, was the dress of him who bestowed all these gorgeous decorations, and in honour of whom these costly robes of ceremonial had been exhibited. Perhaps Napoleon might be of opinion, that a person under the common size, and in his latter days somewhat corpulent, was unfit for the display of rich dresses; or it is more likely he desired to intimate, that although he exacted from others the strict observance of etiquette, he held that the Imperial dignity placed him above any reciprocal obligation towards them.

Perhaps, also, in limiting his personal expenses, and avoiding that of a splendid royal wardrobe, Buonaparte might indulge that love of calculation and order, which we have noticed as a leading point of his character. But his utmost efforts could not carry a similar spirit of economy among the female part of his Imperial family; and it may be a consolation to persons of less consequence to know, that in this respect the Emperor of half the world was nearly as powerless as they may feel themselves to be. Josephine, with all her amiable qualities, was profuse, after the general custom of Creoles, and Pauline de Borghese was no less so. The efforts of Napoleon to limit their expenses, sometimes gave rise to singular scenes. Upon one occasion, the Emperor found in company of Josephine a certain milliner of high reputation and equal expense, with whom he had discharged his wife to have any dealings. Incensed at this breach of his orders, he directed the *marchande des modes* to be conducted to the Bicêtre; but the number of carriages which brought the wives of his principal courtiers to consult her in captivity, convinced him that the popularity of the milliner was too powerful even for his Imperial authority; so he wisely dropped a contention which must have appeared ludicrous to the public, and the artist was set at liberty, to charm and pillage the gay world of Paris at her own pleasure.[327]

On another occasion, the irregularity of Josephine in the article of expense, led to an incident which reminds us of an anecdote in the history of some Oriental Sultan. A creditor of the Empress, become desperate from delay, stopped the Imperial *calèche*, in which the Emperor was leaving St. Cloud, with Josephine by his side, and presented his account, with a request of payment. Buonaparte did as Saladin would have done in similar circumstances—he forgave the man's boldness in consideration of the justice of his claim, and caused the debt to be immediately settled. In fact, while blaming the expense and irregularity which

---

[327] Las Cases, tom. vii., p. 120.

occasioned such demands, his sense of justice, and his family affection, equally inclined him to satisfy the creditor.

The same love of order, as a ruling principle of his government, must have rendered Buonaparte a severe censor of all public breaches of the decencies of society. Public morals are in themselves the accomplishment and fulfilment of all laws; they alone constitute a national code. Accordingly, the manners of the Imperial court were under such regulation as to escape public scandal, if they were not beyond secret suspicion.[328] In the same manner, gambling, the natural and favourite vice of a court, was not practised in that of Buonaparte, who discountenanced high play by every means in his power. But he suffered it to be licensed to an immense and frightful extent, by the minister of police; nor can we give him the least credit when he affirms, that the gambling-houses which paid such immense rents to Fouché, existed without his knowledge. Napoleon's own assertion cannot make us believe that he was ignorant of the principal source of revenue which supported his police. He compounded, on this as on other occasions, with a good-will, in consideration of the personal advantage which he derived from it.

In the public amusements of a more general kind, Buonaparte took a deep interest. He often attended the theatre, though commonly in private, and without eclat. His own taste, as well as political circumstances, led him to encourage the amusements of the stage; and the celebrated Talma, whose decided talents placed him at the head of the French performers, received, as well in personal notice from the Emperor, as through the more substantial medium of a pension, an assurance, that the kindness which he had shown in early youth to the little Corsican student had not been forgotten. The strictest care was taken that nothing should be admitted on the stage which could awaken feelings or recollections unfavourable to the Imperial Government. When the acute wit of the Parisian audience seized on some expression or incident which had any analogy to public affairs, the greatest pains were taken, not only to

---

[328] We again repeat, that we totally disbelieve the gross infamies imputed to Napoleon within his own family, although sanctioned by the evidence of the Memoirs of Fouché. Neither Buonaparte's propensities nor his faults were those of a voluptuary.—S.

prevent the circumstance from recurring, but even to hinder it from getting into general circulation. This secrecy respecting what occurred in public, could not be attained in a free country, but was easily accomplished in one where the public papers, the general organs of intelligence, were under the strict and unremitted vigilance of the government.

There were periods when Buonaparte, in order to gain the approbation and sympathy of those who claim the exclusive title of lovers of liberty, was not unwilling to be thought the friend of liberal opinions, and was heard to express himself in favour of the liberty of the press, and other checks upon the executive authority. To reconcile his opinions (or rather what he threw out as his opinions) with a practice diametrically opposite, was no easy matter, yet he sometimes attempted it. On observing one or two persons, who had been his silent and surprised auditors on such an occasion, unable to suppress some appearance of incredulity, he immediately entered upon his defence. "I am," he said, "at bottom, and naturally, for a fixed and limited government. You seem not to believe me, perhaps because you conceive my opinions and practice are at variance. But you do not consider the necessity arising out of persons and circumstances. Were I to relax the reins for an instant, you would see a general confusion. Neither you nor I, probably, would spend another night in the Tuileries."

Such declarations have often been found in the mouths of those, who have seized upon an unlawful degree of authority over their species. Cromwell was forced to dissolve the Parliament, though he besought the Lord rather to slay him. State necessity is the usual plea of tyrants, by which they seek to impose on themselves and others; and, by resorting to such an apology, they pay that tribute to truth in their language, to which their practice is in the most decided opposition. But if there are any to whom such an excuse may appear valid, what can be, or must be, their sentiments of the French Revolution, which, instead of leading to national liberty, equality, and general happiness, brought the country into such a condition, that a victorious soldier was obliged, contrary to the conviction of his own conscience, to assume the despotic power, and subject the whole empire to the same arbitrary rules which directed the followers of his camp?

The press, at no time, and in no civilized country, was ever so completely enchained and fettered as at this period it was in France. The public journals were prohibited from inserting any article of public news which had not first appeared in the *Moniteur*, the organ of Government; and this, on all momentous occasions, was personally examined by Buonaparte himself. Nor were the inferior papers permitted to publish a word, whether in the way of explanation, criticism, or otherwise, which did not accurately correspond with the tone observed in the leading journal. They might, with the best graces of their eloquence, enhance the praise, or deepen the censure, which characterised the leading paragraph; but seizure of their paper, confiscation, imprisonment, and sometimes exile, were the unfailing reward of any attempt to correct what was erroneous in point of fact, or sophistical in point of reasoning. The *Moniteur*, therefore, was the sole guide of public opinion; and by his constant attention to its contents, it is plain that Napoleon relied as much on its influence to direct the general mind of the people of France, as he did upon the power of his arms, military reputation, and extensive resources, to overawe the other nations of Europe.

Chapter XXXIX

System of Education introduced into France by Napoleon—National University—its nature and objects—Lyceums—Proposed Establishment at Meudon.

The reputation of Buonaparte as a soldier, was the means which raised him to the Imperial dignity; and, unfortunately for himself, his ideas were so constantly associated with war and victory, that peaceful regulations of every kind were postponed, as of inferior importance; and thus war, which in the eye of reason ought always, even when most necessary and justifiable, to be regarded as an extraordinary state into which a nation is plunged by compulsion, was certainly regarded by Napoleon as almost the natural and ordinary condition of humanity. He had been bred on the battle-field, from which his glory first arose. "The earthquake voice of victory," according to the expression of Britain's noble and lost bard, "was to him the breath of life."[329] And although his powerful mind was capable of applying itself to all the various relations of human affairs, it was with war and desolation that he was most familiar, and the tendency of his government accordingly bore an aspect decidedly military.

PUBLIC EDUCATION

The instruction of the youth of France had been the subject of several projects during the Republic; which was the more necessary, as the Revolution had entirely destroyed all the colleges and seminaries of public instruction, most of which were more or less connected with the Church, and had left the nation almost destitute of any public means of education. These schemes were of

---

[329] "The triumph, and the vanity, The rapture of the strife— The earthquake voice of victory, To thee the breath of life." Byron, vol. x., p. 7.

course marked with the wild sophistry of the period. In many cases they failed in execution from want of public encouragement; in others, from want of funds. Still, however, though no fixed scheme of education had been adopted, and though the increasing vice and ignorance of the rising generation was sufficiently shocking, there existed in France two or three classes of schools for different purposes; as indeed it is not to be supposed that so great and civilized a nation could, under any circumstances, tolerate a total want of the means of educating their youth.

The schemes to which we allude had agreed in arranging, that each commune (answering, perhaps, to our parish) should provide a school and teacher, for the purpose of communicating the primary and most indispensable principles of education. This plan had in a great measure failed, owing to the poverty of the communes on whom the expense was thrown. In some cases, however, the communes had found funds for this necessary purpose; and, in others, the expense had been divided betwixt the public body, and the pupils who received the benefit of the establishment. So that these primary schools existed in many instances, though certainly in a precarious and languishing state.

The secondary schools were such as qualified persons, or those who held themselves out as such, had established upon speculation, or by the aid of private contributions, for teaching the learned and modern languages, geography, and mathematics.

There was besides evinced on the part of the Catholic clergy, so soon as the Concordat had restored them to some rank and influence, a desire to resume the task of public education, which, before the Revolution, had been chiefly vested in their hands. Their seminaries had been supported by the public with considerable liberality, and being under the control of the bishop, and destined chiefly to bring up young persons intended for the Church, they had obtained the name of Ecclesiastical Schools.

LYCEUMS

Matters were upon this footing when Buonaparte brought forward his grand project of a National University, composed of a Grand Master, a Chancellor, a treasurer, ten counsellors for life, twenty counsellors in ordinary, and thirty inspectors-general; the whole forming a sort of Imperial council, whose supremacy was to be absolute on matters respecting education. All teachers, and all seminaries of education, were subjected to the supreme authority of the National University, nor could any school be opened without a brevet or diploma from the Grand Master, upon which a considerable tax was imposed. It was indeed the policy of the government to diminish as far as possible the number of Secondary and of Ecclesiastical Schools, in order that the public education might be conducted at the public seminaries, called Lyceums, or Academies.

In these Lyceums the discipline was partly military, partly monastic. The masters, censors, and teachers, in the Lyceums and Colleges, were bound to celibacy; the professors might marry, but in that case were not permitted to reside within the precincts. The youth were entirely separated from their families, and allowed to correspond with no one save their parents, and then only through the medium, and under the inspection, of the censors. The whole system was subjected to the strict and frequent investigation of the University. The Grand Master might dismiss any person he pleased, and such a sentence of dismission disqualified the party receiving it from holding any civil employment.

In the general case, it is the object of a place of learning to remove from the eyes of youth that pomp and parade of war, by which at an early age they are so easily withdrawn from severe attention to their studies. The Lyceums of Buonaparte were conducted on a contrary principle; every thing was done by beat of drum, all the interior arrangements of the boys were upon a military footing. At a period when the soldier's profession held out the most splendid prospects of successful ambition, it was no wonder that young men soon learned to look forward to it as the only line worthy of a man of spirit to pursue. The devotion of the young students to the Emperor, carefully infused into them by their teachers, was farther excited by the recollection, that he was their benefactor for all the means of instruction afforded them; and thus they learned from every circumstance around them, that the first object of their lives was devotion to his service, and that the service required of them was of a military character.

There were in each Lyceum one hundred and fifty exhibitions, or scholarships, of which twenty were of value sufficient to cover the student's full expenses, while the rest, of smaller amount, were called half or three quarter bursaries, in which the parents or relations of the lad supplied a portion of the charge. From these Lyceums, two hundred and fifty of the most selected youth were yearly draughted into the more professional and special military schools maintained by the Emperor; and to be included in this chosen number, was the prime object of every student. Thus, every thing induced the young men brought up at these Lyceums, to look upon a military life as the most natural and enviable course they had to pursue; and thus Buonaparte accomplished that alteration on the existing generation, which he intimated, when he said, "The clergy regard this world as a mere diligence which is to convey us to the next—it must be my business to fill the public carriage with good recruits for my army."

Of the whole range of national education, that which was conducted at the Lyceums, or central schools, was alone supported by the state; and the courses there taught were generally limited to Latin and mathematics, the usual accomplishments of a military academy. Undoubtedly Brienne was in Napoleon's recollection; nor might he perhaps think a better, or a more enlarged course of education necessary for the subjects of France, than that which had advanced their sovereign to the supreme government. But there was a deeper reason in the limitation. Those who, under another system of education, might have advanced themselves to that degree of knowledge which becomes influential upon the mind of the public, or the fortunes of a state, by other means than those of violence, were disqualified for the task by that which they received in the Lyceums; and the gentle, studious, and peaceful youth, was formed, like all the rest of the generation, to the trade of war, to which he was probably soon to be called by the conscription. If the father chose to place his son at one of the Secondary Schools, where a larger sphere of instruction was opened, it was still at the risk of seeing the youth withdrawn from thence and transferred to the nearest Lyceum, if the Directors of the Academy should judge it necessary for the encouragement of the schools which appertained more properly to Government.

Yet Napoleon appears to have been blind to the errors of this system, or rather to have been delighted with them, as tending directly to aid his despotic views. "My university," he was accustomed to say to the very last, "was a masterpiece of combination, and would have produced the most material effect on the public mind." And he was wont on such occasions to throw the blame of its failure on Monsieur Fontanes, the Grand Master, who, he said, afterwards took merit with the Bourbons for having encumbered its operation in some of its most material particulars.

Buonaparte, it must be added, at a later period, resolved to complete his system of national education, by a species of Corinthian capital. He proposed the establishment of an institution at Meudon, for the education of his son, the King of Rome, where he was to be trained to the arts becoming a ruler, in the society of other young princes of the Imperial family, or the descendants of the allies of Napoleon. This would have been reversing the plan of tuition imposed on Cyrus, and on Henry IV., who were bred up among the common children of the peasants, that their future grandeur might not too much or too early obscure the real views of human nature and character. But it is unnecessary to speculate on a system which never was doomed to be brought to experiment; only, we may presume it was intended to teach the young Napoleon more respect to the right of property which his princely companions held in their toys and playthings, than his father evinced towards the crowns and sceptres of his brothers and allies.

WALTER SCOTT

Chapter XL

Military Details—Plan of the Conscription—Its Nature—and Effects— Enforced with unsparing rigour—Its influence upon the general Character of the French Soldiery—New mode of Conducting Hostilities introduced by the Revolution—Constitution of the French Armies, Forced Marches—La Maraude—Its Nature—and Effects—on the Enemy's Country, and on the French Soldiers themselves—Policy of Napoleon, in his personal conduct to his Officers and Soldiers—Altered Character of the French Soldiery during, and after, the Revolution.

THE CONSCRIPTION

We have shown that the course of education practised in France was so directed, as to turn the thoughts and hopes of the youth to a military life, and prepare them to obey the call of the conscription. This means of recruiting the military force, the most formidable ever established in a civilized nation, was originally presented to the Council of Five Hundred in 1798.[330] It comprehended a series of lists, containing the names of the whole youth of the kingdom, from the age of twenty to twenty-five, and empowering government to call them out successively, in such numbers as the exigencies of the state should require. The classes were five in number. The first contained those who were aged twenty years complete, before the commencement of the year relative to which the conscription was demanded, and the same rule applied to the other four classes of men, who had attained the twenty-first, twenty-second, twenty-third, twenty-fourth, and twenty-fifth years successively, before the same period. In practice, however, the second class of conscripts were not called out until the

---

[330] By General Jourdan.

first were actually in service, nor was it usual to demand more than the first class in any one year. But as the first class amounted to 60 or 80,000, so forcible and general a levy presented immense facilities to the government, and was proportionally burdensome to the people.[331]

This law, undoubtedly, has its general principle in the duty which every one owes to his country. Nothing can be more true, than that all men capable of bearing arms are liable to be employed in the defence of the state; and nothing can be more politic, than that the obligation which is incumbent upon all, should be, in the first instance, imposed upon the youth, who are best qualified for military service by the freshness of their age, and whose absence from the ordinary business of the country will occasion the least inconvenience. But it is obvious, that such a measure can only be vindicated in defensive war, and that the conduct of Buonaparte, who applied the system to the conduct of distant offensive wars, no otherwise necessary than for the satisfaction of his own ambition, stands liable to the heavy charge of having drained the very life-blood of the people intrusted to his charge, not for the defence of their own country, but to extend the ravages of war to distant and unoffending regions.

The French conscription was yet more severely felt by the extreme rigour of its conditions. No distinction was made betwixt the married man, whose absence might be the ruin of his family, and the single member of a numerous lineage, who could be easily spared. The son of the widow, the child of the decrepid and helpless, had no right to claim an exemption. Three sons might be carried off in three successive years from the same desolated parents; there was no allowance made for having already supplied a recruit. Those unable to serve were mulcted in a charge proportioned to the quota of taxes which they or their parents contributed to the state, and which might vary from fifty to twelve hundred francs. Substitutes might indeed be offered, but then it was both difficult and expensive to procure them, as the law required that such substitutes should not only have the usual personal

---

[331] Montgaillard, tom. v., p. 139. See also Mounteney's Historical Enquiry relative to Napoleon, p. 20.

qualifications for a military life, but should be domesticated within the same district as their principal, or come within the conscription of the year. Suitable persons were sure to know their own value, and had learned so well to profit by it, that they were not to be bribed to serve without excessive bounties. The substitutes also had the practice of deserting upon the road, and thus cheated the principal, who remained answerable for them till they joined their colours. On the whole, the difficulty of obtaining exemption by substitution was so great, that very many young men, well educated, and of respectable families, were torn from all their more propitious prospects, to bear the life, discharge the duties, and die the death, of common soldiers in a marching regiment.

There was no part of Napoleon's government enforced with such extreme rigour as the levy of the conscriptions.[332] The mayor, upon whom the duty devolved of seeing the number called for selected by lot from the class to whom they belonged, was compelled, under the most severe penalties, to avoid showing the slightest indulgence—the brand, the pillory, or the galleys, awaited the magistrate himself, if he was found to have favoured any individuals on whom the law of conscription had claims. The same laws held out the utmost extent of their terrors against refractory conscripts, and the public functionaries were every where in search of them. When arrested, they were treated like convicts of the most infamous description. Clothed in a dress of infamy, loaded with chains, and dragging weights which were attached to them, they were condemned like galley slaves to work upon the public fortifications. Their relations did not escape, but were often rendered liable for fines and penalties.

But perhaps the most horrible part of the fate of the conscript, was, that it was determined for life. Two or three, even four or five years spent in military service, might have formed a more endurable, though certainly a severe tax upon human life, with its natural prospects and purposes. But the conscription effectually

---

[332] "The Emperor constantly insisted on subjecting the whole nation to the laws of the conscription. 'I am inexorable on the subject of exemption,' said he, one day in the Council of State, 'it would be criminal. How could I acquit my conscience with having exposed the life of one man, for the advantage of another? I do not even think I would exempt my own son.'"—Las Cases, tom. vii., p. 197.

and for ever changed the character of its victims. The youth, when he left his father's hearth, was aware that he was bidding it adieu, in all mortal apprehension, for ever; and the parents who had parted with him, young, virtuous, and ingenuous, and with a tendency, perhaps, to acquire the advantages of education, could only expect to see him again (should so unlikely an event ever take place) with the habits, thoughts, manners, and morals, of a private soldier.

But whatever distress was inflicted on the country by this mode of compulsory levy, it was a weapon particularly qualified to serve Buonaparte's purposes. He succeeded to the power which it gave the government, amongst other spoils of the Revolution, and he used it to the greatest possible extent.

The conscription, of course, comprehended recruits of every kind, good, bad, and indifferent; but chosen as they were from the mass of the people, without distinction, they were, upon the whole, much superior to that description of persons among whom volunteers for the army are usually levied in other countries, which comprehends chiefly the desperate, the reckless, the profligate, and those whose unsettled or vicious habits render them unfit for peaceful life. The number of young men of some education who were compelled to serve in the ranks, gave a tone and feeling to the French army of a very superior character, and explains why a good deal of intellect and power of observation was often found amongst the private sentinels. The habits of the nation also being strongly turned towards war, the French formed, upon the whole, the most orderly, most obedient, most easily commanded, and best regulated troops, that ever took the field in any age or country. In the long and protracted struggle of battle, their fiery courage might sometimes be exhausted before that of the determined British; but in all that respects the science, practice, and usages of war, the French are generally allowed to have excelled their more stubborn, but less ingenious rivals. They excelled especially in the art of shifting for themselves; and it was one in which the wars of Napoleon required them to be peculiarly adroit.[333]

---

[333] Mad. de Staël, tom. ii., p. 351.

The French Revolution first introduced into Europe a mode of conducting hostilities, which transferred almost the whole burden of the war to the country which had the ill-fortune to be the seat of its operations, and rendered it a resource rather than a drain to the successful belligerent. This we shall presently explain.

THE CONSCRIPTION—CORPS D'ARMÉE

At the commencement of a campaign, nothing could be so complete as the arrangement of a French army. It was formed into large bodies, called *corps d'armée*, each commanded by a king, viceroy, mareschal, or general officer of high pretensions, founded on former services. Each corps d'armée formed a complete army within itself, and had its allotted proportion of cavalry, infantry, artillery, and troops of every description. The corps d'armée consisted of from six to ten divisions, each commanded by a general of division. The divisions, again, were subdivided into brigades, of which each, comprehending two or three regiments, (consisting of two or more battalions,) was commanded by a general of brigade. A corps d'armée might vary in number from fifty to eighty thousand men, and upwards; and the general of such a body exercised the full military authority over it, without the control of any one excepting the Emperor himself. There were very few instances of the Emperor's putting the officers who were capable of this high charge under command of each other; indeed, so very few, as might almost imply some doubt on his part, of his commands to this effect being obeyed, had they been issued. This system of dividing his collected forces into separate and nearly independent armies, the generals of which were each intrusted with and responsible for his execution of some separate portion of an immense combined plan, gave great celerity and efficacy to the French movements; and, superintended as it was by the master-spirit which planned the campaign, often contributed to the most brilliant results. But whenever it became necessary to combine two corps d'armée in one operation, it required the personal presence of Napoleon himself.

Thus organised, the French army was poured into some foreign country by forced marches, without any previous arrangement of stores or magazines for their maintenance, and with the purpose of maintaining them solely at the expense of the inhabitants. Buonaparte was exercised in this system; and the combination of great masses, by means of such forced marches, was one great principle of his tactics. This species of war was carried on at the least possible expense of money to his treasury; but it was necessarily at the greatest possible expenditure of human life, and the incalculable increase of human misery. Napoleon's usual object was to surprise the enemy by the rapidity of his marches, defeat him in some great battle, and then seize upon his capital, levy contributions, make a peace with such advantages as he could obtain, and finally return to Paris.

LA MARAUDE

In these dazzling campaigns, the army usually began their march with provisions, that is, bread or biscuit for a certain number of days, on the soldiers' backs. Cattle also were for a time driven along with them, and slaughtered as wanted. These articles were usually provided from some large town or populous district, in which the troops might have been cantoned. The horses of the cavalry were likewise loaded with forage, for the consumption of two or three days. Thus provided, the army set forward on its expedition by forced marches. In a very short time the soldiers became impatient of their burdens, and either wasted them by prodigal consumption, or actually threw them away. It was then that the officers, who soon entertained just apprehensions of the troops suffering scarcity before another regular issue of provisions, gave authority to secure supplies by what was called *la maraude*, in other words, by plunder. To ensure that these forced supplies should be collected and distributed systematically, a certain number of soldiers from each company were despatched to obtain provisions at the villages and farm-houses in the neighbourhood of the march, or of the ground upon which the army was encamped. These soldiers were authorised to compel the inhabitants to deliver their provisions without receipt or payment; and, such being their regular duty, it may be well supposed that they did not confine themselves to provisions, but exacted money and articles of value, and committed many other similar abuses.

THE FRENCH SOLDIERY

It must be owned, that the intellectual character of the French, and the good-nature which is the real ground of their national character, rendered their conduct more endurable under the evils of this system than could have been expected, provided always that provisions were plenty, and the country populous. A sort of order was then observed, even in the disorder of the *maraude*, and pains were taken to divide regularly the provisions thus irregularly obtained. The general temper of the soldiery, when unprovoked by resistance, made them not wholly barbarous; and their original good discipline, the education which many had received, with the habits of docility which all had acquired, prevented them from breaking up into bands of absolute banditti, and destroying themselves by their own irregularities. No troops except the French could have subsisted in the same manner; for no other army is sufficiently under the command of its officers.

But the most hideous features of this system were shown when the army marched through a thinly-peopled country, or when the national character, and perhaps local facilities, encouraged the natives and peasants to offer resistance. Then the soldiers became animated alike by the scarcity of provisions, and irritated at the danger which they sometimes incurred in collecting them. As their hardships increased, their temper became relentless and reckless, and, besides indulging in every other species of violence, they increased their own distresses by destroying what they could not use. Famine and sickness were not long of visiting an army which traversed by forced marches a country exhausted of provisions. These stern attendants followed the French columns as they struggled on. Without hospitals, and without magazines, every straggler who could not regain his ranks fell a victim to hunger, to weather, to weariness, to the vengeance of an incensed peasantry. In this manner, the French army suffered woes, which, till these tremendous wars, had never been the lot of troops in hostilities carried on between civilized nations. Still Buonaparte's object was gained; he attained, amid these losses and sacrifices, and at the expense of them, the point which he had desired; displayed his masses to the terrified eyes of a surprised enemy; reaped the reward of his despatch in a general victory; and furnished new subjects of triumph to the *Moniteur*. So much did he rely upon the celerity of movement, that if an officer asked time to execute any of his commands, it was frequently his remarkable answer—"Ask me for any thing except time." That celerity depended on the uncompromising system of forced marches, without established magazines; and we have described how wasteful it must have been to human life.[334] But when the battle was over, the dead were at rest, and could not complain; the living were victors, and soon forgot their sufferings; and the loss of the recruits who had been wasted in the campaign, was supplied by another draught upon the youth of France, in the usual forms of the conscription.

Buonaparte observed, with respect to his army, an adroit species of policy. His mareschals, his generals, his officers of high rank, were liberally honoured and rewarded by him; but he never treated them with personal familiarity. The forms of etiquette were, upon all occasions, strictly maintained. Perhaps he was of opinion that the original equality in which they had stood with regard to each other, would have been too strongly recalled by a more familiar mode of intercourse. But to the common soldier, who could not misconstrue or intrude upon his familiarity, Buonaparte observed a different line of conduct. He permitted himself to be addressed by them on all suitable occasions, and paid strict attention to their petitions, complaints, and even their remonstrances. What they complained of was, in all instances, inquired into and reformed, if the complaints were just. After a battle, he was accustomed to consult the regiments which had distinguished themselves, concerning the merits of those who had deserved the Legion of Honour, or other military distinction. In these moments of

---

[334] "This is not correct. Activity of movement and rapidity of attack are as conducive to the well-being of mankind, as they are favourable to victory. Where did Sir Walter Scott learn that the system of forced marches pursued by the Emperor Napoleon was always without magazines? On the contrary, his administrative system was admirable, and his calculations on this head worthy of his plans: without the one, the other could not have succeeded."— Louis Buonaparte, p. 54.

conscious importance, the sufferings of the whole campaign were forgotten; and Napoleon seemed, to the soldiery who surrounded him, not as the ambitious man who had dragged them from their homes, to waste their valour in foreign fields, and had purchased victory at the expense of subjecting them to every privation, but as the father of the war, to whom his soldiers were as children, and to whom the honour of the meanest private was as dear as his own.

Every attention was paid, to do justice to the claims of the soldier, and provide for his preferment as it was merited. But with all this encouragement, it was the remark of Buonaparte himself, that the army no longer produced, under the Empire, such distinguished soldiers as Pichegru, Kleber, Moreau, Massena, Desaix, Hoche, and he himself above all, who, starting from the ranks of obscurity, like runners to a race, had astonished the world by their progress. These men of the highest genius, had been produced, as Buonaparte thought, in and by the fervour of the Revolution; and he appears to have been of opinion, that, since things had returned more and more into the ordinary and restricted bounds of civil society, men of the same high class were no longer created. There is, however, some fallacy in this statement. Times of revolution do not create great men, but revolutions usually take place in periods of society when great principles have been under discussion, and the views of the young and of the old have been turned, by the complexion of the times, towards matters of grand and serious consideration, which elevate the character and raise the ambition. When the collision of mutual violence, the explosion of the revolution itself actually breaks out, it neither does nor can *create* talent of any kind. But it brings forth, (and in general destroys,) in the course of its progress, all the talent which the predisposition to discussion of public affairs had already encouraged and fostered; and when that talent has perished, it cannot be replaced from a race educated amidst the furies of civil war. The abilities of the Long Parliament ceased to be seen under the Commonwealth, and the same is true of the French Convention, and the Empire which succeeded it. Revolution is like a conflagration, which throws temporary light upon the ornaments and architecture of the house to which it attaches, but always ends by destroying them.

It is said also, probably with less authority, that Napoleon, even when surrounded by those Imperial Guards, whose discipline had been so sedulously carried to the highest pitch, sometimes regretted the want of the old Revolutionary soldiers, whose war-cry, "Vive la Republique!" identified each individual with the cause which he maintained. Napoleon, however, had no cause to regret any circumstance which referred to his military power. It was already far too great, and had destroyed the proper scale of government in France, by giving the military a decided superiority over all men of civil professions, while he himself, with the habits and reasoning of a despotic general, had assumed an almost unlimited authority over the fairest part of Europe. Over foreign countries, the military renown of France streamed like a comet, inspiring universal dread and distrust; and whilst it rendered indispensable similar preparations for resistance, it seemed as if peace had departed from the earth for ever, and that its destinies were hereafter to be disposed of according to the laws of brutal force alone.

Chapter XLI

Effects of the Peace of Tilsit—Napoleon's views of a State of Peace—Contrasted with those of England—The Continental System—Berlin and Milan Decrees—British Orders in Council—Spain—Retrospect of the Relations of that Country with France since the Revolution—Godoy—His Influence—Character—and Political Views—Ferdinand, Prince of Asturias, applies to Napoleon for Aid—Affairs of Portugal—Treaty of Fontainbleau—Departure of the Prince Regent for Brazil—Entrance of Junot into Lisbon—His unbounded Rapacity—Disturbances at Madrid—Ferdinand detected in a Plot against his Father, and imprisoned—King Charles applies to Napoleon—Wily Policy of Buonaparte—Orders the French Army to enter Spain.

The peace of Tilsit had been of that character, which, while it settled the points of dispute between two rival monarchies, who had found themselves hardly matched in the conflict to which it put a period, left both at liberty to use towards the nations more immediately under the influence of either, such a degree of discretion as their power enabled them to exercise. Such was Napoleon's idea of pacification, which amounted to this:—"I will work my own pleasure with the countries over which my power gives me not indeed the right, but the authority and power; and you, my ally, shall, in recompense, do what suits you in the territories of other states adjoining to you, but over which I have no such immediate influence."

This was the explanation which he put upon the treaty of Amiens, and this was the species of peace which long afterwards he regretted had not been concluded with England. His regrets on that point were expressed at a very late period, in language which is perfectly intelligible. Speaking of France and England, he said, "We have done each other infinite harm—we might have rendered each other infinite service by mutual good understanding. If the school of Fox had succeeded, we would have understood each other—there would only have been in Europe one army and one fleet—we would have governed the world—we would have fixed repose and prosperity every where, either by force or by persuasion. Yes—I repeat how much good we might have done—how much evil we have actually done to each other."[335]

Now, the fundamental principle of such a pacification, which Buonaparte seems to the very last to have considered as the mutual basis of common interest, was such as could not, ought not, nay, dared not, have been adopted by any ministry which England could have chosen, so long as she possessed a free Parliament. Her principle of pacification must have been one that ascertained the independence of other powers, not which permitted her own aggressions, and gave way to those of France. Her wealth, strength, and happiness, do, and must always, consist in the national independence of the states upon the continent. She could not, either with conscience or safety, make peace with a usurping conqueror, on the footing that she herself was to become a usurper in her turn. She has no desire or interest to blot out other nations from the map of Europe, in order that no names may remain save those of Britain and France; nor is she interested in depriving other states of their fleets, or of their armies. Her statesmen must disclaim the idea of governing the world, or a moiety of the world, and of making other nations either happy or unhappy by force of arms. The conduct of England in 1814 and in 1815, evinced this honest and honourable policy; since, yielding much to others, she could not be accused of being herself influenced by any views to extend her own dominion, in the general confusion and blending which arose out of the downfall of the external power of France. That, however, is a subject for another place.

In the meanwhile, France, who, with Russia, had arranged a treaty of pacification on a very different basis, was now busied in gathering in the advantages which she expected to derive from it. In

---

[335] Las Cases, tom. iv., p. 163.

doing so, it seems to have been Buonaparte's principal object so to consolidate and enforce what he called his Continental System, as ultimately to root out and destroy the remaining precarious communications, which England, by her external commerce, continued to maintain with the nations of the continent.

EFFECTS OF THE PEACE OF TILSIT

To attain this grand object, the treaty of Tilsit and its consequences had given him great facilities. France was his own—Holland was under the dominion, nominally, of his brother Louis, but in a great measure at his devotion. His brother Jerome was established in the kingdom of Westphalia. It followed, therefore, in the course of his brother's policy, that he was to form an alliance worthy of his new rank. It has been already noticed that he had abandoned, by his brother's command, Elizabeth Paterson, daughter of a respectable gentleman of Baltimore, whom he had married in 1803. He was now married at the Tuileries to Frederica Catherine, daughter of the King of Wirtemberg.[336]

Prussia, and all the once free ports of the Hanseatic League, were closed against English commerce, so far as absolute military power could effect that purpose. Russia was not so tractable in that important matter as the terms of the treaty of Tilsit, and Napoleon's secret engagements with the Czar, had led him to hope. But Alexander was too powerful to be absolutely dictated to in the enforcement of this anti-commercial system; and, indeed, the peculiar state of the Russian nation might have rendered it perilous to the Czar to enforce the non-intercourse to the extent which Napoleon would have wished. The large, bulky, and heavy commodities of Russia—hemp and iron, and timber and wax, and pitch and naval stores—that produce upon which the Boyards of the empire chiefly depended for their revenue, would not bear the expense of transportation by land; and England, in full and exclusive

---

[336] The marriage took place on the 12th of August, and, a few days after, Jerome was proclaimed king of Westphalia. The constitution of the kingdom was issued on the 15th December, the new monarch's birth-day, who had then completed his twenty-second year; and, on the 21st, Jerome made his public entry into Cassel.

command of the sea, was her only, and at the same time her willing customer. Under various elusory devices, therefore, England continued to purchase Russian commodities, and pay for them in her own manufactures, in spite of the decrees of the French Emperor, and in defiance of the ukases of the Czar himself; and to this Buonaparte was compelled to seem blind, as what his Russian ally could not, or would not, put an end to.

The strangest struggle ever witnessed in the civilized world began now to be maintained, betwixt Britain and those countries who felt the importation of British goods as a subject not only of convenience, but of vital importance, on the one hand, and France on the other; whose ruler was determined that on no account should Britain either maintain intercourse with the continent, or derive the inherent advantages of a free trade. The decrees of Berlin were reinforced by others of the French Emperor, yet more peremptory and more vexatious. By these, and particularly by one promulgated at Milan, 17th December, 1807, Napoleon declared Britain in a state of blockade—all nations whatever were prohibited not only to trade with her, but to deal in any articles of British manufactures.[337] Agents were named in every seaport and trading-town on the part of Buonaparte. There was an ordinance that no ship should be admitted into any of the ports of the continent without certificates, as they were called, of origin; the purpose of which was to show that no part of their cargo was of British produce. These regulations were met by others on the part of Britain, called the Orders in Council.[338] They permitted all neutrals to trade with countries at peace with Great Britain, providing they touched at a British port, and paid the British duties. Neutrals were thus placed in a most undesirable predicament betwixt the two great contending powers. If they neglected the British Orders in Council, they were captured by the cruizers of England, with which the sea was covered. If they paid duties at British ports, they were confiscated, if the fact could be discovered, on arrival at any port under French influence. This led to every species of deception by which the real character of the mercantile transaction could be disguised. False papers, false entries,

---

[337] Annual Register, vol. xlix., p. 779.
[338] For copies of the several Orders in Council, see Hansard's Parliamentary Debates, vol. x., p. 126, and Annual Register, vol. xlix., pp. 745, 746, 754.

false registers, were every where produced; and such were the profits attending the trade, that the most trusty and trusted agents of Buonaparte, men of the highest rank in his empire, were found willing to wink at this contraband commerce, and obtained great sums for doing so. All along the sea-coast of Europe, this struggle was keenly maintained betwixt the most powerful individual the world ever saw, and the wants and wishes of the society which he controlled—wants and wishes not the less eagerly entertained, that they were directed towards luxuries and superfluities.

But it was chiefly the Spanish Peninsula, in which the dominion of its ancient and natural princes still nominally survived, which gave an extended vent to the objects of British commerce. Buonaparte, indeed, had a large share of its profits, since Portugal, in particular, paid him great sums to connive at her trade with England. But at last the weakness of Portugal, and the total disunion of the Royal Family in Spain, suggested to Napoleon the thoughts of appropriating to his own family, or rather to himself, that noble portion of the continent of Europe. Hence arose the Spanish contest, of which he afterwards said in bitterness, "That wretched war was my ruin; it divided my forces—obliged me to multiply my efforts, and injured my character for morality."[339] But could he expect better results from a usurpation, executed under circumstances of treachery perfectly unexampled in the history of Europe? Before entering, however, upon this new and most important era of Napoleon's history, it is necessary hastily to resume some account of the previous relations between France and the Peninsula since the Revolution.

MANUEL DE GODOY—SPAIN

Manuel de Godoy, a favourite of Charles IV. and the paramour of his profligate Queen, was at this time the uncontrolled minister of Spain.[340] He bore the title of Prince of the Peace, or of

---

[339] Las Cases, tom. iii., p. 220.
[340] From the rank of a simple gentleman of the royal guards, Godoy had, through the Queen's influence, been raised to the highest dignities. "There was no jealousy in the Queen's attachment to this minion; she gave him one of the royal family in marriage, but the private life of the favourite continued to be as infamous as the means whereby he had

Peace, as it was termed for brevity's sake, on account of his having completed the pacification of Basle, which closed the revolutionary war betwixt Spain and France. By the subsequent treaty of Saint Ildefonso, he had established an alliance, offensive and defensive, betwixt the two countries, in consequence of which Spain had taken from time to time, without hesitation, every step which Buonaparte's interested policy recommended. But notwithstanding this subservience to the pleasure of the French ruler, Godoy seems in secret to have nourished hopes of getting free of the French yoke; and at the very period when the Prussian war broke out, without any necessity which could be discovered, he suddenly called the Spanish forces to arms, addressing to them a proclamation of a boastful, and, at the same time, a mysterious character, indicating that the country was in danger, and that some great exertion was expected from the Spanish armies in her behalf. Buonaparte received this proclamation on the field of battle at Jena, and is said to have sworn vengeance against Spain.[341] The news of that great victory soon altered Godoy's military attitude, and the minister could find no better excuse for it, than to pretend that he had armed against an apprehended invasion of the Moors. Napoleon permitted the circumstance to remain unexplained. It had made him aware of Godoy's private sentiments in respect to himself and to France, if he had before doubted them; and though passed over without farther notice, this hasty armament of 1806 was assuredly not dismissed from his thoughts.

In the state of abasement under which they felt their government and royal family to have fallen, the hopes and affections of the Spaniards were naturally turned on the heir-apparent, whose succession to the crown they looked forward to as a signal for better things, and who was well understood to be at open variance with the all-powerful Godoy. The Prince of the Asturias, however, does not seem to have possessed any portion of that old heroic pride, and love of independence, which ought to have marked the future King of Spain. He was not revolted at the sway which Buonaparte held in

---

risen. It is said, that there was no way so certain to obtain promotion, as by pandering to his vices; and that wives, sisters, and daughters were offered him as the price of preferment, in a manner more shameful than had ever before been witnessed in a Christian country."— Southey, *History of the Peninsular War*, vol. i., p. 79.
[341] De Pradt, Mémoires sur la Révolution d'Espagne, p. 15.

Europe and in Spain, and, far from desiring to get rid of the French influence, he endeavoured to secure Buonaparte's favour for his own partial views, by an offer to connect his own interest in an indissoluble manner with those of Napoleon and his dynasty. Assisted by some of the grandees, who were most especially tired of Godoy and his administration, the Prince wrote Buonaparte a secret letter, [11th October,] expressing the highest esteem for his person; intimating the condition to which his father, whose too great goodness of disposition had been misguided by wicked counsellors, had reduced the flourishing kingdom of Spain; requesting the counsels and support of the Emperor Napoleon, to detect the schemes of those perfidious men; and entreating, that, as a pledge of the paternal protection which he solicited, the Emperor would grant him the honour of allying him with one of his relations.[342]

In this manner the heir-apparent of Spain threw himself into the arms, or, more properly, at the feet of Napoleon; but he did not meet the reception he had hoped for. Buonaparte was at this time engaged in negotiations with Charles IV., and with that very Godoy whom it was the object of the Prince to remove or ruin; and as they could second his views with all the remaining forces of Spain, while Prince Ferdinand was in possession of no actual power or authority, the former were for the time preferable allies. The Prince's offer, as what might be useful on some future occasion, was for the present neither accepted nor refused. Napoleon was altogether silent. The fate of the royal family was thus in the hands of the Stranger. Their fate was probably already determined. But before expelling the Bourbons from Spain, Napoleon judged it most politic to use their forces in subduing Portugal.

The flower of the Spanish army, consisting of sixteen thousand men, under the Marquis de la Romana, had been marched into the north of Europe, under the character of auxiliaries of France. Another detachment had been sent to Tuscany, commanded by O'Farrel. So far the kingdom was weakened by the absence of her own best troops; the conquest of Portugal was to be made a pretext for introducing the French army to dictate to the whole Peninsula.

---

[342] Southey, vol. i., p. 87.

Portugal was under a singularly weak government. Her army was ruined; the soul and spirit of her nobility was lost; her sole hope for continuing in existence, under the name of an independent kingdom, rested in her power of purchasing the clemency of France, and some belief that Spain would not permit her own territories to be violated for the sake of annihilating an unoffending neighbour and ally.

Shortly after the treaty of Tilsit, the Prince Regent of Portugal was required, by France and Spain jointly, to shut his ports against the English, to confiscate the property of Britain, and to arrest the persons of her subjects wherever they could be found within his dominions. The Prince reluctantly acceded to the first part of this proposal; the last he peremptorily refused, as calling upon him at once to violate the faith of treaties and the rights of hospitality. And the British merchants received intimation, that it would be wisdom to close their commercial concerns, and retire from a country which had no longer the means of protecting them.

In the meantime, a singular treaty was signed at Fontainebleau, for the partition of the ancient kingdom of Portugal. By this agreement, a regular plan was laid for invading Portugal with French and Spanish armies, accomplishing the conquest of the country, and dividing it into three parts. The province of Entre Minho y Douro, with the town of Oporto, was to belong to the King of Etruria (who was to cede his Italian dominions to Napoleon,) with the title of King of Northern Lusitania; another portion, consisting of Alenteyo and the Algarves, was to be given in sovereignty to Godoy, with the title of Prince of the Algarves; and a third was to remain in sequestration till the end of the war.[343] By the treaty of Fontainebleau, Napoleon obtained two important advantages; the first, that Portugal should be conquered; the second, that a great part of the Spanish troops should be employed on the expedition, and their native country thus deprived of their assistance. It is impossible to believe that he ever intended Godoy, or the King of Etruria, should gain any thing by the stipulations in their behalf.

---

[343] This treaty, together with a convention dependent on it, was signed the 27th, and ratified by Napoleon on the 29th of October.

JUNOT ADVANCES UPON LISBON

Junot, one of the most grasping, extravagant, and profligate of the French generals, a man whom Buonaparte himself has stigmatized as a monster of rapacity,[344] was appointed to march upon Lisbon, and intrusted with the charge of reconciling to the yoke of the invaders, a nation who had neither provoked war, nor attempted resistance.

Two additional armies, consisting partly of French and partly of Spaniards, supported the attack of Junot. A French army, amounting to 40,000 men, was formed at Bayonne, in terms of the treaty of Fontainbleau, destined, it was pretended, to act as an army of reserve, in case the English should land troops for the defence of Portugal, but which, it had been stipulated, was on no account to enter Spain, unless such a crisis should demand their presence. It will presently appear what was the true purpose of this army of reserve, and under what circumstances it was really intended to enter the Spanish territory.

Meantime, Junot advanced upon Lisbon with such extraordinary forced marches, as very much dislocated and exhausted his army. But this was of the less consequence, because, aware that he could not make an effectual resistance, the Prince Regent had determined that he would not, by an ineffectual show of defence, give the invaders a pretext to treat Portugal like a conquered country. He resolved at this late hour to comply even with the last and harshest of the terms dictated by France and Spain, by putting the restraint of a register on British subjects and British property; but he had purposely delayed compliance, till little was left that could be affected by the measure. The British Factory, so long domiciliated at Lisbon, had left the Tagus on the 18th of October, amid the universal regret of the inhabitants. The British resident minister, Lord Strangford, although feeling compassion for the force under which the Prince Regent acted, was, nevertheless, under the necessity of considering these unfriendly steps as a declaration against England. He took down the British arms, departed from

---

[344] Las Cases, tom. iv., p. 347.

Lisbon accordingly, and went on board Sir Sidney Smith's squadron, then lying off the Tagus. The Marquis of Marialva was then sent as an ambassador extraordinary, to state to the courts of France and Spain, that the Prince Regent had complied with the whole of their demands, and to request that the march of their forces upon Lisbon should be countermanded. Junot and his army had by this time crossed the frontiers of Portugal, entering, he said, as the friends, allies, and protectors of the Portuguese, come to save Lisbon from the fate of Copenhagen, and relieve the inhabitants from the yoke of the maritime tyrants of Europe.[345] He promised the utmost good discipline on the part of his troops, while, at the same time the constant plunder and exactions of the French were embittered by wanton scorn and acts of sacrilege, which, to a religious people, seemed peculiarly horrible.[346] Nothing, however, retarded the celerity of his march; for he was well aware that it was his master's most anxious wish to seize the persons of the Portuguese royal family, and especially that of the Prince Regent.

ROYAL FAMILY EMBARK FOR BRAZIL

But the Prince, although his general disposition was gentle and compromising, had, on this occasion, impressions not unworthy of the heir of Braganza. He had determined that he would not kiss the dust at the feet of the invader, or be made captive to enhance his triumph. The kingdom of Portugal had spacious realms beyond the Atlantic, in which its royal family might seek refuge. The British ambassador offered every facility which her squadron could afford, and, as is now known, granted the guarantee of Great Britain, that she would acknowledge no government which the invaders might establish in Portugal, to the prejudice of the House of Braganza. The Prince Regent, with the whole royal family, embarked on board the Portuguese vessels of the line, hastily rigged out as they were, and indifferently prepared for sea; and thus afforded modern Europe, for the first time, an example of that species of emigration,

---

[345] Proclamation from Alcantara, Nov. 17.
[346] "As if they had been desirous of provoking the Portuguese to some act of violence which might serve as a pretext for carrying into effect the threats which Junot had denounced, they burnt or mutilated the images in the churches, and threw the wafer to be trodden under foot."—Neves, *Historia de la Guerra contra Nap.*, tom. i., p. 196.

frequent in ancient days, when kings and princes, expelled from their native seats by the strong arm of violence, went to seek new establishments in distant countries. The royal family embarked (27th Nov.) amid the tears, cries, and blessings of the people, from the very spot whence Vasco de Gama loosened his sails to discover for Portugal new realms in the East. The weather was as gloomy as were the actors and spectators of this affecting scene; and the firmness of the Prince Regent was applauded by the nation which he was leaving, aware that his longer presence might have exposed himself to insult, but could have had no effect in ameliorating their own fate.

Junot, within a day's march of Lisbon, was almost frantic with rage when he heard this news. He well knew how much the escape of the Prince, and the resolution he had formed, would diminish the lustre of his own success in the eyes of his master. Once possessed of the Prince Regent's person, Buonaparte had hoped to get him to cede possession of the Brazils; and transmarine acquisitions had for Napoleon all the merit of novelty. The empire of the House of Braganza in the new world, was now effectually beyond his reach; and his general, thus far unsuccessful, might have some reason to dread the excess of his master's disappointment.

Upon the first of December, exhausted with their forced marches, and sufficiently miserable in equipment and appearance,[347] the French vanguard approached the city, and their general might see the retreating sails of the vessels which deprived him of so fair a portion of his prize. Junot, however, was soon led to resume confidence in his own merits. He had been connected with Buonaparte ever since the commencement of his fortunes, which he had faithfully followed. Such qualifications, and his having married a lady named Comnene,[348] who affirmed herself to be descended from the blood of the Greek emperors, was sufficient, he thought, to

---

[347] "Not a regiment, not a battalion, not even a company, arrived entire; many of them were beardless boys, and they came in so pitiable a condition, as literally to excite compassion; foot-sored, bemired and wet, ragged, and hungered, and diseased."—Neves, tom. i., p. 213.

[348] "Her family was from Corsica, and resided in the neighbourhood of mine; they were under great obligations to my mother, not merely for her benevolence towards them, but for services of a more positive nature."—Napoleon, *Las Cases*, tom. iv., p. 349.

entitle him to expect the vacant throne of Lisbon from the hand of his master. In the meantime, he acted as if already in possession of supreme power. He took possession of the house belonging to the richest merchant in the city, and although he received twelve hundred crusadoes a-month for his table, he compelled his landlord to be at the whole expense of his establishment, which was placed on the most extravagant scale of splendour. His inferior officers took the hint, nor were the soldiers slow in following the example. The extortions and rapacity practised in Lisbon seemed to leave all former excesses of the French army far behind. This led to quarrels betwixt the French and the natives; blood was shed; public executions took place, and the invaders, proceeding to reduce and disband the remnant of the Portuguese army, showed their positive intention to retain the kingdom under their own exclusive authority.

This purpose was at last intimated by an official document or proclamation, issued by Junot [1st Feb.] under Buonaparte's orders. It declared, that, by leaving his kingdom, the Prince of Brazil had, in fact, abdicated the sovereignty, and that Portugal, having become a part of the dominions of Napoleon, should, for the present, be governed by the French general-in-chief, in name of the Emperor.[349] The French flag was accordingly displayed, the arms of Portugal every where removed. The property of the Prince Regent, and of all who had followed him, was sequestrated, with a reserve in favour of those who should return before the 15th day of February, the proclamation being published upon the first day of that month. The next demand upon the unhappy country, was for a contribution of forty millions of crusadoes, or four millions and a half sterling;[350] which, laid upon a population of something less than three millions, came to about thirty shillings a-head; while the share of the immense numbers who could pay nothing, fell upon the upper and middling ranks, who had still some property remaining. There was not specie enough in the country to answer the demand; but plate, valuables, British goods, and colonial produce, were received instead of money. Some of the French officers turned jobbers in these last

---

[349] "The House of Braganza has ceased to reign in Portugal, and the Emperor Napoleon wills that this fine country shall be governed entirely in his name, by the general-in-chief of his army."
[350] The edict imposing this contribution was dated from Milan, Dec. 23.

articles, sending them off to Paris, where they were sold to advantage. Some became money-brokers, and bought up paper-money at a discount—so little does the profession of arms retain of its disinterested and gallant character, when its professors become habituated and accustomed depredators.[351]

The proclamation of 2d February, vesting the government of Portugal in General Junot, as the representative of the French Empire, seemed entirely to abrogate the treaty of Fontainbleau, and in fact, really did so, except as to such articles in favour of Napoleon, as he himself chose should remain in force. As for the imaginary princedom of Algarves, with which Godoy was to have been invested, no more was ever said or thought about it; nor was he in any condition to assert his claim to it, however formal the stipulation.[352]

INTRIGUES AT MADRID

While the French were taking possession of Portugal, one of those scandalous scenes took place in the royal family at Madrid, which are often found to precede the fall of a shaken throne.

We have already mentioned the discontent of the Prince of Asturias with his father, or rather his father's minister. We have mentioned that he had desired to ally himself with the family of Buonaparte, in order to secure his protection, but that the Emperor of France had given no direct encouragement to his suit. Still, a considerable party, headed by the Duke del Infantado, and the Canon Escoiquiz, who had been the Prince's tutor,[353] relying upon the general popularity of Ferdinand, seem to have undertaken some cabal, having for its object probably the deposition of the old King and the removal of Godoy. The plot was discovered; the person of the Prince was secured, and Charles made a clamorous appeal to the justice of Napoleon, and to the opinion of the world. He stated that

---

[351] Southey, vol. i., p. 155.
[352] "Fallen from his dreams of royalty, and trembling for his life, he was ready to make any sacrifice which might procure him the protection of France."—Neves, tom. i., p. 313.
[353] And author of an heroic poem on the Conquest of Mexico.

the purpose of the conspirators had been aimed at his life, and that of his faithful minister; and produced, in support of this unnatural charge, two letters from Ferdinand, addressed to his parents, in which he acknowledges (in general terms) having failed in duty to his father and sovereign, and says "that he has denounced his advisers, professes repentance, and craves pardon."[354] The reality of this affair is not easily penetrated. That there had been a conspiracy, is more than probable; the intended parricide was probably an aggravation, of which so weak a man as Charles IV. might be easily convinced by the arts of his wife and her paramour.

So standing matters in that distracted house, both father and son appealed to Buonaparte as the august friend and ally of Spain, and the natural umpire of the disputes in its royal family. But Napoleon nourished views which could not be served by giving either party an effectual victory over the other. He caused his ambassador, Beauharnois, to intercede in favour of the Prince of Asturias. Charles IV. and his minister were alarmed and troubled at finding his powerful ally take interest, even to this extent, in behalf of his disobedient son. They permitted themselves to allude to the private letter from the Prince of Asturias to Napoleon, and to express a hope that the Great Emperor would not permit a rebellious son to shelter himself by an alliance with his Imperial family. The touching this chord was what Buonaparte desired. It gave him a pretext to assume a haughty, distant, and offended aspect towards the reigning King, who had dared to suspect him of bad faith, and had mentioned with less than due consideration the name of a lady of the Imperial house.

Godoy was terrified at the interpretation put upon the remonstrances made by himself and his master, by the awful arbiter of their destiny. Izquierdo, the Spanish ambassador, was directed to renew his applications to the Emperor, for the especial purpose of assuring him that a match with his family would be in the highest degree acceptable to the King of Spain. Charles wrote with his own hand to the same purpose. But it was Napoleon's policy to appear haughty, distant, indifferent, and offended; and to teach the contending father and son, who both looked to him as their judge,

---

[354] Las Cases, tom. iv., p. 198; Southey, vol. i., p. 188; Savary, tom. ii., p. 144.

the painful feelings of mutual suspense. In the meantime, a new levy of the conscription put into his hands a fresh army; and forty thousand men were stationed at Bayonne, to add weight to his mediation in the affairs of Spain.

PROJECTS AGAINST SPAIN

About this period, he did not hesitate to avow to the ablest of his counsellors, Talleyrand and Fouché, the resolution he had formed, that the Spanish race of the House of Bourbon should cease to reign. His plan was opposed by these sagacious statesmen, and the opposition on the part of Talleyrand is represented to have been obstinate.[355] At a later period, Napoleon found it more advantageous to load Talleyrand with the charge of being his adviser in the war with Spain, as well as in the tragedy of the Duke d'Enghien. In Fouché's Memoirs, there is an interesting account of his conversation with the Emperor on that occasion, of which we see room fully to credit the authenticity. It places before us, in a striking point of view, arguments for and against this extraordinary and decisive measure. "Let Portugal take her fate," said Fouché, "she is, in fact, little else than an English colony. But that King of Spain has given you no reason to complain of him; he has been the humblest of your prefects. Besides, take heed you are not deceived in the disposition of the Spaniards. You have a party amongst them now, because they look on you as a great and powerful potentate, a prince, and an ally. But you ought to be aware that the Spanish people possess no part of the German phlegm. They are attached to their laws; their government; their ancient customs. It would be an error to judge of the national character by that of the higher classes, which are there, as elsewhere, corrupted and indifferent to their country. Once more, take heed you do not convert, by such an act of aggression, a submissive and useful tributary kingdom into a second La Vendée."

---

[355] "So far from being opposed to it, M. de Talleyrand even advised it. It was he who dictated all the preliminary steps, and it was with the view of promptly carrying the measure into effect, that he so urgently pressed the conclusion of peace at Tilsit. He was the first who thought of the Spanish expedition; he laid the springs which it was necessary to bring into play to complete the work."—*Mémoires de Savary*, tom. ii., p. 139.

Buonaparte answered these prophetic remarks, by observations on the contemptible character of the Spanish government, the imbecility of the King, and the worthless character of the minister; the common people, who might be influenced to oppose him by the monks, would be dispersed, he said, by one volley of cannon. "The stake I play for is immense—I will continue in my own dynasty the family system of the Bourbons, and unite Spain for ever to the destinies of France. Remember that the sun never sets on the immense Empire of Charles V."[356]

Fouché urged another doubt; whether, if the flames of opposition should grow violent in Spain, Russia might not be encouraged to resume her connexion with England, and thus place the empire of Napoleon betwixt two fires? This suspicion Buonaparte ridiculed as that of a minister of police, whose habits taught him to doubt the very existence of sincerity. The Emperor of Russia, he said, was completely won over, and sincerely attached to him.[357] Thus, warned in vain of the wrath and evil to come, Napoleon persisted in his purpose.

But, ere yet he had pounced upon the tempting prey, in which form Spain presented herself to his eyes, Napoleon made a hurried expedition to Italy. This journey had several motives. One was, to interrupt his communications with the royal family of Spain, in order to avoid being pressed to explain the precise nature of his pretensions, until he was prepared to support them by open force. Another was, to secure the utmost personal advantage which could be extracted from the treaty of Fontainbleau, before he threw that document aside like waste paper; it being his purpose that it should remain such, in so far as its stipulations were in behalf of any others than himself. Under pretext of this treaty, he expelled from Tuscany, or Etruria, as it was now called, the widowed Queen of that territory. She now, for the first time learned, that by an agreement to which she was no party, she was to be dispossessed of her own original dominions, as well as of those which Napoleon himself had

---

[356] Mémoires de Fouché, tom. i., p. 313.
[357] "I am sure of Alexander, who is very sincere. I now exercise over him a kind of charm, independently of the guarantee offered me by those about him, of whom I am equally certain."—Fouché, tom. i., p. 315.

guaranteed to her, and was informed that she was to receive a compensation in Portugal. This increased her affliction. "She did not desire," she said, "to share the spoils of any one, much more of a sister and a friend." Upon arriving in Spain, and having recourse to her parent, the King of Spain, for redress and explanation, she had the additional information, that the treaty of Fontainbleau was to be recognised as valid, in so far as it deprived her of her territories, but was not to be of any effect in as far as it provided her with indemnification.[358] At another time, or in another history, this would have been dwelt upon as an aggravated system of violence and tyranny over the unprotected. But the far more important affairs of Spain threw those of Etruria into the shade.

After so much preparation behind the scenes, Buonaparte now proposed to open the first grand act of the impending drama. He wrote from Italy to the King of Spain, that he consented to the proposal which he had made for the marriage betwixt the Prince of Asturias and one of his kinswomen; and having thus maintained to the last the appearances of friendship, he gave orders to the French army, lying at Bayonne, to enter Spain on different points, and to possess themselves of the strong fortresses by which the frontier of that kingdom is defended.

---

[358] Memoir of the Queen of Etruria, p. 70; Southey, vol. i., p. 193.

CHAPTER XLII

Pampeluna, Barcelona, Montjouy, and St. Sebastians, are fraudulently seized by the French—King Charles proposes to sail for South America—Insurrection at Aranjuez—Charles resigns the Crown in favour of Ferdinand—Murat enters Madrid—Charles disavows his resignation—General Savary arrives at Madrid—Napoleon's Letter to Murat, touching the Invasion of Spain—Ferdinand sets out to meet Napoleon—Halts at Vittoria, and learns too late Napoleon's designs against him—Joins Buonaparte at Bayonne—Napoleon opens his designs to Escoiquiz and Cevallos, both of whom he finds intractable—He sends for Charles, his Queen, and Godoy, to Bayonne—Ferdinand is induced to abdicate the Crown in favour of his Father, who resigns it next day to Napoleon—This transfer is reluctantly confirmed by Ferdinand, who, with his Brothers, is sent to splendid imprisonment at Vallençay—Joseph Buonaparte is appointed to the throne of Spain, and joins Napoleon at Bayonne—Assembly of Notables convoked.

SEIZURE OF SPANISH FORTRESSES

Not a word was spoken, or a motion made, to oppose the entrance of this large French army into the free territories of a friendly power. Neither the King, Godoy, nor any other, dared to complain of the gross breach of the treaty of Fontainbleau, which, in stipulating the formation of the army of reserve at Bayonne, positively provided that it should not cross the frontiers, unless with consent of the Spanish government. Received into the cities as friends and allies, it was the first object of the invaders to possess themselves, by a mixture of force and fraud, of the fortresses and citadels, which were the keys of Spain on the French frontier. The details are curious.

At Pampeluna, [Feb. 9,] a body of French troops, who apparently were amusing themselves with casting snowballs at each other on the esplanade of the citadel, continued their sport till they had an opportunity of throwing themselves upon the drawbridge, possessing the gate, and admitting a body of their comrades, who had been kept in readiness; and the capture was thus effected.[359]

Duhesme, who commanded the French troops detached upon Barcelona, had obtained permission from the Spanish governor to mount guards of French along with those maintained by the native soldiers. He then gave out that his troops were about to march; and, as if previous to their moving, had them drawn up in front of the citadel of the place. A French general rode up under pretence of reviewing these men, then passed forward to the gate, as if to speak to the French portion of the guard. A body of Italian light troops rushed in close after the French officer and his suite; and the citadel was surrendered. Another division summoned the fort of Montjouy, the key, as it may be termed, of Barcelona, which shared the same fate. St. Sebastians was overpowered by a body of French, who had been admitted as patients into the hospital.

Thus the first fruits of the French invasion were the unresisted possession of these four fortresses, each of which might have detained armies for years under its walls.[360]

Nothing could exceed the consternation of the Spanish nation when they saw their frontier invaded, and four of the most impregnable forts in the world thus easily lost and won. There was indignation as well as sorrow in every countenance; and even at this late hour, had Charles and his son attempted an appeal to the spirit of the people, it would have been vigorously answered. But Godoy, who was the object of national hatred, and was aware that he would instantly become the victim of any general patriotic movement, took care to recommend only such measures of safety as he himself

---

[359] Southey, vol. i., p. 196.
[360] Southey, vol. i., p. 201.

might have a personal share in. He had at once comprehended Napoleon's intentions of seizing upon Spain; and could discern no better course for the royal family, than that they should follow the example to which their own invasion of Portugal had given rise, and transport themselves, like the House of Braganza, to their South American provinces. But what in the Prince of Brazil, surrounded by such superior forces, was a justifiable, nay, a magnanimous effort to avoid personal captivity, would have been in the King of Spain the pusillanimous desertion of a post, which he had yet many means of defending.

Nevertheless, upon Godoy's suggestion, the voyage for America was determined on, and troops were hastily collected at Madrid for the sake of securing the retreat of the royal family to Cadiz, where they were to embark. The terror and confusion of the King's mind was artfully increased by a letter from Napoleon, expressing deep resentment at the coldness which Charles, as he alleged, had exhibited on the subject of the proposed match with his house. The intimidated King returned for answer, that he desired nothing so ardently as the instant conclusion of the marriage, but at the same time redoubled his preparations for departure. This effect was probably exactly what Napoleon intended to produce. If the King went off to America, his name might be used to curb the party of the Prince of Asturias; and the chance of influencing the countries where the precious metals are produced, would be much increased, should they fall under the dominion of the weak Charles and the profligate Godoy.

Meantime, the resolution of the king to depart from the royal residence of Aranjuez to Cadiz, with the purpose of going from thence to New Spain, began to get abroad among the people of all ranks. The Council of Castile remonstrated against the intentions of the sovereign. The Prince of Asturias and his brother joined in a strong protest against the measure. The populace, partaking the sentiments of the heir-apparent and council, treated the departure of the king as arising out of some scheme of the detested Godoy, and threatened to prevent it by force. The unfortunate and perplexed monarch changed his opinions, or his language at least, with every new counsellor and every new alarm.

On the 17th of March, the walls of the palace were covered with a royal proclamation, professing his Majesty's intentions to remain with and share the fate of his subjects. Great crowds assembled joyfully beneath the balcony, on which the royal family appeared and received the thanks of their people, for their determination to abide amongst them. But, in the course of that same evening, the movements among the guards, and the accumulation of carriages and baggage, seemed plainly to indicate immediate intentions to set forth. While the minds of the spectators were agitated by appearances so contradictory of the royal proclamation, an accidental quarrel took place betwixt one of the King's body-guard and a bystander, when the former fired a pistol. The literal flash of the weapon could not more effectually have ignited a powder-magazine, than its discharge gave animation at once to the general feelings of the crowd. The few household troops who remained steady, could not check the enraged multitude; a regiment was brought up, commanded by Godoy's brother, but the men made a prisoner of their commanding officer, and joined the multitude. A great scene of riot ensued, the cry was universal to destroy Godoy, and some, it is said, demanded the abdication or deposition of the King. Godoy's house was plundered in the course of the night, and outrages committed on all who were judged his friends and counsellors.

In the morning the tumult was appeased by the news that the King had dismissed his minister. But the crowd continued strictly to search for him, and at length discovered him. He was beaten, wounded, and it was with some difficulty that Ferdinand saved him from instant death, on a promise that he should be reserved for punishment by the course of justice. The people were delighted with their success thus far, when, to complete their satisfaction, the old, weak, and unpopular King, on the 19th March, resigned his crown to Ferdinand, the favourite of his subjects, professing an unconstrained wish to retire from the seat of government, and spend his life in peace and quiet in some remote province. This resolution was unquestionably hurried forward by the insurrection at Aranjuez; nor does the attitude of a son, who grasps at his father's falling diadem, appear good or graceful. Yet it is probable that Charles, in making his abdication, executed a resolution on which he had long meditated,[361] and from which he had chiefly been withheld by the intercession of the Queen and Godoy, who saw in the continuation of the old man's reign the only means to prolong their own power. The abdication was formally intimated to Napoleon, by a letter from the King himself.

MURAT APPROACHES MADRID

While the members of the royal family were distracted by these dissensions, the army of France was fast approaching Madrid, under the command of Joachim Murat, the brother-in-law of Buonaparte. He was at Aranda de Duero upon the day of the insurrection at Aranjuez, and his approach to Madrid required decisive measures on the part of the government. Ferdinand had formed an administration of those statesmen whom the public voice pointed out as the best patriots, and, what was thought synonymous, the keenest opponents of Godoy.[362] There was no time, had there been sufficient spirit in the councils of the new Prince, to request this military intruder to stay upon his road; he was a guest who would have known but too well how to make force supply the want of welcome. But this alarming visitor was, they next learned, to be followed hard upon the heel by one still more formidable. Napoleon, who had hurried back to Paris from Italy, was now setting out for Bayonne, with the purpose of proceeding to Madrid, and witnessing in person the settlement of the Spanish Peninsula.

To render the approach of the Emperor of France yet more appalling to the young King and his infant government, Beauharnois, the French ambassador, made no recognition of Ferdinand's authority, but observed a mysterious and ominous silence, when all the other representatives of foreign powers at

---

[361] "Maria Louisa," said Charles to the Queen, in the presence of Cevallos and of all the other ministers of state, "we will retire to one of the provinces, and Ferdinand, who is a young man, will take upon himself the burden of the government."—Southey, vol. i., p. 206.

[362] "This wretched minion now felt that there are times when despotism itself proves even-handed as justice. He was sent prisoner to the castle of Villa Viciosa: with that measure wherewith he had dealt to others, it was now meted to him; a judicial inquiry into his conduct was ordered, and before any trial—before any inquiry—the whole of his property was confiscated."—Southey, vol. i., p. 220.

Madrid, made their addresses of congratulation to the new sovereign. Murat next appeared, in all the pomp of war; brought ten thousand men within the walls of Madrid, [23d March,] where they were received with ancient hospitality, and quartered more than thrice that number in the vicinity. This commander also wore a doubtful and clouded brow, and while he expressed friendship for Ferdinand, and good-will to his cause, declined any definite acknowledgment of his title as king. He was lodged in the palace of Godoy, supported in the most splendid style, and his every wish watched that it might be attended to. But nothing more could be extracted from him than a reference to Napoleon's determination, which he advised Ferdinand to wait for and be guided by. In the idle hope (suggested by French councils) that a compliment might soothe either the Sultan or the satrap, the sword of Francis I., long preserved in memory of his captivity after the battle of Pavia, was presented to Murat with great ceremony, in a rich casket, to be by his honoured hands transmitted to those of the Emperor of France.[363] The hope to mitigate Buonaparte's severe resolves by such an act of adulation, was like that of him who should hope to cool red-hot iron by a drop of liquid perfume.

But though Murat and Beauharnois were very chary of saying any thing which could commit their principal, they were liberal of their private advice to Ferdinand as his professed friends; and joined in recommending that he should send his second brother, the Infant Don Carlos, to greet Napoleon upon his entrance into Spain, as at once a mark of respect and as a means of propitiating his favour. Ferdinand consented to this, as what he dared not well decline. But when it was proposed that he himself should leave his capital, and go to meet Buonaparte in the north of Spain, already completely occupied by French troops, he demurred, and by the advice of Cevallos, one of the wisest of his counsellors, declined the measure proposed, until, at least, he should receive express information of Napoleon's having crossed the frontier. To meet the French

---

[363] "The Grand Duke of Berg demanded the sword of Francis I. from the arsenal of Madrid. This mode of recovering it was not calculated to soothe the mortification of seeing it transferred to the hands of a conqueror. The Spaniards were sensible to this affront, and it diminished the popularity of the Grand Duke of Berg."—Savary, tom. ii., p. 169.

Emperor in Spain might be courtesy, but to advance into France would be meanness, as well as imprudence.[364]

Meantime, Murat, under pretence of hearing all parties in the family quarrel, opened, unknown to Ferdinand, a correspondence with his father and mother. The Queen, equally attached to her paramour, and filled with unnatural hatred to her son, as Godoy's enemy, breathed nothing but vengeance against Ferdinand and his advisers;[365] and the King at once avowed that his resignation was not the act of his voluntary will, but extorted by compulsion, in consequence of the insurrection of Aranjuez, and its consequences. Thus, the agents of Buonaparte obtained and transmitted to him documents, which, if Ferdinand should prove intractable, might afford ground for setting his right aside, and transacting with his father as still the legitimate possessor of the throne of Spain.

SAVARY—MURAT

A new actor soon appeared on this busy stage. This was Savary, who was often intrusted with Buonaparte's most delicate negotiations.[366] He came, it was stated, to inquire particularly into the character of the insurrection at Aranjuez, and of the old King's abdication. He affected to believe that the explanations which Ferdinand afforded on these subjects, would be as satisfactory to his sovereign as to himself; and having thus opened the young King's heart, by perfectly approving of his cause and conduct, he assumed the language of a friendly adviser, and urged and entreated, by every species of argument, that Ferdinand should meet Buonaparte on the road to Madrid; and the young sovereign, beset with difficulties, saw no resource but in compliance.[367] The capital was surrounded by an army of forty thousand foreigners. The communications of Murat

---

[364] Southey, vol. i., p. 235.
[365] "Every letter was filled with anxious solicitations; of the throne there seemed to be neither thought nor care; with the mob at Aranjuez before her eyes, and the recollection of Marie Antoinette in her heart, this wretched woman was sick of royalty; she asked only an allowance for the King, herself, and Godoy, upon which they might live all three together——a corner in which they might quietly finish their days."—Southey, vol. i., p. 233. See the Letters in Savary, tom. ii., p. 175, and Annual Register, vol. i., p. 240.
[366] For the instructions given by Napoleon to Savary, see his Mémoires, tom. ii., p. 164.
[367] Mémoires de Savary, tom. ii., p. 182; Southey, vol. i., p. 244.

with France were kept open by thirty thousand more; while, exclusive of the Spanish troops, whom the French had withdrawn to distant realms in the character of auxiliaries, the rest of the native forces, dispersed over the whole realm, and in many cases observed and mastered by the French, did not perhaps exceed thirty thousand men. If Ferdinand remained in Madrid, therefore, he was as much under the mastery of the French as he would have been when advancing northward on the journey to meet Buonaparte; while to leave his capital, and raise his standard against France in a distant province, seemed an idea which desperation only could have prompted.

LETTER TO MURAT

Murat, whose views of personal ambition were interested in the complete accomplishment of the subjugation of Spain, seems to have seen no objection remaining when military resistance was placed out of the question. But the penetration of Napoleon went far deeper; and, judging from a letter written to Murat on the 29th March,[368] it seems to have induced him to pause, while he surveyed all the probable chances which might attend the prosecution of his plan. The resignation of Charles IV. had, he observed, greatly complicated the affairs of Spain, and thrown him into much perplexity. "Do not," he continued, "conceive that you are attacking a disarmed nation, and have only to make a demonstration of your troops to subject Spain. The Revolution of the 20th March, when Charles resigned the throne, serves to show there is energy among the Spanish people. You have to do with a *new* people, who will display all the enthusiasm proper to men whose political feelings have not been worn out by frequent exercise. The grandees and clergy are masters of Spain. If they once entertain fear for their privileges and political existence, they may raise levies against us, *en masse*, which will render the war eternal. I have at present partisans;

---

[368] "The Emperor constantly recommended the Grand Duke of Berg to act with the utmost caution. He was no doubt apprehensive of his fits of zeal and ambition; for my departure had been preceded by several couriers, and I had scarcely set out when fresh instructions were despatched. This letter abundantly shows the doubts which existed in Napoleon's mind, and the point of view in which the question presented itself to him."— Savary, tom. ii., p. 169.

but if I show myself in the character of a conqueror, I cannot retain one of them. The Prince of the Peace is detested, because they accuse him of having betrayed Spain to France. The Prince of the Asturias has none of the qualities requisite for a monarch, but that will not prevent their making him out a hero, providing he stands forth in opposition to us. I will have no violence offered to the persons of that family—it is needless to render ourselves unnecessarily odious."

Napoleon, in this remarkable document, touches again on the hazard of a popular war in Spain, and on the dangers arising from the interference of the English; and then proceeds to consider what course his own politics demand. "Shall I go to Madrid, and there exercise the power of a grand protector of the realm of Spain, by deciding between the father and son?—Were I to replace Charles and his minister, they are so unpopular, that they could not sustain themselves three months. On the other hand, Ferdinand is the enemy of France; and to set him on the throne would be to gratify those parties in the state who have long desired the destruction of her authority. A matrimonial alliance would be but a feeble tie of union betwixt us.

"I do not approve of your Highness having so hastily possessed yourself of the capital. You ought to have kept the army at ten leagues distant from Madrid. You could not be sure whether the people and the magistracy would have recognised the young king. Your arrival has powerfully served him, by giving the alarm to the Spaniards. I have commanded Savary to open a communication with the old King, and he will inform you of what passes. In the meantime, I prescribe to you the following line of conduct:—

"You will take care not to engage me to hold any interview with Ferdinand *within Spain*, unless you judge the situation of things such, that I have no alternative save acknowledging him as King. You will use all manner of civility towards the old King, the Queen, and Godoy, and will require that the same honours be rendered to them as heretofore. You will so manage, that the Spaniards may not suspect the course I intend to pursue. This will not be difficult, for I have not fixed upon it myself." He then recommends, that such insinuations be made to all classes, as may best induce them to expect advantages from a more close union with France; exhorts Murat to trust his interests exclusively to his care; hints that Portugal will remain at his disposal; and enjoins the strictest discipline on the part of the French soldiery. Lastly, he enjoins Murat to avoid all explanation with the Spanish generals, and all interference with their order of march. "There must not," he says in one place, "be a single match burnt;" and in another, he uses the almost prophetic expression—"*If war once break out, all is lost.*"[369]

This letter has a high degree of interest, as it tends to show, that not one of the circumstances which attended the Spanish insurrection escaped the prescient eye of Napoleon, although the headlong course of his ambition drove him upon the very perils which his political wisdom had foreseen and delineated. The immense object of adding Spain to his empire, seemed worthy of being pursued, even at the risk of stirring to arms her hardy population, and exciting a national war, which he himself foretold might prove perpetual.

Meantime, to assist the intrigues of Murat, there was carried on a sort of under plot, the object of which was to disguise Napoleon's real intentions, and induce the counsellors of Ferdinand to conclude, that he did not mean to use his power over Spain, save for the attainment of some limited advantages, far short of engrossing the supreme authority, and destroying the independence of the kingdom. With this view, some illusory terms held out had been communicated by Duroc to the Spanish ambassador, Izquierdo, and of which Ferdinand's council had received information. These seemed to intimate, that Napoleon's exactions from Spain might be gratified by the cession of Navarre, and some part of her frontier on the north, in exchange for the whole of Portugal, which, according to Izquierdo's information, Napoleon was not unwilling to cede to Spain. Such an exchange, however objectionable on the ground of policy and morality, would have been regarded as a comparatively easy ransom, considering the

---

[369] Las Cases, tom. iv., p. 203; Savary, tom. ii., p. 169.

disastrous state of Spain, and the character of him who had coiled around the defenceless kingdom the folds of his power.[370]

Under all the influences of hope and fear, conscious helplessness, and supreme dread of Napoleon, Ferdinand took his determination, and announced to his Council of State, [8th April,] his purpose of going as far as Burgos, to meet his faithful friend and mighty ally the Emperor. His absence, he said, would amount to a few days, and he created his uncle, Don Antonio, President, during that time, of the High Council of Government. An effort was made by Ferdinand, previous to his departure, to open a more friendly communication with his father; but the answer only bore that the King was retiring to rest, and could not be troubled.

On the 11th April, in an evil day, and an hour of woe, to use the language of the Spanish romancers, Ferdinand set out on his journey, accompanied by Savary, who eagerly solicited that honour, assuring him that they should meet Buonaparte at Burgos.[371] But at Burgos there were no tidings of the French Emperor, and it was only when he had proceeded as far as Vittoria, that Ferdinand learned Napoleon had but then reached Bourdeaux, and was on his way to Bayonne. He halted, therefore, at Vittoria, where Savary left him, and went on to France, to render an account to his master to what extent his mission had succeeded.

Afraid to advance or to retire, yet feeling ridiculous in the situation where he was, Ferdinand's unpleasant moments spent at Vittoria were not much cheered by private intelligence brought him by Don Mariano Urquijo. This was a Spanish nobleman of considerable talent, who had penetrated the scheme of Napoleon, and came to inform the young King and his counsellors, that the intention of Napoleon was to possess himself of the royal person,

---

[370] Southey, vol. i., p. 240.
[371] "I asked leave to accompany the King, solely for this reason—I had come from Bayonne to Madrid on horseback, which was then the usual mode of travelling in Spain. I had not been long arrived, and it was now necessary to go back, that I might be with the Emperor as soon as Ferdinand; but I did not wish to travel over again the same road in the same manner. I therefore requested the King's grand equery to include in the relays harness and draught-horses for me. He consented; and this is the way in which my carriage happened to be in the suite of the King."—Savary, tom. ii., p. 187.

depose the dynasty of the Bourbons, and name a member of his own family to reign in their stead.

Another Spaniard, Don Joseph Hervas, the brother-in-law of General Duroc, and the intimate friend of Savary, had acquired such strong suspicions of the plot, that his information corroborated that of Urquijo. The astounded sovereign, and his perplexed advisers, could but allege the unlikelihood, that a hero like Napoleon could meditate such treachery. "Men of extraordinary talents," replied Urquijo, "commit great crimes to attain great objects, and are not the less entitled heroes." He offered to go to Bayonne as Ferdinand's ambassador; and advised him even yet to make his escape and retire to some part of his dominions, where, free at least, if not powerful, he might treat with Napoleon on more equal terms.[372]

Ferdinand thought it too late to follow this wise counsel; and, instead of attempting an escape, he wrote a letter to Napoleon, [14th April,] appealing to all that he had done to show himself the devoted friend and ally of France, and endeavouring to propitiate his favour. An answer was instantly returned—[dated Bayonne, 16th April]—containing much that was alarming and ominous. In this the Emperor treated Ferdinand as Prince of Asturias, not King of Spain—censured his earliest measure of writing to himself without his father's knowledge, and, with what seemed a jealous apprehension for the rights of sovereigns, blamed him for availing himself of the arm of the people to shake his father's throne. He intimated, that he had taken the Prince of the Peace under his own protection; hinted that the Prince ought not to rip up the follies of his mother—nay, did not forbear the highly offensive insinuation, that, by exposing her faults, Ferdinand might occasion his own legitimacy to be called in question. Still he assured the Prince of his continued friendship, declared himself anxious to have some personal communication with him on the subject of the revolution of Aranjuez, and intimated, that if the resignation of Charles should

---

[372] Savary, tom. ii., p. 203; Southey, vol. i., p. 249.

appear to have been voluntary, he would no longer scruple to acknowledge King Ferdinand.[373]

Cevallos, before mentioned as one of Ferdinand's wisest counsellors, would fain have prevailed on him to turn back from Vittoria on receiving a letter of such doubtful tenor.[374] Even the people of the town opposed themselves to the prosecution of his rash journey, and went so far as to cut the traces of his mules.[375] Ferdinand, however, proceeded, entered France, and reached Bayonne; placing himself thus in that state of absolute dependence upon the pleasure of the French autocrat, which, as Napoleon had foretold to Murat, could not have had an existence at any spot within the Spanish territory. Ferdinand was now a hostage at least, perhaps a prisoner.

BAYONNE

Buonaparte received the anxious Prince with flattering distinction,[376] invited him to dinner, and treated him with the usual deference exchanged between sovereigns when they meet. But that very evening he sent Savary, by whose encouragement Ferdinand had been deluded to undertake this journey, to acquaint him that the

---

[373] Savary, tom. ii., p. 243; Southey, vol. i., p. 254.

[374] "Ferdinand's counsellors, who were present when I delivered the letter, did not appear satisfied with the manner in which the Emperor expressed himself, because he used the title of royal highness. I felt myself obliged to observe, that the Emperor could not, with propriety, make use of any other address, because, on his part, the recognition was yet a thing to be done; that there were questions still more important than that to be settled between them; and these once adjusted, the rest would follow naturally."—Savary, tom. ii., p. 216.

[375] "I was convinced that all would proceed quietly, when a fierce-looking man, armed, dressed in a way corresponding with his appearance, approached the King's carriage, and with one hand seizing the traces of the eight mules which were harnessed to it, with the other, in which he held a hedgebill, like a sickle, cut with one stroke, the traces of all the mules. The King himself appeared at the window smiling to the multitude, who greeted him with cries of '*Viva Fernando!*' At this moment it struck me, that the scene I witnessed was merely a preconcerted trick."—Savary, tom. ii., p. 248.

[376] "The Prince was received with a salute of artillery from the ramparts, and all the civil and military authorities paid him their respects. The Emperor himself was the first to go and visit him; and his carriage not being ready as soon as he wanted it, he went on horseback. I was present at the interview, during which every thing was as it should be."—Savary, tom. ii., p. 219.

Bourbon dynasty was to cease to reign in Spain, and that the Prince must prepare to relinquish to Napoleon all right over the territories of his ancestors.[377]

ESCOIQUIZ—CEVALLOS

Buonaparte explained himself at length to the Canon Escoiquiz, as the person most likely to reconcile Ferdinand to the lot, which he was determined should be inevitable. The Bourbons, he said, were the mortal enemies of him and of his house; his policy could not permit them to reign in Spain. They were incapable of wise government; and he was determined that Spain should be wisely governed in future, her grievances redressed, and the alliance betwixt her and France placed on an unalterable footing. "King Charles," he said, "is ready to co-operate in such a revolution, by transferring to me his own rights. Let Ferdinand follow his father's wise example, and he shall have the crown of Etruria, and my niece in marriage. Otherwise, I will treat with King Charles exclusively, and all Ferdinand can expect is permission to return to Spain, when hostilities must ensue between us." Escoiquiz justified the insurrection at Aranjuez, and pleaded hard the cause of his former pupil. By protecting Ferdinand, he said, Napoleon might merit and gain the esteem and the affection of Spain; but by an attempt to subject the nation to a foreign yoke, he would lose their affections for ever. Buonaparte set these arguments at defiance. The nobles and higher classes would, he said, submit for security of their property; a few severe chastisements would keep the populace in order. But he declared he was determined on the execution of his plan, should it involve the lives of two hundred thousand men. "The new dynasty," replied Escoiquiz, "will in that case be placed on a volcano—an army of two hundred thousand men will be indispensable to command a country of discontented slaves." The canon was interrupted by Buonaparte, who observed that they could not agree upon their principles, and said he would on the morrow make known his irrevocable determination.

---

[377] Southey, vol. i., p. 262.

To do Napoleon justice, he at no time through this extraordinary discussion made the least attempt even to colour his selfish policy. "I am desirous," he said, "that the Bourbons should cease to reign, and that my own family should succeed them on the throne of Spain." He declared, that this was best both for Spain and France—above all, that he had the power as well as the will to accomplish his purpose. There was never a more unpalliated case of violent and arbitrary spoliation. He argued also with Escoiquiz with the most perfect good-humour, and pulled him familiarly by the ear as he disputed with him. "So then, canon," he said, "you will not enter into my views?"—"On the contrary," said Escoiquiz,[378] "I wish I could induce your Majesty to adopt mine, though it were at the expense of my ears," which Napoleon was at the moment handling somewhat rudely.[379]

With Cevallos the Emperor entered into a more violent discussion, for Buonaparte was as choleric by temperament, as he was upon reflection and by policy calm and moderate. Upon hearing Cevallos, in a discussion with his minister Champagny, insist in a high tone upon the character of the Spaniards, and the feelings they were likely to entertain on the manner in which Ferdinand had been received, he gave loose to his native violence of disposition, accused Cevallos of being a traitor, because having served the old King, he was now a counsellor of his son, and at length concluded with the characteristic declaration—"I have a system of policy of my own.— You ought to adopt more liberal ideas—to be less susceptible on the point of honour, and to beware how you sacrifice the interests of Spain to a fantastic loyalty for the Bourbons."[380]

Cevallos being found as intractable as Escoiquiz, the conduct of the negotiation, if it could be called so on the part of Ferdinand, was intrusted to Don Pedro de Labrador. Labrador, however,

---

[378] "This canon, who had besides a very high opinion of his own talents, did not despair of making an impression on my decisions, by his arguments, and of inducing me to acknowledge Ferdinand, making me a tender, on his own account, of his services to govern, altogether under my control, as effectually as the Prince of the Peace could, under the name of Charles IV.; and it must be owned, that, had I listened to several of his reasons, and adopted some of his ideas, I should have been much better off."—Napoleon, *Las Cases*, tom. iv., p. 199.
[379] Southey, vol. i., p. 262.
[380] Southey, vol. i., p. 269.

insisted on knowing, as an indispensable preliminary, whether King Ferdinand were at liberty; and if so, why he was not restored to his own country? Champagny[381] replied, that such return could scarce be permitted, till the Emperor and he came to an understanding. Cevallos, in his turn, presented a note, expressing on what terms Ferdinand had put himself in the power of Buonaparte, and declaring his master's intention of immediate departure. As a practical answer to this intimation, the guards on the King and his brother were doubled, and began to exercise some restraint over their persons. One of the Infants was even forcibly stopped by a gendarme. The man was punished; but the resentment and despair, shown by the Spaniards of the King's retinue, might have convinced Napoleon how intimately they connected the honour of their country with the respect due to their royal family.

Buonaparte found, by all these experiments, that Ferdinand and his counsellors were likely to be less tractable than he had expected; and that it would be necessary, however unpopular King Charles and still more his wife and minister were in Spain, to bring them once more forward on this singular stage. He therefore sent to Murat to cause the old King, with the Queen and Godoy, to be transported to Bayonne without delay. The arrival of Charles excited much interest in the French assembled at Bayonne, who flocked to see him, and to trace in his person and manners the descendant of Louis XIV. In external qualities, indeed, there was nothing wanting. He possessed the regal port and dignified manners of his ancestors; and, though speaking French with difficulty, the expatriated

---

[381] "I believe this was one of the occasions on which the Emperor was most anxious to have M. de Talleyrand near him, and that he would have sent for him, had he not been afraid of offending M. de Champagny. Cases of this kind often happened to the Emperor. He sometimes offended by mere trifles men who were of an irritable disposition, and, at other times, he sacrificed his own interests through the fear of offending the self-love of a good servant. If M. de Talleyrand had come to Bayonne while there was yet time to bring about an adjustment, the affairs of Spain would have taken a different turn. He would not have been so hasty; for he would have taken care to have many conferences before he committed any thing to writing. M. de Talleyrand had the excellent quality of being quite impassive; when he found that the disposition of the Emperor's mind was not what he thought best suited to the consideration of the subject to which he wished to call his attention, he never said a word about it until he had led him back to that tranquil state which benefited the business. If an order was given in a moment of irritation, he found means to make its execution be evaded; and it seldom happened that he was not thanked for a delay which was almost always attended with good effects."—Savary, tom. ii., p. 221.

monarch, on meeting with Napoleon, showed the easy manners and noble mien of one long accustomed to command all around him.[382] But in spirit and intellect there was a woeful deficiency. Napoleon found Charles,[383] his wife, and minister, the willing tools of his policy; for Godoy accounted Ferdinand his personal enemy; the mother hated him as wicked women have been known to hate their children when they are conscious of having forfeited their esteem; and the King, whose own feelings resented the insurrection of Aranjuez, was readily exasperated to an uncontrollable fit of rage against his son.

Upon his first arrival at Bayonne, Charles loudly protested that his abdication of the 19th March was the operation of force alone; and demanded that his son should repossess him in the crown, of which he had violently deprived him.

The reply of Ferdinand alleged that the resignation of his father had been unquestionably voluntary at the time, and he quoted the old King's repeated declarations to that effect. But he declared, that if they were both permitted to return to Madrid, and summon the Cortes, or body of National Representatives, he was ready to execute in their presence, a renunciation of the rights vested in him by his father's abdication.

In his answer, Charles declared that he had sought the camp of his powerful ally, not as a king in regal splendour, but as an unhappy old man, whose royal office had been taken from him, and even his life endangered by the criminal ambition of his own son. He treated the convocation of the Cortes with contempt. "Every

---

[382] "I was present when Charles alighted from his carriage. He spoke to every body, even to those he did not know; and on seeing his two sons at the foot of the staircase, where they were waiting for him, he pretended not to observe them. He, however, said, as he advanced to the Infantado Don Carlos—'Good morning, Carlos,' and the Queen embraced him. When Ferdinand advanced to embrace him, the King stopped, with an expression of indignation, and then passed on to his apartment."—Savary, tom. ii., p. 223.

[383] "Charles IV. dined with Napoleon on the very day of his arrival. He had some difficulty in ascending the steps leading to the saloon, and he said to the Emperor, who offered him his arm, 'It is because I am so frail that they want to drive me away.' The Emperor replied, 'Oh! oh! we shall see that: let me support you: I have strength enough for us both.' On hearing this, the King stopped, and said, looking at the Emperor, 'I believe and hope so!'"—Savary, tom. ii., p. 224.

thing," he said, "ought to be done by sovereigns for the people; but the people ought not to be suffered to carve for themselves." Finally, he assured his son that the Emperor of France could alone be the saviour of Spain, and that Napoleon was determined that Ferdinand should never enjoy the crown of that kingdom. In different parts of this paternal admonition, Charles accused his son of the crime which existing circumstances rendered most dangerous—of being indisposed towards the interests of France.

Ferdinand replied [3d May] to this manifesto in firm and respectful terms, and appealed, too justly, to the situation he at present stood in, as a proof how unbounded had been his confidence in France. He concluded, that since the conditions he had annexed to his offer of resigning back the crown to his father had given displeasure, he was content to abdicate unconditionally; only stipulating that they should both be permitted to return to their own country, and leave a place where no deed which either could perform would be received by the world as flowing from free-will.[384]

INTERVIEW AT BAYONNE

The day after this letter was written, the unfortunate Ferdinand was summoned to the presence of his parents, where he also found Napoleon himself. The conclave received him sitting; and while the King overwhelmed him with the most outrageous reproaches,[385] the Queen, (the statement appears scarce credible,) in the height of her fury, lost sight of shame and womanhood so far as to tell Ferdinand, in her husband's presence, that he was the son of another man.[386] Buonaparte expressed himself greatly shocked at this scene, in which he compared the Queen's language and deportment to that of a fury on the Grecian stage. The Prince's

---

[384] Southey, vol. i., p. 281-292.—Annual Register, vol. l., pp. 233-236.
[385] "Charles IV. carried constantly in his hand a long cane. He was so enraged, that it sometimes seemed to us he was going to forget himself so far as to use the cane against his son, who maintained all the time a sullen look. We heard the Queen say, 'Why don't you speak? This is always the way with you; for every new folly you have nothing to say.' She approached him, lifting up her hand, as if she meant to give him a slap on the face."—Savary, tom. ii., p. 228.
[386] Southey, vol. i., p. 292.

situation, he owned, moved him to pity; but the emotion was not strong enough to produce any interposition in his favour. This occurred on the 5th of May, 1808. Confused with a scene so dreadful, and at the same time so disgusting, Ferdinand the next day executed the renunciation which had been demanded in such intemperate terms. But the master of the drama had not waited till this time to commence his operations.

Two days before Ferdinand's abdication, that is upon the 4th, his father Charles, acting in the character of King, which he had laid aside at Aranjuez, had named Joachim Murat Lieutenant-General of his kingdom, and President of the Government. A proclamation was at the same time published, in which the Spaniards were particularly and anxiously cautioned against listening to treacherous men, agents of England, who might stir them up against France, and assuring them that Spain had no well-founded hope of safety, excepting in the friendship of the Great Emperor.[387]

On the same day, and without waiting for such additional right as he might have derived from his son's renunciation, Charles resigned all claims on Spain, with its kingdoms and territories, in favour of his friend and faithful ally, the Emperor of the French. To preserve some appearance of attention to external forms, it was stipulated that the cession only took place under the express conditions that the integrity and independence of the kingdoms should be preserved, and that the Catholic religion should be the only one practised in Spain. Finally, all decrees of confiscation or of penal consequences, which had been issued since the revolution of Aranjuez, were declared null and void. Charles having thus secured, as it was termed, the prosperity, integrity, and independence of his kingdom by these articles, stipulates, by seven which follow, for the suitable maintenance of himself and his Queen, his minister the Prince of the Peace, and of others their followers. Rank, income, appanages, were heaped on them accordingly, with no niggard hand; for the prodigality of the King's gift called for some adequate requital.

---

[387] "Trust to my experience, and obey that authority which I hold from God and my fathers! Follow my example, and think that, in your present situation, there is no prosperity or safety for the Spaniards, but in the friendship of the Great Emperor, our ally."

Still the resignation of Ferdinand in Napoleon's favour was necessary to give him some more colourable right, than could be derived from the alienation, by the father, of a crown which he had previously abdicated. Much urgency was used with Ferdinand on the occasion, and for some time firmly resisted. But he found himself completely in Napoleon's power; and the tragedy of the Duke d'Enghien might have taught him, that the Emperor stood on little ceremony with those who were interruptions in his path. His counsellors also assured him, that no resignation which he could execute in his present state of captivity could be binding upon himself or upon the Spanish nation. Yielding, then, to the circumstances in which he was placed, Ferdinand also entered into a treaty of resignation; but he no longer obtained the kingdom of Etruria, or the marriage with Buonaparte's niece, or any of the other advantages held out in the beginning of the negotiation. These were forfeited by his temporary hesitation to oblige the Emperor. A safe and pleasant place of residence, which was not to be absolutely a prison, and an honourable pension, were all that was allowed to Ferdinand, in exchange for his natural birthright, the mighty kingdom of Spain. The Infants, his brothers, who adhered to the same accession which stripped Ferdinand of his heritage, were in like manner recompensed by similar provisions for their holding in future the kind of life which that resignation condemned them to. The palace of Navarre and its dependencies had been assigned to Ferdinand as his residence; but he and his brothers, the Infants, were afterwards conducted to that of Valançay, a superb mansion belonging to the celebrated Talleyrand, who was punished, it was said, by this allocation, for having differed in opinion from his master, on the mode in which he should conduct himself towards Spain. The royal captives observed such rules of conduct as were recommended to them, without dreaming apparently either of escape or of resistance to the will of the victor; nor did their deportment, during the tremendous conflict which was continued in the name of Ferdinand for four years and upwards, ever give Napoleon any excuse for close restraint, or food for ulterior suspicions.

LUCIEN BUONAPARTE

The Spanish royal family thus consigned to an unresisted fate, it only followed to supply the vacant throne by a new dynasty, as Napoleon called it; but, in fact, by some individual closely connected with himself, and absolutely dependent upon him;—much in the manner in which the inferior partners of a commercial establishment are connected with, and subject to, the management of the head of the house. For this purpose, he had cast his eyes on Lucien, who was, after Napoleon, the ablest of the Buonaparte family, and whose presence of mind had so critically assisted his brother at the expulsion of the Council of Five Hundred from Saint Cloud, in a moment when, in the eyes of the bystanders, that of Napoleon seemed rather to waver.

It has been mentioned before, that Lucien had offended Napoleon by forming a marriage of personal attachment; and it is supposed, that on his part, he saw with displeasure the whole institutions and liberties of his native country sacrificed to the grandeur of one man, though that man was his brother. He had been heard to say of Napoleon, "that every word and action of his were dictated by his political system," and "that the character of his politics rested entirely on egotism." Even the proffer of the kingdom of Spain, therefore, did not tempt Lucien from the enjoyments of a private station, where he employed a large income in collecting pictures and objects of art, and amused his own leisure with literary composition. Receiving this repulse from Lucien, Buonaparte resolved to transfer his eldest brother Joseph from the throne of Naples, where, as an Italian, acquainted with the language and manners of the country, he enjoyed some degree of popularity, and bestow on him a kingdom far more difficult to master and to govern. Joachim Murat, Grand Duke, as he was called, of Berg, at present in command of the army which occupied Madrid, was destined to succeed Joseph in the throne which he was about to vacate. It was said that the subordinate parties were alike disappointed with the parts assigned them in this masque of sovereigns. Murat thought his military talents deserved the throne of Spain, and the less ambitious Joseph, preferring quiet to extent of territory, would have willingly remained contented with the less important royalty of Naples. But Napoleon did not permit the will of others to interfere with what he had previously determined, and Joseph was summoned to meet him at Bayonne, and prepared, by instructions communicated to him on the road, to perform without remonstrance his part in the pageant. The purposes of Napoleon were now fully announced to the world. An assembly of Notables from all parts of Spain were convoked, to recognise the new monarch, and adjust the constitution under which Spain should be in future administered.

The place of meeting was at Bayonne; the date of convocation was the 15th of June; and the object announced for consideration of the Notables was the regeneration of Spain, to be effected under the auspices of Napoleon.

But events had already occurred in that kingdom, tending to show that the prize, of which Buonaparte disposed so freely, was not, and might perhaps never be, within his possession. He had indeed obtained, by a course of the most audacious treachery, all those advantages which, after the more honourable success obtained in great battles, had prostrated powerful nations at his feet. He had secured the capital with an army of forty thousand men. The frontier fortresses were in his possession, and enabled him to maintain his communications with Madrid; the troops of the Spanish monarchy were either following his own banner in remote climates, or broken up and scattered in small bodies through Spain itself. These advantages he had possessed over Austria after Austerlitz, and over Prussia after Jena; and in both cases these monarchies were placed at the victor's discretion. But in neither case had he, as now at Bayonne, the persons of the royal family at his own disposal,[388] or had he reduced them to the necessity of

---

[388] "When I had them all assembled at Bayonne, I felt a confidence in my political system, to which I never before had the presumption to aspire. I had not made my combinations, but I took advantage of the moment. I here found the Gordian knot before me, and I cut it. I proposed to Charles IV. and the Queen, to resign the crown of Spain to me, and to live quietly in France. They agreed, I could say, almost with joy, to the proposal. The Prince of Asturias made no extraordinary resistance to the plan; but neither violence nor threats were employed against him. There you have, in very few words, the complete historical sketch of the affair of Spain; whatever may be said, or written on it, must amount to that; and you see, that there could be no occasion for me to have had recourse to paltry tricks, to

becoming his mouth-piece, or organ, in announcing to the people the will of the conqueror. So that, in this very important particular, the advantages which he possessed over Spain were greater than those which Napoleon had obtained over any other country. But then Spain contained within herself principles of opposition, which were nowhere else found to exist in the same extent.

---

falsehoods, to breaches of faith, or violation of engagements."—Napoleon, *Las Cases*, tom. iv., p. 200.

Chapter XLIII

State of morals and manners in Spain—The Nobility—the Middle Classes—the Lower Ranks—the indignation of the People strongly excited against the French—Insurrection at Madrid on the 2d May—Murat proclaims an amnesty, notwithstanding which, many Spanish prisoners are put to death—King Charles appoints Murat Lieutenant-General of the Kingdom, and Ferdinand's resignation of the throne is announced—Murat unfolds the plan of government to the Council of Castile, and addresses of submission are sent to Buonaparte from various quarters—Notables appointed to meet at Bayonne on 15th June—The flame of resistance becomes universal throughout Spain.

MORALS AND MANNERS IN SPAIN

The government of Spain, a worn-out despotism lodged in the hands of a family of the lowest degree of intellect, was one of the worst in Europe; and the state of the nobility, speaking in general, (for there were noble exceptions,) seemed scarce less degraded. The incestuous practice of marrying within the near degrees of propinquity, had long existed, with its usual consequences, the dwarfing of the body, and degeneracy of the understanding. The education of the nobility was committed to the priests, who took care to give them no lights beyond Catholic bigotry. The custom of the country introduced them to premature indulgences, and they ceased to be children, without arriving either at the strength or the intellect of youth.

The middling classes, inhabitants of towns, and those who followed the learned professions, had not been so generally subjected to the same withering influence of superstition and luxury. In many instances, they had acquired good education, and were superior to the bigotry which the ecclesiastics endeavoured to inspire them with; but, mistaking the reverse of wrong for the right, many of these classes had been hurried into absolute scepticism, having renounced altogether the ideas of religion, which better instruction would have taught them to separate from superstition, and having adopted in their extravagance many of the doctrines which were so popular in France at the commencement of the Revolution.

The lower classes of Spain, and especially those who resided in the country, possessed nearly the same character which their ancestors exhibited under the reign of the Emperor Charles V. They were little interested by the imperfections of the government, for the system, though execrable, did not immediately affect their comforts. They lay too low for personal oppression, and as the expenses of the state were supplied from the produce of the American provinces, the Spanish peasants were strangers, in a great measure, to the exactions of the tax-gatherer. Born in a delicious climate, where the soil, on the slightest labour, returned far more than was necessary for the support of the labourer, extreme poverty was as rare as hard toil. The sobriety and moderation of the Spaniard continued to be one of his striking characteristics; he preferred his personal ease to increasing the sphere of his enjoyments, and would rather enjoy his leisure upon dry bread and onions, than toil more severely to gain better fare. His indolence was, however, often exchanged for the most active excitation, and though slow in the labours of the field, the Spaniard was inexhaustible in his powers of travelling through his plains and sierras, and at the end of a toilsome day's journey, seemed more often desirous of driving away his fatigue by the dance, than of recruiting himself by repose. There were many classes of peasantry—shepherds, muleteers, traders between distant provinces—who led a wandering life by profession, and, from the insecure state of the roads, were in the habit of carrying arms. But even the general habits of the cultivators of the soil led them to part with the advantages of civilized society upon more easy terms than the peasantry of a less primitive country. The few and simple rights of the Spaniard were under the protection of the alcalde, or judge of his village, in whose nomination he had usually a vote, and whose judgment was usually satisfactory. If, however, an individual experienced oppression, he took his cloak, sword, and musket, and after or without avenging the real or supposed injury, plunged into the deserts in which the peninsula abounds, joined one of the numerous bands of contraband traders and outlaws by which they were haunted, and did all this without experiencing any violent change, either of sentiment or manner of life.

As the habits of the Spaniard rendered him a ready soldier, his disposition and feelings made him a willing one. He retained, with other traits of his ancestry, much of that Castilian pride, which mixed both with the virtues and defects of his nation. The hours of his indolence were often bestowed on studying the glories of his fathers. He was well acquainted with their struggles against the Moors, their splendid conquests in the New World, their long wars with France; and when the modern Castilian contrasted his own times with those which had passed away, he felt assurances in his bosom, that, if Spain had descended from the high pre-eminence she formerly enjoyed in Europe, it was not the fault of the Spanish people. The present crisis gave an additional stimulus to their natural courage and their patriotism, because the yoke with which they were threatened was that of France, a people to whom their own national character stands in such opposition, as to excite mutual hatred and contempt. Nothing, indeed, can be so opposite as the stately, grave, romantic Spaniard, with his dislike of labour, and his rigid rectitude of thinking, to the lively, bustling, sarcastic Frenchman, indefatigable in prosecution of whatever he undertakes, and calculating frequently his means of accomplishing his purpose, with much more ingenuity than integrity. The bigotry of the Spaniards was no less strikingly contrasted with the scoffing, and, at the same time, proselytizing scepticism, which had been long a distinction of modern France.

To conclude, the Spaniards, easily awakened to anger by national aggression, and peculiarly sensible to such on the part of a rival nation, were yet more irresistibly excited to resistance and to revenge, by the insidious and fraudulent manner in which they had seen their country stript of her defenders, deprived of her frontier fortresses, her capital seized, and her royal family kidnapped, by an ally who had not alleged even a shadow of pretext for such enormous violence.

Such being the character of the Spaniards, and such the provocation they had received, it was impossible that much time should elapse ere their indignation became manifest. The citizens of Madrid had looked on with gloomy suspicion at the course of public events which followed Ferdinand's imprudent journey to Bayonne. By degrees almost all the rest of the royal family were withdrawn thither, and Godoy, upon whose head, as a great public criminal, the people ardently desired to see vengeance inflicted, was also transferred to the same place.[389] The interest excited in the fate of the poor relics of the royal family remaining at Madrid, which consisted only of the Queen of Etruria and her children, the Infant Don Antonio, brother of the old king, and Don Francisco, youngest brother of Ferdinand, grew deeper and deeper among the populace.

On the last day of April, Murat produced an order to Don Antonio,[390] who still held a nominal power of regency, demanding that the Queen of Etruria and her children should be sent to Bayonne. This occasioned some discussion, and the news getting abroad, the public seemed generally determined that they would not permit the last remains of their royal family to travel that road, on which, as on that which led to the lion's den in the fable, they could discern the trace of no returning footsteps. The tidings from thence had become gradually more and more unfavourable to the partisans of Ferdinand, and the courier, who used to arrive every night from Bayonne, was anxiously expected on the evening of April the 30th, as likely to bring decisive news of Napoleon's intentions towards his royal visitor. No courier arrived, and the populace retired for the evening, in the highest degree gloomy and discontented. On the next day (1st of May) the Gate of the Sun, and the vicinity of the Post-office, were crowded with men, whose looks menaced violence, and whose capas, or long cloaks, were said to conceal

---

[389] "The Marquis de Cartellar, to whose custody Godoy had been committed, was instructed to deliver him up, and he was removed by night. Had the people been aware that this minister was thus to be conveyed away from their vengeance, that indignation which soon afterwards burst out would probably have manifested itself now, and Godoy would have perished by their hands."—Southey, vol. i., p. 279.
[390] From his brother King Charles.

arms. The French garrison got under arms, but this day also passed off without bloodshed.

INSURRECTION AT MADRID

On the 2nd of May, the streets presented the same gloomy and menacing appearance. The crowds which filled them were agitated by reports that the whole remaining members of the royal family were to be removed, and they saw the Queen of Etruria and her children put into their carriages, together with Don Francisco, the youngest brother of Ferdinand, a youth of fourteen, who appeared to feel his fate, for he wept bitterly. The general fury broke out at this spectacle, and at once and on all sides, the populace of Madrid assailed the French troops with the most bitter animosity. The number of French who fell was very considerable, the weapons of the assailants being chiefly their long knives, which the Spaniards use with such fatal dexterity.[391]

Murat poured troops into the city to suppress the consequences of an explosion, which had been long expected. The streets were cleared with volleys of grape-shot and with charges of cavalry, but it required near three or four hours' hard fighting to convince the citizens of Madrid, that they were engaged in an attempt entirely hopeless. About the middle of the day, some members of the Spanish Government, joining themselves to the more humane part of the French generals, and particularly General Harispe, interfered to separate the combatants, when there at length ensued a cessation of these strange hostilities, maintained so long with such fury by men almost totally unarmed, against the flower of the French army.

---

[391] "It is certain that, including the peasants shot, the whole number of Spaniards slain did not amount to one hundred and twenty persons, while more than seven hundred French fell. Of the imperial guards seventy men were wounded, and this fact alone would suffice to prove that there was no premeditation on the part of Murat; for if he was base enough to sacrifice his own men with such unconcern, he would not have exposed the select soldiers of the French empire in preference to the conscripts who abounded in his army. The affair itself was certainly accidental, and not very bloody for the patriots, but policy induced both sides to attribute secret motives, and to exaggerate the slaughter."—Napier, vol. i., p. 26.

A general amnesty was proclaimed, in defiance of which Murat caused seize upon and execute several large bands of Spaniards, made prisoners in the scuffle. They were shot in parties of forty or fifty at a time; and as the inhabitants were compelled to illuminate their houses during that dreadful night, the dead and dying might be seen lying on the pavement as clearly as at noon-day. These military executions were renewed on the two or three following days, probably with more attention to the selection of victims, for the insurgents were now condemned by French military courts. The number of citizens thus murdered is said to have amounted to two or three hundred at least.[392] On the 5th May, Murat published a proclamation, relaxing in his severity.

This crisis had been extremely violent, much more so, perhaps, than the French had ever experienced in a similar situation; but it had been encountered with such celerity, and put down with such rigour, that Murat may well have thought that the severity was sufficient to prevent the recurrence of similar scenes. The citizens of Madrid did not again, indeed, undertake the task of fruitless opposition; but, like a bull stupified by the first blow of the axe, suffered their conquerors to follow forth their fatal purpose, without resistance, but also without submission.

News came now with sufficient speed, and their tenor was such as to impress obedience on those ranks, who had rank and title to lose. Don Antonio set off for Bayonne; and on the 7th of May arrived, and was promulgated at Madrid, a declaration by the old King Charles, nominating Murat Lieutenant-General of the kingdom. The abdication of the son, less expected and more mortifying, was next made public, and a proclamation in his name and those of the Infants, Don Carlos and Don Antonio,

---

[392] "In the first moment of irritation, Murat ordered all the prisoners to be tried by a military commission, which condemned them to death; but the municipality representing to him the extreme cruelty of visiting this angry ebullition of the people with such severity, he forbade any executions on the sentence; but forty were shot in the Prado, by direction of General Grouchy, before Murat could cause his orders to be effectually obeyed."—Napier, vol. i., p. 25.

recommended the laying aside all spirit of resistance, and an implicit obedience to the irresistible power of France.[393]

The destined plan of government was then unfolded by Murat to the Council of Castile, who, first by an adulatory address,[394] and then by a deputation of their body despatched personally to Bayonne, hailed the expected resuscitation of the Spanish monarchy as a certain and infallible consequence of the throne being possessed by a relation of the great Napoleon. Other bodies of consequence were prevailed upon to send similar addresses; and one in the name of the city of Madrid, its streets still slippery with the blood of its citizens, was despatched to express the congratulations of the capital.[395] The summons of Murat, as Lieutenant-General of King Charles, and afterwards one from Buonaparte, as possessed of the sovereign power by the cession of that feeble monarch, convoked the proposed meeting of the Notables at Bayonne on 15th June; and the members so summoned began to depart from such places as were under the immediate influence of the French armies, in order to give their attendance upon the proposed convocation.

The news of the insurrection of Madrid, on the 2d May, had in the meantime communicated itself with the speed of electricity to the most remote provinces of the kingdom; and every where, like an alarm-signal, had inspired the most impassioned spirit of opposition to the invaders. The kingdom, from all its provinces, cried out with one voice for war and vengeance; and the movement was so universal and simultaneous, that the general will seemed in a great measure to overcome or despise every disadvantage, which could

---

[393] Southey, vol. i., p. 324.
[394] "Your Imperial Majesty," said they, "who foresees all things, and executes them still more swiftly, has chosen for the provisional government of Spain, a prince educated for the art of government in your own great school. He has succeeded in stilling the boldest storms, by the moderation and wisdom of his measures."
[395] A letter was also transmitted to Napoleon from the Cardinal Archbishop of Toledo, the last of the Bourbons who remained in Spain: "May your Imperial and Royal Majesty," he said, "be graciously pleased to look upon me as one of your most dutiful subjects, and instruct me concerning your high purposes."

arise from the suddenness of the event, and the unprepared state of the country.[396]

MURDER OF SOLANO—PROVISIONAL JUNTAS

The occupation of Madrid might have been of more importance to check and derange the movements of the Spanish nation at large, if that capital had borne exactly the same relation to the kingdom which other metropolises of Europe usually occupy to theirs, and which Paris, in particular, bears towards France. But Spain consists of several separate provinces, formerly distinct sovereignties, which having been united under the same sovereign by the various modes of inheritance, treaty, or conquest, still retain their separate laws; and though agreeing in the general features of the national character, have shades of distinction which distinguish them from each other. Biscay, Galicia, Catalonia, Andalusia, Valencia, and other lesser dominions of Spain, each had their capitals, their internal government, and the means of providing themselves for resistance, though Madrid was lost. The patriotic spirit broke out in all parts of Spain at once, excepting where the French actually possessed large garrisons, and even there the spirit of the people was sufficiently manifest. The call for resistance usually began among the lower class of the inhabitants. But in such instances as their natural leaders and superiors declared themselves frankly for the same cause, the insurgents arranged themselves quietly in the ranks of subordination natural to them, and the measures which the time rendered necessary were adopted with vigour and unanimity. In other instances, when the persons in possession of the authority opposed themselves to the wishes of the people, or gave them reason, by tergiversation and affectation of delay, to believe they were not sincere in the cause of the country, the fury of the people broke out, and they indulged their vindictive temper by the most bloody excesses. At Valencia, in particular, before the insurrection could be organised, a wretched priest, called

---

[396] "The firing on the end of May was heard at Mostoles, a little town about ten miles south of Madrid; and the alcalde, who knew the situation of the capital, despatched a bulletin to the south, in these words: 'The country is in danger; Madrid is perishing through the perfidy of the French; all Spaniards, come to deliver it!' No other summons was sent abroad than this!"—Southey, vol. i., p. 336.

Calvo, had headed the rabble in the massacre of upwards of two hundred French residing within the city, who were guiltless of any offence, except their being of that country. The governor of Cadiz, Solano,[397] falling under popular suspicion, was, in like manner, put to death; and similar bloody scenes signalized the breaking out of the insurrection in different parts of the Peninsula.

Yet among these bursts of popular fury, there were mixed great signs of calmness and national sagacity. The arrangements made for organising their defence, were wisely adopted. The supreme power of each district was vested in a Junta, or Select Committee, who were chosen by the people, and in general the selection was judiciously made. These bodies were necessarily independent in their respective governments, but a friendly communication was actively maintained among them, and by common consent a deference was paid to the Junta of Seville, the largest and richest town in Spain, after Madrid, and whose temporary governors chanced, generally speaking, to be men of integrity and talents.

These provisional Juntas proceeded to act with much vigour. The rich were called upon for patriotic contributions. The clergy were requested to send the church plate to the mint. The poor were enjoined to enter the ranks of the defenders of the country, or to labour on the fortifications which the defences rendered necessary. All these calls were willingly obeyed. The Spanish soldiery, wherever situated, turned invariably to the side of the country, and the insurrection had not broken out many days, when the whole nation assumed a formidable aspect of general and permanent resistance. Let us, in the meantime, advert to the conduct of Napoleon.

---

[397] The mob brought cannon against his house, shattered the doors, and rushed in. Seeing that they were bent upon his death, Solano escaped by the roof, and took shelter in the house of an English merchant, whose lady concealed him in a secret closet. The mistress of the house, Mrs. Strange, in vain endeavoured to save him, by the most earnest entreaties, and by interposing between him and his merciless assailants. She was wounded in the arm; and Solano, as he was dragged away, bade her farewell till eternity! They hauled him towards the gallows, that his death might be ignominious; others were too ferocious to wait for this—they cut and stabbed him, while he resigned himself with composure and dignity to his fate.—See Nellerto, *Mem.*, tom. iii., and Carr's *Travels*, p. 47.

That crisis, of which Buonaparte had expressed so much apprehension in his prophetic letter to Murat—the commencement of that war, which was to be so long in arriving at a close—had taken place in the streets of Madrid on the second of May; and the slaughter of the inhabitants, with the subsequent executions by the orders of Murat, had given the signal for the popular fermentation throughout Spain, which soon attained the extent we have just described.

The news[398] arrived at Bayonne on the very day on which the terrible scene took place between the Queen and her son; and the knowledge that blood had been spilled, became an additional reason for urging Ferdinand to authenticate the cession which Napoleon had previously received from the hand of the weak old king. To force forward the transaction without a moment's delay; to acquire a right such as he could instantly make use of as a pretext to employ his superior force and disciplined army, became now a matter of the last importance; and Cevallos avers, that, in order to overcome Ferdinand's repugnance, Napoleon used language of the most violent kind, commanding his captive to choose betwixt death and acquiescence in his pleasure. The French Emperor succeeded in this point, as we have already shown, and he now proceeded to the execution of his ultimate purpose, without condescending to notice that the people of Spain were a party concerned in this change of rulers, and that they were in arms in all her provinces for the purpose of opposing it.

To the French public, the insurrection of Madrid was described as a mere popular explosion, although, perhaps for the purpose of striking terror, the numbers of the Spanish who fell were exaggerated from a few hundreds to "some thousands of the worst disposed wretches of the capital,"[399] whose destruction was stated to

---

[398] "The Emperor could not restrain his passion on reading these details. Instead of returning home, he went straight to Charles IV. I accompanied him. On entering, he said to the King, 'See what I have received from Madrid. I cannot understand this.' The King read the Grand Duke of Berg's despatch; and no sooner finished it, than with a firm voice, he said to the Prince of the Peace, 'Emanuel, send for Carlos and Ferdinand.' They were in no haste to obey the call; and, in the meantime, Charles IV. observed to the Emperor—'I am much deceived if these youths have not had something to do with this business. I am very vexed, but not surprised at it.'"—Savary, tom. ii., p. 227.
[399] "Plusieurs milliers des plus mauvais sujects du pays."—*Moniteur*.

be matter of joy and congratulation to all good citizens. On the yet more formidable insurrections through Spain in general, the *Moniteur* observed an absolute silence. It appeared as if the French troops had been every where received by the Spanish people as liberators; and as if the proud nation, which possessed so many ages of fame, was waiting her doom from the pleasure of the French Emperor, with the same passive spirit exhibited by the humble republics of Venice or Genoa.

ARRIVAL OF JOSEPH BUONAPARTE

Buonaparte proceeded on the same plan of disguise, and seemed himself not to notice those signs of general resistance which he took care to conceal from the public. We have already mentioned the proceedings of the Assembly of Notables, whom he affected to consider as the representatives of the Spanish nation, though summoned by a foreign prince, meeting within a foreign land, and possessing no powers of delegation enabling them, under any legal form, to dispose of the rights of the meanest hamlet in Spain. Joseph, who arrived at Bayonne on the fifth of June, was recognised by these obsequious personages; received their homage; agreed to guarantee their new constitution, and promised happiness to Spain, while he only alluded to the existence of discontents in that kingdom, by expressing his intention to remain ignorant of the particulars of such ephemeral disturbances.[400]

At length Napoleon, who had convoked this compliant body, thought proper to give them audience before their return to their own country. It is said he was tired of a farce to which few were disposed to give any weight or consequence. At least he was so much embarrassed by a consciousness of the wide distinction between the real condition in which he was placed, and that which he was desirous of being thought to hold, that he lost, on this occasion, his usual presence of mind; was embarrassed in his manner; repeated from time to time phrases which had neither meaning nor propriety; and took a brief adieu of his astonished audience, who were surprised to see how much the consciousness of

---

[400] Southey, vol. i., p. 403.

the evil part he was acting had confused his usual audacity of assertion, and checked the fluency of his general style of elocution.[401]

The brothers then parted, and Joseph prepared to accomplish the destinies shaped out for him by his brother, while Napoleon returned to the capital of his augmented empire. The former did not travel fast or far, although the *Moniteurs* announced nothing save the general joy testified by the Spaniards at his reception, and the serenades performed by the natives on their guitars from night till morning under the windows of their new sovereign. The sounds by which he was in reality surrounded, were of a sterner and more warlike character. The tidings of insurrection, imperfectly heard and reluctantly listened to, on the northern side of the Pyrenees, were renewed with astounding and overpowering reiteration, as the intrusive King approached the scene of his proposed usurpation. He was in the condition of the huntsman, who, expecting that the tiger is at his mercy, and secured in the toils, has the unpleasing surprise of finding him free, and irritated to frenzy. It was judged proper, as Joseph possessed no talents of a military order, that he should remain at Vittoria until the measures adopted by his brother's generals might secure him a free and safe road to the capital. It is singular, that the frontier town which thus saw his early hesitation at entering upon his undertaking, was also witness to its disgraceful conclusion, by the final defeat which he received there in 1813.[402]

No doubts or forebodings attended the return of Napoleon to Paris. The eyes of the French were too much dazzled by the splendid acquisition to the Great Empire, which was supposed to have been secured by the measures taken at Bayonne, to permit them to examine the basis of violence and injustice on which it was to be founded. The union of France and Spain under kindred

---

[401] Southey, vol. i., p. 438.
[402] "From Vittoria, Joseph sent abroad a proclamation. 'I come among you,' he said, 'with the utmost confidence, surrounded by estimable men, who have not concealed from you any thing which they believed to be useful for your interests. Blind passions, deceitful vices, and the intrigues of the common enemy of the continent, whose only view is to separate the Indies from Spain, have precipitated some among you into the most dreadful anarchy. My heart is rent at the thought. Yet this great evil may in a moment cease. Spaniards, unite yourselves! come around my throne! and do not suffer intestine divisions to rob me of the time, and consume the means which I would fain employ solely for your happiness.'"

monarchs, had been long accounted the masterpiece of Louis XIV.'s policy; and the French now saw it, to outward appearance, on the point of accomplishment, at the simple wish of the wonderful man, who had erected France into the Mistress of the World, and whose vigour in forming plans for her yet augmenting grandeur, was only equalled by the celerity with which they were carried into execution.

Buonaparte had indeed availed himself to the utmost of that art of seducing and acting upon the imagination of the French people, in which he accused the Directory of being deficient. He had strung the popular feeling in such a manner, that it was sure to respond to almost every note which he chose to strike upon it. The love of national glory, in itself a praiseworthy attribute, becomes a vice when it rests on success accomplished by means inconsistent with honour and integrity. These unfavourable parts of the picture he kept in shade, while, as an artful picture-dealer, he threw the full lights on those which announced the augmented grandeur and happiness of France. The nation, always willing listeners to their own praises, were contented to see with the eyes of their ruler; and at no period in his life did Buonaparte appear to be in such a genuine degree the pride and admiration of France, as when returning from Bayonne, after having, in his attempt to seize upon the crown of Spain, perpetrated a very great crime, and at the same time committed an egregious folly.

The appearance of brilliant success, however, had its usual effect upon the multitude. In his return through Pau, Thoulouse, Montauban, and the other towns in that district, the Emperor was received with the honours due to a demi-god. Their antique and gloomy streets were arched over with laurels, and strewed with flowers; the external walls of their houses were covered with tapestry, rich hangings, and splendid paintings; the population crowded to meet the Emperor, and the mayors, or prefects, could scarce find language enough to exaggerate what was the actual prevailing tone of admiration towards Napoleon's person. Bourdeaux alone exhibited a melancholy and silent appearance. But Nantes and La Vendée, so distinguished as faithful to the Bourbon cause, seemed to join in the general feeling of the period; and the population of these countries rushed to congratulate him, who had with a strong hand plucked from the throne the last reigning branch of that illustrious house. The gods, says a heathen poet, frequently punish the folly of mortals by granting their own ill-chosen wishes. In the present case, they who rejoiced in the seeming acquisition of Spain to the French empire, could not foresee that it was to cost the lives of a million of Frenchmen; and he who received their congratulations was totally unaware, that he had been digging under his own feet the mine by which he was finally to be destroyed.

Chapter XLIV

Plans of Defence of the Spanish Juntas—defeated by the ardour of the Insurrectionary Armies—Cruelty of the French Troops, and Inveteracy of the Spaniards—Successes of the Invaders—Defeat of Rio Secco—Exultation of Napoleon—Joseph enters Madrid—His reception—Duhesme compelled to retreat to Barcelona, and Moncey from before Valencia—Defeat of Dupont by Castanos at Baylen—His Army surrenders Prisoners of War—Effects of this Victory and Capitulation—Unreasonable Expectations of the British Public—Joseph leaves Madrid, and retires to Vittoria—Defence of Zaragossa.

PLANS OF THE JUNTAS

Surrounded by insurrection, as we have stated them to be, the French generals who had entered Spain entertained no fear but that the experience of their superiority in military skill and discipline, would soon teach the Spaniards the folly of their unavailing resistance. The invading armies were no longer commanded by Murat,[403] who had returned to France, to proceed from thence to take possession of the throne of Naples, vacant by the promotion of Joseph, as in earlier life he might have attained a higher step of military rank, in consequence of regimental succession. Savary, who had, as we have seen, a principal share in directing Ferdinand's mind towards the fatal journey to Bayonne, remained in command at Madrid,[404] and endeavoured, by a general

---

[403] Before Murat had well recovered from a severe attack of the Madrid cholic an intermittent fever supervened, and when that was removed, he was ordered by his physicians to the warm baths of Barèges.
[404] "As some person was immediately wanted to supply the place of the Grand Duke of Berg, he directed me to proceed to Madrid, where I found myself in a more extraordinary

system of vigorous effort in various directions, to put an end to the insurrection, which had now become general wherever the French did not possess such preponderating armed force, as rendered opposition impossible. We can but hint at the character which the war assumed even at the outset, and touch generally upon its more important incidents.

THE INSURRECTIONARY ARMIES

The Spanish Juntas had wisely recommended to their countrymen to avoid general engagements—to avail themselves of the difficulties of various kinds which their country presents to an army of invaders—to operate upon the flanks, the rear, and the communications of the French—and to engage the enemy in a war of posts, in which courage and natural instinct bring the native sharpshooter more upon a level with the trained and practised soldier, than the professors of military tactics are at all times willing to admit. But although this plan was excellently laid down, and in part adhered to, in which case it seldom failed to prove successful, yet on many occasions it became impossible for the Spanish leaders to avoid more general actions, in which defeat and loss were usually inevitable. The character of the insurrectionary armies, or rather of the masses of armed citizens so called, led to many fatal errors of this kind. They were confident in their own numbers and courage, in proportion to their ignorance of the superiority which discipline, the possession of cavalry and artillery, and the power of executing combined and united movements, must always bestow upon regular forces. They were also impatient of the miseries necessarily brought upon the country by a protracted and systematic war of mere defence, and not less unwilling to bear the continued privations to which they themselves were exposed. On some occasions, opposition on the part of their officers to their demand of being led

---

situation than any general officer had ever been placed in. My mission was for the purpose of perusing all the reports addressed to the Grand Duke of Berg, to return answers, and issue orders in every case of emergency; but I was not to affix my signature to any paper; every thing was to be done in the name of General Belliard, in his capacity of chief of the staff of the army. The Emperor adopted this course, because he intended to send the new King forward in a very short time; and felt it to be unnecessary to make any alterations until the King's arrival at Madrid, when I was to be recalled."—Savary, tom. ii., p. 250.

against the enemy, to put an end, as they hoped, to the war, by one brave blow, was construed into cowardice or treachery; and falling under the suspicion of either, was a virtual sentence of death to the suspected person. Sometimes, also, these insurrectionary bodies were forced to a general action, which they would willingly have avoided, either by want of provisions, with which they were indifferently supplied at all times, or by the superior manœuvres of a skilful enemy. In most of the actions which took place from these various causes, the French discipline effectually prevailed over the undisciplined courage of the insurgents, and the patriots were defeated with severe loss.

On these occasions, the cruelty of the conquerors too frequently sullied their victory, and materially injured the cause in which it was gained. Affecting to consider the Spaniards, who appeared in arms to oppose a foreign yoke and an intrusive king, as rebels taken in the fact, the prisoners who fell into the hands of the French were subjected to military execution; and the villages where they had met with opposition were delivered up to the licentious fury of the soldier, who spared neither sex nor age. The French perhaps remembered, that some such instances of sanguinary severity, in the commencement of the Italian campaigns, had compelled the insurgents of Lombardy to lay down their arms, and secured the advantages which Napoleon had gained by the defeat of the Austrian forces. But in Spain the result was extremely different. Every atrocity of this kind was a new injury to be avenged, and was resented as such by a nation at no time remarkable for forgiveness of wrongs. The sick, the wounded, the numerous stragglers of the French army, were, when they fell into the hands of the Spaniards, which frequently happened, treated with the utmost barbarity; and this retaliation hardening the heart, and inflaming the passions of either party as they suffered by it in turn, the war assumed a savage, bloody, and atrocious character, which seemed to have for its object not the subjection, but the extermination of the vanquished.

The character of the country, very unfavourable to the French mode of supporting their troops at the expense of the districts through which they marched, added to the inveteracy of the struggle. Some parts of Spain are no doubt extremely fertile, but there are also immense tracts of barren plains, or unproductive mountains, which afford but a scanty support to the inhabitants themselves, and are totally inadequate to supply the additional wants of an invading army. In such districts the *Marauders*, to be successful in their task of collecting provisions, had to sweep a large tract of country on each side of the line of march—an operation the more difficult and dangerous, that though the principal high-roads through Spain are remarkably good, yet the lateral communications connecting them with the countries which they traverse are of the worst possible description, and equally susceptible of being defended by posts, protected by ambuscades, or altogether broken up, and rendered impervious to an invader. Hence it was long since said by Henry IV., that if a general invaded Spain with a small army, he must be defeated—if with a large one, he must be starved; and the gigantic undertaking of Buonaparte appeared by no means unlikely to fail, either from the one or the other reason.

At the first movement of the French columns into the provinces which were in insurrection, victory seemed every where to follow the invaders. Lefebvre Desnouettes defeated the Spaniards in Arragon on the 9th of June; General Bessières beat the insurgents in many partial actions in the same month, kept Navarre and Biscay in subjection, and overawed the insurgents in Old Castile. These, however, were but petty advantages, compared to that which he obtained, in a pitched battle, over two united armies of the Spaniards, consisting of the forces of Castile and Leon, joined to those of Galicia.

The first of these armies was commanded by Cuesta, described, by Southey,[405] as a brave old man, energetic, hasty, and headstrong, in whose resolute, untractable, and decided temper, the elements of the Spanish character were strongly marked. His army was full of zeal, but in other respects in such a state of insubordination, that they had recently murdered one of the general officers against whom they harboured some rashly adopted suspicions of treachery. The Galician army was in the same disorderly condition; and they also had publicly torn to pieces their

---

[405] History of the Peninsular War, vol. i., p. 453.

general, Filangieri,[406] upon no further apparent cause of suspicion than that he had turned his thoughts rather to defensive than offensive operations. Blake, a good soldier, who enjoyed the confidence of the army, but whose military talents were not of the first order, succeeded Filangieri in his dangerous command, and having led his Galician levies to form a junction with Cuesta, they now proceeded together towards Burgos. The two generals differed materially in opinion. Cuesta, though he had previously suffered a defeat from the French near Cabezon, was for hazarding the event of a battle, moved probably by the difficulty of keeping together and maintaining their disorderly forces; while Blake, dreading the superiority of the French discipline, deprecated the risk of a general action. Bessières left them no choice on the subject. He came upon them, when posted near Medina del Rio Seco, where, on the 14th July, the combined armies of Galicia and Castile received the most calamitous defeat which the Spaniards had yet sustained. The patriots fought most bravely, and it was said more than twenty thousand slain were buried on the field of battle.

July 20.

Napoleon received the news of this victory with exultation. "It is," he said, "the battle of Villa Viciosa. Bessières has put the crown on Joseph's head. The Spaniards," he added, "have now perhaps fifteen thousand men left, with some old blockhead at their head;—the resistance of the Peninsula is ended."[407] In fact, the victory of Medina del Rio Seco made the way open for Joseph to advance from Vittoria to Madrid, where he arrived without molestation. He entered the capital in state, but without receiving any popular greetings, save what the municipal authorities found themselves compelled to offer. The money which was scattered amongst the populace was picked up by the French alone, and by the French

---

[406] "Filangieri, the Governor of Corunna, being called on by a tumultuous crowd to exercise the rights of sovereignty, and to declare war in form against the French, was unwilling to commence such an important revolution upon such uncertain grounds; the impatient crowd instantly attempted his life, which was then saved by the courage of an officer of his staff; but his horrible fate was only deferred. A part of the regiment of Navarre seized him at Villa Franca del Bierzo, planted the ground with their bayonets, and then tossing him in a blanket, let him fall on the points thus disposed, and there leaving him to struggle, they dispersed and retired to their own homes."—Napier, vol. i., p. 37.
[407] Southey, vol. i., p. 481; Napier, vol. i., p. 110.

alone were the theatres filled, which had been thrown open to the public in honour of their new prince.[408]

VALENCIA

In the meantime, however, the advantages obtained by Bessières in Castile seemed fast in the course of being outbalanced by the losses which the French sustained in the other provinces. Duhesme, with those troops which had so treacherously possessed themselves of Barcelona and Figueras, seems, at the outset, to have entertained little doubt of being able not only to maintain himself in Catalonia, but even to send troops to assist in the subjugation of Valencia and Arragon. But the Catalonians are, and have always been, a warlike people, addicted to the use of the gun, and naturally disposed, like the Tyrolese, to act as sharp-shooters. Undismayed by several partial losses, they made good the strong mountain-pass of Bruch and other defiles, and, after various actions, compelled the French general to retreat towards Barcelona, with a loss both of men and character.[409]

An expedition undertaken by Marshal Moncey against Valencia, was marked with deeper disaster. He obtained successes, indeed, over the insurgents as he advanced towards the city; but when he ventured an attack on the place itself, in hopes of carrying it by a sudden effort, he was opposed by all the energy of a general popular defence. The citizens rushed to man the walls—the monks, with a sword in one hand, and a crucifix in the other, encouraged them to fight in the name of God and their King—the very women mingled in the combat, bringing ammunition and refreshments to the combatants.[410] Every attempt to penetrate into the city was found unavailing; and Moncey, disappointed of meeting with the

---

[408] "King Joseph made his entry into Madrid at four in the afternoon, with no other escort than the Emperor's guard. Although his suite was numerous, he was accompanied by no other Spaniard than the Captain-general of Navarre; the ministers and deputies who had left Bayonne in his train had already deserted him. The inhabitants manifested some degree of curiosity, and even gave some signs of approbation; public decorum, however, was not in the least interrupted."—Savary, tom. ii., p. 276.
[409] Napier, vol. i., p. 75.
[410] Southey, vol. i., p. 470; Napier, vol. i., p. 94.

reinforcements which Duhesme was to have despatched him from Barcelona, was obliged to abandon his enterprise, and to retreat, not without being severely harassed, towards the main French army, which occupied Old and New Castile.[411]

It was not common in Napoleon's wars for his troops and generals to be thus disconcerted, foiled, and obliged to abandon a purpose which they had adopted. But a worse and more decisive fate was to attend the division of Dupont, than the disappointments and losses which Duhesme had experienced in Catalonia, and Moncey before Valencia.

So early as Murat's first occupation of Madrid, he had despatched Dupont, an officer of high reputation, towards Cadiz, of which he named him governor. This attempt to secure that important city, and protect the French fleet which lay in its harbours, seems to have been judged by Napoleon premature, probably because he was desirous to leave the passage open for Charles IV. to have made his escape from Cadiz to South America, in case he should so determine. Dupont's march, therefore, was countermanded, and he remained stationary at Toledo, until the disposition of the Andalusians, and of the inhabitants of Cadiz, showing itself utterly inimical to the French, he once more received orders to advance at all risks, and secure that important seaport, with the French squadron which was lying there. The French general moved forward accordingly, traversed the chain of wild mountains called Sierra Morena, which the tale of Cervantes has rendered classical, forced the passage of the river Guadalquiver at the bridge of Alcolea, advanced to, and subdued, the ancient town of Cordoba.[412]

Dupont had thus reached the frontiers of Andalusia; but the fate of Cadiz was already decided. That rich commercial city had embraced the patriotic cause, and the French squadron was in the hands of the Spaniards; Seville was in complete insurrection, and its

---

[411] Moncey could hardly have expected to succeed against the town of Valencia; for, to use Napoleon's words, "a city, with eighty thousand inhabitants, barricadoed streets, and artillery placed at the gates, cannot be *taken by the collar.*"—Napier, vol. i., p. 99.
[412] Savary, tom. ii., p. 255; Napier, vol. i., p. 116.

Junta, the most active in the kingdom of Spain, were organising large forces, and adding them daily to a regular body of ten thousand men, under General Castanos, which had occupied the camp of St. Rocque, near Gibraltar.

If Dupont had ventured onward in the state in which matters were, he would have rushed on too unequal odds. On the other hand, his situation at Cordoba, and in the neighbourhood, was precarious. He was divided from the main French army by the Sierra Morena, the passes of which were infested, and might almost be said to be occupied, by the insurgent mountaineers; and he was exposed to be attacked by the Andalusian army, so soon as their general might think them adequate to the task. Dupont solicited reinforcements, therefore, as well from Portugal as from the French army in the Castiles; such reinforcements being absolutely necessary, not merely to his advancing into Andalusia, but to his keeping his ground, or even effecting a safe retreat. Junot, who commanded in Portugal, occupied at once by the insurrection of the natives of that country, and by the threatened descent of the English, was, as we shall hereafter see, in no situation to spare Dupont the succours he desired. But two brigades, under Generals Vedel and Gobert, joined Dupont from Castile, after experiencing some loss of rather an ominous character, for it could neither be returned nor avenged, from the armed peasantry of the Sierra.

BAYLEN

These reinforcements augmented Dupont's division to twenty thousand men, a force which was thought adequate to strike a decisive blow in Andalusia, providing Castanos could be brought to hazard a general action. Dupont accordingly put himself in motion, occupied Baylen and La Carolina in Andalusia, and took by storm the old Moorish town of Jaen. The sagacious old Spanish general had, in the meantime, been bringing his new levies into order, and the French, after they had possessed themselves of Jaen, were surprised to find themselves attacked there with great vigour and by superior forces, which compelled them, after a terrible resistance, to evacuate the place and retire to Baylen. From thence, Dupont wrote despatches to Savary at Madrid, stating the difficulties of his situation. His men, he said, had no supplies of bread, save from the corn which they reaped, grinded, and baked with their own hands—the peasants, who were wont to perform the country labour, had left their harvest-work to take up arms—the insurgents were becoming daily more audacious—they were assuming the offensive, and strong reinforcements were necessary to enable him either to maintain his ground, or do any thing considerable to annoy the enemy. These despatches fell into the hands of Castanos, who acted upon the information they afforded.

On the 16th July, two large divisions of the Spaniards attacked the French on different points, and, dislodging them from Baylen, drove them back on Menjibar; while Castanos, at the head of a large force, overawed Dupont, and prevented his moving to the assistance of his generals of brigade, one of whom, Gobert, was killed in the action. On the night of the 18th, another battle commenced, by an attempt on the part of the French to recover Baylen. The troops on both sides fought desperately, but the Spaniards, conscious that succours were at no great distance, made good their defence of the village. The action continued the greater part of the day, when, after an honourable attempt to redeem the victory, by a desperate charge at the head of all his forces, Dupont found himself defeated on all points, and so enclosed by the superior force of the Spaniards, as rendered his retreat impossible. He had no resource except capitulation. He was compelled to surrender himself, and the troops under his immediate command, prisoners of war. But, for the division of Vedel, which had not been engaged, and was less hard pressed than the other, it was stipulated that they should be sent back to France in Spanish vessels. This part of the convention of Baylen was afterwards broken by the Spaniards, and the whole of the French army were detained close prisoners. They were led to this act of bad faith, partly by an opinion that the French generals had been too cunning for Castanos in the conditions they obtained—partly from the false idea, that the perfidy with which they had acted towards Spain, dispensed with the obligations of keeping terms with them—and partly at the instigation of Morla, the successor of the unhappy Solano, who scrupled not to recommend to his countrymen that sacrifice of honour to interest, which he himself afterwards practised, in abandoning the cause of his country for that of the intrusive King.[413]

The battle and subsequent capitulation of Baylen, was in itself a very great disaster, the most important which had befallen the French arms since the star of Buonaparte arose—the *furcæ Caudinæ*, as he himself called it, of his military history. More than three thousand Frenchmen had been lost in the action—seventeen thousand had surrendered themselves,[414]—Andalusia, the richest part of Spain, was freed from the French armies—and the wealthy cities of Seville and Cadiz had leisure to employ a numerous force of trained population, and their treasures in support of the national cause. Accordingly, the tidings which Napoleon received while at Bourdeaux, filled him with an agitation similar to that of the Roman Emperor, when he demanded from Varus his lost legions. But the grief and anxiety of Buonaparte was better founded than that of Augustus. The latter lost only soldiers, whose loss might be supplied; but the battle of Baylen dissolved that idea of invincibility attached to Napoleon and his fortunes, which, like a talisman, had so often palsied the councils and disabled the exertions of his enemies, who felt, in opposing him, as if they were predestined victims, struggling against the dark current of Destiny itself. The whole mystery, too, and obscurity, in which Buonaparte had involved the affairs of Spain, concealing the nature of the interest which he held in that kingdom, and his gigantic plan of annexing it to his empire, were at once dispelled. The tidings of Dupont's surrender operated like a whirlwind on the folds of a torpid mist, and showed to all Europe, what Napoleon most desired to conceal—that he was engaged in a national conflict of a kind so doubtful, that it had commenced by a very great loss on the side of France; and that he was thus engaged purely by his own unprincipled ambition. That his armies could be defeated, and brought to the necessity of surrendering, was now evident to Spain and to Europe. The former gathered courage to persist in an undertaking so hopefully begun, while nations, now under the French domination, caught hope for themselves while they watched

---

[413] Southey, vol. i., p. 497; Napier, vol. i., p. 125.
[414] "Dupont surrendered an effective force of 21,000 infantry, forty pieces of cannon, and 2400 cavalry; in short, a full third of the French forces in Spain."—Savary, tom. ii., p. 273.

the struggle; and the spell being broken which had rendered them submissive to their fate, they cherished the prospect of speedily emulating the contest, which they at present only witnessed.

Yet were these inspiriting consequences of the victory of Castanos attended with some counterbalancing inconveniences, both as the event affected the Spaniards themselves, and the other nations of Europe. It fostered in the ranks of Spain their national vice, and excess of presumption and confidence in their own valour; useful, perhaps, so far as it gives animation in the moment of battle, but most hazardous when it occasions inattention to the previous precautions which are always necessary to secure victory, and which are so often neglected in the Spanish armies.[415] In short, while the success at Baylen induced the Spaniards to reject the advice of experience and skill, when to follow it might have seemed to entertain a doubt of the fortunes of Spain, it encouraged also the most unreasonable expectations in the other countries of Europe, and especially in Great Britain, where men's wishes in a favourite cause are so easily converted into hopes. Without observing the various concurrences of circumstances which had contributed to the victory of Baylen, they considered it as a scene which might easily be repeated elsewhere, whenever the Spaniards should display the same energy; and thus, because the patriots had achieved one great and difficult task, they expected from them on all occasions, not miracles only, but sometimes even impossibilities. When these unreasonable expectations were found groundless, the politicians who had entertained them were so much chagrined and disappointed, that, hurrying into the opposite extreme, they became doubtful either of the zeal of the Spanish nation in the cause for which they were fighting, or their power of maintaining an effectual resistance. And thus, to use the scriptural phrase, the love of many waxed cold, and

---

[415] "The moral effect of the battle of Baylen was surprising; it was one of those minor events which, insignificant in themselves, are the cause of great changes in the affairs of nations. Opening as it were a new crater for the Spanish fire, the glory of past ages seemed to be renewed, every man conceived himself a second Cid, and perceived in the surrender of Dupont, not the deliverance of Spain, but the immediate conquest of France. 'We are much obliged to our good friends, the English,' was a common phrase among them, when conversing with the officers of Sir John Moore's army; 'we thank them for their good-will, and we shall have the pleasure of escorting them through France to Calais.' This absurd confidence might have led to great things, if it had been supported by wisdom, activity, or valour; but it was a 'voice, and nothing more.'"—Napier, vol. i., p. 131.

men of a desponding spirit were inclined to wish the aid of Britain withdrawn from a contest which they regarded as hopeless, and that those supplies should be discontinued, on which its maintenance in a great measure depended.

The event of Baylen was not known at Madrid till eight or ten days after it had taken place; but when it arrived, Joseph Buonaparte, the intrusive King, plainly saw that the capital was no longer a safe residence for him, and prepared for his retreat. He generously gave leave to the individuals composing his administration, either to follow his fortunes, or take the national side, if they preferred it;[416] and leaving Madrid, (3d July,) again retired to Vittoria, where, secured by a French garrison, and at no great distance from the frontier, he might in safety abide the events of the war.

SIEGE OF ZARAGOSSA

Another memorable achievement of the Spanish conflict, which served perhaps better than even the victory of Baylen, to evince the character of the resistance offered to the French, was the immortal defence of Zaragossa, the capital of Arragon. This ancient city was defenceless, excepting for the old Gothic, or Roman or Moorish wall, of ten feet high, by which it is surrounded, and which is in most places a mere curtain, without flankers or returning angles of any kind.[417] Its garrison consisted chiefly of the citizens of the place; and its governor, a young nobleman, called Don Joseph Palafox, who was chosen Captain-general because he happened to be in the vicinity, had hitherto been only distinguished by the share he had taken in the frivolous gaieties of the court.[418] The city thus possessing no important advantages of defence, and the French general in Arragon, Lefebvre Desnouettes, having defeated such of the insurgents as had shown themselves in the field, he conceived he had only to advance, in security of occupying the capital of the province. But there never was on earth a defence in which the

---

[416] De Pradt, Mémoire Hist. sur la Rév. de l'Espagne, p. 192.
[417] Napier, vol. i., p. 65.
[418] Southey, vol. i., p. 37.

patriotic courage of the defenders sustained so long, and baffled so effectually, the assaults of an enemy provided with all those military advantages, of which they themselves were totally destitute.

On the 15th of June, the French attempted to carry the place by a *coup-de-main*, in which they failed with great loss. On the 27th, reinforced and supplied with a train of mortars, they made a more regular effort, and succeeded in getting possession of a suburb, called the Terrero. They then began to invest the place more closely, showered bombs on its devoted edifices, and amid the conflagration occasioned by these missiles of destruction, attempted to force the gates of the city at different points. All the Zaragossians rushed to man their defences—condition, age, even sex, made no difference; the monks fought abreast with the laity, and several women showed more than masculine courage.[419]

Lefebvre was incensed by a defence of a place, which, according to all common rules, was untenable. He forgot the rules of war in his turn, and exposed his troops to immense loss by repeatedly attempting to carry the place at the bayonet's point. Meanwhile ammunition ran scarce—but the citizens contrived to manufacture gunpowder in considerable quantities. Famine came—its pressure was submitted to. Sickness thinned the ranks of the defenders—those who survived willingly performed the duty of the absent. It was in vain that the large convent of Santa Engracia, falling into the hands of the besiegers, enabled them to push their posts into the town itself. The French general announced this success in a celebrated summons:—"*Sancta Engracia—Capitulation!*"—"*Zaragossa—war to the knife's blade,*"[420] was the equally

---

[419] "Augustina Zaragoza, a handsome woman of the lower class, about twenty-two years of age, arrived at one of the batteries with refreshments at the time when not a man who defended it was left alive, so tremendous was the fire which the French kept up against it. For a moment the citizens hesitated to re-man the guns. Augustina sprung forward over the dead and dying, snatched a match from the hand of a dead artilleryman, and fired off a six-and-twenty pounder; then jumping upon the gun, made a solemn vow never to quit it alive during the siege."—Southey, vol. ii., p. 14.—Lord Byron states, that when he was at Seville, in 1809, the Maid of Zaragoza was seen walking daily on the Prado, decorated with medals, and orders, by command of the Junta. She has further had the honour of being painted by Wilkie.

[420] "Such be the sons of Spain, and strange her fate They fight for freedom who were never free; A kingless people for a nerveless state, Her vassals combat when their chieftains flee, True to the veriest slaves of treachery: Fond of a land which gave them nought but life,

laconic answer. The threat was made good—the citizens fought from street to street, from house to house, from chamber to chamber—the contending parties often occupied different apartments of the same house—the passages which connected them were choked with dead. After this horrid contest had continued for several weeks, the gallant defence of Zaragossa excited at once the courage and sympathy of those who shared the sentiments of its heroic garrison and citizens, and a considerable reinforcement was thrown into the place in the beginning of August.[421] After this the citizens began to gain ground in all their skirmishes with the invaders; the news of Dupont's surrender became publicly known, and Lefebvre, on the 13th of August, judged it most prudent to evacuate the quarter of the city which he possessed. He blew up the church of Santa Engracia, and set fire to several of the houses which he had gained, and finally retreated from the city which had so valiantly resisted his arms.[422]

The spirit of indomitable courage which the Spaniards manifested on this occasion, has perhaps no equal in history, excepting the defence of Numantium by their ancestors. It served, even more than the victory of Baylen, to extend hope and confidence in the patriotic cause; and the country which had produced such men as Palafox and his followers, was, with much show of probability, declared unconquerable.

It is now necessary to trace the effects which this important revolution produced, as well in England, as in the Portuguese part of the Peninsula.

Pride points the path that leads to liberty; Back to the struggle, baffled in the strife, War, war is still the cry, *'War even to the knife!'* *Childe Harold*, c. i., st. 86.

[421] "Just before the day closed, Don Francisco Palafox, the general's brother, entered the city with a convoy of arms and ammunition, and reinforcement of three thousand men."—Southey, vol. ii., p. 26.

[422] "A hideous and revolting spectacle was exhibited during the action; the public hospital being taken and fired, the madmen confined there issued forth among the combatants, muttering, shouting, singing, and moping, according to the character of their disorder, while drivelling idiots mixed their unmeaning cries with the shouts of contending soldiers."—Napier, vol. i., p. 70.

Chapter XLV

Zeal of Britain with regard to the Spanish struggle—It is resolved to send an Expedition to Portugal—Retrospect of what had passed in that Country—Portuguese Assembly of Notables summoned to Bayonne—Their Singular Audience of Buonaparte—Effects of the Spanish Success on Portugal—Sir Arthur Wellesley—His Character as a General—Despatched at the head of the Expedition to Portugal—Attacks and defeats the French at Roriça—Battle and victory of Vimeiro—Sir Harry Burrard Neale assumes the command, and frustrates the results proposed by Sir Arthur Wellesley from the Battle—Sir Harry Burrard is superseded by Sir Hew Dalrymple—Convention of Cintra—Its Unpopularity in England—A Court of Inquiry is held.

There is nothing more praiseworthy in the British, or rather in the English character for it is they who in this respect give tone to the general feelings of the other two British nations—than the noble candour with which, laying aside all petty and factious considerations, they have at all times united in the same spring-tide of sentiment, when the object in question was in itself heart-stirring and generous. At no time was this unison of sentiment more universally felt and expressed, than when the news became general through Britain that the Spanish nation, the victim of an unparalleled process of treachery, had resolved to break through the toils by which they were enclosed, and vindicate their national independence at the hazard of their lives. "The war," says the elegant historian,[423] to whose labours we are so much indebted in this part of our subject, "assumed a higher and holier character, and men looked to the issue with faith as well as hope." Both these were

---

[423] Southey's History of the Peninsular War, vol. i., p. 444.

the brighter that they seemed to have arisen out of the midnight of scepticism, concerning the existence of public spirit in Spain.

It became the universal wish of Britain, to afford the Spaniards every possible assistance in their honourable struggle. Sheridan declared, that the period had arrived for striking a decisive blow for the liberation of Europe; and another distinguished member of Opposition,[424] having expressed himself with more reserve on the subject, found it necessary to explain, that in doing so he disclaimed the thoughts of abandoning the heroic Spaniards to their fate. But it was with particular interest, that all lovers of their country listened to the manly declaration of Mr. Canning,[425] in which, disclaiming the false and petty policy which made an especial object of what were called peculiarly British interests, he pledged himself, and the Administration to which he belonged, for pursuing such measures as might ensure Spanish success, because it was that which, considering the cause in which she was embarked, comprehended the essential interest not of England only, but of the world. The resolution to support Spain through the struggle, founded as it was on this broad and generous basis, met the universal approbation of the country.

It remained only to inquire in what shape the succours of Britain should be invested, in order to render them most advantageous to the cause of Spanish independence. Most Spaniards seemed to concur with the deputies, who had been hastily despatched to England by the Junta of the Asturias, in declining the assistance of an auxiliary army; "of men," they said, "Spain had more than enough." Arms, ammunition, and clothing, were sent, therefore, with a liberal and unsparing profusion, and military officers of skill and experience were despatched, to assist where their services could be useful to the insurgents. The war with Spain was declared at an end, and the Spanish prisoners, freed from

---

[424] Mr. Whitbread. See Parliamentary Debates, vol. xi., pp. 886, 891. As a farther avowal of these sentiments, Mr. Whitbread addressed a letter, on the situation of Spain, to Lord Holland; "the subject," he said, "being peculiarly interesting to that distinguished nobleman, from the attachment he had formed to a people, the grandeur of whose character he had had the opportunity to estimate."
[425] At that time Secretary of State for foreign affairs.

confinement, clothed, and regaled at the expense of the English, were returned to their country in a sort of triumph.[426]

BRITISH EXPEDITION TO PORTUGAL

The conduct of the Spaniards in declining the aid of British troops, partly perhaps arose out of that overweening confidence which has been elsewhere noted as their great national foible, and might be partly justified by the difficulty of combining the operations of a body of native insurgents with regular forces, consisting of foreigners, professing a different religion, and speaking another language. These objections, however, did not apply with the same force to Portugal, where the subjected state of the country did not permit their national pride, though not inferior to that of the Spaniards, to assume so high a tone; and where, from long alliance, the English, in despite of their being foreigners and heretics, were ever regarded with favour. It was, therefore, resolved to send an expedition, consisting of a considerable body of troops, to assist in the emancipation of Portugal, an operation for which the progress of the Spanish insurrection rendered the time favourable.

PORTUGAL

We left Portugal under the provisional command of General Junot, described by Napoleon himself as one whose vanity was only equalled by his rapacity, and who conducted himself like a tyrant over the unresisting natives, from whom he levied the most intolerable exactions.

There is no access to know in what manner Napoleon intended to dispose of this ancient kingdom. The partition treaty executed at Fontainbleau, which had been made the pretext of occupying Portugal, had never been in reality designed to regulate its destinies, and was neglected on all sides, as much as if it never had existed. Buonaparte subsequently seems to have entertained some

---

[426] Southey, vol. i., p. 451.

ideas of new-modelling the kingdom, which caused him to summon together at Bayonne a Diet, or Assembly of Portuguese Notables, in order to give an ostensible authority to the change which he was about to introduce.

They met him there, according to the summons; and, although their proceedings had no material consequences, yet, as narrated by the Abbé de Pradt, who was present on the occasion, they form too curious an illustration of Buonaparte's mind and manner to be omitted in this place. Having heard with indifference an address pronounced by the Count de Lima, an ancient Portuguese noble, who was President of the deputation, Napoleon opened the business in this light and desultory way:—"I hardly know what to make of you, gentlemen—it must depend on the events in Spain. And then, are you of consequence sufficient to constitute a separate people?—have you enough of size to do so? Your Prince has let himself be carried off to the Brazils by the English—he has committed a great piece of folly, and he will not be long in repenting of it. A prince," he added, turning gaily to the Abbé de Pradt, "is like a bishop—he ought to reside within his charge."—Then again speaking to the Count de Lima, he asked what was the population of Portugal, answering, at the game time, his own question, "Two millions, is it?"—"More than three, Sire," replied the Count.—"Ah—I did not know that—And Lisbon—are there one hundred and fifty thousand inhabitants?"—"More than double that number, Sire."—"Ah—I was not aware of that."

Proceeding through several questions regarding matters in which his information did not seem more accurate, he at length approached the prime subject of the conference. "What do you wish to be, you Portuguese?" he said. "Do you desire to become Spaniards?" This question, even from Napoleon, roused the whole pride of the Portuguese; for it is well known with what ill-will and jealousy they regard the sister-country of the Peninsula, against whom they have so long preserved their independence. The Count de Lima drew up his person to its full height, laid his hand on his sword, and answered the insulting demand by a loud No, which resounded through the whole apartment. Buonaparte was not offended, but rather amused by this trait of national character. He broke up the meeting without entering farther on the business for which it was summoned together, and afterwards told those about his person, that the Count of Lima had treated him with a superb No. He even showed some personal favour to that high-spirited nobleman, but proceeded no farther in his correspondence with the Portuguese deputies. The whole scene is curious, as serving to show how familiar the transference of allegiance, and alienation of sovereignty, was become to his mind, since in the case of a kingdom like Portugal, of some importance were even its ancient renown alone regarded, he could advance to the consideration of its future state with such imperfect knowledge of its circumstances, and so much levity both of manner and of purpose. Kingdoms had become the cards, which he shuffled and dealt at his pleasure, with all the indifference of a practised gamester. The occasion he had for the services of the Portuguese assembly of Notables passed away, and the deputies of whom it had consisted were sent to Bourdeaux, where they resided in neglect and poverty until the general peace permitted them to return to Portugal.

Some hints in Buonaparte's letter to Murat, formerly quoted, might induce one to believe that the crown of the house of Braganza was meant to be transferred to his brows;[427] but he obtained that of Naples, and the fate of Portugal continued undetermined, when the consequences of the Spanish Revolution seemed about to put it beyond the influence of Napoleon.

A movement so general as the Revolution effected in Spain through all her provinces, could not fail to have a sympathetic effect on the sister kingdom of Portugal, on whom the French yoke pressed so much more severely; not merely wounding the pride, and destroying the independence of the country, but leading to the plunder of its resources, and the maltreatment of the inhabitants. The spirit which animated the Spaniards soon showed itself among the Portuguese. Oporto, the second city in the kingdom, after a first attempt at insurrection, which the French, by aid of the timid local authorities, found themselves able to suppress, made a second effort

---

[427] "I will look after your private interests; give yourself no concern about them. Portugal will remain at my disposal. Let no personal project occupy you, or influence your conduct; that would be injurious to my interests, and would injure you still more than me."

with better success, expelled the French from the city and the adjacent country, and placed themselves under the command of a provisional junta, at the head of whom was the Bishop of Oporto. The kindling fire flew right and left in every direction; and at length, wherever the French did not possess a strong and predominating armed force, the country was in insurrection against them. This did not pass without much bloodshed. The French, under command of Loison, marched from the frontier fortress of Almeida, to suppress the insurrection at Oporto; but General Silviera, a Portuguese nobleman, who had put himself at the head of the armed population, managed so to harass the enemy's march, that he was compelled to abandon his intention, and return to Almeida, though his force amounted to four thousand men. At Beja, Leiria, Evora,[428] and other places, the discipline of the French overcame the opposition of the citizens and peasantry; and, in order to strike terror, the bloody hand of military execution was extended against the unfortunate towns and districts. But the inhumanity of the victors only served to increase the numbers and ferocity of their enemies. Men who had seen their houses burned, their vineyards torn up, their females violated, had no further use of life save for revenge; and when either numbers, position, or other advantages, gave the Portuguese an opportunity, it was exercised with premeditated and relentless cruelty.[429]

---

[428] Loison's conduct at Evora was marked by deliberate and sportive cruelty, of the most flagitious kind. The convents and churches afforded no asylum. He promised the archbishop that his property should not be touched, but, after this promise, he, with some of his officers, entered the Episcopal library, took down the books in the hope of discovering valuables behind them, broke off the gold and silver clasps, and, in their wrath at finding so little plunder, tore in pieces a whole pile of manuscripts. They took every gold and silver coin from his cabinet of medals, and every jewel and bit of the precious metals with which the relics were adorned. Loison was even seen in noon-day, to take the archbishop's ring from the table and pocket it. These circumstances are stated by Mr. Southey, on the authority of the archbishop himself.
[429] "In such detestation was Loison held by the Portuguese, that he was scarcely safe from their vengeance when surrounded by his troops. The execrations poured forth at the mere mention of 'the bloody Maneta,' as, from the loss of his hand, he was called, proves that he must have committed many heinous acts."—Napier, vol. i., p. 167.

SIR ARTHUR WELLESLEY

Had Junot been able to employ his full force against the insurgents, it is likely that in so narrow a country this miserable war might have been ended by the despotic efforts of irresistible military force. But the French general had apprehensions from another quarter, which obliged him to concentrate a considerable part of his army, that might otherwise have been disposable for the total subjugation of Portugal. Britain, long excluded from the continent, had assumed, with regard to it, the attitude of the Grecian hero, who, with his lance pointed towards his enemy, surveys his armour of proof from head to foot, in hopes of discovering some rent or flaw, through which to deal a wound. Junot justly argued, that the condition of the peninsula, more especially of Portugal, was such as to invite a descent on the part of the English. In fact, an expedition of ten thousand men had already sailed from Cork, and, what was of more importance than if the force had been trebled, it was placed under the command of Sir Arthur Wellesley, a younger son of the Earl of Mornington, one of those gifted individuals upon whom the fate of the world seems to turn like a gate upon its hinges, or as a vessel is managed by its rudder.

In India, Sir Arthur Wellesley had seen and conducted war upon a large and extended scale, of which no general officer in the European army of England had much comprehension, at least much experience. He was well acquainted with the best mode of supplying armies while in the field. His thoughts had been familiarly exercised in the task of combining grand general movements over extended regions, and his natural genius, deducing the principles of war from the service which he had seen in the East, qualified him to apply them to other countries, and to an enemy of a different description. Formidable in his preparations for battle, and successful in the action itself, he was even more distinguished by the alertness and sagacity which never rested satisfied with a useless victory, but improved to the uttermost the advantages which he had attained, by his own masterly dispositions, and the valour of his troops. His mind was never entirely engrossed by the passing event, how absorbing soever its importance; the past and the future were alike before him; and the deductions derived from a consideration of the whole, were combined, in all their bearings, with a truth and simplicity, which seemed the work of intuition, rather than the exercise of judgment. In fact, the mind of this singular and distinguished man seemed inaccessible to those false and delusive views which mislead ordinary thinkers; his strength of judgment rejected them, as some soils will not produce noxious weeds; and it might be said of him, that on subjects to which he gave his attention, the opinions which he formed, approached, perhaps, as near the perfection of human reason as the fallibility of our nature will permit.

To this prescience of intellect, in itself so rare a quality, was added a decision, which, when his resolution was once formed, enabled Sir Arthur Wellesley to look to the event with a firmness, inaccessible to all the doubts and vacillations to which minds of the highest resolution have been found accessible in arduous circumstances, but which are sure to impair the energy, and exhaust the spirits of others. A frame fitted to endure every species of fatigue and privation, and capable of supplying the want of regular repose by hasty and brief slumbers, snatched as occasion permitted, together with a power of vision uncommonly acute, may be mentioned as tending to complete the qualities of Sir Arthur Wellesley for the extraordinary part to which Providence had destined him. It may be added, that in precision of thought, sagacity of judgment, promptness of decision, and firmness of resolution, there was a considerable resemblance betwixt Napoleon and the English General, destined to be his great rival; and that the characters of both serve to show that the greatest actions are performed, and the greatest objects attained, not by men who are gifted with any rare and singular peculiarities of talent, but by those in whom the properties of judgment, firmness, power of calculation, and rapidity in execution, which ordinary men possess in an ordinary degree, are carried to the highest and most uncommon degree of perfection.

Sir Arthur Wellesley's qualities were well known in India, where, in the brilliant campaign of Assaye, he defeated the whole force of the Mahrattas, and ended triumphantly a long and doubtful war. The following expressions, on his leaving India, occur in the familiar letter of an excellent judge of human character, and who, it is to be hoped, lives to take a natural and just pride in the event of his own prophecy:—"You seem," he wrote to his European correspondent, "to be at a loss for generals in England. There is one now returning from India, who, if you can overcome the objections of precedence and length of service, and place him at once at the head of the British army, is capable of saving England at least, if not Europe, from the dangers which seem thickening around you."—Most fortunately for England, and for Europe, the objections which might have obstructed the rise of another officer in like circumstances, did not operate against Sir Arthur Wellesley in the same degree. His brother, the Marquis Wellesley, distinguished by the talents which had governed and extended our empire in India, had already much interest in our domestic councils, in which, some months afterwards, he held an eminent place.

He was selected at this important crisis to go as ambassador plenipotentiary to Spain, as one on whose wisdom and experience the utmost reliance could be reposed. The Marquis was of course well acquainted with Sir Arthur's talents; and, conscious that in urging his brother's pretensions to high employment in his profession, he was preparing for the arms of Great Britain every chance of the most distinguished success, he requested his assistance as the hand to execute the counsels, which were, in a great measure, to emanate from himself as the head.

The army and the public had become acquainted with Sir Arthur's merits during the brief campaign of Copenhagen—his name already inspired hope and confidence into the country—and when the brother of the Marquis Wellesley received the command of the expedition destined for the peninsula, none hinted that the selection had been made from undue partiality; and subsequent events soon taught the nation, not only that the confidence, so far as reposed in Sir Arthur Wellesley, was perfectly just, but that it ought, in wisdom, to have been much more absolute.

Under these auspices the expedition set sail for the peninsula, and, touching at Corunna, received such news as determined Sir Arthur Wellesley to select Portugal as the scene of his operations, being the point upon which success seemed most likely to influence the general cause. He opened a communication with Oporto, and soon learned the important news of the defeat of Dupont, and the flight of the intrusive King from Madrid. These tidings were of particular importance, because the consequences were likely to find full occupation in Spain for the victorious army of Bessières, which, if left disengaged, might have entered Portugal, and co-operated with Junot. At the same time, a body of British troops, which had been destined to support Castanos, was left disposable by the surrender of Baylen, and, having embarked for Portugal, now joined Sir Arthur Wellesley. Lastly, came the important intelligence, that Sir Arthur's army was to be reinforced immediately with fifteen thousand men, and that Sir Hew Dalrymple was to command in chief. This officer was governor of Gibraltar, and, during the Spanish insurrection, had acted both with wisdom and energy in assisting, advising, and encouraging the patriots; but it is doing him no injury to say, that he does not appear to have had the uncommon combination of talents, both military and political, which, in the present crisis, the situation of commander-in-chief in Portugal peremptorily demanded.

ACTION OF RORIÇA

Assured of these succours, Sir Arthur Wellesley disembarked his army in Mondego bay, and advanced towards Leiria by the sea-coast for the sake of communicating with the fleet, from which they received their provisions. The French generals Laborde and Thomieres were detached from Lisbon to check the progress of the invaders, and Loison, moving from the Alantejo, was in readiness to form a junction with his countrymen. In the meantime, a tumultuary Portuguese army of insurgents commanded by General Freire, an unreasonable and capricious man, (who afterwards lost his life under strong suspicions of treachery to the patriot cause,) first incommoded the British general by extravagant pretensions, and finally altogether declined to co-operate with him. A general of an ordinary character might not unreasonably have been so far disgusted with the conduct of those whom he had come to assist, as to feel diminished zeal in a cause which seemed to be indifferent to its natural defenders. But Sir Arthur Wellesley, distinguished as much by his knowledge of mankind as his military talents, knew how to make allowance for the caprice of an individual called suddenly to a command, for which perhaps his former life had not fitted him, and for the ebb and flow of national spirit in the ranks of an insurgent population. He knew that victory over the French was necessary to obtain the confidence of the Portuguese; and, with an alertness and activity which had prevented the junction of Loison with Laborde, he pushed on to attack (17th August) the latter French general, where he waited the approach of his colleague in a strong position near the town of Roriça. Attacking at once in front and upon the flank, he drove them from their ground, and his victory formed the first permanent and available success obtained by the British army in the eventful Peninsular struggle. Laborde retreated upon Torres Vedras, on which Loison had also directed his course.[430]

The Portuguese insurrection became wide and general on flank and rear, and Junot saw little chance of extinguishing the conflagration, unless he should be able to defeat the English general in a pitched battle. For this purpose he withdrew all the French garrisons except from Lisbon itself, Elvas, Almeida, and Peniche; and, collecting his whole forces, at Vimeiro, near Torres Vedras, determined there to abide the shock of war.

In the meanwhile, Sir Arthur Wellesley had been joined by a part of the promised succours; who, disembarking with difficulty on the dangerous coast, formed a junction with the main body as they marched towards the enemy. It was not an equally fortunate circumstance, that Sir Harry Burrard Neale, an officer of superior rank, also appeared on the coast, and communicated with Sir Arthur Wellesley. The latter explained his plan of engaging the French army, and throwing it back on Lisbon, where an insurrection would instantly have taken place in their rear, and thus Portugal might have been delivered by a single blow. But Sir Harry Burrard, though a brave officer, does not appear to have had that confidence in the

---

[430] Southey, vol. ii., p. 188; Napier, vol. i., p. 204. The loss of the French was 600 killed and wounded; among the latter was Laborde himself. The British also suffered considerably; two lieutenants and nearly 500 men being killed, taken, or wounded.

British soldiery, which they so well deserve at the hands of their leaders. He recommended a defensive system until the arrival of the rest of the succours from England; neither seeing how much, in war, depends upon a sudden and powerful effort, nor considering that the French of all men can best employ to their own advantage, whatever leisure may be allowed them by the timidity or indecision of their enemy.

BATTLE OF VIMEIRO

At this time, however, the difficulties of Junot's situation had determined him on the hazard of a general action; and the armies being already very near each other, the only change occasioned in the course of events by the interposition of the lately arrived British general, was, that Sir Arthur Wellesley, instead of being the assailant, as he had proposed, was, on the memorable 21st August, himself attacked by Junot near the town of Vimeiro. The British amounted to about 16,000 men, but of these not above one half were engaged; the French consisted of about 14,000, all of whom were brought into action.[431] The French attacked in two divisions; that on the left, commanded by Laborde, about five thousand men, and that on the right, under Loison, considerably stronger. The centre, or reserve, was commanded by Kellerman, occupied the space between the attacking divisions, and served to connect them with each other. The battle was interesting to military men, as forming a remarkable example of that peculiar mode of tactics by which the French troops had so often broken through and disconcerted the finest troops of the continent, and also of the manner in which their impetuous valour might be foiled and rendered unavailing, by a steady, active, and resolute enemy.

The favourite mode of attack by the French was, we have often noticed, by formation into massive columns, the centre and rear of which give the head no opportunity to pause, but thrust the leading files headlong forward on the thin line of enemies opposed to them, which are necessarily broken through, as unequal to sustain

---

[431] A French order of battle found upon the field gave a total of 14,000 men present under arms.

the weight of the charging body. In this manner, and in full confidence of success, General Laborde in person, heading a column of better than two thousand men, rushed on the British advanced guard, consisting of the 50th regiment, with some field-pieces, and a single company of sharp-shooters. The regiment, about four hundred men in number, drawn up in line on the brow of a hill, presented an obstacle so little formidable to the heavy column which came against them, that it seemed the very noise of their approach should have driven them from the ground. But Colonel Walker suddenly altering the formation of his regiment, so as to place its line obliquely on the flank of the advancing column, instead of remaining parallel to it, opened a terrible, well-sustained, and irresistible fire, where every ball passing through the dense array of the enemy, made more than one victim, and where the close discharge of grape-shot was still more fatal. This heavy and destructive fire was immediately seconded by a charge with the bayonet, by which the column, unable to form or to deploy, received on their defenceless flank, and among their shattered ranks, the attack of the handful of men whom they had expected at once to sweep from their course. The effect was instantaneous and irresistible; and the French, who had hitherto behaved with the utmost steadiness, broke their ranks and ran, leaving near three-fourths of their number in killed, wounded, and prisoners.[432] The same sort of close combat was general over the field. The brigade of General Fergusson, on the right, was attacked by General Loison with an impetuosity and vigour not inferior to that of Laborde. A mutual charge of bayonets took place; and here, as at Maida, the French advanced, indeed, bravely to the shock, but lost heart at the moment of the fatal encounter. To what else can we ascribe the undeniable fact, that their whole front rank, amounting to three hundred grenadiers, lay stretched on the ground almost in a single instant?[433]

---

[432] After the capitulation of Cintra, General Loison desired to be introduced to Colonel Walker, and congratulated that officer on the steadiness and talent with which he had rendered the defence in line so decidedly superior to Napoleon's favourite measure—the attack in column.—S.

[433] Thiebault, Relation de l'Expédition du Portugal, p. 194; Napier, vol. i., p. 212; Southey, vol. ii., p. 205.

The French were now in full retreat on all sides. They had abandoned their artillery—they were flying in confusion—the battle was won—the victor had only to stretch forth his hand to grasp the full fruits of conquest. Sir Arthur Wellesley had determined to move one part of his army on Torres Vedras, so as to get between the French and the nearest road to Lisbon, while with another division he followed the chase of the beaten army, to whom thus no retreat on Lisbon would remain, but by a circuitous route through a country in a state of insurrection. Unhappily, Sir Arthur Wellesley's period of command was for the present ended. Sir Harry Burrard had landed during the action, and had with due liberality declined taking any command until the battle seemed to be over; when it unhappily occurred to him, in opposition to the remonstrances of Sir Arthur Wellesley, General Fergusson, and other general officers, to interpose his authority for the purpose of prohibiting farther pursuit.[434] He accounted such a measure incautious where the enemy was superior in cavalry, and perhaps entertained too sensitive a feeling of the superiority of French tactics. Thus Vimeiro, in its direct consequences, seemed to be only another example of a victory gained by the English without any corresponding results; one of those numerous instances, in which the soldiers gain the battle from confidence in their own hearts and arms, and the general fails to improve it, perhaps from an equally just diffidence of his own skill and talents.

Meanwhile, Sir Hew Dalrymple, arriving from Gibraltar in a frigate, superseded Sir Harry Burrard, as Sir Harry had superseded Sir Arthur; and thus, within twenty-four hours, the English army had successively three commanders-in-chief.[435] The time of prosecuting the victory was passed away before Sir Hew Dalrymple came ashore—for the French had been able to gain the position of Torres Vedras, from which it had been Sir Arthur Wellesley's chief object to exclude them. That general then knew well, as he

---

[434] Proceedings of the Board of Inquiry; and Napier, vol. i., p. 217.
[435] "Thus, in the short space of twenty-four hours, during which a battle was fought, the army fell successively into the hands of three men, who, coming from different quarters, with different views, habits, and information, had not any previous opportunity of communing even by letter, so as to arrange a common plan of operations."—Napier, vol. i., p. 219.

afterwards showed to the world, what advantage might be taken of that position for the defence of Lisbon.

But Junot had suffered too severely in the battle of Vimeiro, and had too many difficulties to contend with, to admit of his meditating an obstinate defence. The victorious British army was in his front—the insurgents, encouraged by the event of the battle, were on his flanks—the English fleet might operate in his rear—and the populous town of Lisbon itself was not to be kept down without a great military force. Then if the successes in Andalusia were to be followed by similar events, the Spanish armies might invade Portugal, and co-operate with the English. Moved by these circumstances, the French general was induced to propose that evacuation of Portugal, its cities, and fortresses, which was afterwards concluded by the treaty of Cintra.[436] The French, by the articles of that convention, were to be transported to their own country, with their arms, artillery, and property—under which last article they carried off much of the plunder of which they had stripped the Portuguese. A Russian fleet in the Tagus; commanded by Admiral Siniavin, was delivered up to the English, in deposit, as it was termed; so unwilling were we to use towards Russia the language or practice of war, although the countries were in a state of avowed hostilities. In a military point of view, all the British generals concurred in approving of the convention. Sir Arthur Wellesley, who saw better, it may be supposed, than the others, how long the war might be protracted, after the favourable moment of victory had been permitted to pass without being improved, considered the liberation of Portugal, with its sea-coast, its ports, and its fortresses, besides the eastern line of frontier, which offered an easy communication with Spain, as an advantage of the highest importance, and cheaply purchased by the articles granted to Junot.

---

[436] For a copy of the Convention of Cintra, see Annual Register, vol. l., p. 265.

CONVENTION OF CINTRA

But the light in which the people of England saw the Convention of Cintra,[437] was extremely different. It is their nature to nurse extravagant hopes, and they are proportionally incensed when such are disappointed. The public were never more generally united in the reprobation of any measure; and although much of their resentment was founded in ignorance and prejudice, yet there were circumstances in the transaction which justified in some measure the general indignation. The succession of the three generals was compared to the playing of trump-cards at a game of whist; and, whether it was designed or fortuitous, had an air of indecision that was almost ludicrous. Then it was obvious, that the younger and inferior officer of the three had been prevented from following up the victory he had gained, and that this interference had rendered necessary the convention which England seemed determined to consider as injurious to Portugal, and dishonourable to herself. A Court of Inquiry[438] put the proceedings in a more just point of view for the two superior officers, whose error appeared in no degree to have exceeded a mistake in judgment, the fruit of too much caution. But the fierce and loudly expressed resentment on the part of the public[439] produced very important consequences; and though there occurred exceptions, it became comparatively difficult or dangerous, from that period, to propose any one as commander of an expedition whose talents had not pretensions to merit the confidence of the people.

---

[437] "The armistice, the negotiations, the convention itself, and the execution of its provisions, were all commenced, conducted, and concluded, at the distance of thirty miles from Cintra, with which place they had not the slightest connexion, political, military, or local; yet Lord Byron has gravely asserted, in prose and verse, that the convention was signed at the Marquis of Marialva's house at Cintra; and the author of 'The Diary of an Invalid,' improving upon the poet's discovery, detected the stains of the ink spilt by Junot upon the occasion."—Napier.

[438] See Report of the Board of Inquiry, Annual Register, vol. l., p. 272.

[439] See especially Parliamentary Debates, (Feb. 21, 1809,) vol. xii., p. 397.

Chapter XLVI

Duplicity of Buonaparte on his return to Paris—Official Statements in the Moniteur—Reports issued by Champagny, Minister of the Foreign Department—French Relations with the different Powers of Europe—Spirit of Resistance throughout Germany—Russia—Napoleon and Alexander meet at Erfurt on 27th September, and separate in apparent Friendship on 17th October—Actual feelings of the Autocrats—Their joint Letter to the King of Great Britain proposing a general peace on the principle of uti possidetis— Why rejected—Procedure in Spain—Catalonia—Return of Romana to Spain—Armies of Blake, Castanos, and Palafox—Expedition of General Moore—His desponding Views of the Spanish Cause—His Plans—Defeat of Blake—and Castanos—Treachery of Morla—Sir John Moore retreats to Corunna—Disasters on the March—Battle of Corunna, and Death of Sir John Moore.

During no part of his history did Buonaparte appear before the public in a meaner and more contemptible light, than immediately after the commencement of the Spanish revolution. In the deeper disasters of his life, the courage with which he struggled against misfortune, gave to his failing efforts the dignity of sinking greatness; but, on the present occasion, he appeared before France and before Europe in the humiliating condition of one, who had been tempted by selfish greed to commit a great crime, from which he had derived the full harvest of ignominy, without an iota of the expected profit. On the contrary, blinded by the unconscientious desire of acquisition, he had shown himself as shortsighted concerning results, as he was indifferent respecting means.[440] In this, as in other memorable instances, iniquity had brought with it all the consequences of folly.

For some time after his triumphal return to Paris, Buonaparte preserved a total silence on the affairs of the Peninsula, excepting general assurances that all was well;[441] and that the few partial commotions which had been excited by the agents of England, had been every where suppressed by the wisdom of the Grand Council, and the ready concurrence of the good citizens, who saw no safety for Spain save in the renewal of the family compact of the Bourbons, in the more fortunate dynasty of Napoleon. To accredit this state of things, many pieces of news were circulated in the provinces which lay nearest to Spain, tending to depress the spirit and hopes of the insurgents. Thus, M. de Champagny was made to write to the prefect of the department of La Gironde, [8th June,] that George III. of England was dead; that George IV., on succeeding, had made an instant and total change of ministry; and that a general pacification might be instantly expected. The same article, with similar legends, was inserted officially in the Madrid Gazette.[442]

But a system of fiction and imposition resembles an untempered sword-blade, which is not only subject to break at the utmost need of him who wields it, but apt to wound him with the fragments as they spring asunder. The truth began to become too glaring to be concealed. It could not be disguised that the kingdom of Portugal had been restored to independence—that Junot and his army had been driven from Lisbon—that Dupont had surrendered in the south of France—that King Joseph had been expelled from Madrid—and that in almost all the harbours of the Peninsula, which, in the month of March, had been as it were hermetically

---

[440] Gouvion St. Cyr, Journal des Opérations de l'Armée de Catalogne en 1808 et 1809, p. 18.
[441] "The 15th of August was passed in gaiety and amusements, because the affairs of Andalusia had not been made public; and no suspicion was entertained that our customary run of prosperity had received a check. It was only divulged some time afterwards; and it is truly curious to watch how the courtiers, whose trade is any thing else but to fight, criticised those military men who had, on that occasion, clouded with cares that brow, before which the courtiers were all so ready to bend the knee."—Savary, tom. ii., p. 296.
[442] Of June 14th—the very number which contained Napoleon's proclamation of Joseph as King of Spain and the Indies.

sealed against the British shipping and commerce, the English were now received as friends and allies. Nor was it possible to conceal, that these blots on the French arms had all taken place in consequence of the unprincipled ambition, which, not satisfied with disposing of the produce and power of Spain, by using the name of her native princes, had prompted Napoleon to exasperate the feelings of the people by openly usurping the supreme power, and had thus converted a submissive and complaisant ally into a furious and inexorable enemy. It was no easy matter, even for the talents and audacity of Napoleon, to venture before the French nation with an official account of these errors and their consequences, however palliated and modified. Accordingly, we must needs say, that not the confession of a felon, when, compelled to avow his general guilt, he seeks to disguise some of its more atrocious circumstances, and apologise for others, sounds to us more poor and humiliating, than the uncandid, inconsistent, and unmanly exposition which Napoleon was at length compelled to mumble forth in his official document, when the truth could no longer be concealed, and was likely indeed to be circulated even with exaggerations.

STATEMENTS IN THE MONITEUR

Suddenly, on the 4th of September, there appeared in the *Moniteur*, which previously had been chiefly occupied by scientific details, lyrical poetry, or theatrical criticism, a minute and garbled account of the insurrection in Spain. The sanguinary conduct of the insurgents was dwelt upon; the successes obtained by the French armies were magnified; the losses which they had sustained were extenuated or glossed over. Dupont was represented as having behaved like a fool or a traitor. The sufferings of Zaragossa, during the siege, were dwelt upon with emphasis; but on its result the official account remained silent. The most was made of the victory of Medina del Rio Seco, and the retreat of King Joseph from Madrid was ascribed to his health's disagreeing with the air of that capital. There were two reports on the subject of Spanish affairs, both from Champagny, minister of the foreign department, and both addressed to the Emperor. The first was designed to justify the attempt of Napoleon on Spain. It was dated at Bayonne, as far back as the 24th of April, a period when Buonaparte was very little inclined to enter into any reasoning on his right, since, believing he had the power to accomplish his purpose, he did not doubt that the advantage and honour which France would derive from the subjugation of Spain, would sufficiently plead his cause with the Great Nation. But when his first efforts had failed, and further exertions were found inevitably necessary, it became of consequence to render the enterprise popular, by showing that the measures which led to it were founded on policy at least, if not upon moral justice.

CHAMPAGNY'S REPORTS—CONSCRIPTION

To say the truth, the document is contented with arguing the first point. Something is hinted of the Spanish administration having been supposed to nourish hostile purposes towards France, and Godoy's manifesto at the time of the Prussian war is alluded to; but the principle mainly rested upon, and avowed by M. Champagny, is, in plain language, a gross and indecent sophism. "That which policy renders necessary," says the statesman, "justice must of course authorise;" thus openly placing interest in diametrical opposition to that which is honourable or honest; or, in other words, making the excess of the temptation a justification for the immorality of the action. This is the same principle[443] which sends the robber on the high-road, and upon which almost every species of villany is committed, excepting those rare enormities which are practised without any visible motive on the part of the perpetrators. To apply his reasoning to the case, Champagny sets forth the various advantages which France must derive from the more intimate union with Spain—the facilities which such a union afforded for enforcing the continental system against Great Britain—the necessity that Spain should be governed by a prince, on whose faithful attachment France could repose unlimited confidence—and the propriety of recommencing the work which had been the leading object of the policy of Louis the Fourteenth. Having thus shown that the seizing upon the crown and liberties of Spain would be highly advantageous to France, the reporter holds his task accomplished, and resumes his

---

[443] "A principle which the very thief, on his career to the gallows, dares not avow to himself."—Southey, vol. ii., p. 363.

proposition in these remarkable words:—"Policy demands a grand measure from your Majesty—Justice authorises it—the troubles of Spain render it indispensably necessary."

The second report of M. de Champagny held a different and more ominous tone. It was dated Paris, 1st September, and darkly indicated that the gold and machinations of the English had fomented popular intrigues in Spain, which had frustrated the attempt of his Imperial Majesty to render that country happy. The reporter then, in the tone with which a priest addresses the object of his worship, reverentially expostulates with Napoleon, for permitting anarchy to spread over great part of Spain, and for leaving Britain at liberty to say, that her flag, driven from the coasts of the Baltic and of the Levant, floats triumphantly, nevertheless, on the coasts of the kingdom which is the nearest neighbour to France. Having thus indirectly communicated the general fact, that Spain was in insurrection, and that the English fleet rode triumphant on her coasts, the reporter resumes a noble confidence in the power and authority which he was invoking. "No, never, Sire, shall it be thus. Two millions of brave men are ready, if necessary, to cross the Pyrenees, and chase the English from the Peninsula; if the French would combat for the liberty of the seas, they must begin by rescuing Spain from the influence of England."

Much more there is to the same purpose, serving to inform the French people by implication, if not in direct terms, that the Emperor's plans upon Spain had been disconcerted; that he had found unanimous resistance where he had expected unconditional submission; and that the utmost sacrifices would be necessary on the part of France, to enable her ruler to perfect the measures which he had so rashly undertaken. But besides the pressure of Spanish affairs, those of Austria were also hinted at, as requiring France to increase her armies, and stand upon her guard, as that power had been of late sedulously employed in increasing her military strength. The ultimate conclusion founded on these reasonings, was the necessity of anticipating another conscription of eighty thousand men.

The Senate, to whom these reports were sent down, together with a message from the Emperor, failed not to authorise this new draught on the French population; or, it may be said, on her very flesh and life-blood. Like the judge in the drama, but without regret or expostulation, they enforced the demand of the unrelenting creditor. "The court allowed it, and the law did give it."—"The will of France," said these subservient senators, "is the same with the will of her Emperor. The war with Spain is politic, just, and necessary."

Thus armed with all the powers which his mighty empire could give, Napoleon girded himself personally to the task of putting down by force the Spanish insurrection, and driving from the Peninsula the British auxiliaries. But while preparations were making on an immense scale for an enterprise of which experience had now taught him the difficulty, it was necessary for him, in the first place, to ascertain how his relations with the few powers in Europe who had some claim to independence, had been affected by the miscarriage of his Spanish scheme.

Since the treaty of Presburg, by which she lost such a proportion of her power, Austria had lain like a prostrated combatant, whom want, not of will, but of strength, prevents from resuming the contest. In 1806, her friendship became of consequence to Napoleon, then engaged in his contest with Prussia and Russia. The cession of Branau, and some territories about the mouth of the Cattaro, were granted to Austria by France, as in guerdon of her neutrality. But in 1807 and 1808, the government of that country, more vexed and humiliated by the territory and influence which she had lost, than thankful for the importance she had been permitted to retain, began to show the utmost activity in the war department. Abuses were reformed; more perfect discipline was introduced; old soldiers were called to muster; new levies were made on a large scale; armies of reserve were formed, through the Austrian dominions, of the *landwehr* and national guards, and they were subjected to service by conscription, like the militia of England. The Austrian armies of the line were increased to great magnitude. The Hungarian Diet had voted twelve thousand recruits for 1807, and eighty thousand for 1808; while eighty thousand organised soldiers, of whom thirty thousand were cavalry, constituted the formidable reserve of this warlike nation. Every thing seemed to announce war, although the answers of the Court to the remonstrances of France were of the most pacific tendency.

GERMANY

Yet it was not alone the hostile preparations of Austria which seemed to trouble the aspect of Germany. Napoleon had defeated her efforts and defied her armies, when her force was still more imposing. But there was gradually awakening and extending through Germany, and especially its northern provinces, a strain of opinion incompatible with the domination of France, or of any other foreign power, within the ancient empire.

The disappearance of various petty states, which had been abolished in the convulsion of the French usurpation, together with the general system of oppression under which the whole country suffered, though in different degrees, had broken down the divisions which separated the nations of Germany from each other, and, like relations who renew an interrupted intimacy under the pressure of a common calamity, the mass of the people forgot that they were Hanoverians, Hessians, Saxons, or Prussians, to remember that they were all Germans, and had one common cause in which to struggle, one general injury to revenge. Less fiery than the Spaniards, but not less accessible to deep and impassioned feeling, the youth of Germany, especially such as were engaged in the liberal studies, cherished in secret, and with caution, a deep hatred to the French invaders, and a stern resolution to avail themselves of the first opportunity to achieve the national liberty.

The thousand presses of Germany could not be altogether silenced, though the police of Napoleon was unceasingly active in suppressing political publications, wherever they could exercise influence. But the kind of feeling which now prevailed among the German youth, did not require the support of exhortations or reasoning, directly and in express terms adapted to the subject. While a book existed, from the Holy Scriptures down to the most idle romance; while a line of poetry could be recited from the works of Schiller or Goëthe, down to the most ordinary stall ballad—inuendoes, at once secret and stimulating, might be drawn from them, to serve as watch-words, or as war-cries. The prevailing opinions, as they spread wider and wider, began to give rise to mysterious associations, the object of which was the liberation of Germany. That most generally known was called the Bund, or Alliance for Virtue and Justice. The young academicians entered with great zeal into these fraternities, the rather that they had been previously prepared for them by the Burschenschafts, or associations of students, and that the idea of secret councils, tribunals, or machinations, is familiar to the reader of German history, and deeply interesting to a people whose temper is easily impressed by the mysterious and the terrible. The professors of the Universities, in most cases, gave way to or guided these patriotic impressions, and in teaching their students the sciences or liberal arts, failed not to impress on them the duty of devoting themselves to the liberation of Germany, or, as it was now called, Teutonia.[444]

The French, whose genius is in direct opposition to that of the Germans, saw all this with contempt and ridicule. They laughed at the mummery of boys affecting a new sort of national freemasonry, and they gave the principle of patriotic devotion to the independence of Germany the name of Ideology; by which nickname the French ruler used to distinguish every species of theory, which, resting in no respect upon the practical basis of self-interest, could, he thought, prevail with none save hot-brained boys and crazed enthusiasts.

Napoleon, however, saw and estimated the increasing influence of these popular opinions, more justly than might have been inferred from his language. He knew that a government might be crushed, an army defeated, an inimical administration changed, by violence; but that the rooted principle of resistance to oppression diffuses itself the wider the more martyrs are made on its behalf.

---

[444] "A Baron de Nostiz, Stein, the Prussian counsellor of state, Generals Sharnhost and Gneizenau, and Colonel Schill, appear to have been the principal contrivers and patrons of these societies, so characteristic of Germans, who, regular and plodding, even to a proverb, in their actions, possess the most extravagant imaginations of any people on the face of the earth."—Napier, vol. i., p. 316.

The Heir of the Revolution spoke on such subjects the language of the most legitimate of monarchs, and exclaimed against the system of the Tugendbund, as containing principles capable of disorganising the whole system of social society.

The menacing appearance of Austria, and the extension of anti-Gallican principles and feelings through Germany, made it more especially necessary for Buonaparte to secure his hold upon the Emperor of Russia. Trusting little in so important a case to his ministers, Napoleon desired personally to assure himself by a direct communication with the Emperor Alexander, which was willingly acceded to. We have elsewhere assigned some reasons, why such direct conference, or correspondence betwixt sovereigns, tends to degrade their character, without adding any additional security to the faith of their treaties. It is unbecoming their rank to take upon themselves the task of advancing, receding, renouncing, resuming, insisting, and evading, which must occur more or less in all political negotiations. At the same time, they are flattering to princes, as if inferring that they are able to act personally, and free of ministerial control; and in so far have their charms.

CONFERENCES AT ERFURT—SPAIN

Buonaparte and Alexander met at Erfurt on 27th September, with the same appearance of cordiality with which they had parted—their friendship seemed uninjured by a shadow of suspicion. The most splendid festivities celebrated their meeting, and the theatres of Paris sent their choicest performers to enliven the evenings.[445]

---

[445] "The two Emperors passed some days together in the enjoyment of the charms of perfect intimacy, and of the most familiar communications of private life. 'We were,' said Napoleon, 'two young men of quality, who, in their common pleasures, had no secret from each other.' Napoleon had sent for the most distinguished performers of the French theatre. A celebrated actress, Mademoiselle B——, attracted the attention of his guest, who had a momentary fancy to get acquainted with her. He asked his companion whether any inconvenience was likely to be the result. 'None,' answered the latter; 'only,' added he, intentionally, 'it is a certain and rapid mode of making yourself known to all Paris. After tomorrow, post-day, the most minute details will be despatched, and in a short time not a statuary at Paris but will be qualified to give a model of your person from head to foot.'

Amid all these gaieties politics were not neglected, and Buonaparte found his great ally as tractable as at Tilsit. Alexander not only ratified the transactions of Spain, but also the subsequent act, by which Napoleon appropriated to himself the kingdom of Etruria, which, according to the first draught of the Spanish scheme exhibited at Tilsit, was to have been assigned to the disinherited Ferdinand. The Czar stipulated, however, on his own part, that Buonaparte should not in any shape interfere to prevent Russia from aggrandizing herself at the expense of Turkey. He promised, also, to take an ally's share with Buonaparte, if the quarrel with Austria should come to arms. To this indeed he was bound by treaties; nor was there any way of ridding himself from their obligation. The conferences of Erfurt ended on the 17th of October, and, as they had begun, amid the most splendid did festivities. Among these was an entertainment given to the Emperor on the battle-ground of Jena, where Prussia, the hapless ally of Alexander, received such a dreadful blow.

It is probable, however, notwithstanding all the show of cordiality betwixt the Emperors, that Alexander did not require the recollections which this battle-field was sure to inspire, to infuse into his mind some tacit jealousy of his powerful ally. He even already saw the possibility of a quarrel merging between them, and was deeply desirous that Austria should not waste her national strength, by rushing into a contest, in which he would be under the reluctant necessity of acting against her. Neither did Napoleon return from Erfurt with the same undoubting confidence in his imperial ally. The subject of a match between the Emperor of France and one of the Russian Archduchesses had been resumed, and had been evaded, on account, as it was alleged, of the difference in their religions. The objections of the Empress Mother, as well as of the reigning Empress, were said to be the real reasons—objections founded on the character of Napoleon, and the nature of his right to the greatness which he enjoyed.[446] Such a proposal could not be brought forward and rejected or evaded, with how much delicacy soever,

---

The danger of such a kind of publicity appeased the monarch's rising passion; 'for,' observed Napoleon, 'he was very circumspect with regard to that point, and he recollected, no doubt, the old adage, when the mask falls, the hero disappears.'"—Las Cases, tom. ii., p. 219.
[446] Las Cases, tom. ii., p. 220.

without injury to the personal feelings of Napoleon; and as he must have been conscious, that more than the alleged reason of religion entered into the cause of declining his proposal, he must have felt in proportion offended, if not affronted. Still, however, if their cordiality was in any degree diminished, the ties of mutual interest, which bound together these two great autocrats, were as yet sufficient to assure Napoleon of the present assistance of Russia. To confirm this union still farther, and to make their present friendship manifest to the world, the two Emperors joined in a letter to the King of Great Britain, proposing a general peace; and it was intimated that they would admit the basis of *uti possidetis*, which would leave all the contracting powers in possession of what they had gained during the war. The proposal, as must have been foreseen, went off, on Britain demanding that the Spanish government and the King of Sweden should be admitted as parties to the treaty.[447]

But the letter of the Emperors had served its turn, when it showed that the ties between France and Russia were of the most intimate nature; and, confident in this, Napoleon felt himself at liberty to employ the gigantic force which he had already put in preparation, to the subjugation of Spain, and to chasing away the "hideous leopards,"[448] as he was pleased to term the English banners, from the Peninsula.

SPAIN

In the meantime, the Spaniards had not been unfaithful to the cause they had undertaken. They had vested the supreme management of the affairs of their distracted kingdom in a Central or Supreme Junta, which, composed of delegates from all the

---

[447] For the correspondence with the Russian and French governments, relative to the overtures from Erfurt, see Parliamentary Debates, vol. xii., p. 93.

[448] It was one of the minute and childish particulars in which Buonaparte showed a spleen against the British nation, that he would not bear the heraldic achievement, which the English flag had displayed for five hundred years, to be termed Lions, but always called them Leopards. The spirit which this ebullition of spite manifested, could only be compared to that exhibited by the poor citizen, when he revenged himself, as he thought, upon the cognizance of the Earl of Oxford, by calling the nobleman's Swan a Goose.—S.

principal Juntas, fixed their residence at the recovered capital of Madrid, and endeavoured, to the best of their power, to provide for resistance against the invaders. But their efforts, though neither in themselves unwise nor mistimed, were seriously impeded by two great causes, arising both from the same source.

The division of Spain, as already observed, into several disunited and almost unconnected provinces and kingdoms, though it had contributed much to the original success of the insurrection, while each province, regardless of the fate of others, or of the capital itself, provided the means of individual resistance, rendered them, when the war assumed a more general character, unapt to obey the dictates which emanated from the Supreme Junta. General Cuesta, whose devoted and sincere patriotism was frustrated by the haughtiness, self-importance, and insubordination of his character, was the first to set an unhappy example of disobedience to what had been chosen as the residence of the supreme authority. He imprisoned two members of the Supreme Junta, because he thought the choice which had been made of them was derogatory to his own authority, as Captain-General of Castile and Leon, and thus set a perilous example of disunion among the patriots, for which his real energy and love of his country were scarce afterwards sufficient to atone.[449]

But besides this and other instances of personal disregard to the injunctions of the Junta, there was another deep and widely-operating error which flowed from the same source. Each province, according to the high sense which the inhabitants entertained of their individual importance, deemed itself adequate to the protection of its own peculiar territory, and did not, or would not, see the necessity of contributing an adequate proportion of the provincial force to the defence of the nation in general. Those who had shown themselves manfully eager, and often successful, in the defence of their own houses and altars, were more deaf than prudence warranted to the summons which called them to the frontier, to act in defence of the kingdom as a whole. They had accustomed themselves, unhappily, too much to undervalue the immense power by which they were about to be invaded, and did not sufficiently see,

---

[449] Napier, vol. i., p. 303; Southey, vol. ii., p. 300.

that to secure the more distant districts, it was necessary that the war should be maintained by the united force of the realm. What added to this miscalculation, was a point in the national character of which William III. of England, when commanding an allied army to which Spain furnished a contingent, had a century before bitterly complained. "The Spanish generals were so proud of the reputation of their troops and their country," said that experienced warrior, "that they would never allow that they were in want of men, ammunition, guns, or the other necessaries of war, until the moment of emergency came, when they were too apt to be found unprovided in all with which they had represented themselves as being well supplied."

The same unhappy spirit of over-confidence and miscalculation now greatly injured the patriotic cause. Levies and supplies, which it had been determined to raise, were too often considered as completed, when the vote which granted them had been passed, and it was deemed unworthy and unpatriotic to doubt the existence of what the national or provincial council had represented as indispensable. In this manner the Spaniards misled both themselves, and their allies, the British, upon the actual state of their resources; and it followed of course, that British officers, once deceived by their representations in such instances, were disposed to doubt of the reality of their zeal, and to hesitate trusting such representations in future.

Notwithstanding these unhappy errors, the Spanish force, assembled for the defence of the kingdom, was perhaps not inadequate to the task, had they been commanded by a general whose superior energies could have gained him undisputed authority, and who could have conducted the campaign with due attention to the species of warfare which the time and the character of the invading army demanded. But unhappily, no Robert Bruce, no Washington, arose in Spain at this period; and the national defence was committed to men whose military knowledge was of a bounded character, though their courage and zeal admitted of no dispute. Yet favourable incidents occurred to balance these great inconveniences, and for a time the want of unity amongst themselves, and of military talent in the generals, seemed to a certain extent compensated by the courage of the Spanish leaders, and the energy of their followers.

The warlike population of Catalonia are, like the Tyrolese, natural marksmen, who take the field in irregular bodies, called Somatenes, or Miquelets.[450] The inhabitants of this country arose in arms almost universally; and, supported by a small body of four thousand men from Andalusia, contrived, without magazines, military chest, or any of the usual materials necessary to military manœuvres, to raise the siege of Gerona,[451] which had been formed by General Duhesme, and to gain so many advantages over the enemy, that probably, an auxiliary force of English, under such a general as the Earl of Peterborough, adventurous at once and skilful, might, like that gallant leader, have wrested Barcelona, with Monjouy, from the hands of the French, and left the invaders no footing in that important district. The troops might have been supplied from Sicily, where a great British force was stationed, and there was no want of good and experienced officers, competent to the ordinary duties of a general. But that genius, which, freeing itself from the pedantry of professional education, can judge exactly how far insurrectionary allies are to be trusted; that inventive talent, which finds resources where the ordinary aids and appliances are scarce, or altogether wanting, is a gift of very rare occurrence; and unfortunately, there are no means of distinguishing the officers by whom it is possessed, unless chance puts them into a situation to display their qualifications.

Another circumstance favourable for the Spanish cause, was the return of General Romana to Spain, to co-operate in the defence of his country. This nobleman, one of the best soldiers whom Spain had at the time, and a man, besides, of patriotic virtue and excellent talents, commanded that auxiliary body of ten thousand Spanish troops which Buonaparte had prevailed on Godoy to unite with the French army in the north of Europe, in order to secure their absence when he should put his schemes of invasion into execution against their country. These forces, or a large proportion of them,

---

[450] Gouvion St. Cyr says of them that they are the best light troops in Europe.—*Journal*, p. 54.
[451] Southey, vol. ii., p. 323.

were secluded in the isle of Funen, in the Baltic, with a view to conceal from them all that it did not suit Buonaparte should be known of the events which were agitating Spain. Nevertheless, a dexterous and daring agent, a Catholic priest of Scotch extraction, named Robertson, going ashore in disguise, succeeded in opening a communication[452] between the Spanish general and the British admiral Keates, in consequence of which, and by using bold and skilful combinations, Romana was able to extricate the greater part of his troops from the precarious situation in which they were placed, and finally in embarking them for Spain. It was the intention of this judicious officer to have made this little force of nine or ten thousand men the foundation of a regular army, by forming every regiment into a triple battalion. This he was unable to accomplish, but still his body of veterans inspired the Spaniards with hope and trust.

SPANISH ARMIES—OVERTURES OF PEACE

Three armies had been formed in Spain, designed to co-operate with each other; the sum of their numbers was calculated at 130,000 men, but they certainly did not exceed 100,000 at the very utmost. Their commissariat was in a wretched state, and even before the war commenced, the hardships of scarcity were felt in their camps. Three generals, each with independent authority, (an evil of the country and time,) commanded the Spanish armies. Blake, on the western frontier, extended his line from Burgos to Bilboa, disputing the possession of, and finally maintaining himself in, that capital of Biscay. The headquarters of the central army, under Castanos, were as far back as Soria; while the eastern army, under Palafox, extended between Zaragossa and Sanguesa. So that the

---

[452] "Robertson was qualified for this dangerous service by his skill as a linguist. One Spanish verse was given him; to have taken any other credentials might have proved fatal, and there was an anecdote connected with this which would sufficiently authenticate his mission. During Mr. Frere's residence as ambassador in Spain, Romana, who was an accomplished scholar, had recommended to his perusal the Gests of Cid, as one of the most ancient and curious poems in the language. One day he happened to call when Mr. Frere was reading it, and had just made a conjectural emendation in one of the lines: Romana instantly perceived the propriety of the proposed reading, and this line, therefore, when he was reminded of it, would prove that Mr. Robertson had communicated with his friend the British ambassador."—Southey, vol. ii., p. 337.

wings of the army were advanced towards the frontier; and the centre being drawn back, the whole position had the form of a crescent, with the concave side opposed to the enemy. Strongly posted within the position of Northern Spain, which they retained, the French armies, about sixty thousand men strong, lay protected by the fortresses which they occupied, and awaited the approach of Napoleon, with such a predominating force as should enable them to resume the offensive. The co-operation of a British auxiliary force became now an object of the first consequence; and the conduct of Britain had given every reason to expect that she would make in the Spanish cause, exertions to which she had been yet a stranger.

When the two Emperors of France and Russia met at Erfurt, it had been resolved, as we have said, to offer peace to Great Britain, either in some hope that it might have been made upon terms consistent with Buonaparte's pretensions to universal dominion, and Alexander's views upon Turkey, or in order to assume to themselves the credit of a disposition to pacific measures. A letter was accordingly despatched to the King of England, signed by both Emperors, expressive of their wish for a general peace. The official note in which the British administration replied to this overture, declared that the King of England was willing to treat for peace in conjunction with his allies, the King of Sweden, and those now possessing the supreme power in Spain, and exercising it in the name of Ferdinand VII.[453] The admission of any claim in favour of either of these powers, would have interfered with the plans both of France and Russia. The latter had for her object the possession of Finland, and the former judged that peace with England was chiefly desirable for gaining time to overcome all resistance in Spain; but must become useless if the independence of that country was to be stipulated in the treaty. The negotiation, therefore, broke off on these terms, while Britain, by her share in it, showed a manful resolution to identify her cause with that of the Spanish patriots.

---

[453] Parliamentary Debates, vol. xii., p. 97.

SIR JOHN MOORE

The actions of England bore a part with her professions. It was determined, as we have already seen, to reinforce the Portuguese army with an additional force of ten thousand men, and the whole was placed under the command of General Moore, a darling name in the British army, and the only one (excepting the victor of Vimeiro, had his rank in the service permitted the choice) to whom the public would have looked with confidence for the discharge of a trust so unusually weighty. But although the requisite degree of vigour was shown by the English government, yet they were not yet sufficiently accustomed to the necessity of acting with rapidity in executing their resolutions.

The arrival of General Moore's army had been expected so early as the 21st August, by those having best access to know the purposes of Government; yet Sir John Moore and his army were not in motion, to take part in the Spanish cause, till the beginning of October; and every day which was thus lost in unreadiness and indecision was of the most precious import to the cause of Spain. This procrastination could not be imputed to the general, nor even to the Administration. It was the consequence of want of alertness in the different departments, which had been little accustomed to hurry and exertion, and also of the hesitation apt to influence those who venture for the first time on a great and decisive measure. Even when the expedition arrived, there was uncertainty and delay.

Sir John Moore also, in all other respects one of the most eminent military characters, had embraced an unfavourable idea of the event of the Spanish struggle. He saw the faults and imperfections of their system, and they were of a kind which appeared most peculiarly perilous. Independent generals—an unpaid and ill-fed soldiery—a Supreme Junta which could not obtain obedience—were features which argued a speedy and disastrous conclusion to the contest, when opposed to the disciplined army of France, with which General Moore was so well acquainted, and to whose merits he could give the testimony of experience.

His fears, therefore, predominating over his hopes, yet his wishes alike, and his duty, prompting him to do something for the support of the Spanish cause, he was anxious so to direct his efforts, that he might retreat, in case of need, without suffering any considerable loss. For this purpose, it would have been his desire to have carried round the British army to Cadiz, to assist in the defence of Andalusia, where the sea, in case of disaster, would always be open for their retreat. But the English ministers had formed a bolder and more decisive plan of the campaign;—a plan which might have been decisive of the fate even of Buonaparte himself, at least of his Spanish projects of ambition, if either the Spaniards had acted with the skill which distinguished the victors of Baylen, or the enthusiasm which animated the defenders of Zaragossa, or if the British troops had been able to enter into communication with their armies before they were broken and overwhelmed by the Emperor of the French. This plan directed, that the British forces should proceed at once to the north of Spain, where the principal scene of action was necessarily laid, and thus, co-operate with Blake, and the other Spanish armies, which were destined to cover the capital, and withstand the first effort of the invaders. It was left to the judgment of the commander, either to advance into Spain by land from the frontiers of Portugal, or to transport his troops by sea to Corunna, with the purpose of marching through the province of Galicia, and entering in that manner upon the scene of action.

To accomplish the purpose of government, Sir John Moore deemed it most convenient to divide his forces. He sent ten thousand men, under Sir David Baird, by sea to Corunna, and determined to march himself at the head of the rest of the army, about sixteen thousand, to the north of Spain, from the frontiers of Portugal. The general science of war, upon the most extended scale, seems to have been so little understood or practised by the English generals at this time, that, instead of the country being carefully reconnoitred by officers of skill, the march of the army was arranged by such hasty and inaccurate information as could be collected from the peasants. By their report, General Moore was induced to divide his army into five divisions,[454] which were directed to move upon

---

[454] "What 'the general science of war upon an extended scale' may mean, I cannot pretend to say; but that Sir David Baird was sent by the Government from England direct to

Salamanca, where, or at Valladolid, they were to form a junction with the forces of Sir David Baird, expected from Corunna. The advance commenced about the 7th of November; but unhappily ere these auxiliaries appeared on the field, the armies of the Spaniards, whom they were destined to support, were defeated, dispersed, and almost annihilated.

There was no hesitation, no mark of indecision, no loss of precious time, on the part of Napoleon. He traversed the earth, as a comet does the sky, working changes wherever he came.[455] The convention at Erfurt broke up on the 14th October; on the 25th of the same month he opened, in person, the session of the Legislative Body; and on the second following day, he set off for the frontiers of Spain.[456] Here he had prepared, in ample extent, all the means of conquest; for, though trusting, or affecting to trust, a great deal to the influence of his fortune and his star, it was his wise and uniform policy to leave nothing to chance, but always to provide means, adequate to the purpose which he meditated.

Nearly a hundred thousand men had been gradually pouring into the position which the French occupied upon the Ebro.[457] The headquarters at Vittoria, honoured with the residence of the intrusive King, was soon more illustrious by the arrival of Buonaparte himself, a week before the British army had commenced its march from Portugal or Corunna.

To destroy the army of Blake, which lay opposed to the right flank of the French, before the Spanish general could be supported by Sir John Moore's forces, became for Buonaparte a matter of instant and peremptory importance. After some previous fighting, a French division, under Marshal Victor, brought the Spanish general

---

Corunna, and that Sir John Moore was not induced, by the reports of the peasants, to divide his army, may be ascertained by a reference to Sir John Moore's correspondence."—Napier, vol. i., p. 333.

[455] "In a few days I go," he said, "to put myself at the head of my armies, and, with the aid of God, to crown the King of Spain in Madrid, and to plant my eagles on the towers of Lisbon."

[456] "He reached Bayonne, and afterwards Vittoria, with the rapidity of an arrow. He performed the latter journey on horseback in two days, reaching Tolosa on the first, and on the second Vittoria."—Savary, tom. ii., p. 11.

[457] Napier, vol. i., p. 317; Southey, vol. ii., p. 387.

to action at the position of Espinosa. The battle continued for three hours in the evening, and was renewed the next day, when the French turned the Spanish position, and Blake, totally defeated, withdrew from the field with the purpose of making a stand at Reynosa, where he had his supplies and magazines.[458]

Meantime the activity of Buonaparte had struck another fatal blow on a different part of the Spanish defensive line. An army, designed to cover Burgos, and support the right flank of Blake's army, had been formed under the command of the Count de Belvidere, a young nobleman of courage, but without experience. He had under his command some remnants of the old Spanish army of the line, with the Walloons and Spanish guards, and a battalion of students, volunteers from Salamanca and Leon. Here also the French were successful. The youths, whom patriotism had brought to the field, could not be frightened from it by danger. They fell in their ranks, and their deaths spread mourning through many a respectable family in Spain.

Burgos was taken, in consequence of Count Belvidere's defeat; and it was by the same calamity rendered easy for the Duke of Dalmatia [Soult] to co-operate with the French generals, who were operating against the unfortunate Blake, with a view to drive him from his place of refuge at Reynosa. Surrounded on every side, the Spanish general saw no safety for the remnant of his forces, excepting in a retreat to Saint Andero, accomplished under such circumstances of haste and confusion, that his army might be considered as totally disorganised and dispersed. The disasters of Blake were the more to be lamented, that they involved the destruction of that fine body of soldiers whom Romana had led from the Baltic, and who, injudiciously brought into action by single battalions, perished ingloriously among the cliffs at Espinosa.[459]

The whole left wing of the Spanish army of defence, which so lately stretched from Bilboa to Burgos, and in support of which the British forces were advancing, was now totally annihilated, and the

---

[458] Fifth Bulletin of the French Army in Spain; Napier, vol. i., p. 391; Southey, vol. ii., p. 390.
[459] Seventh Bulletin; Southey, vol. ii., p. 393; Jomini, tom. iii., p. 97.

central army, under Castanos, whose left flank was now completely uncovered, was exposed to imminent danger. The veteran would fain have reserved his forces for a more fortunate time, by falling back and avoiding a battle. But he had been joined by Palafox, who had under his independent authority the army of Arragon; and the Supreme Junta, acting in that particular according to the custom of the French Convention, had despatched a commissioner to his camp, to see that that general performed his duty. This official person, with Palafox and other generals, joined in overpowering Castanos's reasoning, and, by the imputations of cowardice and treachery, compelled him to venture an action.[460]

BATTLE OF TUDELA

The battle took place at Tudela, on the 22d November, with all the results which Castanos had dreaded. A great number of Spaniards were killed; guns and baggage were taken; and, for the first time, a considerable number of prisoners fell into the hands of the French.[461] Castanos, with the routed troops of his proportion of the army, escaped to Calatuyud, while Palafox retreated again on the heroic city of Zaragossa, which was destined to suffer further distresses, and acquire additional renown. The road of the invader was now open to Madrid, unless in so far as it might be defended by some forces stationed at the pass of Samosierra, a mountainous defile about ten miles from the city, or as his entrance into the capital might be opposed by the desperate resolution of the citizens themselves. A part of the population placed their hopes on the defence afforded by this defile, not aware how easily, in modern warfare, such passes are either stormed or turned. But most of the citizens assumed the fierce and lowering appearance, which, in the Spaniard, announces an approaching burst of furious violence. Many thousands of peasants arrived from the neighbouring country, to assist, they said, in the defence of the capital; and, animated by the

---

[460] "These great advantages, the result of Napoleon's admirable combinations, the fruits of ten days of active exertion, obtained so easily, and yet so decisive of the fate of the campaign, prove the weakness of the system upon which the Spanish and British governments were at this time acting; if that can be called a system, where no one general knew what another had done—was doing—or intended to do."—Napier, vol. i., p. 394.
[461] Napier, vol. i., p. 401; Seventh Bulletin; Jomini, tom. iii., p. 99.

success of the Zaragossans, menaced war to the knife's point. There were about eight thousand troops of the line in Madrid; resistance was undoubtedly possible, and the people seemed determined upon it. A summons from the Supreme Junta called the inhabitants to arms, and the commencement of the preparations for defence was begun with unanimous vigour. For this purpose the pavement of the streets was taken up and converted into barricadoes; the houses were secured, and loopholed for musketry; and the whole body of the population toiled at erecting batteries, not only in the day-time but by torch-light.

Had Palafox commanded in Madrid, the experiment of resistance would, at all risks, have been attempted. But the governor was Don Thomas Morla, the same who succeeded Solano at Cadiz. His subsequent conduct seems to show, that, despairing of the cause of his country, he already meditated an intended change to the side of the usurper; so that the citizens of Madrid, at the moment when they had recourse to his skill and authority, received neither encouragement nor instructions, nor means of defence. We shall presently see in what manner the generous intentions of the people were cheated and baffled.

THE BRITISH ARMY—MADRID

Amidst the accumulation of disasters which overwhelmed the Spanish cause, Sir John Moore arrived at Salamanca, and Sir David Baird at Astorga, where the latter general halted. The situation of General Moore was extremely embarrassing, and gave him cause for the deepest anxiety. He knew the strength and character of the French armies, and was unwilling to repose too much confidence in the Spaniards, whose wisdom, he contended, was not a wisdom of action or exertion. On the other hand, he well knew the enthusiasm of the English for the Spanish cause, and the high expectations which were founded on his own talents, and on the gallantry of one of the finest armies which ever left Britain; and he felt that something was to be attempted worthy of the character of both. The general voice of the officers and soldiers was also clamorous for being employed. But the defeat of Castanos at Tudela seems to have extinguished the last hope in Sir John Moore's mind, and he at one time determined upon commencing his retreat to Portugal.

Before finally adopting this measure, he thought proper, however, to consult Mr. Frere, the British Minister, whether he thought any good would result from the daring measure of marching on Madrid, instead of retreating to Portugal. The correspondents differed, as might have been expected, from their difference of temperament and habits. Mr. Frere, a scholar and a poet, well known in the world of letters, being attached with enthusiasm to the cause of Spain, was a willing believer in the miracles that might be wrought by the higher and nobler qualities, which found a chord in unison in his own bosom.[462] He advised, as a Spartan would have done, that General Moore should throw all upon the cast, and advance to the succour of Madrid. The general, upon whom the responsibility devolved, viewed the measure in a different light, and his military habits did not permit him to place much confidence in a defence to be maintained by irregular forces against the disciplined armies of France. Yet, urged by his own feelings, and the importunity of the Spanish government, he resolved to try, by an effort against the north-western part of the French army, to answer the double purpose of preventing them from pressing on Romana, who, with indefatigable zeal, was collecting the scattered remains of the Galician army, which had been destroyed under Cuesta, and also of hindering the French from advancing southward to complete the subjugation of the Peninsula.

But while General Moore determined to hazard this bold measure, he saw painfully the danger of drawing upon himself, by adopting it, a predominant force of the enemy, before whom his retreat might be difficult and perilous. Yet he finally ordered Sir David Baird, whose retreat to Corunna was already commenced,

---

[462] "They are resolute," said Mr. Frere, "and I believe every man of them determined to perish with the country; they will not at least set the example, which the ruling powers and higher orders of other countries have exhibited, of weakness and timidity." "I have no hesitation," he added, "in taking upon myself any responsibility which may attach itself to this advice, as I consider the fate of Spain as depending absolutely, for the present, upon the decision which you may adopt. I say, for the present, for such is the spirit and character of the country, that even if abandoned by the British, I should by no means despair of their ultimate success."

again to occupy Astorga, and expressed his intention of hazarding an advance, at whatever risk. But he added these ominous words; "I mean to proceed bridle in hand, for if the bubble bursts, and Madrid falls, we shall have a run for it."[463]

The fate of Madrid was soon decided; but, as is generally believed, not without great treachery on the part of those who had been most apparently zealous for its defence. The passes of Guadarama and Samosierra had fallen into the possession of the French. The latter, on which the people of Madrid had fixed their eyes as on a second Thermopylæ or Roncesvalles, was cleared of its defenders by a charge of Polish lancers! These melancholy tidings, as they were in correspondence with General Moore's expectations, did not prevent his intended movement on the French lines of communication. By this means he might co-operate with General Romana and his army, and if pressed by superior numbers of the French, the retreat lay through Galicia to Corunna, where the transports were attending for the reception of the troops.

RETREAT OF THE BRITISH ARMY

General Moore left Salamanca on the 12th December, and proceeded towards Mayorga, where, on the 20th, he formed a junction with Sir David Baird. Advancing upon Sahagun, the troops received encouragement from a gallant action maintained by the 15th Hussars, five hundred of whom took, cut down, and dispersed, nearly double their own number of French cavalry. All now imagined they were to attack Soult, who had concentrated his forces behind the river Carrion to receive the assault. The British army was in the highest possible spirits, when news were suddenly received that Soult had been considerably reinforced; that Buonaparte was marching from Madrid at the head of ten thousand of his Guards; and that the French armies, who had been marching to the south of Spain, had halted and assumed a direction to the north-west, as if to enclose and destroy the British army.[464] This was exactly the danger

---

[463] Southey, vol. ii., p. 481.
[464] "In my life," says one who was present, "I never witnessed such an instantaneously-withering effect upon any body of living creatures! A few murmurs only were heard, but

which Moore had never ceased to apprehend, even when executing the movement that led to it. A retreat into, if not through Galicia, was the only mode of avoiding the perils by which the British were surrounded. The plan of defending this strong and mountainous province, or at least of effecting a retreat through it with order and deliberation, had been in view for several weeks; Sir David Baird's division of the army passed through it in their advance to Astorga; yet, so imperfect at that time was the British general staff, that no accurate knowledge seemed to have been possessed of the roads through the country, of the many strong military positions which it presents, or of the particular military advantages which it affords for defensive war. Another deficiency, incidental to our service at that period, was the great deficiency of the commissariat department, which had been pointed out so forcibly by Sir Arthur Wellesley, but which had not yet been remedied.[465]

Sufficient exertions in this department might have brought forward supplies from Corunna, and collected those which Galicia itself afforded; and the troops, retiring gradually from position to position, and maintained from their own resources, would have escaped the loss and dishonour of a retreat which resembled a flight in every particular, excepting the terror which accompanies it.

Besides these great deficiencies, a disadvantage of the most distressing kind occurred, from the natural and constitutional aversion of the British army to retrograde movements. Full of hope and confidence when he advances, the English soldier wants the pliability, lightness, and elasticity of character, which enables the Frenchman to distinguish himself during a retreat, by his

---

every countenance was changed, and they who, the minute before, were full of that confidence which ensures victory, were at once deprived of all heart and hope."—Southey, vol. ii., p. 493.

[465] Sir Arthur Wellesley, while exculpating from blame the individuals composing the commissariat of the Portuguese expedition, added these words:—"The fact is, that I wished to draw the attention of the government to this important branch of the public service, which is but little understood in this country. The evils of which I complained, are probably owing to the nature of our political situation, which prevents us from undertaking great military operations, in which the subsistence of armies becomes a subject of serious consideration and difficulty; and these evils consisted in the inexperience of almost every individual, of the mode of procuring, conveying, and distributing supplies." He requested that this explanation might stand in the minutes.—Southey, vol. i., p. 340.—S.

intelligence, discipline, and dexterity. Chafed, sullen, and discontented, the soldiers next became mutinous and insubordinate; and incensed against the Spaniards, by whose want of zeal they thought they had been betrayed, they committed the most unjustifiable excesses on the unresisting inhabitants. Despite the repeated orders of the commander-in-chief, endeavouring to restrain the passions and soothe the irritation of the soldiers, these disgraceful outrages were continued. It is matter of some consolation, that, losing their character for discipline, they retained that for courage. The French, who had pressed on the British rear, near to Benevente, and thrown across the river a large body of the Imperial cavalry, were driven back and defeated on the 29th December; and, leaving General Lefebvre Desnouettes a prisoner, in future were contented with observing, without pressing upon, the English retreat.[466]

At Astorga, 30th December, the commander-in-chief found about 5000 Spaniards under Romana, the relics of the Galician army. These troops wanted clothing, accoutrements, arms, ammunition, and pay—they wanted, in short, every thing, excepting that courage and devotion to the cause of their country, which would have had a better fate, had fortune favoured desert.

The Spanish general still proposed to make a stand at this rallying point; but whatever might be Romana's own skill, and the bravery of his followers, his forces were not of a quality such as to induce Sir John Moore to halt his retreat, which he now directed avowedly upon Corunna.

The scarcity of provisions required forced marches, and combined, with want of general knowledge of the country in a military sense, to hurry forward the soldiers, who too readily took advantage of these irregular movements to straggle and plunder, inflicting on the friendly natives, and receiving from them in return, the mutual evils which are given and received by invaders in an

---

[466] "This news was brought to the Emperor at Valderas, and gave him great pain, owing to the particular value he set upon the chasseurs of the guard. He did not, however, condemn the courageous determination of their colonel, but he regretted that he had not shown more self-command."—Savary, tom. ii., part ii., p. 21.

enemy's country. The weather dark and rainy—the roads blockaded by half-melted snow—the fords become almost impassable—augmented the difficulties of a retreat, resembling that by which a defeated army is forced into a country totally unknown to them, and through which the fugitives must find their way as they can. The baggage of the army, and its ammunition, were abandoned and destroyed. The sick, the wounded, were left to the mercy of the pursuers; and the numbers who in that hour of despair gave way to the national vice of intoxication, added largely to the ineffective and the helpless. The very treasure-chests of the army were thrown away and abandoned. There was never so complete an example of a disastrous retreat.

One saving circumstance, already mentioned, tended to qualify the bad behaviour of the troops; namely, that when a report arose that a battle was to be expected, the courage, nay, the discipline of the soldiers, seemed to revive. This was especially the case on the 6th January, when the French ventured an attack upon our rear-guard near Lugo. So soon as a prospect of action was presented, stragglers hastened to join their ranks—the disobedient became at once subordinate, as if on the parade; and it was made manifest that the call to battle, far from having the natural effect of intimidating to utter dispersion troops already so much disordered, was to the English army the means of restoring discipline, steadiness, and confidence.

The French having declined the proffered engagement, Sir John Moore continued his retreat under the same disadvantageous circumstances, until he arrived at Corunna, the original object of his destination. He was preparing to embark his forces in the transports, which lay prepared for their reception, when his pursuer, Soult, now pressing boldly forward, made it evident that this could not be accomplished unless either by a convention with him, or by the event of a battle, which might disqualify him from opposing the embarkation. Sir John Moore, with the dignity becoming his character, chose the latter alternative, and occupied a position of no great strength in front of the town, to protect the embarkation. The attack was made by the French on the 16th January, in heavy columns, and with their usual vivacity; but it was sustained and repelled on all hands. The gallant general was mortally wounded in the action, just as he called on the 42d Highland regiment to "remember Egypt," and reminded the same brave mountaineers, that though ammunition was scarce, "they had their bayonets."[467]

Thus died on the field of victory, which atoned for previous misfortunes, one of the bravest and best officers of the British army. His body was wrapped in his military cloak, instead of the usual vestments of the tomb; it was deposited in a grave hastily dug on the ramparts of the citadel of Corunna; and the army completing its embarkation upon the subsequent day, their late general was "left alone with his glory."

Thus ended, in the acquisition of barren laurels, plentifully blended with cypress, the campaign, which had been undertaken by so beautiful and efficient an army, under so approved a commander. The delay in sending it to the scene of action was one great cause of its failure, and for that the gallant general, or his memory, cannot be held responsible. Such a force at Salamanca, while the French were unequal in numbers to the Spanish armies, might have had the most important consequences. At a later period, when the patriotic armies were every where defeated, we confess that General Moore, with the ideas which he entertained of the Spaniards, does not seem to us to have been called upon to place the fate of the British army— auxiliaries, it must be observed, not principals in the war—on the same desperate cast by which the natives were compelled to abide. The disasters of the retreat appear to rest on want of knowledge of the ground they were to traverse, and on the deficiency of the commissariat, which, though the army must be entirely dependent on it, was not at that time sufficiently under the control of the commander-in-chief. We owe it to his memory to say, that at the

---

[467] Southey, vol. ii., p. 524. "As the soldiers placed him in a blanket, his sword got entangled, and the hilt entered the wound. Captain Hardinge attempted to take it off, but the dying man stopped him, saying, 'It is as well as it is; I had rather it should go out of the field with me.' And in that manner, so becoming to a soldier, Moore was borne from the fight."—Napier, vol. i., p. 497.

close of his own valuable life, he amply redeemed in his last act the character of the army which he commanded.[468]

---

[468] "Sir John Moore lived to hear that the battle was won. 'Are the French beaten?' was the question which he repeated to every one who came into his apartment; and, addressing his old friend, Colonel Anderson, he said, 'You know that I always wished to die this way.' His strength was fast failing, and life was almost extinct, when, with an unsubdued spirit, he exclaimed, 'I hope the people of England will be satisfied! I hope my country will do me justice!' The battle was scarcely ended, when his corpse, wrapped in a military cloak, was interred by the officers of the staff in the citadel of Corunna. The guns of the enemy paid his funeral honours; and Soult, with a noble feeling of respect for his valour, raised a monument to his memory."—Napier, vol. i., p. 500.

CHAPTER XLVII

General Belliard occupies Madrid—Napoleon returns to France—Cause of his hurried return—View of the Circumstances leading to a Rupture with Austria—Feelings of Russia upon this occasion—Secret intrigues of Talleyrand to preserve Peace—Immense exertions made by Austria—Counter efforts of Buonaparte—The Austrian Army enters Bavaria, 9th April, 1809—Napoleon hastens to meet them—Austrians defeated at Abensberg on the 20th—and at Eckmühl on the 22d—They are driven out of Ratisbon on the 23d—The Archduke Charles retreats into Bohemia—Napoleon pushes forward to Vienna—which, after a brief defence, is occupied by the French on the 12th of May—Retrospect of the events of the War in Poland, Italy, the North of Germany, and the Tyrol—Enterprises of Schill—of the Duke of Brunswick Oels—Movements in the Tyrol—Character and Manners of the Tyrolese—Retreat of the Archduke John into Hungary.

MADRID

Having thus completed the episode of Sir John Moore's expedition, we resume the progress of Napoleon, to whom the successive victories of Reynosa, Burgos, and Tudela, had offered a triumphant path to Madrid. On the 1st of December, his headquarters being at the village of Saint Augustino, he was within sight of that capital, and almost within hearing of the bells, whose hollow and continued toll announced general insurrection, and the most desperate resistance. Nor was the zeal of the people of Madrid inadequate to the occasion, had it been properly directed and encouraged. They seized on the French officer who brought a summons of surrender, and were with difficulty prevented from tearing him to pieces. On the 3d, the French attacked Buen Retiro, a palace which had been fortified as a kind of citadel. A thousand Spaniards died in the defence of this stronghold. On the 4th, Morla opened a capitulation with Napoleon. He and Yriarte, another noble Spaniard, of whom better things had been hoped, came to testify their repentance for the rash part they had undertaken, and to express their sense that the city could in nowise be defended; but, at the same time to state, that the populace and volunteers were resolute in its defence, and that some delay would be necessary, to let their zeal cool, and their fears come to work in their turn.

Buonaparte admitted these deputies to his own presence, and with the audacity which sometimes characterised his language, he read them a lecture on their bad faith,[469] in not observing the treaty of Baylen—on their bad faith, in suffering Frenchmen to be assassinated—on their bad faith, in seizing upon the French squadron at Cadiz. This rebuke was gravely urged by the individual, who had kidnapped the royal family of Spain while they courted his protection as his devoted vassals—who had seized the fortresses into which his troops had been received as friends and allies—who had floated the streets of Madrid with the blood of its population—and, finally, who had taken it upon him to assume the supreme authority, and dispose of the crown of Spain, under no better pretext than that he had the will and the power to do so. Had a Spaniard been at liberty to reply to the Lord of Legions, and reckon with him injury for injury, falsehood for falsehood, drop of blood for drop of blood, what an awful balance must have been struck against him![470]

In the meantime, those citizens of Madrid who had determined on resistance, began to see that they were deserted by such as should have headed them in the task, and their zeal became cooled under the feelings of dismay and distrust. A military convention was finally concluded, in virtue of which General Belliard took possession of the city, on the 4th of December. The

---

[469] "Injustice and bad faith," exclaimed the Emperor, "always recoil upon those who are guilty of either."—*Fourteenth Bulletin.*

[470] "'The Spanish ulcer destroyed me,' was an expression of deep anguish which escaped from Napoleon in his own hour of misfortune."—Napier, vol. i., p. 414.

terms were so favourable, as to show that Buonaparte, while pretending to despise the sort of resistance which the population might have effected, was well pleased, nevertheless, not to drive them to extremity. He then published a proclamation, setting forth his desire to be the regenerator of the Spanish empire. But in case his mild and healing mediation should be again refused, he declared he would treat them as a conquered people, and place his brother on another throne. "I will, in that case, set the crown of Spain on my own head, and I shall know how to make it respected; for God," concluded this extraordinary document, "has given me the power and the will to surmount all difficulties."[471]

VALLADOLID

There were now two operations which nearly concerned Buonaparte. The first was the dispersion of the remaining troops of Castanos, which had escaped the fatal battle of Tudela, and such other armed bodies as continued to occupy the south of Spain. In this the French had for some time an easy task; for the Spanish soldiers, surprised and incensed at their own disasters, were, in many instances, the assassins of their generals, and the generals had lost all confidence in their mutinous followers. But before pursuing his successes in the south, it was Buonaparte's first resolution to detach a part of the French army upon Portugal, by the way of Talavera, and by occupying Lisbon, intercept the retreat of Sir John Moore and his English army. The advance of the English general to Salamanca interfered with this last design. It seemed to Napoleon, that he did not yet possess forces sufficient at the same time to confront and turn back Sir John Moore, and, on the other hand, to enter Portugal and possess himself of Lisbon. The latter part of the plan was postponed. Placing himself at the head of his Guards, Napoleon, as we have seen, directed his march towards Valladolid, and witnessed the retreat of Sir John Moore. He had the pleasure of beholding with his own eyes the people whom he hated most, and certainly did not fear the least, in full retreat, and was observed scarcely ever to have appeared so gay and joyous as during the

---

[471] Nineteenth Bulletin of the French Army in Spain.

pursuit, which the French officers termed the race of Benevente.[472] But he had also the less pleasing spectacle of the skirmish, in which the general commanding the cavalry of his Imperial Guard was defeated, and his favourite, General Lefebvre, made prisoner. He halted with his Guards at Astorga, left Ney with 18,000 men to keep the country in subjection, and assigned to Soult the glorious task of pursuing the English and completing their destruction. We have already seen how far he proved able to accomplish his commission.

Meanwhile, the Emperor himself returned to Valladolid, and from thence set off for France with the most precipitate haste. His last act was to declare his brother Joseph generalissimo over the French armies; yet, notwithstanding this mark of trust and confidence, there is reason to believe that Buonaparte repented already his liberality, in assigning to another, though his own brother, an appanage so splendid, and which was likely to cost so much blood and treasure. Something to this purpose broke out in his proclamation to the people of Madrid; and he was more explicit when speaking confidentially to the Abbé de Pradt, whom, in returning from Benevente, the Emperor met at Valladolid.

They were alone; it was a stormy night; and Buonaparte, opening the window from time to time, to ascertain the possibility of travelling, only turned from it to overwhelm Monsieur de Pradt with questions on the state of the capital which he had just left. The abbé did not disguise their disaffection; and when Napoleon endeavoured to show the injustice of their complaints, by insisting on the blessings he had conferred on Spain, by the diminution of tithes, abolishing feudal servitudes, and correcting other abuses of the old government, De Pradt answered by saying, that the Spaniards did not thank Napoleon for relief from evils to which they were insensible; and that the country was in the situation of the wife of Sganarelle in the farce, who quarrelled with a stranger for interfering with her husband when he was beating her. Buonaparte laughed, and continued in these remarkable words:—"I did not know what Spain was. It is a finer country than I was aware, and I have made Joseph a more valuable present than I dreamed of. But you will see, that by and by the Spaniards will commit some folly,

---

[472] Savary, tom. ii., part ii., p. 20; Twenty-second Bulletin.

which will place their country once more at my disposal. I will then take care to keep it to myself, and divide it into five great viceroyships."[473]

While the favourite of fortune nourished these plans of engrossing and expanding ambition, the eagerness of his mind seems to have communicated itself to his bodily frame; for, when the weather permitted him to mount on horseback, he is said at once, and without halting, save to change horses, to have performed the journey from Valladolid, to Burgos, being thirty-five Spanish leagues, or about seventy English miles and upwards, in the space of five hours and a half.[474]

The incredible rapidity with which Napoleon pressed his return to France, without again visiting Madrid, or pausing to hear the fate of the English army, surprised those around him. Some conjectured that a conspiracy had been discovered against his authority at Paris; others, that a band of Spaniards had devoted themselves to assassinate him; a third class assigned different causes; but it was soon found that the despatch which he used had its cause in the approaching rupture with Austria.[475]

AUSTRIA

This breach of friendship appears certainly to have been sought by Austria without any of those plausible reasons of complaint, on which nations generally are desirous to bottom their

---

[473] De Pradt, p. 211.
[474] "Never did any sovereign ride at such a rate. He ordered his saddle horses to be placed in relays on the road, with a picket of chasseurs at each relay, so as to leave a distance of only three or four leagues from one relay to another. He often made these arrangements himself, and in the utmost secrecy. The horses belonging to the grooms carried portmanteaus with complete changes of dress, and with portfolios containing papers, pens, ink, maps, and telescopes."—Savary, tom. ii., part ii., p. 30.
[475] "The Emperor returned amongst us in a sudden and unexpected manner; whether, as those about him assured me, that a band of Spanish fanatics had sworn to assassinate him (I believed it, and had, on my side, given the same advice;) or whether he was still acted upon by the fixed idea of a coalition in Paris against his authority, I think both these motives united had their weight with him; but they were disguised by referring the urgency of his sudden return to the preparations of Austria."—Fouché, tom. i., p. 330.

quarrels. She did not allege that, with respect to herself or her dominions, France had, by any recent aggression, given her cause of offence. The Abbé de Pradt remarks upon the occasion, with his usual shrewdness, that if Napoleon was no religious observer of the faith of treaties, it could not be maintained that other states acted much more scrupulously in reference to him. Buonaparte himself has alleged, what, in one sense of the word was true, that many of his wars were, in respect to the immediate causes of quarrel, merely defensive on his side. But this was a natural consequence of the style and structure of his government, which, aiming directly at universal empire, caused him to be looked upon by all nations as a common enemy, the legitimate object of attack whenever he could be attacked with advantage, because he himself neglected no opportunity to advance his pretensions against the independence of Europe.

The singular situation of Great Britain, unassailable by his arms, enabled her to avow this doctrine, and to refuse making peace with Napoleon, on terms how favourable soever for England, unless she were at the same time recognised as having authority to guarantee the security of such states as she had a chance of protecting, if she remained at war. Thus, she refused peace when offered, under the condition that France should have Sicily; and, at the period of which we treat, she had again recently declined the terms of pacification proposed by the overture from Erfurt, which inferred the abandonment of the Spanish cause.

This principle of constant war with Buonaparte, or rather with the progress of his ambition, guided and influenced every state in Europe, which had yet any claim for their independence. Their military disasters, indeed, often prevented their being able to keep the flag of defence flying; but the cessions which they were compelled to make at the moment of defeat, only exasperated their feelings of resentment, and made them watch more eagerly for the period, when their own increasing strength, or the weakness of the common enemy, might enable them to resume the struggle. Napoleon's idea of a peace was, as we have elsewhere seen, that the party with whom he treated should derive no more from the articles agreed upon, than the special provisions expressed in his favour. So long, for instance, as he himself observed all points of the treaty of Presburg, the last which he had dictated to Austria, that power, according to his view of the transaction, had no farther right either of remonstrance or intervention, and was bound to view with indifference whatever changes the French Emperor might please to work on the general state of Europe. This was no doubt a convenient interpretation for one who, aiming at universal monarchy, desired that there should be as little interference as possible with the various steps by which he was to achieve that great plan; but it is entirely contradictory of the interpretation put upon treaties by the jurists; and were the jurists of a contrary opinion, it is in diametrical opposition to the feelings of human nature, by which the policy of states, and the conduct of individuals, are alike dictated. Buonaparte being, as his conduct showed him, engaged in a constant train of innovation upon the liberties of Europe, it followed, that the states whom he had not been able entirely to deprive of independence, should, without farther, or more particularly national cause of war, be perpetually on the watch for opportunities to destroy or diminish his terrible authority. In this point of view, the question for Austria to consider was, not the justice of the war, but its expediency; not her right of resisting the common enemy of the freedom of Europe, but practically, whether she had the means of effectual opposition. The event served to show that Austria had over-estimated her own resources.

It is true, that an opportunity now presented itself, which seemed in the highest degree tempting. Buonaparte was absent in Spain, engaged in a distant conquest, in which, besides the general unpopularity of his cause, obstacles had arisen which were strangers to any previous part of his history, and resistance had been offered of a nature so serious, as to shake the opinion hitherto entertained of his invincibility. On the other hand, Austria had instituted in her states organic laws, by which she secured herself the power of being able to call out to arms her immense and military population; and her chief error seems to have been, in not postponing the fatal struggle until these new levies had acquired a better disciplined and more consolidated form. Of this the Emperor of Russia was fully sensible, and, as we have already noticed, he saw with great apprehension Austria's purpose of opposing herself singly to the arms of France; since, however close the intimacy which, for the present, subsisted betwixt Alexander and Napoleon, it was impossible for the former to be indifferent to the vast risk which Europe must incur, should France finally annihilate the independence of Austria. A series of intrigues, of a very singular nature, was accordingly undertaken at Paris, in the hope of preserving peace. Talleyrand, who, perhaps on Napoleon's own account as well as that of France, was unwilling that another great continental war should arise, was active in endeavouring to discover means by which peace might be preserved.[476] In the evening, it was his custom to meet the Counts Metternich and Romanzow at the assemblies of the Prince of Tour and Taxis, and there, totally unknown to Buonaparte, to agitate the means of preventing war;—so certain it is, that even the ablest and most absolute of sovereigns was liable, like an ordinary prince, to be deceived by the statesmen around him. But the ingenuity of these distinguished politicians could find no means of reconciling the interests of Austria—seeing, as she thought, an opportunity of forcing from Napoleon, in his hour of weakness, what she had been compelled to surrender to him in his hour of strength—and those of Buonaparte, who knew that so soon as he should make a single sacrifice to compulsion, he would be held as having degraded that high military reputation which was the foundation of his power. It may reasonably be supposed, that, with the undecided war of Spain on his hands, he would willingly have adjourned the contest; but with him, the sound of the trumpet was a summons to be complied with, in the most complicated state of general embarrassment.

EXERTIONS OF AUSTRIA

The exertions made by Austria on this important occasion were gigantic, and her forces were superior to those which she had been able to summon out at any former period of her history. Including the army of reserve, they were computed as high as five hundred and fifty thousand men, which the Archduke Charles once more commanded in the character of generalissimo.[477] It is said that

---

[476] Jomini, tom. iii., p. 133; Savary, tom. ii., part ii., p. 32.
[477] Jomini, tom. iii., p. 155.

this gallant prince did not heartily approve of the war, at least of the period chosen to commence it, but readily sacrificed his own opinion to the desire of contributing his utmost abilities to the service of his brother and of his country.

Six corps d'armée, each about thirty thousand strong, were destined, under the archduke's immediate command, to maintain the principal weight of the war in Germany; a seventh, under the Archduke Ferdinand, was stationed in Galicia, and judged sufficient to oppose themselves to what forces Russia, in compliance with her engagements to Napoleon, might find herself obliged to detach in that direction; and two divisions, under the Archduke John, were destined to awaken hostilities in the north of Italy, into which they were to penetrate by the passes of Carinthia and Carniola.

Buonaparte had not sufficient numbers to oppose these formidable masses; but he had recourse to his old policy, and trusted to make up for deficiency of general numerical force, by such rapidity of movement as should ensure a local superiority on the spot in which the contest might take place.[478] He summoned out the auxiliary forces of the Confederation of the Rhine, and of the King of Saxony. He remanded many troops who were on their march for Spain, and by doing so virtually adjourned, and, as it proved, for ever, the subjugation of that country. He had already in Germany the corps of Davoust, and of General Oudinot. The garrisons which France had established in Prussia, and in the northern parts of Germany, were drained for the purpose of reinforcing his ranks; but the total amount of his assembled forces was still greatly inferior to those of the Archduke Charles.[479]

On the 9th of April, 1809, the archduke crossed the Inn; and thus a second time Austria commenced her combat with France, by

---

[478] "A conscription was immediately called out; the soldiers were equipped in all haste, and sent off in carriages to their destination. The guard, which was still at Burgos, was ordered to repair to Germany. Never had Napoleon been taken so much by surprise: this war completely astonished him.—'There must,' he said to us, 'be some plans in preparation which I do not penetrate, for there is madness in declaring war against me. They fancy me dead. I expect a courier from Russia: if matters go on there as I have reason to hope they do, I will give them work.'"—Savary, tom. ii., part ii., p. 34.

[479] Jomini, tom. iii., p. 155.

the invasion of Germany. Some confidence was placed in the general discontent which prevailed among the Germans, and especially those of the Confederation of the Rhine, and their hatred of a system which made them on every occasion the instruments of French policy. The archduke averred in his manifesto, that the cause of his brother was that of general independence, not individual aggrandisement; and he addressed himself particularly to those his brothers of Germany, who were now compelled by circumstances to serve in the opposite ranks. Whatever effects might have been produced by such an address, supposing it to have had time to operate, the result was disconcerted by the promptitude, which with Buonaparte was almost always the harbinger of success.

While the Austrian army moved slow, and with frequent halts, encumbered as they were with their baggage and supplies, Napoleon had no sooner learned by the telegraph the actual invasion of Bavaria, than he left Paris on the instant, [11th April,] and hurried to Frankfort; without guards, without equipage, almost without a companion, save the faithful Josephine, who accompanied him as far as Strasbourg, and there remained for some time watching the progress of the campaign, the event of which was destined to have such a melancholy influence on her own happiness.

The Archduke Charles's plan was to act upon the offensive. His talents were undoubted, his army greatly superior in numbers to the French, and favourably disposed, whether for attack or defence; yet, by a series of combinations, the most beautiful and striking, perhaps, which occur in the life of one so famed for his power of forming such, Buonaparte was enabled, in the short space of five days, totally to defeat the formidable masses which were opposed to him.

ACTION OF ABENSBERG

20th April.

Napoleon found his own force unfavourably disposed, on a long line, extending between the towns of Augsburg and Ratisbon, and presenting, through the incapacity it is said of Berthier, an alarming vacancy in the centre, by operating on which the enemy might have separated the French army into two parts, and exposed each to a flank attack.[480] Sensible of the full, and perhaps fatal consequences, which might attend this error, Napoleon determined on the daring attempt to concentrate his army by a lateral march, to be accomplished by the two wings simultaneously. With this view he posted himself in the centre, where the danger was principally apprehended, commanding Massena to advance by a flank movement from Augsburg to Pfaffenhofen, and Davoust to approach the centre by a similar manœuvre from Ratisbon to Neustadt. These marches must necessarily be forced, that of Davoust being eight, that of Massena betwixt twelve and thirteen leagues. The order for this daring operation was sent to Massena on the night of the 17th, and concluded with an earnest recommendation of speed and intelligence. When the time for executing these movements had been allowed, Buonaparte, at the head of the centre of his forces, made a sudden and desperate assault upon two Austrian divisions, commanded by the Archduke Louis and General Hiller. So judiciously was this timed, that the appearance of Davoust on the one flank kept in check those other Austrian corps d'armée, by whom the divisions attacked ought to have been supported; while the yet more formidable operations of Massena, in the rear of the Archduke Louis, achieved the defeat of the enemy. This victory, gained at Abensberg upon the 20th April, broke the line of the Austrians, and exposed them to farther misfortunes.[481] The Emperor attacked the fugitives the next day at

---

[480] Jomini, tom. iii., p. 158. "At Donawert we found the Prince of Neufchatel; but, very shortly after our arrival, the Emperor fell into a passion, which we were at a loss to account for: he was addressing Berthier in these words: 'What you have done appears to me so extraordinary, that, if you were not my friend, I should suspect you of betraying me; for Davoust is really situated at present much more for the convenience of the Archduke Charles than for mine.' This was actually the case: the Prince of Neufchatel had put a wrong construction upon the Emperor's order, and so interpreted it as to expose us to the danger of a most serious disaster at the very commencement of the campaign."—Savary, tom. ii., part ii., p. 49.
[481] Jomini, tom. iii., p. 167; Savary, tom. ii., part ii., p. 57.

Landshut, where the Austrians lost thirty pieces of cannon, nine thousand prisoners, and much ammunition and baggage.[482]

On the 22d April, after this fortunate commencement of the campaign, Buonaparte directed his whole force, scientifically arranged into different divisions, and moving by different routes, on the principal army of the Archduke Charles, which, during these misfortunes, he had concentrated at Eckmühl. The battle is said to have been one of the most splendid which the art of war could display. An hundred thousand men and upwards were dispossessed of all their positions by the combined attack of their scientific enemy, the divisions appearing on the field, each in its due place and order, as regularly as the movements of the various pieces in a game of chess. All the Austrian wounded, great part of their artillery, fifteen stand of colours, and 20,000 prisoners, remained in the power of the French.[483] The retreat was attended with corresponding loss; and Austria, again baffled in her hopes of reacquiring her influence in Germany, was once more reduced to combat for her existence amongst nations.

On the subsequent day, the Austrians made some attempt to protect the retreat of their army, by defending Ratisbon. A partial breach in the ancient walls was hastily effected, but for some time the French who advanced to the storm, were destroyed by the musketry of the defenders. There was at length difficulty in finding volunteers to renew the attack, when the impetuous Lannes, by whom they were commanded, seized a ladder, and rushed forward to fix it himself against the walls. "I will show you," he exclaimed, "that your general is still a grenadier." The example prevailed, the wall was surmounted, and the combat was continued or renewed in the streets of the town, which was speedily on fire. A body of French, rushing to charge a body of Austrians, which still occupied one end of a burning street, were interrupted by some waggons belonging to the enemy's train. "They are tumbrils of powder," cried the Austrian commanding, to the French; "if the flames reach them,

---

[482] "At Landshut the Emperor was fortunately overtaken by Massena, to whom he had written these flattering words, 'Activity, activity!—quickness! I rely upon you.' The marshal, whose zeal was excited by these words, had accelerated his movement, and arrived on the field of battle just at the close of the action."—Savary, tom. ii., part ii., p. 57.
[483] Second Bulletin of the French Army; Jomini, tom. iii., p. 17.

both sides perish." The combat ceased, and the two parties joined in averting a calamity which must have been fatal to both, and finally, saved the ammunition from the flames. At length the Austrians were driven out of Ratisbon, leaving much cannon, baggage, and prisoners, in the hands of the enemy.[484]

In the middle of this last mêlée, Buonaparte, who was speaking with his adjutant, Duroc, observing the affair at some distance, was struck on the toe of the left foot by a spent musket-ball, which occasioned a severe contusion. "That must have been a Tyrolese," said the Emperor coolly; "who has aimed at me from such a distance. These fellows fire with wonderful precision." Those around remonstrated with him for exposing his person; to which he answered, "What can I do? I must needs see how matters go on." The soldiers crowded about him in alarm at the report of his wound; but he would hardly allow it to be dressed, so eager was he to get on horseback and put an end to the solicitude of his army, by showing himself publicly among the troops.[485]

Thus within five days—the space, and almost the very days of the month, which Buonaparte had assigned for settling the affairs of Germany—the original aspect of the war was entirely changed; and Austria, who had engaged in it with the proud hope of reviving her original influence in Europe, was now to continue the struggle for the doubtful chance of securing her existence. At no period in his momentous career, did the genius of Napoleon appear more completely to prostrate all opposition; at no time did the talents of a single individual exercise such an influence on the fate of the universe. The forces which he had in the field had been not only unequal to those of the enemy, but they were, in a military point of view, ill-placed, and imperfectly combined. Napoleon arrived alone, found himself under all these disadvantages, and we repeat, by his

---

[484] Third Bulletin; Jomini, tom. iii., p. 175; Savary, tom. ii., part ii., p. 63.
[485] "I was present at the accident. The Emperor's surgeon, M. Yvan, was immediately sent for, who dressed the wound before us, and before all the soldiers who happened to be near at the time: the more they were ordered to keep off, the nearer they approached. A moment of confusion ensued; which was nothing more than a consequence of the attachment the troops bore him. Had the ball struck the instep, instead of the toe, it must have penetrated the foot. His lucky star was again true to him on this occasion."—Savary, tom. ii., part ii., p. 64.

almost unassisted genius, came, in the course of five days, in complete triumph out of a struggle which bore a character so unpromising.[486] It was no wonder that others, nay, that he himself, should have annexed to his person the degree of superstitious influence claimed for the chosen instruments of Destiny, whose path must not be crossed, and whose arms cannot be arrested.

While the relics of the Archduke Charles's army were on full retreat to Bohemia, Napoleon employed the 23d and 24th of April, to review his troops, and distributed with a liberal hand honours and rewards. It was in this sphere that he was seen to greatest advantage; for although too much of a soldier among sovereigns, no one could claim with better right to be a sovereign among soldiers. It was on this occasion, that, striking a soldier familiarly on the cheek, as he said, "I create you a knight," he asked the honoured party his name. "You ought to know it well," answered the soldier; "since I am the man, who, in the deserts of Syria, when you were in extremity, relieved you from my flask." Napoleon instantly recollected the individual and the circumstance. "I make you," he said "a knight, with an annuity of twelve hundred francs—what will you do with so much money?"—"Drink with my comrades to the health of him that is so necessary to us."

The generals had their share in the Imperial bounty, particularly Davoust, to whose brilliant execution of the manœuvres commanded by Napoleon, the victory was directly to be attributed. He was created Duke of Eckmühl. It was a part of Napoleon's policy, by connecting the names of fields of victory with the titles of those who contributed to acquire it, to ally the recollections of their merits with his own grateful acknowledgment of them. Thus the title of every ennobled marshal was a fresh incentive to such officers as were ambitious of distinction.

---

[486] "On the night of the 22d of April (the eleventh day since his departure from Paris,) the Emperor established his headquarters in a palace which the Archduke Charles had occupied during the whole day: it was, indeed, only at a late hour in the afternoon that the archduke gave up the idea of passing another night there, since we supped off the dishes which had been prepared for himself and suite."—Savary, tom. ii., part ii., p. 61.

RETREAT OF THE AUSTRIANS

After the fatal battle of Eckmühl, the Archduke Charles effected, as we have seen, his retreat into the mountainous country of Bohemia, full of defiles, and highly capable of defence, where he could remodel his broken army, receive reinforcements of every kind, and make a protracted defence, should Napoleon press upon him in that direction. But the victories of these memorable five days had placed the French Emperor in full possession of the right bank of the Danube, and of the high-road to the city of Vienna, which is situated on the same side of the river. True to his principle of striking directly at the heart of his antagonist, Napoleon determined to march on the metropolis of Austria, instead of pursuing the archduke into the mountains of Bohemia.[487] By the latter course, the war might have been long protracted, a contingency which it was always Napoleon's policy to avoid; and, alarmed for the preponderance which France was about to acquire, Russia herself, now acting tardily and unwillingly as the ally of Napoleon, might have assumed a right of mediating, which she had strength enough to enforce if it should be declined.

On the other hand, the Austrian General Hiller, defeated at Landshut, and cut off from communication with the archduke, had been able to unite himself with a considerable reserve, and assumed the mien of defending the high-road to the capital. Buonaparte had thus an enemy of some consequence in front, while the army of Charles might operate from Bohemia upon the communications in his rear; and a universal national insurrection of the Tyrolese threatened not only entirely to expel the French and Bavarians from their mountains, but even to alarm Bavaria herself. Insurrections were also beginning to take place all through Germany, of a character which showed, that, had the tide of war turned against France, almost all the north of Germany would have been in arms against her. These dangers, which would have staggered a man of less determination, only confirmed Napoleon in his purpose of compelling Austria to make peace, by descending the Danube, and effecting a second occupation of her capital.

---

[487] Jomini, tom. iii., p. 177.

All was shortly in motion for the intended enterprise. General Hiller, too weak to attempt the defence of the Inn, retreated to Ebersberg, a village with a castle upon the river Traun, which was in most places unfordable, and had elevated rocky banks, scarped by the hand of Nature. One bridge communicating with the town, was the only mode of approaching the position, which, viewed in front, seemed almost impregnable. It was occupied by Hiller with more than thirty thousand men, and a formidable train of artillery. He trusted to be able to maintain himself in this strong line of defence, until he should renew his communications with the Archduke Charles, and obtain that prince's co-operation in the task of covering Vienna, by defending the course of the Danube.

Upon the 3d of May, the position of Ebersberg was attacked by Massena, and stormed after a most desperate resistance, which probably cost the victors as many men as the vanquished. The hardiness of this attack has been censured by some military critics, who pretend, that if Massena had confined his front attack to a feint, the Austrian general would have been as effectually dislodged, and at a much cheaper rate, by a corresponding movement upon his flank, to be executed by General Lannes, who passed the river Traun at Wels for that purpose. But Massena, either from the dictates of his own impetuous disposition, or because he had understood the Emperor's commands as positively enjoining an attack, or that he feared Lannes might be too late in arriving, when every moment was precious, because every moment might re-establish the communication between the archduke and Hiller—attempted and succeeded in the desperate resolution of disposting the Austrian general by main force.[488]

General Hiller retreated to Saint Polten, then crossed the Danube by the bridge at Mautern, which he destroyed after his passage, and, marching to form his junction with the Archduke Charles, left the right side of the Danube, and consequently the high-road to Vienna, open to the French. Napoleon moved forward with a steady yet rapid pace, calculating upon gaining the advance necessary to arrive at the Austrian capital before the archduke, yet at

---

[488] Fifth Bulletin of the Grand French Army; Savary, tom. ii., part ii., p. 68; Jomini, tom. iii., p. 181.

the same time marching without precipitation, and taking the necessary measures for protecting his communications.

VIENNA

The city of Vienna, properly so called, is surrounded by the ancient fortifications which withstood the siege of the Turks in 1683. The suburbs, which are of great extent, are surrounded by some slighter defences, but which could only be made good by a large army. Had the archduke, with his forces, been able to throw himself into Vienna before Buonaparte's arrival under its walls, no doubt a formidable defence might have been made.[489] The inclination of the citizens was highly patriotic. They fired from the ramparts on the advance of the French, and rejected the summons of surrender. The Archduke Maximilian was governor of the place, at the head of ten battalions of troops of the line, and as many of Landwehr, or militia.

A shower of bombs first made the inhabitants sensible of the horrors to which they must necessarily be exposed by defensive war. The palace of the Emperor of Austria was in the direct front of this terrible fire. The Emperor himself, and the greater part of his family, had retired to the city of Buda in Hungary; but one was left behind, confined by indisposition, and this was Maria Louisa, the young archduchess, who shortly afterwards became Empress of France. On intimation to this purpose being made to Buonaparte, the palace was respected, and the storm of these terrible missiles directed to other quarters.[490] The intention of defending the capital was speedily given up. The Archduke Maximilian, with the troops of the line, evacuated the city; and, on the 12th, General O'Reilly, commanding some battalions of landwehr, signed the capitulation with the French.

Napoleon did not himself enter Vienna; he fixed—for the second time—his headquarters at Schoenbrun, a palace of the Emperor's, in the vicinity of the capital.

---

[489] Savary, tom. ii., part ii., p. 73.
[490] De Bourrienne, tom. viii., p. 190.

In the meanwhile, the Archduke Charles, unable to prevent the fall of Vienna, was advancing to avenge it. In the march which he made through Bohemia, he had greatly increased his army; and the events in the north of Germany and the Tyrol had been so dangerous to French influence, that it required all the terrors of the battle of Eckmühl to keep the unwilling vassals of the conqueror in a state of subjection. Before, therefore, we trace the course of remarkable events which were about to take place on the Danube, the reader is requested to take a brief view of the war on the Polish frontier, in Italy, in the north of Germany, and in the Tyrol; for no smaller portion of the civilized world was actually the scene of hostilities during this momentous period.

In Poland, the Archduke Ferdinand threw himself into the Grand Duchy of Warsaw, as the part of Poland which formerly belonged to Prussia; obtained possession of Warsaw itself, and pressed northward with such vivacity, that, while Prince Poniatowski was hardly able to assemble a small defensive army between the Narew and the Vistula, the archduke approached Thorn, and was in a situation to summon Prussia to arms. The call would doubtless have been readily obeyed, had the Archduke Charles obtained any shadow of success in the commencement of the campaign. But the French had possession of all the most important Prussian fortresses, which rendered it imprudent, indeed almost impossible, for that power to offer any effectual means of resistance, until the arms of Austria should assume that decided preponderance, which they were not on this occasion doomed to attain.[491]

SCHILL—KATT—DUKE OF BRUNSWICK OELS

The feeling of indignation against the foreign yoke had, however, penetrated deeply into the bosom of the Prussians. The doctrines of the Tugend-bund had been generally received among the higher and middling classes—the lower listened to the counsels only of their own patriotism and courage. The freedom of Europe—the independence of Germany—the delivery of Prussia from a foreign bondage—the obtaining security for what was most

---

[491] Jomini, tom. iii., p. 236.

dear and valuable to mankind, determined Schill, a Prussian major of hussars, to attempt, even without the commands of his King, the liberation of his country.

During the former unhappy war, Schill, like Blucher, conducted himself with the most patriotic devotion, and had, when courage and conduct were rare, been distinguished by both in his service as a partisan officer. On the present occasion, his attempt may be likened to a rocket shot up into the firmament, which, by its descent upon a magazine, may give rise to the most appalling results; or which, bursting in empty space, is only remembered by its brief and brilliant career. Chance allotted to Schill the latter and more unfavourable conclusion; but his name must be enrolled in the list of those heroes who have ventured their lives to redress the wrongs of their country, and the remembrance of whose courage often forms the strongest impulse to others to reassume the heroic undertaking, for which they themselves have struggled in vain.

The movement which this daring soldier had projected, was connected with a plan of general insurrection, but was detected by a premature discovery. Colonel Doernberg, an officer of the Westphalian guard, was engaged in the conspiracy, and had undertaken to secure the person of Jerome Buonaparte. His scheme was discovered; and among his papers were found some which implicated Schill in these insurrectionary measures. Jerome, of course, made his complaint to the King of Prussia, who was in no capacity to refuse to deliver up the accused officer. Obliged thus to precipitate his plan of insurrection, Schill put himself at the head of his regiment, which was animated by his own spirit, and marched out of Berlin to proclaim the independence of his country. He showed the utmost speed and dexterity in his military manœuvres, and soon assembled a small army of 5000 or 6000 men, sufficient to take possession of various towns, and of the little fortress of Domitz.

Katt, another insurgent, placed himself at the head of an insurrection in Cassel; and a yet more formidable leader, distinguished alike by his birth, his bravery, and his misfortunes, appeared in the field. This was the Duke of Brunswick Oels, son of him who was mortally wounded at Jena. The young prince had ever since before his eyes the remembrance of his father, to whom Buonaparte's enmity would not permit even the leisure of an hour to die in his own palace. The breaking out of the war betwixt France and Austria seemed to promise him the road to revenge. The duke contracted with Austria to levy a body of men, and he was furnished by England with the means to equip and maintain them. His name, his misfortunes, his character, and his purpose, tended soon to fill his ranks; the external appearance of which indicated deep sorrow, and a determined purpose of vengeance. His uniform was black, in memory of his father's death; the lace of the cavalry was disposed like the ribs of a skeleton; the helmets and caps bore a death's head on their front.

The brave young soldier was too late in appearing in the field. If he could have united his forces with those of Schill, Doernberg, Katt, and the other insurgents, he might have effected a general rising in the north; but the event of Eckmühl, and the taking of Vienna, had already checked the awakening spirit of Germany, and subsequent misfortunes tended to subdue, at least for the time, the tendency to universal resistance which would otherwise certainly have been manifested. It was about the middle of May when the Duke of Brunswick advanced from Bohemia into Lusatia, and by that time the corps of Schill and others were existing only as separate bands of partisans, surrounded or pursued by the adherents of France, to whom the successes of Buonaparte had given fresh courage.

General Thielman opposed himself to the duke, at the head of some Saxon troops, and was strong enough to prevent his forcing his way into the middle of Germany, where his presence might have occasioned great events. Still, however, though the plans of the insurgents had been thus far disappointed or checked, their forces remained on foot, and formidable, and the general disposition of the nation in their favour rendered them more so.

THE TYROLESE

While the insurrectional spirit which animated the Germans smouldered in some places like subterranean fire, and partially showed itself by eruptions in others, the mountains of the Tyrol were in one general blaze through their deepest recesses. Those wild regions, which had been one of the oldest inheritances of Austria, had been torn from her by the treaty of Presburg, and conferred on the new kingdom of Bavaria. The inclination of the inhabitants had not been consulted in this change. The Austrians had always governed them with a singular mildness and respect for their customs; and had thus gained the affection of their Tyrolese subjects, who could not therefore understand how an allegiance resembling that of children to a parent, should have been transferred, without their consent, to a stranger sovereign, with whom they had no tie of mutual feeling. The nation was the more sensible of these natural sentiments, because the condition of the people is one of the most primitive in Europe. The extremes of rank and wealth are unknown in those pastoral districts; they have almost no distinction among their inhabitants; neither nobles nor serfs, neither office-bearers nor dependents; in one sense, neither rich nor poor. As great a degree of equality as is perhaps consistent with the existence of society, is to be found in the Tyrol. In temper they are a gay, animated people, fond of exertion and excitation, lovers of the wine-flask and the dance, extempore poets, and frequently good musicians. With these are united the more hardy qualities of the mountaineer, accustomed to the life of a shepherd and huntsman, and, amidst the Alpine precipices, often placed in danger of life, while exercising one or other of the occupations. As marksmen, the Tyrolese are accounted the finest in Europe; and the readiness with which they obeyed the repeated summons of Austria during former wars, showed that their rustic employments had in no respect diminished their ancient love of military enterprise. Their magistrates in peace, and leaders in war, were no otherwise distinguished from the rest of the nation than by their sagacity and general intelligence; and as these qualities were ordinarily found among inn-keepers, who, in a country like the Tyrol, have the most general opportunities of obtaining information, many of that class were leaders in the memorable war of 1809. These men sometimes could not even read or write, yet in general, exhibited so much common sense and presence of mind, such a ready knowledge of the capacity of the troops they commanded, and of the advantages of the country in which they served, that they became formidable to the best generals and the most disciplined soldiers.[492]

In the beginning of April these ready warriors commenced their insurrection, and in four days, excepting in the small fortress of Kufstein, which continued to hold out, there was not a Frenchman or Bavarian in the Tyrol, save those who were prisoners. The history of that heroic war belongs to another page of history. It is enough here to say, that scarcely supported by the Austrians, who had too much to do at home, the Tyrolese made, against every odds, the most magnanimous and obstinate defence. It was in vain that a French army, led by Lefebvre, marched into the country, and occupied Inspruck, the capital. The French were a second time compelled by these valiant mountaineers to retreat with immense loss; and if Austria could have maintained her own share of the contest, her faithful provinces of Tyrol and the Vorarlberg must on their side have come off victors.[493]

But the disasters of the Archduke Charles, as they had neutralized the insurrections in Germany, and rendered of no comparative avail the victories of the Tyrolese, so they also checked the train of success which had attended the movements of the Archduke John in Italy, at the commencement of the war. We have already said, that the safety and honour of Austria being, as it was thought, sufficiently provided for by the strength of the main army, this young prince had been despatched into Italy, as the Archduke Ferdinand into Poland, to resuscitate the interest of their House in their ancient dominions. Eugene, the son-in-law of Buonaparte, and his viceroy in Italy, was defeated at Sacile upon the 15th of April, by the Archduke John, and compelled to retire to Caldiero on the Adige. But ere the Austrian prince could improve his advantages, he received the news of the defeat at Eckmühl, and the peril in which

---

[492] The Austrians censured the want of tactics of the Tyrolese. Some poetical sharpshooter defended his countrymen by an epigram, of which the following is a translation:— "It is but chance, our learn'd tacticians say, Which without science gains the battle day; Yet would I rather win the field by chance, Than study tactics, and be beat by France."—S.
[493] Jomini, tom. ii., p. 232.

Vienna was placed. He was, therefore, under the necessity of retreating, to gain, if possible, the kingdom of Hungary, where the presence of his army might be of the most essential consequence. He was in his turn pursued by Prince Eugene, to whom the Austrian retreat gave the means of uniting himself with the French force in Dalmatia, from which he had been separated, and thus enabled him to assume the offensive with forces much augmented.[494]

Thus the mighty contest was continued, with various events, from the shores of the Baltic to those of the Adriatic, and from the eastern provinces of Germany to those of Hungary. But the eyes of all men, averted from the more remote and subordinate scenes of the struggle, were now turned towards the expected combat betwixt Buonaparte and the Archduke Charles, which it was easily predicted must soon take place under the walls of Vienna, and decide, it was then apprehended for ever, the future fate, perhaps the very existence, of the empire of Austria.

---

[494] Jomini, tom. iii., p. 224-232.

Chapter XLVIII

Position of the French and Austrian Armies after the Battle of Eckmühl—Napoleon crosses the Danube—Great Conflict at Asperne, when victory was claimed by both parties—Battle of Wagram fought 6th July—Armistice concluded at Znaim—Close of the Career of Schill and the Duke of Brunswick Oels—Defence of the Tyrol—Its final unfortunate result—Growing resistance throughout Germany—Its effects on Buonaparte—He publishes a singular Manifesto in the Moniteur.

PASSAGE OF THE DANUBE

We left Napoleon concentrating his army near Vienna, and disposing it so as to preserve his communications with France, though distant and precarious. He occupied the city of Vienna, and the right bank of the Danube. The Archduke Charles now approached the left bank of the same river, which, swollen by the spring rains, and the melting of snow on the mountains, divided the two hostile armies as if by an impassable barrier. In the year 1805, when Napoleon first obtained possession of Vienna, the bridges over the Danube were preserved, which had enabled him to press his march upon Koutousoff and the Russians. This time he had not been so fortunate. No bridge had been left unbroken on the Danube, whether above or below Vienna, by which he might push his forces across the river, and end the war by again defeating the Austrian archduke. At the same time, the hours lost in indecision were all unfavourable to the French Emperor. Charles expected to be joined by his brothers, and, being in his own country, could subsist with ease; while Napoleon, in that of an enemy, could expect no recruits, and might have difficulty in obtaining supplies. Besides, so long as an Austrian army was in the field, the hopes of Germany remained unextinguished. The policy, therefore, of Buonaparte determined him to pursue the most vigorous measures, by constructing a bridge over the Danube, and crossing it at the head of his army, with the purpose of giving battle to the archduke on the left bank.

The place originally selected for this bold enterprise was at Nussdorf, about half a league above Vienna, where the principal stream passes in a full but narrow channel under the right bank, which is there so high as to command the opposite verge of the river, and affords, therefore, the means of protecting the passage. But above five hundred men having been pushed across, with the view of re-establishing the old bridge which had existed at Nussdorf in 1805, were attacked and cut off by the Austrians, and this point of passage was in consequence abandoned.

Napoleon then turned his thoughts to establishing his intended bridge at the village of Ebersdorf, on the right bank, opposite to which the channel of the Danube is divided into five branches, finding their course amongst islands, one of which, called the island of Lobau, is extremely large. Two of these branches are very broad. The islands are irregular in their shape, and have an alluvial character. They exhibit a broken and diversified surface, partly covered with woods, partly marshy, and at times overflowed with water. Here Napoleon at length determined to establish his bridge, and he collected for that purpose as many boats and small craft as he could muster, and such other materials as he could obtain. The diligence of the engineer officer, Aubry, was distinguished on this occasion.

The French were obliged to use fishers' caissons filled with bullets, instead of anchors, and to make many other substitutions for the accomplishment of their objects. They laboured without interruption; for the Austrians, though they made various demonstrations upon Krems and Linz, as if they themselves meant to cross the Danube above Vienna, yet did nothing to disturb Napoleon's preparation for a passage at Ebersdorf, although troops might have been easily thrown into the island of Lobau, to dispute the occupation, or to interrupt the workmen. It is impossible to suppose the Archduke Charles ignorant of the character of the ground in the neighbourhood of his brother's capital; we must therefore conjecture, that the Austrian general had determined to let Buonaparte accomplish his purpose of passing the river, in order to have the advantage of attacking him when only a part of his army had crossed, and of compelling him to fight with the Danube in his rear, which, in case of disaster, could only be repassed by a succession of frail and ill-constructed bridges, exposed to a thousand accidents. It is doing the archduke no discredit to suppose he acted on such a resolution, for we shall presently see he actually gained the advantages we have pointed out, and which, could they have been prosecuted to the uttermost, would have involved the ruin of Buonaparte and his army.

The materials having been brought together from every quarter, Napoleon, on the 19th May, visited the isle of Lobau, and directed that the completion of the bridge should be pressed with all possible despatch. So well were his orders obeyed, that, on the next day, the troops were able to commence their passage, although the bridge was still far from being complete. They were received by skirmishers on the left bank; but as these fell back without any obstinacy of resistance, it became still more obvious that the archduke did not mean to dispute the passage, more especially as he had not availed himself of the important means of doing so which the locality presented.[495]

At the point where the extremity of the last bridge of the chain (for there were five in number, corresponding to the five streams,) touched the left bank of the Danube, the French troops, as they passed over, entered upon a little plain, extending between the two villages of Asperne and Essling. Asperne lies farthest to the left, a thousand toises distant from the bridge; Essling is at the other extremity of the plain, about one thousand five hundred toises from the same point. The villages, being built of mason-work, with gardens, terraces, and court-yards, formed each a little fortified place, of which the churchyard of Asperne, and a large granary at Essling, might be termed the citadels. A high-road, bordered by a deep ditch, extended between these two strong posts, which it

---

[495] Tenth Bulletin of the French Army; Savary, tom. ii., part ii., p. 78; Jomini, tom. iii., p. 188-196.

connected as a curtain connects two bastions. This position, if occupied, might indeed be turned on either flank, but the character of the ground would render the operation difficult.

Still farther to the right lay another village, called Enzersdorf. It is a thousand toises from Asperne to Essling, and somewhat less from Essling to Enzersdorf. Before these villages rose an almost imperceptible ascent, which extended to two hamlets called Raschdorf and Breitenlee, and on the left lay the wooded heights of Bisamberg, bounding the landscape in that direction. Having passed over near thirty thousand infantry, with about six thousand horse, Napoleon directed a redoubt to be constructed to cover the extremity of the bridge on the left side. Meantime, his troops occupied the two villages of Asperne and Essling, and the line which connected them.

The reports brought in during the night were contradictory, nor could the signs visible on the horizon induce the generals to agree concerning the numbers and probable plans of the Austrians. On the distant heights of Bisamberg many lights were seen, which induced Lannes and others to conceive the enemy to be there concentrated. But much nearer the French, and in their front, the horizon also exhibited a pale streak of about a league in length, the reflected light of numerous watch-fires, which the situation of the ground prevented being themselves seen.

From these indications, while Lannes was of opinion they had before them only a strong rear-guard, Massena, with more judgment, maintained they were in presence of the whole Austrian army. Napoleon was on horseback by break of day on the 21st, to decide by his own observation; but all the ground in front was so thickly masked and covered by the Austrian light cavalry, as to render it vain to attempt to reconnoitre. On a sudden, this living veil of skirmishers was withdrawn, and the Austrians were seen advancing with their whole force, divided into five columns of attack, headed by their best generals, their numbers more than double those of the French, and possessing two hundred and twenty pieces of artillery. The combat commenced by a furious attack on the village of Asperne, which seemed only taken that it might be retaken, only retaken that it might be again lost. The carnage was dreadful; the obstinacy of the Austrians in attacking, could not, however, overcome that of the French in their defence. Essling was also assaulted by the Austrians, though not with the same pertinacity; yet many brave men fell in its attack and defence.

The battle began about four afternoon; and when the evening approached, nothing decisive had been done. The Archduke brought his reserves, and poured them in successive bodies upon the disputed village of Asperne. Every garden, terrace, and farm-yard, was a scene of the most obstinate struggle. Waggons, carts, harrows, ploughs, were employed to construct barricades. As the different parties succeeded on different points, those who were victorious in front were often attacked in the rear by such of the other party as had prevailed in the next street. At the close of the day, Massena remained partially master of the place, on fire as it was with bombs, and choked with the slain. The Austrians, however, had gained possession of the church and churchyard, and claimed the superiority on the left accordingly.

BATTLE OF ESSLING

Essling was the object, during the last part of this bloody day, of three general attacks; against all which the French made decisive head. At one time, Lannes, who defended the post, was so hard pressed, that he must have given way, had not Napoleon relieved him and obtained him breathing time, by a well-timed though audacious charge of cavalry. Night separated the combatants.

The French could not in any sense be said to have been beaten; but it was an unusual thing for them, fighting under Napoleon's eye, to be less than completely victorious. The Austrians could as little be called victors; but even the circumstance of possessing themselves of the most important part of Asperne, showed that the advantage had been with, rather than against them; and both armies were affected with the results of the day, rather as they appeared when compared with those of their late encounters, than as considered in their own proper character. The feeling of the

Austrians was exultation; that of the French not certainly discouragement, but unpleasant surprise.

On the 22d, the work of carnage recommenced. Both armies had received reinforcements during the night—Napoleon from the left bank, the Archduke from reserves in his rear. The French had at first the advantage—they recovered the church of Asperne, and made a number of Austrians prisoners in the village. But the attacks on it were presently renewed with the same fury as on the preceding day. Napoleon here formed a resolution worthy of his military fame. He observed that the enemy, while pressing on the village of Asperne, which was the left-hand point of support of the French position, kept back, or, in military language, refused the right and centre of his line, which he was therefore led to suppose were weakened for the purpose of supporting the assault upon Asperne. He determined, for this reason, to advance the whole French right and centre, to assail the Austrian position on this enfeebled point. This movement was executed in echellon, advancing from the French right. Heavy masses of infantry, with a numerous artillery, now advanced with fury. The Austrian line was forced back, and in some danger of being broken. Regiments and brigades began to be separated from each other, and there was a danger that the whole centre might be cut off from the right wing. The Archduke Charles hastened to the spot, and in this critical moment discharged at once the duty of a general and of a common soldier. He brought up reserves, replaced the gaps which had been made in his line by the fury of the French, and seizing a standard, himself led the grenadiers to the charge.

At this interesting point, the national accounts of the action differ considerably. The French despatches assert, that, notwithstanding the personal gallantry of their general, the Austrians were upon the point of a total defeat. Those of the Archduke, on the contrary, affirm that the resistance of the Austrians was completely successful, and that the French were driven back on all points.[496] All agree, that just at this crisis of the combat, the bridge

---

[496] "Asperne was ten times taken, lost, and again conquered. Essling, after repeated attacks, could not be maintained. At eleven at night the villages were in flames, and we remained

which Buonaparte had established over the Danube was swept away by the flood.

This opportune incident is said, by the Austrian accounts, to have been occasioned by fire-ships sent down the river. The French have denied the existence of the fire-ships, and, always unwilling to allow much effect to the result of their adversaries' exertions, ascribe the destruction of the floating bridge to the trunks of trees and vessels borne down by a sudden swell of the Danube.[497] General Pelet,[498] indeed admits, with some reluctance, that timber frames of one or more windmills, filled with burning combustibles, descended the river. But whether the Austrians had executed the very natural plan of launching such fire-works and driftwood on the stream, or whether, as the ancient heathen might have said, the aged and haughty river shook from his shoulders by his own exertions the yoke which the strangers had imposed on him, the bridge was certainly broken, and Buonaparte's army was extremely endangered.[499]

He saw himself compelled to retire, if he meant to secure, or rather to restore, his communication with the right bank of the Danube. The French movement in retreat was the signal for the Austrians' advance. They recovered Asperne; and had not the French fought with the most extraordinary conduct and valour, they must have sustained the greatest loss. General Lannes, whose behaviour had been the subject of admiration during the whole day, was mortally wounded by a ball, which shattered both his legs. Massena sustained himself in this crisis with much readiness and presence of mind; and the preservation of the army was chiefly attributed to him. It is said, but perhaps falsely, that Napoleon himself showed on this occasion less alertness and readiness than was his custom.

---

masters of the field of battle. The most complete victory crowned our army."—*Austrian Official Bulletin.*—See *Supplement to the London Gazette, 11th July.*
[497] Tenth Bulletin of the French Army; Jomini, tom. iii., pp. 303, 214; Savary, tom. ii., part ii., p. 82; Rapp, p. 123.
[498] Mémoires sur la Guerre de 1809.
[499] "The enemy had a complete view of our body in its whole extent; and contriving to fill with stones the largest boats they could find, they sent them down the current. This contrivance proved but too successful."—Savary, tom. ii., part ii., p. 85.

DEATH OF LANNES

At length, the retreat of the French was protected by the cannon of Essling, which was again and again furiously assaulted by the Austrians. Had they succeeded on this second point, the French army could hardly have escaped, for it was Essling alone which protected their retreat. Fortunately for Buonaparte, that end of the bridge which connected the great isle of Lobau with the left bank on which they were fighting still remained uninjured, and was protected by fortifications. By this means he was enabled to draw back his shattered army during the night into the great island, evacuating the whole position which he had held on the right bank. The loss of both armies was dreadful, and computed to exceed twenty thousand men on each side, killed and wounded. General St. Hilaire, one of the best French generals, was killed in the field, and Lannes, mortally wounded, was brought back into the island. He was much lamented by Buonaparte, who considered him as his own work. "I found him," he said, "a mere swordsman, I brought him up to the highest point of talent. I found him a dwarf, I raised him up into a giant." The death of this general, called the Roland of the army, had something in it inexpressibly shocking. With both his legs shot to pieces, he refused to die, and insisted that the surgeons should be hanged who were unable to cure a mareschal and Duke de Montebello. While he thus clung to life, he called upon the Emperor, with the instinctive hope that Napoleon at least could defer the dreadful hour, and repeated his name to the last, with the wild interest with which an Indian prays to the object of his superstition.[500] Buonaparte showed much and creditable emotion at beholding his faithful follower in such a condition.[501]

---

[500] "He twined himself round me with all he had left of life; he would hear of no one but me, he thought but of me, it was a kind of instinct."—Napoleon, *Las Cases*, tom. ii., p. 353. On the 31st May, Napoleon wrote to Josephine—"La perte Duc de Montebello, qui est mort ce matin, m'a fort affligé. *Ainsi tout finit!!* Si tu peux contribuer à consoler la pauvre Maréchale, fais-le."—*Lettres à Joséphine*, tom. ii., p. 67.

[501] "The Emperor perceived a litter coming from the field of battle, with Marshal Lannes stretched upon it. He ordered him to be carried to a retired spot, where they might be alone and uninterrupted: with his face bathed in tears, he approached and embraced his dying friend."—Savary, tom. ii., part i., p. 87.

The news of this terrible action flew far and wide, and was represented by the Austrians as a glorious and complete victory. It might have well proved so, if both the villages of Asperne and Essling could have been carried. As it was, it cannot properly be termed more than a repulse, by which the French Emperor's attempt to advance had been defeated, and he himself driven back into an island, and cut off by an inundation from the opposite bank, on which his supplies were stationed; and so far, certainly, placed in a very precarious condition.

The hopes and wishes of all Europe were opposed to the domination of Buonaparte; and Hope, it is well known, can build fair fabrics on slighter foundations than this severe check afforded. It had been repeatedly prophesied, that Napoleon's fortune would some time or other fail in one of those hardy measures, and that by penetrating into the depth of his enemy's country, in order to strike a blow at his capital, he might engage himself beyond his means of recovery, and thus become the victim of his own rashness. But the time was not yet arrived which fate had assigned for the fulfilment of this prophecy. More activity on the part of the Austrian prince, and a less vigorous development of resources and energy on that of Napoleon, might have produced a different result; but, unhappily, the former proved less capable of improving his advantage, than the latter of remedying his disasters.

THE DANUBE

On the morning of the 23rd, the day after the bloody battle of Asperne, Buonaparte, with his wounded, and the remnant of his forces, was cooped up in the marshy island of Lobau, and another nearer to the left bank, called Enzersdorf, from the village of that name. This last island, which served as an outwork to the larger, is separated from the left bank, which was occupied by the Austrians, only by a small channel of twenty toises in breadth. The destruction of the bridges had altogether divided Buonaparte from the right bank, and from his rear, under Davoust, which still remained there.[502] The nature of the ground, on the left side of the Danube, opposite to the isle of Enzersdorf, admitted cannon being placed to command the passage, and it is said that General Hiller ardently pressed the plan of passing the stream by open force at that point, and attacking successively the islands of Enzersdorf and Lobau, and offered to answer with his head for its success. The extreme loss sustained by the Austrian army on the two preceding days, appears to have been the cause that this proposal was rejected. It has been also judged possible for Prince Charles to have passed the Danube, either at Presburg or higher up, and thus placed himself on the right bank, for the purpose of attacking and destroying the reserves which Buonaparte had left at Ebersdorf under Davoust, and from which he was separated by the inundation. Yet neither did the Archduke adopt this plan, but, resuming the defensive, from which he had only departed for a few hours, and concluding that Napoleon would, on his part, adopt the same plan which he had formerly pursued, the Austrian engineers were chiefly engaged in fortifying the ground between Asperne and Essling, while the army quietly awaited till it should suit Napoleon to renew his attempt to cross the Danube.

With unexampled activity, Buonaparte had assembled materials, and accomplished the re-establishment of his communications with the right bank, by the morning of the second day after the battle. Thus was all chance destroyed of the Austrians making any farther profit of the interruption of his communications. With equal speed, incessant labour converted the isle of Lobau into an immense camp, protected by battering cannon, and secured either from surprise or storm from the Austrian side of the river; so

---

[502] "The two arms of the Danube which traversed the island, and had hitherto been found dry, or at least fordable, had become dangerous torrents, requiring hanging bridges to be thrown over them. The Emperor crossed them in a skiff, having Berthier and myself in his company. When arrived on the bank of the Danube, the Emperor sat down under a tree, and, being joined by Massena, he formed a small council, in order to collect the opinion of those about him as to what had best be done under existing circumstances. Let the reader picture to himself the Emperor sitting between Massena and Berthier on the bank of the Danube, with the bridge in front, of which there scarcely remained any vestige, Davoust's corps on the other side of the broad river, and, behind, in the island of Lobau itself, the whole army separated from the enemy by a mere arm of the Danube, thirty or forty toises broad, and deprived of all means of extricating himself from this position, and he will admit that the lofty and powerful mind of the Emperor could alone be proof against discouragement."—Savary, tom. ii., part ii., p. 88.

that Hiller's plan became equally impracticable. The smaller islands were fortified in the like manner; and, on the first of July, Buonaparte pitched his headquarters[503] in the isle of Lobau, the name of which was changed to Napoleon Island, as in an immense citadel, from which he had provided the means of sallying at pleasure upon the enemy. Boats, small craft, and means to construct, on a better plan than formerly, three floating bridges, were prepared and put in order in an incredibly short space of time.[504] The former bridge, repaired so strongly as to have little to fear from the fury of the Danube, again connected the islands occupied by the French with the left-hand bank of that river; and so imperfect were the Austrian means of observation, though the campaign was fought within their own country, whose fate depended upon its issue, that they appear to have been ignorant of the possibility of Napoleon's using any other means of passage than this identical original bridge, which debouched betwixt Asperne and Essling; and they lost their time in erecting fortifications under that false impression. Yet certainly a very little inquiry might have discovered that the French Emperor was constructing three bridges, instead of trusting to one.

For several weeks afterwards, each army was receiving reinforcements. The Austrian and Hungarian nobles exerted themselves to bring to the field their vassals and tenantry; while Buonaparte, through every part of Germany which was subject to his direct or indirect influence, levied additional forces, for enabling him to destroy the last hope of their country's independence.

More powerful and numerous auxiliary armies also approached the scene of action from the north-eastern frontier of Italy, from which the Archduke John, as we have already mentioned, was retiring, in order, by throwing his army into Hungary, to have

---

[503] "Malevolence has delighted in representing the Emperor as of a mistrustful character; and yet on this occasion, where ill-intentioned men might have made any attempt upon his person, his only guard at headquarters was the Portuguese legion, which watched as carefully over him as the veterans of the army of Italy could have done."—Savary, tom. ii., part ii., p. 91.

[504] "General Bertrand, the Emperor's aide-de-camp, was the officer who executed this splendid work. He was one of the best engineer officers that France could boast of since the days of Vauban. The exhaustless arsenal of Vienna had supplied us with a profusion of timber, and also with cordage, iron, and with forty engines to drive the piles in."—Savary, tom. ii., part ii., p. 93.

an opportunity of co-operating with his brother, the Archduke Charles. He came, but not unpursued or unmolested. Prince Eugene Beauharnois, at the head of the army which was intended to sustain the Archduke John's attack in Italy, joined to such forces as the French had in Dalmatia, followed the march of the Austrians, brought them to action repeatedly, gained advantages over them, and finally arrived on the frontiers of Hungary as soon as they did. Here the town of Raab ought to have made some protracted defence, in order to enable the Archduke John to co-operate with his younger brother Regnier, another of this warlike family, who was organising the Hungarian insurrection. But the same fatality which influenced every thing else in this campaign, occasioned the fall of Raab in eight days, after the Austrian prince had been worsted in a fight under its walls.[505] The Italian army of Eugene now formed its junction with the French; and the Archduke John, crossing the Danube at Presburg, advanced eastward, for the purpose of joining the Archduke Charles. But it was not the purpose of Napoleon to permit this union of forces.

On the 5th of July, at ten o'clock at night, the French began to cross from the islands in the Danube to the left-hand bank.[506] Gun-boats, prepared for the purpose, silenced some of the Austrian batteries; others were avoided, by passing the river out of reach of their fire, which the French were enabled to do by the new and additional bridges they had secretly prepared.

BATTLE OF WAGRAM

At daylight on the next morning, the Archduke had the unpleasing surprise to find the whole French army on the left bank of the Danube, after having turned all the fortifications which he had formed for the purpose of opposing their passage, and which were thus rendered totally useless. The villages of Essling and

---

[505] Nineteenth Bulletin of the French army; Jomini, tom. iii., p. 248; Savary, tom. ii., part ii., p. 105.
[506] "The island of Lobau was a second valley of Jehosophat; men who had been six years asunder met here on the banks of the Danube for the first time since that long separation; 150,000 infantry, 750 pieces of cannon, and 300 squadrons of cavalry, constituted the Emperor's army."—Savary, tom. ii., part ii., p. 109.

Enzersdorf had been carried, and the French line of battle was formed upon the extremity of the Archduke's left wing, menacing him, of course, both in flank and rear. The Archduke Charles endeavoured to remedy the consequences of this surprise by outflanking the French right, while the French made a push to break the centre of the Austrian line, the key of which position was the village of Wagram. Wagram was taken and retaken, and only one house remained, which was occupied by the Archduke Charles, when night closed the battle, which had been bloody and indecisive. Courier after courier were despatched to the Archduke John, to hasten his advance.

On the next day, being the 6th July, was fought the dreadful battle of Wagram, in which, it is said, that the Archduke Charles committed the great military error of extending his lines, and weakening his centre. His enemy was too alert not to turn such an error to profit. Lauriston, with a hundred pieces of cannon, and Macdonald,[507] at the head of a chosen division, charged the Austrians in the centre, and broke through it. Napoleon himself showed all his courage and talents, and was ever in the hottest of the action, though the appearance of his retinue drew on him showers of grape, by which he was repeatedly endangered.[508]

At length the Austrian army seems to have fallen into disorder; the left wing, in particular, conducted itself ill; cries of alarm were heard, and the example of precipitate flight was set by those who should have been the last to follow it, when given by others. The French took twenty thousand prisoners; and so complete was the discomfiture, that though the Archduke John came up with a part of his army before the affair was quite over, so

---

[507] "On the day after the battle, Napoleon, on passing by Macdonald, held out his hand to him, saying, 'Shake hands, Macdonald—no more enmity between us—we must henceforth be friends; and, as a pledge of my sincerity, I will send you your marshal's staff, which you so gloriously earned in yesterday's battle.'"—Savary, tom. ii., part ii., p. 128.

[508] "Out of seventy-two hours of the 4th, 5th, and 6th July, the Emperor was at least sixty hours on horseback. In the height of the danger, he rode in front of the line upon a horse as white as snow (it was called the Euphrates, and had been sent to him as a present from the Sophi of Persia.) He proceeded from one extremity of the line to the other, and returned at a slow pace: it will easily be believed, that shots were flying about him in every direction. I kept behind, with my eyes riveted upon him, expecting at every moment to see him drop from his horse."—Savary, tom. ii., part ii., p. 120.

little chance was there of redeeming the day, that he was glad to retire from the field unnoticed by the enemy.[509]

All hope of farther resistance was now abandoned by the Austrian princes and government; and they concluded an armistice with Buonaparte at Znaim, by which they agreed to evacuate the Tyrol, and put the citadels of Brunn and Gratz into the hands of Napoleon, as pledges for their sincerity in desiring a peace.[510]

With this armistice sunk all the hopes of the gallant Tyrolese, and of the German insurgents, who had sought by force of arms to recover the independence of their country. But the appearance of these patriots on the stage, though productive of no immediate result of importance, is worthy of particular notice as indicative of a recovery of national spirit, and of an awakening from that cold and passive slavery of mind, which makes men as patient under a change of masters, as the dull animal who follows with indifference any person who has the end of his halter in his hand. We, therefore, referring to what we have said of the revival of public feeling in Germany, have briefly to notice the termination of the expeditions of Schill and the Duke of Brunswick, together with the insurrection of the Tyrolese.

The career of the gallant Schill had long since closed. After traversing many parts of Germany, he had failed in augmenting his little force of about 5000 men, against whom Jerome Buonaparte had assembled a large army from all points. In his marches and skirmishes, Schill displayed great readiness, courage, and talent; but so great were the odds against him, that men looked on, wondered, and praised his courage, without daring to espouse his cause. Closely pursued, and often nearly surrounded, by bodies of Dutch, of Westphalians, and of Danes, Schill was at length obliged to throw himself into some defensive position, where he might wait the assistance of Great Britain, either to prosecute his adventure, or to effect his escape from the Continent. The town of Stralsund presented facilities for this purpose, and, suddenly appearing before it on the 25th of May, he took possession of the place; repaired, as

---

[509] Twenty-fifth Bulletin; Jomini, tom. iii., p. 267; Savary, tom. ii., part ii., p. 117.
[510] Twenty-seventh Bulletin.

well as he could, its ruined fortifications, and there resolved to make a stand.

But the French saw the necessity of treading out this spark, which might so easily have excited a conflagration. A large force of Dutch and Danish troops advanced to Stralsund on the 31st May, and in their turn forced their way into the place. Schill, with his brave companions, drew up in the market-place, and made a most desperate defence, which might even have been a successful one, had not Schill himself fallen, relieved by death from the yoke of the oppressor. The King of Prussia had from the beginning disavowed Schill's enterprise; and when the capture of Vienna rendered the Austrian cause more hopeless, he issued a proclamation against him and his followers, as outlaws. Availing themselves of this disavowal and denunciation, the victorious French and their vassals proceeded to inflict on the officers of Schill the doom due to unauthorised robbers and pirates—a doom which, since the days of Wallace and Llewellyn, has been frequently inflicted by oppressors on those by whom their tyranny has been resisted.

THE DUKE OF BRUNSWICK OELS

Schill's career was nearly ended ere that of the Duke of Brunswick began. Had it been possible for them to have formed a junction, the result of either enterprise might have been more fortunate. The young duke, while he entered into alliance with Austria, and engaged to put himself at the head of a small flying army, declined to take rank in the Imperial service, or appear in the capacity of one of their generals. He assumed the more dignified character of a son, bent to revenge his father's death; of a Prince of the Empire, determined to recover by the sword the inheritance of which he had been forcibly deprived by the invasion of strangers. Neither his talents nor his actions were unequal to the part which he assumed. He defeated the Saxons repeatedly, and showed much gallantry and activity. But either from the character of the Austrian general, Am Endé, who should have co-operated with the duke, or from some secret jealousy of an ally who aspired to personal independence, the assistance which the duke should have received from the Austrians was always given tardily, and sometimes altogether withheld at the moment of utmost need.[511]

Nevertheless, the Duke of Brunswick occupied temporarily, Dresden, Leipsic, Lindenau—compelled the intrusive King of Westphalia to retreat, and at the date of the armistice of Znaim, was master of a considerable part of Franconia. There, of course, terminated the princely adventurer's career of success, as he was, in consequence of the terms of that convention, entirely abandoned by the Austrian armies. Being then at Schleitz, a town in Upper Saxony, the Duke of Brunswick, instead of listening to the timid counsellors who advised him to capitulate with some one of the generals commanding the numerous enemies that surrounded him, resolved to cut his way through them, or die in the attempt, rather than tamely lay down the arms he had assumed for the purpose of avenging his father's death and the oppression of his country.

Deserted by many of his officers, the brave prince persevered in his purpose, dispersed some bodies of cavalry that lay in his way, and marched upon Halberstadt, which he found in possession of some Westphalian infantry, who had halted there for the purpose of forming a junction with the French general Reubel. Determined to attack this body before they could accomplish their purpose, the duke stormed the gates of the place, routed the Westphalians, and made prisoners upwards of sixteen hundred men; while the citizens welcomed him with shouts of "Long live the Duke of Brunswick!—Success to the sable Yagers!"

From Halberstadt he proceeded to Wolfenbuttel, and thence to Brunswick, the capital of his father's states, and of his own patrimony. The hopeless state in which they saw their young duke arrive, did not prevent the citizens from offering their respect and their services, though certain that in doing so they were incurring the heavy hatred of those, who would be again in possession of the government within a very short period.

The duke left his hereditary dominions the next day, amid the regrets of the inhabitants, openly testified by gestures, good wishes,

---

[511] Le Royaume de Westphalie, par un Témoin Oculaire, p. 66; Mémoires de Rapp, p. 123.

and tears; and forcing his way to the shores of the Baltic, through many dangers, had at length the good fortune to embark his Black Legion for Britain, undishonoured by submission to the despot who had destroyed his father's house. His life, rescued probably from the scaffold, was reserved to be laid down in paving the way for that great victory, in which the arms of Germany and of Brunswick were fully avenged.[512]

RISING IN THE TYROL

The defence of the Tyrol, which fills a passage in history as heroic as that which records the exploits of William Tell, was also virtually decided by the armistice of Znaim. Not that this gallant people abandoned their cause, because the Austrians, in whose behalf they had taken arms, had withdrawn their forces, and yielded them up to their fate. In the month of July, an army of 40,000 French and Bavarians attacked the Tyrol from the German side; while from Italy, General Rusca, with 18,000 men, entered from Clagenfurth, on the eastern side of the Tyrolese Alps. Undismayed by this double and formidable invasion, they assailed the invaders as they penetrated into their fastnesses, defeated and destroyed them. The fate of a division of 10,000 men belonging to the French and Bavarian army, which entered the Upper Innthal, or Valley of the Inn, will explain in part the means by which these victories were obtained.

The invading troops advanced in a long column up a road bordered on the one side by the river Inn, there a deep and rapid torrent, where cliffs of immense height overhang both road and river. The vanguard was permitted to advance unopposed as far as Prutz, the object of their expedition. The rest of the army were therefore induced to trust themselves still deeper in this tremendous pass, where the precipices, becoming more and more narrow as they advanced, seemed about to close above their heads. No sound but of the screaming of the eagles, disturbed from their eyries, and the roar of the river, reached the ears of the soldier, and on the precipices, partly enveloped in a lazy mist, no human forms showed

---

[512] Le Royaume de Westphalie, par un Témoin Oculaire; Jomini, tom. iii., p. 287.

themselves. At length the voice of a man was heard calling across the ravine, "Shall we begin?"—"No," was returned in an authoritative tone of voice, by one who, like the first speaker, seemed the inhabitant of some upper region. The Bavarian detachment halted, and sent to the general for orders; when presently was heard the terrible signal, "In the name of the Holy Trinity, cut all loose!" Huge rocks, and trunks of trees, long prepared and laid in heaps for the purpose, began now to descend rapidly in every direction, while the deadly fire of the Tyrolese, who never throw away a shot, opened from every bush, crag, or corner of rock, which could afford the shooter cover. As this dreadful attack was made on the whole line at once, two-thirds of the enemy were instantly destroyed; while the Tyrolese, rushing from their shelter, with swords, spears, axes, scythes, clubs, and all other rustic instruments which could be converted into weapons, beat down and routed the shattered remainder. As the vanguard, which had reached Prutz, was obliged to surrender, very few of the ten thousand invaders are computed to have extricated themselves from the fatal pass.

But not all the courage of the Tyrolese, not all the strength of their country, could possibly enable them to defend themselves, when the peace with Austria had permitted Buonaparte to engage his whole immense means for the acquisition of these mountains. Austria too—Austria herself, in whose cause they had incurred all the dangers of war—instead of securing their indemnity by some stipulations in the treaty, sent them a cold exhortation to lay down their arms. Resistance, therefore, was abandoned as fruitless; Hofer, chief commander of the Tyrolese, resigned his command, and the Bavarians regained the possession of a country which they could never have won back by their own efforts. Hofer, and about thirty chiefs of these valiant defenders of their country, were put to death, in poor revenge for the loss their bravery had occasioned. But their fame, as their immortal spirit, was beyond the power of the judge alike and executioner; and the place where their blood was shed, becomes sacred to the thoughts of freedom, as the precincts of a temple to those of religion.[513]

REVOLUTIONARY MOVEMENTS

Buonaparte was particularly aware of the danger around him from that display of national spirit, which, commencing in Spain, exhibited itself in the undertakings of Schill and the Duke of Brunswick, and blazed forth in the defence of the Tyrol. He well knew the character of these insurrections to be awful indications, that in future wars he would not only have the enmity of the governments to encounter, but the hatred of the people; not merely the efforts of the mercenary soldier, whose power may be great, yet can always be calculated, but the resistance of the population at large, which cannot be made subject to any exact means of computation, and which amid disorder, and even flight, often finds a road to safety and to revenge.

It was Napoleon's policy, of course, to place in an odious and false point of view, every call which the sovereigns of Europe made on the people of that continent, exciting them to rise in their own defence, and stop the French plan of extended and universal dominion. Every summons of this kind he affected to regard with horror, as including Jacobinical and anti-social principles, and tending to bring back all the worst horrors of the French Revolution. There is a very curious paper in the *Moniteur*, upon the promises of liberty and exhortations to national union and national vengeance, which were circulated at this period in Germany. These were compared with the cries of Liberty and Equality, with which the French Republicans, in the early days of the Revolution, sapped the defences and seduced the feelings of the nations whom they afterwards attacked, having made their democratic doctrines the principal means to pave the way for the success of their arms. The *Moniteur*, therefore, treats such attempts to bring the people forward in the national defence, as similar to the use of poisoned weapons, or other resources inconsistent with the laws of civilized war.

---

[513] Geschichte Andreas Hofer, Leipsic, 1817; Jomini, tom. iii., p. 290; Savary, tom. ii., part ii., p. 143.

General Pelet,[514] also, the natural admirer of the sovereign whose victories he had shared, has the same sacred horror at invoking the assistance of a nation at large to defend its independence. He inveighs vehemently against the inexpedience and the impolicy, nay, the ingratitude, of lawful princes employing revolutionary movements against Napoleon, by whom the French Revolution, with all the evils which its duration boded to existing monarchies, had been finally ended. He asks, what would have been the state of the world had Napoleon in his turn inflamed the popular feelings, and excited the common people, by democratical reasoning, against the existing governments? a sort of reprisals which he is stated to have held in conscientious horror. And the cause of civilisation and good order is invoked, as endangered by a summons to a population to arm themselves against foreign invasion. These observations, which are echoes of expressions used by Napoleon himself, belong closely to our subject, and require some examination.

In the first place, we totally deny that an invitation to the Spanish, the Tyrolese, or the Germans, or any other people, whom a victorious enemy has placed under a foreign yoke, has any thing whatever in common with the democratic doctrines which instigated the lower classes, during the French Revolution, to plunder the rich, banish the distinguished, and murder the loyal and virtuous.

Next, we must point out the extreme inconsistency betwixt the praise assigned to Napoleon as the destroyer of revolutionary practices, the friend and supporter of tottering thrones, and that which is at the same time claimed for him by himself and his advocates, as the actual Messias of the principles of the said Revolution, whose name was to be distinguished by posterity, as being connected with it.[515] Where could be the sense, or propriety,

---

[514] Mémoires sur la Guerre de 1809.
[515] "Sir Walter confounds the object of the Revolution with its horrors. Napoleon may well have said uncontradicted, 'that from him would date the era of representative governments'—that is to say, of monarchical governments, but founded upon the laws. He might have added, without contradiction or exaggeration, that he had put an end to the atrocities of the Revolution and to popular fury, the renewal of which he prevented. Impartial posterity will, perhaps, reproach my brother with not having kept an even way between the weakness of Louis XVI. and an inflexible firmness: it will reproach him with not having confided the preservation of the rights and the newly-obtained advantages of the nation to fundamental and stable laws, instead of making them rest on his own

or consistency, of such a rant as the following, in the mouth of one, who, provoked by the example of the allies to appeal to revolutionary principles, yet considered them as too criminal and too dangerous to be actually resorted to in retaliation?—"The great principles of our Revolution, these great and beautiful truths, must abide for ever; so much have we interwoven them with glory, with monuments, with prodigies. Issued from the bosom of the French tribune; decorated with the laurels of victory; greeted with the acclamations of the people, &c. &c. &c., they must ever govern. They will be the faith, the religion, the morality, of all nations in the universe. And that memorable era, whatever can be said to the contrary, will ally itself with me; for it was I who held aloft the torch, and consecrated the principles of that epoch, and whom persecution now renders its victim." Surely these pretensions, which are the expressions of Napoleon himself, are not to be reconciled with his alleged regard to the preservation of the ancient governments of Europe, and the forbearance for which he claims credit, in having refused to employ against these tottering thrones the great lever of the Revolution.

But the truth is, that no such forbearance existed; for Buonaparte, like more scrupulous conquerors, failed not to make an advantage to himself of whatever civil dissensions existed in the nations with whom he was at war, and was uniformly ready to support or excite insurrections in his enemy's country. His communications with the disaffected in Ireland, and in Poland, are sufficiently public; his intrigues in Spain had their basis in exciting the people against their feudal lords and royal family; and, to go no farther than this very war, during which it was pretended he had abstained from all revolutionary practices against the Austrians, he published the following address to the people of Hungary:— "Hungarians, the moment is come to revive your independence. I offer you peace, the integrity of your territory, the inviolability of your constitutions, whether of such as are in actual existence, or of those which the spirit of the time may require. I ask nothing from

---

existence: but I am greatly deceived if it will confirm the predictions of Sir Walter. I believe that it will divide the good and the advantages of the French Revolution from its excesses and horrors, the end and suppression of which it will attribute to Napoleon."—Louis Buonaparte, p. 58.

you; I only desire to see your nation free and independent. Your union with Austria has made your misfortune; your blood has flowed for her in distant regions; and your dearest interests have always been sacrificed to those of the Austrian hereditary estates. You form the finest part of the empire of Austria, yet you are treated as a province. You have national manners, a national language, you boast an ancient and illustrious origin. Reassume then your existence as a nation. Have a king of your own choice, who will reside amongst you, and reign for you alone. Unite yourselves in a national Diet in the fields of Racos, after the manner of your ancestors, and make me acquainted with your determination."

After reading this exhortation, it will surely not be believed, that he by whom it was made felt any scruple at exciting to insurrection the subjects of an established government. If the precise language of republican France be not made use of, it must be considered, first, that no one would have believed him, had he, the destroyer of the French republic, professed, in distinct terms, his purpose to erect commonwealths elsewhere; secondly, that the republican language might have excited recollections in his own army, and among his own forces, which it would have been highly imprudent to have recalled to their mind.

The praise so gratuitously assumed for his having refused to appeal to the governed against the governors, is, therefore, in the first place, founded on an inaccurate statement of the facts; and, next, so far as it is real, Napoleon's forbearance has no claim to be imputed to a respect for the rights of government, or a regard for the established order of society, any more than the noble spirit of patriotism and desire of national independence, which distinguished Schill, Hofer, and their followers, ought to be confounded with the anti-social doctrines of those stern demagogues, whose object was rapine, and their sufficing argument the guillotine.

APPENDIX

No. I

INSTRUCTIONS BY NAPOLEON TO TALLEYRAND, PRINCE OF BENEVENTUM

This very singular memorandum contains the instructions given by Napoleon to Talleyrand, concerning the manner in which he wished him to receive Lord Whitworth, then about to quit Paris, under the immediate prospect of the war again breaking out. He did not trust, it seems, to that accomplished statesman the slightest circumstance of the conference; "although," as Talleyrand himself observed, as he gave to the Duke of Wellington the interesting document, in Napoleon's own handwriting, "if I could be trusted with any thing, it must have been the mode of receiving and negotiating with an ambassador." From the style of the note, it seems that the warmth, or rather violence, which the first consul had thrown into the discussion at the levée, did not actually flow from Napoleon's irritated feelings, but was a calculated burst of passion, designed to confound and overwhelm the English nobleman, who proved by no means the kind of person to be shaken with the utmost vehemence. It may be also remarked, that Napoleon, while he was desirous to try the effect of a cold, stern, and indifferent mode of conduct towards the English minister, was yet desirous, if that should not shake Lord Whitworth's firmness, that Talleyrand, by reference to the first consul, should take care to keep open the door for reconciliation.

The various errors in orthography, as *fait* for *fais* or *faites*, *dit* for *dis* or *dites*, are taken from the original.

"St. Cloud, à 4½.

"Je reçois votre lettre qui m'a été remise à la Malmaison. Je desire que la conference ne se tourne pas en partage. Montez-vous y froid, altier, et même un peu fier.

"Si la notte comtient le mot *ultimatum*, fait[516] lui sentir que ce mot renferme celui de guerre, que cette manière de negocier et d'un supérieur à un inférieur. Si la notte ne comtient pas ce mot, fait[517] qu'il le mette, en lui observant qu'il faut enfin savoir à quoi nous en tenir—que nous sommes las de cet état d'anxiété—que jamais on n'obtiendra de nous ce que l'on *a obtenu des dernières années des Bourbons,—que nous ne sommes plus ce peuple qui recevra un Commissaire à Dunquerque*; que, l'ultimatum remis, tout deviendra rompût.

"Effrayez le sur les suites de cette remise. S'il est *inebranlable*, accompagnez le dans votre salon ...[518] de vous quitter dit lui, mais le Cap et l'Isle de Gorée, sont ils évacués?—radoucissez un peu la fin de la conference, et invitez le à revenir avant d'écrire à sa cour, enfin que vous puissiez lui dire l'impression qu'elle a fait sur moi, qu'elle pourrait être diminué par les mesures de ces evacuations du Cap et de l'Isle de Gorée."

TRANSLATION.

St. Cloud, half-past four.

I received your letter, which was brought to me at Malmaison. I request that the conference do not go into dialogue. Show yourself cold, lofty, even a little haughty.

If his note contains the word *ultimatum*, make him sensible that that word imports war, since such a manner of negotiating only takes place betwixt a superior and an inferior. If the note does not

---

[516] Fais.
[517] Fais.
[518] Illegible.

contain that word, contrive to make him insert it, by observing to him that it is necessary at length we should know upon what footing we are to stand with respect to each other; that we are weary of this state of anxiety; that they will never obtain from us those advantages which they extorted during the latter part of the reign of the Bourbons; that we are no longer the same people who received an English commissary at Dunkirk; that the *ultimatum* being rejected, all treaty will be broken off.

Alarm him upon the consequences of that rejection. If he remains still immovable, accompany him into your saloon ... and at the moment of his departure, ask him incidentally, "By the way, the Cape and the Island of Goree, are they evacuated?" Soften your tone a little towards the end of the conference, and invite him to return before writing to his court. At last, you may hint that the unfavourable impression he has made on me may possibly be diminished by the evacuation of the Cape and the Isle of Goree.

No. II

FURTHER PARTICULARS CONCERNING THE ARREST, TRIAL, AND DEATH OF THE DUKE D'ENGHIEN

This most melancholy history appears to deserve farther notice than we had it in our power to bestow, without too long interrupting the course of our narrative. It has been, and must for ever remain, the most marked and indelible blot upon the character of Napoleon Buonaparte. "A young prince," says the author of a well-reasoned dissertation on this subject, "in the flower of his age, treacherously seized in a neutral country, where he reposed under the protection of the law of nations, dragged into France, brought before judges, who had no pretension to assume that character, accused of supposed crimes, deprived of the assistance of a legal advocate or defender, put to death by night in the ditches of a state-prison;—so many virtues misconstrued, so many fond hopes crushed in the bud, will always render that catastrophe one of the most revolting acts which absolute power has been tempted to consummate."

The Duke d'Enghien was one of the most active and determined of the exiled princes of the House of Bourbon, to whom the emigrants and the Royalists who remained within France were alike devotedly attached. He was master of many of their secrets; and in July 1799, when the affairs of the Republic were in a very perilous state, and the Royalists were adjusting a general rising through all the south of France, his name was used upon the following extraordinary occasion.

A former member of the Representation, known as much by his character as a Royalist, as by his worth and probity, requested a private interview with General Bernadotte, then minister at war. The audience being granted by the minister, with whom he had some connexion, the representative entered into a long argument to prove what could not be denied—the disastrous and dangerous state of

France, and then proceeded thus: "The republican system being no longer able to support itself, a general movement is about to take place for the restoration of the King, and is so well organised, that it can scarce fail to be successful. The Duke d'Enghien, lieutenant-general of the royal army, is at Paris at this very moment while I speak to you, and I am deputed by one of his most faithful adherents, to make known these circumstances to General Bernadotte. The prince esteems you, confides his safety to your loyalty, reckons on your assistance, and is ready to grant any conditions which you may attach to your services." Bernadotte replied to this unexpected communication, "That the Duke d'Enghien should have no reason to repent the confidence which he had reposed in him: but that the loyalty which the duke had ascribed to him prevented his complying with the prince's wishes and request." He proceeded to state, that his own fame and personal interests were alike interested in his adherence to a government sprung from the will of the people; and that he was incapable of violating his oath of fidelity, or overthrowing the constitution to which he had sworn. "Make haste," he continued, "to convey my sentiments to him who sent you; tell him they are sincere and unalterable. But let him know, that for three days I will keep the secret which I have just learned, most profoundly. During that time he must find means of placing himself in security, by repassing the frontiers: but on the fourth morning, the secret will be mine no longer. This very morning, the term of three days will commence; make haste—and remember that the least imprudence on your part will be attended with fatal consequences."

It was afterwards ascertained that the deputy was mistaken, when he averred that the Duke d'Enghien was in Paris. It was pretty certain that he had never crossed the Rhine, and only waited the favourable reply of the minister at war to make the attempt. But in the light in which the case was presented to Bernadotte, his generous and firm conduct does not the less honour that eminent person, especially when contrasted with that of Napoleon. There might have been a strong temptation, and even a show of right, to have seized on the unfortunate Prince, supposing him to be in Paris, negotiating plans against the existing government, and tempting the fidelity of their principal ministers;—there could be none to kidnap him in foreign parts, when, however it might be suspected, it could not be shown by proof, that the unfortunate duke was concerned in any of the political intrigues which were laid to his charge. The tottering state of public affairs requiring so much vigilance and vigour on the part of the government, might also have been pleaded in excuse of Bernadotte, had he delivered up the Duke d'Enghien to dungeon or scaffold; while Napoleon, on the contrary, took the unhappy prince's life at a moment when his own power was so firmly established, as rather to incur danger than to acquire safety by the indulgence of a cruel revenge. The above anecdote, not, we believe, generally known, may be relied upon as authentic.

Napoleon, four years later, adopted towards the unfortunate prince that line of severity with which the world is acquainted. His broad vindication uniformly was stated to be, that the duke had offended against the laws of the country, and that, to put a stop to conspiracies, he had, from the beginning, determined to let the law take its course against him. He alleged, as we shall hereafter notice, various pleas in palliation or excuse; but his chief defence uniformly consisted in an appeal to the laws; and it is therefore just to the memory of Napoleon and his victim, that we should examine whether, in a legal sense, the procedure against the Duke d'Enghien is vindicated in whole or in part. The labours of Monsieur Dupin, the learned author of a pamphlet already quoted, have furnished us with an excellent work on this subject.

The case of the unfortunate duke must always be admitted to be a hard one. This is not denied by Buonaparte himself; and, on that account, it is the more necessary to the vindication of those upon whom his fate depended, to bring their procedure within the pale of the law. We are not now talking of reconciling the tragedy to the general rules of justice, generosity, or humanity; but in resigning the arguments which these afford, we are the more entitled to expect that the procedure which we impugn should, however harsh or cruel, be at least in strict conformity with the existing laws of France at the time, and such as could be carried on and vindicated by daylight, and in an open court. This is surely limiting our inquiry to the narrowest possible ground; and we shall prosecute the subject by examining the process in detail.

ARREST OF THE DUKE D'ENGHIEN

Every arrest, to be legal, must be so in three points of view: 1. As to the place where it is made; 2. concerning the person whom it regards; 3. in respect of the grounds on which it proceeds.

The duke was residing in the territories of the Elector of Baden, a sovereign prince who had not ventured to afford him that refuge without consulting the French governor on the subject, and who was authorised to believe that his affording hospitality to the unfortunate prince would afford no cause of rupture with his powerful neighbour. The acquiescence of the French government affords too much reason to suppose, that the measure afterwards adopted had been for some time premeditated; and that there was a secret design of detaining the victim within reach of the blow which they had already resolved to strike, when they should see convenient. Whether this was the case or no, the Duke d'Enghien was residing under protection of the law of nations, which proclaims the inviolability of the territories of one state by the soldiers of another, unless in case of war openly declared. It would be wasting arguments to show that the irruption of the French troops into the territory of Baden, and the seizure of the prince and his retinue, were directly contrary to public law, and could only be compared to an incursion of Algerines or robbers. Thus the place of arrest was highly and evidently illegal.

The charge on which the arrest was granted did not improve its legality. The only laws which could be referred to as applicable to the occasion, are those of 28th March, 1793, and of 25 Brumaire, An III. tit. 5, sect. i., art 7. By these, it is provided that *emigrants*, who have carried arms against France, shall be arrested, *whether in France, or in any hostile or conquered country*, and judged within twenty-four hours, by a commission of five members, to be named by the chief of the état major of the division of the army quartered in the district where they are found. A third law extended this order to all emigrants of every description, *arrested within the territory of the Republic*; but provided that the court should consist of seven persons, instead of five, to be named by the general commanding the division in which the arrest was made. These ferocious laws had in practice been so far modified, that it was laid down in the law books, that although, speaking strictly, they continued to exist, yet "the government always limited to deportation the sentence of such emigrants as were arrested within the French territory."[519] Before reviving them in their utmost severity against a single individual, it was therefore doubly incumbent to show that the party arraigned fell within these charges.

By no force of construction could the Duke d'Enghien be brought under the influence of these laws. He was not, properly speaking, an emigrant, nor did he possess the qualities of such. He was a Prince of France—as such declared an alien, and banished for ever from France. But, what is much more to the purpose, the Duke d'Enghien was neither found within France, nor in the precincts of any hostile or conquered country; but brought by force from a territory neutral to, and friendly in its relations with, France; and that without legal warrant, and by main force. Buonaparte took credit to himself for having prevented the execution of these laws against emigrants who had been forced on the shore of France by tempest, and had thereby come under the letter, though not the spirit, of the law. How much more ought the Duke d'Enghien's case to have been excepted, who was only within France by the force exercised on his person, and, instead of being arrested within the territory, as the law required, was arrested in a neutral country, and brought into France against his will? The arrest was therefore, so far as respected the person on whom it was used, an act of illegal violence; and not less so considering the grounds on which it proceeded, since there was no charge founded on any existing law.

INCOMPETENCY OF THE COURT

A military commission was assembled at Paris, to take under trial the Duke d'Enghien, accused of having borne arms against the Republic—of having been, and of still being in the pay of England—and, lastly, of having taken part in the conspiracies against the safety of the Republic, both external and internal.

---

[519] *Nouveau Repertoire de Jurisprudence, au mot Commission.*

Mons. Dupin, by the most decisive arguments and authorities, shows, that although the military commission might possibly be competent judges in the case of bearing arms against France, or receiving pay from England, yet the trial of a criminal accused of political conspiracy, was totally beyond the power of a court-martial, and could only be taken cognizance of by the regular tribunals. He quotes decisions of the minister of justice upon this point of jurisprudence, and concludes by applying to the military commission the well-known brocard of law, *Nullus major defectus, quam potestatis.*

IRREGULARITIES IN THE PROCEDURE

I. The procedure took place at the dead of night, contrary to the laws of France and every civilized country. The worn-out and exhausted criminal was roused at midnight from the first sleep he had been permitted to enjoy for three nights, and called in to place himself on defence for his life, whilst, through fatigue of body and mind, he could scarcely keep himself awake.

He answered to their interrogatories in a manly and simple manner; and by the French order of process, his answers ought to have been read over to him, and he should have been called upon for his remarks upon the exactitude with which they had been taken down; but nothing of this kind was proposed to the Duke d'Enghien.

II. The French law enjoins, that after closing the interrogatory, the reporter should require of the accused person to make choice of a friend for the purpose of conducting his defence. The accused, it further declares, shall have the selection amongst all the persons present, and failing his making such a choice, the reporter shall select a defender to act on his behalf. No such choice was allowed to the Duke d'Enghien; and, indeed, it would have been to little purpose; nor was any legal assistant assigned to him in terms of the law. The law presumes an open court at a legal hour, and held in broad daylight. It would have been but an additional insult to have required the duke to select a friend of a defender among the gendarmes, who alone were bystanders in the castle of Vincennes, or at the hour of midnight. Contrary, therefore, to the privilege of accused persons by the existing law of France, the accused had no benefit either of legal defence, or friendly assistance.

DEFECTS OF THE SENTENCE

The trial itself, though it deserves not the name, took place on the day after the interrogatory, or more properly on the night of that day, being what was then called the 30th Ventose;—like the previous interrogation, at the hour of midnight. The whole castle of Vincennes was filled with gendarmes, and Savary was in the actual command. He has published that he was led there by curiosity, though the hour was midnight, and the place so strictly guarded against every person, saving those who were to be officially concerned, that even one of the officers, who had been summoned, had considerable difficulty in procuring admission. We shall presently see if his presence and conduct indicated the part of a mere bystander; for the vindication which he was pleased to publish, drew forth that of General Hullin, president of the military commission, who has informed us of several important circumstances which had escaped the memory of the Duke of Rovigo, but which bear, nevertheless, very much on the point at issue.

The court being constituted duly, the warrant was read, which contained the charge against the prisoner. It accused him, 1. Of having fought against France; 2. Of being in the pay of England; 3. Of plotting with the latter power against the internal and external safety of the Republic. Of the *two first* counts, as they may be termed, of the indictment, we have already shown that they could not be rendered cognizable under any law then existing in France, unless qualified by the additional circumstance, that the emigrant accused had been found either within France, or in a country hostile to, or which had been subdued by France, which could not be stated to be the case of the Duke d'Enghien. Respecting the *third* count, the military commission were not legally competent to try it; the courts ordinary of France alone had the alleged crime within their jurisdiction. Nevertheless, in mockery of the form, as well as the essence of law, the court proceeded upon the trial upon two points of accusation, which were irrelevant, and upon a third, which was incompetent.

The mock trial, when brought on, was a mere repetition of the interrogatory which the duke had been previously subjected to. We are now to give an abstract of both interrogatories, only premising that within their limits must be found the whole head and front of the offences charged. The guilt of the accused must either be proved from thence, or his innocence must be acknowledged; the sole evidence produced, or attempted to be brought forward, on the trial, being the answers of the duke.

Upon the first examination, the following admissions were made by the accused. The duke avowed his name, birth, and quality; his exile from France, and the campaigns which he had made with the emigrant army under his grandfather, the Prince of Condé. He stated the various countries which he had inhabited since the army of Condé was disbanded, and that he had resided at Ettenheim for two years and a half, by permission of the elector. Interrogated, if he had ever been in England, or if that government had made him any allowance? He answered, he had never been in that country; but that England did allow him an annuity, which was his only means of support. Interrogated, what were his reasons for residing at Ettenheim? He answered, that he had thoughts of settling at Fribourg in the Brisgaw, as a pleasanter place of residence, and had only remained at Ettenheim on account of the elector's indulging him with full liberty of hunting, to which amusement he was very partial. Interrogated, if he kept up any correspondence with the French princes of his family who were at London, and if he had seen them lately? He replied, that he naturally kept up a correspondence with his grandfather ever since he had left him at Vienna, after the disbanding of his army; but had not seen him since that period;—that he also corresponded with his father, (Duke of Bourbon,) but had not seen him since 1794 or 1795. Interrogated, what rank he occupied in the army of Condé? He answered, commandant of the vanguard; and that when the army was received into Prussia, and divided into two corps, he was made colonel of one of them. These admissions might have been deduced or presumed from the simple fact, that the individual before them was the Duke d'Enghien, whose history and military services were sufficiently known.

The subsequent part of the examination consisted in an attempt to implicate the accused in the conspiracy of Georges, Pichegru, and Moreau. The reader will see how far his answers make the charge good.

"Interrogated, if he knew General Pichegru, and if he had any connexion or intercourse with him? Replied, I do not know him; I have never, I believe, seen him; I have had no conversation with him; I am glad I have not been acquainted with him, if the story told be true respecting the vile means which he proposed making use of."

"Interrogated, if he knew General Dumouriez, or had any connexion with him? Answered, that he knew him no more than the other—he had never seen him."

"Interrogated, if, after the peace, he had not kept up a correspondence in the interior of the Republic? Replied, I have written to some friends that are still attached to me, who had fought along with me, both on their affairs and my own. These correspondences were not of the character which I conceive to be alluded to."

The report further bears, that when the process-verbal was closed, he expressed himself thus:—"Before signing the process-verbal, I make with urgency the request, to have a particular audience of the First Consul. My name, my rank, my manner of thinking, and the horror of my situation, make me hope he will not refuse my desire."

In the second interrogatory, in presence of the military commission, the duke adhered to what he had said in his preceding examination, with the sole additional circumstance, that he was ready to renew the war, and to take service in the approaching hostilities betwixt England and France.

The commission, as appears from record of their proceedings, received no other evidence of any kind whatever, whether written or oral, and undertook the task which they knew was expected from them, of extracting reasons for awarding a capital punishment out of a confession from which nothing could be drawn by any ordinary process of reasoning, save that the accused person had been in arms against France, and was willing to be so again—but in open warfare, and in the hope of recovering what he considered as the rights of his family—a case which could not be brought under the penalty of death, except under the laws of 28th March, 1793, and of 25th Brumaire, An. III., where the capital punishment is limited, as we have repeatedly said, to emigrants taken within the limits of France, or of countries hostile to her, or subjected by her arms. The avowal that the duke had a pension from England did not infer that he was in her military pay, nor, indeed, did he in fact hold that allowance on any other conditions than as an alimentary provision allowed by the generous compassion of the British nation. Neither could he be found guilty upon his candid avowal that he was willing, or even desirous, to enter into the English service; for, supposing the actually doing so were a crime, the mere intention to do so could not be construed into one, since men are in this world responsible only for their actions, not for their thoughts, or the unexecuted purposes of their mind. No other evidence was adduced excepting the report of an officer of police, or state spy, sent to watch the Duke d'Enghien's movements, who declared that the Duke d'Enghien received many emigrants at his table, and that he was frequently absent for several days without his (the spy's) being able to discover where he went; but which suspicious facts were sufficiently explained, by his having the means of giving some assistance to his distressed companions, and his long hunting parties in the Black Forest, in which he was wont to pass many days at a time. A report from Shee, the prefect of the Lower Rhine, was also read; but neither Savary nor Hullin mention its import, nor how it was converted into evidence, or bore upon the question of the Duke d'Enghien's guilt or innocence. Hullin also mentions a long report from the counsellor of state, Real, where the affair, with all its ramifications, was rendered so interesting, that it seemed the safety of the state, and the existence of the government, depended on the judgment which should be returned. Such a report could only argue the thirst of the government for the poor young man's blood, and exhibit that open tampering with the court, which they were not ashamed to have recourse to, but certainly could not constitute evidence in the cause.

But both Savary and Hullin are disposed to rest the reason of the condemnation upon the frank and noble avowal of the prisoner, which, in their opinion, made it imperative on the court to condemn him. He uniformly maintained, that "'he had only sustained the right of his family, and that a Condé could never enter France save with arms in his hands. My birth,' he said, 'my opinions, must ever render me inflexible on this point.' The firmness of his answers reduced the judges," continues Hullin, "to despair. Ten times we gave him an opening to retract his declarations, but he still persisted in them immovably. 'I see,' he said, 'the honourable intention of the members of the commission, but I cannot resort to the means of safety which they indicate.'" And being acquainted that the military commissioners judged without appeal; "I know it," he replied, "and I do not disguise from myself the danger which I incur. My only request is, to have an interview with the First Consul." It is sufficiently plain, that the gallant bearing of the prince, so honourable to himself, brought him under no law by which he was not previously affected. But it did much worse for him in a practical sense. It avowed him the open enemy of Buonaparte, and placed each judge under the influence of such reasoning as encouraged Sir Piers Exton to the murder of a deposed prince at the hint of a usurper.[520]

The doom of the prisoner had been fixed from the moment he crossed the drawbridge of that gloomy state prison. But it required no small degree of dexterity to accommodate the evidence to the law, so as to make out an ostensible case of guilt, which should not carry absurdity and contradiction on its very front. This was the more difficult, as it is an express legal form in French courts-martial, that it shall express upon its record the exact fact for which death is to be inflicted, and the precise article of the law

---

[520] "Did'st thou not mark the king, what words he spake? Have I no friend will rid me of this living fear? Have I no friend? quoth he: he spake it twice, And, speaking it, he wistfully looked on me; As who should say—I would, thou wert the man, That would divorce this terror from my heart; Meaning, the king at Pomfret.—Come, let's go; I am the king's friend, and will rid his foe."

under which the sentence is awarded. The military commission had much more trouble in placing the record upon a plausible footing, than they found in going through the brief forms of such a trial as they were pleased to afford the accused. They experienced the truth of the observation, that it is much more easy to commit a crime than to justify it.

VERDICT

The first difficulty which occurred was to apply the verdict to the indictment, to which it ought to be the precise answer, since it would be monstrous to find a man guilty of a crime different from that of which he stood accused; as, for example, to find a man guilty of theft, when he had been charged with murder, or *vice versa*. The judges of this military commission had, at the same time, the additional difficulty of reconciling the verdict with the evidence which had been adduced, as well as with the accusations laid. If the reader will take the trouble to peruse the following copy of the record, with our observations, which we have marked by italics, they will see how far the military court of Vincennes had been able to reconcile their verdict with the act of accusation, and with the sentence.

The verdict bears: "The voices being collected on each of the underwritten questions, beginning with the younger, and ending with the president; the court declares Louis Antoine de Bourbon, Duke de Enghien,—

"1. Unanimously guilty of having borne arms against the French Republic."—*This is in conformity with the accusation, and the evidence; therefore, so far regular.*

"2. Unanimously guilty of having offered his services to the English government, the enemy of the French Republic."—*This is not in conformity to the charge. The duke only said he was willing to join the English in the new war, not that his services had been either offered or accepted. The former was a matter of intention, the latter would have been a point of fact.*

"3. Unanimously guilty of having received and accredited agents of the said English government, of having procured them means of intelligence in France, and of having conspired with them against the internal and external safety of the Republic."—*The facts alluded to in this clause of the verdict may be considered as contained by implication in the general charge in the accusation, that the duke plotted with England. But certainly they are not there stated in the precise and articulate manner in which a charge which a man must answer with his life ought to be brought against him. As to evidence, there is not, in the examination of the duke, the slightest word to justify the finding him guilty of such an offence. Not a question was put, or an answer received, respecting the plot with England, or the duke's accession to and encouragement of them.*

"4. Unanimously guilty of having placed himself at the head of a large collection of French emigrants, and others, formed in the frontiers of France, in the county of Fribourg and Baden, paid by England."—*There is not a word of such a charge in the accusation or indictment, nor was the slightest evidence of its existence brought forward before the court, or inquired into upon the duke's examination.*

"5. Unanimously guilty of having had communications with the town of Strasburg, tending to excite insurrection in the neighbouring departments, for the purpose of a diversion in favour of England."—*There is no mention of this charge in the accusation—there is no mention of it in the evidence.*

"6. Unanimously guilty of being one of the favourers and accomplices of the conspiracy carried on by the English against the life of the First Consul; and intending, in the event of such conspiracy, to enter France."—*There is no mention of this charge in the act of accusation or indictment. The evidence on the subject goes distinctly to disprove the charge. The Duke d'Enghien said he did not know Pichegru, and had no connexion with him; and added, that he rejoiced at the circumstance, if it was true that the general aimed at success by means so horrible.*

The result of the whole is, that this most liberal commission, in answer to the three charges, brought in a verdict upon six points of indictment; and that, on applying the evidence to the verdict, not one of the returns is found supported by evidence, the first excepted; of the other five, of which three at least are gratuitously introduced into the charge, four are altogether unsupported by the evidence, and the sixth is not only unsupported, but disproved, being in direct contradiction to the only testimony laid before the commissioners.

SENTENCE

Having drawn up their verdict, or answer to the act of accusation, with so little regard either to the essence or forms of justice, this unconscientious court proceeded to the sentence, which, according to the regular form, ought to bear an express reference to the law by which it was authorised. But to discover such a law, must be inevitably a work of some difficulty; and, in the mean time, the devoted victim still lived. The record of the court-martial bore the date, *two in the morning*;[521] so that *two hours* had already elapsed upon the trial and subsequent proceedings, and it was destined the sun should not rise on the devoted head of the young Bourbon. It was, therefore, necessary that he should be immediately found guilty and executed, as all that was considered the direct object for which the court was convened. It would be time enough to consider after he was no more, under what law he had suffered, and to fill up the blanks in the sentence accordingly. One would have thought such a tragedy could never have taken place in a civilized age and country; seven French officers, claiming to be esteemed men of honour by profession, being the slavish agents. It must, one would say, have occurred at Tripoli or Fez, or rather among the Galla and Shangalla, the Agows, or the Lasta of Abyssinia. But here is the sentence to speak for itself:—

"The prisoner having withdrawn, the court being cleared, deliberating with closed doors, the president collected the votes of the members; beginning with the *junior*, and voting himself the last, the prisoner was unanimously found guilty; and in pursuance of the———*blank*———article of the law of———*blank*———to the

---

[521] A sense of shame caused these words to be erased, but the operation has left them still legible. The attempt at concealment shows the sense of guilt, without hiding the crime.

following effect————————[two or three lines left blank for inserting the law which should be found applicable]————————condemned to suffer the punishment of death. *Ordered that the judge-advocate should see the present sentence executed,* IMMEDIATELY."

Most laws allow at least a few days of intervention betwixt sentence and execution. Such an interval is due to religion and to humanity; but in France it was also allowed for the purpose of appeal. The laws, 25 Brumaire, An. VI., and 27 Ventose, An. VIII., permitted appeals from the judgments of courts-martial. The decree of the 17 Messidor, An. XII., permitting no appeal from military sentences, was not then in existence; but if it had, even that severe and despotic enactment allowed prisoners some brief space of time betwixt this world and the next, and did not send a human being to execution until the tumult of spirits, incidental to a trial for life and death, had subsided, and his heart had ceased to throb betwixt hope and fear. Twenty-four hours were permitted betwixt the court of justice and the scaffold—a small space in ordinary life, but an age when the foot is on the brink of the grave. But the Duke d'Enghien was ordered for instant execution.

Besides the blanks in the sentence of this court, as originally drawn up, which made it a mockery of all judicial form, there lay this fatal error to the sentence, that it was not signed by the greffier, or clerk of court.

We do the judges the credit to believe that they felt for the accused, and for themselves; saw with pity the doom inflicted, and experienced shame and horror at becoming his murderers. A final attempt was made by General Hullin to induce the court to transfer to Buonaparte the request of the prisoner. He was checked by Savary. "It will be *inopportune*," said that officer, who, leaning on the back of the president's chair, seems to have watched and controlled the decisions of the court. The hint was understood, and nothing more was said.

We have given one copy of the sentence of the court-martial. It was not the only one. "Many draughts of this sentence were tried," says Hullin; "among the rest, the one in question: but after we had signed it, we doubted (*and with good reason*) whether it were regular; and, therefore, caused the clerk make out a new draught, grounded chiefly on a report of the privy-counsellor, Real, and the answers of the Prince. This second draught was the true one, and ought alone to have been preserved."

This second draught has been preserved, and affords a curious specimen of the cobbling and trumping up which the procedure underwent, in hopes it might be rendered fit for public inspection. Notwithstanding what the president says was intended, the new draught contains no reference to the report of Shee, or the arguments of Real, neither of which could be brought into evidence against the duke. The only evidence against him, was his owning the character of a prince of the blood, an enemy by birth, and upon principle, to the present government of France. His sole actual crime, as is allowed by Monsieur Savary himself, consisted in his being the Duke d'Enghien; the sole proof was his own avowal, without which it was pretended the commissioners would not have found him guilty.

To return to the new draught of this sentence. It agrees with the original draught, in so far as it finds the duke guilty of *six* criminal acts upon a charge which only accused him of *three*. But there is a wide distinction in other respects. The new draught, though designed to rest (according to Hullin's account) upon the report of the privy-counsellor, Real, and the answers of the prince, takes no notice of either. It does make an attempt, however, to fill up the blanks of the first copy, by combining the sentence with three existing laws; but how far applicable to the case under consideration, the reader shall be enabled to judge.

Article II. 1st Brumaire, An. V. Every individual, of whatever rank, quality, or profession, convicted of being a spy for the enemy, shall be punished with death.—*The Duke d'Enghien had neither been accused nor convicted of being a spy for the enemy.*

Article I. Every plot against the Republic shall be punished with death.—*There was no evidence that the Duke was engaged in any plot; he positively denied it on his examination.*

Article II. *All conspiracies or plots tending to disturb* the state by a civil war—to arm the citizens against each other, or against lawful authority, shall be punished with death.—*Here the same want of evidence applies.*

Upon the whole, it appears that the law could neither be so moulded as to apply to the evidence, nor the evidence so twisted as to come under the law—the judges were obliged to suppress the one or the other, or to send their sentence forth with a manifest contradiction on the face of it.

But this second draught of the sentence was so far conforming to the law, that it was signed by the greffier or clerk of court, which was not the case with the former. It was also more indulgent towards the accused; for the order for immediate execution was omitted, and its place supplied by the following details:—

"It is enjoined to the capitaine rapporteur instantly to read the present judgment to the condemned person in presence of the guard assembled under arms.

"Ordered that the president and the reporter use their diligence according to the legal forms, in despatching copies of this procedure to the minister at war, the great judge, minister of justice, and to the general in chief, governor of Paris."

By the interposition of these legal forms, the commissioners unquestionably desired to gain some time, to make interest with Buonaparte that he might not carry his cruel purpose into execution. This has been explained by the president of the court-martial, General Hullin himself, who, blind, aged and retired from the world, found himself obliged, on the appearance of Savary's vindication of his share in the murder of the Duke d'Enghien, to come forward, not to vindicate his conduct, but, while expressing his remorse for the share he really had in the tragedy, to transfer the principal charge to the superior officer, who was present during the whole trial, to overawe, it would seem, and to control the court. His account is in these words:—

"Scarcely was it (the sentence) signed, when I began a letter to Napoleon, in which I conveyed to him, in obedience, to the unanimous wish of the court, the desire expressed by the prince of an interview with the first consul; and farther, to conjure the first consul to remit the punishment, which the severity of our situation did not permit us to elude. It was at this moment that a man interfered, [Savary,] who had persisted in remaining in the court-room, and whom I should name without hesitation, if I did not recollect that, even in attempting a defence for myself, it does not become me to accuse another. 'What are you doing there?' said this person, coming up to me. 'I am,' I replied, 'writing to the first consul, to convey to him the wish of the prisoner, and the recommendation of the court.'—'You have done your business,' said he, taking the pen out of my hand, 'and what follows is mine.' I confess that I thought at the moment, and so did several of my colleagues, that he meant to say, that the conveying of these sentiments to the first consul was his business. His answer, thus understood, left us still the hope that the recommendation would reach the first consul. I only recollect, that I even at the moment felt a kind of vexation at seeing thus taken out of my hands, the only agreeable circumstance of the painful situation in which I was placed. Indeed, how could we imagine, that a person had been placed about us with an order to violate all the provisions of the law? I was in the hall, outside the council-room, conversing about what had just occurred. Several knots of persons had got into private conversation. I was waiting for my carriage, which not being permitted (any more than those of the other members) to come into the inner court of the castle, delayed my departure and theirs. We were ourselves shut in, and could not communicate with those without, when an explosion took place—a terrible sound, which struck us to the hearts, and froze them with terror and fright. Yes, I swear, in the name of myself and my colleagues, that this execution was not authorised by us; our sentence directed that copies of the sentence should be sent to the minister of war, the grand judge, and the general Governor of Paris. The latter alone could, according to law, direct the execution; the copies were not yet made; they would occupy a considerable portion of the day. On my return to Paris, I should have waited on the governor—on the first consul; who knows what might have happened?—but all of a sudden, this terrific explosion informed us that the prince was no more. We know not whether he [Savary] who thus hurried on this dreadful execution, had orders for doing so. If he had not, he alone is responsible; if he had, the court, which knew nothing of these orders, which, itself was kept in confinement—the court, whose last resolution was in favour of the prince, could neither foresee nor prevent the catastrophe."

EXECUTION

The gallant young prince, therefore, was cut off in the flower of his age, and, so far as we can see, on no evidence whatever, excepting that he was a son of the house of Bourbon, the enemy, by his birth, of the temporary Governor of France, but his public and declared enemy, who had never owed duty to him, and who had not been taken engaged in any active proceedings against him. The descendant of the great Condé was condemned to a bloody death, by a court, the judges of which were themselves prisoners, at the hour when thieves and murderers deal with their victims, and upon an unproved accusation tried by incompetent judges.

The research of the lawyer must go beyond the prince's nameless and bloody tomb to inquire into the warrant by which he was consigned to it. Was it by virtue of the first or of the second draught of that sentence, which the military erudition found so much difficulty in cobbling up into the form of a legal sentence? We suppose it must have been in virtue of the *first* draught, because *that* commands instant execution. If this conjecture is allowed, the Duke d'Enghien was executed in virtue of a document totally deficient in solemnity, since that first remains blank in its most essential parts, and is not signed by the greffier or clerk of court—a formality expressly enjoined by law.

If, again, we suppose that the *second*, not the *first* copy of the sentence, was the warrant made use of, the proceeding to execution will be found not less illegal. For that second draught, though it exhibits no blanks, and is signed by the greffier, and is so far more formal than the first, gives no authority for *instant* execution of the sentence. On the contrary, it enjoins the usual legal delays, until the copies should be made out and sent to the various officers of state mentioned in the warrant itself. The effect of this delay might have probably been the saving of the unfortunate prince's life; for if Paris had not heard of his death at the same time with his arrestment, it is not likely that Buonaparte would have braved public opinion, by venturing on concluding his nocturnal tragedy by a daylight catastrophe. But, laying that consideration aside, it is enough for a lawyer to pronounce, that such sentence, executed in a manner disconforming from its warrant, is neither more nor less than A MURDER; for as such are construed in the laws of every civilized country, those cases in which the prompt will of the executioner anticipates the warrant of the judge.

GENERAL VIEW OF THE PROCEDURE

Looking over this whole procedure, with the eyes of one accustomed to juridical reasoning, it is impossible to resist the conviction, that a train of more gross inconsistencies, practised with a more barefaced audacity, or for a worse purpose, does not stain and disgrace the page of history. The arrest was against the law of nations; the constitution of the court was against the military law; the mode of conducting the trial was against the law of France; the sentence was contrary to the forms of every civilized nation; the execution was a contravention of the laws of God and man. It would be absurd to term the slaughter of the Duke d'Enghien a murder committed by the sword of justice, unless we understand Hogarth's parody of that allegorical figure, with one eye open, one scale depressed with a bribe, and a butcher's knife in her hand instead of the even-swayed sword.

Having endeavoured to trace this bloody and cruel proceeding in a legal point of view, we must, before leaving the subject, consider what apologies have been set up against the black charge which arises out of the details.

The first of these screens would have been doubly convenient, providing it could have been rendered plausible. It amounted to the transference of the more active part of the guilt from Napoleon himself to Talleyrand, whom it would have been delicious revenge to have overwhelmed with the odium of a crime which must have made an impassable gulf between the ex-imperial minister and the restored royal family. Napoleon therefore repeatedly hinted and expressed, that the measure of the Duke d'Enghien's death had been thrust upon him by the advice of Talleyrand, and that, without giving the matter due consideration, he had adopted the course recommended to him. It was afterwards still more broadly averred, that Talleyrand had intercepted a letter written by the prince from Strasburg, begging his life, and offering, in grateful return, to serve Napoleon in his armies. This boon Napoleon intimates he might have granted, if Talleyrand had delivered the letter; but by intercepting it, that statesman became the actual murderer of the unfortunate prince.

There are two modes of considering every allegation, that is, according to the presumptive, or the positive and direct evidence brought in support of it. If we look at the former, we cannot discern the shadow of a motive why Talleyrand, however unprincipled we may suppose him, should have led his master into the commission of a great and odious crime, of which he was likely to have the whole unpopularity thrown upon himself, so soon as it should be found too heavy for his principal. Talleyrand was a politician; but so far as we have ever heard, possessed of no bloodthirsty disposition, and being himself descended from a noble family, was unlikely, to say the least, to urge the catastrophe of a young prince, against whom, or his family, he is never believed to have had any especial enmity. On the other hand, if we suppose him guided to the step by foolish and misguided zeal for Buonaparte's own interest, we traduce Talleyrand's mental capacity as much in the one case, as we should do his natural disposition in the other. No man knew better than the Prince of Beneventum, that power is, in enlightened nations, dependent on public opinion, and that the blood of an innocent and high-spirited enemy might indeed stain his master's throne, but could not cement its basis.—Again, if we regard the spirit displayed by the Duke d'Enghien upon his mock trial, when he declared he would not recall his avowed enmity to the French, in conformity to the hints thrown out by the court-martial, how is it possible that the same individual can be supposed capable of having, two days before, crouched to Buonaparte for his life; or how are we to reconcile his having offered to accept service under the first consul, with his declaration that it did not become a Condé to enter France, save with arms in his hands? We must suppose him a madman, if, having endeavoured to creep to Buonaparte's favour by the means of submission, he should have assumed an air of contumacy and defiance towards the judges who were to report his conduct on his trial to the first consul. The existence of the letter, and the fact of its being intercepted by Talleyrand, is, therefore, disproved as far as it can be, both by the character of the alleged writer, and of the minister for foreign affairs.

But, farther, it is disproved not only by reasoning *à priori*, but directly and from the state of facts, as far as negative evidence possibly can go. The whole proceedings against the Duke d'Enghien took place under the Counsellor of State, Real, and was managed entirely by the police; those safe, silent agents, who acted by immediate directions from the supreme head of the government, like the mutes of the seraglio, and were not liable to the control of any subordinate minister. Talleyrand never interfered, nor indeed had an opportunity of interfering, in it.

It was an officer of the police who was sent to inquire into the state of things at Ettenheim; and his report was made *not* to Talleyrand, not even to his proper chief, Real—but to Buonaparte himself. This is proved by Savary's own narrative, who says expressly, that "the first inspector of the gendarmerie received the report from the officer, and carried it himself to the first consul, instead of giving it to M. Real." The troops employed in the act of seizing the Duke d'Enghien, were also gendarmes, that is, policemen; and had a letter been written by their prisoner at Strasburg, or any where else, it would certainly have gone, like the report above mentioned, to the first consul, and not to Talleyrand to the foreign department. *2dly*, There is a sad, but minute memorial of his imprisonment, kept by the duke as a sort of diary. In this record is no mention of his having written such a letter. *3dly*, As the Baron St. Jacques, secretary to the unfortunate prince, was with his master constantly until the duke was taken from Strasburg, he was in a situation to offer a formal testimony against the very allegation of such a letter having been written, since he must have become acquainted with it, if it had any real existence. *4thly*, The gendarmes who collected the duke's few papers, and made an inventory of them, would not have failed to secure such a document, if, as we said before, there had been such a document to secure.

For all these reasons, the story of the suppressed letter must be considered, from beginning to end, as an absolute fiction, invented to absolve Napoleon of what he felt was generally considered as a great crime, and to transfer the odium to Talleyrand, whose active offices in behalf of the royal family, his former master could neither forget nor forgive.

But the story of the letter was not the only one to which Napoleon had recourse to qualify the public indignation, which was so generally directed against him as the author of this unhappy deed.

In the examination of the persons who were arrested on account of accession to the conspiracy of Pichegru and Georges, it appeared, according to a very apocryphal statement by Napoleon, that a person occasionally appeared among the conspirators, of noble mien and distinguished manners, to whom the principal conspirators showed such symptoms of homage and deference as are paid only to princes. "He appeared," says Savary, "36 years of age, his hair was fair, his forehead open, of a middle stature and size. When he entered the apartment, all present, even Messrs. de Polignac and De Riviere, rose and remained standing in his presence." The police considered who this mysterious personage could be, and agreed it must be the Duke d'Enghien. To the impression this supposed discovery made on the mind of the first consul, was to be imputed, according to his own account and General Savary's, the mission of the police officer to Strasburg, as already mentioned. The report of the spy concerning the frequent absences of the Duke d'Enghien from Ettenheim, was held sufficient to identify him with the mysterious stranger at Paris—the resolution to kidnap him was formed and executed; and although no circumstances occurred to show that he had been in Paris, or to identify him with the incognito above alluded to, and although they were not even at the trouble of confronting the duke with the persons who described that individual, to see if they could recognise them to be one and the same; yet he was put to death, we are called upon to believe, upon the conviction that he was the visitor and friend of Georges Cadoudal, and the person in whose presence all the world testified such profound respect. Hardly, however, had the duke been huddled into his bloody grave, than we are told it was discovered that the mysterious personage so often alluded to, was no other than Pichegru; and the blame of keeping up the mistake in the first consul's mind is imputed to Talleyrand, who is destined to be the scape-goat in every version of the story which comes from Napoleon or his favourers.

We submit that no author of a novel or romance, when compelled, at the conclusion of his tale, to assign a reason for the various incidents which he has placed before the reader, ever pressed into his service a string of such improbable and inconsistent circumstances. Was it credible that a prince of the blood, supposing him to have ventured to Paris during the consulate, and mingled with a band of conspirators, would have insisted upon, or would have permitted, the honours of his rank, and thus have betrayed his character to those who did not profess to know more of him than from that circumstance only? The very mention of a line of conduct so improbable, ought to have made the legend suspected at the very outset. Secondly, How could a mistake possibly occur betwixt the person of the Duke d'Enghien and that of General Pichegru? The former was fair, with light-coloured hair; the latter was dark, with a high-coloured complexion, and dark hair. The duke was slight and elegant in his form; Pichegru was stout-made, robust, and athletic. The prince was but just turned of thirty; Pichegru was forty years of age and upwards. There was scarcely a point of similarity between them. Thirdly, How was it possible for those circumstances to have occurred which occasioned the pretended mistake? Under what imaginable character was Pichegru to have commanded the respects paid to a prince of the blood, and that not only from the Chouan Georges, but from the Messieurs De Polignac and De Riviere, who, it is pretended, remained uncovered in his presence? Lastly, On the voluminous trial of Georges, which was published in the *Moniteur*, though several of his band were brought to bear witness against him, there was no evidence whatever of royal honours being rendered either to him or any one else. So that the whole legend seems to have been invented, *ex post facto*, as a screen, and a very frail one, behind which Napoleon might shelter himself. It is evident, indeed, even by his own most improbable account, that if the Duke d'Enghien died in consequence of a blunder, it was one which a moment's consideration must have led every one to doubt, and which a moment's inquiry would have explained, and that Napoleon's credulity can only be imputed to his determination to be deceived. How Talleyrand could have contributed to it, is not intimated; but General Savary informs us that the consul exclaimed—"Ah! wretched Talleyrand, what hast thou made me do!" This apostrophe, if made at all, must have been intended to support a future charge against his minister; for as to being led by the nose by Talleyrand, in a matter where his own passions were so deeply interested, it is totally inconsistent with all that is recorded of Napoleon, as well as with the character, and even the private interest, of his minister.

After this tedious dissertation, the reader may perhaps desire to know the real cause of the extraordinary outrage. Napoleon's interest seemed no way, or very slightly, concerned, as the sufferer was, of all the Bourbon family, the farthest removed from the succession to the throne. The odium which the deed was to occasion, without any corresponding advantage, was, it might have seemed, to the politic and calculating spirit which Napoleon usually evinced, a sufficient reason for averting an unnecessary outrage; nor was his temper by any means of that ferocious quality which takes delight in causing misery, or in shedding blood.

All these things admitted, we must remind our readers, that, as Napoleon was calm and moderate by policy, he was also by temperament fierce and ardent, and had in his blood a strain of the wild and revengeful disposition, for which his native Corsica has been famous since the days of the ancients. The temptation was strong on the present occasion. He felt himself exposed to the danger of assassination, to which his nerves seem to have been peculiarly sensible; he knew that the blow would be aimed by the partisans of the royal family; and he suspected that they were encouraged by the exiled princes. In such a case, what is the principle of the savage state, or that which approaches next to it? A North American Indian, injured by one white trader who escapes his vengeance, retaliates on the first European who falls within his power. A Scotch Highlander, wronged by an individual of another clan, took vengeance on the first of the sept which he happened to meet. The Corsicans are not less ruthless and indiscriminate in their feuds, which go from father to son, and affect the whole family, without the resentment being confined to the particular persons who have done the wrong. Upon this principle the first consul seems to have acted, when, conceiving his life aimed at by the friends of the Bourbons, he sprung like a tiger at the only one of the family who was within his reach and his power. The law of nations and those of society were alike forgotten in the thirst of revenge; and, to gratify an immediate feeling of vengeance, he stained his history with a crime of which no time can wash away the infamy.

The tendency to violence, arising out of a fierce and semi-barbaric resentment and love of revenge, might perhaps have shown itself in more instances than actually occurred, had it not been for Napoleon's policy, and his respect for public opinion, which would not have borne many such acts of vindictive cruelty. But though he was able in general to subdue this peculiar temper, he could not disguise it from those by whom he was closely observed. When some one, in the presence of Mounier, pronounced a eulogium upon Napoleon, and concluded by defying any of the listeners to produce a parallel character—"I think I could find something like him," said Mounier, "*among the Montenegrins.*"

END OF VOLUME THIRD

www.ingramcontent.com/pod-product-compliance
Lightning Source LLC
Chambersburg PA
CBHW060310230426
43663CB00009B/1656